Smart and Agile Cybersecurity for IoT and IIoT Environments

Qasem Abu Al-Haija
Jordan University of Science and Technology, Jordan

A volume in the Advances in Information Security,
Privacy, and Ethics (AISPE) Book Series

Published in the United States of America by
IGI Global
Information Science Reference (an imprint of IGI Global)
701 E. Chocolate Avenue
Hershey PA, USA 17033
Tel: 717-533-8845
Fax: 717-533-8661
E-mail: cust@igi-global.com
Web site: http://www.igi-global.com

Library of Congress Cataloging-in-Publication Data

CIP DATA PROCESSING

2024 Information Science Reference
ISBN(hc): 9798369334515
ISBN(sc): 9798369350621
eISBN: 9798369334522

British Cataloguing in Publication Data
A Cataloguing in Publication record for this book is available from the British Library.

The views expressed in this book are those of the authors, but not necessarily of the publisher.

For electronic access to this publication, please contact: eresources@igi-global.com.

Advances in Information Security, Privacy, and Ethics (AISPE) Book Series

Manish Gupta
State University of New York, USA

ISSN:1948-9730
EISSN:1948-9749

Mission

As digital technologies become more pervasive in everyday life and the Internet is utilized in ever increasing ways by both private and public entities, concern over digital threats becomes more prevalent.

The **Advances in Information Security, Privacy, & Ethics (AISPE) Book Series** provides cutting-edge research on the protection and misuse of information and technology across various industries and settings. Comprised of scholarly research on topics such as identity management, cryptography, system security, authentication, and data protection, this book series is ideal for reference by IT professionals, academicians, and upper-level students.

Coverage

- Risk Management
- Global Privacy Concerns
- Internet Governance
- Technoethics
- IT Risk
- Privacy-Enhancing Technologies
- Information Security Standards
- Tracking Cookies
- Network Security Services
- Computer ethics

IGI Global is currently accepting manuscripts for publication within this series. To submit a proposal for a volume in this series, please contact our Acquisition Editors at Acquisitions@igi-global.com or visit: http://www.igi-global.com/publish/.

The Advances in Information Security, Privacy, and Ethics (AISPE) Book Series (ISSN 1948-9730) is published by IGI Global, 701 E. Chocolate Avenue, Hershey, PA 17033-1240, USA, www.igi-global.com. This series is composed of titles available for purchase individually; each title is edited to be contextually exclusive from any other title within the series. For pricing and ordering information please visit http://www.igi-global.com/book-series/advances-information-security-privacy-ethics/37157. Postmaster: Send all address changes to above address.

Titles in this Series

For a list of additional titles in this series, please visit: www.igi-global.com/book-series

Machine Learning and Cryptographic Solutions for Data Protection and Network Security
J. Anitha Ruth (SRM Institute of Science and Technology, Vadapalani, India) Vijayalakshmi G. V. Mahesh (BMS Institute of Technology and Management, India) P. Visalakshi (Department of Networking and Communications, College of Engineering and Technology, SRM Institute of Science and Technology, Katankulathur, India) R. Uma (Sri Sairam Engineering College, Chennai, India) and A. Meenakshi (SRM Institute of Science and Technology, Vadapalani, India)
Engineering Science Reference • copyright 2024 • 526pp • H/C (ISBN: 9798369341599) • US $355.00 (our price)

Global Perspectives on the Applications of Computer Vision in Cybersecurity
Franklin Tchakounté (University of Ngaoundere, Cameroon) and Marcellin Atemkeng (Rhodes University, South Africa)
Engineering Science Reference • copyright 2024 • 306pp • H/C (ISBN: 9781668481271) • US $250.00 (our price)

Enhancing Security in Public Spaces Through Generative Adversarial Networks (GANs)
Sivaram Ponnusamy (Sandip University, Nashik, India) Jilali Antari (Ibn Zohr Agadir University, Morocco) Pawan R. Bhaladhare (Sandip University, Nashik, India) Amol D. Potgantwar (Sandip University, Nashik, India) and Swaminathan Kalyanaraman (Anna University, Trichy, India)
Information Science Reference • copyright 2024 • 409pp • H/C (ISBN: 9798369335970) • US $325.00 (our price)

Blockchain Applications for Smart Contract Technologies
Abdelkader Mohamed Sghaier Derbali (Taibah University, Saudi Arabia)
Engineering Science Reference • copyright 2024 • 349pp • H/C (ISBN: 9798369315118) • US $290.00 (our price)

Emerging Technologies for Securing the Cloud and IoT
Amina Ahmed Nacer (University of Lorraine, France) and Mohammed Riyadh Abdmeziem (Ecole Nationale Supérieure d'Informatique, Algeria)
Information Science Reference • copyright 2024 • 361pp • H/C (ISBN: 9798369307663) • US $275.00 (our price)

Investigating and Combating Gender-Related Victimization
Gabriela Mesquita Borges (University of Lusíada, Portugal) Ana Guerreiro (University of Maia, Portugal & School of Criminology, Faculty of Law, University of Porto, Portugal) and Miriam Pina (School of Criminology, Faculty of Law, University of Porto, Portugal & Faculté de Droit, des Sciences Criminelles et d'administration Publique, Université de Lausanne, Switzerland)

701 East Chocolate Avenue, Hershey, PA 17033, USA
Tel: 717-533-8845 x100 • Fax: 717-533-8661
E-Mail: cust@igi-global.com • www.igi-global.com

Titles in this Series

For a list of additional titles in this series, please visit: www.igi-global.com/book-series

Information Science Reference • copyright 2024 • 279pp • H/C (ISBN: 9798369354360) • US $265.00 (our price)

701 East Chocolate Avenue, Hershey, PA 17033, USA
Tel: 717-533-8845 x100 • Fax: 717-533-8661
E-Mail: cust@igi-global.com • www.igi-global.com

Table of Contents

Ammar Odeh, Princess Sumaya University for Technology, Jordan
Anas Abu Taleb, Princess Sumaya University for Technology, Jordan
Tareq Alhajahjeh, De Montfort University, UK
Francisco Aparicio-Navarro, De Montfort University, UK

Ahmed Mahfouz, Faculty of Computer Studies, Arab Open University (AOU), Oman &
Computer Science Department, Minia University, Egypt

Stéphanie Chollet, Laboratoire de Conception et d'Intégration des Systèmes, France
Arthur Desuert, Laboratoire de Conception et d'Intégration des Systèmes, France
David Hély, Laboratoire de Conception et d'Intégration des Systèmes, France
Laurent Pion, Laboratoire de Conception et d'Intégration des Systèmes, France

Shahad Ammar Al-Tamimi, Prince Sumaya University for Technology, Jordan
Qasem Abu Al-Haija, Jordan University of Science and Technology, Jordan

Walaa R. Ayyad, Jordan University of Science and technology, Jordan
Qasem Abu Al-Haija, Jordan University of Science and Technology, Jordan
Hussein M. K. Al-Masri, Yarmouk University, Jordan & American University of the Middle
East, Kuwait

Akash Bag, Amity University, India
Parul Sinha, Amity University, India

Abdullah S. Alshra'a, University of Erlangen-Nuremberg, Germany
Mamdouh Muhammad, University of Erlangen-Nuremberg, Germany
Reinhard German, University of Erlangen-Nuremberg, Germany

Ajay B. Gadicha, P.R. Pote Patil College of Engineering and Management, India
Vijay B. Gadicha, P.R. Pote Patil College of Engineering and Management, India

Mohammad Zuhair, P.R. Pote Patil College of Engineering and Management, India
Vishal A. Ingole, P.R. Pote Patil College of Engineering and Management, India
Sachin S. Saraf, P.R. Pote Patil College of Engineering and Management, India

Khadiga Eltira, University of Benghazi, Libya
Abdelhamid Younis, University of Benghazi, Libya
Raed Mesleh, German Jordanian University, Jordan

Detailed Table of Contents

Chapter 1
    Abdullah S. Alshraa, University of Erlangen-Nuremberg, Germany
    Loui Al Sardy, University of Erlangen-Nuremberg, Germany
    Mahdi Dibaei, University of Erlangen-Nuremberg, Germany
    Reinhard German, University of Erlangen-Nuremberg, Germany

As the integration of the internet of things (IoT) and industrial internet of things (IIoT) technologies continues to increase across various industries, ensuring strong cybersecurity measures becomes essential. In smart and agile cybersecurity for IoT and IIoT environments, foundational principles like risk management, security controls, governance, and a code of ethics are required. Risk management involves proactively identifying and mitigating potential threats, and ensuring the resilience of interconnected systems against cyber-attacks and vulnerabilities. Similarly, robust security controls, including encryption protocols and access management tools, provide essential layers of defense, safeguarding sensitive data and preventing unauthorized access. Furthermore, effective governance structures establish clear responsibility and guide policy implementation, enabling adherence to regulatory requirements and organizational objectives. Eventually, a strict code of ethics emphasizes the ethical imperatives basics in cybersecurity practices, enabling integrity, transparency, and respect for privacy rights. Through a comprehensive study of these topics, this chapter aims to provide readers with the necessary knowledge and strategies to steer the complexity of cybersecurity in IoT and IIoT environments efficiently, enabling resilience and adaptability against evolving threats.

Chapter 2
    Akashdeep Bhardwaj, University of Petroleum and Energy Studies, India

The meteoric rise of the internet of things (IoT) and industrial internet of things (IIoT) is reshaping our world, ushering in an era of hyper-connectivity and automation. This interconnected landscape, however, presents a significant paradigm shift in the cybersecurity landscape. This chapter delves into the unique challenges that this interconnected world presents, outlining the vulnerabilities inherent in IoT/IIoT environments and the evolving tactics employed by attackers to exploit them. The sheer scalability of these ecosystems presents a significant challenge. Billions of devices are projected to be online in the coming years, creating a vast and ever-expanding attack surface. This chapter explores some of the most common attack vectors employed by malicious actors. One prevalent threat is the formation of botnets. By compromising devices, attackers can create a distributed network with immense processing power. This processing power can then be harnessed for a variety of malicious purposes, such as launching denial-of-service (DoS) attacks or generating spam emails.

Chapter 3

Ivonne Kuma Nketia, University of Ghana, Ghana
Winfred Yaokumah, University of Ghana, Ghana
Justice Kwame Appati, University of Ghana, Ghana

This chapter conducts a comprehensive empirical review of internet of things (IoT) botnet detection to identify gaps in the literature. An empirical analysis of literature work related to IoT botnet detection is conducted. A state-of-the-art review of works done on IoT botnet detection is synthesized. This review is based on classifying the subcategories of IoT botnet detection, including honeypot and intrusion detection techniques, specifically host and network-based IDSs. This is further broken down into anomaly, signature, and hybrid-based approaches. Anomaly-based detections include machine learning techniques and deep learning techniques. Other detection methods include distributed techniques (software defined networking [SDN] and blockchain), graph theory approach, and domain name service (DNS) techniques. Finally, the chapter recommends future research directions in IoT security and the application of deep learning techniques.

Chapter 4
Wasswa Shafik, School of Digital Science, Universiti Brunei Darussalam, Gadong, Brunei
Darussalam & Dig Connectivity Research Laboratory (DCRLab), Kampala, Uganda

Agile security in the ever-changing field of cybersecurity encompasses the ability to adjust and react to emerging threats. This chapter explores the fundamental elements, benefits, methods of implementation, difficulties, and upcoming developments in the field of agile security. Agile security strengthens organizational defenses, allowing for flexibility, efficiency, and effective risk reduction. This chapter provides organizations with practical insights and best practices for effective adoption by thoroughly examining popular frameworks and techniques. It effectively explores the various difficulties encountered and offers strategic remedies, accompanied by practical examples showcasing successful executions. Finally, the study provides a brief insight into the future by examining advanced technologies and predicting their influence on agile security methodologies. In a nutshell, this chapter acts as a guide, highlighting the significance of agile security and encouraging additional investigation and adoption within organizational security policies.

Chapter 5
Akashdeep Bhardwaj, University of Petroleum and Energy Studies, India

The ever-expanding world of IoT and IIoT devices necessitates a robust and adaptable security framework to safeguard these interconnected systems. This chapter outlines the core principles for building such a framework, emphasizing proactive and continuous protection strategies for vulnerability analysis, malware detection, and anomaly detection. The framework foundation lies in conducting thorough risk assessments. By identifying potential vulnerabilities in devices, networks, and protocols, we can prioritize mitigation efforts and the use of secure protocols like TLS (transport layer security) and DTLS (datagram transport layer security) for encrypting data transmission, protecting sensitive information from unauthorized access. Anomaly detection systems identify deviations from normal behavior, while intrusion prevention systems (IPS) actively block malicious network activity. However, security cannot be an afterthought. This chapter emphasizes the importance of integrating security considerations throughout the development lifecycle of IoT/IIoT devices.

Ammar Odeh, Princess Sumaya University for Technology, Jordan
Anas Abu Taleb, Princess Sumaya University for Technology, Jordan
Tareq Alhajahjeh, De Montfort University, UK
Francisco Aparicio, De Montfort University, UK
Sara Hamed, Princess Sumaya University for Technology, Jordan
Nizar Al Daradkeh, Princess Sumaya University for Technology, Jordan
Nasser Ali Al-Jarallah, University of Almaarefa, Saudi Arabia

The chapter explores the critical aspects of data privacy and compliance within the rapidly expanding field of the internet of things (IoT). As IoT devices proliferate across consumer, industrial, and healthcare sectors, they bring with them significant challenges related to data security, privacy, and regulatory compliance. The integration of these devices into daily life raises substantial concerns about personal privacy, data breaches, and the ethical use of collected data. This discussion delves into the mechanisms IoT uses to collect, process, and store data; the associated privacy risks; and the comprehensive strategies necessary to mitigate these risks while ensuring compliance with global data protection regulations.

Ammar Odeh, Princess Sumaya University for Technology, Jordan
Anas Abu Taleb, Princess Sumaya University for Technology, Jordan
Tareq Alhajahjeh, De Montfort University, UK
Francisco Aparicio-Navarro, De Montfort University, UK

This chapter delves into the fundamental and advanced aspects of cryptography, an essential discipline for securing information in our digital age. It outlines the core concepts including encryption, decryption, ciphers, keys, and algorithms, which safeguard data integrity, confidentiality, and accessibility. The discussion extends to the distinctions between symmetric and asymmetric cryptography, their specific applications in various sectors, and the role of cryptographic hash functions in ensuring data integrity. Additionally, the chapter explores recent advancements such as quantum cryptography and the implications of artificial intelligence in cryptographic solutions. It also addresses the societal and technological impacts of robust cryptographic practices, balancing security needs with ethical and legal considerations. This comprehensive overview underscores the critical role of cryptography in protecting digital interactions and data in an increasingly interconnected world.

Ahmed Mahfouz, Faculty of Computer Studies, Arab Open University (AOU), Oman &
Computer Science Department, Minia University, Egypt

This chapter delves deep into the issue of user authentication in the environment of the internet of things (IoT) and industrial internet of things (IIoT). It's a journey defined by security implications, presented trends, and analyzed conventional practices, all of which set the stage for further examination. The authors explore the challenges and limitations of involving user authentication in the context of interacting ecosystems, and then they dive into the exciting world of the latest advancements aimed at ensuring higher security and privacy. These include blockchain-based tools, multi-modal authentication, and zero-trust paradigms. Also, they navigate the legislative landscape, provide compliance recommendations, and provide relevant tips for the establishment of strong authentication practices. Through captivating case studies and real-world applications, they draw a clear picture of the importance of user authentication in safeguarding IoT and IIoT systems against evolving cyber threats.

Chapter 9

Stéphanie Chollet, Laboratoire de Conception et d'Intégration des Systèmes, France
Arthur Desuert, Laboratoire de Conception et d'Intégration des Systèmes, France
David Hély, Laboratoire de Conception et d'Intégration des Systèmes, France
Laurent Pion, Laboratoire de Conception et d'Intégration des Systèmes, France

Connected devices have become increasingly prevalent in the daily lives of human users, forming the basis of smart spaces designed to provide valuable services, such as remote control of users' homes or efficient energy usage in large buildings. However, they also pose significant challenges, particularly in terms of security. This chapter aims to clearly define these challenges, focusing on device authentication, data confidentiality, and integrity. It begins by outlining a classical architecture for connecting devices and applications in commercial or industrial smart spaces. Various facets of this framework are explored, emphasizing the security requisites. The authors then delve into several key points of this architecture and explore the associated security needs. Current technologies are introduced, along with proof of concept from recent research work, including the promising physically unclonable function (PUF) technology, which offers a cost-effective hardware primitive for enhancing security in connected devices.

Chapter 10

Shahad Ammar Al-Tamimi, Prince Sumaya University for Technology, Jordan
Qasem Abu Al-Haija, Jordan University of Science and Technology, Jordan

In the digital era, supply chain security (SCS) is paramount for companies, governments, and consumers. Technological advancements, notably IoT and blockchain, enhance supply chain safety and transparency. Blockchain ensures data integrity and traceability, reducing fraud. IoT devices enable real-time monitoring for proactive risk management. Networked sensors provide asset data for preventive maintenance and route optimization. ML and AI algorithms detect security issues, while UAVs and self-driving vehicles enhance logistics. Automated last-mile delivery mitigates human risk. The chapter explores blockchain's role in SCS, addresses challenges, and discusses future advancements to bolster global resilience.

Chapter 11

Walaa R. Ayyad, Jordan University of Science and technology, Jordan
Qasem Abu Al-Haija, Jordan University of Science and Technology, Jordan
Hussein M. K. Al-Masri, Yarmouk University, Jordan & American University of the Middle
East, Kuwait

Human factors (HFs) play a primary role in cybersecurity. They can either improve the efficiency of security measures or produce susceptibilities that hackers can exploit. Hackers manipulate human error, making an organization's digital content attackable. Employee behavior, decision-making, and communication are all conducive factors that can result in security breaches. In cybersecurity, the human element should be addressed and addressed. Therefore, it's crucial to acknowledge the value of human factors and take integral steps to diminish the associated risks. It is necessary to reduce the hazard of such occurrences to safeguard an organization from data breaches and conserve its reputability and financial security. This protects sensitive data, secures unauthorized access, and prevents malicious performers. This chapter highlights the significance of the human factor in cybersecurity and urges us to take it seriously.

Chapter 12

Akash Bag, Amity University, India
Parul Sinha, Amity University, India

The growth of internet of things (IoT) devices across industries has brought advances but also revealed security risks and digital forensic challenges. This chapter examines IoT security threats, student understanding of them and their remedies, and IoT forensic examination issues. The research highlights the need for user training in IoT security, identifies prevalent dangers including malware and DDoS attacks, and highlights mitigation solutions through a synergistic literature analysis and comprehensive survey. It explores IoT forensics, its core processes, its crucial importance, and the many obstacles that hinder digital investigations in the IoT ecosystem. This chapter adds to the body of information on IoT device security, emphasizes user awareness, and highlights the challenges of IoT forensics.

Chapter 13

Abdullah S. Alshra'a, University of Erlangen-Nuremberg, Germany
Mamdouh Muhammad, University of Erlangen-Nuremberg, Germany
Reinhard German, University of Erlangen-Nuremberg, Germany

The incorporation of information and communication technologies (ICT) into power grids has brought a new generation in energy management, known as smart grids. This digital transformation has also raised new challenges to cybersecurity. This chapter presents the architecture and cybersecurity interplay within smart grids, highlights the need to secure critical infrastructure, and outlines the security requirements and the importance of availability, integrity, and confidentiality. Also, it discovers potential cyber-threats and vulnerabilities inherent in smart grids and analyzes historical incidents to provide insight into real-world implications. Moreover, the strategies for safeguarding smart grids components, such as supervisory control and data acquisition (SCADA) and industrial control systems (ICS), are discussed, alongside a unified framework to address privacy concerns. Finally, the chapter predicts future trends, identifies pioneering issues, and draws tracks for continuous research and development to strengthen smart grids' resilience against evolving threats.

Chapter 14

Ajay B. Gadicha, P.R. Pote Patil College of Engineering and Management, India
Vijay B. Gadicha, P.R. Pote Patil College of Engineering and Management, India
Mohammad Zuhair, P.R. Pote Patil College of Engineering and Management, India

Vishal A. Ingole, P.R. Pote Patil College of Engineering and Management, India
Sachin S. Saraf, P.R. Pote Patil College of Engineering and Management, India

In today's dynamic and interconnected digital landscape, traditional cybersecurity approaches are proving insufficient against evolving threats. This chapter explores emerging technologies that are driving smart and agile cybersecurity solutions. The authors examine how these innovations are reshaping security practices to adapt to modern challenges efficiently and effectively.

Khadiga Eltira, University of Benghazi, Libya
Abdelhamid Younis, University of Benghazi, Libya
Raed Mesleh, German Jordanian University, Jordan

This chapter proposes computationally secure physical layer wireless communication for multiple–input multiple–output (MIMO) systems. The algorithm presented is applicable across various MIMO configurations and resistant to attacks. It relies on accurate knowledge of wireless channel characteristics and channel reciprocity. Both transmitter and legitimate receiver generate a permutation vector based on channel fading paths to create the security key. The vast number of potential combinations makes decryption nearly infeasible. Additionally, secrecy rate analysis is introduced, considering space modulation techniques (SMTs) and spatial multiplexing (SMX) MIMO approaches, evaluating mutual information and average bit error rate (ABER) at both ends. Various SMTs schemes including space shift keying (SSK), spatial modulation (SM), and quadrature spatial modulation (QSM) are examined to validate the derived formulations.

Preface

Welcome to *Securing the Future: Smart and Agile Cybersecurity for IoT and IIoT Environments*. As editors of this groundbreaking reference book, we are thrilled to present an arsenal of insights and strategies aimed at fortifying the interconnected world against the relentless tide of cyber threats.

In today's digital landscape, the proliferation of Internet of Things (IoT) and Industrial Internet of Things (IIoT) devices has unlocked boundless opportunities for innovation and efficiency. Yet, this connectivity also unveils a daunting array of cybersecurity challenges that demand nothing short of ingenious and nimble solutions.

This edited volume stands as a beacon of empowerment for cybersecurity professionals, IT practitioners, business leaders, and enthusiasts alike. Whether you're a seasoned expert navigating the turbulent waters of cyber defense or an eager newcomer seeking to arm yourself against emerging threats, 'Securing the Future' is your indispensable companion in the quest for digital resilience.

Across its sixteen meticulously crafted chapters, this book delves deep into the heart of cybersecurity for IoT and IIoT environments. From laying the groundwork with a comprehensive introduction to IoT and IIoT, to unveiling cutting-edge strategies such as intelligent threat detection and agile security measures, each chapter is a veritable treasure trove of knowledge and tactics to shield your digital assets against adversaries.

But 'Securing the Future' is not merely a compendium of theoretical musings. No, it is a practical roadmap illuminated by real-world case studies, actionable implementation guides, and visionary insights into emerging technologies and future trends. Dive into the critical realms of data privacy, cryptographic solutions, network security, incident response, human factors, supply chain security, and collaborative information sharing, and emerge armed with the tools of a digital guardian.

As editor, I extend heartfelt gratitude to the visionary contributors who have generously shared their expertise and experiences. Together, we have forged a formidable arsenal in the ongoing battle for digital sovereignty.

Embrace the challenge. Embrace the opportunity. Embrace 'Securing the Future.' Within these pages lie the keys to unlocking a safer, more resilient digital future. Let us stand together as guardians of the connected realm and forge ahead towards a brighter tomorrow.

This edited reference book delves into the intricacies of cybersecurity in the realm of interconnected devices, offering insights, strategies, and solutions to tackle the evolving threats in IoT and IIoT ecosystems.

Chapter 1: Security Principles in Smart and Agile Cybersecurity for IoT and IIoT Environments

Authored by Abdullah Alshraa, Loui Al Sardy, Mahdi Dibaei, and Reinhard German, this chapter lays the groundwork for effective cybersecurity by elucidating foundational principles such as risk management, security controls, governance, and ethics. By understanding these principles, readers gain the necessary knowledge and strategies to navigate the complexities of cybersecurity in IoT and IIoT environments with resilience and adaptability.

Chapter 2: Evolving Threat Landscape in IoT and IIoT Environments

Authored by Akashdeep Bhardwaj, this chapter delves into the dynamic and evolving threat landscape shaping IoT and IIoT ecosystems. It explores the vulnerabilities inherent in interconnected environments and analyzes the tactics employed by malicious actors to exploit them. By understanding the evolving threats, readers can better fortify their systems against potential cyber-attacks.

Chapter 3: A Comprehensive Review of Internet-of-Things (IoT) Botnet Detection Techniques

Authored by Ivonne Nketia, Winfred Yaokumah, and Justice Kwame Appati, this chapter provides a comprehensive review of IoT botnet detection techniques. By synthesizing state-of-the-art research, it offers insights into detecting and mitigating botnet threats, enabling proactive measures to safeguard IoT ecosystems.

Chapter 4: Agile Security Strategies

Authored by Wasswa Shafik, this chapter explores agile security strategies essential for adapting to evolving threats in the cybersecurity landscape. By examining practical tools and frameworks, it equips organizations with the flexibility and resilience needed to mitigate risks effectively and stay ahead of emerging threats.

Chapter 5: Building a Smart Security Framework for IoT/IIoT

Authored by Akashdeep Bhardwaj, this chapter emphasizes the importance of a robust security framework for IoT and IIoT environments. By outlining proactive protection strategies and prioritizing vulnerability analysis, readers gain insights into safeguarding sensitive data and preventing unauthorized access. The chapter highlights the significance of integrating security considerations throughout the development lifecycle to ensure comprehensive protection.

Chapter 6: Data Privacy and Compliance in IoT

Authored by Ammar Odeh, Anas Abu Taleb, Tareq Alhajahjeh, Francisco Aparicio, Sara Hamed, Nizar Al Daradkeh, and Nasser Ali Al-Jarallah, this chapter explores the critical aspects of data privacy and compliance in the expanding IoT landscape. It addresses concerns regarding data security, privacy rights, and regulatory compliance, offering comprehensive strategies to mitigate risks while ensuring adherence to global data protection regulations.

Chapter 7: Cryptographic Solutions

Authored by Ammar Odeh, Anas Abu Taleb, Tareq Alhajahjeh, and Francisco Aparicio-Navarro, this chapter delves into the fundamental concepts of cryptography and its role in securing digital interactions. By exploring encryption techniques, key management, and recent advancements such as quantum cryptography, readers gain insights into robust cryptographic practices essential for protecting data integrity and confidentiality.

Chapter 8: User Authentication in the IoT and IIoT Environment

Authored by Ahmed Mahfouz, this chapter examines the challenges and advancements in user authentication within IoT and IIoT ecosystems. By exploring blockchain-based tools, multi-modal authentication, and zero-trust paradigms, readers gain valuable insights into enhancing security and privacy measures to combat evolving cyber threats effectively.

Chapter 9: Security of Connected Devices: Challenges and Solutions

Authored by Stéphanie Chollet, Arthur Desuert, David Hély, and Laurent Pion, this chapter addresses the security challenges associated with connected devices in smart spaces. By exploring device authentication, data confidentiality, and integrity, readers gain a deeper understanding of the security requisites for safeguarding interconnected systems against cyber threats.

Chapter 10: Supply Chain Security, Technological Advancements, and Future Trends

Authored by Shahad AL-Tamimi and Qasem Abu Al-Haija, this chapter explores the critical role of supply chain security (SCS) in the digital era. By leveraging technological advancements like IoT and blockchain, organizations can enhance transparency and mitigate risks in their supply chains. The chapter provides insights into real-time monitoring, predictive analytics, and the integration of AI and ML algorithms to fortify supply chain resilience.

Chapter 11: Human Factors in Cybersecurity

Authored by Walaa Ayyad, Qasem Al-Haija, and Hussein Al-Masri, this chapter highlights the significance of human factors in cybersecurity. By addressing employee behavior, decision-making processes, and communication strategies, organizations can reduce vulnerabilities and mitigate security breaches. The chapter underscores the importance of integrating human-centric approaches into cybersecurity policies to safeguard sensitive data and maintain organizational integrity.

Chapter 12: Forensic Approaches to Cybersecurity Challenges

Authored by Akash Bag and Parul Sinha, this chapter examines forensic approaches to cybersecurity challenges in the IoT ecosystem. By analyzing security threats, user awareness, and forensic examination techniques, readers gain insights into mitigating risks and conducting effective digital investigations. The chapter emphasizes the need for user training and proactive security measures to combat evolving cyber threats effectively.

Chapter 13: Cybersecurity Strategies for Smart Grids

Authored by Abdullah Alshra'a and Mamdouh Muhammad, this chapter explores cybersecurity strategies for smart grids. By highlighting security requirements, potential cyber threats, and incident response frameworks, readers gain insights into safeguarding critical infrastructure against cyber attacks. The chapter emphasizes the importance of continuous research and development to enhance smart grid resilience and mitigate emerging threats.

Chapter 14: ZTA-DEVSECOPS: Strategies for Cybersecurity in IoT and IIoT Environments

Authored by Ajay Gadicha, Vijay Gadicha, Mohammad Zuhair, Vishal Ingole, and Sachin Saraf, this chapter discusses emerging technologies and strategies for cybersecurity in IoT and IIoT environments. By integrating AI, ML, and zero-trust architecture (ZTA), organizations can adapt to modern cyber threats and enhance security postures. The chapter provides insights into proactive threat detection, automated incident response, and identity-centric security models.

Chapter 15: Securing Wireless MIMO Systems: Computational Insights

Authored by Khadiga Eltira, Abdelhamid Younis, and Raed Mesleh, this chapter proposes computationally secure physical layer wireless communication for MIMO systems. By leveraging accurate channel characteristics and permutation-based encryption techniques, organizations can enhance data security and confidentiality in wireless communication networks. The chapter explores space modulation techniques and evaluates their efficacy in mitigating security risks in MIMO systems.

These chapters offer valuable insights and strategies for fortifying cybersecurity in IoT and IIoT environments, emphasizing proactive risk management, user awareness, and technological innovations. Stay tuned for further exploration into cybersecurity best practices and emerging trends.

As we come to the culmination of this groundbreaking reference book, *Securing the Future: Smart and Agile Cybersecurity for IoT and IIoT Environments*, it is with great pride and gratitude that we reflect on the wealth of insights and strategies shared within its pages.

In today's digital landscape, the interconnected world of IoT and IIoT devices presents boundless opportunities for innovation and efficiency. Yet, alongside these opportunities comes a formidable array of cybersecurity challenges that demand ingenious and nimble solutions. Through the collective efforts of our esteemed contributors and editors, this volume stands as a beacon of empowerment for cybersecurity professionals, IT practitioners, business leaders, and enthusiasts alike.

Each of the sixteen meticulously crafted chapters serves as a testament to our commitment to providing practical solutions to the complex challenges of cybersecurity in IoT and IIoT environments. From foundational principles and evolving threat landscapes to advanced cryptographic solutions and forensic approaches, this book traverses the breadth and depth of cybersecurity with unparalleled depth and clarity.

But beyond theoretical musings, "Securing the Future" offers a practical roadmap illuminated by real-world case studies, actionable implementation guides, and visionary insights into emerging technologies and future trends. It is our fervent hope that readers will find within these pages the tools and inspiration to navigate the turbulent waters of cyber defense and emerge as guardians of the connected realm.

As we extend our heartfelt gratitude to the visionary contributors who have generously shared their expertise and experiences, we invite you to embrace the challenge, the opportunity, and the future. Together, let us stand as guardians of the digital frontier and forge ahead towards a safer, more resilient digital future.

Qasem Abu Al-Haija

Jordan University of Science and Technology, Jordan

Chapter 1
Security Principles in Smart and Agile Cybersecurity for IoT and IIoT Environments

Abdullah S. Alshraa
University of Erlangen-Nuremberg, Germany

Loui Al Sardy
https://orcid.org/0000-0002-8461-5154
University of Erlangen-Nuremberg, Germany

Mahdi Dibaei
https://orcid.org/0000-0001-5110-6110
University of Erlangen-Nuremberg, Germany

Reinhard German
University of Erlangen-Nuremberg, Germany

ABSTRACT

As the integration of the internet of things (IoT) and industrial internet of things (IIoT) technologies continues to increase across various industries, ensuring strong cybersecurity measures becomes essential. In smart and agile cybersecurity for IoT and IIoT environments, foundational principles like risk management, security controls, governance, and a code of ethics are required. Risk management involves proactively identifying and mitigating potential threats, and ensuring the resilience of interconnected systems against cyber-attacks and vulnerabilities. Similarly, robust security controls, including encryption protocols and access management tools, provide essential layers of defense, safeguarding sensitive data and preventing unauthorized access. Furthermore, effective governance structures establish clear responsibility and guide policy implementation, enabling adherence to regulatory requirements and organizational objectives. Eventually, a strict code of ethics emphasizes the ethical imperatives basics in cybersecurity practices, enabling integrity, transparency, and respect for privacy rights. Through a comprehensive study of these topics, this chapter aims to provide readers with the necessary knowledge and strategies to steer the complexity of cybersecurity in IoT and IIoT environments efficiently, enabling resilience and adaptability against evolving threats.

DOI: 10.4018/979-8-3693-3451-5.ch001

1. INTRODUCTION

The expansion of IoT and IIoT technologies has supported various industries to have interconnected devices and systems, as shown in Figure 1, utilizing network connectivity to seamlessly integration. sensors are on the top of the interconnected ecosystem, which plays an important role in collecting real-time data from the physical world. These sensors range from simple temperature or motion detectors to more complicated devices measuring environmental parameters, machine performance, or even human health metrics. The existence of IoT and IIoT technologies raise the efficiency and precision of automation to unprecedented levels. Thus, industries now automate repetitive tasks, optimize resource allocation, and streamline workflows, leading to increased productivity and cost savings. Monitoring tools support remote tracking and management of equipment, assets, and processes and provide insights enabling better proactive decision-making and troubleshooting. Furthermore, IoT integration has improved quality control processes by coupling real-time monitoring of production lines with data analytics, early detection of defects or variations from quality standards, reducing waste, and ensuring product consistency. In addition, IoT-enabled solutions have supported safety measures in various systems, from smart surveillance systems to wearable devices equipped with emergency alert functionalities, which help prevent accidents and enable a rapid response in case of emergencies.

Figure 1. IoT and IIoT Devices

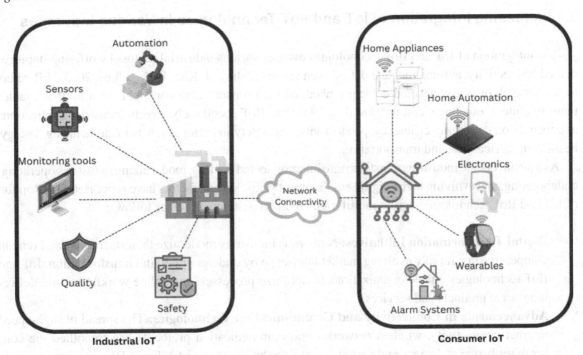

Regarding home applications and automation, IoT allows users to create smart homes equipped with interconnected devices offering convenience, energy efficiency, and more security. Many examples start from smart thermostats that optimize energy usage to connected devices that can be controlled remotely. Likewise, electronics manufacturers utilize IoT to create interconnected devices that seamlessly communicate and coordinate. Also, Wearable devices, a product of IoT technology, are transforming personal health and fitness monitoring by allowing individuals to track their activity levels, critical signs, and overall wellness in real-time. With the adoption of IoT, alarm systems have also evolved, providing homeowners and businesses with advanced features such as remote monitoring, customizable alerts, and integration with other smart devices for comprehensive security solutions.

These technologies offer unprecedented automation levels, efficiency, and data insights, driving innovation and transforming traditional processes (Hromada, Costa, Santos, & Rabadão, 2023). However, along with these advancements appear many significant security challenges. Therefore, Ensuring the integrity, confidentiality, and availability of data in IoT and IIoT environments is essential in particular with the interconnected nature, the critical operations industrial, and extensive amounts of sensitive information. Security breaches in these environments can have severe consequences, ranging from financial losses to reputational and physical damage (Dibaei et al., 2020).

Thus, designing security principles is important to handle the raised challenges posed by IoT and IIoT environments. Adhering to these principles is also necessary to build a strong and agile cybersecurity capable of addressing evolving threats and challenges in these environments. Consequently, organizations can enhance the resilience and security of their smart and agile systems by incorporating these principles into their cybersecurity strategy. Thus, safeguarding the organization against potential cyber threats, and ensuring the trust and reliability of IoT deployments.

1.1 Increasing Integration of IoT and IIoT Technologies in Various Industries

The integration of IoT and IIoT technologies evolves various industrial sectors by offering unprecedented connectivity, automation, and data-driven understanding (J. Kim, Park, & Lee, 2023). IoT refers to the network of interconnected devices embedded with sensors, actuators, and software that enables them to collect, exchange, and analyze data while the IIoT specifically targets industrial applications and focuses on enhancing efficiency, productivity, and safety in sectors such as manufacturing, energy, healthcare, agriculture, and transportation.

As a result, classic industries transform into interconnected devices, modernizing industries operating, collaborating, and evolving in the digital era. In recent years, several factors have supported the adoption of IoT and IIoT technologies across multifarious industries, summarized as follows:

- **Digital Transformation Initiatives:** Numerous industries modernize their operations and remain competitive in a rapidly evolving market landscape by undergoing digital transformation. IoT and IIoT technologies enable organizations to optimize processes, streamline workflows, and deliver innovative products and services.
- **Advancements in Connectivity and Communication Technologies:** The spread of high-speed internet connectivity, wireless networks, and communication protocols has smoothed the connectivity between devices and systems, forming the backbone of IoT and IIoT ecosystems. This infrastructure enables real-time data transmission and remote monitoring/control capabilities.
- **Cost Reducing and Efficiency Advancements:** Cost-effective alternatives to traditional methods of monitoring, control, and resource management are offered by IoT and IIoT solutions. Industries can optimize resource utilization, minimize downtime, and improve operational efficiency by employing sensors, actuators, and intelligent algorithms.

- **Data-driven Decision Making:** The amount of data generated by IoT and IIoT devices supplies useful understandings of operational performance, consumer behavior, and market trends. By implementing advanced analytics, machine learning, and artificial intelligence techniques, industries extract actionable intelligence to navigate informed decision-making and strategic planning.
- **Enhanced Safety and Security:** Safety and security are considered major concerns in industrial settings. IoT and IIoT technologies offer developed monitoring, predictive maintenance, and safety protocols to mitigate risks, control accidents, and ensure compliance with regulatory standards. Additionally, cybersecurity measures are implemented to protect critical infrastructure against cyber threats.

1.2 Importance of the CIA Triad

Ensuring integrity, confidentiality, and availability is important in protecting IoT and IIoT ecosystems (Garah, Mbarek, & Kirgizov, 2022; Litvinov et al., 2023). Therefore, security principles act as the foundation for robust cybersecurity strategies, safeguarding sensitive information, mitigating risks, and maintaining the trust of stakeholders. Data integrity refers to the accuracy, consistency, and reliability of information throughout its life-cycle. In IoT and IIoT environments, where data is the raw material of operations, any vulnerabilities to its integrity can have hurtful consequences. Security principles such as data validation, encryption, and access controls play a key role in preserving data integrity. Thus, organizations strive to implement cryptographic techniques such as digital signatures and hashing algorithms to verify the authenticity and integrity of data transmitted between devices and systems. Moreover, robust access controls guarantee that only authorized entities can modify or access sensitive data, reducing the risk of unauthorized tampering or manipulation. These security measures not only support data reliability in addition, support confidence in the accuracy of understandings derived from IoT and IIoTgenerated data (Abbas & Merad-Boudia, 2022).

On the other side, Data Confidentiality is essential in protecting exposed information from unauthorized revelation or access. When data streams cross many networks and interfaces, confidentiality maintenance generates an influential challenge. Security principles such as encryption, authentication, and data masking are critical in protecting data confidentiality. Encryption mechanisms such as end-to-end encryption and secure communication protocols, guarantee that data stays unreadable to unauthorized players even if intercepted during transmission. Also, strong authentication mechanisms (i.e. Multifactor Authentication and Biometric Verification) authenticate the identities of users and appliances by preventing unauthorized access to confidential data. Likewise, data masking techniques (i.e. Tokenization and Anonymization) mitigate the risk of data disclosure by replacing sensitive information with encrypted values to keep the organization's utility far from legitimate objectives (Hossayni, Khan, & Crespi, 2021). As a result, organizations can mitigate the risk of data breaches and protect the privacy of individuals and entities associated with IoT and IIoT deployments.

Besides, Data availability represents the ability to access and utilize the information whenever needed. Once real-time decision-making depends on the continuous flow of data, ensuring data availability is vital for operational resilience. Accordingly, data availability is beneficial for redundancy, fault tolerance, and disaster recovery planning. Organizations can mitigate the impact of hardware failures, network disruptions, or cyberattacks on data availability by implementing redundant systems and failover mechanisms. Also, organizations can handle issues that may compromise data availability using proactive monitoring and predictive analytics which enable early detection of potential threats or anomalies. Moreover, organizations utilize robust disaster recovery plans having data backups and recovery procedures to provide prompt restoration of services in the event of catastrophic events or cyber incidents.

As the threat landscape resumes to grow, compliance with security principles stays essential in ensuring the resilience and reliability of IoT and IIoT ecosystems. Following the three security principles pillars, which are widely known as the CIA Triad, organizations establish a strong foundation for protecting their information assets from different threats and guaranteeing the confidentiality, integrity, and availability of their data and systems. By implementing a holistic technique containing encryption, access controls, authentication mechanisms, redundancy, and disaster recovery planning, organizations will mitigate risks, protect sensitive information, and maintain the trust of stakeholders.

2. RISK MANAGEMENT

2.1 Major Threats and Continuous Assessment

Figure 2. Threats of Connectivity and Automation of IoT and IIoT

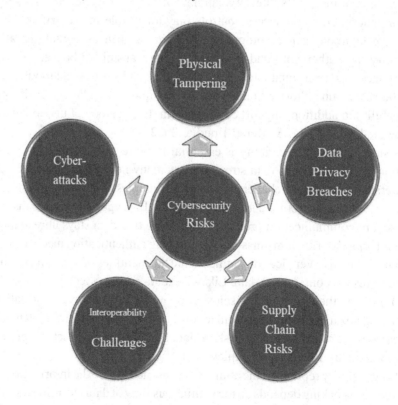

Connectivity and automation of IoT and IIoT technologies might bring along diverse threats and vulnerabilities, especially since every connected device would be a potential entry point for malicious users. Thus, various types of threats and vulnerabilities pose significant risks varying from traditional cybersecurity risks to unique challenges inherent to interconnected devices and industrial systems that impact the security and integrity of connected devices, systems, and data. Therefore, understanding the diverse nature of threats and vulnerabilities is essential for developing robust security systems proper to the risks encountered by IoT and IIoT environments (Liu et al., 2019). The following shortlist includes some of the major threats (Dhirani, Armstrong, & Newe, 2021):

- **Cyber-Attacks:** Malicious actors exploit vulnerabilities in IoT and IIoT devices and networks to launch cyber-attacks such as malware infections, distributed denialof-service (DDoS) attacks, and phishing campaigns. These attacks can compromise data confidentiality, disrupt operations, and cause financial losses (Duo, Zhou, & Abusorrah, 2022).
- **Physical Tampering:** Physical access to IoT devices or industrial control systems (ICS) can enable malicious users to manipulate hardware components, tamper with sensors or actuators, and compromise the integrity of data or processes. Physical tampering poses significant risks in critical infrastructure sectors such as energy, transportation, and healthcare (Pathak, Saguna, Mitra, & Åhlund, 2021).
- **Data Privacy Breaches:** IoT devices generate and transmit vast amounts of sensitive data including personal information, proprietary business data, and operational telemetry. Hence, these devices are attractive targets for data breaches, because unauthorized access to this data leads to privacy violations, identity theft, and regulatory non-compliance (Tawalbeh, Muheidat, Tawalbeh, & Quwaider, 2020; Kang, Dibaei, Luo, Yang, & Zheng, 2020; Kang et al., 2021).
- **Supply Chain Risks:** Supply chain risks arise with the interconnected nature of IoT ecosystems, where compromised components, firmware, or software updates might bring vulnerabilities into the system. Here, the adversary can exploit weaknesses in the supply chain to penetrate networks, compromise devices, or inject malicious applications (Birkel & Hartmann, 2020).
- **Interoperability Challenges:** Integration of heterogeneous devices and legacy systems in IoT deployments often results in interoperability challenges, creating opportunities for misconfigurations, protocol vulnerabilities, and communication errors. Adversaries may exploit incompatibilities between devices or protocols to disrupt services or bypass security controls (Albouq et al., 2022).

On top of the above, new vulnerabilities could be discovered, and novel attack vectors arise with alarming frequency. Accordingly, the need for a proactive and adaptive approach to risk management and continuous risk assessment is critical. Sometimes, traditional risk assessments may become outdated rapidly since new vulnerabilities appear or threat actors design innovative attack techniques. The Stay Ahead of Emerging Threats principle concentrates on continuous monitoring of intelligence sources and vulnerability databases. Also, organizations should rely on security advisories to identify and mitigate emerging risks promptly.

Adapt to Changing Environments represents another principle, where IoT and IIoT ecosystems are subject to constant changes and have potential security implications such as system updates, device deployments, and network expansions. Thereby, Ongoing risk assessments are requested to evaluate the impact of changes on the organization's security and revise security controls accordingly.

Similarly, the Address Operational Shifts principle handles the operational modifications that might influence the risk landscape within organizations such as new business processes, technological innovations, or regulatory requirements. Continuous risk assessment helps organizations assess the implications of these shifts on security objectives. Furthermore, Improve Incident Response Preparedness principle focuses on maintaining a current understanding of risks to enhance incident response preparedness by identifying potential attack vectors, understanding the potential impact of security incidents, and developing response plans suitable to specific threats and vulnerabilities. On the other hand, Threat Modeling, Vulnerability Assessment, and Asset Prioritization techniques help organizations proactively identify potential threats and vulnerabilities, which allows for timely mitigation strategies, risk identification, and robust cybersecurity practices in IoT and IIoT environments. These techniques complement each other and provide organizations with a comprehensive approach to risk identification. Threat Modeling applies systematically identifying potential threats to a system, understanding their potential impacts and assessing the possibility of their occurrence. Threat Modeling helps organizations analyze their systems from an attacker's perspective, identifying entry points, attack vectors, and potential weaknesses. Common approaches to threat modeling include STRIDE (Spoofing, Tampering, Repudiation, Information Disclosure, Denial of Service, Elevation of Privilege) and DREAD (Damage, Reproducibility, Exploitability, Affected Users, Discoverability) (R. Khan, McLaughlin, Laverty, & Sezer, 2017; K. H. Kim, Kim, & Kim, 2022). While, Vulnerability Assessment scans systems, networks, and applications for known vulnerabilities and has automated tools to identify vulnerabilities such as unpatched software, misconfigured systems, or insecure network protocols. Eventually, Asset Prioritization identifies and categorizes critical assets within an organization's infrastructure based on their value and importance to business operations. Hence, the organization allocates resources effectively and focuses its risk management efforts on guarding the most critical components.

2.2 Risk Mitigation Strategies

Once risks are identified and assessed, the organizations implement certain strategies to mitigate them. These strategies contain different methods, including risk avoidance, risk transfer, risk reduction, and risk acceptance (Verma, Pokharna, & Mishra, 2022; Alagappan, Andrews, Venkatachary, D, & Raj, 2022).

Risk Avoidance, the method involves actions to eliminate or reduce the possibility of specific risks occurring. This may include suspending or avoiding certain activities, processes, or technologies showing big security risks. For example, an organization may avoid using an IoT device or platform known to have critical vulnerabilities or lack acceptable security features. Although risk avoidance may be an effective strategy for mitigating high-impact risks, it may also have trade-offs such as limiting functionality or innovation. While Risk Transfer works typically through insurance or contractual agreements to shift the financial consequences of risks to third-party vendors, insurers, or partners who have the resources and expertise to manage them effectively. For example, organizations buy cybersecurity insurance policies to cover possible losses resulting from security breaches or data breaches. However, risk transfer does not eliminate risks.

In Risk Reduction, the organization aims to reduce vulnerabilities and strengthen defenses by running rules and measures against the possible impact of identified risks. Thus, risk reduction utilizes technical controls such as firewalls, intrusion detection systems, encryption, and access controls to protect against unauthorized access, data breaches, and cyber-attacks. Also, Risk reduction utilizes policies, procedures, and training programs to raise awareness among employees and stakeholders about security best practices and protocols. With a dissimilar method, Risk Acceptance has acknowledged and tolerated certain risks without taking additional mitigation measures. This may be a deliberate decision based on factors such as cost-benefit analysis, risk appetite, and organizational priorities. For example, organizations may choose to accept certain low-impact risks if the cost of mitigation outweighs the potential benefits. However, it is essential for organizations to carefully evaluate the implications of risk acceptance and ensure that it aligns with their overall risk management strategy.

2.3 Integration of Risk Management Into Organizations Practices

Accordingly, organizations should work to integrate risk management processes into the security frameworks to effectively identify, assess, and mitigate risks in IoT and IIoT environments. This integration ensures that security efforts are compatible with the organization's objectives and risk tolerance levels. Several key steps can facilitate the seamless integration of risk management into security practices (Popescu, Popescu, & Prostean, 2021):

- **Establishment of Clear Policies and Procedures** that outline the roles, responsibilities, and processes related to risk management. These documents serve as a guide for employees, ensuring consistency and accountability in risk management activities.
- **Alignment with Business Objectives** by understanding the assets, and processes, and involving stakeholders, Hence, security teams can prioritize risk mitigation efforts effectively.
- **Integration with Security Frameworks** should facilitate compliance with regulatory requirements and industry standards in addition to ensuring that security initiatives are comprehensive and well-coordinated with established security frameworks such as ISO/IEC 27001, NIST Cybersecurity Framework, or COBIT.
- **Cross-Functional Collaboration**, where security teams should work closely with stakeholders from IT, operations, legal, and compliance departments to identify and address risks holistically. This collaborative approach enhances the organization's ability to anticipate and mitigate emerging threats.
- **Continuous Monitoring and Improvement**, where Organizations should establish mechanisms for continuous risk assessment, incorporating feedback from security incidents, audits, and changes in the business environment. Regular reviews of security policies, controls, and procedures ensure that the organization remains resilient to evolving threats.

3. SECURITY CONTROLS

Security controls have an essential role in protecting connected devices, networks, and data against cyber threats (Mnasri, 2022). Security controls contain many measures and mechanisms to guard IoT and IIoT ecosystems against unauthorized access, data breaches, and malicious behaviors. As IoT and IIoT devices increase across industries such as healthcare, manufacturing, transportation, and smart cities, the need for robust security controls becomes essential for ensuring the integrity, confidentiality, and availability of sensitive information and infrastructure in interconnected environments.

3.1 Illustration of Access Control Mechanisms

Access control regulates who can access what resources in a system and contains three main components: authentication, authorization, and accounting (AAA), each serving a specific role in managing access to sensitive information and functionalities within IoT and IIoT environments.

Authentication verifies the identity of users or devices trying to access a system or resource and ensures that only authorized entities are granted access while preventing unauthorized access. This mechanism commonly has three methods as follows (Qiu et al., 2020; Karatas & Akbulut, 2018):

*   Password-based Authentication: Users provide a username and password combination to authenticate themselves. However, passwords are vulnerable to brute-force attacks and password guessing.
*   Multi-factor Authentication (MFA): To enhance security, MFA adds further layers of verification and requires users to present multiple forms of identification. For example, a password, security token, biometric data (e.g., fingerprint, facial recognition), or one-time codes sent via SMS or email.
*   Certificate-based Authentication: Certificates issued by trusted Certificate Authorities (CAs) are used to authenticate devices or users. This method ensures the authenticity of entities based on cryptographic certificates, reducing the reliance on passwords and enhancing security.

After the Authentication completes, the Authorization mechanism specifies the actions and resources that authenticated users or devices can access within a system. That includes the permissions and privileges associated with different user roles or groups, ensuring the user access is only to the resources necessary to perform their tasks. This mechanism commonly has the following methods (J. A. Khan, 2024):

*   Role-based Access Control (RBAC): RBAC is a permission management system that assigns access rights to users based on predefined roles within an organization. Each user is assigned a specific role that corresponds to their job responsibilities, and access rights are granted based on these roles. RBAC simplifies access management by standardizing permissions across user groups, which streamlines the administration process. To implement RBAC, organizations should take the following steps: define roles, assign users to roles, administer roles, and define rolebased access control policies. Following these steps will ensure that access control systems are effective, efficient, and secure, providing robust protection against unauthorized access.
*   Attribute-based Access Control (ABAC): ABAC dynamically evaluates different attributes to make access control decisions. These attributes include user attributes such as role, department, and clearance level, resource attributes such as sensitivity and classification, and environmental attributes such as time of access and location. The implementation of ABAC requires a strict identification of relevant attributes, the designing of access control policies using logical expressions that incorporate attribute-based rules, the implementation of an access control decision engine, and the enforcement of policies in real-time. With ABAC, the organization can be confident that access requests are evaluated based on the most relevant attributes and environmental context, ensuring that only authorized access is granted while preventing unauthorized access.

During the user interacts with the system, Accounting (AAA) (Known as auditing or accountability) mechanism tracks and logs all user activities in the system and records its relevant information such as login attempts, resource access, and system changes, facilitating forensic analysis, compliance auditing, and incident response. The AAA framework includes three components (Paolini et al., 2020):

- Authentication Logging records the details of authentication events, including successful and failed login attempts, as well as the authentication method used. These logs can help detect and investigate unauthorized access attempts and security breaches.
- Authorization Logging logs the access control decisions made by the system, including the permissions granted or denied for specific resources. These logs provide visibility into access patterns and help identify anomalous behavior or policy violations.
- Accounting Logging is used to track user activities and system events, such as file modifications, configuration changes, and network traffic. These logs facilitate compliance with regulatory requirements, support incident response efforts, and aid in forensic investigations.

3.2 Overview of Encryption Techniques

In IoT and IIoT environments, where huge amounts of sensitive data are transmitted and stored, encryption is important to ensure confidentiality and integrity. Encryption protects data by converting it into an unreadable format, which can only be decrypted with the correct decryption key. Symmetric and asymmetric encryption are two primary encryption methods generally utilized in IoT and IIoT security.

Figure 3. Encryption Techniques: (a) Symmetric Encryption, (b) Asymmetric Encryption

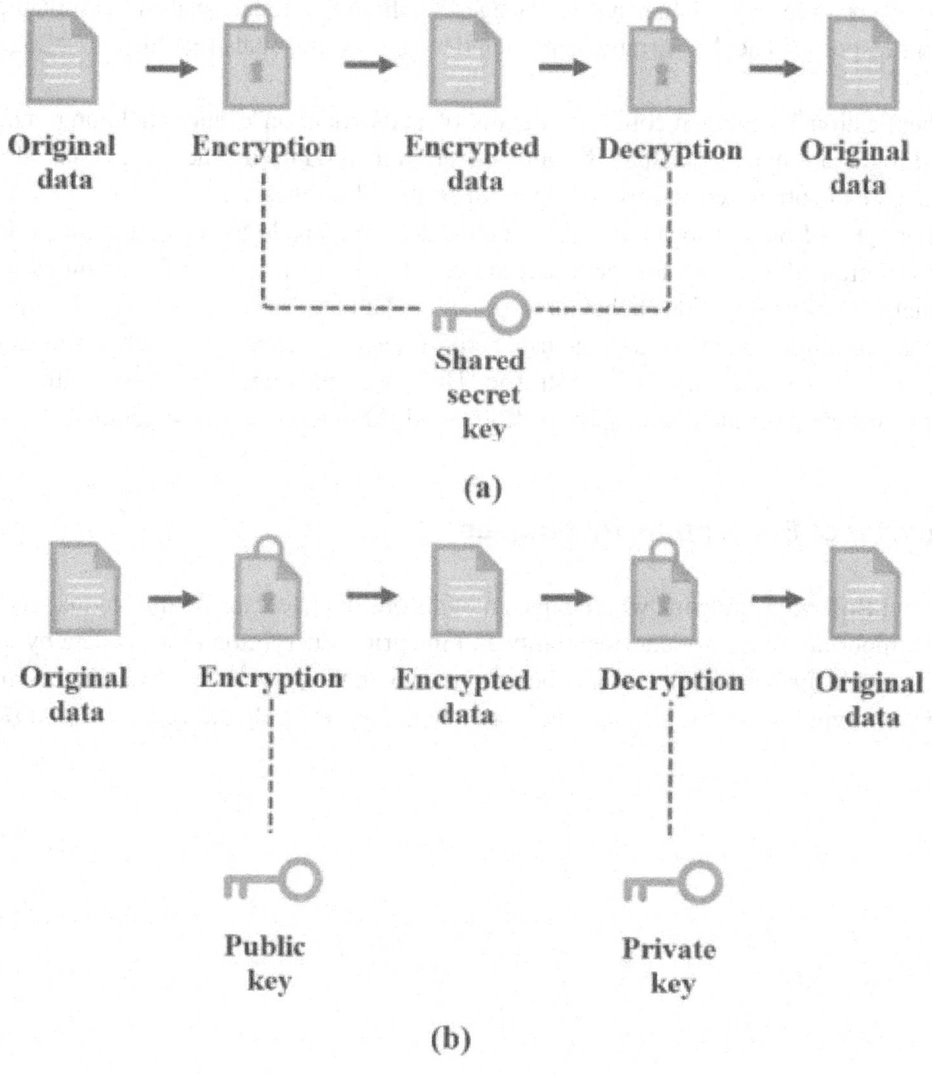

Symmetric Encryption, also called secret key encryption, employs a single shared key to encrypt and decrypt data. But, the single key must remain away from unauthorized access. Popular symmetric encryption algorithms include Advanced Encryption Standard (AES), Data Encryption Standard (DES), and Triple DES (3DES) (Ramachandra et al., 2022; Vuppala, Roshan, Nawaz, & Ravindra, 2020). Whereas, Asymmetric Encryption, also known as public-key encryption, utilizes a pair of keys: a public key and a private key. The public key is shared publicly and utilized for encryption, while the private key is saved secret and used for decryption. Thus, the data encrypted with the public key can only be decrypted with the corresponding private key (Figure 3). Common asymmetric encryption algorithms include RSA (Rivest-Shamir-Adleman), Diffie-Hellman, and Elliptic Curve Cryptography (ECC) (Alhassan, Mahama, & Alhassan, 2022; Alshra'a & Seitz, 2021; Ullah et al., 2023). Sometimes, organizations employ a combination of symmetric and asymmetric encryption techniques to have robust encryption solutions and protect sensitive data and communications in IoT and IIoT deployments.

Despite the advantages of IoT and IIoT technologies, unique security challenges and vulnerabilities appear that organizations must address proactively. By implementing effective security controls, organizations can mitigate common security challenges and vulnerabilities associated with IoT and IIoT deployments. For instance, different Secure communication protocols are utilized to counter the challenge of Insecure Communication Protocols to encrypt data exchanged between IoT devices and backend systems, such as Transport Layer Security (TLS) and Datagram Transport Layer Security (DTLS). Moreover, implement secure communication channels, such as Virtual Private Networks (VPNs), to protect data in transit.

3.3 Best Practices for Implementing Security Controls

Based on the above, Organizations can establish firm foundations for security in interconnected environments. By adhering to these foundations, organizations enhance security conditions, mitigate risks, and protect critical assets and data from cyber threats. In general, the following points represent best practices for implementing security controls in IoT and IIoT deployments (Phelps, 2022; Barrera, Bellman, & van Oorschot, 2022):

- **End-to-end Encryption** ensures that data stays confidential and secure, even if intercepted by unauthorized parties.
- **Authentication and Access Control** verifies the identity of users and devices accessing IoT and IIoT systems. Besides, organizations implement access controls based on the principle of least privilege to restrict access to sensitive resources.
- **Secure Device Provisioning and life-cycle Management** Ensure that IoT and IIoT devices are securely equipped and managed during deployment. therefore, the organization must utilize secure onboarding devices, apply security updates and patches, and withdraw devices when no longer in use.
- **Secure Configuration Management** according to security best practices and industry standards. Further, the organization must disable unneeded services and features, adjust default passwords, and apply access controls to decrease the attack surface.
- **Continuous Monitoring and Incident Response** help in detecting and responding to security incidents in real-time. Thus, mitigating the consequence of security breaches and minimizing downtime.
- **Vendor Risk Management** It is important to conduct thorough security assessments of IoT and IIoT vendors and suppliers. This ensures the realization of the required security standards, in addition to establishing contractual agreements outlining security expectations and responsibilities, including data protection and incident response.
- **Participants Awareness and Training** by educating employees, partners, and stakeholders regarding security best practices and potential risks. Also, Providing frequent training sessions and awareness programs about a culture of security awareness.

Similarly, Weak Authentication and Authorization challenges must be handled by implementing robust authentication mechanisms, such as certificate-based authentication or biometric authentication, to verify the identity of users and devices or enforce granular access controls based on the principle of least privilege to restrict unauthorized access to sensitive resources.

Lack of Device Security is another challenge imposed to protect IoT devices from physical and cyber threats. So, the organization must conduct device-level security measures, such as secure boot, tamper detection, and hardware-based security features, and apply security updates and patches regularly to address known vulnerabilities and mitigate emerging threats. Data Privacy and Protection Implement data encryption and anonymization techniques to protect sensitive information collected and processed by IoT devices. Adhere to data protection regulations, such as the General Data Protection Regulation (GDPR) and the California Consumer Privacy Act (CCPA), to ensure compliance and protect user privacy.

Likewise, the Supply Chain Risks and Insufficient Monitoring and Incident Response challenges force organizations and their administration to address these common security challenges and vulnerabilities through effective security controls. Consequently, organizations can enhance the resilience of their IoT and IIoT deployments and mitigate the risks associated with interconnected ecosystems.

4. CYBERSECURITY GOVERNANCE

4.1 Governance Frameworks in IoT and IIoT and Its Elements

Governance frameworks present structured methodologies and guidelines for establishing, implementing, and monitoring security controls and practices within organizations (Galaitsi, Trump, & Linkov, 2020). Therefore, they are extremely important in providing organizations with structured approaches for managing risks, ensuring compliance, and driving security initiatives. These governance frameworks suggest valuable guidance and best practices for establishing robust security systems and ensuring the confidentiality, integrity, and availability of data and systems in IoT and IIoT environments (Sedrati, Mezrioui, & Ouaddah, 2023; Qishun, 2023; Sedrati, Mezrioui, & Ouaddah, 2022).

In an environment that depends on IoT and IIoT, several major governance frameworks provide comprehensive frameworks for managing security risks and ensuring the resilience of connected environments. The ISO/IEC 27001, for example, contains policies, procedures, organizational structures, and technologies to manage information security risks effectively. It represents standards and systematic strategy for information security management, presenting a framework for establishing, implementing, maintaining, and continuously enhancing an Information Security Management System (ISMS) (Achmadi, Suryanto, & Ramli, 2018). Another example, NIST Cybersecurity Framework, developed by the National Institute of Standards and Technology (NIST), provides a common language for organizations to evaluate and manage cybersecurity risks, enabling them to align their cybersecurity measures with business purposes and regulatory requirements. A further example, COBIT (Control Objectives for Information and Related Technologies) developed by ISACA for governing and managing enterprise IT governance and management practices (Talab & Flayyih, 2023).

Typically, all the mentioned Governance frameworks have several essential elements that support security initiatives and ensure the effectiveness of security controls, as the following:

* **Policies and Procedures** define policies and procedures that summarize the organization's strategy for managing security risks, establishing standards, and implementing compliance with regulatory requirements. Consequently, these policies supply clear guidelines for security-related activities in the organization.

- **Risk Management** has processes for identifying, estimating, mitigating, and monitoring security risks and supplies methodologies and tools for achieving risk assessments, prioritizing risks, and implementing suitable risk countermeasures.
- **Roles and Responsibilities** define roles and responsibilities for individuals and stakeholders involved in managing security in the organization. for instance, assigning accountability for security-related activities, establishing reporting lines, and fostering a culture of security awareness and accountability.
- **Compliance and Assurance:** Governance frameworks provide mechanisms for monitoring and ensuring compliance with applicable requirements, and performing internal and external audits to evaluate the effectiveness of security controls.
- **Monitoring and Measurement Element** provides metrics and performance indicators for evaluating the effectiveness of security initiatives, identifying areas for improvement, and verifying compliance with security objectives and requirements.

4.2 Significance of Governance in Security for IoT and IIoT

On the one hand, The governance structure establishes the basis for a complete and coordinated technique for cybersecurity. In the IoT and IIoT environment, the organization must define clear roles, responsibilities, and accountability for security stakeholders (Alnahdi & Albalawi, 2023; Almalki, Alnahdi, & Albalawi, 2023). The Role Definition clarifies the roles of individuals and teams responsible for cybersecurity, including IT professionals, security analysts, compliance officers, and executives. Each role should have specific responsibilities and authority levels to ensure effective coordination and decision-making. The Responsibility Assignment gives specific security-related tasks and duties to relevant personnel based on their expertise and job functions. Hence, confirming all aspects of cybersecurity, including risk management, incident response, compliance, and security awareness, are adequately addressed. Also, the Accountability Framework holds individuals and teams accountable for their security-related actions and decisions. Therefore, the Accountability Framework defines performance metrics, conducts regular assessments, and implements consequences for non-compliance or security breaches.

On the other hand, effective governance structures ensure that security strategies are aligned with broader business objectives and priorities of organizations. For that, the organization relies on Business-Driven Risk Management to integrate security risk management practices into strategic planning processes to identify, assess, and mitigate risks that may influence business operations, financial performance, and reputation. Furthermore, the organization relies on Strategic Decision Making involving security leaders in strategic decision-making processes to ensure that security considerations are integrated into business initiatives (i.e. new product development, mergers and acquisitions, and digital transformation projects). This approach allows organizations to predict and address security implications early in the first stages, reducing the probability of high-cost security incidents. Also, the organization must adhere to Regulatory Compliance and Corporate Governance, which ensures compliance with relevant regulations, industry standards, and corporate governance requirements by aligning security practices with legal and regulatory obligations.

4.3 Ensuring Compliance and Regulatory Requirements

It is crucial to comply with regulatory requirements and industry standards when implementing IoT and IIoT solutions (Rizvi, Campbell, & Alden, 2020). Such deployments are subject to numerous regulations and compliance standards aimed at protecting data privacy, ensuring security, and mitigating risks. It is essential for organizations deploying IoT and IIoT solutions to understand and adhere to these regulations to avoid legal and financial consequences, protect consumer rights, and maintain trust and reputation (Dibaei & Ghaffari, 2017; Ivanchenko, Lepeshkina, Kulguskina, & Giniyatullin, 2022). Some of the key regulatory frameworks and standards relevant to IoT and IIoT security include: General Data Protection Regulation (GDPR), California Consumer Privacy Act (CCPA), Industry-Specific Regulations (ISR), and International Standards (Baik, 2020; Tankard, 2016; Palagashvili & Suarez, 2020).

The GDPR is one of the regulatory frameworks and standards relevant to IoT and IIoT security (Allegue, Rhahla, & Abdellatif, 2020). The GDPR implemented by the European Union (EU), demands strict requirements for the protection of personal data. Organizations collecting and processing personal data in IoT and IIoT environments must comply with GDPR principles, including data minimization, purpose limitation, and accountability (Tankard, 2016). Another regulatory framework, the CCPA, was implemented to enhance privacy rights and consumer protection for residents of the state of California in the United States. It provides consumers with rights regarding their personal information and sets duties on businesses that collect and process personal data that involve the collection of personal data from California residents.

The Industry-Specific Regulations where many industries, including healthcare, finance, and transportation, have specific regulations that govern the security and privacy of data. Organizations operating in these sectors must comply with industry-specific regulations, such as the Health Insurance Portability and Accountability Act (HIPAA) in healthcare or the Payment Card Industry Data Security Standard (PCI DSS) in finance (Moore & Frye, 2020; Seaman, 2020). Moreover, The International Standards where international organizations like the International Organization for Standardization (ISO) and the National Institute of Standards and Technology (NIST) publish guidelines and standards for cybersecurity and data protection. Adhering to internationally recognized standards, such as ISO/IEC 27001 for information security management or the NIST Cybersecurity Framework, demonstrates a commitment to best practices in IoT and IIoT security (White & Sjelin, 2022; Malatji, 2023).

4.4 Ensuring Compliance With Data Protection Regulations and Industry Standards

Organizations typically adopt the following strategies to ensure compliance with data protection regulations and industry standards in IoT and IIoT deployments, mitigate legal and regulatory risks, and protect the privacy and security of data collected and processed in an interconnected environment (Hamdani et al., 2021; Kasse, Xu, Devrieze, & Bai, 2019):

1. Conducting Regulatory Assessments: This involves examining data protection laws, industry regulations, and contractual obligations to specify appropriate regulatory requirements and evaluate the organization's compliance status.

2. Implementing Privacy by Design: This requires combining privacy and data protection principles into the design and development of IoT and IIoT solutions from the beginning. A Privacy by Design approach is adopted to emphasize data minimization, user consent, transparency, and security throughout the product lifecycle.

3. Establishing Data Governance Frameworks: This involves developing and implementing data governance frameworks that define policies, procedures, and controls for managing and protecting data in IoT and IIoT environments. This includes establishing data classification schemes, access controls, data retention policies, and incident response procedures.

4. Implementing Security Controls: Security controls and measures should be deployed to protect data and mitigate risks, in compliance with regulatory requirements and industry standards. Encryption, access controls, secure authentication mechanisms, intrusion detection systems, and regular security assessments are some of the security controls that can be deployed.

5. Providing Employee Training and Awareness: Employees and stakeholders must be educated about their roles and responsibilities in maintaining compliance with data protection regulations and industry standards. Training on privacy best practices, security awareness, and incident response procedures should be provided to promote a culture of compliance and vigilance.

6. Conducting Regular Audits and Assessments: Regular audits, assessments, and compliance reviews should be conducted to evaluate the effectiveness of security controls and ensure ongoing compliance with regulatory requirements and industry standards. This includes internal audits, third-party assessments, and vulnerability scans to identify and remediate compliance gaps.

5. CODE OF ETHICS IN IOT AND IIOT

5.1 Ethical Responsibilities in Cybersecurity

The integration of IoT and IIoT technologies into critical infrastructure, healthcare systems, transportation networks, and smart cities is increasing rapidly (Tzafestas, 2018). It is important to consider ethical implications and shape the societal influence of these innovations. A Code of Ethics can provide a framework for individuals and organizations involved in the design, implementation, and operation of IoT and IIoT systems. Such a code should emphasize principles of integrity, confidentiality, and professionalism. By establishing clear expectations and standards of conduct for stakeholders, a Code of Ethics can foster a culture of ethical behavior, transparency, and accountability. Security professionals always work to ensure integrity, confidentiality, and availability of data. They are authorized with the critical mission of safeguarding against cyber threats. Thus, they must obligate to different ethical considerations, such as the following:

*   **Protection of Privacy** consideration for individuals' rights to guarantee that personal data collected and processed by IoT and IIoT systems is managed ethically and legally. This includes implementing measures to anonymize or pseudonymize data, obtaining user consent for data collection and processing, and limiting access to sensitive information.

*   **Transparency and Accountability**, with the transparency consideration, the security professionals should disclose their actions and decisions, supplying clear descriptions of security measures and their implications for stakeholders. While, with accountability consideration, security profession-

als should be responsible for their actions, security incidents, and breaches and work to mitigate their impact.

- **Integrity and Honesty** are core values that guide security professionals to act with sincerity and truthfulness in all aspects of their work, avoiding conflicts of interest and refraining from engaging in unethical or dishonest behavior.
- **Professional Competence** which demands the security professionals to continuously learn, train, and grow their skills. That also includes staying informed about up-to-date threats, best practices, and industry standards.
- **Respect for Law and Regulations**, hence security professionals have to follow the relevant laws, regulations, and industry standards related to cybersecurity and data protection.
- **Ethical Decision-Making** compels security professionals to prioritize ethical considerations and values while making decisions if there are ethical difficulties or conflicts of interest. Therefore, security professionals must consider the possible impact of their actions on stakeholders, society, and the environment, and aim to uphold ethical principles and values.

The Code of Ethics highlights several essential security principles such as integrity, confidentiality, and professionalism, which are the basis of ethical behavior and practices for securing information assets (Shahraki & Haugen, 2018). Therefore, security professionals maintain ethical standards during developing a secure and reliable IoT and IIoT ecosystem, creating trust and confidence among users, stakeholders, and the general public. In addition, promoting ethical practices is important for cultivating a culture of responsibility, integrity, and trust in IoT and IIoT systems. Strategies such as training and education initiatives, and establishing codes of conduct and professional standards for ethical security practices are important in promoting ethical behavior among security practitioners. Investing in these initiatives empowers security practitioners to navigate ethical challenges and promote ethical behavior in IoT and IIoT environments.

For instance, comprehensive training and education initiatives equip professionals with the required knowledge, skills, and ethical principles. These initiatives usually include specialized Ethics training programs concentrating on ethical considerations in cybersecurity. In addition, real-world examples and difficulties can be used as Case studies and scenarios to engage participants and encourage critical thinking and ethical decision

making. Moreover, Role-Based Training or tailored programs for different job functions, addressing specific ethical challenges faced by security analysts, engineers, managers, and executives, should also be provided. On another side, Continuous Learning Opportunities such as workshops, seminars, and online courses should also be provided to stay updated on emerging ethical issues. Also, Certification and accreditation programs such as CISSP (Certified Information Systems Security Professional), CEH (Certified Ethical Hacker), and CISM (Certified Information Security Manager) should be available to support practitioners in validating their expertise in ethical hacking and information security governance (Marquardson & Elnoshokaty, 2020; Sinha & Arora, 2020).

5.2 Integrating Ethics into Organizations' Security Culture

Integrating ethics into the security culture of organizations is essential for supporting a culture of integrity, transparency, and ethical decision-making in IoT and IIoT environments. By integrating ethical principles into organizational values, policies, and practices, organizations follow responsible behavior, mitigate risks, and build high trust with stakeholders.

5.2.1 Establishing Codes of Conduct and Professional Standards

Establishing codes of conduct and professional standards supports ethical security practices and steers the behavior of security practitioners in IoT and IIoT ecosystems. Codes of conduct summarize the ethical principles, values, and expected behaviors that individuals and organizations should uphold, while professional standards define the competencies, responsibilities, and ethical responsibilities of security professionals. Therefore, the practitioners must consider some keys for establishing codes of conduct and professional standards like Collaborative Development Process which includes stakeholders across the organization in developing codes of conduct and professional standards such as security teams, legal experts, human resources, and executive leadership. This collaboration guarantees that the resulting guidelines reflect the organization's values, culture, and ethical priorities. Another Kay shows Clear Articulation of Ethical Principles and Values supporting the organization's approach to cybersecurity in IoT and IIoT environments, emphasizing principles such as integrity, confidentiality, transparency, accountability, and respect for privacy, and providing alignment with industry standards and regulatory requirements.

Moreover, Practical Guidance and Examples key illustrates the implementation method of ethical principles in different scenarios and contexts in addition to the usage of case studies, scenarios, and best practices to demonstrate ethical decision-making processes and facilitate adherence to ethical standards in day-to-day operations. Similarly, the key of Training and Awareness Initiatives ensures widespread understanding and adoption among security practitioners by integrating codes of conduct and professional standards into training and awareness initiatives, Offering training sessions, workshops, and resources that emphasize key ethical considerations and promote ethical behavior in cybersecurity practices. Also, Enforcement and Compliance Mechanisms key establishes mechanisms for monitoring, enforcing, and assessing compliance with codes of conduct and professional standards in addition to defining consequences for violations of ethical principles and provides channels for reporting ethical concerns or breaches of conduct in a confidential and non-retaliatory manner.

Following the aforementioned keys, Organizations can promote responsible cybersecurity practices by formulating a culture of ethics and integrity among their security practitioners. One way to achieve this is by establishing codes of conduct and professional standards, which mainly serve to build trust, maintain credibility, and foster ethical leadership in the digital reality. By following these guidelines, security practitioners can uphold ethical principles and contribute to a safer digital world in IoT and IIoT environments. Furthermore, Organizations must strengthen a culture of integrity and ethical decision-making to construct a strong security culture in IoT and IIoT environments by the following:

- **Leadership Commitment:** Leadership plays a crucial role in setting the tone for ethical behavior and decision-making within organizations. Senior executives and managers should demonstrate a strong commitment to ethics and integrity, leading by example and championing ethical principles in all aspects of their leadership.

- **Clear Ethical Guidelines:** Establish clear ethical guidelines, policies, and codes of conduct that articulate the organization's values, principles, and expectations regarding ethical behavior in cybersecurity practices. These guidelines should emphasize the importance of integrity, honesty, transparency, and accountability in all interactions and decisions.
- **Ethical Decision-Making Frameworks:** Provide security practitioners with frameworks and tools for ethical decision-making, such as ethical decision trees, decision matrices, or scenario-based training exercises. These resources help individuals navigate ethical dilemmas, assess potential risks and consequences, and make informed and ethical choices in challenging situations.
- **Training and Awareness Programs:** Offer training and awareness programs that educate employees about ethical considerations and obligations in cybersecurity. Use case studies, real-world scenarios, and interactive workshops to illustrate ethical principles in action and promote discussions about ethical decision-making in IoT and IIoT environments.
- **Recognition and Reward Systems:** Recognize and reward individuals and teams that demonstrate exemplary ethical behavior and decision-making in security practices. Establish incentives, awards, or recognition programs that celebrate ethical leadership, integrity, and adherence to ethical principles, reinforcing desired behaviors and values.
- **Ethical Role Models:** Highlight and celebrate ethical role models within the organization who exemplify integrity, professionalism, and ethical conduct in their work. Share success stories, testimonials, and examples of ethical behavior to inspire and motivate others to uphold ethical standards in their practices.

5.2.2 Encouraging Open Communication and Reporting of Ethical Concerns

Encouraging open communication and reporting ethical concerns is important for identifying and addressing ethical issues and breaches in security practices early. Besides, this is particularly important in IoT and IIoT environments as it can prevent potential harm and uphold ethical standards and values. Hence, the organization fosters trust, transparency, and integrity which enhances its reputation and credibility among stakeholders and the broader community. Therefore, Organizations can promote transparency, accountability, and ethical behavior by the following steps:

- **Establishing Reporting Mechanisms** such as ethics hotlines, anonymous reporting channels, or whistle-blower policies, enable employees to report ethical concerns or violations of ethical standards without fear of retaliation. Ensure that reported concerns are promptly investigated and addressed fairly and impartially.
- **Promoting Psychological Safety** involves creating an environment where employees are more comfortable speaking up about ethical concerns or challenging decisions that may compromise ethical principles. To achieve this, it is important to encourage open dialogue, active listening, and constructive feedback. This fosters an environment where diverse perspectives and dissenting opinions are valued and respected.

- **Training on Reporting Procedures** Provides training and guidance on reporting procedures and ethical reporting channels to ensure employees understand how to raise ethical concerns effectively and confidentially. Educate employees about their rights and protections as whistle-blowers and the organization's commitment to non-retaliation against those who report in good faith.

- **Responsive and Supportive Leadership** that demonstrate leadership's commitment to ethical conduct by promptly addressing reported ethical concerns, investigating allegations thoroughly, and taking appropriate remedial actions to address any identified violations or misconduct. Provide support and protection to employees who report ethical concerns, reassuring them of their importance in upholding ethical standards and values.

- **Continuous Improvement and Feedback** from employees about the effectiveness of reporting mechanisms and the organization's responsiveness to ethical concerns. The organization might use the feedback to identify areas for improvement, enhance reporting processes, and strengthen the organization's culture of ethics and accountability over time.

6. CONCLUSION AND FUTURE DIRECTIONS

Researchers are currently concentrating on addressing the challenges posed by the rapidly growing landscape of connected devices and systems in IoT and IIoT environments (Job & Paul, 2022). Likely, the most important research area is to develop advanced *Threat Intelligence and Detection* tools tailored specifically for IoT and IIoT environments by leveraging machine learning, artificial intelligence, and data analytics to detect anomalous behavior and potential security breaches in real-time (Sadhwani, Modi, Muthalagu, & Pawar, 2024; Nazir et al., 2024). Alike, *Blockchain and Distributed Ledger Technologies* enhances the security and integrity of IoT and IIoT systems. Research must explore how blockchain can be leveraged to establish trust, secure data transactions, and enable decentralized authentication and access control mechanisms in IoT and IIoT environments (Tyagi, 2024; Ali, Li, & Yousafzai, 2024; Chatziamanetoglou & Rantos, 2024). Also, there is a growing need for automation and orchestration solutions to streamline security operations and response processes. Research develop *Security Automation and Orchestration* methods to automate threat detection, incident response, and remediation workflows to enhance the agility and efficiency of cybersecurity operations in IoT and IIoT environments.

Apart from that, researchers must explore novel strategies for *Edge Computing Security* to secure edge devices, edge networks, and edge computing platforms, including secure bootstrapping, secure communication protocols, and lightweight encryption algorithms optimized for resource-constrained devices. Moreover, Research considers *Privacy-Preserving Technologies* and designs privacy-enhancing protocols, secure data aggregation techniques, and anonymization methods to protect sensitive data while still enabling valuable insights to be gleaned from IoT-generated data. Similarly, Researchers are exploring ways to enhance *Resilience and Robustness* of IoT and IIoT systems against cyber-attacks, physical tampering, and natural disasters. This includes developing adaptive security measures, redundancy mechanisms, and failover strategies to ensure continuous operation and data integrity in the face of unforeseen disruptions. It is worth mentioning that more efforts to develop *Standardization and Interoperability* protocols promote interoperability and compatibility among various IoT and IIoT devices, platforms, and ecosystems while ensuring robust security.

In terms of future directions and the essential trends, *Zero Trust Security Paradigm* and *Secure Supply Chain Management* could be included. The *Zero Trust Security Paradigm* will earn more attraction, wherein strict access controls, continuous authentication, and micro-segmentation are applied to IoT and IIoT environments to mitigate the risk of insider threats and lateral movement of attackers. Besides, *Secure Supply Chain Management* will become increasingly important to verify the integrity and authenticity of IoT devices, components, and software throughout their lifecycle.

Ultimately, the expansion of employed IoT and IIoT and how these technologies are being operated in different industries improve the importance of ensuring that the transmitted and saved data is safe, secure, and available when it is needed. Accordingly, this chapter covers different topics, starting with risk management. This means understanding and evaluating risks and ensuring that security frameworks are in place to manage those risks. The chapter briefs security control issues, like access control and encryption. It concentrates on common security challenges and how to handle and mitigate risks effectively. Governance frameworks are also important in IoT and IIoT security. This means confirming that everyone knows their roles and responsibilities and that security strategies are aligned with business goals. It is also important to follow regulatory requirements and industry standards. In the next section, the chapter shows the Code of Ethics in IoT and IIoT by showing that security professionals need to be ethical and how follow certain standards. This includes training and education, and everyone obeys ethical practices.

Overall, the chapter covers important issues for securing IoT and IIoT environments and discusses current research and future directions in IoT and IIoT cybersecurity.

REFERENCES

Abbas, M. M., & Merad-Boudia, O. R. (2022). *On ensuring data integrity in data aggregation protocols in iot environments.* IEEE. 10.1109/ICAEE53772.2022.9962093

Achmadi, D., Suryanto, Y., & Ramli, K. (2018). *On developing information security management system (isms) framework for iso 27001-based data center. 2018 international workshop on big data and information security (iwbis).*

Alagappan, A., Andrews, L. J. B., & Venkatachary, S. K. (2022, December 23). D, S., & Raj, R. A. (2022). Cybersecurity risks mitigation in the internet of things. *International Journal for Research in Applied Science and Engineering Technology*, 1–6. Advance online publication. 10.1109/CISCT55310.2022.10046549

Albouq, S. S., Abi Sen, A. A., Almashf, N., Yamin, M., & Alshanqiti, A. (2022). A survey of interoperability challenges and solutions for dealing with them in iot environment. *IEEE Access : Practical Innovations, Open Solutions*, 10, 36416–36428. 10.1109/ACCESS.2022.3162219

Alhassan, A.-B., Mahama, A.-H., & Alhassan, S. (2022). *Residue architecture enhanced audio data encryption scheme using the rivest, shamir, adleman algorithm.* The Research Institute of Advanced Engineering Technology.

Ali, S., Li, Q., & Yousafzai, A. (2024). Blockchain and federated learning-based intrusion detection approaches for edge-enabled industrial iot networks: A survey. *Ad Hoc Networks*, 152, 103320. 10.1016/j.adhoc.2023.103320

Allegue, S., Rhahla, M., & Abdellatif, T. (2020). *Toward gdpr compliance in iot systems.* Springer. 10.1007/978-3-030-45989-5_11

Almalki, L. S., Alnahdi, A. K., & Albalawi, T. F. (2023). The roles of stakeholders in internet of things: A theoretical framework. In *2023 1st international conference on advanced innovations in smart cities (icaisc)* (pp. 1–6). IEEE.

Alnahdi, A., & Albalawi, T. (2023). Role-driven clustering of stakeholders: A study of iot security improvement. *Sensors (Basel)*, 23(12), 5578. Advance online publication. 10.3390/s2312557837420743

Alshra'a, A. S., & Seitz, J. (2021). Towards applying ipsec between edge switches and end users to counter ddos attacks in sdns. In *2021 IEEE 23rd int conf on high performance computing & communications; 7th int conf on data science & systems; 19th int conf on smart city; 7th int conf on dependability in sensor, cloud & big data systems & application (hpcc/dss/smartcity/dependsys)* (pp. 1545–1551). 10.1109/HPCC-DSS-SmartCity-DependSys53884.2021.00229

Baik, J. S. (2020). Data privacy against innovation or against discrimination?: The case of the california consumer privacy act (ccpa). *Telematics and Informatics*, 52, 52. 10.1016/j.tele.2020.101431

Barrera, D., Bellman, C., & van Oorschot, P. C. (2022). Security best practices: A critical analysis using iot as a case study. *ACM Transactions on Privacy and Security*. 10.1145/3563392

Birkel, H. S., & Hartmann, E. (2020). Internet of things–the future of managing supply chain risks. *Supply Chain Management*, 25(5), 535–548. 10.1108/SCM-09-2019-0356

Chatziamanetoglou, D., & Rantos, K. (2024). Cyber threat intelligence on blockchain: A systematic literature review. *Computers*, 13(3), 60. 10.3390/computers13030060

Dhirani, L. L., Armstrong, E., & Newe, T. (2021). Industrial iot, cyber threats, and standards landscape: Evaluation and roadmap. *Sensors (Basel)*, 21(11), 3901. 10.3390/s21113901 34198727

Dibaei, M., & Ghaffari, A. (2017). Tsis: A trust-based scheme for increasing security in wireless sensor networks. *Majlesi Journal of Electrical Engineering*, 11(4), 45–52.

Dibaei, M., Zheng, X., Jiang, K., Abbas, R., Liu, S., Zhang, Y., Xiang, Y., & Yu, S. (2020). Attacks and defences on intelligent connected vehicles: A survey. *Digital Communications and Networks*, 6(4), 399–421. 10.1016/j.dcan.2020.04.007

Duo, W., Zhou, M., & Abusorrah, A. (2022). A survey of cyber attacks on cyber physical systems: Recent advances and challenges. *IEEE/CAA Journal of Automatica Sinica*, 9(5), 784–800.

Galaitsi, S., Trump, B. D., & Linkov, I. (2020). Governance for the internet of things: Striving toward resilience. *Modeling and Design of Secure Internet of Things*, 371–381.

Garah, A., Mbarek, N., & Kirgizov, S. (2022). *An architecture for confidentiality self-management in the internet of things*. Academic Press.

Hamdani, R. E., Mustapha, M., Amariles, D. R., Troussel, A., & Meeùs, S., & Krasnashchok, K. (2021). A combined rule-based and machine learning approach for automated gdpr compliance checking. In *Proceedings of the eighteenth international conference on artificial intelligence and law* (pp. 40–49). Academic Press.

Hossayni, H., Khan, I., & Crespi, N. (2021). Privacy-preserving sharing of industrial maintenance reports in industry 4.0. In *2021 IEEE fourth international conference on artificial intelligence and knowledge engineering (aike)* (pp. 17–24). IEEE.

Hromada, D., Costa, R. L. C., Santos, L., & Rabadão, C. (2023). Security aspects of the internet of things. In *Research anthology on convergence of blockchain, internet of things, and security* (pp. 67–87). IGI Global.

Ivanchenko, N. S., Lepeshkina, D., Kulguskina, M., & Giniyatullin, A. (2022). Internet of things and compliance control. *Vestnik Rossijskoj akademii estestvennyh nauk*. 10.52531/1682-1696-2022-22-2-116-122

Job, D., & Paul, V. (2022). Challenges, security mechanisms, and research areas in iot and iiot. *Internet of things and its applications*, 523–538.

Kang, J. J., Dibaei, M., Luo, G., Yang, W., Haskell-Dowland, P., & Zheng, X. (2021). An energy-efficient and secure data inference framework for internet of health things: A pilot study. *Sensors (Basel)*, 21(1), 312. 10.3390/s21010312 33466416

Kang, J. J., Dibaei, M., Luo, G., Yang, W., & Zheng, X. (2020). A privacypreserving data inference framework for internet of health things networks. In *2020 IEEE 19th international conference on trust, security and privacy in computing and communications (trustcom)* (pp. 1209–1214). IEEE.

Karatas, G., & Akbulut, A. (2018). Survey on access control mechanisms in cloud computing. *Journal of Cyber Security and Mobility*, 1–36.

Kasse, J. P., Xu, L., Devrieze, P., & Bai, Y. (2019). Verifying for compliance to data constraints in collaborative business processes. In *Collaborative networks and digital transformation: 20th IFIP WG 5.5 working conference on virtual enterprises, pro-ve 2019, Turin, Italy, september 23–25, 2019, proceedings 20* (pp. 259–270). 10.1007/978-3-030-28464-0_23

Khan, J. A. (2024). Role-based access control (rbac) and attribute-based access control (abac). In *Improving security, privacy, and trust in cloud computing* (pp. 113–126). IGI Global. 10.4018/979-8-3693-1431-9.ch005

Khan, R., McLaughlin, K., Laverty, D., & Sezer, S. (2017). *Stride-based threat modeling for cyber-physical systems. 2017 IEEE pes innovative smart grid technologies conference Europe (isgt-europe).*

Kim, J., Park, J., & Lee, J.-H. (2023). *Analysis of recent iiot security technology trends in a smart factory environment. 2023 international conference on artificial intelligence in information and communication (icaiic).*

Kim, K. H., Kim, K., & Kim, H. K. (2022). Stride-based threat modeling and dread evaluation for the distributed control system in the oil refinery. *ETRI Journal*, 44(6), 991–1003. 10.4218/etrij.2021-0181

Litvinov, E., Llumiguano, H., Santofimia, M. J., Del Toro, X., Villanueva, F. J., & Rocha, P. (2023). Code integrity and confidentiality: An active data approach for active and healthy ageing. *Sensors (Basel)*, 23(10), 4794. 10.3390/s2310479437430708

Liu, S., Dibaei, M., Tai, Y., Chen, C., Zhang, J., & Xiang, Y. (2019). Cyber vulnerability intelligence for internet of things binary. *IEEE Transactions on Industrial Informatics*, 16(3), 2154–2163. 10.1109/TII.2019.2942800

Malatji, M. (2023). *Management of enterprise cyber security: A review of iso/iec 27001: 2022. 2023 international conference on cyber management and engineering (cymaen).*

Marquardson, J., & Elnoshokaty, A. (2020). Skills, certifications, or degrees: What companies demand for entry-level cybersecurity jobs. *Information Systems Education Journal*, 18(1), 22–28.

Mnasri, S. (2022). *A new secure architecture for the access control of resources in iot networks. 2022 international conference on emerging trends in computing and engineering applications (etcea).* IEEE.

Moore, W., & Frye, S. (2020). Review of hipaa, part 2: Limitations, rights, violations, and role for the imaging technologist. *Journal of Nuclear Medicine Technology*, 48(1), 17–23. 10.2967/jnmt.119.22782731604900

Nazir, A., He, J., Zhu, N., Wajahat, A., Ullah, F., Qureshi, S., Ma, X., & Pathan, M. S. (2024). Collaborative threat intelligence: Enhancing iot security through blockchain and machine learning integration. *Journal of King Saud University. Computer and Information Sciences*, 36(2), 101939. 10.1016/j.jksu-ci.2024.101939

Palagashvili, L., & Suarez, P. (2020). *Technology startups and industry-specific regulations.* Fraser Institute.

Paolini, A., Scardaci, D., Liampotis, N., Spinoso, V., Grenier, B., & Chen, Y. (2020). Authentication, authorization, and accounting. *Towards Interoperable Research Infrastructures for Environmental and Earth Sciences: A Reference Model Guided Approach for Common Challenges*, 247–271.

Pathak, A. K., Saguna, S., Mitra, K., & Åhlund, C. (2021). Anomaly detection using machine learning to discover sensor tampering in iot systems. In *ICC 2021-IEEE international conference on communications* (pp. 1–6). 10.1109/ICC42927.2021.9500825

Phelps, R. P. (2022). *On security best practices, systematic analysis of security advice, and internet of things devices*. Carleton University., 10.22215/etd/2022-15268

Popescu, T. M., Popescu, A., & Prostean, G. (2021). Leaders' perspectives on iot security risk management strategies in surveyed organizations relative to iotsrm2. *Applied Sciences (Basel, Switzerland)*, 11(19), 9206. Advance online publication. 10.3390/app11199206

Qishun, Z. (2023). Enhancing reliability of iot adoption in e-government: A conceptual framework. *Journal of DigitainabilityRealism & Mastery*, 2(05), 38–44.

Qiu, J., Tian, Z., Du, C., Zuo, Q., Su, S., & Fang, B. (2020). A survey on access control in the age of internet of things. *IEEE Internet of Things Journal*, 7(6), 4682–4696. 10.1109/JIOT.2020.2969326

Ramachandra, M. N., Srinivasa Rao, M., Lai, W. C., Parameshachari, B. D., Ananda Babu, J., & Hemalatha, K. L. (2022). An efficient and secure big data storage in cloud environment by using triple data encryption standard. *Big Data and Cognitive Computing*, 6(4), 101. 10.3390/bdcc6040101

Rizvi, S., Campbell, S., & Alden, K. (2020). *Why compliance is needed for internet of things? In 2020 international conference on software security and assurance (icssa)*. IEEE.

Sadhwani, S., Modi, U. K., Muthalagu, R., & Pawar, P. M. (2024). Smartsentry: Cyber threat intelligence in industrial iot. *IEEE Access : Practical Innovations, Open Solutions*, 12, 34720–34740. 10.1109/ACCESS.2024.3371996

Seaman, J. (2020). *Pci dss: an integrated data security standard guide*. Apress. 10.1007/978-1-4842-5808-8

Sedrati, A., Mezrioui, A., & Ouaddah, A. (2022). Iot governance: A state of the art and a comparative analysis. In *2022 13th international conference on information and communication systems (icics)* (pp. 76–81). IEEE. 10.1109/ICICS55353.2022.9811219

Sedrati, A., Mezrioui, A., & Ouaddah, A. (2023). Iot-gov: A structured framework for internet of things governance. *Computer Networks*, 233, 109902. Advance online publication. 10.1016/j.comnet.2023.109902

Shahraki, A., & Haugen, Ø. (2018). Social ethics in internet of things: An outline and review. *2018 IEEE Industrial Cyber-Physical Systems (ICPS)*, 509–516.

Sinha, S., & Arora, D. Y. (2020). Ethical hacking: the story of a white hat hacker. *International Journal of Innovative Research in Computer Science & Technology*.

Talab, H. R., & Flayyih, H. H. (2023). An empirical study to measure the impact of information technology governance under the control objectives for information and related technologies on financial performance. *International Journal of Professional Business Review*, 8(4), 25.

Tankard, C. (2016). What the gdpr means for businesses. *Network Security*, 2016(6), 5–8. 10.1016/ S1353-4858(16)30056-3

Tawalbeh, L., Muheidat, F., Tawalbeh, M., & Quwaider, M. (2020). Iot privacy and security: Challenges and solutions. *Applied Sciences (Basel, Switzerland)*, 10(12), 4102. 10.3390/app10124102

Tyagi, A. K. (2024). Blockchain and artificial intelligence for cyber security in the era of internet of things and industrial internet of things applications. In *Ai and blockchain applications in industrial robotics* (pp. 171–199). IGI Global.

Tzafestas, S. G. (2018). Ethics and law in the internet of things world. *Smart Cities, 1*(1), 98–120.

Ullah, S., Zheng, J., Din, N., Hussain, M. T., Ullah, F., & Yousaf, M. (2023). Elliptic curve cryptography; applications, challenges, recent advances, and future trends: A comprehensive survey. *Computer Science Review*, 47, 100530. 10.1016/j.cosrev.2022.100530

Verma, S., Pokharna, M., & Mishra, V. (2022). Identifying and analyzing risk mitigation strategies in iot devices using light weight symmetric encryption algorithms. *International Journal for Research in Applied Science and Engineering Technology*, 10(9), 638–646. Advance online publication. 10.22214/ ijraset.2022.46697

Vuppala, A., Roshan, R. S., Nawaz, S., & Ravindra, J. (2020). An efficient optimization and secured triple data encryption standard using enhanced key scheduling algorithm. *Procedia Computer Science*, 171, 1054–1063. 10.1016/j.procs.2020.04.113

White, G. B., & Sjelin, N. (2022). The nist cybersecurity framework. In *Research anthology on business aspects of cybersecurity* (pp. 39–55). IGI Global. 10.4018/978-1-6684-3698-1.ch003

Chapter 2
Evolving Threat Landscape in IoT and IIoT Environments

Akashdeep Bhardwaj
https://orcid.org/0000-0001-7361-0465
University of Petroleum and Energy Studies, India

ABSTRACT

The meteoric rise of the internet of things (IoT) and industrial internet of things (IIoT) is reshaping our world, ushering in an era of hyper-connectivity and automation. This interconnected landscape, however, presents a significant paradigm shift in the cybersecurity landscape. This chapter delves into the unique challenges that this interconnected world presents, outlining the vulnerabilities inherent in IoT/IIoT environments and the evolving tactics employed by attackers to exploit them. The sheer scalability of these ecosystems presents a significant challenge. Billions of devices are projected to be online in the coming years, creating a vast and ever-expanding attack surface. This chapter explores some of the most common attack vectors employed by malicious actors. One prevalent threat is the formation of botnets. By compromising devices, attackers can create a distributed network with immense processing power. This processing power can then be harnessed for a variety of malicious purposes, such as launching denial-of-service (DoS) attacks or generating spam emails.

1. INTRODUCTION

The meteoric rise of the IoT (What Is the Internet of Things (IoT) & Why Is It Important?, n.d.) and IIoT (Team, n.d.) is reshaping our world, ushering in an era of hyper-connectivity and automation. This interconnected landscape, however, presents a significant paradigm shift in the cybersecurity landscape. This chapter delves into the unique challenges that this interconnected world presents, outlining the vulnerabilities inherent in IoT/IIoT environments and the evolving tactics employed by attackers to exploit them. Unlike traditional Information Technology (IT) (Traditional IT Systems, n.d.) infrastructure with a well-defined perimeter, IoT/IIoT ecosystems are characterized by convergence, blurring the lines between IT and Operational Technology (OT) (The Rise of Operational Technology, n.d.) systems. This conver-

DOI: 10.4018/979-8-3693-3451-5.ch002

gence creates a sprawling network of interconnected devices, ranging from simple sensors embedded in everyday objects to complex industrial machines that control critical infrastructure.

IoT and its industrial cousin, the IIoT, haven't been around for that long. While the seeds were planted with early inventions like the telegraph and the internet itself, the true concept of IoT emerged in the late 1990s. Early precursors to IoT existed. In the 1980s, a now-famous Coca-Cola vending machine at Carnegie Mellon University was connected to the internet, allowing users to see if drinks were cold and stocked before venturing out. However, widespread connectivity awaited advancements in wireless technologies like Wi-Fi and cellular networks, which arrived in the early 2000s. The term IoT was coined in 1999 by Kevin Ashton, who envisioned a world where everyday objects could communicate with each other. This period saw the development of the first truly connected devices for consumers, laying the groundwork for smart homes and remote appliance control. As connectivity boomed, so did security worries. Early IoT devices often lacked robust security features, making them vulnerable to hacking. This raised concerns about data privacy, with potential attackers able to access personal information or even take control of devices. The IIoT took hold alongside consumer IoT. Factories and industrial facilities began deploying connected sensors and machines to improve efficiency and automation. However, the stakes in industrial settings are much higher. A hacked IIoT system could disrupt critical infrastructure, cause physical harm, or even lead to environmental damage.

Cybersecurity threats in the IoT and IIoT space continue to evolve. As devices become more sophisticated and interconnected, attackers develop new techniques to exploit vulnerabilities. The vast number of connected devices also creates a massive attack surface for malicious actors.

The sheer scalability of the IT and OT ecosystems presents a significant challenge. Billions of devices are projected to be online in the coming years, creating a vast and ever-expanding attack surface. These devices, however, are often not designed with security as a primary concern. Resource constraints often limit their processing power, and they might lack the robust security features typically found in traditional IT systems. Additionally, the nature of these devices often deployed in remote locations or embedded within physical systems can make it difficult to implement and maintain security updates. This combination of factors limited processing power, weak security protocols, and infrequent updates creates a breeding ground for vulnerabilities that attackers can exploit. Cybercriminals are constantly refining their tactics to exploit the vulnerabilities inherent in IoT/IIoT environments. This chapter explores some of the most common attack vectors employed by malicious actors. One prevalent threat is the formation of botnets. By compromising devices, attackers can create a distributed network with immense processing power. This processing power can then be harnessed for a variety of malicious purposes, such as launching Denial-of-Service (DoS) attacks or generating spam emails.

Ransomware (Al-Hawawreh et al., 2024) is a major threat which encrypts critical data on connected devices, attackers can disrupt operations and hold businesses or even critical infrastructure hostage, demanding a ransom payment for decryption. The consequences of a successful ransomware attack on an IIoT system can be particularly devastating, potentially causing significant financial losses, operational downtime, and even physical damage. Beyond digital threats, the interconnected nature of IoT/IIoT systems also introduces the risk of physical tampering. By gaining direct access to devices, attackers can manipulate sensors, inject malicious code, or even cause physical damage to disrupt operations or steal sensitive data. The potential consequences of these threats are not merely theoretical.

Another critical area of focus is data privacy. The vast amount of data collected by IoT devices raises concerns about how this information is used, stored, and protected. Several international regulations play a crucial role in safeguarding user privacy as discussed below.

- General Data Protection Regulation (GDPR) is the regulation implemented by the European Union (EU) in 2018, sets a high bar for data protection. It applies to any organization processing the personal data of EU citizens, regardless of location. For IoT devices that collect user data, GDPR mandates transparency in data collection practices, strong user consent requirements, and robust security measures to protect sensitive information.

- California Consumer Privacy Act (CCPA) and California Privacy Rights Act (CPRA): Inspired by the GDPR, California enacted the CCPA in 2018 and the CPRA in 2020. These regulations grant California residents similar rights to access, delete, and opt-out of the sale of their personal data. Like the GDPR, the CCPA and CPRA have a significant impact on companies that collect data from California residents, including those involved in the development and deployment of IoT devices.

- Security Frameworks and Standards: While regulations like GDPR and CCPA focus on data privacy, a separate set of standards define best practices for securing IoT and IIoT environments. These standards provide a blueprint for manufacturers, developers, and users to follow, fostering a more secure ecosystem.

- ISO/IEC 27000 Series: This series of international standards, published by the International Organization for Standardization (ISO) and the International Electrotechnical Commission (IEC), provides a comprehensive framework for information security management. The standard outlines best practices for risk assessment, access control, data encryption, and other critical security controls. Applying these principles to the design, development, and deployment of IoT and IIoT solutions significantly enhances security.

- ETSI EN 303 645: This standard, developed by the European Telecommunications Standards Institute (ETSI), specifically addresses security requirements for consumer IoT devices. It mandates secure boot processes, software updates, and secure communication protocols. By adhering to this standard, manufacturers can build more secure devices and reduce the attack surface for malicious actors.

- NIST SP 800-161: The National Institute of Standards and Technology (NIST) in the United States has published special publications focused on IoT security. NIST SP 800-161 provides recommendations for supply chain security, identity management, and device hardening. These guidelines help ensure that best practices are implemented throughout the lifecycle of an IoT device, from design to deployment.

These international standards and regulations are having a profound impact on the way IoT and IIot devices are developed and deployed. Regulations like GDPR are forcing manufacturers to consider data privacy from the very beginning of the design process. This means built-in features for user consent, data minimization, and secure data storage are becoming essential components of any IoT device. Standards like ETSI EN 303 645 mandate specific security features. This incentivizes manufacturers to invest in secure boot processes, strong encryption, and regular software updates for their devices. NIST SP 800-161 emphasizes the importance of securing the entire supply chain for IoT devices. This ensures that vulnerabilities aren't introduced at any stage of the manufacturing and distribution process. Regulations like GDPR require transparency in data collection practices. This fosters accountability among manufacturers and incentivizes them to be more upfront about the data their devices collect and how it's used.

The chapter explores real-world examples of successful cyberattacks on IoT/IIoT systems. Breaches in critical infrastructure, such as power grids or transportation systems, can have a cascading effect, disrupting essential services and jeopardizing public safety. Even seemingly innocuous devices, such as smart home gadgets, can be compromised and used as a springboard for launching attacks on broader networks. These real-world examples serve as a stark reminder of the urgency for a proactive and agile approach to cybersecurity in this dynamic environment. Traditional security measures designed for IT systems, with a focus on perimeter defence, may not be sufficient to address the unique challenges of IoT/IIoT environments.

2. RELATED WORK

Industrial control systems integrate into vital industrial sectors that have an impact on our daily lives and monitor, automate, and run complex infrastructure and operations. These systems have transitioned from being specialized and independent to centralized corporate infrastructure with the introduction of networking and automation. Although this has made it easier to monitor and manage everything using conventional detection techniques, networks are now vulnerable to behavior-based cybersecurity assaults due to the use of Web Application Firewalls or Intrusion Detection Systems. Such assaults modify the processes and control flow, and they have the nefarious potential to completely change how these systems operate. This study (Bhardwaj et al., 2020) examines the efficacy of signature-based detection techniques and focuses on using process analytics to identify threats in industrial control infrastructure systems. The suggested study offers a pattern recognition technique called "Capturing-the-Invisible," or CTI, to identify behavior-based attacks being carried out in real-time and uncover hidden processes in industrial control device logs.

IoT and devices with internet access are being used more frequently as a result of greater internet connectivity. These Internet of Things gadgets are starting to form Industry 4.0's core. They are more susceptible to cyberattacks because of their reliance on IoT devices. IoT devices are frequently used in hostile environments, faced with energy-starved challenges, and faced with low computing costs. The crucial IoT ecosystem is more vulnerable to cyberattacks as a result of all these restrictions, which also make it difficult to implement accurate intrusion detection systems (IDSs) in IoT devices. This study (Computers, n.d.) introduces a unique feature selection approach and a new lightweight IDS to address the issues of accuracy and computational cost. The proposed strategy chooses the feature in the dataset with the highest statistical dependence and entropy reduction based on information theory models. With various classifiers, this feature selection technique also demonstrated a decrease in training time of 26-73% and an increase in performance metrics. When tested using the CICIDS2018 dataset, the suggested IDS with the algorithm demonstrated accuracy, precision, recall, and F1-Score of greater than 99%. In comparison to the most recent published studies, the suggested IDS is competitive in terms of accuracy, precision, recall, and training duration. The UNSWNB15 dataset demonstrated consistent performance from the proposed IDS.

While linking various communication devices was the primary function of the Internet in the early 2000s, in recent years, the emphasis has shifted to connecting objects to the Internet. An intricate network of devices, sensors, and things makes up the majority of the Internet of Things ecosystem, despite the fact that these items and equipment are not clearly categorized online. These objects use the current cloud infrastructure and are managed by people. These gadgets offer advantages to improve the comfort of our life. Smart wearables, smart cities, smart grids, industrial IoT, linked cars, smart homes, smart healthcare, and smart retail are some of the IoT domains. Human-to-IoT, IoT-to-IoT, and IoT-to-traditional systems designs are all included in various IoT models. Generally, the architecture establishes a connection with the unprotected Internet. This has made a number of important concerns visible, which could result in cybersecurity assaults against IoT devices. The architecture, protocols, or IoT connectivity were never designed to withstand modern cybersecurity threats. IoT devices have constrained memory, storage, networks, and processing power. The authors of this study (Bhardwaj et al., 2021) provide a novel IoT attack methodology called IAF, concentrating on how IoT threats affect IoT applications and service levels. Additionally, the authors suggested a comprehensive attack taxonomy that would categorize different IoT ecosystem threats.

Robot-based systems and procedures have incorporated data security and efficiency into a wide range of industries, including internet services, manufacturing, logistics, agriculture, and healthcare. There has been an increase in clever hacks that target corporate and industrial robotic systems in particular. As soon as industrial units deploy organization integration, internet of things, and internet, these threats take effect. For cyber-physical systems (CPS) with industrial components and embedded sensors that process information logs and processes, this research (Bhardwaj, Alshehri, Kaushik et al, 2022) created security criteria-based indices. The authors suggested an attack tree-based security architecture that accounts for the critical exploitable flaws needed to carry out the assaults, but does not encompass every CPS device. Using logs and data from a sensor indices device library, this study categorized every physical device and integrated sensor. This study used a two-phase procedure to mimic real-time vulnerability exploitation on CPS robotic systems utilizing the suggested architecture. This verifies that, in the event of a real-time cyberattack, the integrated sensor and physical nodes' improved data security output is validated by the intelligent monitor and controller system health monitor. This research used telnet pivoting and cross-site scripting to replicate common cyberattacks on cyber-physical controller systems. Using a tree-based attack method, the authors compiled known and new vulnerabilities and took advantage of them. The average time it takes for hackers with varying levels of expertise to break into CPS systems and devices was determined by the authors.

In order to replicate assaults aimed at compromising node and sensor data, the authors (Bhardwaj, Kaushik, Bharany, Elnaggar et al, 2022) constructed an attack scenario. In order to circumvent compromise detection, this research suggests a system with algorithms that creates automated malicious commands that adhere to device protocol requirements. Using three distinct house setting simulations, the authors tested attack detection and used the F1-Score as the metric for Accuracy of Detection, Ease of Precision, and Attack Recall. The K-Nearest Neighbor, Multilayer Perceptron, Logistic Regression, Random Forest, and linear Support Vector Classifier models were employed to produce the findings for anomaly detection of IoT logs and communications. The attack results showed false-negative replies for several models as well as false-positive responses with and without the suggested framework. Precision, Accuracy, F1-Score, and Recall were computed as attack-detection performance models in this study. Ultimately, the authors assessed a variety of abnormalities and contrasted them with the fraudulently generated log messages in order to assess the effectiveness of the suggested IoT communication protocol attack framework.

The Internet of Things has completely changed a number of facets of our daily lives, including cutting-edge healthcare services, automation and control over our living environments, and much more. Our lives have undergone drastic, disruptive changes as a result of the integration of digital Internet of things (IoT) devices and sensors with industrial systems, home appliances, and online services in the real world. These "things" on the Internet, or IoT, are generally accepted by the industry and by consumers at home. Nevertheless, the inherent and intrinsic consequences for security and privacy of data are not assessed. Industrial IoT (IIoT) security is still in its early stages. Although broad security goals can be addressed by techniques from security and privacy research, attacks on industrial equipment persist. This study (Bhardwaj, Kaushik, Bharany, Rehman et al, 2022) investigated the vulnerabilities of IIoT ecosystems as interconnected infrastructures of digital and physical systems interacting with the domains, rather than just as isolated nodes. In order to examine the threats on IIoT application settings, the authors provide a novel threat model approach. In order to assess privacy issues at the application level, the authors identified sensitive data flows inside IIoT devices and investigated device exchanges at the physical level. Ecosystems are unstable as a result of these two dangers. In addition, the writers examined the security of digital and physical realms.

The total security flaws or security lapses in the device, operating system, related software, and local infrastructure are added up to determine the threat surface area of Internet of Things devices. This compiles all known and unknown risks that could expose the device, data, hosted apps, logs, and logs. Device vulnerabilities can reduce the exposed threat surface area by minimizing the exposed portions of the device surface. In order to compute the maturity and severity levels of a device compromise, this research (Bhardwaj, Kaushik, Dagar et al, 2023) first maps all the devices inside the ecosystem, measures the possible threat surface area based on exposure indicators for each layer, and then identifies the threat vectors. To reevaluate and recalculate the maturity and severity levels, the authors suggest new measurements. Stakeholders involved in the design, implementation, and security ecosystem of smart devices might benefit from a new security viewpoint offered by newly disclosed threat surface elements, which are based on new measurements.

The Internet of Things (IoT) has become popular because to its ease of use, convenience, and intelligence. Lately, the industry has become more interested in user-favorite devices. An unprecedented number of IoT endpoints, including devices in our homes, are now connected to external networks as a result of the growing adoption of this technology. Usually, this kind of firmware is closed source and heterogeneous. Because security flaws affect systems more quickly and extensively, it is more difficult to identify and assess them at the firmware level. A number of similarity-based firmware security detection methods and instruments have emerged as prominent areas of research in recent years. The main priorities for IoT security equipment, especially IoT cameras, are security threats and issues. One of the areas of device security that has historically received the least attention is the firmware, making it vulnerable to unscrupulous actors. A novel twelve-step procedure for doing firmware analysis and security evaluation of Smart IoT-based camera devices was developed in this research (Bhardwaj, Kaushik, Bharany et al, 2023).

Applications and a bootloader on Internet of Things devices are in charge of setting up the hardware and installing the operating system or firmware. Making sure the bootloader is secure is essential to preventing malicious firmware or applications from being installed on the device. Utilizing digital signature verification to make sure that only approved firmware may be loaded into the device is one method to strengthen the bootloader's security. Furthermore, putting in place secure boot procedures like a chain of trust helps guard against manipulation during the boot process and stop unwanted access to the device's firmware. The most important stage in guaranteeing the security and integrity of these devices is the firmware bootloader and application dataflow taint analysis and security evaluation of IoT devices, which forms the basis of our research (Bhardwaj, Vishnoi, Bharany et al, 2023). This procedure aids in locating weak points and possible entry points for attackers, and it offers a framework for creating successful restoration plans.

In addition to improving our daily lives, smart home devices have introduced a disruptive and innovative Internet-based ecosystem. However, they have also forced private information from inside our houses into external public sources. Attacks and threats directed towards IoT deployments have only grown in the last few years. Although there have been many suggestions for securing home automation systems, our home IoT platforms are not completely safe from cybersecurity risks. The Internet of Things (IoT) network was the target of firmware, brute force, and denial-of-service (DoS) attacks that were successful in taking down the device in less than a minute. These attack efforts were examined in this research (Bhardwaj et al., 2024). Brute Force methods for the HTTP, SSH, Telnet, and FTP protocols were used to break weak passwords, and an unidentified service port was used to expose backdoor access. On Internet of Things devices, a cross-site scripting vulnerability was found that might enable the installation of malicious software. Additionally, the authors used the unidentified services to expose backdoors, obtain private device information, and possibly even add additional ports or rules to transform the Internet of Things devices into routers from which they could attack other devices. The authors present an IoT-based intrusion detection and prevention system to secure smart home network devices in order to identify and counteract such attempts. The authors contrasted the suggested framework with prior studies that were comparable in terms of precision, accuracy, recall, and F-measure. The suggested model exceeds all other existing models, with a high detection percentage of 95% for malicious attack packets, compared to other models' claimed detection percentages of 58% and 71%.

3. UNIQUE CHALLENGES OF INDUSTRIAL SYSTEMS

IoT and IIoT represent a paradigm shift, connecting billions of devices and creating a highly interconnected ecosystem. While this connectivity offers immense potential for automation, efficiency, and data-driven decision making, it also introduces unique challenges to security. Unlike traditional IT systems, IoT and IIoT environments present a complex attack surface with diverse devices, communication protocols, and OT often lagging in security measures.

One of the primary challenges is the sheer scale and diversity of interconnected devices. These devices can range from simple sensors to complex industrial controllers, each with varying levels of processing power, memory, and security capabilities. This heterogeneity makes it difficult to implement a one-size-fits-all security approach. Additionally, legacy systems integrated with newer IoT devices create vulnerabilities as older systems might have weaker security protocols or lack essential security features. Consider a connected factory with sensors monitoring temperature, pressure, and machine performance. An attacker might target a low-powered sensor with a simple exploit, gaining access to the network and potentially pivoting to more critical industrial control systems (ICS). Pseudo-code for Industrial Exploit is presented in Table 1.

Table 1. Pseudo-code for Industrial Exploit

```
def exploit_sensor(sensor_ip):
# Send a malformed packet to exploit a vulnerability in the sensor's firmware
send_packet(sensor_ip, exploit_data)
# If successful, gain access to the sensor and potentially the network
if exploit_successful():
access_granted = True
return access_granted
```

Many IoT and IIoT devices rely on lightweight communication protocols like Bluetooth Low Energy (BLE) or proprietary protocols designed for low power consumption and limited bandwidth. These protocols often prioritize efficiency over robust security features such as encryption and authentication. This creates opportunities for attackers to eavesdrop on communication, inject malicious commands, or manipulate data in transit. A smart thermostat connected to a home network might use a simple protocol to communicate temperature data. An attacker could intercept this communication and gain access to the thermostat settings, potentially disrupting the home's climate control. Algorithm for eavesdropping communication is presented in Table 2.

Table 2. Algorithm for Eavesdropping Communication

```
def eavesdrop_communication(target_device, protocol):
# Monitor network traffic for communication between the target device and its server
capture_packets(protocol)
# Analyze captured packets to extract data or identify potential vulnerabilities
analyze_packets(captured_data)
# If exploitable data is found, exploit the vulnerability
if exploit_found():
exploit_vulnerability(extracted_data)
```

Many IoT devices have limited processing power, memory, and battery life. Implementing complex security solutions on these devices can be challenging due to resource constraints. Legacy systems integrated with IoT devices might not have been designed with security in mind, creating vulnerabilities that are difficult or expensive to patch. A connected agricultural irrigation system utilizes older control panels for pump management. These panels lack robust security features, making them susceptible to brute-force attacks or manipulation by unauthorized users.

The evolving nature of the threat landscape poses a significant challenge. Attackers are constantly developing new techniques to exploit vulnerabilities in IoT and IIoT devices. Traditional security measures might not be effective against these evolving threats. New vulnerabilities are always discovered in IoT sensor-based operating systems. Attackers quickly develop exploits targeting this vulnerability, potentially compromising millions of devices before a patch is available.

Example 1: Buffer Overflow Vulnerability

Buffer overflow vulnerability (Bhardwaj et al., 2020) occurs when more data is written to a buffer than it can hold, potentially overwriting adjacent memory locations. This vulnerability could allow attackers to inject malicious code and potentially gain control of the sensor. Security researchers discovered the flaw during a routine penetration test and responsibly reported it to the vendor.

Imagine a temperature sensor in a building automation system running a vulnerable operating system. An attacker discovers a buffer overflow vulnerability in the system's network communication code. They craft a malicious packet containing specially crafted data that overflows a buffer and injects code to manipulate sensor readings. This could lead to disrupting building climate control or potentially triggering a false fire alarm. Buffer overflow vulnerabilities can have a severe impact on IIoT systems. They can allow attackers to manipulate sensor data, disrupt operations, or even cause physical damage. Table 3 presents the pseudo-code for Buffer Overflow in IoT Sensors.

Table 3. Pseudo-code for Buffer Overflow in IoT Sensors

```
def process_data(data):
buffer = [0] * 100 # Fixed-size buffer
for byte in data:
buffer.append(byte) # Vulnerable line - potential overflow
```

Algorithm steps for Buffer Overflow:

i Attacker sends a packet containing legitimate data followed by a carefully crafted sequence of bytes exceeding the buffer size.
ii The vulnerable code attempts to write all received data to the fixed-size buffer, causing a buffer overflow.
iii The attacker's crafted bytes overwrite the buffer's return address, redirecting program execution to the injected malicious code.
iv The injected code takes control of the device, allowing the attacker to manipulate sensor readings or perform other malicious actions.

Example 2: Integer Overflow Vulnerability

Integer overflow vulnerability (Butt et al., 2022) occurs when a mathematical operation results in a value exceeding the maximum representable value by the data type. This can lead to unexpected behavior and potentially code execution. This flaw allows attackers (Howell, 2024) to manipulate sensor readings and potentially compromise the safety of critical infrastructure. Security researchers identified and reported the issue to the vendor, who promptly issued a patch.

Consider a pressure sensor in an industrial pipeline monitoring system. The sensor OS has a vulnerability where a critical calculation involving pressure readings overflows an integer variable. An attacker exploits this to send a specially crafted message that overflows the variable, causing a jump in the program flow to a malicious code section. This code could manipulate pressure readings, potentially masking a real pressure build-up and leading to a safety hazard. Integer overflow vulnerabilities can lead to unexpected behavior in IIoT systems. In safety-critical applications, this can have serious consequences, potentially causing malfunctions or even physical damage. Table 4 presents the pseudo-code for Integer Overflow.

Table 4. Pseudo-code for Integer Overflow

```
def calculate_pressure(data):
pressure = int(data)
pressure += 1000 # Vulnerable line - potential overflow for high data values
if pressure > MAX_PRESSURE:
# Handle high pressure (may not trigger due to overflow)
...
return pressure
```

Algorithm steps for Integer Overflow:

i The attacker sends a message containing a pressure value slightly below the maximum representable integer.
ii The vulnerable code adds 1000 to the pressure value, causing an integer overflow.
iii Due to the overflow, the pressure variable wraps around to a very low value, bypassing the high-pressure check.
iv The program continues execution, potentially allowing the attacker to inject malicious code or manipulate sensor readings.

Strategies for Mitigating Evolving Threats:

- Secure by Design: Security should be considered throughout the entire lifecycle of an IoT device, from design and development to deployment and maintenance. This includes implementing secure coding practices, incorporating robust encryption and authentication mechanisms, and regularly testing for vulnerabilities.
- Least Privilege: Devices should have the minimum level of access required to perform their designated functions. This principle helps to limit the damage caused by a successful attack.
- Network Segmentation: Segmenting the network into different zones based on device type and function can help to isolate compromised devices and prevent lateral movement within the network.
- Continuous Monitoring: Continuously monitor network traffic and device activity for suspicious behavior. Anomaly detection systems can be used to identify potential threats in real-time.
- Patch Management: Regularly update device firmware and software with the latest security patches. This is crucial to eliminate vulnerabilities exploited by attackers.
- Secure Communication Protocols: Use secure communication protocols such as TLS (Transport Layer Security) or DTLS (Datagram Transport Layer Security) to encrypt data in transit and ensure message integrity. These protocols help to prevent eavesdropping, data manipulation, and unauthorized access.
- Secure Boot and Secure Enclave: Implement secure boot mechanisms to prevent unauthorized code from being loaded onto devices. Additionally, utilize secure enclave technology to isolate sensitive data and cryptographic operations, further enhancing security.

- User Authentication and Authorization: Implement strong user authentication and authorization mechanisms to control access to devices and data. Multi-factor authentication (MFA) is recommended as an additional layer of security.
- Threat Intelligence: Stay informed about the latest threats targeting IoT and IIoT devices. Utilize threat intelligence feeds to identify potential vulnerabilities and implement proactive security measures.
- Incident Response Planning: Develop a comprehensive incident response plan that outlines the steps to be taken in case of a security breach. This plan should include procedures for identifying, containing, eradicating, and recovering from a cyberattack.
- Addressing Legacy Systems: While securing legacy systems can be challenging, several strategies can be employed:

  - Segmentation: Isolate legacy systems from newer IoT devices to minimize the attack surface and prevent compromised devices from impacting critical systems
  - Port Control: Restrict network access to legacy systems by limiting inbound and outbound traffic to only authorized ports and protocols.
  - Vulnerability Assessment and Patching: Regularly assess legacy systems for vulnerabilities and prioritize patching critical vulnerabilities as soon as possible.

The interconnected nature of IoT and IIoT environments presents unique security challenges. By adopting a security-by-design approach, implementing the strategies outlined above, and continuously adapting to the evolving threat landscape, organizations can mitigate these challenges and build secure and resilient IoT/IIoT deployments.

4. ATTACK VECTORS IN IT/OT

The ever-growing landscape of IoT and IIoT devices presents a complex and evolving threat landscape. These interconnected systems offer a treasure trove of data and control capabilities, making them a prime target for malicious actors. This chapter explores new attack vectors exploiting vulnerabilities in these environments, along with the evolving tactics of prominent threat actor groups. Traditionally, cyberattacks focused on compromising IT infrastructure like servers and workstations. However, the explosion of IoT and IIoT devices introduces new attack surfaces with unique vulnerabilities. Emerging attack vectors are:

- Supply Chain Attacks: Attackers are increasingly targeting the supply chain of IoT and IIoT devices. This involves compromising a manufacturer's systems or processes to introduce malware or backdoors during the development or manufacturing stage. Once deployed, these devices become a backdoor for attackers to gain access to the target network or manipulate sensor data at the source. In 2020, a large-scale supply chain attack targeted a company that supplied GPS trackers for various industries. The attackers compromised the manufacturer's build server and injected malicious firmware into the trackers. This allowed them to track the location of targeted vehicles and potentially steal sensitive data.

Denial-of-Service (DoS) Attacks on OT: While DoS attacks are not new, their application to OT systems in IIoT environments poses a significant threat. Attackers can target critical infrastructure by overwhelming devices with junk traffic, disrupting their normal operation. This can have severe consequences, impacting power grids, manufacturing processes, or essential services. In 2021, a large-scale botnet attacks targeted wind farms across several countries. The attackers coordinated a DoS attack on the wind turbines' control systems, causing them to disconnect from the grid and disrupt power generation. Table 5 presents the Distributed Denial of Service algorithm.

Table 5. DDoS Algorithm

```
def ddos_attack(target_ip, attack_duration):
while time < attack_duration:
send_junk_traffic(target_ip)
```

- Man-in-the-Middle (MitM) Attacks on Encrypted Channels: The increasing use of encryption protocols in IoT and IIoT communication doesn't guarantee complete security. Sophisticated attackers might exploit vulnerabilities in encryption algorithms or key management practices to intercept data flowing between devices. This allows them to steal sensitive information or inject malicious commands into the network. In 2019, researchers discovered a vulnerability in a popular TLS implementation used in some IoT devices. This vulnerability, known as 'RoLBack', could potentially allow attackers to decrypt communication between devices and steal sensitive data like sensor readings or control commands.
- Side-Channel Attacks: These attacks exploit unintended information leaks from devices, such as power consumption or electromagnetic radiation. By analysing these leaks, attackers can potentially extract sensitive information like encryption keys or device functionality. Researchers have demonstrated side-channel attacks on smart meters, extracting encryption keys by analyzing the device's power consumption patterns during cryptographic operations. This could allow attackers to tamper with energy usage data or manipulate billing information. Pseudo code for side channel attacks is presented in Table 6.

Table 6. Pseudo-code for Side Channel Attack

```
def side_channel_attack(device, data_to_extract):
monitor_power_consumption(device)
while not data_extracted(monitored_data):
# Analyze power consumption patterns to extract information leaks
analyze_power_data(monitored_data)
return extracted_data
```

- Attacks on Machine Learning (ML) Models: As IIoT systems increasingly leverage machine learning for tasks like anomaly detection or predictive maintenance, they become vulnerable to attacks targeting these models. Poisoning training data or manipulating model inputs can lead to erroneous outputs, impacting decision-making and potentially causing operational disruptions.

Researchers have shown how adversarial machine learning attacks can be manipulated to exploit a predictive maintenance model in an industrial setting. By injecting subtly altered sensor data into the training data, attackers can cause the model to incorrectly predict healthy equipment as failing, triggering unnecessary maintenance shutdowns, and disrupting production. Table 7 presents the presudo code for training the data.

Table 7. Pseudo-code for Training Data

```
def poison_training_data(training_data, attack_vector):
for data_point in training_data:
if is_target_data(data_point):
manipulate_data(data_point, attack_vector)
return poisoned_data
```

The threat landscape is further complicated by the evolving tactics of various threat actor groups. Here's a glimpse into some prominent groups and their motivations:

- Nation-State Actors: Nation-state actors are increasingly targeting critical infrastructure in IIoT environments for espionage or disruption purposes. They possess sophisticated capabilities and resources, making them a serious threat to national security. In 2016, a cyberattack believed to be orchestrated by a nation-state actor targeted the Ukrainian power grid, causing widespread blackouts. This attack highlighted the vulnerability of critical infrastructure to cyberattacks and the potential for significant disruption by nation-state actors.
- Cybercriminal Groups: Financial gain is a primary motivator for many cybercriminal groups. They target IoT devices to steal sensitive data, disrupt operations for ransom, or launch large-scale botnet attacks. Ransomware attacks targeting connected medical devices pose a significant threat. In 2021, a cybercriminal group launched a ransomware attack against a healthcare provider, encrypting data on medical devices and disrupting patient care until a ransom was paid.
- Hacktivist Groups: Hacktivist groups are often motivated by ideology or activism. They might target IoT devices to disrupt operations of companies they disagree with or raise awareness about a particular cause. In 2020, a hacktivist group targeted a network of smart thermostats, causing widespread disruption to home heating systems as a form of protest.
- Insider Threats: Disgruntled employees or individuals with authorized access can pose a significant threat to IoT and IIoT security. They can leverage their insider knowledge to bypass security controls and gain unauthorized access to sensitive data or manipulate critical systems. In 2018, a disgruntled employee at a casino gained access to the building management system through an IoT device. The employee used this access to manipulate the temperature controls, causing discomfort for patrons and disrupting casino operations.

5. RANSOMWARE ATTACKS ON INDUSTRIAL SYSTEMS

The rise of ransomware attacks has become a defining threat of the digital age, and industrial systems are increasingly becoming prime targets. Unlike traditional IT systems, industrial control systems (ICS) often lack robust security measures, making them vulnerable to encryption and disruption by ransomware actors. This chapter delves into the growing threat of ransomware in IIoT environments, exploring real-time examples, attack methodologies, and potential mitigation strategies.

Ransomware attacks on industrial systems often follow a multi-stage process:

i Initial Compromise: Attackers gain initial access to the network through various means, such as phishing campaigns, exploiting vulnerabilities in unpatched software, or targeting internet-facing devices.

ii Lateral Movement: Once inside the network, attackers use various techniques to move laterally, compromising additional systems and escalating their privileges.

iii Identifying Targets: Attackers identify and target critical industrial control systems within the network.

iv Deployment and Encryption: Ransomware is deployed on these systems, encrypting critical data and disrupting operations.

v Ransom Demand: Attackers issue a ransom demand, threatening to keep the data encrypted or release it publicly unless the ransom is paid.

Ransomware actors are drawn to industrial systems for several reasons:

- High Impact: Disruptions to industrial operations can have significant financial consequences for companies. Production downtime, product spoilage, and reputational damage create a high pressure to pay ransom demands.

- Limited Redundancy: Many industrial systems rely on legacy equipment and lack robust backup and recovery mechanisms. This limited redundancy makes them more susceptible to the pressure of restoring operations quickly, even if it means paying a ransom.

- Convergence of IT and OT: The increasing convergence of IT and OT networks creates a larger attack surface for ransomware actors. By compromising a single IT system, attackers can potentially gain access to critical industrial control systems.

In 2021, a major oil pipeline operator in the United States fell victim to a ransomware attack. The attack disrupted pipeline operations, leading to fuel shortages and price hikes across the country. The company ultimately paid a significant ransom to regain control of their systems. In 2020, a ransomware attack targeted a large-scale water treatment facility. Attackers gained initial access through a phishing email and then moved laterally through the network until they reached the control systems for the water treatment process. They encrypted critical data related to water treatment operations and demanded a ransom in exchange for the decryption key. This attack highlighted the potential impact of ransomware on critical infrastructure and the disruption it can cause to essential services. Table 8 presents the pseudo code for ransomware attack.

Table 8. Pseudo-code for Ransomware Attack

```
def deploy_ransomware(target_system):
# Establish connection to the target system
connect(target_system)
# Download and execute ransomware payload
download_payload()
execute_payload()
# Encrypt target data
encrypt_data(target_system)
# Display ransom message
display_ransom_message()
```

Algorithm steps involved are:

i.   Attackers launch a phishing campaign targeting employees with access to the network.

ii. An employee clicks a malicious link in a phishing email, unknowingly downloading malware onto their device.

iii. The malware exploits a vulnerability in the employee's device and establishes a foothold on the network.

iv. Attackers use the compromised device to move laterally through the network, identifying and exploiting additional vulnerabilities.

v.   Once they reach critical industrial control systems, attackers deploy the ransomware payload, encrypting data and disrupting operations.

vi. A ransom message is displayed demanding payment in exchange for the decryption key.

Mitigating the risk of ransomware attacks on industrial systems requires a multi-layered approach:

- Network Segmentation: Segmenting the network to isolate critical ICS from less secure IT systems can limit the attacker's ability to move laterally and reach control systems.

- Patch Management: Regularly update device firmware and software with the latest security patches to address known vulnerabilities that attackers might exploit to gain initial access.

- Strong Passwords and Access Control: Implement strong password policies and enforce least privilege access control to limit the damage caused by compromised credentials.

- User Education and Awareness: Train employees on cybersecurity best practices, including identifying phishing attempts and avoiding suspicious links or email attachments.

- Backups and Disaster Recovery: Maintain regular backups of critical data and have a well-defined disaster recovery plan that outlines the steps to recover from a ransomware attack. This minimizes downtime and reduces the pressure to pay a ransom.

- Cybersecurity Assessments and Threat Intelligence: Conduct regular cybersecurity assessments to identify vulnerabilities in the system and stay informed about the latest ransomware threats targeting industrial systems.

- Zero-Trust Security: Implementing a zero-trust security model can further enhance security. This approach assumes no device or user is inherently trustworthy and requires continuous verification before granting access to critical systems. A large manufacturing company implemented a zero-trust security model for its industrial control systems. The model required multi-factor authentication and continuous monitoring of user activity. This approach helped prevent a ransomware attack when an attacker gained access to an employee's device through a phishing email. The zero-trust security measures prevented the attacker from moving laterally and deploying ransomware on the control systems.

- Advanced Threat Detection and Response (AT&DR): Utilizing advanced threat detection and response solutions can help organizations identify and respond to ransomware attacks in real-time. These solutions can detect suspicious activity indicative of ransomware deployment and potentially stop the attack before critical data is encrypted.

The battle against ransomware is an ongoing arms race. As attackers develop new techniques, organizations need to continuously adapt their security posture. By implementing a comprehensive security strategy, staying informed about the latest threats, and fostering a culture of cybersecurity awareness among employees, organizations can build resilience against ransomware attacks and protect their critical industrial systems.

6. PHYSICAL TAMPERING ATTACKS

The interconnected nature of IoT and IIoT environments extends beyond the digital realm. Physical access to devices and systems introduces another layer of vulnerability - the risk of physical tampering attacks. Unlike cyberattacks that exploit software weaknesses, physical tampering attacks involve directly manipulating hardware components or altering physical security measures. This chapter explores the growing concern of physical tampering in IIoT environments, examining real-world examples, attack methodologies, and strategies for mitigating these threats.

Several factors motivate individuals to physically tamper with industrial systems and devices:

- Industrial Espionage: Competitors might seek to steal proprietary information or intellectual property by tampering with control systems or extracting data from devices.
- Disruption and Sabotage: Disgruntled employees, activists, or criminals might tamper with systems to disrupt operations, cause damage, or create safety hazards.
- Data Manipulation: Tampering with sensors or other data acquisition devices can lead to manipulated data being fed into the system, potentially impacting decision-making and control processes.
- Covert Operations: In some cases, physical tampering might be used as part of a larger cyberattack strategy. Attackers could tamper with devices to establish a foothold in the network or bypass security controls.

In 2010, the Stuxnet worm, a sophisticated cyberattack believed to be orchestrated by a nation-state, targeted Iranian nuclear facilities. While Stuxnet itself was a software attack, it's believed that physical tampering might have been used to disable safety mechanisms within the centrifuges, allowing the malware to cause more significant damage.

Physical tampering attacks can take various forms, depending on the attacker's skill level, access, and objectives, the methods include:

- Direct Hardware Modification: Attackers might physically modify hardware components like circuit boards or memory chips to alter their functionality or steal sensitive data.
- Data Port Manipulation: Tampering with data ports or cables can allow attackers to intercept or modify data flowing between devices.

- Covert Hardware Implants: Sophisticated attackers might implant malicious hardware devices within systems to gain unauthorized access or manipulate data.
- Environmental Manipulation: Tampering with the physical environment surrounding devices, such as temperature or humidity, can potentially exploit vulnerabilities or cause malfunctions.

In 2014, a group of hackers gained physical access to a casino's thermostat system. They manipulated the thermostats to cause discomfort for patrons, hoping to disrupt operations and potentially force the casino to close. This incident highlights how seemingly minor physical tampering can have significant consequences as shown in Table 9.

Table 9. Pseudo-code for Sensor Tempering

```
def modify_sensor_reading(sensor, target_value):
# Gain physical access to the sensor
access_sensor(sensor)
# Identify component responsible for reading data (illustrative)
modify_resistor_value(sensor_component, target_value)
# This modification alters the sensor's output to reflect the target value
```

Algorithm steps include the following:

i Attacker gains physical access to a critical sensor in an industrial system (through infiltration, social engineering, etc.).

ii The attacker identifies the component within the sensor responsible for reading data (e.g., a resistor).

iii Using specialized tools or techniques, the attacker modifies the component's value, altering the sensor's output.

iv The tampered sensor now transmits manipulated data to the system, potentially impacting control processes or decision-making.

The consequences of a successful physical tampering attack can be severe:

- Operational Disruptions: Tampering with control systems can disrupt critical processes, leading to production downtime and financial losses.
- Safety Hazards: In some cases, tampering can create safety hazards, such as equipment malfunctions or environmental incidents.
- Data Integrity Issues: Altered sensor readings or manipulated data can lead to inaccurate information being used for decision-making, potentially compromising safety or efficiency.
- Loss of Intellectual Property: Attackers might steal sensitive information or proprietary control algorithms through physical tampering.

7. PROPOSED SECURE FRAMEWORK (ZTSF)

Traditional security approaches in IIoT often rely on perimeter defenses like firewalls and intrusion detection systems (IDS). While these play a role, they have limitations:

- Static Defenses: Attackers can exploit vulnerabilities in perimeter defenses or find ways to bypass them altogether.
- Limited Visibility: Traditional approaches might not provide complete visibility into all devices and communication within the network, especially with the growing number and diversity of devices in IIoT.
- Lack of Granularity: Perimeter controls offer a one-size-fits-all approach, which might not be suitable for the varying security needs of different devices and systems within an IIoT environment.

The ever-expanding attack surface of IIoT environments necessitates a paradigm shift in security strategies. Traditional perimeter-based defenses struggle to address the dynamic nature of interconnected devices and the evolving tactics of attackers. This chapter proposes a unique secure framework - the Zero-Trust Segmentation Framework (ZTSF) - specifically designed to mitigate attacks on industrial systems and devices within IIoT environments. ZTSF leverages the principles of zero trust and network segmentation to create a multi-layered defense specifically tailored to the dynamic nature of IIoT. Here's a breakdown of the core principles:

- Zero Trust: No device or user is inherently trusted within the network. Continuous verification and authorization are required for any access attempt.
- Segmentation: The network is divided into micro-segments, isolating critical industrial control systems (ICS) from less secure devices and IT systems.

Imagine a large power generation facility. Traditionally, a firewall might be used to protect the entire network. However, the ZTSF would segment the network. One segment would isolate the critical ICS responsible for controlling power generation. Another segment would house less critical IT systems used for administrative tasks. This segmentation minimizes the potential damage if an attacker gains access to a less secure device, as they would be restricted from reaching the critical ICS.

ZTSF implements several layers of security to create a holistic defense:

- Microsegmentation: Network segmentation is taken a step further by creating micro-segments that isolate individual devices or groups of devices with similar functionality. This minimizes the blast radius of a potential attack.
- Continuous Authentication and Authorization (CaaA): All access attempts, regardless of source (user or device), are continuously authenticated and authorized before granting access. This ensures only authorized devices and users can access specific resources within the network, the proposed pseudo code for secure framework is shown in Table 10.

Table 10. Pseudo-code ZTSF

```
def access_control(device, request):
# Verify device identity and authorization level
verify_device_credentials(device)
# Check if request is authorized for the device's segment and access level
if authorized(request, device_segment, device_access_level):
grant_access(device, request)
else:
deny_access(device)
```

- Least Privilege Access Control: The principle of least privilege is strictly enforced. Devices and users are granted only the minimum level of access required to perform their designated functions. This minimizes the potential damage caused by compromised credentials.
- Policy-Based Security: Security policies are defined to govern access control, data flow, and device behavior within each micro-segment. This allows for granular control over security measures based on the specific needs of each segment.
- Continuous Monitoring and Threat Detection: Advanced threat detection and response (AT&DR) solutions are deployed to continuously monitor network activity for suspicious behavior that might indicate an attack.

Example: A manufacturing facility implements the ZTSF. Sensors on the production line are placed in a micro-segment isolated from the network management systems used by IT staff. This ensures that even if an attacker compromises a device used for network management, they wouldn't be able to access or manipulate the critical sensors controlling the production line.

ZTSF offers several advantages over traditional security approaches:

- Reduced Attack Surface: Micro-segmentation limits the potential impact of an attack by restricting lateral movement within the network.
- Enhanced Visibility: Continuous monitoring provides deeper insights into network activity, allowing for faster detection and response to threats.
- Granular Control: Policy-based security allows for tailored security measures based on the specific needs of each device and segment.
- Improved Resilience: ZTSF creates a more resilient network architecture, better equipped to withstand attacks and minimize potential damage.
- Network Assessment: A comprehensive network assessment is crucial to identify critical assets, understand device communication flows, and determine segmentation strategies.
- Technology Selection: Selecting the right security technologies to implement micro-segmentation, CaaA, and continuous monitoring is essential. Software-defined networking (SDN) and network function virtualization (NFV) can play a significant role in enabling micro-segmentation and dynamic policy enforcement.
- Policy Development: Security policies need to be established to define access control rules, data flow restrictions, and device behavior within each micro-segment.
- Integration and Automation: Security solutions should be integrated to enable automated threat detection, response, and policy enforcement across the network.

- User Training and Awareness: Educating users on the ZTSF principles and secure practices within the new security framework is crucial for its success.

Example: A chemical manufacturing plant decides to implement the ZTSF. The first step involves a network assessment to identify critical control systems for chemical processing. Next, the network is segmented, isolating these critical systems from other devices like human-machine interface (HMI) terminals and engineering workstations. Security policies are defined to restrict communication between segments and enforce least privilege access control. Finally, the security team integrates SIEM and threat intelligence solutions to monitor network activity for suspicious behavior and enable a swift response to potential attacks.

ZTSF is a dynamic framework that needs continuous improvement as technologies and threats evolve. Here are some key considerations for the future:

- Integration with IoT Security Standards: As new IoT security standards emerge, like those from the Industrial Internet Consortium (ICII), the ZTSF should be adaptable to incorporate these standards and best practices.
- Zero-Trust Identity and Access Management (ZT-IAM): Integrating ZT-IAM solutions can further strengthen access control mechanisms within the ZTSF by focusing on identity verification and authorization beyond just devices.
- Leveraging ML for Threat Detection: Utilizing machine learning algorithms for anomaly detection within network traffic can enhance the ZTSF's ability to identify and respond to novel threats.

8. FUTURE SCOPE

The dynamic world of IoT and IIoT security is constantly evolving, with ongoing research exploring innovative solutions to address emerging threats. Potential predictions and exciting research directions to consider are:

- **AI-powered Security:** Artificial intelligence (AI) and machine learning (ML) hold immense potential for enhancing IoT/IIoT security. AI systems can analyze vast amounts of data to detect anomalies, identify suspicious behavior, and predict potential attacks. This proactive approach could revolutionize threat detection and response, allowing systems to learn and adapt to ever-changing threatscapes.
- **Blockchain for Secure Data Management:** Blockchain technology, known for its secure distributed ledger system, could play a crucial role in securing data exchange within the IoT/IIoT ecosystem. By creating a tamper-proof record of transactions, blockchain can ensure data integrity and prevent unauthorized access. This technology could be particularly valuable for securing sensitive industrial data collected by IIoT devices.
- **Zero-Trust Security Models:** The traditional perimeter-based security model might not be enough for the complex and interconnected world of IoT. Zero-trust security models, where every device and user must be continuously authenticated before granting access, are gaining traction. This approach can significantly reduce the attack surface and minimize the potential damage from breaches.

- **Quantum Challenge:** The rise of quantum computing presents a significant challenge for current encryption methods used in IoT/IIoT security. Quantum computers can potentially break the encryption algorithms that safeguard data communication. Research is ongoing to develop post-quantum cryptography (PQC) algorithms that are resistant to attacks from quantum computers. Securing the future of IoT/IIoT will require a proactive transition to PQC standards.
- **Security by Design:** The concept of "security by design" will continue to be paramount. Security considerations need to be embedded throughout the entire lifecycle of an IoT/IIoT device, from initial design to development, deployment, and maintenance. This holistic approach will ensure that security is not an afterthought but a fundamental principle guiding the development of all connected devices.

The future of IoT/IIoT security is brimming with exciting possibilities. From leveraging AI and blockchain to embracing zero-trust models and preparing for the quantum challenge, the security landscape is constantly adapting. By prioritizing security by design and fostering ongoing research in these critical areas, we can build a more secure and trustworthy foundation for the interconnected world of the future.

CONCLUSIONS AND REMARKS

By adopting a proactive and multifaceted approach, organizations can mitigate the risks associated with IoT/IIoT deployments and ensure the secure and reliable operation of these interconnected systems in the years to come. ZTSF presents a unique and adaptable security framework specifically designed to address the challenges of securing IIoT environments. By combining zero-trust principles with micro-segmentation, continuous monitoring, and policy-based controls, the ZTSF offers a holistic defense against a wide range of threats targeting industrial systems and devices. As IIoT continues to evolve, so too must security strategies. The ZTSF provides a strong foundation for building a resilient and secure future for industrial automation and control systems.

REFERENCES

Al-Hawawreh, M., Alazab, M., Ferrag, M. A., & Hossain, M. S. (2024, March). Securing the Industrial Internet of Things against ransomware attacks: A comprehensive analysis of the emerging threat landscape and detection mechanisms. *Journal of Network and Computer Applications*, 223, 103809. 10.1016/j.jnca.2023.103809

Bhardwaj, A., Alshehri, M. D., Kaushik, K., Alyamani, H. J., & Kumar, M. (2022, March). Secure framework against cyber attacks on cyber-physical robotic systems. *Journal of Electronic Imaging*, 31(06). Advance online publication. 10.1117/1.JEI.31.6.061802

Bhardwaj, A., Bharany, S., Abulfaraj, A. W., Osman Ibrahim, A., & Nagmeldin, W. (2024, March). Fortifying home IoT security: A framework for comprehensive examination of vulnerabilities and intrusion detection strategies for smart cities. *Egyptian Informatics Journal*, 25, 100443. 10.1016/j.eij.2024.100443

Bhardwaj, A., Kaushik, K., Bharany, S., Elnaggar, M. F., Mossad, M. I., & Kamel, S. (2022, September). Comparison of IoT Communication Protocols Using Anomaly Detection with Security Assessments of Smart Devices. *Processes (Basel, Switzerland)*, 10(10), 1952. 10.3390/pr10101952

Bhardwaj, A., Kaushik, K., Bharany, S., & Kim, S. K. (2023, December). Forensic analysis and security assessment of IoT camera firmware for smart homes. *Egyptian Informatics Journal*, 24(4), 100409–100409. 10.1016/j.eij.2023.100409

Bhardwaj, A., Kaushik, K., Bharany, S., Rehman, A. U., Hu, Y.-C., Eldin, E. T., & Ghamry, N. A. (2022, November). IIoT: Traffic Data Flow Analysis and Modeling Experiment for Smart IoT Devices. *Sustainability (Basel)*, 14(21), 14645. 10.3390/su142114645

Bhardwaj, A., Kaushik, K., Dagar, V., & Kumar, M. (2023, August). Framework to measure and reduce the threat surface area for smart home devices. *Advances in Computational Intelligence*, 3(4), 16. Advance online publication. 10.1007/s43674-023-00062-2

Bhardwaj, A., Kumar, M., Stephan, T., Shankar, A., Ghalib, M. R., & Abujar, S. (2021, October). IAF: IoT Attack Framework and Unique Taxonomy. *Journal of Circuits, Systems, and Computers*, 31(02), 2250029. Advance online publication. 10.1142/S0218126622500293

Bhardwaj, A., Vishnoi, A., Bharany, S., Abdelmaboud, A., Ibrahim, A. O., Mamoun, M., & Nagmeldin, W. (2023, December). Framework to perform taint analysis and security assessment of IoT devices in smart cities. *PeerJ. Computer Science*, 9, e1771. 10.7717/peerj-cs.177138192478

Bhardwaj, F., Al-Turjman, F., Kumar, M., Stephan, T., & Mostarda, L. (2020). Capturing-the-Invisible (CTI): Behavior-Based Attacks Recognition in IoT-Oriented Industrial Control Systems. *IEEE Access : Practical Innovations, Open Solutions*, 8, 104956–104966. 10.1109/ACCESS.2020.2998983

Butt, M. A., Ajmal, Z., Khan, Z. I., Idrees, M., & Javed, Y. (2022, July). An In-Depth Survey of Bypassing Buffer Overflow Mitigation Techniques. *Applied Sciences (Basel, Switzerland)*, 12(13), 6702. 10.3390/app12136702

Computers. (n.d.). *Efficient, Lightweight Cyber Intrusion Detection System for IoT Ecosystems Using MI2G Algorithm.* https://www.mdpi.com/2073-431X/11/10/142/review_report

Howell, J. (2024). *An Overview of Integer Overflow Attacks*. 101 Blockchains. https://101blockchains .com/integer-overflow-attacks/

Team, N. (n.d.). *IIoT Explained: Examples, Technologies, Benefits and Challenges*. https://www.emqx .com/en/blog/iiot-explained-examples-technologies-benefits-and-challenges

The Rise of Operational Technology: Why Businesses Need to Focus on OT Now More Than Ever. (n.d.). https://www.linkedin.com/pulse/rise-operational-technology-ot-why-businesses-need-focus-padam-kafle/

Traditional IT Systems: A Comprehensive Analysis of Their Drawbacks. (n.d.). https://www.linkedin .com/pulse/traditional-systems-comprehensive-analysis-drawbacks-muntakim-pwvqc/

What Is the Internet of Things (IoT) & Why Is It Important? (n.d.). IMD business school for management and leadership courses. https://www.imd.org/reflections/internet-of-things/

Chapter 3
A Comprehensive Review of Internet–of–Things (IoT) Botnet Detection Techniques

Ivonne Kuma Nketia
ⓘ http://orcid.org/0009-0003-8320-2475
University of Ghana, Ghana

Winfred Yaokumah
ⓘ http://orcid.org/0000-0001-7756-1832
University of Ghana, Ghana

Justice Kwame Appati
ⓘ http://orcid.org/0000-0003-2798-4524
University of Ghana, Ghana

ABSTRACT

This chapter conducts a comprehensive empirical review of internet of things (IoT) botnet detection to identify gaps in the literature. An empirical analysis of literature work related to IoT botnet detection is conducted. A state-of-the-art review of works done on IoT botnet detection is synthesized. This review is based on classifying the subcategories of IoT botnet detection, including honeypot and intrusion detection techniques, specifically host and network-based IDSs. This is further broken down into anomaly, signature, and hybrid-based approaches. Anomaly-based detections include machine learning techniques and deep learning techniques. Other detection methods include distributed techniques (software defined networking [SDN] and blockchain), graph theory approach, and domain name service (DNS) techniques. Finally, the chapter recommends future research directions in IoT security and the application of deep learning techniques.

DOI: 10.4018/979-8-3693-3451-5.ch003

1. INTRODUCTION

The internet has been a vital tool for sharing information and connecting computers worldwide for many years. It has enabled devices to share resources and information due to their interconnectivity (Partridge, 2016). The Internet of Things (IoT) concept emerged in the early 1990s at the MIT Auto-ID Centre (Ben-Daya et al., 2019), introducing the idea that different objects could be interconnected. Kevin Ashton, the Centre's head at the time, coined the term "Internet of Things" in 1999 (Greengard, 2015). According to Ben-Daya et al. (2019), the IoT is a system where everyday objects like cars and refrigerators are linked through the internet. They can automatically detect, monitor, and interact with each other within and across networks, enabling portability, availability, surveillance, and resource sharing. By 2025, the Cisco research team projected that there will be 75.3 billion IoT devices that are connected to the internet (Yastrebova et al., 2018). Numerous security issues affect IoT devices, including inconsistent manufacturing standards and patch oversight flaws spurred on by IoT software developers. Critical challenges include the physical management of security concerns and users' inexperience because of their ignorance of security issues related to IoT devices (Gyamfi & Jurcut, 2022).

A botnet, which is made up of thousands of hacked IoT devices, can be used for various kinds of attacks, such as leading DDoS attacks and phishing schemes (Putman et al., 2018). IoT devices have limited resources, such as little memory and computing power (Wazzan et al., 2021). IoT botnets have a serious worldwide impact, as evidenced by their ranking as the seventh most dangerous cyber threat in the world in 2018 by the European Union Agency for Network and Information Security (ENISA) (Marinos & Lourenço, 2018). They adversely affect the economy. For instance, In July 2017, an attack was launched on a power system that supplies electricity to the United Kingdom and Ireland. The cyberattack was able to breach power management systems so that they could cut off a portion of the electrical grid resulting in a halt of several systems. This resulted in significant financial loss to the states (Arman et al., 2022). Aside from the financial loss to the economy, IoT botnet attacks also affect the economy as they can shut down power grid systems and bring a nation's power supply to a standstill. An example of this was seen in the city of Ivano-Frankivsk, which has a population of 100,000 people. A denial-of-service attack caused the city to lose power for six hours (Yilmaz & Uludag, 2017). Also, during the middle of the Finland winter in the city of Lappeenranta, a targeted DDoS attack shut off the heat and hot water systems in two apartment complexes (Arman et al., 2022).

IoT technology has various applications in different industries. In the healthcare sector, IoT can be used for monitoring patients' adherence to medication, telemedicine services, and patient well-being notifications. Sensors can be used both on outpatients and inpatients, as well as dental Bluetooth devices and toothbrushes to provide information after use and for patient monitoring. IoT components like RFID, Bluetooth, and Wi-Fi can be utilized to significantly improve vital signs such as pulse rate, temperature, heart rate, blood level, and several other essential measuring and monitoring approaches for vital body operations (Hussein, 2019). In the urban setting, IoT technology is used to create smart cities. IoT sensors and monitoring equipment are integrated into smart cities and connected to the internet, allowing for the gathering of information that can be used to manage sewage systems, power plants, and other facilities. Smart cities can be used for energy management, water distribution, urban security, and environmental monitoring. Smart cities collect and analyze data through the Internet of Things to engage directly with city structures (Gomathi et al., 2018).

Wearable technology is also a popular use of IoT. Wearables are devices that can be worn or carried on the human body, and they can detect and transmit information about the user. Wearables provide fitness, medical, and recreational information (Gomathi et al., 2018). Smart agriculture involves various technologies to improve the quality and efficiency of farming. In the field of transport and logistics, roads and railroads are increasingly equipped with sensors, actuators, and computing power. As advanced roads, trains, buses, and bicycles become available, drivers and passengers can input essential information to enable easier navigation and enhance security. (Singh & Singh, 2019).

In this chapter, we present a state-of-the-art review of IoT botnet detection techniques. Our review is based on a classification of subcategories of IoT botnet detection, which include honeypot techniques, intrusion detection techniques (specifically host and network-based IDSs), and anomaly, signature, and hybrid-based approaches. Anomaly-based detections comprise machine learning and deep learning techniques. Other detection methods include distributed techniques (like Software Defined Networking (SDN) and blockchain), graph theory approach, and Domain Name Service (DNS) techniques. Figure 1 illustrates the various approaches to IoT botnet detection which are discussed in this chapter.

Figure 1. IoT Botnet detection techniques

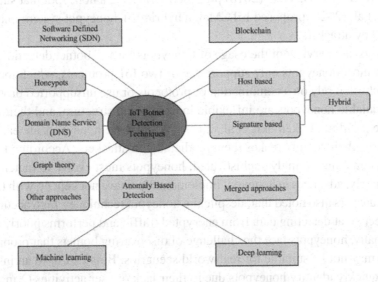

2. IOT BOTNET DETECTION APPROACHES

2.1 Honeypot Techniques

A honeypot is a tool that lures attackers to study their attack methods by gathering information about them (Anirudh et al., 2017). As explained by Malik (2020), the purpose of a honeypot is to collect information and knowledge about an attack, which is then logged for further investigation. Honeypots entice attacks in various ways such as organizing specific hosts, network services, or data, recording attack behavior, assessing the attacker's tools and tactics, and inferring their goal and motive (Zhang et al., 2020). According to Wang et al. (2018), honeypots can be classified into three groups based on their level of interaction. High-interaction honeypots involve the actual or real-world deployment of the honeypot. Low-interaction honeypots simulate the system or protocol. Lastly, medium-interaction honeypots are a hybrid of high and low-interaction honeypots (Wang et al., 2018).

Two studies proposed high-interaction honeypots to detect attacks on IoT devices. Zhang et al. (2020) built a honeypot that simulates real-world IoT devices and can handle SOAP service communication. Guarnizo et al. (2017) proposed SIPHON, a honeypot architecture that uses IoT devices linked to the internet via wormholes. They documented numerous brute-force login attempts, with some of them succeeding. Other studies proposed the use of honeypots for IoT devices. Wang & Wu (2019) created high-interaction honeypots to attract IoT attacks. Xu et al. (2021) proposed HoneyIoT, a robust IoT honeypot system, which discovered over 12,500 fraudulent connections and 3,423 different login attempts during a real-world industrial experiment. Hakim et al. (2018) created U-PoT, a honeypot architecture for IoT devices that use the UPnP protocol. They found that it could mimic an actual IoT device, but it could be improved to support other protocols. Researchers have proposed various IoT honeypot systems to gather data on attacks targeting IoT devices. Dowling et al. (2017) created a ZigBee honeypot to analyze SSH attack vectors. Wang et al. (2018) proposed ThingPot, a honeypot that supports the entire IoT platform. Wang et al. (2020) proposed IoTCMal, a hybrid IoT honeypot system that identifies malware families operated by attackers.

Table 1 presents an overview of the usage of honeypots for IoT botnet detection. From the analysis, it was found that most honeypots only support one or two IoT protocols, which makes them incapable of detecting attacks that rely on a combination of protocols or use unsupported protocols. Additionally, most publicly available honeypots are inflexible in design and structure, and their development cycles and servicing are peculiar (Tsikerdekis et al., 2019). While these honeypots are easily accessible to cybersecurity experts, their rigidity makes them predictable to attackers. According to Xing et al. (2021), as IoT botnets become increasingly sophisticated, honeypots must evolve to match their anti-detection tactics. Unfortunately, advances in honeypot implementation have not kept up with the growing range of IoT botnets. The authors also noted that, despite the honeypot technique's high accuracy in botnet detection, it is not effective at detecting data from encrypted traffic and performs poorly in identifying novel attacks. Additionally, honeypots face the challenge of discovering botnets that propagate through social engineering and may not be suitable for real-world scenarios. Bots that have an in-built anti-honeypot feature can also quickly identify honeypots due to their lack of user activities (Xing et al., 2021).

Table 1. Studies using the honeypot approach

Reference	Method	Pros	Cons
Zhang et al. (2020)	Supports SOAP technology	Simulates real-world IoT devices	Does not support other IoT protocols
Guarnizo et al. (2017)	High interaction honeypot	Had 400 brute force login attempts with 11 successful	Expensive to set up and maintain, real damage can affect the operating system
Hakim et al. (2018)	Supports UPnP protocol	Can mimic an actual IoT device	Does not support other IoT protocols
Dowling et al. (2017)	Supports Zigbee protocol	Attackers engaged in it	Does not support other IoT protocols

continued on following page

Table 1. Continued

Reference	Method	Pros	Cons
Wang et al. (2018)	Supports the entire IoT platform	Discovered 5 types of attack vectors	Inefficient at detecting data coming from encrypted traffic
Wang et al. (2020)	Hybrid interaction honeypot	Identified 8 malware families	May be unable to detect novel attacks

2.2 IoT Intrusion Detection Techniques

Intrusion Detection Systems (IDSs) are designed to track and identify any attempts at unauthorized access on a single device, such as an IoT device, or across the entire network. There are two categories of IDSs: Host-based IDS (HIDS) and Network-based IDS (NIDS) (Alrashdi et al., 2019). IoT NIDS monitors, captures, and examines network traffic to detect harmful data within packets. It observes both external and internal network traffic, as well as data transfer between IoT network devices. On the other hand, IoT HIDS is installed on individual IoT devices and only monitors data packets sent by that device. It alerts the administrator if any unusual network activity is detected (Jahwar & Ameen, 2021). IoT IDSs can evaluate the type and quality of attacks and identify intrusions (Dhir & Kumar, 2020). Intrusion Detection Systems use three approaches: signature-based detection, anomaly-based detection, and hybrid-based detection. IoT intrusion detection studies are reviewed under these subcategories.

2.2.1 Host-Based Approaches

In Bezerra et al.'s (2019) study, a technique called IoTDS was presented for detecting botnets in IoT devices. This technique used one-class classifiers that only model benign device activity to detect anomalies without requiring manual labeling. Unlike Myridakis et al. (2020), which used power supply as the only feature for detection, IoTDS collected features from the device's CPU usage and temperature, memory usage, and number of ongoing processes to evaluate the device's behavior. This approach eliminated the use of data from network traffic. The results showed that IoTDS had strong predictive performance for various botnets. The best-ranked algorithm, the Local Outlier Factor, achieved a mean F1 score of 94%.

Breitenbacher et al. (2019) proposed HADES-IoT, a Host-based Anomaly Detection System for IoT, which uses a whitelist created during profiling and a system call interception approach with minimal performance overhead. Hsiao et al. (2017) relied on statistical features and risk assessment to identify bot-infected hosts. Myridakis et al. (2020) presented a circuit that collects data from the device's power source to detect real-time malicious activities with a 100% success rate, but the evaluation results were limited. Arshad et al. (2020) suggest that incorporating the intrusion detection module in an IoT device leads to a significant increase in processing overhead, which can be detrimental for low-powered devices. As an alternative, their proposed systems focus on monitoring individual device events, but this approach can cause device overload and communication channel congestion (Arshad et al., 2020). Table 2 presents a concise overview of host-based methods for detecting IoT botnets.

Table 2. Studies using the host-based approach

Reference	Method	Pros	Cons
Bezerra et al. (2019)	Collects features from the device's Central Processing Unit (CPU) usage and other ongoing processes to evaluate the device's behavior,	Has strong predictive performance for various botnets	Increases the processing overhead at the IoT device
Breitenbacher et al. (2019)	Uses a whitelist created during profiling, minimal performance overload	May be used on a vast scope of IoT devices	Searching in the white list takes an hour for each device, computational overload
Hsiao et al. (2017)	Relied on the botnet life-cycle to detect each infected host	Can successfully detect the bot process activity even with other active ongoing processes	Congests the communication channel
Myridakis et al. (2020)	A circuit that is connected in line with the device's power source	The success rate of 100%.	Only power supply was considered as a physical feature

2.2.2 Signature-Based Approaches

Signature-based approaches are used for detecting intrusions, which involve keeping databases of known attack signatures. These databases are used to compare actions against stored information to identify known threats with high accuracy, requiring fewer resources to detect intrusions.

Habibi et al. (2017) introduced Heimdall, which is a whitelist-based intrusion detection approach designed for IoT devices. Heimdall's dynamic profile learning abilities are intended for usage on routers that serve as IoT gateways and provide unified protection across all devices behind the router. The authors built and tested a comprehensive prototype, demonstrating that uninfected devices continue to function normally while harmful activity from infected devices is quickly stopped, all with minimal overhead. However, using an IP-based whitelisting strategy for profiling and policy compliance would hamper the devices' normal operation as the IP address for a valid destination server is likely to change often. Ben Said et al. (2018) compared syntactic and behavioral analysis techniques to detect Mirai botnet samples. Both techniques were evaluated on a collection of over 500 Mirai samples, with behavioral analysis proving to be more efficient. It had an F0.5-score of about 99.41% compared to syntactic analysis, which had an F0.5 score of 98.61%.

NURSE is a tool developed by Estalenx and Gañán (2021) for detecting IoT-related malware intrusions in private home networks. It uses rule-based detection components to trigger alerts and evaluates IoT traffic using an ARP spoofing mechanism. NURSE effectively detects malware infected IoT devices with an accuracy of 86.7% based on device network behavior and accessed destinations. Although signature-based approaches are easy to deploy, they have the disadvantage of being unable to detect new, undiscovered, or upcoming threats. Whitelists must be updated regularly to keep up with the ever-growing plethora of IoT botnets (Wazzan et al., 2021). Table 3 summarizes works using signature-based approaches for IoT botnet detection.

Table 3. Studies using signature-based approaches

Reference	Method	Pros	Cons
Habibi et al. (2017)	Whitelist-based intrusion detection approach for routers	Has a low overhead	Hampers the devices' normal operation Constant list update
Ben Said et al. (2018)	Uses syntactic and behavioral analysis	Has null false positives on the sample testing set	Limited to Mirai samples
Estalenx and Gañán (2021)	Uses a set of rule-based detection components to trigger alerts.	Has an accuracy of 86.7%, based on device network behavior	Unable to detect upcoming threats

2.2.3 Hybrid Approaches

Hybrid approaches combine both anomaly and signature-based techniques for intrusion detection. Sedjelmaci et al. (2017) proposed a game-theoretic technique that initiates anomaly detection only when a new attack signature is likely to emerge. This approach results in a balance between detection, false positive rates, and energy usage. The authors claim that their hybrid detection technique outperforms existing anomaly detection techniques as it uses low energy consumption to detect malicious attacks while ensuring high detection and low false positive rates. According to the simulation results, this hybrid method achieved detection rates of about 93% and false positive rates of about 2%.

On the other hand, Arshad et al. (2019) designed a hybrid intrusion detection framework called COLIDE for IoT networks. The framework combines host and network-based intrusion detection at the node level and the edge router level. The authors proposed using signature-based intrusion detection at the nodes and anomaly-based intrusion detection at the edge router. This is accomplished via the Detection Engine module, which correlates alerts received from both approaches. The authors concluded that the COLIDE framework is effective in terms of energy consumption and processing overheads, and it achieves high performance in an IoT environment. However, both approaches have limitations when it comes to zero-day attacks. This is due to the need to subject each IoT device to both signature and anomaly-based detection systems, which results in increased computational overhead. Table 4 summarizes the hybrid-based works for IoT botnet detection.

Table 4. Summary of Related Studies Using Hybrid Approach

Reference	Method	Pros	Cons
Sedjelmaci et al. (2017)	Game theoretic technique	High detection and low false positive rates of about 93% and 2% respectively.	Increased computational overhead
Arshad et al. (2019)	Relies on the node level and the edge router.	Attaining high performance in an IoT environment	Increased computational overhead

2.3 Anomaly-Based Approaches

Anomaly-based detection is a method of comparing typical or standard activities to observed events to discover noteworthy variances (Zarpelão et al., 2017). This technique involves observing certain parameters such as ports used in data traffic, increased network latency, or high volumes of traffic (De Neira et al., 2020). Machine learning and deep learning techniques are extensively employed for intrusion detection in general and specifically for IoT. The key benefit of the anomaly detection approach is that it provides a high detection rate as it can detect zero-day attacks, that is, new attacks that have never been encountered before (Sedjelmaci et al., 2017). However, the biggest disadvantage is the considerable computational overhead necessary to model normal behavior.

Machine learning approaches are further grouped into four categories: supervised, semi-supervised, unsupervised, and reinforcement learning techniques. Under anomaly-based detection, machine learning and deep learning techniques are reviewed and discussed. Supervised techniques focus on using a labeled set of data to train an algorithm that acts as the optimal function for defining the input data selection. Thus, suitable outputs that correspond to the data, as well as known inputs, are provided for the learning (Dalal, 2020).

2.3.1 Machine Learning Methods

Prokofiev et al. (2018) proposed a logistic regression model to detect IoT botnets during their propagation stage with 97.30% accuracy. In contrast, De Neira et al. (2020) introduced ANTE, a framework with an average accuracy of 99.87% to detect botnets in the early stages proactively. Kumar and Lim (2019) introduced EDIMA for detecting IoT malware network activity during the scanning and infecting phase, with the k-NN classifier performing the best. However, EDIMA has a drawback as it can't detect malware capable of bypassing the scanning and infecting phase.

Several studies have employed machine learning techniques to detect botnet attacks in IoT environments using datasets such as N-BaIoT and BoTIoT. Abbasi et al. (2021) proposed two feature extraction and classification approaches based on Logistic Regression and Artificial Neural Networks, achieving a high level of classification accuracy. Bagui et al. (2021) used three machine-learning classifiers and achieved outstanding results using the N-BaIoT dataset. Tzagkarakis et al. (2019) proposed an IoT botnet attack detection approach, centered on a sparsity representation framework. Shafiq et al. (2021), Injadat et al. (2020), and Yaokumah et al. (2021) used the BoTIoT dataset in the evaluation of their work, achieving success rates higher than 96%. Some studies have proposed machine learning models to identify and detect attacks on IoT networks. Injadat et al. (2020) and Yaokumah et al. (2021) used the BoTIoT dataset to evaluate their models, which showed high accuracy and resilience in detecting botnet attacks and IoT malware. Liu et al. (2020), Desai et al. (2020), and Doshi et al. (2018) also used different datasets to evaluate their models and obtained high accuracies and efficiencies in detecting network intrusions and DoS attacks on IoT devices. However, some studies had limitations such as a smaller dataset, manual feature engineering, and the use of only one dataset.

Researchers have used supervised and deep learning models to detect IoT botnet and network attacks. The IoT Network Intrusion Detection dataset was used in many of these studies. Random Forest was found to be the most effective model for detecting and classifying attacks. Other general intrusion detection datasets were also used, such as UNSW-NB15 and NIMS. The proposed ensemble technique by Moustafa et al. (2019) showed a greater detection rate and a lower false positive rate. The AD-IoT system by Alrashdi et al. (2019) also used Random Forest and achieved a maximum classification accuracy of 99.34%. Studies have employed semi-supervised and unsupervised machine learning techniques to detect IoT botnets. Desai et al. (2021) integrated supervised and unsupervised machine learning algorithms to detect new incoming attacks in network traffic. Naveed and Wu (2020) presented a neural network-based approach that uses a self-organizing map (SOM) for IoT botnet detection. Naveed et al. (2020) introduced Dytokinesis, and Haseeb et al. (2020) used clustering to sort captured attacks and construct a model.

In reinforcement learning, Ngo et al. (2021) developed a Printable String Information (PSI)-graph machine learning model to detect IoT botnets and evaluate the model's effectiveness against adversarial attacks created by reinforcement learning. Table 5 shows a summary of machine learning works under IoT botnet detection. Although machine learning works demonstrated good results, they require manual feature engineering, and hence, deep learning methods were developed to overcome this. Table 6 also shows the advantages and disadvantages of some machine learning works discussed.

Table 5. Studies using Machine learning works

Reference	Purpose	Classifier	Dataset	Performance metrics	Results
Prokofiev et al. (2018)	Detect IoT botnets during their propagation stage	Logistic regression model	100 botnets collected	Accuracy Precision Recall F-Measure	A-97.3% P-94% R-98% F- 96%
De Neira et al. (2020)	Anticipate botnet signals at the early stages	Autonomous ML	ISOT HTTP Botnet CTU-13 CICDDoS2019	Accuracy Precision	A-99.87% P- 100%
Kumar and Lim (2019)	Detect IoT botnets at the scanning and infection stages	Naïve Bayes Random Forest K-NN	Gateway traffic collected	Accuracy Precision Recall F-Measure	A-94.44% P-92% R-100% F- 96%
Abbasi et al. (2021)	Detect IoT botnets during their propagation stage	Logistic Regression (LR) and Artificial Neural Network (ANN).	N-BaIoT	Accuracy	A- 99.98%
Bagui et al. (2021)	Evaluate botnet traffic in an IoT environment	Used SVM, LR, and RF	N-BaIoT	Accuracy Precision Recall F-Measure	A-99% P-94% R-98% F- 96%
Tzagkarakis et al. (2019)	Detect harmful network traffic at the IoT edge	Sparsity representation framework	N-BaIoT	Accuracy Recall F-Measure	-
Shafiq et al. (2021)	Harmful traffic detection in the IoT environment	Proposed a new feature selection metric called CorrAUC	BoTIoT	Accuracy	A-96%
Injadat et al. (2020)	Detect botnet attacks in IoT networks	Fusion of B0-GP and DT	BoTIoT	Accuracy Precision Recall F-Measure	A-99.99% P-99.0% R-100% F- 100%
Yaokumah et al. (2021)	Examine the performance of machine learning models for identifying IoT malware	LR NB DT KNN SVM NN RF BG ST	BoTIoT	Accuracy Precision Recall F-Measure	A-100% P-100% R-100% F- 100%

continued on following page

Table 5. Continued

Reference	Purpose	Classifier	Dataset	Performance metrics	Results
Liu et al. (2020)	Use underlying network behavior to distinguish anomalies from normal flow traffic	LR SVM KNN RF XGB	IoT Network Intrusion	Accuracy F1-Score Recall	A-90% F1-84% R-84.4%
Desai et al. (2020)	Detect IoT and other network attacks	RF DT SVM PCA	IoT Network Intrusion	Accuracy	A-99.97%
Hegde et al. (2020)	Detect botnet activity in IoT network traffic	DT RF Multi-class DF Multi-class NN Two-class NN	IoT-23	Accuracy	A-99.9%
Doshi et al. (2018)	Differentiate regular traffic from DoS attack traffic across consumer IoT devices	KN SVM DT RF NN	An experimental consumer IoT device network	Accuracy Precision F1-Score Recall	A-99.9% P- 99.9% R-96.94% F1-99.5%
Moustafa et al. (2019)	Curb harmful botnet attacks against DNS, MQTT and HTTP	ANN DT NB (AdaBoost Ensemble)	UNSW-NB15 and NIMS	Accuracy False positive rate Detection rate	-
Abbasi et al. (2021)	Investigate datasets for IoT intrusion	LR ANN	N-BaIoT	Accuracy Precision Recall F1-score	A-99.98% P- 99.9% R-96.96% F1-99.92%
Alrashdi et al. (2019	Detect infected IoT devices at fog nodes	RF	UNSW-NB15	Accuracy	A-99.34%
Bahsi et al. (2018)	Use feature selection to reduce the number of features used to detect IoT bots	DT	N-BaIoT	Accuracy	A-99.9%
Gurulakshmi and Nesarani (2018)	Evaluate IoT malware and decrease the packet destination	SVM KNN	large number of IoT devices	Accuracy	A-97%
Desai et al. (2021)	Detect new incoming attacks in network traffic	RF	IoT Network Intrusion	Accuracy	A-99.97%
Naveed and Wu (2020)	Zero-day and real-time attack detection	NN	N-BaIoT	Accuracy False positive rate False Negative rate	-
Haseeb et al. (2020)	Evaluation of captured attacks to find the links	Clustering	Medium interaction honeypot on a public network	-	Recommend a 20-feature set for analysis
Ngo et al. (2021)	Detect IoT botnets and evaluate effectiveness against adversarial attacks	SVM DT RF	Manually assembled	Accuracy	A-94.1%

Table 6. Pros and Cons of the Machine Learning Methods

Pros	Cons
Good accuracy results	Manual feature engineering
	Some works use inconclusive datasets which limit the knowledge scope of the model

2.3.2 Deep Learning Techniques

Numerous works have been carried out on IoT botnet detection using deep learning techniques. In this regard, Meidan et al. (2018) presented N-BaIoT, a network-based method of anomaly detection for IoT that captures network behavior snapshots and employs deep learning techniques, particularly deep autoencoders. The authors designed the system to learn the normal behaviors of IoT by capturing statistical features that record behavioral snapshots of harmless IoT traffic. For each device, a deep autoencoder is trained, and the snapshots are compressed using the deep autoencoder. If the autoencoder fails to reconstruct a snapshot, it is a clear indication that the observed behavior is unusual. The approach was tested on nine commercial IoT devices that were compromised with Mirai and Bashlite botnets, and the results showed that the proposed strategy could quickly and accurately detect attacks as they were taking place from compromised IoT devices in a botnet.

Moreover, Sriram et al. (2020), Karaca and Cetin (2021), Rahmantyo et al. (2021), and Liu et al. (2019) evaluated the works done using the N-BaIoT dataset. Sriram et al. (2020) presented a botnet detection method based on deep learning that operates on network traffic flows. The botnet detection system collects network traffic flows, transforms them into connection records, and employs a deep learning model to detect attacks coming from infected IoT devices. Several experiments were performed on N-BaIoT and BoTIoT datasets to find the best deep-learning model. The authors stated that their suggested deep learning model outperformed existing machine learning models. However, the authors acknowledged one significant drawback, which is the fact that the analysis relied only on features derived from the network traffic flow, instead of analyzing the entire network payload data.

Karaca and Cetin (2021) conducted a study to evaluate the efficiency of a one-dimensional CNN (1DCNN) model in detecting botnet attacks. They tested the CNN model against other models that used the same dataset and reported their findings for each IoT device. The proposed CNN model showed the best performance and had an accuracy rate of 97.98% in identifying botnet attacks on the Provision PT 838 Security Camera. The CNN model outperformed other models such as K-Nearest Neighbors, Gaussian Naive Bayes, Artificial Neural Networks, and Support Vector Machines. However, since they only tested the CNN model on one device from the N-BaIoT dataset, the scope of their work was limited. Similarly, in a study by Rahmantyo et al. (2021), they also used a 1DCNN to detect botnet attacks. They proposed a deep residual 1DCNN model for botnet traffic detection and provided an algorithm for data processing and training of the IoT botnet detection model. The dataset was assessed for data processing, training, and running tests, and the framework was optimized with various optimizers. The Deep residual 1DCNN was compared against LSTM, CNN with RNN, and other models with different optimizers. According to their findings, the Deep Residual 1DCNN with Adam optimizer performed the best, with a training accuracy of 88.67%, validation accuracy of 88.67%, and test accuracy of 88.53%.

Ullah and Mahmoud (2021) developed an anomaly-based intrusion detection system for IoT networks using a 1D, 2D, and 3D CNN approach. They created a multi-classification model with a convolutional neural network to classify various types of cyberattacks and differentiate them from typical network traffic. The proposed framework was evaluated using several intrusion detection datasets, and their models demonstrated high accuracy compared to existing deep learning approaches. Other researchers such as Popoola et al. (2021) and Sriram et al. (2020) also used the BoTIoT dataset for their studies. Liang and Znati (2019) proposed an LSTM-based DDoS detection technique that outperformed conventional machine learning techniques. Popoola et al. (2021) presented a hybrid deep learning model, LAE-BLSTM, for effective botnet detection in IoT environments. McDermott et al. (2018) also employed BLSTM but coupled with RNN for IoT botnet detection, and the bidirectional approach was found to be more progressive in the long run, albeit with higher computational costs.

Several studies, including those by Hussain et al. (2020, 2021), Karaca and Cetin (2021), Rahmanctyo et al. (2021), Liu et al. (2019), and Panda et al. (2021), have utilized CNN detection strategies to identify network traffic. For instance, Liu et al. (2019) used a CNN to differentiate benign traffic from various types of attack traffic with 99.57% accuracy. Hussain et al. (2020, 2021) suggested CNN-based methodologies to detect DoS and DDoS attacks with high accuracy. Panda et al. (2021) combined machine learning and deep learning approaches to achieve 100% accuracy with no false alarm rate in network intrusion detection. Table 7 shows a summary of deep learning methods for IoT botnet detection. So far, deep learning has had the best performance results, however for lightweight. IoT devices may be computationally expensive. Table 8 also shows the advantages and disadvantages of this method.

Table 7. Studies using Deep learning methods

Reference	Purpose	Classifier	Dataset	Performance metrics	Results
Sriram et al. (2020)	Botnet detection on network traffic flows	DNN	N-BaIoT	Accuracy Precision Recall F-Measure	A-100% P-100% R-100% F- 100%
Karaca and Cetin (2021)	Identifying botnet attacks on each IoT device	1DCNN	N-BaIoT (One device)	Accuracy	A-97.98%
Rahmantyo et al. (2021)	Botnet traffic detection with various optimizers	1DCNN	N-BaIoT	Accuracy	A-88.67%
Ullah and Mahmoud (2021)	Anomaly-based intrusion detection system for IoT networks	1D,2D,3D	BoTIoT IoT Network Intrusion IoT-23	Accuracy Precision Recall F-Measure	A-99.9% P-99.9% R-99.9% F- 99.9%
Popoola et al. (2021)	Effective botnet detection in IoT environments	LAE-BLSTM	BoTIoT	Accuracy	A-97.29%
Liang and Znati (2019)	Identify DDoS attacks	LSTM	CICIDS 2017	Precision Recall F-1 Score	P-99% R-99% F-99%
McDermott et al. (2018)	Identification and conversion of packets using. Word embedding	RNN-BLSTM	Manually assembled	Accuracy	A-98.66%
Hussain et al. (2020)	Convert a dataset of non-image network traffic into image format	CNN	CICD- DoS2019	Accuracy	A-99.9%
Hussain et al. (2021)	Prevent and also detect IoT botnet attacks	CNN	Manually collected	Accuracy Precision Recall F-	A-98.89% P-99.01% R-98.74% F-98.87%
Panda et al. (2021)	Early detection of IoT botnets	CNN	UNSW-NB15	Accuracy	A-100%

Table 8. Pros and Cons of the Deep Learning Methods

Pros	Cons
Excellent accuracy results	Computationally expensive
	Some works use inconclusive datasets which limit the knowledge scope of the model

2.4 Graph-Based Approaches

Graph-based techniques are mathematical models that represent the relationship between different components of a network. These models can be created based on the behavior of executable files, including control flow, call and code graphs, or on the behavior of nodes in network traffic, such as IP-domain mapping relations, classification, and detection. Two studies, conducted by Ngo et al. (2021) and Yassin et al. (2019), utilized graph theory in their IoT botnet detection strategies. Ngo et al. (2021) proposed a strategy that utilized graph-theoretic features to detect IoT botnets. To test their proposed methods, the authors gathered a dataset of binary files from IoTPOT and VirusShare, which were divided into two categories: IoT benign and botnet samples. The authors used six machine learning classifiers to evaluate their proposed graph-theoretic features and found that Random Forest (RF) was the most effective at detecting IoT botnet malware with an accuracy of 94.84 percent. Yassin et al. (2019) employed a graph-theoretical technique to identify malicious registry data altered by IoT botnet actions, specifically Mirai. By creating dependency graphs of similar and dissimilar patterns of different botnets, the authors were able to identify malware variant characteristics. The study focused only on Mirai and did not consider other types of IoT malware, both known and unknown. Table 9 summarizes works based on the graph approach for IoT botnet detection.

Table 9. Studies using the graph approach

Reference	Method	Pros	Cons
Ngo et al. (2021)	Graph-theoretic features by the extraction of PSI graph	Good accuracy of 94.94%	Some important features may be missing
Yassin et al. (2019)	Using a dependency graph	Derived an attack pattern for the Mirai botnet	Focused on only the Mirai botnet and only registry information

2.5 Blockchain and Software-Defined Networking Approaches

Blockchain was initially intended to record encrypted financial transactions, which were monitored by all parties involved, such as Bitcoin and other cryptocurrencies. All transactions are explicit, and any modifications can be traced and detected with ease. Using blockchain technology for IoT botnet detection involves leveraging smart contracts, digital signatures, reward systems, and other technologies to achieve trustworthy information exchange or polling among multiple detectors. The blockchain paradigm has been used in literature for IoT botnet detection. Falco et al. (2019) used a "friendly" botnet that works through the Bitcoin blockchain. Their technology is compatible with different devices, such as industrial IoT, and has already been put to the test on CCTV cameras, smart meters, and routers. NeuroMesh was able to shut down the Mirai botnet and stop rogue processes from executing. However, individual devices were tested, and not full networks of systems that require distinct load balancing methods and greater scale distributed computing.

Sagirlar et al. (2018) introduced AutoBotCatcher, a method for detecting P2P IoT botnets. The goal of AutoBotCatcher is to detect botnets by dynamically assessing communities of IoT devices based on their network traffic flows. AutoBotCatcher uses a permissioned Byzantine Fault Tolerant (BFT) blockchain, in which device manufacturers and security regulators participate in the consensus process. On the mutual contact graph of IoT devices, blockchain is used for adaptive network-based botnet community detection. The suggested architecture by Kumar et al. (2019) segregated the network into multiple Autonomous Systems (AS), via which host connectivity is formed. Blockchains are used to preserve and exchange a record of Internet Protocol (IP) addresses of various hosts linked to an AS that has been detected as malicious. The proposed technique is tested using a custom-built simulator to identify an appropriate figure for the malicious threshold. The findings demonstrated that the proposed approach can achieve a true detection rate of up to 95%.

Lekssays et al. (2021) introduced PAutoBotCatcher, a botnet detection tool based on community behavior study across peers run by various actors. PAutoBotCatcher used blockchain technology to provide immutability and openness across actors. The authors created a series of optimization methods, including caching detection output and pre-processing shared network traffic, to enhance persistent detection while maintaining high accuracy. Furthermore, the authors used a variety of privacy-preserving measures to prevent devices from being re-identified throughout the botnet detection process. The system can handle well over 15,000 nfps, and blockchain contributes a 1,168-second overhead for the testing scenario under evaluation. The authors concluded that blockchain can be used to achieve dynamic detection of botnets.

In a research paper by Spathoulas et al. (2019), an extension of the work done by Giachoudis et al. (2019) was presented. The study aimed to identify distributed denial of service (DDoS) attacks executed by IoT device botnets through the use of lightweight agents deployed at various Internet of Things (IoT) installations. The authors utilized a blockchain smart contract to regulate the information stream, ensuring the integrity of both the operation and the information. The findings showed that the detection of the network behavior of a DDoS attack is feasible if several agents work together.

Similarly, Golomb et al. (2018) introduced CIoTA, a lightweight system that employs the blockchain paradigm to undertake distributed and collaborative anomaly detection for resource-constrained devices. Using self-attestation and consensus across IoT devices, CIoTA leverages blockchain to progressively update a trustworthy anomaly detection model. The authors tested CIoTA on a distributed IoT simulation platform, comprising forty-eight Raspberry Pis, and the findings demonstrated that the proposed methodology can improve the security of individual devices as well as the security of the entire network. However, one drawback of CIoTA was identified, which is the requirement of a separate chain to be published for each hardware, making it impractical for industrial environments. While blockchain can enable multiple parties to work together to detect botnets (Wazzan et al., 2021), it is not lightweight because the proof of work procedure has a high cost due to the intense use of resources. Moreover, generating a block increases the throughput and latency (Cui et al., 2019). Table 10 shows a summary of blockchain works under IoT botnet detection.

Table 10. Studies using Blockchain

Reference	Method	Pros	Cons
Falco et al. (2019)	Bitcoin Technology	Able to shut down the Mirai botnet	Individual devices have only been tested
Sagirlar et al. (2018)	Permissioned Byzantine Fault Tolerant (BFT) blockchain	Performs community detection on IoT traffic	Lacks privacy protection
Ahmed et al. (2019)	Multiple Autonomous Systems	Had a true detection rate of up to 95%.	Heavyweight because the proof of work procedure
Lekssays et al. (2021)	Use blockchain technology to provide immutability and openness across actors.	Privacy-preserving blockchain IoT detection	High throughput and latency
Spathoulas et al. (2019)	Lightweight agents deployed at IoT devices, using a blockchain smart contract	Works well when several agents work together	Heavyweight because the proof of work procedure
Golomb et al. (2018)	Distributed and collaborative anomaly detection	Improve the security of individual devices	It requires a separate chain to be published for each hardware

Software-defined networking (SDN) is a networking paradigm that modifies traditional network design by placing all control operations in one location and making centralized choices. Controllers, which conduct control decision functions as they route packets, are the brains of SDN architecture. The ability to make routing decisions centrally improves network performance (Paliwal et al., 2018). The division of control and data planes achieved by SDN technology is commonly utilized to develop multiple security detection methods and strategies to reduce attacks (Xing et al., 2021).

Some research papers employed SDN for IoT botnet detection and these are discussed in further detail. Ozcelik et al. (2017) used Mirai as a case study to provide an edge-oriented detection technique for DDoS attacks in IoT leveraging SDN and Fog techniques. SDN was employed as a flexible approach for defining new flow rules and updating them dynamically as needed. Although ECESID is designed to detect Mirai variations, it may be readily set up and extended to detect additional Botnet threats. In this context, the authors also utilized fog computing to assist ECESID. The suggested methodology revealed that DDoS attacks from IoT can be controlled and curbed via SDN. Hamza et al. (2018) used MUD and SDN to create an intrusion detection system for IoT devices. They converted MUD policies from 28 consumer IoT devices into flow rules and tested the system's performance using traces collected over several months. Ceron et al. (2019) proposed a method for managing IoT malware traffic using SDN. Wazzan et al. (2021) suggested that SDN may not be the best choice for IoT botnet detection due to the possibility of a single point of failure. Table 11 shows a summary of SDN works under IoT botnet detection.

Table 11. Studies using SDN

Paper	Method	Pros	Cons
Ozcelik et al. (2017)	SDN and fog computing	Controls and curbs DDoS attacks via SDN	Cannot always curb zero-day attacks
Hamza et al. (2018)	SDN and MUD conversion into rules	Can identify voluminous internal and external attacks	SDN presents a single point of failure
Ceron et al. (2019)	SDN controller performs network functions	Stops attacks to target systems	SDN presents a single point of failure

2.6 Domain Name Service (DNS) Approaches

Domain Name System (DNS) technology uses globally dispersed hierarchical name servers on a worldwide scale to map domain names to IP addresses (Kim & Reeves, 2020). This technology has been employed in some IoT botnet detection strategies as discussed. Dwyer et al (2019) proposed a DNS-based profiling strategy using real datasets of Mirai-like botnet traffic activity gathered on honeypots that are dispersed worldwide. The authors demonstrated how using DNS information from a single DNS record can help with profiling IoT-based botnets. Additionally, the authors demonstrated the applicability of the strategy by testing the created feature set against a variety of Machine Learning (ML) classifiers. Their result findings revealed that the suggested feature set can greatly cut botnet detection time while also retaining a high accuracy average of 99% on the random forest model.

On the other hand, Lysenko et al. (2020) also proposed an approach for detecting IoT attacks centered on DNS traffic analysis. The approach is heuristic and also proactive. It was dependent on the collection of a set of features that could detect the existence of IoT attacks. The attack detection framework's methodology is founded on the collection of cyberattack features from networks and the development of feature vectors. Semi-supervised fuzzy c-means clustering, Support Vector Machine, and Artificial Immune System classification techniques were used as classification algorithms. The test findings revealed that applying the SVM produced the best outcome. With false positives ranging from 0.015 to 0.31%, the efficacy of the SVM approach is in the range of 96.06 to 98.01%.

Rosenthal et al. (2020) proposed The Anomaly and Reputation Technique (ARBA), an algorithm for detecting malicious IoT hosts in sizable great-scale DNS traffic. It consisted of two primary components. The first component compared previous and new domains requested by the host to determine the host's infection status. Afterward, the isolation forest is then used to detect anomalies in the host. The second component classified harmful domains that each suspected host queries. This stage involved the use of both black- and whitelists, proceeded by feature extraction and the use of a trained random forest classification algorithm to process the results. ARBA was further implemented in a real-time production setting. The authors showed that ARBA can be used in a production environment and that it can detect malicious and suspicious behaviors that are done across DNS in real time. However, since the massive amounts of traffic that occur in network environments are computationally expensive, most DNS traffic monitoring systems are not real-time (Thanh et al., 2021). Table 12 shows a summary of DNS works under IoT botnet detection.

Table 12. Studies using DNS

Reference	Method	Pros	Cons
Dwyer et al (2019)	DNS profiling using records	Achieves 99% accuracy on RF classifier	Only focused on records
Lysenko et al. (2020)	Traffic analysis	Detection of suspicious behaviors	Lacks inclusion of new IoT attack features
Rosenthal et al. (2020)	Anomaly and Reputation-based	Can detect malicious behaviors in DNS real-timeline	Systems are mostly not real-time

2.7 Merged Approaches

The evolution of botnets has led to the emergence of diversified platforms, concealed communications, and intelligent control. As a result, a single abnormal behavior detection method is no longer adequate to meet the current requirements. Multi-agent and multi-technology combined detection methods have been developed to address this challenge. Multi-technology refers to the use of multiple algorithms or technologies (Xing et al., 2021). Meanwhile, multi-agent technology uses more than one agent in its detection approach. In their research, Giachoudis et al. (2019) proposed a distributed multi-agent approach to IoT security. They used lightweight agents in large-scale IoT installations to enable joint and cooperative efforts in detecting security events and avoiding potential attacks. The authors conducted a simulation to evaluate the performance of their methodology. Specifically, their approach mitigates the impact of distributed denial of service attacks performed by botnets of IoT devices. According to the authors, the findings show that when many agents work together, the likelihood of detecting the network behavior of a DDoS attack is high. However, in real-life scenarios, coordination between agents does not always work out as smoothly as expected.

Other multi-technology approaches combine honeypots with machine learning techniques (Vishwakarma & Jain, 2019). Vishwakarma and Jain (2019) proposed a honeypot-based IoT malware detection strategy that employed machine learning techniques. They used data collected by the IoT virtual honeypot as a dataset for efficient and agile machine learning model training. This study specifically employed an unsupervised machine learning approach. The authors explained that the combined method of honeypot and unsupervised machine learning can be used as a productive starting point for countering zero-day DDoS Attacks, which have recently surfaced as a major difficulty in protecting IoT from DDoS Attacks.

Several proposed methods for IoT botnet detection using hybrid AI-based honeynets and machine learning techniques have been suggested in recent years. Miller et al. (2020) suggested a multi-layer approach consisting of ISP architecture, advanced detection methods, and user education. Lee et al. (2021) suggested a model for botnet detection and classification in smart factories using machine learning algorithms. Trajanovski and Zhang (2021) proposed a honeypot with a sandbox known as the IoT-BDA framework. Memos and Psannis (2020) also proposed a hybrid AI-based honeynet for improved IoT botnet detection. These proposed models have not been implemented in real life, and a comparative analysis has not been performed to determine their efficiency. The drawback of the proposed model is similar to that of (Nguyen et al., 2018); in cases of concealment and encryption by botnets, detection cannot be achieved. Table 13 shows a summary of merged approaches under IoT botnet detection.

Table 13. Studies using merged methods

Reference	Method	Pros	Cons
Giachoudis et al. (2019)	An agent for each IoT installation	High likelihood of network behavior detection	Expensive setup
Vishwakarma and Jain (2019)	Honeypot and ML	Identification of zero-day attacks	Anti-honeypot strategies by attackers
Memos and Psannis (2020)	Honeypot, cloud, and ML	Identification of zero-day attacks	Anti-honeypot strategies by attackers

continued on following page

Table 13. Continued

Reference	Method	Pros	Cons
Lee et al. (2021)	Honeypot, R-studio, and Weka ML	R-studio performs better for botnet detection	The model requires further optimization
Trajanovski and Zhang (2021)	Honeypot and sandbox	Acquired over 4000 IoT botnet samples	May evade new anti-honeypot strategies
Sudheera et al. (2021)	Network traffic, a security manager, and ML	Outperforms baselines	Involves manual feature engineering
Ashraf et al. (2021)	SDN and 3 ML classifiers	Curb DDoS attacks before they reach target destinations.	SDN presents a single point of failure
Swarna and Ratna (2020)	ML and DL	LSTM best performing	Computationally expensive
Ghazi and Rachid (2020)	Signature and anomaly IDS, ANN	Achieves accuracy of 94.4%	Constant update of the attack list
Nguyen et al. (2018)	Graph and DL (PSI and CNN)	Achieves accuracy of 92% and F-score of 94%	Computationally expensive
Ngo et al. (2021)	Graph and ML	Achieves accuracy of 99%	Computationally expensive

2.8 Other Approaches

Myridakis et al. (2021) proposed a circuit that detects abnormal behaviors in IoT devices and achieved a 100% success rate. However, it only considers one physical feature for detection. Mudgerikar et al. (2020) presented a system-level IDS E-Spion suitable for resource-constrained IoT devices which achieved detection rates of over 78%, 97%, and 99% respectively. Frank et al. (2017) proposed a device hardening concept to secure devices from becoming malicious bots as part of the Mirai botnet, but it is limited to the Mirai botnet. Sajjad et al. (2020) proposed a mechanism for detecting and resolving firmware vulnerabilities before creating a device's Manufacturer Usage Description (MUD) profile. Ibrahim et al. (2019) developed US-AID, a collective attestation mechanism for large networks to isolate infected devices. Yilmaz and Uludag (2017) proposed a general security architecture for the Smart Grid's information-gathering subsystems and created the MIAMI-DIL intrusion detection system. Le & Ngo (2020) focused on creating a practical and effective sandbox, known as V-Sandbox, for IoT Botnet dynamic analysis performance.

Several research works have been conducted on IoT security. Al-Duwairi et al. (2020) presented an IoT botnet DDoS detection and mitigation system that monitors particular packet types such as TCP SYN, ICMP, and DNS packets emerging from infected IoT devices. Shah and Venkatesa (2019) introduced a strategy known as "login puzzle" to prevent the large-scale takeover of IoT devices. Yamaguchi (2020) expanded on Botnet Defense Technology (BDS) to combat malicious botnets. Khaing et al. (2020) investigated network forensics to detect DoS or DDoS flooding attacks on IoT devices. Neisse et al. (2017) proposed a method for improving IoT device certification. Al-Kasas007sbeh et al. (2020) presented a Fuzzy Rule Interpolation-based detection technique for IoT botnet threats. Mahmoud and Ullah (2020) implemented a flow-based abnormal activity detection method with two levels for IoT networks. Table 14 presents a summary of other methods for IoT botnet detection.

Table 14. Studies using other methods

Reference	Method	Pros	Cons
Myridakis et al. (2021)	Circuit in series with IP camera power source	100% success	Only one attribute is considered
Mudgerikar et al. (2020)	Baseline profile using system data	78%,97%, and 99% detection rates	Other IoT variants aside Mirai left out
Frank et al. (2017)	Hardening and detection scripts	Identify and terminate infections in a regulated environment	Tested on only one IoT device, regulated. environment does not give an accurate evaluation
Sajjad et al. (2020)	MUD profile	Increased security	Impractical for some IoT devices
Ibrahim et al. (2019)	Isolation from the network	Viability of technique	Infeasible in some instances
Yilmaz and Uludag (2017)	Isolation from the network	Viability of technique	Infeasible in some instances
Shah and Venkatesa (2019)	Login puzzle	Reduces attack time	Uniform password
Yamaguchi (2020)	White hat botnets	Included other IoT variants aside from Mirai	No implementation
Neisse et al. (2017)	Model and policy-based	Successfully applied to M2M systems	Further work on other IoT systems
Al-Kasassbeh et al. (2020)	Fuzzy Rule Interpolation	95.4% detection rate	Generation of higher false positive instances
Mahmoud and Ullah (2020)	Flow-based detection	100% and 99% accuracy for two levels	Datasets were imbalanced which affected the results

3. EVALUATION OF APPROACHES

Upon review of the various IoT botnet detection methods, Table 15 summarizes the advantages and disadvantages of each method. However, honeypots are efficient at detecting botnets, and attackers. Keep developing anti-honeypot strategies to combat honeypots. Some honeypots are also expensive to set up and cannot read encrypted traffic. Thus, honeypots alone are not a great choice for IoT botnet detection. Host-based detection methods which are only on the. Host devices have limited detection capabilities. Signature-based methods are excellent at detecting known attacks; however, the lists need constant updates and this method cannot. Combat zero-day attacks since it relies on a list of known signatures. Hybrid attacks, despite high detection rates are computationally expensive.

On the other hand, graph theory methods were limited to only one type of IoT botnet or one source of data such as the registry, and this limits the efficiency of findings. Distributed methods such as blockchain and SDN have shown efficiency in IoT botnet detection, however, due to proof-of-concept, blockchain is resource-intensive. Some blockchain works also presented privacy concerns for the parties involved. The SDN controller presents a single point of failure which creates security challenges. Although merged methods have excellent results, they are computationally expensive as IoT devices are lightweight. The same issue is faced by deep learning methods, which so far have presented the best performance results for IoT botnet detection. Machine learning methods that have good performance results rely on manual feature engineering, hence the most recent works have employed deep learning over machine learning. Table 15 shows a summary of the approaches discussed and their advantages and disadvantages.

Table 15. Evaluation of IoT botnet detection methods

Approach	Pros	Cons
Honeypot	Efficient at detecting malware	Anti-honeypot strategies
Host-based	Efficient at host attack detection	Cannot detect network traffic attacks
Signature-based	Low overhead Detects known attacks	Constant list update Unable to detect zero-day. Attacks
Hybrid	High detection rates	High computational overhead
Machine learning	Good accuracy results	Manual feature engineering
Deep learning	Excellent performance results	Computationally expensive for lightweight IoT devices
Graph theory	High pattern recognitions	Limited data for evaluation
DNS	Good detection of suspicious events	Systems are mostly not real-time
Blockchain	Multiple parties detect botnets by working together	High throughput and latency Resource intensive
SDN	Facilitates IoT botnet detection	SDN controller is a single point of failure
Merged	Excellent results	Computationally expensive

4. EMERGING TECHNOLOGIES OF IOT BOTNET DETECTION

There are some emerging trends and technologies that are showing remarkable influence in the field of IoT botnets. A few of these are discussed below.

4.1 5G Networks

The fifth generation of mobile communication systems, also known as 5G, encourages the use of mobile networks to run and integrate computing. and smart devices in addition to people coverage. With a maximum data transfer rate of 35.46 Gbps, 5G outperforms 4G in terms of speed coverage (Wazid et al., 2021). These 5G networks are less expensive and offer greater capacity, reduced latency, and improved coverage. Despite these advantages of 5G for IoT, 5G is expected to speed up the Internet of Things rapid growth, posing new security issues (Lefoane et al., 2022). Ghorbani et. al. (2020) explained that because 5G technology can build essential infrastructure, stronger security will be needed. For instance, 5G can carry more data and reduce latency while transporting critical information, therefore it should be able to guarantee data fidelity across the transmission channel (Ghorbani et al., 2020). Potential security issues may arise in the 5G central network components when an IoT device with inadequate security is linked to the network (Kim et al., 2022).

In today's cellular network, for instance, 4G, a DDoS attack can affect only one service. These DDoS attacks as previously stated can stem from IoT botnets. On the other hand, in 5G networks, services associated with the same virtual network may be jeopardized if a malevolent hacker seizes control and initiates a DDoS attack. Furthermore, a distributed denial of service (DDoS) attack might become increasingly severe in 5G networks, and it could potentially impact other installations if they utilize one tunneling protocol (Moudoud et al., 2022). Thus, methods to address these concerns can be considered in future work under 5G-IoT.

4.2 Edge Computing

Deploying computational resources nearer to end devices, that is, towards the edge of the network, is known as edge computing. It is an enticing strategy to meet the latency and bandwidth requirements of IoT (Bhardwaj et al., 2018). Forwarding computationally demanding operations to a cloud center could cause a delay because it takes time to send, analyze, and receive an enormous quantity of data. Edge computing was developed to swiftly complete the required computational workload in the network edge devices to get around this restriction. A quicker response time can be achieved by placing threat detection closer to end devices; at the edge, as opposed to the cloud. (Huong et al., 2021) . A reduction in latency time is achieved by eliminating redundant data transmission when raw data generated by Internet of Things (IoT) devices is processed, stored, and transferred at edge nodes through edge computing (Xu et al., 2020).

Nevertheless, the edge has restricted computational resources and experiences little network traffic. Unlike the elastic cloud, the edge is unable to scale the resources required for mitigation or to capture the aggregate network traffic necessary for IoT-DDoS detection (Bhardwaj et al., 2018). Because of the inherent communication cost, deploying AI-DL models on edge nodes for effective intrusion detection is not feasible due to their higher computing and memory needs. (Aldaej et al., 2023). In addition, because the edge layer itself requires security protection, it also widens the attack areas. Since most edge nodes may not be managed by a robust staff of security experts and may not be situated in a physically safe environment, securing the edge layer is not an easy endeavor when compared to cloud data centers (Sha et al., 2020).

A significant element of security is still required for the communication pathways that link end devices to the edge. Yet given the significant resource constraints at the IoT end devices, it is challenging and needs to be further explored.

4.3 Blockchain

Blockchain offers a distributed system for storage and computation. The smart contract token allows users to connect to the system after they have successfully authenticated themselves on a blockchain once (Xu et al., 2020). The prerequisites for safety for IoT infrastructure can be met by the qualities of high availability, tamper resistance, and transparency (Cui et al., 2019).

Given its interoperability between IoT devices, data block capacity to trace IoT data, and the integrity of digital signatures and asymmetric encryption methods, among other cryptographic techniques, blockchain is also well-suited for the Internet of Things (Dai et al., 2019). However, given that any blockchain node can access data stored in the blockchain, privacy issues merit serious consideration (Xu et al., 2020). Because miners must continuously execute hashing to add a block to the chain, the Proof of Work (PoW) mining process is very resource-intensive. Thus, more work needs to be done to take advantage of the merits of blockchain for IoT while addressing these challenges.

5. CONCLUSION AND FUTURE RESEARCH DIRECTIONS

Based on the review discussed, the chapter suggests several future research directions in IoT security to enhance botnet detection and overall cybersecurity. Some of the key recommendations include:

- Application of Deep Learning Techniques: Further exploration and utilization of deep learning techniques for IoT botnet detection to improve accuracy and efficiency.
- Enhanced Anomaly Detection: Continued research on anomaly-based detection methods, including machine learning and deep learning, to better identify and respond to abnormal IoT device behaviors.
- Exploration of Distributed Techniques: Further investigation into distributed techniques such as Software Defined Networking (SDN) and blockchain for IoT botnet detection to leverage their potential benefits.
- Graph Theory Approaches: Continued research on graph theory methods for IoT botnet detection to enhance pattern recognition capabilities and improve efficiency.
- Real-Time DNS Techniques: Development of real-time Domain Name Service (DNS) techniques for detecting suspicious events in IoT networks to enhance proactive threat detection.
- Integration of IoT Security Measures: Integration of IoT security measures into existing frameworks and protocols to strengthen overall cybersecurity in IoT and IIoT environments.

By focusing on these future research directions, the IoT community can advance the field of IoT security and develop more robust strategies for detecting and mitigating botnet attacks in connected environments.

REFERENCES

Abbasi, F., Naderan, M., & Alavi, S. E. (2021). Anomaly detection in the Internet of Things using feature selection and classification based on Logistic Regression and Artificial Neural Networks on N-BaIoT dataset. *Proceedings of 2021 5th International Conference on Internet of Things and Applications, IoT 2021*. 10.1109/IoT52625.2021.9469605

Al-Duwairi, B., Al-Kahla, W., AlRefai, M. A., Abdelqader, Y., Rawash, A., & Fahmawi, R. (2020). SIEM-based detection and mitigation of IoT-botnet DDoS attacks. *Iranian Journal of Electrical and Computer Engineering*, 10(2), 2182–2191. 10.11591/ijece.v10i2.pp2182-2191

Al Hayajneh, A., Bhuiyan, M. Z. A., & McAndrew, I. (2020). Improving Internet of Things (IoT) security with software-defined networking (SDN). *Computers*, 9(1), 1–14. 10.3390/computers9010008

Al-Kasassbeh, M., Almseidin, M., Alrfou, K., & Kovacs, S. (2020). Detection of IoT-botnet attacks using fuzzy rule interpolation. *Journal of Intelligent & Fuzzy Systems*, 39(1), 421–431. 10.3233/JIFS-191432

Aldaej, A., Ahanger, T. A., & Ullah, I. (2023). Deep learning-inspired IOT-IDS mechanism for edge computing environments. *Sensors (Basel)*, 23(24), 9869. 10.3390/s2324986938139716

Alrashdi, I., Alqazzaz, A., Aloufi, E., Alharthi, R., Zohdy, M., & Ming, H. (2019). AD-IoT: Anomaly detection of IoT cyberattacks in the smart city using machine learning. *2019 IEEE 9th Annual Computing and Communication Workshop and Conference, CCWC 2019*, 305–310. 10.1109/CCWC.2019.8666450

Angrishi, K. (2017). *Turning Internet of Things(IoT) into the Internet of Vulnerabilities (IoV) : IoT Botnets*. Academic Press.

Arshad, J., Azad, M. A., Abdellatif, M. M., Ur Rehman, M. H., & Salah, K. (2019). COLIDE: A collaborative intrusion detection framework for the Internet of Things. *IET Networks*, 8(1), 3–14. 10.1049/iet-net.2018.5036

Ashraf, J., Moustafa, N., Bukhshi, A. D., & Javed, A. (2021). Intrusion Detection System for SDN-enabled IoT Networks using Machine Learning Techniques. *Proceedings - IEEE International Enterprise Distributed Object Computing Workshop, EDOCW*, 46–52. 10.1109/EDOCW52865.2021.00031

Ashton, K. (2009). That 'Internet of things' thing. *RFID Journal*, 22(7), 97–114.

Bagui, S., Wang, X., & Bagui, S. (2021). Machine Learning Based Intrusion Detection for IoT Botnet. *International Journal of Machine Learning and Computing*, 11(6), 399–406. 10.18178/ijmlc.2021.11.6.1068

Bahsi, H., Nomm, S., & La Torre, F. B. (2018). Dimensionality Reduction for Machine Learning Based IoT Botnet Detection. *2018 15th International Conference on Control, Automation, Robotics and Vision, ICARCV 2018*, 1857–1862. 10.1109/ICARCV.2018.8581205

Bastos, G., Meira, W., Marzano, A., Fonseca, O., Fazzion, E., Hoepers, C., Steding-Jessen, K., Marcelo, C. H. P. C., Cunha, I., & Guedes, D. (2019). Identifying and Characterizing Bashlite and Mirai CC Servers. *Proceedings - IEEE Symposium on Computers and Communications*, 1–6. 10.1109/ISCC47284.2019.8969728

Ben Said, N., Biondi, F., Bontchev, V., Decourbe, O., Given-Wilson, T., Legay, A., & Quilbeuf, J. (2018). Detection of Mirai by Syntactic and Behavioral Analysis. *Proceedings - International Symposium on Software Reliability Engineering, ISSRE*, 224–235. https://doi.org/10.1109/ISSRE.2018.00032

Bhardwaj, K., Miranda, J. C., & Gavrilovska, A. (2018). Towards {IoT-DDoS} Prevention Using Edge Computing. *USENIX workshop on hot topics in edge computing (HotEdge 18)*.

Bilal, D., Rehman, A.-U., & Ali, R. (2018). Internet of Things (IoT) Protocols: A Brief Exploration of MQTT and CoAP. *International Journal of Computer Applications*, 179(27), 9–14. 10.5120/ijca2018916438

Breitenbacher, D., Homoliak, I., Aung, Y. L., & Tippenhauer, N. O. (2019). *HADES-IoT : A Practical Host-Based Anomaly Detection System for IoT Devices*. Academic Press.

Çelik, Ö. (2018). A Research on Machine Learning Methods and Its Applications. *Journal of Educational Technology and Online Learning*, 1(3), 25–40. 10.31681/jetol.457046

Ceron, J. M., Steding-Jessen, K., Hoepers, C., Granville, L. Z., & Margi, C. B. (2019). Improving IoT botnet investigation using an adaptive network layer. *Sensors (Basel)*, 19(3), 1–16. 10.3390/s1903072730754667

Chen, M., Wan, J., & Li, F. (2012). Machine-to-machine communications: Architectures, standards, and applications. *KSII Transactions on Internet and Information Systems*, 6(2), 480–497. 10.3837/tiis.2012.02.002

Chitralekha, G., & Roogi, J. M. (2021). A Quick Review of ML Algorithms. *Proceedings of the 6th International Conference on Communication and Electronics Systems, ICCES 2021*. 10.1109/ICCES51350.2021.9488982

Cui, P., Guin, U., Skjellum, A., & Umphress, D. (2019). Blockchain in IoT: Current Trends, Challenges, and Future Roadmap. *Journal of Hardware and Systems Security*, 3(4), 338–364. 10.1007/s41635-019-00079-5

Dai, H.-N., Zheng, Z., & Zhang, Y. (2019). Blockchain for Internet of things: A survey. *IEEE Internet of Things Journal*, 6(5), 8076–8094. 10.1109/JIOT.2019.2920987

Dalal, K. R. (2020). Analyzing the Role of Supervised and Unsupervised Machine Learning in IoT. *Proceedings of the International Conference on Electronics and Sustainable Communication Systems, ICESC 2020, Icesc*, 75–79. 10.1109/ICESC48915.2020.9155761

De Neira, A. B., Araujo, A. M., & Nogueira, M. (2020). Early botnet detection for the Internet and the Internet of Things by autonomous machine learning. *Proceedings - 2020 16th International Conference on Mobility, Sensing, and Networking, MSN 2020*, 516–523. 10.1109/MSN50589.2020.00087

Desai, M. G., Shi, Y., & Suo, K. (2020). IoT Bonet and Network Intrusion Detection using Dimensionality Reduction and Supervised Machine Learning. *2020 11th IEEE Annual Ubiquitous Computing, Electronics and Mobile Communication Conference, UEMCON 2020*, 316–322. 10.1109/UEMCON51285.2020.9298146

Desai, M. G., Shi, Y., & Suo, K. (2021). *A Hybrid Approach for IoT Botnet Attack Detection*. 10.1109/IEMCON53756.2021.9623102

Dhir, S., & Kumar, Y. (2020). Study of machine and deep learning classifications in cyber-physical systems. *Proceedings of the 3rd International Conference on Smart Systems and Inventive Technology, ICSSIT 2020, Icssit*, 333–338. 10.1109/ICSSIT48917.2020.9214237

Doshi, R., Apthorpe, N., & Feamster, N. (2018). Machine learning DDoS detection for consumer Internet of Things devices. *Proceedings - 2018 IEEE Symposium on Security and Privacy Workshops, SPW 2018, MI*, 29–35. 10.1109/SPW.2018.00013

Dowling, S., Schukat, M., & Melvin, H. (2017). A ZigBee honeypot to assess IoT cyberattack behavior. *2017 28th Irish Signals and Systems Conference, ISSC 2017*. 10.1109/ISSC.2017.7983603

Dwyer, O. P., Marnerides, A. K., Giotsas, V., & Mursch, T. (2019). Profiling IoT-based botnet traffic using DNS. *2019 IEEE Global Communications Conference, GLOBECOM 2019 - Proceedings*. 10.1109/GLOBECOM38437.2019.9014300

El Ghazi, A., & Moulay Rachid, A. (2020). Machine learning and data mining methods for hybrid IoT intrusion detection. *Proceedings of 2020 5th International Conference on Cloud Computing and Artificial Intelligence: Technologies and Applications, CloudTech 2020*. https://doi.org/10.1109/CloudTech49835.2020.9365895

Estalenx, A., & Gañán, C. H. (2021). *NURSE : eNd-UseR IoT malware detection tool for Smart homEs*. Academic Press.

Falco, G., Li, C., Fedorov, P., Caldera, C., Arora, R., & Jackson, K. (2019). NeuroMesh: IoT security enabled by a blockchain-powered botnet vaccine. *ACM International Conference Proceeding Series, Part F1481*, 1–6. 10.1145/3312614.3312615

Frank, C., Nance, C., Jarocki, S., Pauli, W. E., & Madison, S. D. (2017). Protecting IoT from Mirai botnets; IoT device hardening. *Proceedings of the Conference on Information Systems Applied Research ISSN, 2167*, 1508.

Gharami, S., Prabadevi, B., & Bhimnath, A. (2019). Semantic analysis - Internet of things, the study of past, present, and future of IoT. *Electronic Government, 15*(2), 144–165. 10.1504/EG.2019.098668

Ghorbani, H., Mohammadzadeh, M. S., & Ahmadzadegan, M. H. (2020, April). DDoS Attacks on the IoT Network with the Emergence of 5G. In *2020 International Conference on Technology and Entrepreneurship-Virtual (ICTE-V)* (pp. 1-5). IEEE. 10.1109/ICTE-V50708.2020.9113779

Giachoudis, N., Damiris, G. P., Theodoridis, G., & Spathoulas, G. (2019). Collaborative agent-based detection of DDoS IoT botnets. *Proceedings - 15th Annual International Conference on Distributed Computing in Sensor Systems, DCOSS 2019*, 205–211. 10.1109/DCOSS.2019.00055

Golomb, T., Mirsky, Y., & Elovici, Y. (2018). *CIoTA: Collaborative Anomaly Detection via Blockchain*. 10.14722/diss.2018.23003

Gomathi, R. M., Krishna, G. H. S., Brumancia, E., & Dhas, Y. M. (2018). A Survey on IoT Technologies, Evolution and Architecture. *2nd International Conference on Computer, Communication, and Signal Processing: Special Focus on Technology and Innovation for Smart Environment, ICCCSP 2018, Icccsp*, 1–5. 10.1109/ICCCSP.2018.8452820

Goudarzi, A., Ghayoor, F., Waseem, M., Fahad, S., & Traore, I. (2022). A survey on IOT-enabled smart grids: Emerging, applications, challenges, and outlook. *Energies*, 15(19), 6984. 10.3390/en15196984

Grover, A., & Berghel, H. (2011). A Survey of RFID Deployment and Security Issues. *Journal of Information Processing Systems*, 7(4), 561–580. 10.3745/JIPS.2011.7.4.561

Guarnizo, J., Tambe, A., Bhunia, S. S., Ochoa, M., Tippenhauer, N. O., Shabtai, A., & Elovici, Y. (2017). SIPHON: Towards scalable high-interaction physical honeypots. *CPSS 2017 - Proceedings of the 3rd ACM Workshop on Cyber-Physical System Security, Co-Located with ASIA CCS 2017*, 57–68. 10.1145/3055186.3055192

Gurulakshmi, K., & Nesarani, A. (2018). Machine Learning_algorithm_prespective.pdf. *2018 2nd International Conference on Trends in Electronics and Informatics (ICOEI)*, 1052–1057.

Gyamfi, E., & Jurcut, A. (2022). Intrusion detection in Internet of Things systems: A review on Design Approaches Leveraging Multi-Access Edge Computing, machine learning, and datasets. *Sensors (Basel)*, 22(10), 3744. 10.3390/s2210374435632153

H., Z., A., H., & M., M. (2015). Internet of Things (IoT): Definitions, Challenges, and Recent Research Directions. *International Journal of Computer Applications, 128*(1), 37–47. 10.5120/ijca2015906430

Habibi, J., Midi, D., Mudgerikar, A., & Bertino, E. (2017). Heimdall: Mitigating the Internet of Insecure Things. *IEEE Internet of Things Journal*, 4(4), 968–978. 10.1109/JIOT.2017.2704093

Hakim, M. A., Aksu, H., Uluagac, A. S., & Akkaya, K. (2018). U-PoT: A Honeypot Framework for UPnP-Based IoT Devices. *2018 IEEE 37th International Performance Computing and Communications Conference, IPCCC 2018*. 10.1109/PCCC.2018.8711321

Hamza, A., Gharakheili, H. H., & Sivaraman, V. (2018). Combining MUD policies with SDN for IoT intrusion detection. *IoT S and P 2018 - Proceedings of the 2018 Workshop on IoT Security and Privacy, Part of SIGCOMM 2018*, 1–7. 10.1145/3229565.3229571

Haseeb, J., Mansoori, M., Al-Sahaf, H., & Welch, I. (2020). IoT attacks: Features identification and clustering. *Proceedings - 2020 IEEE 19th International Conference on Trust, Security and Privacy in Computing and Communications, TrustCom 2020*, 353–360. 10.1109/TrustCom50675.2020.00056

Hegde, M., Kepnang, G., Al Mazroei, M., Chavis, J. S., & Watkins, L. (2020). Identification of Botnet Activity in IoT Network Traffic Using Machine Learning. *2020 International Conference on Intelligent Data Science Technologies and Applications, IDSTA 2020, 1*, 21–27. 10.1109/IDSTA50958.2020.9264143

Hsiao, S., Mattox, S., Park, T., Selvaraj, S., & Tam, A. (2017). *BotRevealer: Behavioral Detection of Botnets based on Botnet Life-cycle*. IS e C Ure.

Huong, T. T., Bac, T. P., Long, D. M., Thang, B. D., Binh, N. T., Luong, T. D., & Phuc, T. K. (2021). Lockedge: Low-complexity cyberattack detection in IoT edge computing. *IEEE Access : Practical Innovations, Open Solutions*, 9, 29696–29710. 10.1109/ACCESS.2021.3058528

Hussain, F., Abbas, S. G., Husnain, M., Fayyaz, U. U., Shahzad, F., & Shah, G. A. (2020). IoT DoS and DDoS Attack Detection using ResNet. *Proceedings - 2020 23rd IEEE International Multi-Topic Conference, INMIC 2020*. 10.1109/INMIC50486.2020.9318216

Hussain, F., Abbas, S. G., Pires, I. M., Tanveer, S., Fayyaz, U. U., Garcia, N. M., Shah, G. A., & Shahzad, F. (2021). A Two-Fold Machine Learning Approach to Prevent and Detect IoT Botnet Attacks. *IEEE Access : Practical Innovations, Open Solutions*, 9, 163412–163430. 10.1109/ACCESS.2021.3131014

Hussein, A. R. H. (2019). Internet of Things (IoT): Research challenges and future applications. *International Journal of Advanced Computer Science and Applications*, 10(6), 77–82. 10.14569/IJACSA.2019.0100611

Ibrahim, A., Sadeghi, A. R., & Tsudik, G. (2019). US-AID: Unattended scalable attestation of IoT devices. *Proceedings of the IEEE Symposium on Reliable Distributed Systems, 2019-Octob*, 21–30. 10.1109/SRDS.2018.00013

Injadat, M. N., Moubayed, A., & Shami, A. (2020). Detecting Botnet Attacks in IoT Environments: An Optimized Machine Learning Approach. *Proceedings of the International Conference on Microelectronics, ICM, 2020-Decem.* 10.1109/ICM50269.2020.9331794

Jahwar, A. F., & Ameen, S. Y. (2021). A Review of Cybersecurity based on Machine Learning and Deep Learning Algorithms. *Journal of Soft Computing and Data Mining*, 2(2), 14–25. 10.30880/jscdm.2021.02.02.002

Juels, A. (2006). RFID security and privacy: A research survey. *IEEE Journal on Selected Areas in Communications*, 24(2), 381–394. 10.1109/JSAC.2005.861395

Karaca, K. N., & Cetin, A. (2021). Botnet Attack Detection Using Convolutional Neural Networks in the IoT Environment. *2021 International Conference on Innovations in Intelligent Systems and Applications, INISTA 2021 - Proceedings.* 10.1109/INISTA52262.2021.9548445

Karim, A., Salleh, R., Shiraz, M., Shah, S. A. A., Awan, I., & Anuar, N. B. (2014). Botnet detection techniques: Review, future trends, and issues. *Journal of Zhejiang University: Science C*, 15(11), 943–983. 10.1631/jzus.C1300242

Khaing, M. S., Thant, Y. M., Tun, T., Htwe, C. S., & Thwin, M. M. S. (2020). IoT Botnet Detection Mechanism Based on UDP Protocol. *2020 IEEE Conference on Computer Applications, ICCA 2020.* 10.1109/ICCA49400.2020.9022832

Kim, T. H., & Reeves, D. (2020). A survey of domain name system vulnerabilities and attacks. *Journal of Surveillance, Security, and Safety*, 34–60. https://doi.org/10.20517/jsss.2020.14

Kim, Y. E., Kim, M. G., & Kim, H. (2022). Detecting IoT Botnet in 5G Core Network Using Machine Learning. *Computers, Materials & Continua*, 72(3), 4467–4488. 10.32604/cmc.2022.026581

Koroniotis, N., Moustafa, N., Sitnikova, E., & Turnbull, B. (2019). Towards the development of realistic botnet dataset in the Internet of Things for network forensic analytics: Bot-IoT dataset. *Future Generation Computer Systems*, 100, 779–796. 10.1016/j.future.2019.05.041

Kulkarni, A. A., Mishra, P. K., Tripathy, B. K., & Panda, M. (2018). A Security Survey on Internet of Things. *International Journal on Computer Science and Engineering*, 6(6), 1227–1233. 10.26438/ijcse/v6i6.12271233

Kumar, A., & Lim, T. J. (2019). EDIMA: Early Detection of IoT Malware Network Activity Using Machine Learning Techniques. *IEEE 5th World Forum on Internet of Things, WF-IoT 2019 - Conference Proceedings*, 289–294. 10.1109/WF-IoT.2019.8767194

Le, H. V., & Ngo, Q. D. (2020). V-Sandbox for Dynamic Analysis IoT Botnet. *IEEE Access : Practical Innovations, Open Solutions*, 8, 145768–145786. 10.1109/ACCESS.2020.3014891

Lee, S., Abdullah, A., Jhanjhi, N. Z., & Kok, S. H. (2021). Honeypot Coupled Machine Learning Model for Botnet Detection and Classification in IoT Smart Factory – An Investigation. *MATEC Web of Conferences, 335*, 04003. 10.1051/matecconf/202133504003

Lefoane, M., Ghafir, I., Kabir, S., & Awan, I. U. (2022). Unsupervised learning for feature selection: A proposed solution for botnet detection in 5g networks. *IEEE Transactions on Industrial Informatics*, 19(1), 921–929. 10.1109/TII.2022.3192044

Lekssays, A., Landa, L., Carminati, B., & Ferrari, E. (2021). PAutoBotCatcher: A blockchain-based privacy-preserving botnet detector for the Internet of Things. *Computer Networks*, 200, 108512. Advance online publication. 10.1016/j.comnet.2021.108512

Liang, X., & Znati, T. (2019). A long short-term memory-enabled framework for DDoS detection. *2019 IEEE Global Communications Conference, GLOBECOM 2019 - Proceedings*. 10.1109/GLOBECOM38437.2019.9013450

Liu, J., Liu, S., & Zhang, S. (2019). Detection of IoT botnet based on deep learning. *Chinese Control Conference, CCC*, 8381–8385. 10.23919/ChiCC.2019.8866088

Liu, Z., Thapa, N., Shaver, A., Roy, K., Yuan, X., & Khorsandroo, S. (2020). Anomaly detection on lot network intrusion using machine learning. *2020 International Conference on Artificial Intelligence, Big Data, Computing and Data Communication Systems, IcABCD 2020 - Proceedings*, 3–7. 10.1109/icABCD49160.2020.9183842

Locke, D. (2010). Mq telemetry transport (mqtt) v3. 1 protocol specification. *IBM DeveloperWorks Technical Library, 15*.

Lysenko, S., Bobrovnikova, K., Savenko, O., & Shchuka, R. (2020). Technique for cyberattack detection based on DNS traffic analysis. *CEUR Workshop Proceedings*, 2732, 171–182.

Mahmoud, Q. H., & Ullah, I. (2020). A two-level flow-based anomalous activity detection system for IoT networks. *Electronics (Basel)*, 9(3), 530. Advance online publication. 10.3390/electronics9030530

Majumder, A., Goswami, J., Ghosh, S., Shrivastawa, R., Mohanty, S. P., & Bhattacharyya, B. K. (2017). Pay-Cloak: A Biometric Back Cover for Smartphone with Tokenization Principle for Cashless Payment. *IEEE Consumer Electronics Magazine*, 6(2), 78–88. 10.1109/MCE.2016.2640739

Marinos, L., & Lourenço, M. (2018). ENISA Threat Landscape Report 2018 15 Top Cyberthreats and Trends. In *European Union Agency For Network and Information Security*. Issue January., 10.2824/622757

McDermott, C. D., Majdani, F., & Petrovski, A. V. (2018). Botnet Detection in the Internet of Things using Deep Learning Approaches. *Proceedings of the International Joint Conference on Neural Networks, 2018-July*. 10.1109/IJCNN.2018.8489489

Meidan, Y., Bohadana, M., Mathov, Y., Mirsky, Y., Shabtai, A., Breitenbacher, D., & Elovici, Y. (2018). N-BaIoT-Network-based detection of IoT botnet attacks using deep autoencoders. *IEEE Pervasive Computing*, 17(3), 12–22. 10.1109/MPRV.2018.03367731

Memos, V. (2020). *AI-Powered Honeypots for Enhanced IoT Botnet Detection*. Academic Press.

Miller, B., Alabama, N., & College, C. (2020). a Multi-Layer Approach To Detecting and Preventing IoT-Based Botnet Attacks. *Issues in Information Systems*, 21(3), 168–178. 10.48009/3_iis_2020_168-178

Moudoud, H., Khoukhi, L., & Cherkaoui, S. (2020). Prediction and detection of fdia and DDoS attacks in 5g enabled iot. *IEEE Network*, 35(2), 194–201. 10.1109/MNET.011.2000449

Moustafa, N., Turnbull, B., & Choo, K. K. R. (2019). An ensemble intrusion detection technique based on proposed statistical flow features for protecting network traffic of the Internet of Things. *IEEE Internet of Things Journal*, 6(3), 4815–4830. 10.1109/JIOT.2018.2871719

Mudgerikar, A., Sharma, P., & Bertino, E. (2020). Edge-Based Intrusion Detection for IoT Devices. *ACM Transactions on Management Information Systems*, 11(4), 1–21. Advance online publication. 10.1145/3382159

Myridakis, D., Myridakis, P., & Kakarountas, A. (2020). Intrusion Detection and Botnet Prevention Circuit for IoT Devices. *SEEDA-CECNSM 2020 - 5th South-East Europe Design Automation, Computer Engineering, Computer Networks, and Social Media Conference*, 2020–2023. 10.1109/SEEDA-CECNSM49515.2020.9221789

Myridakis, D., Myridakis, P., & Kakarountas, A. (2021). A power dissipation monitoring circuit for intrusion detection and botnet prevention on IoT devices. *Computation (Basel, Switzerland)*, 9(2), 1–11. 10.3390/computation9020019

Naveed, K., & Wu, H. (2020). Poster: A Semi-Supervised Framework to Detect Botnets in IoT Devices. *IFIP Networking 2020 Conference and WorkshopsNetworking*, 2020, 649–651.

Naveed, K., Wu, H., & Abusaq, A. (2020). Dytokinesis: A Cytokinesis-Inspired Anomaly Detection Technique for IoT Devices. *Proceedings - Conference on Local Computer Networks, LCN, 2020-Novem*, 373–376. 10.1109/LCN48667.2020.9314856

Ngo, Q. D., Nguyen, H. T., Nguyen, V. D., Dinh, C. M., Phung, A. T., & Bui, Q. T. (2021). Adversarial Attack and Defense on Graph-based IoT Botnet Detection Approach. *3rd International Conference on Electrical, Communication and Computer Engineering, ICECCE 2021*, 12–13. 10.1109/ICEC-CE52056.2021.9514255

Ngo, Q. D., Nguyen, H. T., Tran, H. A., & Nguyen, D. H. (2021). IoT Botnet detection is based on the integration of static and dynamic vector features. *ICCE 2020 - 2020 IEEE 8th International Conference on Communications and Electronics*, 540–545. 10.1109/ICCE48956.2021.9352145

Ngo, Q. D., Nguyen, H. T., Tran, H. A., Pham, N. A., & Dang, X. H. (2021). Toward an approach using graph-theoretic for IoT botnet detection. *ACM International Conference Proceeding Series*, 1. 10.1145/3468691.3468714

Nguyen, H. T., Ngo, Q. D., & Le, V. H. (2018). IoT Botnet Detection Approach Based on PSI graph and DGCNN classifier. *2018 IEEE International Conference on Information Communication and Signal Processing, ICICSP 2018, Icsp*, 118–122. 10.1109/ICICSP.2018.8549713

Ozcelik, M., Chalabianloo, N., & Gur, G. (2017). Software-Defined Edge Defense Against IoT-Based DDoS. *IEEE CIT 2017 - 17th IEEE International Conference on Computer and Information Technology*, 308–313. 10.1109/CIT.2017.61

Panda, M., Mousa, A. A. A., & Hassanien, A. E. (2021). Developing an Efficient Feature Engineering and Machine Learning Model for Detecting IoT-Botnet Cyber Attacks. *IEEE Access : Practical Innovations, Open Solutions*, 9, 91038–91052. 10.1109/ACCESS.2021.3092054

Popoola, S. I., Adebisi, B., Ande, R., Hammoudeh, M., & Atayero, A. A. (2021). Memory-efficient deep learning for botnet attack detection in IoT networks. *Electronics (Basel)*, 10(9), 4944–4956. 10.3390/electronics10091104

Prokofiev, A. O., Smirnova, Y. S., & Surov, V. A. (2018). A method to detect Internet of Things botnets. *Proceedings of the 2018 IEEE Conference of Russian Young Researchers in Electrical and Electronic Engineering, ElConRus 2018, 2018-Janua*, 105–108. https://doi.org/10.1109/EIConRus.2018.8317041

Putman, C. G. J., Abhishta, & Nieuwenhuis, L. J. (2018). Business model of a botnet. *2018 26th Euromicro International Conference on Parallel, Distributed and Network-Based Processing (PDP)*. https://doi.org/10.1109/pdp2018.2018.0007

Rahmantyo, D. T., Erfianto, B., & Satrya, G. B. (2021). *Deep Residual CNN for Preventing Botnet Attacks on The Internet of Things*. Advance online publication. 10.1109/IC2IE53219.2021.9649314

Rodriguez-Gomez, R. A., Macia-Fernandez, G., & Garcia-Teodoro, P. (2013). Survey and taxonomy of botnet research through life-cycle. *ACM Computing Surveys*, 45(4), 1–33. Advance online publication. 10.1145/2501654.2501659

Rosenthal, G., Kdosha, O. E., Cohen, K., Freund, A., Bartik, A., & Ron, A. (2020). ARBA: Anomaly and Reputation Based Approach for Detecting Infected IoT Devices. *IEEE Access : Practical Innovations, Open Solutions*, 8, 145751–145767. 10.1109/ACCESS.2020.3014619

Sagirlar, G., Carminati, B., & Ferrari, E. (2018). AutoBotCatcher: Blockchain-based P2P botnet detection for the Internet of Things. *Proceedings - 4th IEEE International Conference on Collaboration and Internet Computing, CIC 2018*, 1–8. 10.1109/CIC.2018.00-46

Sajjad, S. M., Yousaf, M., Afzal, H., & Mufti, M. R. (2020). EMUD: Enhanced manufacturer usage description for IoT botnet prevention on home wifi routers. *IEEE Access : Practical Innovations, Open Solutions*, 8, 164200–164213. 10.1109/ACCESS.2020.3022272

Sedjelmaci, H., Senouci, S. M., & Taleb, T. (2017). An accurate security game for low-resource IoT devices. *IEEE Transactions on Vehicular Technology*, 66(10), 9381–9393. 10.1109/TVT.2017.2701551

Sha, K., Yang, T. A., Wei, W., & Davari, S. (2020). A survey of Edge Computing-based designs for IOT Security. *Digital Communications and Networks*, 6(2), 195–202. 10.1016/j.dcan.2019.08.006

Shafiq, M., Tian, Z., Bashir, A. K., Du, X., & Guizani, M. (2021). CorrAUC: A Malicious Bot-IoT Traffic Detection Method in IoT Network Using Machine-Learning Techniques. *IEEE Internet of Things Journal*, 8(5), 3242–3254. 10.1109/JIOT.2020.3002255

Shah, T., & Venkatesan, S. (2019). A method to secure IoT devices against botnet attacks. In *Lecture Notes in Computer Science (including subseries Lecture Notes in Artificial Intelligence and Lecture Notes in Bioinformatics): Vol. 11519 LNCS*. Springer International Publishing. 10.1007/978-3-030-23357-0_3

Spathoulas, G., Giachoudis, N., Damiris, G. P., & Theodoridis, G. (2019). Collaborative blockchain-based detection of distributed denial of service attacks based on Internet of things botnets. *Future Internet*, 11(11), 226. Advance online publication. 10.3390/fi11110226

Sriram, S., Vinayakumar, R., Alazab, M., & Soman, K. P. (2020). Network flow-based IoT botnet attack detection using deep learning. *IEEE INFOCOM 2020 - IEEE Conference on Computer Communications Workshops, INFOCOM WKSHPS 2020*, 189–194. 10.1109/INFOCOMWKSHPS50562.2020.9162668

Sudheera, K. L. K., Divakaran, D. M., Singh, R. P., & Gurusamy, M. (2021). ADEPT: Detection and Identification of Correlated Attack Stages in IoT Networks. *IEEE Internet of Things Journal*, 8(8), 6591–6607. 10.1109/JIOT.2021.3055937

Swarna Sugi, S. S., & Ratna, S. R. (2020). Investigation of machine learning techniques in an intrusion detection system for IoT network. *Proceedings of the 3rd International Conference on Intelligent Sustainable Systems, ICISS 2020*, 1164–1167. 10.1109/ICISS49785.2020.9315900

Trajanovski, T., & Zhang, N. (2021). An Automated and Comprehensive Framework for IoT Botnet Detection and Analysis (IoT-BDA). *IEEE Access : Practical Innovations, Open Solutions*, 9, 124360–124383. 10.1109/ACCESS.2021.3110188

Tyagi, A. K., & Aghila, G. (2011). A Wide Scale Survey on Botnet. *International Journal of Computer Applications*, 34(9), 9–22.

Tzgkarakis, C., Petroulakis, N., & Ioannidis, S. (2019). Botnet attack detection at the IoT edge is based on sparse representation. *Global IoT Summit, GIoTS 2019 - Proceedings*. 10.1109/GIOTS.2019.8766388

Ullah, I., & Mahmoud, Q. H. (2021). Design and Development of a Deep Learning-Based Model for Anomaly Detection in IoT Networks. *IEEE Access : Practical Innovations, Open Solutions*, 9, 103906–103926. 10.1109/ACCESS.2021.3094024

Vishwakarma, R., & Jain, A. K. (2019). A honeypot with a machine learning-based detection framework for defending IoT-based botnet DDoS attacks. *Proceedings of the International Conference on Trends in Electronics and Informatics, ICOEI 2019, Icoei*, 1019–1024. 10.1109/ICOEI.2019.8862720

Wang, B., Dou, Y., Sang, Y., Zhang, Y., & Huang, J. (2020). IoTCMal: Towards A Hybrid IoT Honeypot for Capturing and Analyzing Malware. *IEEE International Conference on Communications*. 10.1109/ICC40277.2020.9149314

Wang, H., & Wu, B. (2019). SDN-based hybrid honeypot for attack capture. *Proceedings of 2019 IEEE 3rd Information Technology, Networking, Electronic and Automation Control Conference, ITNEC 2019, Itnec*, 1602–1606. 10.1109/ITNEC.2019.8729425

Wang, M., Santillan, J., & Kuipers, F. (2018). *ThingPot: an interactive Internet-of-Things honeypot.* Academic Press.

Wazid, M., Das, A. K., Shetty, S., Gope, P., & Rodrigues, J. J. (2021). Security in 5G-enabled Internet of Things communication: Issues, challenges, and future research roadmap. *IEEE Access : Practical Innovations, Open Solutions*, 9, 4466–4489. 10.1109/ACCESS.2020.3047895

Wazzan, M., Algazzawi, D., Bamasaq, O., Albeshri, A., & Cheng, L. (2021). Internet of Things botnet detection approaches: Analysis and recommendations for future research. *Applied Sciences (Basel, Switzerland)*, 11(12), 5713. Advance online publication. 10.3390/app11125713

Xing, Y., Shu, H., Zhao, H., Li, D., & Guo, L. (2021). Survey on Botnet Detection Techniques: Classification, Methods, and Evaluation. *Mathematical Problems in Engineering*, 2021, 1–24. Advance online publication. 10.1155/2021/6640499

Xu, Y., Jiang, Y., Yu, L., & Li, J. (2021). Brief industry paper: Catching IoT malware in the wild using HoneyIoT. *Proceedings of the IEEE Real-Time and Embedded Technology and Applications Symposium, RTAS*, 433–436. 10.1109/RTAS52030.2021.00045

Xu, Z., Liu, W., Huang, J., Yang, C., Lu, J., & Tan, H. (2020). Artificial Intelligence for securing IOT services in Edge computing: A survey. *Security and Communication Networks*, 2020, 1–13. 10.1155/2020/8872586

Yamaguchi, S. (2020). Botnet Defense System and Its Basic Strategy against Malicious Botnet. *2020 IEEE International Conference on Consumer Electronics - Taiwan, ICCE-Taiwan 2020*, 1–2. 10.1109/ICCE-Taiwan49838.2020.9258257

Yaokumah, W., Appati, J. K., & Kumah, D. (2021). Machine Learning Methods for Detecting Internet-of-Things (IoT) Malware. *International Journal of Cognitive Informatics and Natural Intelligence*, 15(4), 1–18. 10.4018/IJCINI.286768

Yassin, W., Abdullah, R., Abdollah, M. F., Mas, Z., & Bakhari, F. A. (2019). *An IoT Botnet Prediction Model Using Frequency-based Dependency Graph : Proof-of-concept.* Academic Press.

Yastrebova, A., Kirichek, R., Koucheryavy, Y., Borodin, A., & Koucheryavy, A. (2018). Future Networks 2030: Architecture & Requirements. *2018 10th International Congress on Ultra Modern Telecommunications and Control Systems and Workshops (ICUMT)*. 10.1109/ICUMT.2018.8631208

Yilmaz, Y., & Uludag, S. (2017). Mitigating IoT-based cyberattacks on the smart grid. *Proceedings - 16th IEEE International Conference on Machine Learning and Applications, ICMLA 2017*, 517–522. 10.1109/ICMLA.2017.0-109

Zarpelão, B. B., Miani, R. S., Kawakani, C. T., & de Alvarenga, S. C. (2017). A survey of intrusion detection in Internet of Things. *Journal of Network and Computer Applications*, 84(January), 25–37. 10.1016/j.jnca.2017.02.009

Zhang, W., Zhang, B., Zhou, Y., He, H., & Ding, Z. (2020). An IoT Honeynet Based on Multiport Honeypots for Capturing IoT Attacks. *IEEE Internet of Things Journal*, 7(5), 3991–3999. 10.1109/JIOT.2019.2956173

Chapter 4
Agile Security Strategies

Wasswa Shafik
http://orcid.org/0000-0002-9320-3186

School of Digital Science, Universiti Brunei Darussalam, Gadong, Brunei Darussalam & Dig Connectivity Research Laboratory (DCRLab), Kampala, Uganda

ABSTRACT

Agile security in the ever-changing field of cybersecurity encompasses the ability to adjust and react to emerging threats. This chapter explores the fundamental elements, benefits, methods of implementation, difficulties, and upcoming developments in the field of agile security. Agile security strengthens organizational defenses, allowing for flexibility, efficiency, and effective risk reduction. This chapter provides organizations with practical insights and best practices for effective adoption by thoroughly examining popular frameworks and techniques. It effectively explores the various difficulties encountered and offers strategic remedies, accompanied by practical examples showcasing successful executions. Finally, the study provides a brief insight into the future by examining advanced technologies and predicting their influence on agile security methodologies. In a nutshell, this chapter acts as a guide, highlighting the significance of agile security and encouraging additional investigation and adoption within organizational security policies.

INTRODUCTION

The notion of agile security signifies a fundamental change in cybersecurity techniques, which is particularly relevant in the current dynamic and ever-changing threat landscape (Rindell et al., 2018). Agile security refers to a flexible and proactive strategy for reducing risks in a constantly evolving environment with dynamic threats. Agile security differs from traditional security models by focusing on a dynamic, iterative, and flexible approach. It enables organizations to quickly adapt and respond to new threats instead of solely strengthening their defenses (Kagombe et al., 2021). It is a mental attitude that recognizes the unavoidable occurrence of breaches and prioritizes resilience, highlighting the capacity to identify, react to, and recover from incidents efficiently (Bell et al., 2017).

The importance of agile security resides in its ability to adapt promptly to the ever-changing landscape of cyber threats. As technology progresses swiftly, the dangers are getting increasingly sophisticated, varied, and uncertain (Merkow, 2021). Agile security acknowledges this fact by prioritizing ongoing surveillance, flexible defenses, and swift response systems. It effectively explores the various difficulties

DOI: 10.4018/979-8-3693-3451-5.ch004

encountered and offers strategic remedies, accompanied by practical examples showcasing successful executions. This method guarantees that security measures stay pertinent and efficient in response to developing threats rather than depending on fixed, outmoded defenses that can rapidly become obsolete (Reddivari, 2022).

Furthermore, agile security is strongly aligned with the principles of agile development, fostering cooperation, adaptability, and incremental enhancements. It seamlessly incorporates security practices into the development lifecycle, promoting a culture of security awareness throughout all stages of software or product development (Or, 2009). This integration improves both the security posture and operational efficiency by minimizing conflicts between security protocols and development deadlines. The importance of agile security goes beyond technical issues; it is a strategic approach that recognizes the interdependence of technology, individuals, and procedures (Nägele et al., 2023).

The need to embrace agile security strategies (ASS) arises from the recognition that conventional tactics frequently fall behind the adaptability of contemporary threats. Traditional security mechanisms face challenges in adapting to the wide range and complexity of modern cyber threats (Oyetoyan et al., 2017). Agile security, on the other hand, represents a proactive and adaptable approach that involves a constant process of monitoring, acquiring knowledge, and promptly addressing dangers as they arise (Raschke et al., 2014). It promotes a change of thinking, acknowledging that breaches are inevitable and emphasizing the importance of resilience and quick recovery as essential elements of cybersecurity, security methodologies in agile development as illustrated in Figure 1. The emergence of interconnected systems, cloud technologies, and the widespread use of connected devices has made traditional security methods insufficient (He et al., 2022).

Figure 1. Security Methodologies in Agile Development (Credit: Exalate)

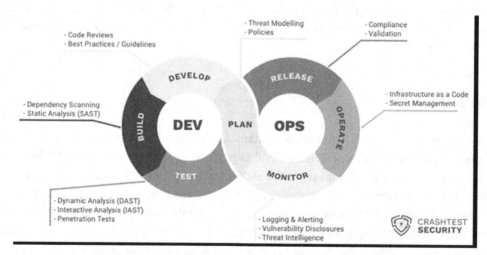

Study Motivation

Gaining comprehension and effectively applying ASS provides an opportunity to navigate the intricacies of contemporary cybersecurity environments. This journey explores the combination of technology, innovation, and resilience. It provides an opportunity to understand the essential principles of adaptability and responsiveness that are necessary for protecting against advanced cyber-attacks. This study path is not solely focused on gaining knowledge but rather on adopting a mindset that promotes ongoing learning, proactive risk mitigation, and the implementation of forward-looking initiatives to safeguard our digital ecosystems. It offers a profound and impactful experience, enabling users to become agents of change in protecting digital environments from constantly changing dangers.

Chapter Contributions

This chapter presents the following contributions.

- This chapter aims to provide a precise explanation of agile security in the context of cybersecurity, highlighting its dynamic character and importance.
- Provide an in-depth examination of the fundamental elements and principles that make up agile security methods, facilitating comprehensive comprehension.
- Emphasizing the concrete advantages of implementing agile security, including its ability to improve flexibility, efficiency, and risk reduction.
- Providing practical guidance and expert advice on how to effectively adopt agile security frameworks and techniques, with a specific emphasis on concrete steps for enterprises.
- Identifying prevalent difficulties in implementing agile security measures and proposing efficient solutions to overcome them.
- Demonstrating tangible instances and triumphs of firms that have proficiently executed agile security, offering pragmatic illustrations of its implementation.
- Exploring upcoming technologies and their possible influence on adaptable security measures, providing insights into the changing environment.
- Finally, it enhances the ongoing discussion in cybersecurity by aggregating and delivering extensive knowledge on agile security tactics.

Chapter Organization

Section 2 illustrates the understanding of agile security in the realm of cybersecurity, which refers to the approach of adapting and responding swiftly to emerging threats and vulnerabilities. It involves the implementation of flexible and dynamic security measures that can effectively counteract evolving cyber risks. Section 3 presents agile security benefits, examining the ways in which agile security facilitates the ability to adjust and respond to ever-changing threats. Elucidate the manner in which it improves reaction time and optimizes resource allocation. Section 4 illustrates implementing agile security and examines widely used frameworks DevSecOps and agile approaches that are implemented in security procedures. Section 5 presents the challenges and solutions, identifies the challenges encountered while implementing agile security procedures, and provides effective solutions and tactics to overcome these barriers. Section 6 showcases achievement stories of officialdoms implementing agile security strategies. Section 7 presents the future trends and discusses how technologies like machine learning, artificial intelligence, or blockchain could impact agile security.

UNDERSTANDING AGILE SECURITY

Agile Security in the realm of cybersecurity refers to a shift away from conventional, unchanging protection strategies towards a flexible and responsive approach (Daneva & Wang, 2018). Essentially, it signifies a change in thinking, recognizing that cyber dangers are continuously changing and requiring a flexible reaction instead of depending entirely on inflexible, predetermined security measures (Bartsch, 2011; Woody, 2013). This strategy incorporates the fundamental tenets of agility as presented in Figure 2, which are frequently observed in software development, and places emphasis on adaptability, cooperation, and ongoing enhancement within security protocols (Singh et al., 2021).

Figure 2. Selected Categorized Entities of Agile Security Strategy

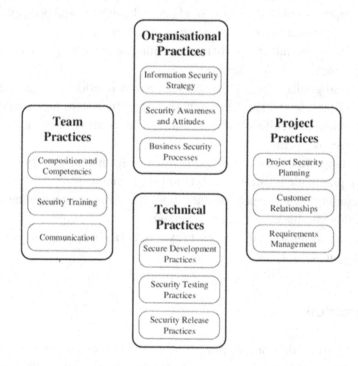

Agile Security prioritizes a proactive and iterative strategy for identifying and addressing threats. Instead of adopting a passive approach, it entails ongoing surveillance and prompt evaluation to detect and resolve weaknesses or irregularities inside the system quickly (Villamizar et al., 2020). By adopting a proactive approach, security teams are able to identify and address possible issues before they develop into major breaches. It cultivates a culture characterized by flexibility and the ability to recover quickly from difficulties (Sonia & Banati, 2014). Agile Security recognizes that breaches can happen even with strong protections rather than only concentrating on avoiding them. Hence, it underscores the significance of prompt recuperation and adjustment, guaranteeing that systems can quickly recover from occurrences, restricting harm, and decreasing the duration of inactivity (Jabangwe et al., 2019; Riisom et al., 2018).

Agile Security closely corresponds with agile development approaches such as DevSecOps[1], seamlessly incorporating security measures into the software development lifecycle (Ghani et al., 2014). This integration guarantees that security is not neglected, but rather a basic aspect is considered from the outset, therefore minimizing vulnerabilities and optimizing the whole development process (Baca & Carlsson, 2011). Therefore, agile security refers to a proactive, adaptable, and collaborative approach that involves continuous monitoring, rapid reaction, and resilience-building mechanisms to counter the always-changing cyber threats successfully (Mihelič et al., 2023).

Essential Elements of Agile Security Strategies

Continuous Monitoring

Continuous monitoring is an essential component of ASS, which involves ongoing and immediate supervision of systems and networks to identify abnormalities or possible risks (Khaim et al., 2016). This continuous examination guarantees that any departures from typical conduct are swiftly recognized and resolved. Automated monitoring systems continuously track system activity and identify abnormal trends that may suggest a security compromise (Villamizar et al., 2018). The significance of continuous monitoring resides in its capacity to promptly identify security issues, enable quick responses, and minimize possible harm by resolving threats before they worsen (Moyón et al., 2020).

Rapid Response Mechanisms

ASS emphasize promptly addressing identified risks or breaches. This entails implementing pre-established response protocols, deploying automated incident response systems, and maintaining well-prepared teams capable of swiftly addressing security incidents (Kumar & Jolly, 2019; Shafik, 2023a). Having playbooks that provide detailed instructions for responding to a breach allows security teams to limit and minimize the consequences quickly and effectively (Tøndel et al., 2019). The significance of rapid response mechanisms is paramount—they reduce the timeframe for attackers, restrict the scope of harm, and facilitate the prompt restoration of systems to their regular state (Moyon et al., 2020).

Adaptive Defenses

ASS promote the use of flexible defenses that respond to new threats as they arise. This entails consistently updating security procedures, utilizing threat intelligence, and utilizing knowledge gained from previous incidents to strengthen defenses (Tøndel et al., 2022). One possible illustration is the implementation of automatic patch management systems that rapidly update vulnerabilities throughout the network. The influence of adaptive defenses is significant as it guarantees the continued effectiveness of security measures against ever-changing threats, hence decreasing the probability of successful attacks (Tøndel & Cruzes, 2022).

Cross-Functional Collaboration

This factor highlights the importance of fostering collaboration among various departments within a business, specifically between security teams and other operational units such as development or operations. DevSecOps approaches, for example, promote collaboration between developers and security teams at every stage of the software development process (López et al., 2022). The impact is substantial as it dismantles isolated departments, fosters collective accountability for security, and guarantees the integration of security issues at every phase of the development process. This coordination improves the overall security stance while reducing vulnerabilities resulting from fragmented initiatives (Jin et al., 2021).

Agile Governance and Compliance

ASS promotes the use of governance and compliance frameworks that can easily adjust and respond to changes. Agile governance, as opposed to strict regulatory compliance, entails adaptable structures that may handle evolving security needs (Nozari & Ghahremani Nahr, 2022)—for example, employing agile approaches to guarantee that compliance upgrades are smoothly incorporated into security protocols (Chang et al., 2022). The impact is the maintenance of compliance that stays in line with the changing security requirements, avoiding any potential discrepancies between regulatory obligations and the implemented security measures (Rindell et al., 2018).

Continuous Improvement

ASS are mostly centered around the concept of continuous improvement. This process includes fostering a culture of continuous assessment, extracting lessons from incidents, and progressively enhancing security practices (Kagombe et al., 2021). For instance, performing post-mortems following security incidents to pinpoint areas for enhancement and subsequently implementing appropriate modifications. The impact is the progressive enhancement of security measures, which continuously strengthen in response to emerging threats, ensuring a proactive stance in an ever-evolving threat environment (Bell et al., 2017).

AGILE SECURITY MERITS

This section provides the benefits of ASS, discussing how agile security enables adaptability, amongst other factors in securing operations, depicting merits and possible impacts.

Flexibility and Adaptability

The main advantage of ASS is their inherent flexibility and adaptation to the ever-changing cyber scene. This method allows for the swift adaptation of security measures in order to address new threats or modifications in the organizational architecture (Bell et al., 2017). Implementing agile approaches in security operations enables prompt updates to security procedures upon the discovery of new vulnerabilities. This flexibility guarantees that security measures are up-to-date and efficient (Reddivari, 2022). The positive impact refers to a proactive defensive system that can quickly respond to emerging threats without causing major disturbances to the general operating flow, as presented in Figure 3. This system ensures a strong security posture that can withstand developing cyber hazards (Or, 2009).

Figure 3. Key Features of Agile Strategy Management

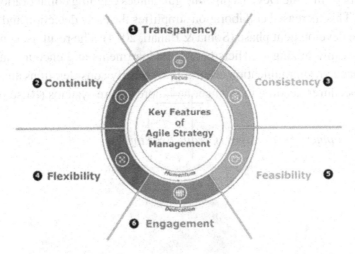

Efficiency in Response Time

ASS greatly improves the speed at which security problems are addressed. Organizations can promptly identify, examine, and alleviate threats by incorporating automated systems for detection and response (Oyetoyan et al., 2017). Utilizing automated incident response systems may rapidly confine and neutralize security intrusions, as demonstrated by this case. The impact is a decrease in the duration that risks remain within the network, hence decreasing the potential harm caused by prolonged exposure to cyber-attacks (Raschke et al., 2014). This improved response time efficiency enhances the organization's prompt and effective risk mitigation.

Effective Risk Mitigation

ASS reduce risks efficiently. Organizations can effectively identify vulnerabilities by adopting a proactive approach and consistently monitoring their systems. This enables them to address any flaws promptly before they can be maliciously exploited (He et al., 2022). Using threat intelligence technologies to identify possible threats enables proactive risk mitigation strategies. The impact entails a decrease in the probability and intensity of security incidents, hence lowering the organization's vulnerability to cyber threats (Daneva & Wang, 2018). This efficient risk reduction enhances the robustness of the security position, instilling assurance in stakeholders and safeguarding vital assets.

Enhanced Collaboration and Communication

ASS promote improved teamwork and communication among various teams in an organization, specifically between security, development, and operational units (Bartsch, 2011). For example, incorporating security practices into the DevOps pipeline guarantees ongoing collaboration between developers and security teams. This increased collaboration simplifies the early detection and resolution of security problems during the development phase (Sonia & Banati, 2014). The result is a unified and coordinated approach to security, minimizing conflicts between departments and encouraging a culture of shared accountability. Enhanced communication ensures that security considerations are seamlessly integrated into operational procedures, leading to stronger and more secure systems (Riisom et al., 2018).

Figure 4. Agile Development Percentages (Credit: Briskinfosec)

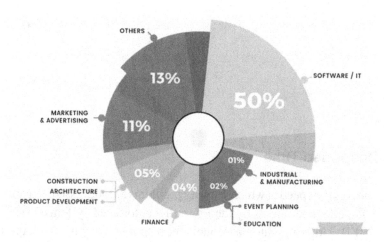

In today's digital landscape, even amidst the ongoing epidemic, numerous companies strive to address challenges in adhering to their current operational framework. To address this issue, we made the decision to enhance the performance of the current model that we typically utilize in the office. We adhere to the widely adopted spiral model, which requires slight adjustments to function effectively in the virtual environment (Khaim et al., 2016). "Similar to the Japanese culture, we typically allocate 60-70% of our time during meetings to comprehending and initiating work based on the given requirements[2]." Agile methodology is implemented across many sectors, despite its initial development by the information technology team.

Improved Resource Allocation

ASS enhances resource allocation by prioritizing efforts on security measures with significant impact. Using risk-based assessments enables businesses to prioritize security measures according to anticipated threats and their potential impact on vital assets (Ghani et al., 2014). This method guarantees the effective allocation of resources, focusing efforts on areas where they may generate the most substantial enhancements in security. The impact is a highly efficient security strategy that optimizes resource allocation and strengthens defenses against the most relevant threats (Baca & Carlsson, 2011). This optimization enables enterprises to strike a harmonious equilibrium between expenditures in security and the avoidance of risks, thus boosting their overall cybersecurity stance without incurring needless expenses (Khaim et al., 2016).

Enhanced Regulatory Compliance

ASS facilitate the attainment and preservation of regulatory compliance through the incorporation of agile governance methods. Implementing agile approaches in compliance management guarantees that security measures are consistently updated to comply with ever-changing regulatory standards (Villa-mizar et al., 2018). This strategy guarantees that compliance stays in line with ever-changing security requirements. The result is an efficient compliance procedure that eliminates any potential discrepancies between regulatory requirements and implemented security measures, hence minimizing risks associated with compliance and ensuring the firm continuously adheres to industry standards (Moyón et al., 2020). This alignment fosters confidence among stakeholders and reduces legal or reputational risks linked to non-compliance.

AGILE SECURITY IMPLEMENTATION

This section presents an examination of widely used frameworks and agile approaches implemented in security procedures and identifies practical measures for firms to deploy agile security successfully.

Integration of Agile Methodologies

Agile Security integrates agile methodologies with security practices. Initially, it is imperative for organizations to promote collaboration and shared responsibility across their security, development, and operational teams (Moyón et al., 2020). It is necessary to dismantle barriers and promote transparent communication and collaboration. Security protocols should incorporate automated testing, continuous integration, and deployment pipelines. Security is integrated into the development process by automating security checks and tests (Kumar & Jolly, 2019). Forming cross-functional teams that consist of both security professionals and developers enables them to have a comprehensive understanding of security concerns and effectively implement secure coding practices (Valdés-Rodríguez et al., 2023). By implementing these measures and incorporating agile methodologies into security protocols, companies may establish a cohesive ecosystem where security is an inherent component of the development process (Van Der Heijden et al., 2018).

Agile Governance and Adaptive Policies

Efficient implementation of Agile Security necessitates the presence of flexible governance and responsive policies. Organizations ought to embrace more flexible security measures. Continuous security policy evaluations and changes are necessary to reflect emerging threats and advancements in technology (Rindell et al., 2018). Organizations can effectively manage resources and concentrate on critical areas by prioritizing security measures according to risk. An effective incident response plan, along with playbooks, ensures prompt and uniform security incident responses (Kagombe et al., 2021).

Agile frameworks that incorporate compliance management ensure adherence to legal obligations and effectively adapt to evolving security demands. Agile governance enables companies to implement security policies that are up-to-date, adaptable, and efficient in countering contemporary threats (Bell et al., 2017).

Continuous Training and Skill Development

To successfully adopt Agile Security, it is crucial to allocate resources towards ongoing training and skill enhancement for security staff (Tøndel et al., 2022). Organizations want to offer frequent training sessions, workshops, and certifications to ensure that security personnel remain well-informed about the most current security trends, technologies, and procedures. Continuing education guarantees that security staff possess the requisite abilities to adjust to changing threats and proficiently execute flexible security measures (López et al., 2022). In addition, cultivating a culture of ongoing learning motivates security workers to remain proactive and imaginative when addressing cybersecurity threats.

Embrace Iterative Approach and Feedback Loops

Executing Agile Security requires a systematic and repetitive strategy, as well as strong feedback mechanisms. Organizations should embrace an iterative attitude, wherein security measures are consistently evaluated, enhanced, and enhanced further (Jin et al., 2021). This includes performing routine security assessments, penetration testing, and vulnerability scanning to detect vulnerabilities. Implementing feedback loops enables the gathering of valuable insights from security incidents, operational experiences, and user input (Nozari & Ghahremani Nahr, 2022). These observations guide modifying and improving security measures, resulting in stronger defense systems that adapt to real-world situations and evolving threats.

Data-Driven and Threat Intelligence Decision-Making

The deployment of Agile Security entails utilizing threat intelligence and making decisions based on data analysis. By integrating threat intelligence tools, organizations may actively collect and analyze data on emerging threats, attack trends, and vulnerabilities (Chang et al., 2022). The utilization of data in decision-making enables the prioritization of security measures and the allocation of resources based on well-informed judgments. Furthermore, employing analytics and metrics to evaluate the efficacy of security measures aids in detecting deficiencies and opportunities for enhancement (Peyman et al., 2021). Organizations may enhance their security measures against both existing and emerging threats by utilizing data-driven tactics to make well-informed decisions.

Establish Key Performance Indicators and Metrics

To successfully implement Agile Security, it is crucial to create Key Performance Indicators (KPIs) and appropriate metrics to assess the effectiveness of security measures (Rindell et al., 2018). Quantifiable metrics of security performance can be obtained by defining key performance indicators (KPIs) such as mean time to detect (MTTD), mean time to respond (MTTR), or the number of vulnerabilities closed within a specific timeframe (Merkow, 2021). Furthermore, monitoring metrics associated with the prevention or mitigation of successful security incidents aid in assessing the effectiveness of security measures. Consistently evaluating these KPIs and metrics allows firms to monitor advancement, pinpoint areas for enhancement, and showcase the significance of agile security procedures to stakeholders (Reddivari, 2022).

CHALLENGES AND SOLUTIONS

This section presents some identified challenges, shows the impacts, and suggests possible solutions, as discussed below.

Complexity of Implementation

The implementation of ASS sometimes faces problems stemming from the intricate nature of integrating with pre-existing systems and processes. The problem has a noticeable effect on traditional workflows, necessitating substantial adaptations and restructurings (Rindell et al., 2018). The intricacy of this situation may also result in opposition from teams familiar with conventional security methods. In order to tackle this issue, organizations should allocate resources towards thorough planning and gradual implementation tactics (Kagombe et al., 2021). To prevent disruptions, it is crucial to conduct comprehensive assessments of current systems, identify possible integration points, and gradually implement agile security measures (Merkow, 2021). In addition, promoting transparent communication and delivering comprehensive training to employees on the advantages and procedures of agile security helps mitigate opposition and guarantee a more seamless transition (Reddivari, 2022).

Resource Limitations

Agile Security implementation has substantial obstacles due to resource constraints, such as budget limitations and a scarcity of experienced individuals. The impact is evident in the form of possible deficiencies in security measures or insufficient response skills when confronted with emerging threats (Nägele et al., 2023). To address these difficulties, companies can allocate resources strategically by prioritizing expenditures in security measures that have a significant impact. Introducing automation in applicable areas can mitigate resource constraints by optimizing procedures and minimizing the necessity for manual involvement (Raschke et al., 2014). Engaging in collaboration with external suppliers can provide access to specialized expertise and allow for the outsourcing of specific security responsibilities.

Cultural Shift and Resistance

The successful application of agile approaches can be hindered by resistance to change from traditional security practices. This resistance might result in a dearth of support from crucial stakeholders or hesitancy among teams to adopt novel methodologies (He et al., 2022). To tackle this difficulty, it is necessary to foster a culture that values transparency while highlighting the advantages of adaptability and cooperation in security measures. To overcome reluctance and promote a security culture in line with agile principles, it is beneficial to promote active involvement from all levels of the business, create platforms for open debate and feedback, and highlight successful examples of agile security implementation (Bartsch, 2011).

Balancing Speed and Security

Striking a balance between velocity and safeguarding presents a notable obstacle in the execution of agile security. The inherent rapidity of agile approaches may cause security to be seen as an obstacle to speed, perhaps leading to the disregard of crucial security safeguards (Singh et al., 2021). On the other hand, an excessively cautious approach could hinder the flexibility of development cycles. To tackle this difficulty, it is necessary to include security seamlessly into the development process without hindering agility. Integrating security checkpoints into the development pipeline, adopting automated security testing, and utilizing DevSecOps principles facilitate the combination of speed and security (Tøndel & Cruzes, 2022). Promoting a mentality that regards security as a facilitator rather than an obstacle to agility can assist in achieving a harmonious equilibrium between swift development and strong security protocols.

CASE STUDIES OF AGILE SECURITY STRATEGIES

This section showcases some identified case studies of organizations implementing ASS.

Netflix

Netflix[3] is widely recognized for successfully utilizing ASS. They adopt a culture that values constant innovation and flexibility, ensuring that their security measures are in line with agile approaches (Tøndel et al., 2022). Through the integration of security into their DevOps pipeline, they have achieved the automation of security inspections and the seamless incorporation of security measures into their development processes. By employing this method, Netflix promptly detect and resolve weaknesses, guaranteeing that security does not impede but rather becomes an essential component of their agile development processes (Tøndel & Cruzes, 2022). Their success is attributed to their adeptness in maintaining an equilibrium between velocity and protection, all the while ensuring the security of a vast and ever-changing streaming platform.

Airbnb

Airbnb[4] implements ASS to safeguard its online marketplace, with a primary emphasis on proactive identification of threats and prompt reaction procedures. They employ automated monitoring techniques that consistently evaluate their systems for potential threats (Peyman et al., 2021). The success of Airbnb can be attributed to its adeptness in promptly adjusting and addressing developing risks, thereby guaranteeing a safe atmosphere for both hosts and visitors. Their strategy prioritizes the incorporation of security at every stage of their product development process, guaranteeing that security measures progress in tandem with the expansion of their platform (Reddivari, 2022).

Salesforce

Salesforce[5] implements ASS by adopting a comprehensive approach to security across their cloud-based services. They utilize DevSecOps methodologies to include security in their software development lifecycle. The key to Salesforce's successful implementation of agile security rests in its prioritization of collaboration between its security and development teams (Shafik, 2023b). This relationship enables the prompt detection and resolution of security concerns, guaranteeing a strong and secure platform for their clients while consistently improving their security position (Bell et al., 2017).

Capital One

Capital One[6] has adopted agile security measures to enhance its banking services. By integrating security into their DevOps practices, they have embraced an agile mindset, allowing them to establish protocols for continuous monitoring and swift response (Merkow, 2021). Capital One's success in implementing agile security can be attributed to its proactive strategy in identifying and responding to threats. They effectively manage risks while maintaining the flexibility necessary in a competitive financial environment. This is achieved by implementing automation and fostering a culture that promotes collective accountability for ensuring secure operations.

Microsoft

Microsoft[7] has effectively executed ASS by integrating security into their software development processes. They utilize threat modeling, a proactive methodology that detects potential security risks and weaknesses during the design phase (Bell et al., 2017). By implementing this technique, Microsoft proactively tackles security problems at an early stage of the development process, hence minimizing the chances of vulnerabilities being present in the final product. Microsoft maintains a strong security stance for its products and services by incorporating security measures at every stage of its development process (Oyetoyan et al., 2017). This approach instills trust in their users and allows them to respond to changing threats.

Etsy

Etsy[8], a digital marketplace, utilizes ASS to safeguard its online platform. Their main emphasis is on conducting ongoing security testing and prioritizing security solutions based on risk assessment. Etsy's success is attributed to its capacity to promptly address security incidents by using well-defined incident response methods (Chang et al., 2022; Jun et al., 2021). Etsy cultivates a dynamic security environment by embracing a culture of learning and improvement, where incidents serve as valuable lessons that enhance their security posture (Oyetoyan et al., 2017). Their dedication to actively preventing threats and quickly responding showcases the efficacy of agile security in upholding a secure platform for consumers and vendors.

Google

Google has incorporated ASS by integrating security measures into its development lifecycle. They employ automation extensively to detect and resolve security problems. Google's achievement in implementing agile security is credited to its strong security culture, which prioritizes collaboration, innovation, and ongoing learning. Google efficiently enhances the security of its services and products by utilizing machine learning and advanced analytics to detect anomalies and potential threats (Oyetoyan et al., 2017; Kalinaki et al., 2024). Google's security strategy[9] is characterized by its flexible approach, which allows it to take proactive measures against constantly changing cyber threats. This strategy effectively protects the extensive range of platforms and services offered by Google[10].

FUTURE RESEARCH TRENDS

This section examines how the incorporation of these technologies into ASS will contribute to the future development of a stronger and more flexible defense against the always-changing threat landscape.

Artificial Intelligence in Agile Security

AI enhances the ability to detect hazards by examining large quantities of data to discover trends, irregularities, and possible dangers promptly. The capacity to acquire knowledge and adjust enables the proactive detection and reduction of security vulnerabilities. AI-powered systems streamline incident response, facilitating swift and flexible responses to security problems. These systems can independently handle and control threats, resulting in shorter response times and limiting the consequences of security breaches (Oyetoyan et al., 2017; Shafik, 2023c). Artificial intelligence enables the use of predictive analytics to forecast possible security vulnerabilities by analyzing historical data and current patterns. This feature allows for preventative actions and strategic security planning, in line with the flexible approach of responding to changing threats.

Machine Learning Impact on Agile Security

Machine learning algorithms are highly effective in identifying anomalies in network traffic or system behavior, which is a crucial component of agile security[11]. Machine learning-based anomaly detection systems improve the ability to identify and respond to threats at an early stage (Or, 2009). Machine learning assists in prioritizing vulnerabilities by evaluating their severity and probable consequences. This aids security teams in effectively allocating resources and prioritizing key security measures. Utilizing machine learning algorithms, behavioral analysis is employed to detect anomalies in user or system behavior, hence enhancing user authentication and access control methods in ASS.

Blockchain's Influence on Agile Security

The immutable ledger of blockchain[12] guarantees the integrity of data, hence minimizing the possibility of unauthorized alterations or tampering of data. The decentralized design of the system improves both the security and reliability of the data (Moyón et al., 2020). Blockchain-powered identity management systems provide improved authentication and authorization procedures. Decentralized identities and smart contracts enhance security protocols in a dynamic setting (Or, 2009). Blockchain ensures transparency and traceability in security transactions, which is essential for preserving audit trails and upholding the integrity of security protocols in ASS (Oyetoyan et al., 2017).

Blockchain for Supply Chain Security

The utilization of blockchain in supply chain security entails establishing unalterable and easily comprehensible records of transactions and data transfers inside supply networks. Through the utilization of blockchain technology, enterprises may guarantee the integrity of the supply chain data, validating the genuineness of products and tracing their trajectory (Jabangwe et al., 2019). The decentralized and tamper-resistant ledger improves supply chain security, especially in ASS, where quick responses and reliability in data interchange are crucial. The capacity of blockchain to offer complete visibility and ensure safe data sharing is in line with the agile principles of adaptation and resilience in safeguarding supply chains from various threats (Moyón et al., 2020).

Machine Learning-Enabled Security Automation

Machine learning enhances security automation by enabling intelligent decision-making in automated security operations. Machine learning algorithms independently adjust to changing threats, enhancing security operations without the need for continuous human involvement. This automation simplifies repetitive security chores, enabling security personnel to concentrate on more intricate threats and strategic enhancements to protection (Jabangwe et al., 2019). ML-powered automation in ASS ensures prompt and efficient response to security incidents, hence improving the overall security posture.

Artificial Intelligent-Powered Threat Hunting

The function of AI in threat hunting is utilizing machine learning algorithms to actively search for prospective threats that may bypass conventional security measures. By consistently examining network behaviors and trends, AI-powered threat hunting can detect advanced threats, hence decreasing the amount of time attackers spend within the network. This approach is in line with agile security since it prioritizes the proactive identification of threats and the swift response to manage risks efficiently (Jabangwe et al., 2019; Riisom et al., 2018).

KEY TAKEAWAYS AND CONCLUSION

The study on ASS reveals a new way of thinking in the ever-changing digital world. It emphasizes the importance of being adaptable and taking proactive actions to protect against constantly changing cyber threats; other key insights from the study are presented.

* ASS prioritizes adaptability and reaction to changing cyber threats, moving away from inflexible and unchanging protection techniques.

- Efficient implementation requires the seamless integration of agile approaches such as DevSecOps into security processes, promoting collaboration and iterative enhancements.
- Uninterrupted surveillance and prompt reaction systems are essential. Implementing automated systems for identifying and addressing potential threats allows for preventative measures to minimize the effect of security incidents.
- The challenges encompass intricacies in integration, constraints in resources, cultural transformations, and the need to strike a balance between speed and security. Successful implementation of these challenges necessitates rigorous planning, training, and cultural alignment.
- Technologies such as AI, blockchain, and ML, as discussed above, have a substantial impact on agile security. They improve the ability to identify and respond to potential dangers, streamline operations through automation, and establish secure frameworks that cannot be altered or controlled by a single authority.
- It is crucial to prioritize the establishment of a culture that promotes ongoing learning, feedback loops, and incremental improvements. Studying and analyzing incidents helps to enhance security measures.
- The cooperation among diverse teams and the establishment of efficient communication channels are crucial. By dismantling silos, there is a collective accountability for security throughout the organization.
- The core principles of agile security are prioritizing risks, allocating resources efficiently, and implementing proactive measures to mitigate risks.
- Finally, implementing agile governance frameworks guarantees adherence to regulations while accommodating changing security requirements, hence avoiding discrepancies between mandated regulations and implemented security measures.

CONCLUSION

The insights derived from ASS suggest that the future of cybersecurity will be characterized by ongoing adaptation and the seamless integration of technology. The advancement of security procedures relies on adopting agile approaches, utilizing cutting-edge technology such as AI, ML, and blockchain, and promoting a culture of collaboration and ongoing enhancement. In the future, the combination of these factors will lead to the creation of security frameworks that can quickly adjust to constantly evolving threats. Generative artificial intelligence and existing ML advancement will enhance threat identification and response by automating procedures and improving predictive analytics to mitigate risks proactively. The immutable and decentralized characteristics of blockchain technology will bring about a significant transformation in ensuring data integrity and securing transactions, especially inside supply chains. Nevertheless, the future necessitates tackling issues such as ethical artificial intelligence, the ability of blockchain to handle large-scale operations, and finding a balance between speed and security. The current study focuses on the importance of innovation, ethical concerns, and the smooth incorporation of emerging technologies into the agile security framework to strengthen enterprises against future, increasingly advanced cyber-attacks.

REFERENCES

Baca, D., & Carlsson, B. (2011). Agile development with security engineering activities. *Proceedings - International Conference on Software Engineering.* 10.1145/1987875.1987900

Bartsch, S. (2011). Practitioners' perspectives on security in agile development. *Proceedings of the 2011 6th International Conference on Availability, Reliability and Security, ARES 2011.* 10.1109/ARES.2011.82

Bell, L., Brunton-Spall, M., Smith, R., & Bird, J. (n.d.). *Agile Application Security: Enabling Security in a Continuous Delivery Pipeline.* O'Reilly Media, Inc. https://www.oreilly.com/library/view/agile-application-security/9781491938836/

Chang, V., Golightly, L., Modesti, P., Xu, Q. A., Doan, L. M. T., Hall, K., Boddu, S., & Kobusińska, A. (2022). A Survey on Intrusion Detection Systems for Fog and Cloud Computing. *Future Internet*, 14(3), 89. Advance online publication. 10.3390/fi14030089

Daneva, M., & Wang, C. (2018). Security requirements engineering in the agile era: How does it work in practice? *Proceedings - 2018 1st International Workshop on Quality Requirements in Agile Projects, QuaRAP 2018.* 10.1109/QuaRAP.2018.00008

Ghani, I., Azham, Z., & Jeong, S. R. (2014). Integrating software security into the agile-Scrum method. *KSII Transactions on Internet and Information Systems*, 8(2), 646–663. Advance online publication. 10.3837/tiis.2014.02.019

He, Y., Zamani, E. D., Lloyd, S., & Luo, C. (2022). Agile incident response (AIR): Improving the incident response process in healthcare. *International Journal of Information Management*, 62, 102435. Advance online publication. 10.1016/j.ijinfomgt.2021.102435

Jabangwe, R., Kuusinen, K., Riisom, K. R., Hubel, M. S., Alradhi, H. M., & Nielsen, N. B. (2019). Challenges and Solutions for Addressing Software Security in Agile Software Development. *International Journal of Systems and Software Security and Protection*, 9(1), 1–17. Advance online publication. 10.4018/IJSSSP.2018010101

Jin, H., Li, Z., Zou, D., & Yuan, B. (2021). DSEOM: A Framework for Dynamic Security Evaluation and Optimization of MTD in Container-Based Cloud. *IEEE Transactions on Dependable and Secure Computing*, 18(3), 1. Advance online publication. 10.1109/TDSC.2019.2916666

Kagombe, G. G., Mwangi, R. W., & Wafula, J. M. (2021). Achieving Standard Software Security in Agile Developments. *ACM International Conference Proceeding Series.* https://doi.org/10.1145/3484399.3484403

Khaim, R., Naz, S., Abbas, F., Iqbal, N., & Hamayun, M. (2016). A Review of Security Integration Technique in Agile Software Development. *International Journal of Software Engineering and Its Applications*, 7(3), 49–68. Advance online publication. 10.5121/ijsea.2016.7304

Kumar, S., & Jolly, A. (2019). Secure software development by integrating security activities with agile activities. *International Journal of Advanced Science and Technology*, 28(15).

López, L., Burgués, X., Martínez-Fernández, S., Vollmer, A. M., Behutiye, W., Karhapää, P., Franch, X., Rodríguez, P., & Oivo, M. (2022). Quality measurement in agile and rapid software development: A systematic mapping. *Journal of Systems and Software*, 186, 111187. Advance online publication. 10.1016/j.jss.2021.111187

Merkow, M. S. (2021). *Practical Security for Agile and DevOps*. 10.1201/9781003265566

Mihelič, A., Vrhovec, S., & Hovelja, T. (2023). Agile Development of Secure Software for Small and Medium-Sized Enterprises. *Sustainability (Basel)*, 15(1), 801. Advance online publication. 10.3390/su15010801

Moyon, F., Almeida, P., Riofrio, D., Mendez, D., & Kalinowski, M. (2020). Security Compliance in Agile Software Development: A Systematic Mapping Study. *Proceedings - 46th Euromicro Conference on Software Engineering and Advanced Applications, SEAA 2020*. 10.1109/SEAA51224.2020.00073

Moyón, F., Méndez, D., Beckers, K., & Klepper, S. (2020). How to Integrate Security Compliance Requirements with Agile Software Engineering at Scale? Lecture Notes in Computer Science (Including Subseries Lecture Notes in Artificial Intelligence and Lecture Notes in Bioinformatics), 12562 LNCS. 10.1007/978-3-030-64148-1_5

Nägele, S., Korn, L., & Matthes, F. (2023). Adoption of Information Security Practices in Large-Scale Agile Software Development: A Case Study in the Finance Industry. *ACM International Conference Proceeding Series*. 10.1145/3600160.3600170

Nozari, H., & Ghahremani Nahr, J. (2022). The Impact of Blockchain Technology and The Internet of Things on the Agile and Sustainable Supply Chain. *International Journal of Innovation in Engineering*, 2(2), 33–41. Advance online publication. 10.59615/ijie.2.2.33

Or, E. (2009). *Security Development Lifecycle for Agile Development*. Development. https://www.blackhat.com/presentations/bh-dc-10/Sullivan_Bryan/BlackHat-DC-2010-Sullivan-SDL-Agile-wp.pdf

Oyetoyan, T. D., Jaatun, M. G., & Cruzes, D. S. (2017). A Lightweight Measurement of Software Security Skills, Usage and Training Needs in Agile Teams. *International Journal of Secure Software Engineering*, 8(1), 1–27. Advance online publication. 10.4018/IJSSE.2017010101

Peyman, M., Copado, P. J., Tordecilla, R. D., Martins, L. D. C., Xhafa, F., & Juan, A. A. (2021). Edge computing and iot analytics for agile optimization in intelligent transportation systems. *Energies*, 14(19), 6309. Advance online publication. 10.3390/en14196309

Raschke, W., Zilli, M., Baumgartner, P., Loinig, J., Steger, C., & Kreiner, C. (2014). Supporting evolving security models for an agile security evaluation. *2014 IEEE 1st International Workshop on Evolving Security and Privacy Requirements Engineering, ESPRE 2014 - Proceedings*. 10.1109/ESPRE.2014.6890525

Reddivari, S. (2022). An Agile Framework for Security Requirements: A Preliminary Investigation. *Proceedings - 2022 IEEE 46th Annual Computers, Software, and Applications Conference, COMPSAC 2022*. 10.1109/COMPSAC54236.2022.00076

Riisom, K. R., Hubel, M. S., Alradhi, H. M., Nielsen, N. B., Kuusinen, K., & Jabangwe, R. (2018). Software security in agile software development: A literature review of challenges and solutions. *ACM International Conference Proceeding Series, Part F147763*. 10.1145/3234152.3234189

Rindell, K., Hyrynsalmi, S., & Leppänen, V. (2018). Aligning security objectives with agile software development. *ACM International Conference Proceeding Series, Part F147763*. 10.1145/3234152.3234187

Shafik, W. (2023a). A Comprehensive Cybersecurity Framework for Present and Future Global Information Technology Organizations. In *Effective Cybersecurity Operations for Enterprise-Wide Systems* (pp. 56–79). IGI Global., 10.4018/978-1-6684-9018-1.ch002

Shafik, W. (2023b). Cyber security perspectives in public spaces: Drone case study. *Handbook of Research on Cybersecurity Risk in Contemporary Business Systems*. 10.4018/978-1-6684-7207-1.ch004

Shafik, W. (2023c). Making Cities Smarter: IoT and SDN Applications, Challenges, and Future Trends. *Opportunities and Challenges of Industrial IoT in 5G and 6G Networks*. 10.4018/978-1-7998-9266-3.ch004

Singh, N., Patel, P., & Datta, S. (2021). A survey on security and human-related challenges in agile software deployment. *Proceedings - 2021 International Conference on Computational Science and Computational Intelligence, CSCI 2021*. 10.1109/CSCI54926.2021.00365

Sonia, A. S., & Banati, H. (2014). FISA-XP: An Agile-based Integration of Security Activities with Extreme Programming. *Software Engineering Notes*, 39(3). Advance online publication. 10.1145/2597716.2597728

Tøndel, I. A., & Cruzes, D. S. (2022). Continuous software security through security prioritisation meetings. *Journal of Systems and Software*, 194, 111477. Advance online publication. 10.1016/j.jss.2022.111477

Tøndel, I. A., Cruzes, D. S., Jaatun, M. G., & Sindre, G. (2022). Influencing the security prioritisation of an agile software development project. *Computers & Security*, 118, 102744. Advance online publication. 10.1016/j.cose.2022.102744

Tøndel, I. A., Jaatun, M. G., Cruzes, D. S., & Williams, L. (2019). Collaborative security risk estimation in agile software development. *Information and Computer Security*, 26(4), 508–535. Advance online publication. 10.1108/ICS-12-2018-0138

Valdés-Rodríguez, Y., Hochstetter-Diez, J., Díaz-Arancibia, J., & Cadena-Martínez, R. (2023). Towards the Integration of Security Practices in Agile Software Development: A Systematic Mapping Review. *Applied Sciences (Basel, Switzerland)*, 13(7), 4578. Advance online publication. 10.3390/app13074578

Van Der Heijden, A., Broasca, C., & Serebrenik, A. (2018). An empirical perspective on security challenges in large-scale agile software development. *International Symposium on Empirical Software Engineering and Measurement*. 10.1145/3239235.3267426

Villamizar, H., Kalinowski, M., Garcia, A., & Mendez, D. (2020). An efficient approach for reviewing security-related aspects in agile requirements specifications of web applications. *Requirements Engineering*, 25(4), 439–468. Advance online publication. 10.1007/s00766-020-00338-w

Villamizar, H., Kalinowski, M., Viana, M., & Fernández, D. M. (2018). A systematic mapping study on security in agile requirements engineering. *Proceedings - 44th Euromicro Conference on Software Engineering and Advanced Applications, SEAA 2018*. https://doi.org/10.1109/SEAA.2018.00080

Woody, C. (2013). *Agile Security – Review of Current Research and Pilot Usage.* SEI White Paper. https://insights.sei.cmu.edu/documents/366/2013_019_001_70236.pdf

ENDNOTES

[1]   https://www.ibm.com/topics/devsecops

[2]   https://www.briskinfosec.com/

[3]   https://www.netflix.com/

[4]   https://www.airbnb.com/

[5]   https://www.salesforce.com/

[6]   https://www.capitalone.com/

[7]   https://www.microsoft.com/en-us/

[8]   https://www.etsy.com/

[9]   https://safety.google/security-privacy/

[10]   https://www.google.com/

[11]   https://www.veracode.com/security/agile-security

[12]   https://www.blockchain.com/

Chapter 5
Building a Smart Security Framework for IoT/IIoT

Akashdeep Bhardwaj

https://orcid.org/0000-0001-7361-0465

University of Petroleum and Energy Studies, India

ABSTRACT

The ever-expanding world of IoT and IIoT devices necessitates a robust and adaptable security framework to safeguard these interconnected systems. This chapter outlines the core principles for building such a framework, emphasizing proactive and continuous protection strategies for vulnerability analysis, malware detection, and anomaly detection. The framework foundation lies in conducting thorough risk assessments. By identifying potential vulnerabilities in devices, networks, and protocols, we can prioritize mitigation efforts and the use of secure protocols like TLS (transport layer security) and DTLS (datagram transport layer security) for encrypting data transmission, protecting sensitive information from unauthorized access. Anomaly detection systems identify deviations from normal behavior, while intrusion prevention systems (IPS) actively block malicious network activity. However, security cannot be an afterthought. This chapter emphasizes the importance of integrating security considerations throughout the development lifecycle of IoT/IIoT devices.

1. INTRODUCTION

Internet of Things (IoT) (What is the Internet of Things?) and the Industrial Internet of Things (IIoT) (What is Industrial Internet of Things)?) represent a paradigm shift in how we interact with the world around us. By embedding sensors and actuators into everyday objects and industrial machinery, we create a network of interconnected devices capable of collecting, transmitting, and analysing vast amounts of data. This interconnectedness promises significant advancements in various domains, from smart homes and wearable health trackers to automated factories and intelligent transportation systems. However, this interconnectedness also introduces new security challenges that demand robust and adaptable security frameworks.

The sheer scale of the IoT/IIoT landscape is a major security concern. Billions of devices are projected to be connected to the internet in the coming years, creating a vast attack surface for malicious actors. Unlike traditional computers, many IoT/IIoT devices are resource-constrained, with limited processing

DOI: 10.4018/979-8-3693-3451-5.ch005

power and memory. This makes it difficult to implement complex security measures and keep software up to date with the latest security patches. Additionally, the heterogeneity of devices and communication protocols within the IoT/IIoT ecosystem creates compatibility challenges, making it harder to establish a unified security posture.

In 2015, researchers demonstrated the ability to remotely hack a Jeep Cherokee's (The Groundbreaking 2015 Jeep Hack Changed Automotive Cybersecurity) entertainment system, allowing them to control steering, brakes, and other critical functions. This incident exposed the vulnerability of connected vehicles and the potential for attackers to disrupt transportation networks or cause physical harm to passengers. The security threats facing IoT/IIoT devices go beyond data breaches and device manipulation. Botnets, large networks of compromised devices, can be used to launch denial-of-service attacks, overwhelming servers, and disrupting critical infrastructure. Additionally, these devices can be used as stepping stones for attackers to gain access to more secure networks.

The foundation of a secure IoT/IIoT ecosystem is laid during the development process. Insecure coding practices, weak authentication mechanisms, and the lack of proper security testing can introduce vulnerabilities that attackers can exploit. Furthermore, the rapid development cycle of many IoT/IIoT devices often prioritizes functionality over security, neglecting the importance of secure coding practices and vulnerability assessments. Despite the challenges, securing the IoT/IIoT landscape is not an insurmountable task. A smart security framework, built upon proactive and continuous protection strategies, is essential for safeguarding these interconnected systems. This framework should include a comprehensive risk assessment process to identify potential vulnerabilities in devices, networks, and protocols. By prioritizing mitigation efforts based on the identified risks, organizations can optimize their security posture.

Hardening devices by implementing secure configurations, enforcing strong passwords, and maintaining a diligent patching schedule is crucial for minimizing the attack surface. Additionally, securing communication channels with encryption protocols like TLS (Transport Layer Security) and DTLS (Datagram Transport Layer Security) protects sensitive data from unauthorized access. Constant vigilance is key in the dynamic threat landscape of IoT/IIoT. Anomaly detection systems can identify deviations from normal device behavior, while intrusion prevention systems actively block malicious network activity. These systems play a vital role in detecting and responding to security threats in real-time.

Building security into the design of IoT/IIoT devices from the ground up is a proactive approach known as 'Security-by-design'. This approach emphasizes secure coding practices, secure development methodologies, and thorough vulnerability assessments throughout the development lifecycle. By integrating security considerations at every stage, organizations can create inherently resilient devices less susceptible to cyberattacks. The future of IoT/IIoT holds immense potential for innovation and progress. However, this potential can only be fully realized if we address the security challenges head-on. By implementing a smart security framework characterized by proactive measures, continuous monitoring, and a "security-by-design" philosophy, we can build a more secure and trustworthy IoT/IIoT landscape. The security landscape surrounding IoT/IIoT is constantly evolving, with new threats and vulnerabilities emerging alongside technological advancements. The key areas demanding ongoing attention are:

- Supply Chain Attacks: The interconnected nature of the global supply chain creates opportunities for attackers to introduce vulnerabilities at an early stage. Malicious actors can compromise software development tools, hardware components, or firmware updates, impacting a wide range of devices downstream. Mitigating this risk requires robust security practices throughout the entire supply chain, from component manufacturers to device vendors.

- Artificial Intelligence (AI) and Machine Learning (ML) Security: The integration of AI and ML algorithms into IoT/IIoT devices presents both opportunities and challenges for security. While AI can be used to develop advanced threat detection systems, these algorithms themselves can be vulnerable to manipulation by attackers. Securing AI models and ensuring the integrity of training data is crucial for preventing adversarial attacks that exploit these systems.

- Convergence of IT and OT Systems: The convergence of Information Technology (IT) and Operational Technology (OT) systems in industrial settings creates new security risks. OT systems, traditionally isolated from the internet, are now increasingly interconnected, making them vulnerable to cyberattacks that can disrupt critical infrastructure. Security frameworks for IIoT environments need to bridge the gap between IT and OT security best practices.

- Privacy Concerns: The vast amount of data collected by IoT/IIoT devices raises significant privacy concerns. User data needs to be protected from unauthorized access, use, or disclosure. Implementing robust data anonymization techniques and enforcing strict data governance policies are essential for ensuring user privacy.

- Standardization and Regulations: The fragmented nature of the IoT/IIoT ecosystem, with its diverse device types and communication protocols, hinders the development of a unified security approach. Standardization efforts and the development of clear regulations are crucial for establishing a baseline level of security across the industry.

While technology plays a vital role in securing the IoT/IIoT landscape, the human factor remains a critical element. Security awareness training for users and developers is essential for promoting responsible practices and identifying potential security risks. Additionally, establishing a culture of security within organizations, where security is considered a top priority, is key to fostering a proactive approach to cyber threats. Securing the ever-expanding IoT/IIoT landscape requires a collaborative approach that brings together stakeholders from various sectors. Governments, industry leaders, security researchers, and consumers all have a role to play. By sharing knowledge, best practices, and threat intelligence, we can build a more robust and resilient IoT/IIoT ecosystem.

2. EVOLUTION OF IOT SECURITY & SOCIETAL IMPACT OF IOT BREACHES

IoT has revolutionized how we interact with the world around us. From smart homes and wearables to industrial automation and connected cities, the sheer number and variety of interconnected devices have ushered in an era of unprecedented efficiency and convenience. However, this interconnectedness also creates a vast and often vulnerable attack surface for cybercriminals. This section delves into the evolution of IoT security, highlighting its nascent beginnings, the wake-up call from early attacks, and the ongoing efforts to fortify the landscape.

The early days of IoT, roughly the mid-2000s to the late 2010s, were characterized by a rapid proliferation of devices with security as an afterthought. The focus was on functionality and connectivity, often at the expense of robust security measures. This resulted in several shortcomings. Many devices shipped with pre-configured usernames and passwords that were either well-known or easily guessable. The infamous Mirai botnet attack of 2016 exploited this by compromising millions of devices with default logins, launching a massive Distributed Denial-of-Service (DDoS) attack that crippled major internet services. Early IoT devices often lacked the ability to receive firmware updates, leaving them vulnerable to newly discovered exploits. Unencrypted communication between devices and the cloud exposed sensitive data to interception.

These early vulnerabilities became a stark reminder of the importance of security in the IoT ecosystem. The large-scale attacks of the late 2010s served as a wake-up call for the industry. Regulatory bodies, governments, and industry leaders began collaborating to address the glaring security gaps. Organizations like the IETF (Internet Engineering Task Force) and the Zigbee Alliance developed standardized security protocols for IoT communication, such as DTLS (Datagram Transport Layer Security) and Secure Neighbor Discovery. A paradigm shift emerged towards integrating security considerations throughout the entire product lifecycle, from design inception to manufacturing and deployment. Initiatives like PSA Certified (Platform Security Architecture) emerged to provide standardized security certifications for IoT devices and chipsets, ensuring baseline levels of protection. These efforts aimed to lay a foundation for a more secure future for the IoT landscape.

The fight for secure IoT is an ongoing process. As attackers become more sophisticated, new threats and vulnerabilities continue to emerge. Hackers are increasingly targeting vulnerabilities in the software supply chain to compromise multiple devices at once. The SolarWinds attack of 2020 highlighted the potential for widespread damage through such attacks. IoT botnets are becoming more complex and targeted, capable of launching denial-of-service attacks, stealing data, or disrupting critical infrastructure. Machine learning is being used by attackers to automate vulnerability discovery and exploit development, making it even harder to stay ahead of the curve.

However, the industry is not standing still and some of the promising advancements in IoT security are:

- Zero-Trust Architecture: This approach assumes no device or user is inherently trustworthy and requires continuous verification throughout the network.
- Blockchain Technology: Blockchain can be used to create tamper-proof audit trails for device activity and ensure data integrity.
- Secure Enclaves: These hardware-based secure execution environments isolate critical security functions from the rest of the device, making them more resistant to tampering.

These cutting-edge solutions offer hope for a more secure future of IoT, but constant vigilance and adaptation remain crucial. The evolution of IoT security showcases a continuous struggle between convenience and protection. We've moved from a largely unsecured wild west to a frontier with fortified defenses, but the battle is far from over. By understanding the past, present, and future threats, we can build smart security frameworks for the ever-evolving landscape of IoT/IIoT.

The consequences of IoT/IIoT security breaches extend far beyond compromised devices and stolen data. They can have a significant ripple effect, impacting economies, societies, and even individual lives. Understanding these broader impacts strengthens the case for robust security frameworks in the interconnected world of IoT. Data breaches can lead to hefty financial losses for businesses. This includes costs associated with:

- Incident Response: Identifying the breach, containing the damage, and restoring systems can be a resource-intensive process.

- Regulatory Fines: Non-compliance with data protection regulations can result in significant fines, depending on the severity of the breach and the jurisdiction.
- Reputational Damage: Security breaches can erode consumer trust and damage a company's reputation, leading to lost sales and decreased brand value.
- Disruption of Operations: Depending on the nature of the attack, compromised systems and data can disrupt critical business operations, leading to lost productivity and revenue.

A study by IBM found that the average cost of a data breach in 2023 was $4.35 million (Cost of a Data Breach, 2023), highlighting the substantial financial burden breaches place on businesses. These costs are not isolated to individual companies; they can have a cascading effect on entire industries. For example, a large-scale cyberattack on a critical infrastructure provider could disrupt entire supply chains, leading to widespread economic losses.

The fear of security breaches can deter businesses from investing in IoT technologies. Companies may be hesitant to adopt connected solutions if they perceive the security risks to outweigh the potential benefits. This can hinder innovation and slow down the overall growth of the IoT market. IoT devices collect a vast amount of personal data, from home energy consumption patterns to health information worn on fitness trackers. Security breaches can expose this sensitive data to unauthorized individuals, leading to privacy violations and identity theft. This can have a significant impact on individuals' sense of security and well-being. Frequent security breaches can erode public trust in IoT technologies. Consumers may become hesitant to adopt smart home devices or connect themselves to the internet of things if they perceive the risks to be too high. This can hinder the overall adoption and social integration of IoT technologies.

Security breaches in certain sectors, such as industrial automation or connected healthcare devices, can have severe safety implications. For example, hackers could gain control of critical infrastructure, leading to disruptions in power grids or transportation systems. In healthcare, compromised medical devices could potentially harm patients. The interconnected nature of IoT means that a seemingly minor security breach in one device can have cascading consequences for public safety and well-being. Successful IoT security breaches can embolden cybercriminals and encourage them to target more devices and systems. This creates a continuous cycle of attack and defense, requiring constant vigilance and adaptation from security professionals. Cyberattacks on critical infrastructure can have geopolitical implications. If a nation-state is suspected of being behind an attack, it can escalate tensions between countries and potentially lead to retaliatory actions.

Security should not be seen as a cost center but as an investment in the future of IoT. Just as we wouldn't build a house without a foundation, we shouldn't deploy IoT devices without a robust security framework. Strong security can significantly reduce the costs associated with data breaches. A focus on security can help to build consumer trust and encourage wider adoption of IoT technologies. Effective security can help to prevent disruptions to critical business operations. By prioritizing security, we can create a win-win situation for businesses

3. LITERATURE REVIEW

A novel technique for textual data deduplication was presented by Ghassabi et al. (2024). It used a hybrid approach that combines client-side and cloud-side deduplication methods to achieve significant compression rates without compromising data security. This lightweight preprocessing and client-side deduplication makes it suited for resource-constrained devices like IoT devices. It is also made to withstand side-channel assaults. The efficacy and obtained compression rates of approximately 66% are demonstrated in experimental assessments on the Touchdown dataset, which consists of handwritten navigation directions for routes. This considerably reduces storage needs while maintaining the secrecy of textual data. Large-scale data management systems may see considerable cost savings and increased efficiency as a result of this large decrease in storage requirements.

An explainable AI framework was presented by Namrata et al. (2024) to improve anomaly detection in Internet of Things systems. The first of this framework's two primary components is the AI-based anomaly detection of IoT systems, which uses two kinds of AI methods—single and ensemble—to detect anomalies in intelligent IoT systems. Finding anomalous data (from deployed sensors or network traffic between IoT devices) is the goal of this kind of anomaly detection. Secondly, we do feature importance analysis to determine the primary features that AI models may use to detect abnormalities in Internet of Things systems.

An online RL-based system that learns appropriate MTD methods to mitigate diverse zero-day assaults in SBC was proposed by Huertas Celdrán et al. (2024). The framework takes into account RL to learn MTD strategies that mitigate each dangerous condition and behavioral fingerprinting to represent the states of SBCs. It has been implemented using a Raspberry Pi serving as a spectrum sensor in an actual Internet of Things crowdsensing situation. Various instances of ransomware, rootkits, and command-and-control malware have infiltrated the Raspberry Pi, allowing it to choose from four MTD methods that are now in use. Experiments showed that the framework could learn appropriate MTD approaches to mitigate all assaults (except from a dangerous rootkit) with little CPU usage, less than 1 MB of storage, and about 10% of RAM.

In order to explore their integration within the IoT space, Solis et al. (2024) carried out a Systematic Literature Review. They did this by carefully assessing the state-of-the-art through the analysis of 40 papers against 38 extraction criteria, which covered technical aspects unique to FC, BC, FL, or their integration. The results cover data processing, privacy, and security issues in the Internet of Things and provide insights on the benefits, difficulties, possibilities, and limitations of this integration. This work contributes to the field's knowledge development by addressing a research gap and explicitly investigating FC, BC, and FL interoperability across architectural levels. To set itself apart from other research endeavors, this study provides a unique architecture for integrating FL and BC within FC contexts for IoT applications along with an extensive synthesis of the literature. It also suggests future research directions, highlights research gaps, and provides insightful analysis of the state of the field. Readers may obtain tailored information on FC-BC-FL integration with the help of the framework and literature synthesis offered, which facilitates the development and execution of reliable IoT solutions.

4. SMART RISK ASSESSMENT AND CONSUMER IOT

While the overall security framework is crucial, consumer IoT devices present unique challenges due to their widespread adoption and user base. Many consumers lack the technical expertise to understand complex security configurations or even identify potential security risks. This makes them more susceptible to social engineering attacks and phishing scams. Consumer IoT devices often prioritize ease of use over robust security features. Complex authentication processes can deter users, making them more likely to opt for weak passwords or skip updates altogether. Smart home devices collect a vast amount of data, from energy consumption patterns to routine movements. Consumers might not be fully aware of what data is being collected, how it's used, or who has access to it.

Security configurations should be intuitive and user-friendly. Pre-configured strong passwords with easy-to-remember recovery options can strike a balance between usability and protection. Automatic security updates and patch installations are essential to address newly discovered vulnerabilities. Users should be notified of updates but not burdened with the manual installation process. Device manufacturers should collect only the data essential for device functionality. Consumers should have clear and easily accessible information about data collection practices, including how data is stored, used, and shared with third parties. Security should be embedded into the design of consumer IoT devices from the very beginning. This could include features like anonymized data collection or user-controlled data deletion options.

Since many consumer IoT devices are controlled through mobile applications, it's critical to ensure the apps themselves are secure. This includes implementing secure code development practices, regular security audits, and strong authentication mechanisms for user logins. Industry-wide standards for consumer IoT security can help ensure a baseline level of protection. Consumer certification programs can further guide purchasing decisions by highlighting devices that meet specific security requirements. Educating consumers about the importance of IoT security and best practices for secure usage is crucial. Easy-to-understand information campaigns can empower consumers to make informed decisions and protect themselves from cybersecurity threats. By tailoring the security framework to address these specific consumer IoT concerns, we can create a more secure and trustworthy smart home environment. This fosters wider adoption and user confidence in the transformative potential of this technology.

Risk assessment serves as the foundation for a proactive IIoT security strategy. By understanding your vulnerabilities, you can prioritize mitigation efforts and build a more robust defense against cyber threats. Smart risk assessment encompasses a combination of methodologies, tools, and best practices tailored to address the specific vulnerabilities of IoT/IIoT devices. The foundation of any security strategy lies in understanding the potential threats. A comprehensive risk assessment process helps identify vulnerabilities in devices, networks, and protocols within the IoT/IIoT ecosystem. Frameworks like STRIDE (Spoofing, Tampering, Repudiation, Information Disclosure, Denial-of-Service, Elevation of Privilege) provide a structured approach to risk assessment. Consider a smart lock on a home door. For Risk assessment using STRIDE to identify potential vulnerabilities:

- Spoofing: An attacker could spoof the owner's credentials to gain unauthorized access.
- Tampering: The physical lock mechanism could be tampered with, bypassing the electronic access control.
- Information Disclosure: Communication between the lock and smartphone app could be intercepted, revealing the lock status.

- Denial-of-Service: A DoS attack could prevent authorized users from unlocking the door.

The core principles of a smart security framework are presented below.

- Proactive Threat Identification: Risk assessments go beyond simply reacting to known threats. They proactively analyze your IIoT environment, pinpointing potential weaknesses before they can be exploited. This allows you to address vulnerabilities and mitigate risks before they disrupt operations or compromise sensitive data.
- Prioritization of Security Efforts: IIoT environments can be complex, with a multitude of devices, networks, and protocols. Risk assessments help prioritize where to focus your security efforts. By identifying the most critical assets and the vulnerabilities posing the highest risk, you can allocate resources effectively.
- Understanding Potential Impact: Not all vulnerabilities are created equal. Risk assessments help you understand the potential impact of a successful attack on each vulnerability. This allows you to prioritize remediation efforts based on the severity of potential consequences, such as production downtime, data breaches, or safety hazards.
- Data-Driven Decision Making: Risk assessments rely on data collected from your IIoT environment. This data provides valuable insights into device behavior, network traffic, and potential security gaps. With this data-driven approach, you can make informed decisions about security investments and prioritize vulnerabilities based on real-world threats.
- Regulatory Compliance: Many industries have specific regulations regarding cybersecurity. Risk assessments can help you demonstrate compliance with these regulations by providing a documented process for identifying and managing risks in your IIoT environment.

Pseudo code for Risk Assessment algorithm: This pseudo code in Table 1 outlines a simplified risk assessment function. It takes the device, network, and protocol as inputs and iterates through vulnerability databases for each element. The function then returns a list of identified risks.

Table 1. Risk Assessment Function

```
function risk_assessment(device, network, protocol):
risks = []
# Analyze device vulnerabilities
for vulnerability in device_vulnerability_database:
if vulnerability.applicable(device):
risks.append(vulnerability)
# Analyze network vulnerabilities
for weakness in network_security_assessment:
risks.append(weakness)
# Analyze protocol vulnerabilities
for flaw in protocol_security_analysis:
risks.append(flaw)
return risks
```

4.1 Device Hardening

Once vulnerabilities are identified, the next step is to harden devices by minimizing their attack surface. This involves implementing a combination of security measures:

- Secure Configurations: Disabling unnecessary functionalities and services within the device reduces the potential attack vectors.
- Strong Password Enforcement: Enforcing complex password requirements and regular password changes minimizes the risk of unauthorized access.
- Diligent Patch Management: A process for deploying security patches promptly addresses known vulnerabilities and exploits.

Example, Security cameras in an IIoT environment can be hardened by:
- Disabling remote access features when not in use.
- Setting a strong password for the camera's web interface.
- Configuring the camera to receive automatic firmware updates.

4.2 Secure Communication Channels

Securing communication channels protects sensitive data transmitted between devices. This is achieved by utilizing encryption protocols like Transport Layer Security (TLS) or Datagram Transport Layer Security (DTLS). These protocols establish a secure connection, encrypting data in transit, ensuring only authorized parties can decrypt it.

Pseudo code for TLS encryption function: This pseudo code in Table 2 represents TLS encryption function. It takes the data to be encrypted and the encryption key as inputs. In a real-world implementation, a TLS library would handle the secure connection establishment, key exchange, and data encryption processes.

Table 2. TLS Encryption Function

```
function encrypt_data(data, key):
# Simulate connection establishment and key exchange with TLS handshake
encrypted_data = data
# Replace with actual TLS encryption library functions
return encrypted_data
```

Securing communication between a wearable health tracker and a cloud server storing patient data is crucial. TLS encryption ensures that sensitive medical information remains confidential during transmission.

4.3 Continuous Monitoring and Threat Detection

Constant vigilance is key in the dynamic threat landscape of IoT/IIoT. A smart security framework employs continuous monitoring and threat detection mechanisms to identify and respond to security incidents promptly. The steps include:

- Data Collection and Preprocessing:

  o Continuously collect data from various sources in the IIoT environment (e.g., sensor readings, network traffic logs, device logs).

  ° Preprocess the data to extract relevant features and normalize it for consistency.

- Anomaly Detection:

  ° Implement anomaly detection algorithms to identify deviations from normal behavior patterns.
  ° Utilize a combination of statistical analysis, machine learning techniques, and rule-based systems.

- Threat Analysis:

  ° Investigate potential threats flagged by the anomaly detection system.
  ° Analyze the context of the anomaly (e.g., device type, data source, severity) to determine potential threat categories (e.g., malware, unauthorized access).

- Alerting and Mitigation:

  ° Generate alerts for identified threats based on severity and potential impact.
  ° Implement automated or manual mitigation actions depending on the threat type (e.g., isolating compromised devices, blocking suspicious network traffic).

Table 3 presents thes pseudocode for continuous monitoring and threat detection. This pseudocode provides a high-level overview. Specific implementations will involve choosing appropriate data sources, anomaly detection models, and mitigation actions based on the chosen programming language and IIoT environment. The model variable represents a pre-trained anomaly detection model specifically suited for IIoT data. Security personnel should regularly review and update the anomaly detection models to adapt to evolving threats. By implementing continuous monitoring and threat detection, organizations can proactively identify and respond to potential security incidents in their IIoT environments.

Table 3. Continuous Monitoring and Threat Detection

```
# Define functions for data collection, preprocessing, and anomaly detection
def collect_data():
# Collect data from various sources in the IIoT environment
def pre_process_data(data):
# Extract relevant features, normalize data
def detect_anomalies(data, model):
# Utilize pre-trained anomaly detection model (e.g., Isolation Forest)
# Identify anomalies based on deviation from expected behavior
# Return a list of potential anomalies with severity scores
# Main loop for continuous monitoring
while True:
data = collect_data()
preprocessed_data = pre_process_data(data)
anomalies = detect_anomalies(preprocessed_data, model)
# Analyze anomalies and trigger actions based on severity
for anomaly in anomalies:
threat_analysis(anomaly) # Analyze context and categorize threat
# Define function for threat analysis and mitigation
def threat_analysis(anomaly):
# Analyze anomaly details (device, data source, severity)
# Categorize potential threat type (e.g., malware, unauthorized access)
# Trigger mitigation actions based on threat category and severity
# (e.g., isolate device, block traffic, trigger investigation)
```

The key improvements from implementing this pseudo code are:

- Continuous Data Collection: Continuously monitors the IIoT environment for real-time threat detection.
- Data Preprocessing: Ensures consistency and improves the effectiveness of anomaly detection algorithms.
- Multi-pronged Anomaly Detection: Combines statistical analysis, machine learning, and rule-based systems for comprehensive threat identification.
- Threat Analysis and Categorization: Provides context to anomalies and helps prioritize mitigation actions.
- Alerting and Mitigation: Triggers automated or manual responses based on the severity and type of threat.

4.4 Anomaly Detection Systems (ADS)

ADS systems analyse historical data on device behavior, network traffic patterns, and resource usage. Significant deviations from established baselines can indicate a potential attack or malfunction. Imagine a smart refrigerator that monitors its internal temperature and energy consumption. An anomaly detection system can analyse historical data and identify unusual spikes in temperature or sudden increases in energy usage. These deviations could indicate a malfunctioning component, or a potential cyberattack attempting to disrupt the refrigerator's operation.

4.5 Intrusion Prevention Systems (IPS)

IPS systems actively monitor network traffic for suspicious patterns and signatures associated with known attacks. When an IPS identifies a potential threat, it can take steps to block the attack, such as dropping malicious packets or blocking connections from suspicious sources.

Pseudo code for Signature-based IDS: This pseudo code in Table 4 outlines signature-based intrusion detection system. It takes a network packet as input and iterates through a database of known attack signatures. If a match is found, the function returns True, indicating a potential intrusion attempt. Real-world IPS implementations use more sophisticated techniques like anomaly detection in conjunction with signature-based analysis.

Table 4. Signature-based Intrusion Detection System

```
function detect_intrusion(packet):
for signature in known_attack_signatures:
if signature.matches(packet):
return True
return False
```

The smart security framework outlined above provides a comprehensive approach to securing the ever-evolving IoT/IIoT landscape. By combining risk assessment, device hardening, secure communication channels, continuous monitoring, and a security-by-design philosophy, we can proactively mitigate security risks and build a more trustworthy connected ecosystem. This requires collaboration across various stakeholders:

- Device Manufacturers: Prioritizing security throughout the development lifecycle and ensuring ongoing maintenance of devices.
- Cloud Service Providers: Implementing robust security measures to protect user data.
- Standardization Bodies: Developing baseline security requirements for different components of the ecosystem.
- Governments: Enacting regulations that promote secure development practices and responsible data handling.
- Consumers: Making informed choices by demanding security features in IoT/IIoT devices and following best practices for securing their own devices.

By working together, we can unlock the immense potential of the IoT/IIoT revolution while ensuring a secure future where the benefits of interconnected devices outweigh the risks. As we embrace a connected world, let proactive security remain at the forefront, safeguarding our data, privacy, and critical infrastructure in the age of the Internet of Things.

5. RISK ASSESSMENT MODEL

Risk assessment is a crucial step in any project or situation where potential threats could impact success. The STRIDE model provides a structured framework for identifying, analysing, and prioritizing these risks. This methodology leverages the power of graphs to visualize interconnected risks, making the assessment process more efficient and insightful.

Risk assessment methodology process involves the following steps:

i Define the System and Scope: The first step involves clearly defining the system or project under evaluation. This includes outlining its components, functionalities, and intended use. Next, establish the scope of the assessment; what specific aspects of the system will be scrutinized for potential risks?

ii Identify Risks using STRIDE: STRIDE stands for Spoofing, Tampering, Repudiation, Information Disclosure, Denial-of-Service, and Elevation of Privilege. Each category represents a potential threat to a system's security:

- º Spoofing: Impersonating a legitimate user or system to gain unauthorized access.
- º Tampering: Modifying data, code, or system configurations without authorization.
- º Repudiation: Denying involvement in actions taken within the system.
- º Information Disclosure: Unauthorized access to confidential information.
- º Denial-of-Service (DoS): Preventing authorized users from accessing system resources.
- º Elevation of Privilege: Gaining unauthorized access to higher levels of system privileges.

For each STRIDE category, brainstorm potential risks specific to your system. Consider how an attacker could exploit vulnerabilities to fulfil that category's threat. Imagine a web application for online banking. A potential "Spoofing" risk could be unauthorized users creating fake login credentials to access accounts.

iii Constructing the Risk Graph: Now that you have identified potential risks, leverage the power of graphs to visualize their relationships. A risk graph is a network where nodes represent individual risks, and edges depict connections between them as follows:

- º Create a node for each identified risk.
- º Analyze how risks can influence each other. For example, a successful 'Spoofing' attack could lead to "Information Disclosure" if the attacker gains access to sensitive data.
- º Draw an edge between connected risks, with the thickness of the edge representing the strength of the connection (higher connection = greater impact).

iv Risk Analysis and Prioritization: With the risk graph established, we can move on to analyze and prioritize the identified risks. Two key factors here are crucial – the first factor is the Likelihood which is the probability of a specific risk occurring. Impact: The severity of the consequences if the risk materializes.

Pseudocode for Risk Analysis using Risk scoring algorithm helps prioritize mitigation efforts as displayed in Table 5. One common approach is multiplying the likelihood and impact ratings to obtain a risk score. Higher scores indicate risks requiring immediate attention. Consider the 'Spoofing' risk in the online banking application. The likelihood might be rated as 'medium' due to existing security measures. However, the impact could be 'high' as unauthorized access could lead to financial losses. The resulting risk score would be 'medium-high', highlighting the need for implementing stronger authentication methods.

Table 5. Risk Analysis Function

Function AnalyzeRisk(risk):
Assign likelihood rating (low, medium, high) based on historical data, system vulnerabilities, and threat landscape.
Estimate impact rating (low, medium, high) based on potential damage (financial loss, data breach, reputational damage).
*Calculate risk score: likelihood rating * impact rating*
Return risk score

v Risk Mitigation and Monitoring: Based on the risk analysis, prioritize the identified risks according to their scores. Develop mitigation strategies for high-scoring risks. These strategies may involve implementing security controls, enhancing user training, or establishing incident response plans. Graph Algorithms for mitigation to identify critical nodes in the risk graph, representing risks with high connectivity or scores. Focusing mitigation efforts on these critical nodes can have a cascading effect, reducing the overall risk profile of the system. Example when analyzing the risk graph for the online banking application might reveal that mitigating the 'Spoofing' risk (critical node) reduces the likelihood of 'Information Disclosure' as they are connected. By prioritizing strong authentication, both risks are simultaneously addressed.

vi Continuous Monitoring and Improvement: Risk assessment is an iterative process. The risk landscape is constantly evolving, so continuous monitoring is essential. Regularly review the risk graph, update likelihood and impact ratings, and adapt mitigation strategies as needed. Consider using automated tools for continuous monitoring and integrate them with the risk assessment process.

Benefits of using Graphs in Risk Assessment:

- Improved Visualization: Risk graphs provide a clear visual representation of interconnected threats, aiding in a more holistic understanding of the risk landscape.
- Enhanced Analysis: Edges in the graph highlight dependencies and cascading effects, enabling you to predict how a single risk can trigger others.
- Effective Prioritization: By analyzing node connectivity and risk scores, you can prioritize mitigation efforts towards the most critical vulnerabilities.
- Identification of Hidden Risks: Hidden connections between seemingly unrelated risks can be revealed through the graph, leading to a more comprehensive analysis.

This methodology for risk assessment using STRIDE with graphs provides a powerful tool for any security professional or project manager. By utilizing the strengths of structured risk identification, visual representation, and prioritization algorithms, you can ensure proactive risk management and the security of your systems. Remember, constant monitoring and adaptation are key to keeping your risk assessment relevant and effective in today's ever-changing technological landscape.

6. PROPOSED SECURITY FRAMEWORK

The chapter presents a unique security framework designed to detect device and application vulnerabilities, anomalies and malware attacks in IIoT environments. It combines traditional security techniques with Machine Learning (ML) for a proactive approach. for Industrial IoT (IIoT). The framework operates across three layers: Device, Network, and Management. The central hub collects and analyzes data from all layers and ML integration uses anomaly detection algorithms to identify suspicious activities.

Data Flow:

- Device Layer: Sensors and embedded devices collect data and send it to the network layer.
- Network Layer: Network devices (e.g., gateways, routers) forward data to the Security Hub.
- Management Layer: Security software manages access control, encryption, and firmware updates.
- Security Hub: Analyzes data from all layers using:
- Traditional Techniques: Signature-based intrusion detection, vulnerability scanning.
- Machine Learning: Anomaly detection algorithms learn normal behavior and flag deviations.

The vulnerability assessment for IIoT Environments approach combines automated and manual techniques for a comprehensive vulnerability assessment in IIoT environments. The steps involve:

The following functions are presented in Table 6 for Vulnerability Scanning:

- get_device_list function: Not shown here, retrieves a list of all connected devices in the IIoT environment.
- scanner variable: Represents a chosen vulnerability scanner compatible with IIoT devices.
- get_configuration function: Not shown here, retrieves configuration details from devices and applications.

Table 6. Vulnerability Scanning

```
# Define functions for device interaction and vulnerability scanning
def get_device_info(device_id):
# Retrieve device details (e.g., OS, firmware version)
def scan_for_vulnerabilities(device, scanner):
# Utilize a vulnerability scanner (e.g., OpenVAS, Nessus) specific for IIoT devices
# Scan the device for known vulnerabilities based on retrieved device information
# Return a list of identified vulnerabilities with severity levels
# Loop through devices
for device_id in get_device_list():
device_info = get_device_info(device_id)
vulnerabilities = scan_for_vulnerabilities(device_info, scanner)
# Process identified vulnerabilities (store, prioritize)
```

Table 7 presents the pseudocode for Configuration Review.

Table 7. Configuration Review

```
# Define functions for configuration analysis
def check_password_strength(password):
# Implement password strength checks
def analyze_configuration(config):
# Review configuration files for security best practices violations (e.g., weak passwords)
# Return a list of identified configuration issues and severity
# Loop through devices/applications
for target in get_targets():
config = get_configuration(target)
issues = analyze_configuration(config)
# Process identified configuration issues (store, prioritize)
```

The key improvements when using this framrwork include:

- Combines automated scanning with manual penetration testing for broader coverage.
- Analyzes device and application configurations for security weaknesses.
- Integrates threat modeling to prioritize vulnerabilities based on potential impact.

Threat Modeling techniques: Not explicitly shown here, but can involve tools like STRIDE or Trike.
Remember: This is a high-level representation. The actual implementation will involve specific tools, libraries, and tailoring the pseudocode to the chosen programming language and IIoT environment.
Pseudocode for Anomaly Detection is presented in Table 8.

Table 8. Anamoly Detection

```
# Train Machine Learning Model on historical data
TrainModel(data)
# Continuously monitor data streams
while True:
# Receive data from a layer
data = receiveData()
# Predict normalcy of data using trained model
prediction = predictNormal(data, model)
# If anomaly detected
if not prediction:
# Trigger investigation and mitigation procedures
triggerMitigation(data)
```

High level algorithm steps are presented as:

i. Data Preprocessing: Clean and normalize data from all layers for consistency.
ii. Feature Engineering: Extract relevant features from the data (e.g., sensor readings, network traffic patterns).
iii. Model Training: Train an unsupervised Machine Learning model (e.g., Isolation Forest) on historical data to identify normal behavior patterns.
iv. Anomaly Detection: Continuously analyze data streams from all layers. The model flags deviations from the learned normal behavior as potential anomalies.
v. Mitigation: Upon anomaly detection, the system triggers predefined mitigation actions based on the type and severity of the anomaly. This could include:

   o Isolating compromised devices.

     °   Blocking suspicious network traffic.

     °   Alerting security personnel.

The process steps include:

- System Deployment: Install security agents on all devices and deploy network monitoring tools.
- Data Collection and Training: Collect historical data from all layers and train the Machine Learning model.
- Continuous Monitoring: Continuously monitor data streams and analyze them for anomalies.
- Mitigation and Response: Implement automated or manual mitigation procedures based on the detected anomalies.
- Security Improvement: Refine the Machine Learning model based on new data and emerging threats.

An intricate pseudocode for advanced level anomaly detection incorporating data pre-processing and anomaly scoring is presented in Table 9.

Table 9. Advanced Anamoly Detection

```
# Define functions for data pre-processing
def normalize_data(data):
# Implement normalization techniques (e.g., min-max scaling)
def extract_features(data):
# Extract relevant features based on data type (e.g., sensor readings, network traffic)
# Define function for anomaly detection using Isolation Forest
def anomaly_detection(data, model):
# Pre-process data
normalized_data = normalize_data(data)
features = extract_features(normalized_data)
# Predict anomaly score using Isolation Forest
anomaly_score = predict_anomaly(features, model)
return anomaly_score
# Main loop for continuous monitoring
while True:
# Receive data from a layer
data = receiveData()
# Calculate anomaly score
score = anomaly_detection(data, model)
# Define anomaly threshold based on historical data analysis
if score > threshold:
# Flag anomaly and assign severity based on score (Low, Medium, High)
anomaly = {
"type": "data", # Can be "device", "network", based on data source
"severity": get_severity(score),
"data": data
}
# Trigger investigation and mitigation procedures based on anomaly details
trigger_mitigation(anomaly)
```

This framework focuses on data-level anomalies which can be expanded to detect device or network-level anomalies by analyzing specific data patterns and provides the following improvements:

- Data Pre-processing: Includes normalization and feature extraction for better model performance.

- Isolation Forest Integration: predict_anomaly function leverages Isolation Forest to generate anomaly scores.
- Anomaly Scoring and Thresholding: Anomaly score reflects the "outlier-ness" of the data. A threshold defines the boundary between normal and anomalous behavior.
- Severity Levels: Anomaly score helps categorize the severity (Low, Medium, High) for prioritizing
- Anomaly Object: Captures details like anomaly type, severity, and associated data for comprehensive investigation.

The pseudocode incorporates multiple techniques involving several functions as presented in Table 10 for malware detection in IIoT environments.

- get_device_list function: Not shown here, retrieves a list of all connected devices in the IIoT environment.
- known_signatures variable: Stores a database of known malware signatures for comparison.
- ml_models variable: Represents pre-trained Machine Learning models for behavior-based anomaly detection.
- trigger_mitigation function: Not shown here, initiates actions based on the detected malware type and severity (e.g., quarantining infected devices, updating firmware).

Table 10. Malware Detection

```
# Define functions for data collection and pre-processing
def collect_data(device_id):
# Collect data from various sources (e.g., sensor readings, logs, system calls) for the device
def pre_process_data(data):
# Extract relevant features (e.g., CPU usage, network traffic patterns)
# Apply anomaly detection techniques (e.g., statistical analysis, clustering)
# Generate pre-processed data with identified potential anomalies
# Define functions for malware detection using different approaches
def signature_based_detection(data, signatures):
# Compare data features against known malware signatures
# Return a list of potential malware matches
def behavior_based_detection(data, models):
# Analyze data for deviations from expected device behavior patterns
# Utilize pre-trained Machine Learning models for anomaly scoring
# Return an anomaly score and potential malware category
# Main loop for continuous monitoring
while True:
# Iterate through devices in the IIoT environment
for device_id in get_device_list():
data = collect_data(device_id)
preprocessed_data = pre_process_data(data)
# Combine results from different detection methods
potential_malware = []
potential_malware.extend(signature_based_detection(preprocessed_data, known_signatures))
anomaly_score, category = behavior_based_detection(preprocessed_data, ml_models)
if anomaly_score > threshold:
potential_malware.append({"type": "behavioral", "category": category, "score": anomaly_score})
# Evaluate combined potential malware findings
if potential_malware:
# Trigger investigation and mitigation procedures based on findings
trigger_mitigation(device_id, potential_malware)
```

The key enhancements include:

- Data Collection: Gathers data from various sources like sensor readings, logs, and system calls for a more comprehensive view.
- Multi-pronged Detection: Combines signature-based and behavior-based detection for improved accuracy.
- Signature-based detection identifies known malware based on pre-defined signatures.
- Behavior-based detection analyzes deviations from expected behavior patterns using Machine Learning models.
- Anomaly Scoring: Anomaly scores from behavior-based detection help prioritize potential threats.
- Combined Findings: Evaluates results from both detection methods for a more robust assessment.
- Device Iteration: Iterates through all devices in the IIoT environment for comprehensive monitoring.

This security framework can provide the following benefits:

- Proactive threat detection through Machine Learning.
- Multi-layered approach for comprehensive security.
- Automated mitigation actions for faster response.
- Continuous learning and improvement.

7. USE CASES IN SMART HOMES

The allure of smart homes is undeniable. From voice-controlled lighting to automated thermostats, these interconnected devices promise convenience and enhanced comfort. However, the convenience often comes at a cost to security. As more and more devices become connected to the internet, vulnerabilities emerge, exposing our homes to potential breaches. This exposes not only our privacy but also our physical safety. Few real-world examples of security vulnerabilities in smart home IoT devices are discussed below that highlight the need for robust security measures:

Use Case #1: Mirai Botnet

In 2016, the world witnessed the devastating impact of the Mirai botnet. This large-scale botnet, comprised of compromised IoT devices, primarily low-powered home devices like webcams and routers, launched a series of distributed denial-of-service (DDoS) attacks against major internet service providers and companies like Twitter, Netflix, and Reddit. These attacks overwhelmed the targets with a flood of traffic, rendering them inaccessible to legitimate users. The Mirai botnet exploited default credentials and weak security protocols on these smart devices. Hackers easily scanned for vulnerable devices using automated tools and infected them with malware that turned them into controllable bots. The botnet's attack highlighted the potential for weaponized smart devices and the devastating consequences of neglecting security in the IoT landscape.

Use Case #2: Smart Lock Vulnerabilities

Smart locks offer the convenience of keyless entry, but some models have shown critical flaws. In 2017, researchers discovered vulnerabilities in a popular smart lock brand that allowed them to bypass authentication and unlock doors remotely. The vulnerability lay in the way the lock communicated with the smartphone app, allowing attackers to intercept the communication and unlock the door using readily available tools. This incident demonstrates the importance of choosing smart locks with robust encryption protocols and regularly updating firmware to address known vulnerabilities. Additionally, using two-factor authentication can add an extra layer of security, requiring not just the password but also a temporary code sent to the user's phone, further mitigating unauthorized access.

Use Case 3: Baby Monitor Breach

Baby monitors are a valuable tool for parents, allowing them to check on their children remotely. However, some models have been targeted by hackers, raising concerns about privacy violation and potential stalking. In 2019, reports emerged of hackers gaining access to baby monitor feeds, allowing them to spy on families in their most private moments. The vulnerabilities exploited by hackers often involved weak password practices or insecure communication protocols. Leaving the default password on a baby monitor is akin to leaving your front door unlocked; it simply invites trouble. Choosing strong, unique passwords and opting for monitors with secure encryption features can significantly reduce the risk of unauthorized access.

Use Case #4: Smart TV Malware

Smart TVs are not immune to security threats. In 2020, researchers identified malware targeting specific smart TV models. This malware could hijack the TV, displaying unwanted content, stealing personal information, or even launching further attacks on other devices connected to the same network. These vulnerabilities often stemmed from insecure app stores pre-installed on smart TVs, where malicious apps could masquerade as legitimate ones, tricking users into downloading them. This highlights the importance of only installing apps from trusted sources on smart TVs and keeping the TV's firmware updated to address security flaws.

Use Case #5: Voice Assistant Hijacking

Voice assistants are increasingly prevalent in smart homes, facilitating hands-free control of various devices. However, these assistants are not foolproof against hijacking attempts. In 2021, a study revealed vulnerabilities in several popular voice assistants that allowed attackers to exploit wake-word confusion or use voice spoofing techniques to trick the assistants into performing unauthorized actions.

These vulnerabilities could potentially allow attackers to control your smart home devices, change settings, or even eavesdrop on your conversations. Strong authentication methods, such as user voice recognition, can help mitigate voice spoofing risks. Additionally, users should be cautious about the information they share with voice assistants and exercise common sense when setting commands.

These are just a few examples of security vulnerabilities in smart home IoT devices. As the smart home market expands, so too does the attack surface. Tips for securing the smart homes are:

- Prioritize Security: Don't prioritize convenience over security when choosing smart home devices. Research the security features of devices before purchasing and choose ones with robust encryption protocols and a history of addressing vulnerabilities through firmware updates.
- Patch and Update Regularly: Just like your computer and phone, smart home devices need regular firmware updates to address known vulnerabilities.
- Embrace Strong Passwords and Two-Factor Authentication: Resist the temptation to use default passwords on your smart home devices. Create strong, unique passwords for each device and consider enabling two-factor authentication where available. This adds an extra layer of security, requiring a temporary code sent to your phone in addition to the password, making it more difficult for unauthorized access.
- Minimize Attack Surface: Not every device needs to be connected to the internet. Consider the functionality of your smart home devices and only connect those that require internet access. For example, a simple light switch might not need internet connectivity if it can be controlled locally. Limiting internet-connected devices reduces the potential attack surface and makes your smart home network more secure.
- Separate Smart Home Network: Creating a separate network specifically for your smart home devices can help isolate them from other devices on your home network, potentially containing sensitive data like your computer or work laptop. This segmentation can limit the potential damage if a smart home device is compromised.
- Secure Your Home Wi-Fi Network: The foundation of your smart home security lies in a robust Wi-Fi network. Utilize strong encryption protocols like WPA3 (if supported by your router) and disable features like Guest Wi-Fi when not in use. Additionally, consider changing the default administrator password on your router to something more complex.
- Stay Informed and Vigilant: The world of cybersecurity is constantly evolving. Stay informed about the latest vulnerabilities in smart home devices by subscribing to security advisories from reputable sources or following security researchers on social media. Additionally, be vigilant about unusual activity on your smart home devices and report any suspicious behavior to the device manufacturer or relevant authorities.

The convenience and benefits of smart homes are undeniable. However, security concerns should not be an afterthought. By prioritizing robust security measures, choosing devices with strong security features, and implementing a layered approach to protection, we can create safer and more secure smart home environments. As the industry matures, manufacturers have a responsibility to prioritize security by design in their devices, implementing secure coding practices, regular vulnerability assessments, and timely security patches. Governments can also play a role by creating regulations that mandate minimum security standards for smart home devices. By working together, users, manufacturers, and policymakers can create a future where smart homes offer convenience with a strong foundation of security, allowing us to reap the benefits of interconnected living without compromising our privacy and safety.

8. USE CASES IN INDUSTRIAL ENVIRONMENTS

The Industrial Internet of Things (IIoT) and Smart IoT are revolutionizing industries, enabling automation, remote monitoring, and data-driven decision making. However, this interconnectedness comes with a significant downside: security vulnerabilities. These vulnerabilities can expose critical infrastructure, disrupt operations, and even pose safety hazards. Few real-world examples of security vulnerabilities in industrial and smart IoT devices are discussed below that highlight the need for robust security measures in these interconnected environments:

Use Case #1 TRITON/TRISIS

In 2017, the cybersecurity industry was shaken by the discovery of the TRITON/TRISIS malware. This sophisticated malware specifically targeted safety instrumented systems (SIS) used in industrial control systems (ICS) of critical infrastructure, such as power plants and chemical facilities. The malware could manipulate safety logic, potentially leading to catastrophic events like equipment malfunctions or explosions. The TRITON/TRISIS attack was a wake-up call for the industry. It demonstrated the potential for targeted attacks on critical infrastructure and the devastating consequences of compromising safety systems. The attack also highlighted the need for stricter security measures in ICS environments, including segmentation, network monitoring, and vulnerability management of industrial control systems.

Use Case #2: Stuxnet Worm

Stuxnet worm, discovered in 2010, remains a landmark example of a sophisticated cyberattack targeting physical infrastructure. This worm specifically targeted Siemens programmable logic controllers (PLCs) used in Iranian nuclear facilities. Stuxnet could manipulate control processes, potentially causing damage to centrifuges used in uranium enrichment. While the exact origin of Stuxnet remains a mystery, it is widely believed to be a nation-state sponsored attack. This incident highlighted the vulnerabilities in industrial control systems and the potential for cyberattacks to disrupt critical infrastructure and national security. The Stuxnet attack spurred increased awareness and international collaboration on securing critical infrastructure against cyber threats.

Use Case #3: Jeep Hack

In 2015, researchers demonstrated a remote hack on a Jeep Cherokee, showcasing the vulnerabilities of connected vehicles. By exploiting weaknesses in the vehicle's entertainment system, the researchers could gain control of critical functions like steering, acceleration, and brakes. This incident exposed the security risks associated with connected vehicles and the potential for attackers to cause accidents or even take physical control of vehicles. The Jeep hack pushed the automotive industry to prioritize cybersecurity. Manufacturers are now investing heavily in secure communication protocols and in-vehicle security features to mitigate the risks of remote attacks on connected vehicles. As autonomous vehicles become a reality, ensuring robust cybersecurity in these vehicles will be paramount.

Use Case #4: WannaCry Ransomware Attack

In 2017, the WannaCry ransomware attack wreaked havoc globally, affecting hospitals, businesses, and government agencies. This ransomware attack exploited a vulnerability in Microsoft Windows, encrypting data on infected systems and demanding ransom payments for decryption. This attack exposed the interconnectedness of critical infrastructure and the potential for widespread disruption caused by ransomware attacks targeting IIoT and smart IoT devices. WannaCry attack highlighted the importance of patching vulnerabilities promptly and maintaining up-to-date software on all devices, including industrial control systems and other potentially vulnerable IoT devices within critical infrastructure. Additionally, organizations need robust backup and recovery plans to mitigate the impact of ransomware attacks.

Use Case #5: Hacking of Smart Meters

Smart meters, used to monitor and manage energy consumption, are becoming increasingly common. However, these devices have also been targeted by hackers. In 2016, researchers demonstrated the ability to hack into smart meters and manipulate energy consumption data. While the potential for direct control of energy grids through smart meter vulnerabilities is still debated, such attacks could disrupt energy supplies or even provide attackers with valuable insights into grid operations that could be used in future attacks. This incident highlights the need for robust security measures in smart meters and other intelligent grid devices to ensure the reliability and security of energy infrastructure.

These are just a few examples of the security vulnerabilities that threaten industrial and smart IoT devices. To address these challenges, a multifaceted approach is needed as presented below:

- Security by Design: Manufacturers need to prioritize security throughout the lifecycle of a device, from design to development and deployment. This includes secure coding practices, vulnerability assessments, and secure communication protocols.
- Patching and Updates: Regular patching and updates are crucial for addressing vulnerabilities in IIoT and smart IoT devices. Organizations deploying these devices need to have a process in place for timely updates and vulnerability management.
- Network Segmentation: Segmenting networks that connect critical infrastructure to IIoT and smart IoT devices can limit the potential damage if a device is compromised. This compartmentalization can prevent attackers from gaining access to critical systems within the network.
- Network Monitoring and Intrusion Detection: Continuously monitoring network traffic for suspicious activity and deploying intrusion detection systems (IDS) can help identify and prevent cyberattacks on industrial control systems and other vulnerable devices.
- Risk Assessments and Threat Modeling: Regularly conducting risk assessments and threat modeling exercises can help organizations identify potential security vulnerabilities and prioritize mitigation efforts based on the risks involved.
- Security Awareness Training: Providing security awareness training to personnel working with IIoT and smart IoT devices can help them identify and report suspicious activity, reducing the risk of human error contributing to a security breach.

- Collaboration and Information Sharing: Collaboration between government agencies, industry leaders, and security researchers is crucial for sharing information about new threats and vulnerabilities. Open communication facilitates a coordinated response to cyber threats targeting critical infrastructure.
- Regulation and Standards: Developing and enforcing regulations and security standards for IIoT and smart IoT devices will raise the bar for security in these technologies. Government regulations can incentivize manufacturers to prioritize security features and hold them accountable for vulnerabilities in their products.

Industrial Internet of Things and Smart IoT offer tremendous benefits for various industries. However, these benefits must be balanced with robust security measures. By prioritizing security by design, implementing best practices, and fostering collaboration, we can create a future where these technologies operate securely, driving innovation without jeopardizing the safety and security of critical infrastructure. The onus lies on all stakeholders involved, from manufacturers to end-users and government agencies, to prioritize cybersecurity in industrial and smart IoT environments. By working together, we can build a more secure future for interconnected systems, ensuring they remain a valuable tool for progress without compromising the safety and reliability of critical infrastructure.

9. FUTURE DIRECTIONS

The landscape of IoT/IIoT security is constantly evolving. As new technologies emerge and attackers develop more sophisticated techniques, our security frameworks need to adapt and improve. Further development of standardized security protocols and frameworks is crucial for ensuring interoperability between devices from different manufacturers. This will simplify security management and create a more unified defense against cyber threats. As quantum computing advances, current encryption methods might become vulnerable. Research and development of quantum-resistant cryptography solutions is vital to ensure the long-term security of IoT/IIoT devices. Artificial Intelligence for Security:** Leveraging artificial intelligence and machine learning for threat detection and prevention can significantly enhance security posture. AI-powered systems can analyze network traffic in real-time, identify anomalies, and proactively respond to potential attacks.

Blockchain technology can play a pivotal role in securing data exchange within the IoT ecosystem. Its immutable ledger system can ensure data integrity, provenance, and tamper-proof storage, mitigating risks associated with data breaches. Continuous education and awareness campaigns are crucial to foster a culture of security among all stakeholders, including device manufacturers, developers, system administrators, and end-users. Empowering users with knowledge of best practices will strengthen the overall security posture of the IoT ecosystem. By focusing on these future directions, researchers, developers, and policymakers can contribute to building a more secure and resilient IoT/IIoT landscape. This collaborative effort is essential for ensuring the continued growth and safe adoption of this transformative technology.

CONCLUSION

The increasing landscape of interconnected devices in IoT and IIoT environments demands a proactive and multifaceted security approach. This chapter has outlined the fundamental principles for constructing a robust security framework, emphasizing continuous protection and vulnerability mitigation. By laying the groundwork with comprehensive risk assessments, we can pinpoint potential weaknesses in devices, networks, and protocols, allowing for prioritized remediation efforts. Hardening devices through secure configurations, strong passwords, and consistent patching schedules strengthens the overall security posture. Securing communication channels with robust protocols like TLS and DTLS safeguards sensitive data in transit. Anomaly detection systems and Intrusion Prevention Systems (IPS) act as vigilant guardians, identifying and thwarting abnormal behavior and malicious network activity.

However, security cannot be an afterthought. This chapter underscores the paramount importance of integrating security considerations throughout the entire development lifecycle of IoT/IIoT devices. By embracing a "security-by-design" philosophy, we can build inherent resilience into these systems from the very beginning. By implementing these core principles, organizations can establish a smart and adaptable security framework, effectively shielding their IIoT environments from the ever-evolving threats lurking in the digital landscape. Remember, security is an ongoing journey, not a destination. Continuous monitoring, adaptation, and personnel training are essential for maintaining a robust defense against cyberattacks and ensuring the safety and integrity of interconnected systems.

REFERENCES

Erwin, B. (2021). The Groundbreaking 2015 Jeep Hack Changed Automotive Cybersecurity. Fractional CISO - Virtual CISO. https://fractionalciso.com/the-groundbreaking-2015-jeep-hack-changed-automotive -cybersecurity/

Ghassabi, K., & Pahlevani, P. (2024). DEDUCT: A Secure Deduplication of Textual Data in Cloud Environments. *IEEE Access : Practical Innovations, Open Solutions*, 12, 70743–70758. 10.1109/AC-CESS.2024.3402544

Gillis, A. (n.d.). What is IIoT (Industrial Internet of Things)? Definition from TechTarget.com. IoT Agenda. https://www.techtarget.com/iotagenda/definition/Industrial-Internet-of-Things-IIoT

Huertas Celdrán, A., Miguel Sánchez Sánchez, P., von der Assen, J., Schenk, T., Bovet, G., Martínez Pérez, G., & Stiller, B. (2024). RL and Fingerprinting to Select Moving Target Defense Mechanisms for Zero-Day Attacks in IoT. *IEEE Transactions on Information Forensics and Security*, 19, 5520–5529. 10.1109/TIFS.2024.3402055

IBM. (2023). Cost of a Data Breach 2023. IBM. https://www.ibm.com/reports/data-breach

Namrita Gummadi, A., Napier, J. C., & Abdallah, M. (2024). XAI-IoT: An Explainable AI Framework for Enhancing Anomaly Detection in IoT Systems. *IEEE Access : Practical Innovations, Open Solutions*, 12, 71024–71054. 10.1109/ACCESS.2024.3402446

Oracle. (2022). What is the Internet of Things (IoT)? https://www.oracle.com/in/internet-of-things/what -is-iot

Solis, W. V., Marcelo Parra-Ullauri, J., & Kertesz, A. (2024). Exploring the Synergy of Fog Computing, Blockchain, and Federated Learning for IoT Applications: A Systematic Literature Review. *IEEE Access : Practical Innovations, Open Solutions*, 12, 68015–68060. 10.1109/ACCESS.2024.3398034

Chapter 6
Data Privacy and Compliance in IoT

Ammar Odeh
https://orcid.org/0000-0002-9929-2116
*Princess Sumaya University for
Technology, Jordan*

Anas Abu Taleb
*Princess Sumaya University for
Technology, Jordan*

Tareq Alhajahjeh
De Montfort University, UK

Francisco Aparicio
De Montfort University, UK

Sara Hamed
*Princess Sumaya University for
Technology, Jordan*

Nizar Al Daradkeh
*Princess Sumaya University for
Technology, Jordan*

Nasser Ali Al-Jarallah
University of Almaarefa, Saudi Arabia

ABSTRACT

The chapter explores the critical aspects of data privacy and compliance within the rapidly expanding field of the internet of things (IoT). As IoT devices proliferate across consumer, industrial, and healthcare sectors, they bring with them significant challenges related to data security, privacy, and regulatory compliance. The integration of these devices into daily life raises substantial concerns about personal privacy, data breaches, and the ethical use of collected data. This discussion delves into the mechanisms IoT uses to collect, process, and store data; the associated privacy risks; and the comprehensive strategies necessary to mitigate these risks while ensuring compliance with global data protection regulations.

INTRODUCTION

In today's interconnected world, the Internet of Things (IoT) represents a significant evolution in how technology integrates into every aspect of daily life. IoT refers to the network of physical objects—'things'—embedded with sensors, software, and other technologies to connect and exchange data with other devices and systems over the internet. These objects range from ordinary household items like refrigerators and thermostats to sophisticated industrial tools. What makes IoT uniquely influential is not merely the

DOI: 10.4018/979-8-3693-3451-5.ch006

internet connectivity of these devices but their ability to gather, analyze, and act on data, often without human intervention (Pasquier et al., 2018; Subahi & Theodorakopoulos, 2018).

Defining IoT and Its Relevance Today

IoT is a transformative force across many sectors, driving innovations that enhance efficiency, improve real-time decision-making, and increase the overall quality of life. In the consumer sector, IoT technology can be seen in smart home devices that enhance domestic security, manage energy use, and contribute to home health monitoring, offering unprecedented convenience and efficiency. In agriculture, IoT devices monitor soil moisture and weather conditions, directly informing watering and harvesting operations, significantly improving crop yields and resource usage. In healthcare, IoT applications range from remote patient vital signs monitoring to advanced sensors that can predict and alert healthcare providers about potential health crises before they occur (Abu Al-Haija, Odeh, & Qattous, 2022; Abu Taleb, Abu Al-Haija, & Odeh, 2023; Chaudhuri, 2016; Lindmeier & Mühling, 2020; Mittelbach & Fischlin, 2021).

The relevance of IoT today extends beyond mere convenience; it plays a crucial role in data-driven decision-making. For instance, in urban planning and smart city applications, IoT devices provide data that helps in traffic management, pollution control, and infrastructure maintenance, making cities more sustainable, safer, and more efficient. IoT drives the fourth industrial revolution in industries by enabling automation, real-time monitoring of equipment, predictive maintenance, and supply chain logistics, enhancing productivity and safety (Barati, Rana, Petri, & Theodorakopoulos, 2020).

Overview of the Importance of Data Privacy and Compliance in IoT

As much as IoT proliferates in utility and efficiency, it raises significant challenges, particularly concerning data privacy and compliance. Each IoT device serves as a potential entry point for security threats and is a repository of sensitive data, including personal information, proprietary business information, or critically sensitive data like healthcare records.

Data privacy in IoT involves managing personal data in legally and ethically acceptable ways. As IoT devices collect immense amounts of data, often without explicit user consent or awareness, the risk of privacy breaches increases. For example, smart home devices can collect data about personal habits, living conditions, and even confidential conversations. If such data is not handled correctly, it could be misused for invasive advertising, identity theft, or worse, leading to significant privacy violations (Wright, 2019).

Compliance is another critical aspect, encompassing the regulatory requirements that IoT devices must meet to ensure privacy, security, and data protection. Different regions have different laws and regulations governing data protection, such as the General Data Protection Regulation (GDPR) in the European Union, which imposes strict rules on data handling, including IoT data. Compliance is about adhering to laws and building trust with consumers and other stakeholders by demonstrating commitment to data security and ethical data use.

Ensuring compliance and protecting privacy in IoT is particularly challenging because of the diverse and distributed nature of the devices. Each device may fall under different regulatory jurisdictions depending on its location, purpose, and nature of the data it collects. Moreover, the scale of data collected by thousands, if not millions, of IoT devices complicates data management, making it harder to ensure all data is handled correctly by applicable laws and regulations (Abu Al-Haija et al., 2022; Raghunandan, Gagnani, Amarendra, & Santhosh Krishna, 2020; Subahi & Theodorakopoulos, 2018; Wright, 2019).

The importance of data privacy and compliance in the IoT sector cannot be overstated. It is fundamental for protecting individual rights and ensuring the sustainability of IoT solutions in privacy-sensitive areas. Without robust privacy measures and strict compliance with data protection laws, the very benefits that IoT promises could lead to significant risks and liabilities.

As IoT grows and evolves, understanding its implications on data privacy and compliance becomes crucial. The balance between leveraging the capabilities of IoT and protecting the privacy of individuals is delicate. It requires a proactive approach to security, regular updates to compliance measures, and a commitment to ethical standards. By addressing these challenges head-on, stakeholders can harness the full potential of IoT while minimizing the risks associated with data privacy and security. Ensuring robust privacy and compliance frameworks will protect users and enhance the trust and reliability of IoT technologies, paving the way for their wider acceptance and integration into more aspects of our lives (Ahmad, Li, & Luo, 2022; Baloyi & Kotzé, 2020; Varadharajan & Bansal, 2016).

DATA PRIVACY IN IOT

Data privacy includes a person's right to manage personal information and establishes guidelines for its usage, sharing, and security. Within the Internet of Things (IoT) framework, this refers to an abundance of internet-connected gadgets, from commonplace domestic objects to highly advanced industrial instruments. The capacity of Internet of Things (IoT) devices to network and communicate allows them to send, receive, and analyze data on their own. Because of the volume and sensitive nature of the data being handled, data privacy is becoming increasingly important due to the ongoing data transmission and storage. Strong data privacy in the Internet of Things necessitates addressing broad issues with the gathering, processing, sharing, and protecting private and sensitive data against breaches and illegal access (Abroshan, 2021; Abu Al-Haija, Alohaly, & Odeh, 2023; Abu Al-Haija et al., 2022; Abu Taleb et al., 2023; Ahmad et al., 2022; Al-Shabi, 2019; Alshowkan, Elleithy, Odeh, & Abdelfattah, 2013; Anwar, Apriani, & Adianita, 2021; Avesani et al., 2019).

Types of Data Collected by IoT Devices

IoT devices collect various types of data, each with specific privacy considerations:

1. **Personal Data:** This refers to any information that may be used to identify a person, directly or indirectly. Examples of this information include names, addresses, and even the precise locations monitored by cellphones and smartwatches. Devices in the personal fitness and health sectors collect biometric and physical activity data and associate it with user profiles (Barati, Petri, & Rana, 2019).

2. **Sensitive Data:** This category includes information that might substantially affect an individual if handled improperly or made public. IoT applications in the healthcare industry, for example, gather patient health information and data about living circumstances and personal behaviors, which smart home devices may collect. Due to the sensitive nature of this material, very strict handling and security protocols are required (Tawalbeh, Muheidat, Tawalbeh, & Quwaider, 2020).

3. **Operational Data**: This comprises performance metrics, ambient factors, and other non-personal details about the IoT device's operating features. When combined with personal data, this non-identifying data might provide indirect insights into the preferences and behavior of the user (Onyebueke et al., 2023).

Privacy Risks in IoT

The pervasive nature of IoT introduces several privacy risks:

- **Surveillance and Tracking**: IoT devices' constant data collection and monitoring capabilities raise the possibility of inadvertent surveillance, in which specific personal preferences and habits are recorded and examined without the user's express agreement (Sinha, Park, Sinha, & Park, 2017).
- **Data Breaches**: Many Internet of Things (IoT) devices are susceptible to assaults that might result in serious data breaches because of their interdependence and sometimes insufficient protection. In addition to jeopardizing privacy, these violations can harm a person's finances and reputation (Borangiu, Trentesaux, Thomas, Leitão, & Barata, 2019; Chaudhuri, 2016; Dhanda, Singh, & Jindal, 2020).
- **Inadequate Consent Mechanisms**: IoT deployments frequently suffer from unclear or insufficient user consent mechanisms regarding data collection and processing. This erodes trust and poses challenges in meeting the stringent requirements of data privacy regulations (Goldreich, 2019; Hammad, Sagheer, Ahmed, & Jamil, 2020; Jatoth, Gangadharan, Fiore, & Buyya, 2019; Keshta & Odeh, 2021).
- **Third-Party Data Sharing**: Several parties are usually involved in the Internet of Things ecosystem, such as service providers, app developers, and device makers, all of whom may have access to the gathered data. The complicated chain of data custody might make it difficult to implement privacy laws since it can be unclear who has access to the data and for what purposes (Kuznetsov et al., 2021).
- **Long-term Data Storage**: IoT devices create enormous volumes of data that may be retained for extended periods, increasing the risk of unwanted access or data leaks. Data retention for long periods raises questions regarding potential privacy violations and their future usage (Alhalafi & Veeraraghavan, 2019).

Mitigating Data Privacy Risks in IoT

Effective strategies to mitigate these risks include:

- **Enhanced Security Measures**Putting into practice cutting-edge security measures, such as strong encryption techniques, secure device boot procedures, and routine software and firmware upgrades, may help protect IoT devices from cyberattacks and unwanted access.
- **Data Minimization**: Privacy hazards may be considerably decreased by following the data minimization principle, which calls for just gathering the information required for a given purpose and keeping it only for as long as necessary.

- **Transparent Consent Practices**: Transparency is improved, and users are given more authority to make decisions about their data by creating simple and intuitive consent procedures that tell users about the types of data that are collected, how they are used, and who they may share them with [8].
- **Regulatory Compliance**: It is essential to abide by privacy rules and regulations, such as the California Consumer Privacy Act (CCPA) in the United States and the General Data Protection Regulation (GDPR) in the European Union. To preserve privacy in the context of the Internet of Things, these policies uphold essential concepts like user permission, data minimization, and transparency.
- **Privacy by Design**: Privacy is a core part of technology development rather than an afterthought, and privacy considerations are ensured in the design and architecture of IoT systems from the very beginning. This strategy increases user confidence and complies with legal requirements and data protection best practices (Loukil, Ghedira-Guegan, Boukadi, & Benharkat, 2018).

KEY PRIVACY CHALLENGES IN IOT

The Internet of Things (IoT) is revolutionizing how we interact with technology, with billions of devices connected and communicating. This vast network, however, introduces significant privacy challenges that must be addressed to safeguard user data and maintain trust in IoT systems. This section explores four critical areas of concern: scale and scope, data security, data minimization, and user consent and transparency.

Scale and Scope

The scale and scope of IoT are unprecedented, with forecasts suggesting that by 2025, over 75 billion IoT devices will be in operation. This explosion of connected devices presents a unique set of privacy challenges, primarily due to the massive volume of data these devices generate and collect. Each device, from smart thermostats to fitness trackers, continuously gathers personal information, creating a detailed digital footprint of an individual's activities, preferences, and behaviors. This data aggregation across various devices and platforms can lead to significant risks, including unauthorized data access and misuse, if not managed properly. The challenge is protecting this vast amount of data and managing it in a way that respects user privacy across diverse systems and jurisdictions.

Data Security

IoT devices often suffer from inadequate security measures, partly due to their diverse range and capabilities, which make standardization difficult. Many IoT devices are built with cost and convenience in mind rather than security, leading to vulnerabilities at various points—from the device itself to the data transmission and storage phases. For instance, many devices cannot be patched or updated, which leaves them open to exploits long after a vulnerability is discovered. Moreover, the interconnected nature of these devices means that compromising one device can potentially provide a gateway to infiltrate entire networks, thereby multiplying the risks and potential damage. Strengthening these vulnerabilities requires better security practices at the design and manufacturing stages and ongoing management throughout the device lifecycle.

Data Minimization

Data minimization is a key principle that challenges the traditional 'collect it all' mindset, urging only the collection of data that is directly necessary for the intended purpose of the IoT application. However, implementing this principle in IoT is complex due to the fact that many devices have passive and pervasive data collection mechanisms. For instance, a smart home assistant may need to 'listen' continuously for activation commands, but this functionality could lead to the unintentional capture of private conversations. Addressing this challenge involves designing systems that intelligently determine which data is essential for functionality and which is extraneous and can, therefore, be disregarded or never collected. This protects user privacy and reduces the burden on storage and processing, enhancing efficiency.

User Consent and Transparency

Ensuring informed user consent and maintaining transparency are fundamental in managing privacy in IoT. However, the complexity and opacity of IoT systems can make it difficult for users to understand what data is being collected, how it is being used, and with whom it is being shared. Moreover, obtaining meaningful consent is challenging when interactions with devices are passive or continuous. For effective consent, users must be provided with clear, concise, and accessible information about data practices. Additionally, consent should be easy to give and just as easy to withdraw. Transparency can be improved through user-friendly privacy notices and real-time data access reports that allow users to see what data is collected and how it is used.

REGULATORY LANDSCAPE

As the Internet of Things (IoT) expands, comprehensive regulatory frameworks to manage and protect the massive amounts of data generated become imperative. This section provides an overview of the global regulatory landscape that governs IoT, discusses specific laws and regulations relevant to the field, and highlights the differing compliance requirements across various regions.

Overview of Global Regulatory Frameworks Affecting IoT

The regulatory frameworks governing IoT are as diverse as the technology, spanning numerous jurisdictions, each with its own rules and standards. Globally, these regulations aim to address the common challenges IoT poses, such as data security, privacy protection, and cross-border data flows. However, the absence of a unified global standard for IoT security and privacy means businesses and consumers must navigate a complex patchwork of regional laws.

Specific Laws and Regulations

Several key laws and regulations have emerged as benchmarks in the IoT space:

General Data Protection Regulation (GDPR) in Europe: GDPR is one of the world's most stringent privacy and security laws. It imposes obligations onto organizations anywhere, so long as they target or collect data related to people in the EU. GDPR has set a high standard with its stringent consent requirements, data subject rights, and penalties for non-compliance, influencing IoT operations worldwide.

California Consumer Privacy Act (CCPA) in California, USA: The CCPA gives California residents the right to know about the personal information a business collects about it and its purposes. This law also allows consumers to sue companies if the privacy guidelines are violated, even if there is no breach.

Personal Information Protection and Electronic Documents Act (PIPEDA) in Canada: PIPEDA governs how private sector organizations collect, use, and disclose personal information during commercial business. It also provides guidelines on the security of IoT devices.

These laws, among others, are pivotal in shaping how IoT devices are developed, marketed, and managed across borders.

Differences in Compliance Requirements Across Regions

Compliance with IoT regulations can vary significantly from one region to another, impacting how companies design and deploy IoT solutions globally:

Europe vs. United States: While Europe's GDPR heavily emphasizes user consent and stringent data protection measures, U.S. laws like the CCPA offer a slightly more flexible approach, focusing on transparency and giving consumers control over their personal information. The U.S. lacks a federal privacy law akin to GDPR, leading to a more fragmented regulatory landscape.

Asia-Pacific: Countries like Japan and South Korea have robust IoT frameworks that blend stringent data protection with innovative technology policies. However, other parts of Asia have less stringent or evolving policies, leading to a varied regulatory landscape that can be challenging for multinational IoT deployments.

Navigating the regulatory landscape for IoT requires a keen understanding of these diverse frameworks and the ability to adapt IoT practices to comply with regional laws. For IoT to truly realize its potential, policymakers, and businesses must work together to create harmonized regulations that facilitate innovation while protecting consumer privacy and enhancing security. The ongoing development and harmonization of IoT regulations will be crucial as the technology becomes increasingly integrated into the fabric of daily life (Loukil et al., 2018; Odeh, Elleithy, Alshowkan, & Abdelfattah, 2013; Onyebueke et al., 2023).

COMPLIANCE STRATEGIES FOR IOT

In an era where interconnected devices are embedded into the fabric of daily life, ensuring compliance with regulatory frameworks is crucial for the success and safety of Internet of Things (IoT) systems. This section discusses effective strategies for maintaining compliance, focusing on data protection by design, the necessity of regular audits and updates, and the implementation of role-based access control.

Data Protection by Design

Data Protection by Design is a principle that advocates for integrating data protection features directly into the development and design of IoT technologies. This approach helps comply with laws like the GDPR, which explicitly requires Data Protection by Design and enhances user trust in IoT systems. The strategies for embedding privacy can include the following:

Minimizing data collection: Only collect data essential for the specific purposes of the IoT device or service.

Encrypting data: Implement strong encryption for data at rest and in transit to protect it from unauthorized access.

Privacy settings: Offer users robust and intuitive privacy settings by default, ensuring they have control over their data.

Anonymization: Where possible, anonymize data to prevent association with specific individuals, reducing privacy risks.

These techniques should be considered from the earliest stages of IoT product and service design, ensuring they are fundamental rather than supplementary components of technology development.

Regular Audits and Updates

Regular audits and updates are essential to maintaining security and compliance. IoT devices are often deployed in vast numbers and may operate continuously without direct human oversight, making them vulnerable to evolving threats.

Security updates: Developers should provide regular software updates to address new vulnerabilities. A seamless and secure update system should be established to protect devices against potential exploits.

Compliance audits: Regular audits help ensure IoT systems comply with applicable privacy laws and industry regulations. These audits should assess IoT systems' technical and procedural aspects, including how data is collected, stored, and processed.

Implementing these practices will help identify potential compliance issues and security vulnerabilities before they can be exploited, reducing the risk of breaches and non-compliance penalties.

Role-Based Access Control

Role-based Access Control (RBAC) restricts system access to authorized users based on their role within an organization. In the context of IoT, RBAC is crucial for:

Limiting access: By defining roles and associated permissions, organizations can ensure that individuals only have access to the information necessary for their job functions. This minimizes the risk of accidental or malicious data breaches.

Enhancing security: Implementing RBAC helps create a more secure IoT environment by reducing the number of potential attack points. Fewer people with access to critical systems means a smaller chance of those systems being compromised.

Simplifying management: RBAC systems make it easier to manage user permissions, especially in large organizations or systems with multiple types of IoT devices.

Effective compliance in IoT requires a proactive approach, embedding privacy and security measures from the design phase to the ongoing management of devices. By incorporating Data Protection by Design, conducting regular audits and updates, and implementing RBAC, organizations can meet regulatory requirements and strengthen the trust of users and partners. These strategies are critical in harnessing the full potential of IoT technologies while safeguarding against the increasing risks in a connected world.

CASE STUDIES

Understanding how real-world applications handle data privacy and compliance is crucial in the complex landscape of Internet of Things (IoT) deployments. This section presents a series of case studies that illustrate successful strategies and notable failures in IoT implementations, offering valuable insights into effective data management and regulatory compliance.

Case Study 1: Smart City Initiatives

Example: Singapore's Smart Nation Initiative Singapore's Smart Nation initiative is a prime example of IoT success. It utilizes a network of sensors and cameras across the city to optimize everything from traffic management to waste collection and public safety. The initiative prioritizes data privacy and security in its operations, implementing robust data protection measures in line with Singapore's Personal Data Protection Act (PDPA) (Neirotti, De Marco, Cagliano, Mangano, & Scorrano, 2014).

Successes

Integrated Security Framework: Singapore developed a holistic security framework that includes technology, processes, and policies to safeguard personal data.
Public Engagement: The government actively involves the public in its data privacy discussions, ensuring transparency and building trust.

Lessons Learned

The importance of integrating privacy and security from the outset of IoT project planning.
The value of public engagement in gaining trust and compliance.

Case Study 2: Consumer IoT Products

Example: Smart Home Devices Smart home devices like Amazon Echo and Google Nest have transformed everyday living. However, they have also faced scrutiny over privacy concerns, particularly regarding data collection and the potential for eavesdropping.

Failures

Data Breaches: Incidents of unauthorized access to consumer data have raised serious privacy concerns.
Lack of Transparency: Consumers have often been unaware of the extent of data collection and its uses.

Successes

Regular Updates: Following the backlash, companies improved their privacy policies and now offer regular firmware updates to enhance security.

Enhanced User Controls: Companies have introduced more robust user controls for data management and device operation, improving transparency.

Lessons Learned

Continuous improvement in privacy practices is crucial.

Transparency and user control are key to maintaining consumer trust.

Case Study 3: Industrial IoT (IIoT)

Example: Predictive Maintenance in Manufacturing IoT devices are widely used in manufacturing for predictive maintenance. Sensors collect data from equipment to predict failures before they occur, significantly reducing downtime and maintenance costs.

Successes

Data Minimization: Only relevant data necessary for predictive analytics is collected, adhering to data minimization principles.

Strong Access Controls: Access to sensitive data is tightly controlled, with role-based access ensuring that only essential personnel can view or process data.

Failures

Complex Compliance Landscapes: Some deployments have struggled with varying compliance requirements across different countries, complicating data management.

Lessons Learned

There is a need for an adaptable compliance strategy that can adjust to various regulatory environments.

Role-based access controls are effective in managing data privacy risks.

Case Study 4: Healthcare IoT

Example: Remote Patient Monitoring Systems IoT devices are increasingly used in healthcare for remote patient monitoring, providing real-time data to healthcare providers, and improving patient outcomes.

Successes

Encrypted Data Transmission: Data transmitted from IoT devices to healthcare providers is encrypted, ensuring patient confidentiality.

Compliance with Health Regulations: IoT deployments in healthcare rigorously adhere to health-specific regulations like HIPAA in the U.S., ensuring compliance.

Failures

Data Integrity Issues: Some systems have faced challenges regarding the accuracy and integrity of the data collected, affecting patient care.

Lessons Learned

Ensuring data integrity is as crucial as protecting data privacy.

Compliance with sector-specific regulations is essential for successful deployment.

The diverse range of IoT applications across different sectors highlights varied approaches to handling data privacy and compliance. These case studies demonstrate that while there are challenges and failures, successful strategies often include robust data protection measures, regular updates, transparency, and strict compliance with regulations. Learning from the successes and failures of these real-world examples provides crucial insights for future IoT deployments, emphasizing the need for comprehensive privacy strategies tailored to specific sector needs and regulatory requirements.

EMERGING TRENDS AND FUTURE DIRECTIONS (AMMAR ODEH)

The integration of Artificial Intelligence (AI) and Machine Learning (ML) into the Internet of Things (IoT) is revolutionizing how we interact with our devices and manage data. As these technologies evolve, they raise significant privacy and compliance issues, necessitating careful consideration of the regulatory landscape. This essay explores the role of AI and ML in enhancing privacy and compliance in IoT systems and predicts future challenges and opportunities that could shape the regulatory framework.

Integration of AI With IoT

AI and ML are not merely supporting technologies in the IoT ecosystem; they are becoming integral to its core functionality. IoT devices equipped with AI capabilities can process and analyze data directly at the source—a concept known as edge computing. This reduces latency, conserves bandwidth, and, crucially, minimizes the volume of data that needs to be transferred, thereby enhancing data privacy.

Enhancing Privacy and Compliance

Data Minimization: By analyzing data locally on IoT devices, less information must be transmitted over networks, reducing exposure to potential data breaches. For example, a smart home device with ML capabilities can process data internally, only sending essential information to the cloud for further action, thus minimizing the data footprint.

Automated Compliance: AI can automate the enforcement of compliance policies by identifying and classifying sensitive data. For instance, AI algorithms can ensure that personally identifiable information (PII) collected by IoT devices is handled by GDPR guidelines, automatically encrypting data or anonymizing personal details before they are stored or transmitted.

Anomaly Detection: AI enhances security in IoT networks by continuously learning normal network behaviors and quickly identifying anomalies that could signify breaches or non-compliance. For instance, unexpected data flows or unauthorized access to device controls can be flagged and addressed immediately.

Predicting Future Challenges and Opportunities

Regulatory Challenges

Constant Evolution: The rapid advancement of AI and IoT technologies presents a significant challenge for regulators. Regulations may become outdated as soon as they are implemented, failing to address new privacy concerns that arise from technological innovations.

Global Standards: Developing uniform regulations that span multiple jurisdictions is increasingly complex as IoT deployments cross international boundaries. This lack of standardization can lead to regulatory conflicts and hinder the global deployment of IoT solutions.

Opportunities for Improvement

AI in Regulatory Development: AI can assist regulators by analyzing the potential impacts of proposed regulations, processing public feedback, and simulating outcomes. This could lead to more informed, effective, and adaptable regulatory frameworks.

Public Trust and Adoption: Enhanced privacy and compliance measures driven by AI can help build public trust in IoT technologies. As trust increases, so does adopting these technologies, which can drive further innovation and improvement.

The balance between technological advancement and privacy rights is delicate. Proactive, adaptive regulatory measures that can keep pace with technological developments will be crucial in safeguarding individual privacy while fostering innovation. Reflecting on these points, it becomes clear that the future of IoT is not only on technological advancements but also on the evolution of regulatory frameworks that support these advancements while protecting the fundamental rights of individuals.

ETHICAL CONSIDERATIONS IN AI-ENABLED IOT

Ethical considerations become paramount as AI and IoT become more embedded in everyday life. The autonomous nature of AI-driven decisions, especially when personal data is involved, raises significant moral questions. Key among these are concerns about bias, privacy, and accountability:

Bias in AI Algorithms: AI systems are only as unbiased as the data on which they are trained. In IoT applications, biased data can lead to discriminatory outcomes, such as unfair treatment in smart healthcare devices or biased decision-making in AI-driven hiring processes via IoT platforms. Addressing these biases requires rigorous algorithm testing and transparency in AI deployments.

Privacy Concerns: While AI can enhance privacy through data minimization and anomaly detection, it poses risks. The capability of AI to infer additional personal information from seemingly innocuous data can lead to unintended privacy breaches. Thus, privacy-enhancing technologies (PETs) must evolve alongside AI to mitigate these risks.

Accountability: Establishing clear accountability for AI-driven decisions is crucial. In IoT environments, where multiple AI systems may interact, pinpointing responsibility when things go wrong can be challenging. Developing frameworks for accountability that include clear guidelines on liability and redress mechanisms is essential for fostering trust and confidence in AI-IoT integrations.

The Role of Emerging Technologies in Shaping Future IoT Deployments

Emerging technologies such as Quantum Computing and Blockchain offer promising enhancements to AI and IoT ecosystems, potentially addressing some of the current limitations and risks:

Quantum Computing: Quantum computing could revolutionize AI's capabilities by processing information at unprecedented speeds. For IoT, this means faster data analysis and more complex problem-solving in real-time, dramatically increasing the efficiency and effectiveness of AI algorithms used in everything from traffic management to energy conservation.

Blockchain: Blockchain technology can enhance IoT security and transparency. By creating decentralized and tamper-proof records of data transactions, blockchain can secure IoT data transfers, ensure data integrity, and improve trust in IoT ecosystems. For example, blockchain can provide a transparent and secure record of product journeys from manufacture to sale in supply chain management.

Reflecting further on the integration of AI and IoT, it becomes evident that while these technologies offer profound benefits, they also necessitate a sophisticated approach to ethical, privacy, and compliance challenges. The future of IoT will likely be shaped by a combination of advanced technologies and enhanced regulatory frameworks that together address these challenges while promoting innovation.

To thrive in this future, stakeholders across the IoT ecosystem must continuously dialogue about the ethical implications of AI and IoT. Moreover, they must actively participate in developing technologies like blockchain and quantum computing that can provide robust solutions to the complex privacy and security problems in IoT networks.

As we consider the balance between technological advancement and privacy rights, it is clear that our ability to harness the full potential of IoT and AI will depend not only on technological innovation but also on our commitment to ethical standards and comprehensive regulatory oversight. Ensuring that these technologies are developed and deployed in ways that respect and enhance our shared social values will be crucial for their success and acceptance.

SUMMARY

The chapter defines the Internet of Things (IoT) as a network of interconnected devices that collect and exchange data. It emphasizes its transformational impact across healthcare, agriculture, and urban development. The relevance of IoT today is highlighted by its capabilities to enhance efficiency and decision-making processes through real-time data analysis.

A significant portion of the chapter discusses IoT's privacy and security challenges. The vast amounts of data collected by IoT devices pose risks such as unauthorized access and potential misuse of personal information. The chapter outlines specific privacy concerns related to surveillance, tracking, data breaches, and the inadequacies of consent mechanisms in IoT deployments.

To address these issues, the chapter advocates for robust privacy and compliance frameworks that incorporate principles such as data minimization and transparency. It emphasizes the importance of 'Privacy by Design' as a proactive approach in IoT system development, ensuring that privacy and compliance are considered at every stage of the design and operational process.

Furthermore, the chapter examines the regulatory landscape, noting the variations in compliance requirements across different regions and the challenges posed by the lack of a unified global standard. It discusses key regulations such as the General Data Protection Regulation (GDPR) in the European Union and the California Consumer Privacy Act (CCPA) in the United States. It underscores their impact on IoT operations and the necessity for IoT systems to adapt to these legal frameworks.

The chapter concludes by stressing the delicate balance between advancing IoT technological capabilities and protecting individual privacy rights. It calls for ongoing adjustments to regulatory measures and a continuous commitment to ethical standards to ensure the sustainability and acceptance of IoT technologies in society.

REFERENCES

Abroshan, H. (2021). A hybrid encryption solution to improve cloud computing security using symmetric and asymmetric cryptography algorithms. *International Journal of Advanced Computer Science and Applications*, 12(6), 31–37. 10.14569/IJACSA.2021.0120604

Abu Al-Haija, Q., Alohaly, M., & Odeh, A. (2023). A lightweight double-stage scheme to identify malicious DNS over HTTPS traffic using a hybrid learning approach. *Sensors (Basel)*, 23(7), 3489. 10.3390/s2307348937050549

Abu Al-Haija, Q., Odeh, A., & Qattous, H. (2022). PDF malware detection based on optimizable decision trees. *Electronics (Basel)*, 11(19), 3142. 10.3390/electronics11193142

Abu Taleb, A., Abu Al-Haija, Q., & Odeh, A. (2023). Efficient Mobile Sink Routing in Wireless Sensor Networks Using Bipartite Graphs. *Future Internet*, 15(5), 182. 10.3390/fi15050182

Ahmad, J., Li, F., & Luo, B. (2022). *Iotprivcomp: A measurement study of privacy compliance in iot apps.* Paper presented at the European Symposium on Research in Computer Security. 10.1007/978-3-031-17146-8_29

Al-Shabi, M. A. (2019). A survey on symmetric and asymmetric cryptography algorithms in information security. *International Journal of Scientific and Research Publications*, 9(3), 576–589. 10.29322/IJSRP.9.03.2019.p8779

Alhalafi, N., & Veeraraghavan, P. (2019). *Privacy and Security Challenges and Solutions in IOT: A review.* Paper presented at the IOP conference series: Earth and environmental science. 10.1088/1755-1315/322/1/012013

Alshowkan, M., Elleithy, K., Odeh, A., & Abdelfattah, E. (2013). *A new algorithm for three-party Quantum key distribution.* Paper presented at the Third International Conference on Innovative Computing Technology (INTECH 2013). 10.1109/INTECH.2013.6653692

Anwar, M. R., Apriani, D., & Adianita, I. R. (2021). Hash Algorithm In Verification Of Certificate Data Integrity And Security. *Aptisi Transactions on Technopreneurship*, 3(2), 181–188. 10.34306/att.v3i2.212

Avesani, P., McPherson, B., Hayashi, S., Caiafa, C. F., Henschel, R., Garyfallidis, E., & Olivetti, E. (2019). The open diffusion data derivatives, brain data upcycling via integrated publishing of derivatives and reproducible open cloud services. *Scientific Data*, 6(1), 69. 10.1038/s41597-019-0073-y31123325

Baloyi, N., & Kotzé, P. (2020). *Data privacy compliance benefits for organisations–A cyber-physical systems and internet of things study.* Paper presented at the Information and Cyber Security: 18th International Conference, ISSA 2019, Johannesburg, South Africa. 10.1007/978-3-030-43276-8_12

Barati, M., Petri, I., & Rana, O. F. (2019). *Developing GDPR compliant user data policies for internet of things.* Paper presented at the 12th IEEE/ACM International conference on utility and cloud computing. 10.1145/3344341.3368812

Barati, M., Rana, O., Petri, I., & Theodorakopoulos, G. (2020). GDPR compliance verification in Internet of Things. *IEEE Access : Practical Innovations, Open Solutions*, 8, 119697–119709. 10.1109/ACCESS.2020.3005509

Borangiu, T., Trentesaux, D., Thomas, A., Leitão, P., & Barata, J. (2019). *Digital transformation of manufacturing through cloud services and resource virtualization* (Vol. 108). Elsevier.

Chaudhuri, A. (2016). Internet of things data protection and privacy in the era of the General Data Protection Regulation. *Journal of Data Protection & Privacy*, 1(1), 64–75.

Dhanda, S. S., Singh, B., & Jindal, P. (2020). Lightweight cryptography: A solution to secure IoT. *Wireless Personal Communications*, 112(3), 1947–1980. 10.1007/s11277-020-07134-3

Goldreich, O. (2019). On the foundations of cryptography. In *Providing sound foundations for cryptography: on the work of Shafi Goldwasser and Silvio Micali* (pp. 411-496). Academic Press.

Hammad, B. T., Sagheer, A. M., Ahmed, I. T., & Jamil, N. (2020). A comparative review on symmetric and asymmetric DNA-based cryptography. *Bulletin of Electrical Engineering and Informatics*, 9(6), 2484–2491. 10.11591/eei.v9i6.2470

Jatoth, C., Gangadharan, G., Fiore, U., & Buyya, R. (2019). SELCLOUD: A hybrid multi-criteria decision-making model for selection of cloud services. *Soft Computing*, 23(13), 4701–4715. 10.1007/s00500-018-3120-2

Keshta, I., & Odeh, A. (2021). Security and privacy of electronic health records: Concerns and challenges. *Egyptian Informatics Journal*, 22(2), 177–183. 10.1016/j.eij.2020.07.003

Kuznetsov, A., Oleshko, I., Tymchenko, V., Lisitsky, K., Rodinko, M., & Kolhatin, A. (2021). Performance analysis of cryptographic hash functions suitable for use in blockchain. *International Journal of Computer Network & Information Security*, 13(2), 1–15. 10.5815/ijcnis.2021.02.01

Lindmeier, A., & Mühling, A. (2020). *Keeping secrets: K-12 students' understanding of cryptography*. Paper presented at the 15th Workshop on Primary and Secondary Computing Education. 10.1145/3421590.3421630

Loukil, F., Ghedira-Guegan, C., Boukadi, K., & Benharkat, A. N. (2018). *Towards an end-to-end IoT data privacy-preserving framework using blockchain technology*. Paper presented at the Web Information Systems Engineering–WISE 2018: 19th International Conference, Dubai, United Arab Emirates. 10.1007/978-3-030-02922-7_5

Mittelbach, A., & Fischlin, M. (2021). *The theory of hash functions and random oracles. An Approach to Modern Cryptography*. Springer Nature. 10.1007/978-3-030-63287-8

Neirotti, P., De Marco, A., Cagliano, A. C., Mangano, G., & Scorrano, F. (2014). Current trends in Smart City initiatives: Some stylised facts. *Cities (London, England)*, 38, 25–36. 10.1016/j.cities.2013.12.010

Odeh, A., Elleithy, K., Alshowkan, M., & Abdelfattah, E. (2013). *Quantum key distribution by using public key algorithm (RSA)*. Paper presented at the Third International Conference on Innovative Computing Technology (INTECH 2013). 10.1109/INTECH.2013.6653697

Onyebueke, A. E., Emmanuel, S., Mu'awuya Dalhatu, A. S. A., Mazadu, L. E. I. J., Ifeanyi, O. C., & Eyitayo, A. (2023). *Data privacy and compliance in cloud-based iot systems: A security assessment*. Paper presented at the African-European Regional Governance & Development Conference.

Pasquier, T., Singh, J., Powles, J., Eyers, D., Seltzer, M., & Bacon, J. (2018). Data provenance to audit compliance with privacy policy in the Internet of Things. *Personal and Ubiquitous Computing*, 22(2), 333–344. 10.1007/s00779-017-1067-4

Raghunandan, K., Gagnani, L., Amarendra, K., & Santhosh Krishna, B. (2020). Product key activation for software products using Collatz Conjuncture and asymmetric key cryptography. *Materials Today: Proceedings*. https://doi. . MATPR, 907org/10.1016/J

Sinha, S. R., Park, Y., Sinha, S. R., & Park, Y. (2017). Dealing with security, privacy, access control, and compliance. *Building an Effective IoT Ecosystem for Your Business*, 155-176.

Subahi, A., & Theodorakopoulos, G. (2018). *Ensuring compliance of IoT devices with their Privacy Policy Agreement.* Paper presented at the 2018 IEEE 6th International Conference on Future Internet of Things and Cloud (FiCloud). 10.1109/FiCloud.2018.00022

Tawalbeh, L., Muheidat, F., Tawalbeh, M., & Quwaider, M. (2020). IoT Privacy and security: Challenges and solutions. *Applied Sciences (Basel, Switzerland)*, 10(12), 4102. 10.3390/app10124102

Varadharajan, V., & Bansal, S. (2016). Data security and privacy in the internet of things (iot) environment. *Connectivity Frameworks for Smart Devices: The Internet of Things from a Distributed Computing Perspective*, 261-281.

Wright, S. A. (2019). *Privacy in iot blockchains: with big data comes big responsibility.* Paper presented at the 2019 IEEE International Conference on Big Data (Big Data). 10.1109/BigData47090.2019.9006341

Chapter 7
Cryptographic Solutions

Ammar Odeh
https://orcid.org/0000-0002-9929-2116
Princess Sumaya University for Technology, Jordan

Anas Abu Taleb
Princess Sumaya University for Technology, Jordan

Tareq Alhajahjeh
De Montfort University, UK

Francisco Aparicio-Navarro
De Montfort University, UK

ABSTRACT

This chapter delves into the fundamental and advanced aspects of cryptography, an essential discipline for securing information in our digital age. It outlines the core concepts including encryption, decryption, ciphers, keys, and algorithms, which safeguard data integrity, confidentiality, and accessibility. The discussion extends to the distinctions between symmetric and asymmetric cryptography, their specific applications in various sectors, and the role of cryptographic hash functions in ensuring data integrity. Additionally, the chapter explores recent advancements such as quantum cryptography and the implications of artificial intelligence in cryptographic solutions. It also addresses the societal and technological impacts of robust cryptographic practices, balancing security needs with ethical and legal considerations. This comprehensive overview underscores the critical role of cryptography in protecting digital interactions and data in an increasingly interconnected world.

INTRODUCTION TO CRYPTOGRAPHY

Cryptography is the scientific practice of safeguarding information by converting it into a secure format. The term "cryptography" originates from the Greek terms 'Kryptos,' which means concealed, and 'graphene,' which means to write. This approach, essential for ensuring digital security, guarantees that individuals can only access information with the required authorization. With the increasing scope

DOI: 10.4018/979-8-3693-3451-5.ch007

of the digital world, the significance of cryptography has risen significantly, becoming crucial in protecting personal data, financial information, and national security.

The importance of cryptography in digital security cannot be overemphasized. Amidst a time characterized by frequent data breaches and prevalent cyber dangers, cryptographic methods employ encryption to safeguard sensitive data. Consequently, the data remains incomprehensible and immune to misuse even if intercepted. Cryptography protects data by preventing unauthorized access and guarantees data integrity by confirming the integrity and authenticity of the information transmitted, ensuring it remains unaltered and free from tampering or corruption (Zhang et al., 2019).

Cryptography has been practiced for thousands of years, developing into many types and levels of intricacy. Historically, cryptography was predominantly employed in politics and military tactics. An early instance of cryptography may be traced back to ancient Egypt, approximately in 1900 BCE. During this time, hieroglyphs were employed in an unorthodox arrangement on a tomb to conceal the inscriptions' true significance. The primary objective of this method was to obfuscate the genuine importance of the message from the general observer while remaining comprehensible to a limited group of individuals (Sharafi et al., 2019, Dhanda et al., 2020).

As civilizations progressed, the techniques of cryptography also evolved. The ancient Greeks made significant contributions to the history of cryptography through the utilization of the scytale by the Spartan military. The scytale was a device used to encode communications by wrapping a strip of parchment around a baton of a specific diameter, ensuring that the message could only be deciphered by using a baton of the same diameter. This straightforward yet efficient technique emphasizes the strategic application of cryptography in military operations and international relations (Ott and Peikert, 2019, Abroshan, 2021).

During the Roman era, Julius Caesar employed a replacement cipher, currently referred to as the Caesar Cypher, to convey messages to his generals. This technique entailed displacing the letters of the alphabet by a predetermined number of positions. It was groundbreaking in its era due to its straightforwardness and efficiency in ensuring secure communication (Sadhu et al., 2022).

During the Renaissance, more advanced cryptography techniques were developed in response to the increasing complexity of political and economic affairs. During this period, polyalphabetic ciphers were created, which employ numerous cipher alphabets to encode a message. One of the most prominent examples is the Vigenère Cypher, which offered a method for encrypting alphabetical text by a straightforward version of polyalphabetic substitution.

The arrival of the 20th century and the ensuing digital era revolutionized cryptography by incorporating mathematical theory and computer science, creating contemporary cryptographic methods. This era signifies the shift from mechanical and analog systems to the digital applications that are prevalent today, including symmetric and asymmetric encryption methods. The advent of computers and the Internet created a demand for increasingly sophisticated cryptographic solutions due to the widespread use of digital communication.

The Enigma machine, employed by Germany during World War II and its subsequent decipherment by Allied cryptographers, emphasized the pivotal significance of cryptography in national security and warfare. After the war, the focus was changed to developing cryptographic techniques that might effectively protect governmental and non-governmental communications in the growing digital world.

Encryption plays a crucial role in safeguarding electronic transaction identification information and guaranteeing the confidentiality of online interactions. In the era of digital advancements, the field of cryptography is constantly evolving to meet the demands of enhancing security measures and combating new cyber threats. Cryptography is crucial in safeguarding information, which is of utmost importance.

As it progresses, it consistently safeguards, verifies, and fortifies the digital realm, serving as the foundation of contemporary information security systems.

FUNDAMENTAL CONCEPTS OF CRYPTOGRAPHY

Cryptography is an essential discipline within the field of information security, serving as the bedrock for secure communications in the digital age. Its fundamental concepts—encryption, decryption, cipher, key, and algorithm—are critical to understanding how cryptographic systems protect data. Additionally, the types of cryptography, such as symmetric and asymmetric cryptography, and the role of cryptographic hash functions play pivotal roles in various security applications (Martin, 2020; Goldreich, 2019).

INTRODUCTION TO CRYPTOGRAPHIC TECHNIQUES

Cryptography is an essential discipline within the field of information security, serving as the bedrock for secure communications in the digital age. Its fundamental concepts—encryption, decryption, cipher, key, and algorithm—are critical to understanding how cryptographic systems protect data.

Encryption and Decryption

Encryption converts plaintext, readable data into ciphertext, which is scrambled and appears random. This transformation is done using a cipher and a key, making the information unintelligible to anyone who does not have the key.

Decryption: The inverse process where ciphertext is converted back into plaintext, allowing authorized users to retrieve the original information. These processes ensure that data can be securely transmitted or stored, inaccessible to unauthorized users.

Cipher and Key

Cipher: A method or algorithm for performing encryption and decryption. The cipher uses a specific set of well-defined steps during encryption and decryption.

Key: A piece of information that determines the functional output of a cryptographic algorithm. In essence, the key configures the cipher to process the text, making the key an integral part of securing the data.

Cryptographic Algorithms

An algorithm is a procedure or formula for solving a problem based on conducting a sequence of specified actions. Cryptography algorithms are designed to create ciphers that can effectively encrypt and decrypt data, using keys to vary the data output and ensure security. The strength of cryptographic security largely depends on the algorithm's robustness and the key's secrecy.

Types of Cryptography: Symmetric vs. Asymmetric

Symmetric Cryptography: Uses the same key for both encryption and decryption. This type requires that both the sender and the recipient have secure access to the secret key, which can be challenging to manage, especially over large networks or insecure channels. Symmetric key algorithms, such as the Advanced Encryption Standard (AES), are widely used to efficiently process large amounts of data quickly. (Al-Shabi, 2019)

Asymmetric Cryptography: Uses two keys, one for encryption (public key) and one for decryption (private key). These keys are mathematically linked: whatever is encrypted with the public key can only be decrypted by its corresponding private key, and vice versa. This method helps solve the key distribution problem by allowing the public key to be openly distributed and keeping the private key secret. Common asymmetric key algorithms include RSA and Elliptic Curve Cryptography (ECC)(Al-Shabi, 2019, Hammad et al., 2020).

Cryptographic Hash Functions

Cryptographic hash functions accept an input (or 'message') and return a fixed-size string of bytes, typically a digest unique to each unique input. Hashes are commonly used to verify data integrity, as even a small change in the input will produce a significantly different output. This property is vital for secure data transmission and storage, ensuring that any alteration of data can be detected. Hash functions such as SHA-256 are central in various security protocols, including digital signatures and data integrity checks(Tchórzewski & Jakóbik, 2019).

Understanding these fundamental cryptography concepts is essential for implementing secure systems that protect information and communications in our increasingly digital world. Each component, from encryption to hash functions, plays a specific role in safeguarding data from unauthorized access and tampering, thus maintaining confidentiality, integrity, and availability.(Lindmeier and Mühling, 2020)

Cryptographic hash functions are a cornerstone of digital security, used to verify the integrity of data across many applications, from securing passwords to ensuring that a file has not been altered during transmission.

A hash function takes an input, or 'message,' and produces a fixed-size string of bytes, typically called a hash or a digest. This process involves running the input data through a complex algorithm that outputs a unique hash value distinctly representative of the input data(Kuznetsov et al., 2021). One of the critical properties of a cryptographic hash function is that it is deterministic—meaning that the same input will always produce the same output. Furthermore, a strong hash function ensures that it is computationally infeasible to:

- Generate the original input by knowing the hash value (pre-image resistance).
- Find two different inputs that produce the same output (collision resistance).
- Make changes to the input without changing the output (avalanche effect).

Common Uses of Hash Functions

Cryptographic hash functions are fundamental tools in cybersecurity, utilized across various applications to ensure data integrity and authenticity. These functions, by design, convert input data of any size into a fixed-size string of bytes, commonly referred to as a hash. This section explores the common uses of hash functions, shedding light on how they secure digital communications, validate data integrity, and provide the backbone for numerous security protocols. Whether employed in securing passwords, facilitating digital signatures, or anchoring the structure of blockchain technology, hash functions play a pivotal role in safeguarding our digital interactions(Odeh et al., 2020, Shen et al., 2019).

Data Integrity Checks: Hash functions create a unique data fingerprint. If two files have the same hash value, one can be confident they are identical. This is essential for verifying software downloads or ensuring data has not been tampered with during transmission(Anwar et al., 2021).

Password Storage: Instead of storing passwords directly, systems store the hash of a password. When a user logs in, the system hashes the entered password and compares it to the stored hash. This method keeps actual passwords hidden, even from administrators of the systems.

Digital Signatures: Hash functions are also used in digital signatures, which provide a way to verify the authenticity of digital messages or documents. The signature process involves hashing the message and encrypting the hash with a private key. The recipient can verify the signature by decrypting it with the corresponding public key and then comparing the resultant hash.

Key Properties of Cryptographic Hash Functions

Deterministic: A hash function is deterministic, meaning it will always produce the same hash for the same input, regardless of how often it is executed. This consistency is vital for verifying data integrity over time.

Fast Computation: The function should generate the hash value quickly. This is crucial for systems that process large volumes of data where performance and speed are essential.

Pre-image Resistance: It should be computationally infeasible to generate the original input by knowing its hash value. This property is crucial for security, ensuring that even if the hash is exposed, the actual data remains protected.

Small Changes Produce Big Differences: Known as the avalanche effect; this property ensures that even the slightest change in input dramatically changes the hash. This sensitivity is critical for security systems to detect alterations in data.

Collision Resistance: It should be hard to find two different inputs that produce the same hash output. Ensuring this property prevents attackers from substituting a legitimate piece of data with another with the same hash(Kuznetsov et al., 2021).

Applications of Cryptographic Hash Functions

Verifying Data Integrity: Hash functions verify the integrity of data sent over insecure networks. Users can determine whether the data has been altered in transit by comparing hashes calculated before and after transmission.

Secure Password Storage: Storing passwords as hashes rather than plain text can protect user data even if security breaches occur. Websites often hash user passwords and compare stored hash values to those generated during user logins to authenticate identity.

Digital Signatures: In digital signatures, hash functions are used to ensure the authenticity and integrity of a message. The message hash is encrypted with a private key to create a signature that can be verified by decrypting it with the corresponding public key and comparing it to the message's hash computed upon receipt.

Blockchain Technology: Hash functions secure blockchain transactions and maintain the integrity of the data within each block. By hashing transaction details along with the previous block's hash, blockchains create a secure, unalterable chain.

Anti-Tamper Mechanisms: Software and hardware can employ hash functions to detect unauthorized modifications. By regularly checking the hashes of its components against known good hashes, a system can detect and react to tampering attempts.

These versatile applications highlight the importance of cryptographic hash functions in maintaining security and integrity across various digital platforms and technologies. As digital interactions and dependencies increase, the role of cryptographic hash functions will continue to grow, evolving to meet emerging security challenges in an increasingly connected world(Mittelbach & Fischlin, 2021).

ADVANCES IN CRYPTOGRAPHIC KEY MANAGEMENT

Key management is a critical aspect of cryptography that involves handling and safeguarding cryptographic keys throughout their lifecycle. Effective key management ensures the security and integrity of the cryptographic keys used for encryption, decryption, and authentication. This section explores the recent advances in cryptographic key management, highlighting the importance of modern techniques and systems designed to enhance digital data security.

Key Lifecycle Management

The lifecycle of a cryptographic key includes its generation, distribution, storage, usage, rotation, and eventual destruction.

Figure 1. Key Lifecycle Management

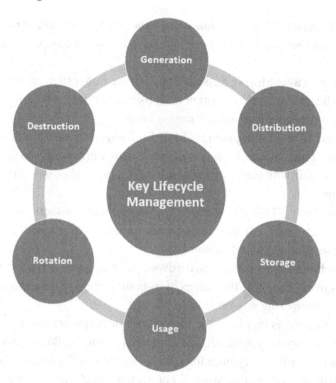

Each stage in the lifecycle presents unique challenges and requires secure practices to prevent unauthorized access and misuse:

Generation: Keys must be generated securely using random or pseudorandom number generators that meet established security standards to ensure the unpredictability of the keys.

Distribution: Securely distributing keys to intended users while preventing interception is crucial. Techniques such as public key infrastructure (PKI) and key exchange algorithms (e.g., Diffie-Hellman) facilitate safe key distribution.

Storage: Keys must be stored securely using hardware security modules (HSMs) or encrypted databases to protect them from theft or unauthorized access.

Usage: Managing how and when keys are used is critical to prevent unauthorized use. Access controls and audit logs are often implemented to monitor key usage.

Rotation: Regularly updating or rotating keys helps mitigate the risk of key compromise over time. Automated systems are increasingly used to manage the rotation process.

Destruction: Properly destroying keys when they are no longer needed or have been compromised is essential to prevent unauthorized use. This involves ensuring that keys are irretrievably deleted or wiped from all storage locations.

Automated Key Management Systems

Advances in technology have led to the development of automated key management systems (KMS), which streamline the management of cryptographic keys. These systems automate many aspects of the key lifecycle, reducing the potential for human error and enhancing the efficiency and security of cryptographic operations. KMS solutions often integrate with existing hardware and software infrastructure, providing a centralized platform for managing keys across various applications and systems(Ramteke & Dongre, 2022).

Integration With Cloud Services

As businesses increasingly move data and applications to the cloud, managing cryptographic keys in cloud environments has become critical. Cloud service providers now offer built-in key management services that allow users to manage and control their encryption keys while leveraging the scalability and accessibility of cloud computing. These services provide robust security features, such as key isolation, logging, and regular audits, to protect keys against external attacks and insider threats(Keshta and Odeh, 2021, Borangiu et al., 2019).

Challenges and Considerations

Despite advancements, cryptographic key management still faces several challenges:

Scalability: As organizations grow and deploy more encrypted services, scaling key management practices to keep up with increased demand without compromising security is challenging.

Compliance: Adhering to regulatory requirements related to data protection and privacy (e.g., GDPR, HIPAA) requires meticulous key management practices, often necessitating regular reviews and updates to key management policies.

Complexity: The increasing complexity of IT environments, with multiple clouds and a mix of on-premises and remote resources, complicates key management strategies.

Advances in cryptographic key management are vital for maintaining the security of digital communications and storage in an increasingly interconnected world. Organizations can enhance their security posture by adopting modern key management practices and technologies, ensuring that their data remains protected against evolving threats. As the digital landscape continues to expand, the importance of robust cryptographic key management will only grow, highlighting the need for ongoing research and development in this essential area of cybersecurity(Avesani et al., 2019; Abu Al-Haija et al., 2023).

SYMMETRIC KEY ALGORITHMS

` Symmetric key algorithms use the same key for encrypting and decrypting information, making them a cornerstone of practical cryptography. This section outlines three widely used symmetric algorithms: DES, AES, and Blowfish(Odeh, 2020; Jatoth et al., 2019).

DES (Data et al.): Developed in the 1970s, DES was one of the first encryption standards widely adopted. It encrypts data in 64-bit blocks using a 56-bit key through transformations and substitutions. While DES was innovative in its time, its relatively short key length has made it susceptible to brute-force attacks, leading to its decline in favor of more secure alternatives.

AES (Advanced et al.): AES was introduced to overcome the limitations of DES. It encrypts data in 128-bit blocks and is available in key sizes of 128, 192, or 256 bits, providing strong protection against attacks. AES encryption involves multiple rounds of processing that include substitutions, permutations, and mixing the input plaintext with the keys, making it the standard choice for numerous security protocols.

Blowfish: Designed as a fast and flexible replacement for DES, Blowfish has a block size of 64 bits and supports a wide range of key lengths from 32 to 448 bits. The algorithm is known for its efficiency and effectiveness, especially in systems where changing the encryption key frequently is not a problem.

Use Cases and Applications in Modern Technology

Symmetric algorithms are crucial across various applications due to their operational efficiency:

Data Encryption: AES is the standard encryption technique for securing sensitive data, and it is used widely across government and private sectors to protect classified and sensitive information.

Financial Transactions: Blowfish is particularly valued in financial sectors for encrypting transactions, thanks to its strong encryption capabilities and efficiency in systems where keys can be regularly rotated.

VPN and Internet Security: Symmetric algorithms like AES are foundational for securing VPN tunnels, providing fast and secure means to encrypt data transmitted over the Internet, ensuring information confidentiality and integrity.

Mobile Device Encryption

In the realm of mobile computing, symmetric algorithms such as AES are extensively used to secure data on mobile devices. This encryption helps protect personal and corporate information stored on smartphones and tablets against unauthorized access, loss, or theft. The adoption of these encryption methods by mobile operating systems like iOS and Android underscores their importance in the consumer technology space, where they ensure the confidentiality of user data while maintaining optimal device performance.

Cloud Storage Security

Cloud services rely on symmetric encryption to protect data at rest and in transit. Providers like AWS, Google Cloud, and Microsoft Azure utilize AES encryption to secure files stored on their servers. This practice allows users to safely store sensitive information in the cloud, assuring that their data is shielded from external breaches and internal vulnerabilities. Encrypting data before it leaves the user's device and decrypting it only when authorized users access it adds a layer of security in multi-tenant cloud environments.

Digital Media Streaming

Symmetric encryption plays a pivotal role in the secure streaming of digital media. Services like Netflix and Spotify use AES to encrypt streaming content, protect copyright, and prevent unauthorized access. This encryption ensures that media is only viewable by subscribers and is not intercepted during transmission, providing a secure and compliant method for distributing copyrighted content.

Database Security

Databases storing sensitive information, such as personal data, financial details, or health records, employ symmetric encryption to ensure data privacy and protection against data breaches. Encryption at the database level safeguards against potential insider threats and external attacks, making it a fundamental security measure for organizations handling high-stakes information.

Gaming Security

In the gaming industry, symmetric encryption is used to secure in-game transactions and protect user data. Online games that support purchases and store sensitive user information leverage algorithms like AES to encrypt this data, ensuring that player details and payment information are kept secure from potential threats.

Backup and Disaster Recovery

For backup and disaster recovery processes, symmetric encryption ensures that all backed-up data remains secure and is only accessible to authorized users. Whether the data is stored on physical devices or offsite in cloud environments, encryption is a critical defense against data theft or exposure during recovery following a cybersecurity incident or physical disaster.

Strengths and Weaknesses in Practical Scenarios

While symmetric algorithms are integral to secure communication, they present both advantages and challenges:

Strengths

Efficiency: These algorithms quickly perform encryption and decryption processes, making them suitable for environments with limited computational resources.

Ease of Implementation: Algorithms like Blowfish are simple to implement, reducing the risk of encryption errors.

Weaknesses

Key Distribution: The major drawback is the key distribution requirement. The sender and receiver need access to the same secret key, which must be shared and stored securely.

Scalability Issues: In large networks, managing symmetric keys becomes cumbersome as the number of participants increases, making it less scalable without sophisticated key management strategies.

Security Concerns: Older algorithms like DES are vulnerable to modern attack techniques, though newer algorithms like AES provide robust security against various attacks.

In conclusion, symmetric key algorithms are vital for their speed and efficiency in secure data transmission, yet they require careful key management and modernization to address evolving security threats.

ASYMMETRIC KEY ALGORITHMS

Public Key Infrastructure (PKI) is a framework to secure communications and transactions over unsecured networks, such as the Internet. PKI utilizes asymmetric cryptography to provide both public and private keys. The public key is available to everyone and can encrypt messages or verify signatures. In contrast, the private key remains confidential and is used to decrypt messages or sign information. This system underpins various security protocols by enabling secure, encrypted communications between parties without prior sharing of secret keys(Kokoris Kogias et al., 2020, Raghunandan et al., 2020).

RSA (Rivest-Shamir-Adleman): RSA is one of the first practical public-key cryptosystems widely used for secure data transmission. It works because it is easy to multiply large numbers but difficult to factorize their product. The security of RSA derives from the challenge of factoring the product of two large prime numbers.

ECC (Elliptic et al.): ECC offers the same level of security as RSA but uses smaller key sizes, resulting in faster processing and lower resource consumption. It uses the mathematics of elliptic curves over finite fields. It provides a more efficient approach to key generation and encryption, making it suitable for mobile environments and devices with limited computational power.

Diffie-Hellman Key Exchange: This algorithm allows two parties to jointly establish a shared secret key over an insecure channel without having previously exchanged secret information. It is fundamental to creating a secure channel for private communication over public networks.

REAL-WORLD APPLICATIONS AND THEIR SECURITY IMPLICATIONS

Asymmetric algorithms are integral to numerous applications across various sectors, enhancing both the security and integrity of communications:

Digital Signatures and Certificates: PKI and digital signatures secure emails, documents, and software by verifying the source's authenticity and the content's integrity. Digital certificates issued by Certificate Authorities (CA) help establish the legitimacy of websites by authenticating their identities(Dulac-Arnold et al., 2019; Xie et al., 2019).

Secure Online Transactions: E-commerce sites, financial institutions, and payment gateways use SSL/TLS protocols, often employing RSA or ECC, to secure transactions. This ensures that sensitive information like credit card numbers is encrypted and confidential.

Encrypted Communications: Applications such as messaging apps and email services use asymmetric cryptography to ensure that only the intended recipient can read the messages sent.

Security Implications

While asymmetric cryptography significantly enhances security, it is not without challenges:

Key Management: Managing the public and private keys in asymmetric cryptography, especially ensuring the security of private keys, is critical.

Computational Cost: Asymmetric encryption processes are more computationally intensive than symmetric methods, which can be a limiting factor in resource-constrained environments.

Vulnerability to Quantum Attacks: Algorithms like RSA and ECC could be vulnerable to future attacks by quantum computers, potentially breaking these cryptosystems through advanced factorization capabilities.

Asymmetric key algorithms provide a robust framework for securing digital communications and transactions, playing a crucial role in the architecture of modern cybersecurity solutions. Their ability to facilitate secure key exchange and authentication over insecure channels makes them indispensable in today's digital age, albeit with considerations for their computational demand and evolving security threats.

CRYPTOGRAPHIC PROTOCOLS

Cryptographic protocols such as SSL/TLS, SSH, and IPSec are essential for securing network communications. SSL (Secure et al.) and TLS (Transport et al.) are protocols used primarily to secure internet connections, safeguarding data exchanged between two endpoints by preventing eavesdropping, tampering, and message forgery. SSH (Secure Shell) is used for secure remote login and other secure network services over an unsecured network. IPSec (Internet et al.) secures Internet Protocol communications by authenticating and encrypting each IP packet in a data stream(Zeadally et al., 2021, Abu Taleb et al., 2023).

HOW THESE PROTOCOLS EMPLOY CRYPTOGRAPHIC ALGORITHMS TO SECURE DATA

- **SSL/TLS**: These protocols use asymmetric cryptography for key exchange (e.g., RSA, ECC, Diffie-Hellman) during the handshake phase, establishing a secure connection without prior key exchange. Once a safe connection is established, symmetric encryption (e.g., AES) provides data confidentiality.
- **SSH**: SSH employs a combination of asymmetric and symmetric encryption, hashing, and digital signatures. It starts with a public key mechanism for authentication followed by symmetric key encryption for the session, ensuring the connection setup's security and the speed of encrypted data transfer.

- **IPSec**: This protocol suite offers a choice of cryptographic algorithms for various functions; it can use AES or Blowfish for encryption, RSA for key management, and MD5 or SHA for integrity checks. IPSec operates at the IP layer, securing almost any application traffic across an IP network.

CRYPTOGRAPHIC HASH FUNCTIONS

Explore SHA, MD5, and Their Applications in Integrity Verification

Cryptographic hash functions are algorithms that take an input (or 'message') and return a fixed-size string of bytes. The output hash is a "digest" that uniquely represents the input data.

- **SHA (Secure et al.):** SHA is used extensively in various security applications and protocols, including TLS and SSL, PGP, SSH, and IPSec. SHA-256, a variant of SHA, is widely used for its robust security features. The SHA family ensures data integrity by producing a unique hash value from which the original data cannot be easily reconstructed.
- **MD5 (Message et al. 5):** Although now considered vulnerable and unsuitable for further use in security applications due to its susceptibility to hash collisions, MD5 was once widely used for integrity checks. It produces a 128-bit hash value used in various applications to ensure data is not altered.

IMPACT OF HASH FUNCTIONS ON DATA SECURITY AND INTEGRITY

Hash functions impact data security by verifying data integrity without exposing the original data(-Fomichev et al., 2022). This capability is critical in the detection of data tampering or corruption:

- **Integrity Verification**: By comparing the computed hash of received data with an expected hash value, recipients can determine whether the data has been altered during transmission.
- **Password Storage:** Hashing passwords before storing them in a database protects user credentials even if an unauthorized party accesses the storage system. Since hashes are irreversible, the original passwords remain concealed.
- **Digital Signatures:** Hash functions are also used to create digital signatures, which provide a means to verify the authenticity of digital documents analogous to a handwritten signature but appropriate for non-repudiation in the digital realm.

Cryptographic hash functions are crucial for maintaining data security and integrity across various applications, ensuring that data remains unchanged from its source and verifying the authenticity of digital messages. Despite the vulnerabilities of some hash functions, ongoing development in cryptographic practices continues to enhance their effectiveness in securing digital data.

RECENT ADVANCES IN CRYPTOGRAPHY

Quantum cryptography represents a significant leap forward in the field, utilizing the principles of quantum mechanics to enhance security in the transmission of information. Unlike classical encryption methods, which rely on complex mathematical problems to secure data, quantum cryptography is based on the physical properties of particles at quantum scales, such as photons(Portmann & Renner, 2022).

One of the most promising applications of quantum cryptography is Quantum Key Distribution (QKD). QKD uses quantum mechanics to securely distribute keys between two parties without any risk of interception. Any attempt to eavesdrop on the quantum key will inevitably disturb the quantum states of the particles involved, alerting the parties to the presence of an interloper. This method theoretically provides a level of security that is impossible to breach with current technology(Bennett et al., 1992; Odeh et al., 2013).

Quantum cryptography's potential extends beyond just ultra-secure communication. It could fundamentally change the data security landscape, especially as quantum computing becomes more practical and widespread. This advance prompts both excitement and concern, as quantum computers could potentially break many of the cryptographic protocols currently in use today, such as RSA and ECC, which are based on the difficulty of factoring large numbers or computing discrete logarithms(Alshowkan et al., 2013).

The Emergence of Homomorphic Encryption

Homomorphic encryption is a form of encryption that allows computations to be performed on cipher-texts, generating an encrypted result that, when decrypted, matches the result of operations performed on the plaintext. This revolutionary technique enables secure data processing without exposing the underlying data, offering significant benefits for privacy-preserving computations in cloud computing environments.

The primary advantage of homomorphic encryption lies in its ability to allow data to be used for computation without compromising its confidentiality. This has applications in various fields, including financial services, healthcare, and machine learning, where third-party services can process and analyze sensitive data without exposing the actual data. For example, a financial institution could encrypt client data and send it to a cloud service for analysis, receiving encrypted results that can only be decrypted and understood by the institution(Yousuf et al., 2020).

Cryptographic Solutions for Blockchain and Cryptocurrencies

Blockchain technology and cryptocurrencies such as Bitcoin rely heavily on cryptographic algorithms to secure transactions and maintain user anonymity. At the heart of blockchain technology lies the concept of a decentralized ledger that is both transparent and immutable, which is maintained by cryptographic hashes.

Each block in a blockchain contains a cryptographic hash of the previous block, a timestamp, and transaction data. This structure creates a chain of blocks, with each consecutive block reinforcing the ones before it. Such a setup ensures that once data is recorded in a blockchain, it cannot be altered retroactively without altering all subsequent blocks and the collaboration of the network majority.

Cryptocurrencies use cryptographic algorithms not only to create proof of work systems but also to secure wallets. Digital wallets store encrypted keys needed for transaction signing and blockchain interactions, emphasizing cryptography's role in ensuring the security and integrity of digital currencies.

The ongoing development of cryptographic solutions for blockchain is also exploring more advanced concepts, including zero-knowledge proofs, which allow a party to prove the truth of a statement without revealing any additional information. This development is crucial for enhancing privacy and security in blockchain applications.

These recent advancements in cryptography demonstrate the field's dynamic nature and critical role in shaping the future of digital security and privacy. As technology evolves, so will cryptographic techniques, which must constantly adapt to new security challenges and computational capabilities.

CRYPTOGRAPHIC AUTHENTICATION MECHANISMS

Authentication is a critical aspect of security in computing and network systems, where it verifies the identity of a user, machine, software component, or any other entity. In cryptography, authentication mechanisms ensure that information is accessible only to those correctly identified and authorized to have access. This section delves into various cryptographic techniques to achieve robust authentication, including digital signatures, certificates, and biometric encryption, exploring their applications, benefits, and potential vulnerabilities(Somsuk & Thakong, 2020).

Digital Signatures and Certificates

Digital Signatures: A digital signature is one of the most powerful tools in cryptographic authentication, verifying the authenticity of digital messages or documents. It involves using a private key to create a signature on a document, which anyone with the corresponding public key can then verify. This process confirms the sender's identity and ensures the document's integrity since any alteration after signing invalidates the signature.

Certificates: Digital certificates are another vital component of cryptographic authentication. A certificate is a digital document that uses a digital signature to bind a public key with an identity (e.g., a name or an organization). Certificates are issued by a trusted entity known as a Certificate Authority (CA). They play a crucial role in secure communications in networks, especially in systems like HTTPS, where they authenticate the identities of websites to users.

Biometric Encryption

Biometric Encryption: This method uses an individual's unique biological characteristics to encrypt and decrypt data. Common biometric features include fingerprints, facial recognition, iris scans, and voice recognition. The primary advantage of biometric encryption is that it binds information access directly to the user's physical traits, which are significantly harder to forge or steal than traditional passwords.

Multi-Factor Authentication (MFA)

MFA: Multi-factor authentication combines two or more independent credentials to create a layered defense and make it more difficult for an unauthorized person to access a target such as a physical location, computing device, network, or database. MFA can include something the user knows (password), something the user has (security token), and something the user is (biometric verification). By integrating these layers, MFA provides a higher level of security, making unauthorized access more challenging(Sharafi et al., 2019).

Challenges in Cryptographic Authentication

Security Vulnerabilities: Despite the robustness of cryptographic authentication methods, they are not without vulnerabilities. Digital signatures, for instance, depend on the security of the private key. If a private key is compromised, so is the security of the digital signatures created with it. Similarly, biometric systems must carefully protect the data they collect to prevent identity theft(Kokoris Kogias et al., 2020; Zeadally et al., 2021).

Management and Scalability: Managing cryptographic keys and certificates can be complex, especially in large organizations. The overhead associated with distributing, revoking, and renewing certificates and ensuring the secure storage of private keys can be substantial.

User Acceptance and Privacy Concerns: Biometric encryption raises significant privacy issues, requiring collecting and storing sensitive personal data. Users may be reluctant to adopt biometric authentication systems because they fear how their data will be used and protected.

Future Directions in Cryptographic Authentication

Advanced Cryptographic Techniques: As computational power increases and attackers become more sophisticated, advanced cryptographic techniques will be necessary to stay ahead. Post-quantum cryptography, which involves developing systems that are secure against both quantum and classical computers, and zero-knowledge proofs, which allow one party to prove to another that they know a value without revealing any information apart from the fact that they know that value, are examples of where cryptographic authentication may head in the future(Sharafi et al., 2019).

Integration with Emerging Technologies: Integrating cryptographic authentication methods with emerging technologies such as blockchain and Internet of Things (IoT) devices presents new opportunities for enhancing security. For instance, blockchain can provide a decentralized and tamper-proof infrastructure for managing digital identities and biometric data, potentially alleviating privacy concerns.

Regulatory and Ethical Considerations: As cryptographic authentication methods become more intertwined with daily life, regulatory and ethical considerations will increasingly emerge. Ensuring these technologies are used responsibly and not infringe on individual rights will be crucial. This exploration of cryptographic authentication mechanisms illustrates their critical role in securing digital identities and transactions, highlighting both the potential and challenges of these technologies in the face of evolving threats and opportunities. As the digital landscape expands, developing and refining cryptographic authentication methods will remain a dynamic and essential field of study(Kokoris Kogias et al., 2020).

CHALLENGES IN CRYPTOGRAPHY

Cryptography, the art and science of securing communications, faces many challenges that evolve as rapidly as the technology and the threats themselves. From the complex issues of key management and the looming threat of quantum computing, which could potentially unravel current cryptographic protections, to the dense thicket of legal and ethical considerations surrounding its use, the field of cryptography must constantly adapt. These technical challenges involve significant legal and societal dimensions, influencing how cryptography is implemented and regulated globally. As we delve deeper into the specifics of these challenges, it becomes clear that the future of cryptography will depend on balancing robust security measures with responsible practices that respect legal standards and ethical norms(Shen et al., 2019; Tchórzewski & Jakóbik, 2019; Yousuf et al., 2020).

Key Management and Quantum Computing Threats

- **Key Management:** One of the most significant challenges in cryptography is key management, which involves the generation, storage, distribution, use, and destruction of cryptographic keys. Effective key management is critical because the security of encrypted data directly depends on the protection of the keys used to encrypt and decrypt it. Managing these keys without introducing vulnerabilities can be highly complex in large organizations or systems with numerous encryption keys. Poor key management practices can lead to compromised keys, unauthorized access, and data breaches. Systems must ensure that keys are as secure as the data they protect, using secure storage solutions such as hardware security modules (HSMs), strict access controls, and regular key rotation policies.

- **Quantum Computing Threats:** The rise of quantum computing presents a dual-edged sword in the field of cryptography. While quantum computers offer the potential for significant advancements in processing power, they also seriously threaten the security of current cryptographic algorithms. Quantum computers can potentially break many current cryptographic systems by exploiting their ability to solve problems like integer factorization and discrete logarithms—computationally infeasible problems for classical computers. This capability could undermine the security of public-key infrastructures and other security protocols relying on these problems for protection, such as RSA and ECC. Cryptographers are actively researching quantum-resistant algorithms, which can withstand attacks from quantum computers, under initiatives like the Post-Quantum Cryptography (PQC) project by the National Institute of Standards and Technology (NIST).

Legal and Ethical Considerations in the Use of Cryptography

- **Legal Issues:** The use of cryptography intersects with various legal issues, particularly in privacy, surveillance, and national security. Governments worldwide have diverse laws regarding the use and export of cryptographic technology. Some countries impose restrictions on the strength of encryption products that can be imported or exported, while others require backdoors to be built into systems for law enforcement access. These legal requirements can conflict with the privacy rights of individuals and the security needs of corporations, creating a complex legal landscape for using encryption.

- **Ethical Considerations:** The moral implications of cryptography are also significant. While encryption can protect privacy and secure communications, it can also be used for malicious purposes, such as hiding illegal activities or protecting data involved in criminal acts. The ethical use of cryptography balances the benefits of securing legitimate information while preventing its use for harmful purposes. Furthermore, deploying encryption methods that include backdoors for government access raises ethical questions about the right to privacy and the potential for abuse of such access.

The challenges facing cryptography are technical and encompass broader legal and ethical considerations. Effective cryptographic solutions must, therefore, navigate these complexities, ensuring robust protection against evolving threats while adhering to the legal frameworks and moral norms of the societies in which they operate. As cryptography continues to grow, so will its challenges. It requires ongoing innovation and thoughtful debate among technologists, policymakers, and legal experts to ensure its responsible use in protecting information and privacy in the digital age(Goldreich, 2019; Kokoris Kogias et al., 2020; Lindmeier & Mühling, 2020; Odeh, 2020; Portmann & Renner, 2022).

FUTURE TRENDS AND PREDICTIONS

As we navigate through the digital age, the role of cryptography in securing our virtual landscapes continues to expand. The rapid evolution of technology enhances our ability to protect sensitive data and presents new challenges and opportunities for cryptographic methods. In this section, we explore how the impending advancements in technology, particularly the integration of artificial intelligence (AI), are poised to reshape the future of cryptography. This analysis will delve into the anticipated developments in cryptographic practices, the potential impact of these technologies, and the innovative applications they might enable.

Advancements in Technology Shaping the Future of Cryptography

The future of cryptography is closely tied to advancements in various technological fields. One of the most significant influences is the development of quantum computing. Unlike classical computing, quantum computers leverage the principles of quantum mechanics to perform calculations at speeds unattainable today, offering the potential to solve complex cryptographic algorithms that are currently considered secure. This development is prompting a surge in research into quantum-resistant cryptography, focusing on creating algorithms that can withstand the power of quantum computing. Such cryptographic methods are not only necessary to protect against future threats but also essential for maintaining the confidentiality, integrity, and availability of information in a post-quantum world.

Moreover, as more devices connect to the Internet and each other, the field of cryptography must adapt to the unique challenges of securing vast amounts of data transmitted across these networks. The growth of the Internet of Things (IoT) and 5G technology will require new cryptographic solutions that can operate efficiently at scale and with limited power consumption. Lightweight cryptography addresses these needs by providing secure cryptographic protocols suitable for less powerful devices, ensuring broad adoption and robust security in a hyper-connected environment.

The Role of AI in Cryptographic Solutions

AI is set to play a transformative role in the field of cryptography. AI-driven cryptographic solutions can enhance the security of data systems through automated and adaptive security protocols that evolve in response to emerging threats. For instance, AI algorithms can analyze patterns in encryption traffic to identify and react to potential cyber-attacks in real time. This proactive approach to security, which leverages the learning capabilities of AI, could drastically reduce human errors in data protection and improve the efficiency of cryptographic operations.(Abroshan, 2021, Abu Taleb et al., 2023, Anwar et al., 2021, Dulac-Arnold et al., 2019)

Additionally, AI can assist in optimizing cryptographic processes by determining the most effective algorithms and key management strategies based on the specific requirements and behaviors of the system. This application of AI increases the security level and optimizes the performance of cryptographic systems, making encryption more accessible and cost-effective for a broader range of applications.

AI is also being explored for its potential to create new forms of cryptographic keys and algorithms. Through techniques like genetic algorithms and neural networks, AI can help design cryptographic keys that are harder to predict and breach, thereby enhancing the overall security of encrypted data. Furthermore, AI could potentially automate the encryption process, selecting and implementing the most appropriate encryption methods based on the data type and sensitivity, simplifying the user experience, and enhancing security measures.

Predictions for Cryptography's Future

Looking ahead, we can expect several key developments in the field of cryptography:

Integration of Cryptography with Blockchain Technology: As blockchain platforms gain prominence, integrating advanced cryptographic techniques will be crucial for ensuring the security and efficiency of these decentralized systems.

Increased Regulatory and Ethical Standards: With the global nature of digital data and its inherent risks, there will likely be an increase in regulatory oversight concerning cryptographic practices, focusing on privacy, data protection, and cyber-resilience.

Widespread Adoption of Zero-Knowledge Proofs: These cryptographic protocols enable the sharing information between parties without revealing the actual data, a crucial feature for privacy-preserving technologies.

The future of cryptography is a fascinating convergence of tradition and innovation, where established practices meet groundbreaking technological advances. As we continue to witness these developments, it is clear that cryptography will remain at the forefront of digital security, adapting to protect against both current and future threats. The integration of AI and advancements in quantum-resistant cryptography is just the beginning of what promises to be a dynamic evolution in the quest to secure the digital world.

Reflection on the Societal and Technological Impacts of Strong Cryptography

Strong cryptography profoundly impacts societal and technological landscapes, serving as the linchpin for secure communications in our increasingly digital world. As we delve deeper into the age of information, the role of cryptography in protecting privacy, securing transactions, and safeguarding national security cannot be overstated.

Implementing robust cryptographic systems empowers individuals with the confidence to engage in digital interactions without fear of unauthorized access or identity theft. For instance, e-commerce, online banking, and confidential communications rely heavily on encryption to protect sensitive data from cybercriminals. This security is crucial for maintaining individual privacy and preserving the integrity of financial systems and personal communications. Moreover, in regimes where freedom of speech is not guaranteed, strong cryptography enables citizens to communicate freely and organize without fear of government surveillance, embodying a tool for civil liberty and personal safety.

Technologically, strong cryptography stimulates innovation by providing a secure foundation for developing new applications and services. As businesses and governments increasingly depend on digital solutions, the need for advanced cryptographic measures becomes more critical. This necessity drives technological advancement, pushing researchers and developers to innovate continuously in digital security. Furthermore, as Internet of Things (IoT) devices proliferate, strong cryptography is essential for ensuring that they operate securely, protecting the data they generate and their networks.

However, the widespread use of strong cryptography also presents challenges, particularly in law enforcement and national security. The same tools that protect privacy and secure communications can also shield illegal activities, including terrorism and cybercrime, from detection. This dual-use nature of cryptography necessitates ongoing dialogue and cooperation between technology providers, users, and regulatory bodies to strike a balance between security and accessibility.

CONCLUSIONS AND REMARKS

This chapter explored the essential discipline of cryptography, highlighting its pivotal role in safeguarding information in the digital age. We discussed the foundational concepts of cryptography, including encryption, decryption, ciphers, keys, and algorithms. Each component is crucial in creating secure communication channels and protecting data from unauthorized access and tampering.

We delved into symmetric and asymmetric cryptography, illustrating their applications in various sectors such as government, financial services, and personal data protection. Symmetric cryptography, characterized by its efficiency and speed, is ideal for scenarios where large volumes of data need secure processing. In contrast, asymmetric cryptography solves the key distribution problem by using a pair of keys, enhancing security for communications over insecure channels.

The chapter also covered cryptographic hash functions, underscoring their importance in ensuring data integrity and supporting security protocols like digital signatures and password storage. Advances in cryptographic key management were discussed, emphasizing modern techniques that ensure the security and integrity of cryptographic keys across their lifecycle.

Additionally, we examined the integration of emerging technologies such as AI and quantum computing in cryptography, predicting how these advancements could shape the future of cryptographic practices. The potential of AI to enhance cryptographic solutions and the development of quantum-resistant algorithms to counter the threats posed by quantum computing were highlighted.

REFERENCES

Abroshan, H. (2021). Using symmetric and asymmetric cryptography algorithms, a hybrid encryption solution to improve cloud computing security. *International Journal of Advanced Computer Science and Applications,12*, 31–37.

Abu Al-Haija, Q., Alohaly, M., & Odeh, A. (2023). Using a hybrid learning approach, a lightweight double-stage scheme to identify malicious DNS over HTTPS traffic. *Sensors (Basel)*, 23, 3489. 10.3390/s2307348937050549

Abu Taleb, A., Abu Al-Haija, Q., & Odeh, A. (2023). Efficient Mobile Sink Routing in Wireless Sensor Networks Using Bipartite Graphs. *Future Internet*, 15(5), 182. 10.3390/fi15050182

Al-Shabi, M. A. (2019). A survey on symmetric and asymmetric cryptography algorithms in information security. *International Journal of Scientific and Research Publications*, 9(3), 576–589. 10.29322/IJSRP.9.03.2019.p8779

Alshowkan, M., Elleithy, K., Odeh, A., & Abdelfattah, E. (2013). A new algorithm for three-party Quantum key distribution. *Third International Conference on Innovative Computing Technology (INTECH 2013)*, 208-212. 10.1109/INTECH.2013.6653692

Anwar, M. R., Apriani, D., & Adianita, I. R. (2021). Hash Algorithm In Verification Of Certificate Data Integrity And Security. *Aptisi Transactions on Technopreneurship*, 3(2), 181–188. 10.34306/att.v3i2.212

Avesani, P., Mcpherson, B., Hayashi, S., Caiafa, C. F., Henschel, R., Garyfallidis, E., Kitchell, L., Bullock, D., Patterson, A., Olivetti, E., Sporns, O., Saykin, A. J., Wang, L., Dinov, I., Hancock, D., Caron, B., Qian, Y., & Pestilli, F. (2019). The open diffusion data derivatives, brain data upcycling via integrated publishing of derivatives, and reproducible open cloud services. *Scientific Data*, 6(1), 69. 10.1038/s41597-019-0073-y31123325

Bennett, C. H., Bessette, F., Brassard, G., Salvail, L., & Smolin, J. (1992). Experimental quantum cryptography. *Journal of Cryptology*, 5(1), 3–28. 10.1007/BF00191318

Borangiu, T., Trentesaux, D., Thomas, A., Leitão, P., & Barata, J. (2019). *Digital transformation of manufacturing through cloud services and resource virtualization*. Elsevier. 10.1016/j.compind.2019.01.006

Dhanda, S. S., Singh, B., & Jindal, P. (2020). Lightweight cryptography: A solution to secure IoT. *Wireless Personal Communications*, 112(3), 1947–1980. 10.1007/s11277-020-07134-3

Dulac-Arnold, G., Mankowitz, D., & Hester, T. 2019. Challenges of real-world reinforcement learning. *arXiv preprint arXiv:1904.12901*.

Fomichev, V., Bobrovskiy, D., Koreneva, A., Nabiev, T., & Zadorozhny, D. (2022). Data integrity algorithm based on additive generators and hash function. *Journal of Computer Virology and Hacking Techniques*, 18(1), 31–41. 10.1007/s11416-021-00405-y

Goldreich, O. 2019. On the foundations of cryptography. *Providing sound foundations for cryptography: on the work of Shafi Goldwasser and Silvio Micali*. Academic Press.

Hammad, B. T., Sagheer, A. M., Ahmed, I. T., & Jamil, N. (2020). A comparative review on symmetric and asymmetric DNA-based cryptography. *Bulletin of Electrical Engineering and Informatics*, 9(6), 2484–2491. 10.11591/eei.v9i6.2470

Jatoth, C., Gangadharan, G., Fiore, U., & Buyya, R. (2019). SELCLOUD: A hybrid multi-criteria decision-making model for selection of cloud services. *Soft Computing*, 23(13), 4701–4715. 10.1007/s00500-018-3120-2

Keshta, I., & Odeh, A. (2021). Security and privacy of electronic health records: Concerns and challenges. *Egyptian Informatics Journal*, 22(2), 177–183. 10.1016/j.eij.2020.07.003

Kokoris Kogias, E., Malkhi, D., & Spiegelman, A. (2020). Asynchronous Distributed Key Generation for Computationally-Secure Randomness, Consensus, and Threshold Signatures. *Proceedings of the 2020 ACM SIGSAC Conference on Computer and Communications Security*, 1751-1767. 10.1145/3372297.3423364

Kuznetsov, A., Oleshko, I., Tymchenko, V., Lisitsky, K., Rodinko, M., & Kolhatin, A. (2021). Performance analysis of cryptographic hash functions suitable for use in blockchain. *International Journal of Computer Network & Information Security*, 13(2), 1–15. 10.5815/ijcnis.2021.02.01

Lindmeier, A., & Mühling, A. (2020). Keeping secrets: K-12 students' understanding of cryptography. *Proceedings of the 15th Workshop on Primary and Secondary Computing Education*, 1-10. 10.1145/3421590.3421630

Martin, K. (2020). *Cryptography: The key to digital security, how it works, and why it matters*. WW Norton & Company.

Mittelbach, A., & Fischlin, M. (2021). *The theory of hash functions and random oracles. An Approach to Modern Cryptography*. Springer Nature. 10.1007/978-3-030-63287-8

Odeh, A. (2020). Taxonomy of Cluster-Based Target Tracking System in Wireless Sensor Networks. *International Journal of Sensors, Wireless Communications and Control*, 10(5), 649–658. 10.2174/2210327910999200606230150

Odeh, A., Elleithy, K., Alshowkan, M., & Abdelfattah, E. (2013). Quantum key distribution by using public key algorithm (RSA). *Third International Conference on Innovative Computing Technology (INTECH 2013)*, 83-86. 10.1109/INTECH.2013.6653697

Odeh, A., Keshta, I. & Abdelfattah, E. (2020). *Efficient detection of phishing websites using multilayer perceptron*. Academic Press.

Ott, D., & Peikert, C. (2019). Identifying research challenges in post quantum cryptography migration and cryptographic agility. *arXiv preprint arXiv:1909.07353*.

Portmann, C., & Renner, R. (2022). Security in quantum cryptography. *Reviews of Modern Physics*, 94(2), 025008. 10.1103/RevModPhys.94.025008

Raghunandan, K., Gagnani, L., Amarendra, K. & Santhosh Krishna, B. (2020). Product key activation for software products using Collatz Conjuncture and asymmetric key cryptography. *Materials Today: Proceedings*. https://doi. . MATPR, 907org/10.1016/J

Ramteke, B., & Dongre, S. (2022). IoT Based Smart Automated Poultry Farm Management System. *2022 10th International Conference on Emerging Trends in Engineering and Technology-Signal and Information Processing (ICETET-SIP-22)*, 1-4.

Sadhu, P. K., Yanambaka, V. P., & Abdelgawad, A. (2022). Internet of things: Security and solutions survey. *Sensors (Basel)*, 22(19), 7433. 10.3390/s2219743336236531

Sharafi, M., Fotouhi-Ghazvini, F., Shirali, M., & Ghassemian, M. (2019). A low power cryptography solution based on chaos theory in wireless sensor nodes. *IEEE Access : Practical Innovations, Open Solutions*, 7, 8737–8753. 10.1109/ACCESS.2018.2886384

Shen, W., Qin, J., Yu, J., Hao, R., Hu, J., & Ma, J. (2019). Data integrity auditing without private key storage for secure cloud storage. *IEEE Transactions on Cloud Computing*, 9(4), 1408–1421. 10.1109/TCC.2019.2921553

Somsuk, K., & Thakong, M. (2020). Authentication system for e-certificate by using RSA's digital signature. *TELKOMNIKA*, 18(6), 2948–2955. 10.12928/telkomnika.v18i6.17278

Tchórzewski, J. & Jakóbik, A. (2019). Theoretical and experimental analysis of cryptographic hash functions. *Journal of Telecommunications and Information Technology*, 125-133.

Xie, K., Yang, D., Ozbay, K., & Yang, H. (2019). Use of real-world connected vehicle data in identifying high-risk locations based on a new surrogate safety measure. *Accident; Analysis and Prevention*, 125, 311–319. 10.1016/j.aap.2018.07.00229983165

Yousuf, H., Lahzi, M., Salloum, S. A. & Shaalan, K. (2020). Systematic review on fully homomorphic encryption scheme and its application. *Recent Advances in Intelligent Systems and Smart Applications*, 537-551.

Zeadally, S., Das, A. K., & Sklavos, N. (2021). Cryptographic technologies and protocol standards for Internet of Things. *Internet of Things : Engineering Cyber Physical Human Systems*, 14, 100075. 10.1016/j.iot.2019.100075

Zhang, L., Xiong, H., Huang, Q., Li, J., Choo, K.-K. R., & Li, J. (2019). Cryptographic solutions for cloud storage: Challenges and research opportunities. *IEEE Transactions on Services Computing*, 15(1), 567–587. 10.1109/TSC.2019.2937764

Chapter 8
User Authentication in the IoT and IIoT Environment

Ahmed Mahfouz

Faculty of Computer Studies, Arab Open University (AOU), Oman & Computer Science Department, Minia University, Egypt

ABSTRACT

This chapter delves deep into the issue of user authentication in the environment of the internet of things (IoT) and industrial internet of things (IIoT). It's a journey defined by security implications, presented trends, and analyzed conventional practices, all of which set the stage for further examination. The authors explore the challenges and limitations of involving user authentication in the context of interacting ecosystems, and then they dive into the exciting world of the latest advancements aimed at ensuring higher security and privacy. These include blockchain-based tools, multi-modal authentication, and zero-trust paradigms. Also, they navigate the legislative landscape, provide compliance recommendations, and provide relevant tips for the establishment of strong authentication practices. Through captivating case studies and real-world applications, they draw a clear picture of the importance of user authentication in safeguarding IoT and IIoT systems against evolving cyber threats.

1. INTRODUCTION

The Internet of Things (IoT) and the Industrial Internet of Things (IIoT) have revolutionized technology, interconnecting devices, sensors, and systems to collect, exchange, and analyze data for automation and innovation (Boyes et al., 2018). Adding the IoT to the industrial applications such as cyber-physical systems (CPS) transformed them into smart and intelligent devices. Using the IoT has extended the network connectivity and computing capabilities to objects, facilitating data generation, exchange, and consumption with a decreasing of human intervention. In the context of IIoT, the IoT technologies is used in industrial settings to fulfill industry-specific objectives (Hazra et al., 2021). So, we can define the IIoT as the as the use of IoT technologies in manufacturing, emphasize the integration of smart objects

DOI: 10.4018/979-8-3693-3451-5.ch008

within CPS, cloud or edge computing platforms, and the real-time, autonomous exchange and analysis of process, product, or service information (Kumar & Agrawal, 2023).

The evolving IoT and IIoT ecosystem has an impact on how we engage with our industrial environment (Sisinni et al., 2018). Innovations in edge computing, connectivity, and data analytics are driving major breakthroughs on the Internet of Things and IIoT (Kumar & Agrawal, 2023). Every area of our life and business is being impacted by IoT and IIoT technology. from wearable technology and smart homes to smart factories and industrial automation. Artificial Intelligence, machine learning and cloud computing introduces a set of innovative possibilities for automation, predictive maintenance, and real-time decision-making (Adi et al., 2020; Al-Garadi et al., 2020; Kumar & Agrawal, 2023; Xiao et al., 2018). Furthermore, the Low-Power technologies and the spread of networks like 5G increased the scalability of deploying IoT and IIoT systems (Khanh et al., 2022). As the devolvement of these technologies, they hold the potential to change the industries, optimize processes, and enhance the quality of life for individuals around the globe (Jiang et al., 2018).

The significance of security in IoT and IIoT cannot be neglected, given the pervasive connectivity and sensitive data exchanged within these ecosystems (Tawalbeh et al., 2020). With millions of interconnected devices collecting and transmitting data, the risk of cyber threats and attacks is heightened, posing significant challenges to the integrity and privacy of information (Sengupta et al., 2020). One of the foundational pillars of IoT and IIoT security is user authentication – the process of verifying the identity of individuals or devices seeking access to resources within these ecosystems (Lee, 2020). As seen in figure 1, user authentication in the IoT and IIoT environment plays a crucial role in ensuring the security and integrity of connected systems. With the proliferation of interconnected devices and the exchange of sensitive data, robust authentication mechanisms are essential to verify the identity of users and devices accessing these ecosystems (Liang et al., 2020; C. Shi et al., 2021). Traditional authentication methods, such as passwords and tokens, are often insufficient to address the unique challenges posed by IoT and IIoT, including device heterogeneity, resource constraints, and scalability requirements (Lien & Vhaduri, 2023). As a result, novel approaches to user authentication, such as biometrics, multi-factor authentication, and device attestation, are being explored to enhance security without compromising usability (Abuhamad et al., 2021; Masud et al., 2022; C. Shi et al., 2017; Vhaduri & Poellabauer, 2019).

Figure 1. The IoT and IIoT environments contain different components such as robots, controls, could, and data analysis tools. All these components are accessible through computing machines with a user authentication interface

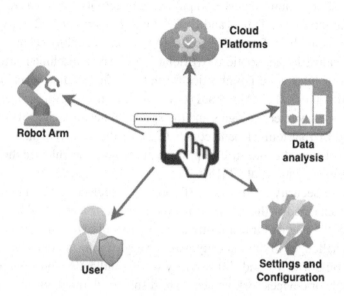

To further contextualize the unique security challenges in IoT and IIoT environments, it is essential to highlight the distinct differences from traditional IT systems. IoT and IIoT ecosystems are characterized by a vast array of interconnected devices, often with limited computational resources and varying security capabilities. Unlike traditional IT systems, these environments operate in diverse and often harsh conditions, making standardized security protocols difficult to implement uniformly. The heterogeneous nature of devices, coupled with real-time data processing and critical infrastructure dependencies, amplifies the complexity of ensuring robust user authentication. These challenges necessitate innovative and adaptive security measures tailored specifically for the dynamic and resource-constrained landscape of IoT and IIoT, underscoring the critical need for specialized authentication strategies explored in this chapter.

2. CURRENT PRACTICES AND CHALLENGES

This section presents the current landscape of user authentication practices within IoT and IIoT environments. It examines the common methods and techniques utilized for verifying the identity of users and devices accessing interconnected systems. From traditional password-based authentication to more advanced biometric and token-based approaches (Al-Naji & Zagrouba, 2020; Bojinov & Boneh, 2011; Harbach et al., 2016; Owusu et al., 2012). It also explores the strengths, limitations, and practical implications of each method (Lee, 2020; Lien & Vhaduri, 2023; Sengupta et al., 2020; Tawalbeh et al., 2020). Additionally, it addresses the challenges inherent in implementing user authentication in the context of IoT and IIoT, including device heterogeneity, scalability issues, and resource constraints (Khanh et al., 2022; Lien & Vhaduri, 2023; Tawalbeh et al., 2020; Zimmermann & Gerber, 2020).

2.1. Traditional Authentication Methods

Traditional authentication methods are foundational techniques used to verify the identity of users accessing systems or devices. These methods rely on factors such as knowledge, possession, or inherence to authenticate users (Al-Naji & Zagrouba, 2020; Lien & Vhaduri, 2023). Traditional authentication methods include password-based authentication, PIN-based authentication, and pattern-based authentication, which involves drawing a pattern on a touch screen. Additionally, token-based authentication (Bojinov & Boneh, 2011) utilizes physical or virtual tokens to generate one-time passwords or cryptographic keys for authentication. These methods have been widely used for decades but may pose security risks if not implemented correctly (Lee, 2020; Mamdouh et al., 2021; Tawalbeh et al., 2020). Traditional authentication methods serve as the cornerstone of user verification in IoT and IIoT environments and will be discussed in detail in the subsequent points, highlighting their strengths, weaknesses, and practical considerations for implementation.

2.1.1. Password-Based Authentication

Password-based authentication remains one of the most utilized methods for user verification in IoT and IIoT environments. This approach involves users providing a secret combination of characters, known only to them, to gain access to devices, systems, or networks. Despite its widespread use, password-based authentication presents inherent security risks (Harbach et al., 2016; Lee, 2020; Owusu et al., 2012; Zimmermann & Gerber, 2020), including vulnerability to brute force attacks, password guessing, and credential theft (Andriotis et al., 2013; Khan et al., 2016; Sengupta et al., 2020). Moreover, the proliferation of IoT devices with limited resources may introduce additional challenges in securely managing passwords, such as storage constraints and susceptibility to eavesdropping attacks (Feng et al., 2024; Sengupta et al., 2020).

2.1.2. PIN-Based Authentication

PIN-based authentication is a widely implemented method for user verification in IoT and IIoT environments. This approach involves users inputting a numeric code, typically four to six digits, to authenticate themselves and gain access to devices, systems, or networks. While PIN-based authentication offers simplicity and ease of use, it presents certain security challenges, including susceptibility to brute force attacks and unauthorized access attempts (Lien & Vhaduri, 2023; Mamdouh et al., 2021; Sisinni et al., 2018; Tawalbeh et al., 2020; Von Zezschwitz et al., 2013). Moreover, the integration of PIN-based authentication in IoT and IIoT systems requires careful consideration of factors such as device limitations, storage constraints, and potential interception risks (Abu Waraga et al., 2020; Lee, 2020).

2.1.3. Pattern-Based Authentication

Pattern-based authentication presents an alternative for user verification within the IoT and IIoT environments. Unlike traditional alphanumeric passwords or numeric PINs, pattern-based authentication involves users drawing a unique pattern on a touchscreen device, typically connecting a series of dots in a specific sequence (Ian Jermyn and Alain Mayer and Fabian Monrose and Michael K. Reiter and Aviel Rubin, 1999; Li et al., 2015). This method offers several advantages, including ease of use, intuitive interaction, and the potential for enhanced user experience (Khan et al., 2019). By leveraging familiar touchscreen gestures, such as swiping or tapping, pattern-based authentication aims to simplify the authentication process, particularly on mobile and touchscreen-enabled IoT devices (Tolosana et al., 2020). However, like any authentication mechanism, pattern-based authentication is facing some challenges. Security concerns arise regarding the interception and replication of patterns, as well as the potential for unauthorized access if patterns are observed or guessed. Furthermore, the effectiveness of pattern-based authentication may vary depending on factors such as screen size, and resolution (Zaidi et al., 2021).

2.1.4. Token-Based authentication.

Token-based authentication is a prevalent method used to verify user identity and secure access to systems and resources in various digital environments, including IoT and IIoT. This approach involves the use of tokens, which can be physical or virtual, to generate and validate authentication credentials (Dammak et al., 2019; Ebrahimpour & Babaie, 2024). Physical tokens may include smart cards, USB tokens, or key fobs, while virtual tokens often take the form of cryptographic keys or one-time passwords (OTPs) generated by authentication apps or sent via SMS (Bojinov & Boneh, 2011; Dammak et al., 2019; Smith & Hans, 2004). Token-based authentication offers several advantages, including enhanced security using dynamic and time-sensitive credentials, reduced reliance on static passwords, and support for multi-factor authentication (MFA) approaches. However, challenges such as token management, distribution, and potential loss or theft of physical tokens must be addressed to ensure the effectiveness and usability of token-based authentication in IoT and IIoT environments (Saqib & Moon, 2023). Despite these challenges, token-based authentication remains a robust and widely adopted method for securing access to IoT and IIoT systems, providing a crucial layer of defense against unauthorized access and data breaches.

2.2. Biometric Authentication Methods

Biometric authentication methods offer a promising avenue for enhancing security and usability within the IoT and IIoT ecosystems (Lien & Vhaduri, 2023). This subsection explores various biometric authentication techniques utilized in IoT and IIoT environments, including fingerprint recognition, iris recognition, and face recognition. By leveraging the unique physiological traits of individuals (J. Zhang et al., 2023), these methods provide a robust means of verifying user identities, mitigating the vulnerabilities associated with traditional authentication mechanisms. Through an in-depth examination of each biometric authentication method, this subsection aims to illustrate their strengths, limitations, implementation considerations, and potential applications in securing connected devices and systems in IoT and IIoT contexts (W. Yang et al., 2021).

2.2.1. Fingerprint Recognition

Fingerprint recognition is one of the most widely used biometric authentication methods in IoT and IIoT environments. This technology leverages the unique patterns of ridges and valleys on an individual's finger to verify their identity. The process involves capturing a fingerprint image using a fingerprint scanner sensor, extracting distinctive features from the image, and comparing these features against stored templates to allow or deny access to specific individuals (W. Yang et al., 2021). It has some advantages such as high accuracy, ease of use, and difficulty to forge and .it is particularly well-suited for environments where quick and reliable authentication is essential. However, fingerprint recognition is suffering from a set of challenges. Environmental factors such as dust, oil, and moisture can affect the quality of the captured fingerprint image, potentially leading to false rejections or false acceptances. The quality of the fingerprint sensor also plays a crucial role in the system's overall performance. Low-resolution sensors may fail to capture sufficient detail, resulting in higher error rates. Moreover, the technology is vulnerable to spoofing attacks if an attacker can replicate the fingerprint patterns using materials like silicone or gelatin (Abu Waraga et al., 2020). In the context of IoT and IIoT, fingerprint recognition can be applied in various scenarios, such as securing access to smart homes, industrial control systems, and personal devices. For instance, in a smart home setting, fingerprint recognition can be used to unlock doors, access control panels, or authenticate users for various smart appliances. In industrial environments, it can secure access to machinery, control systems, and sensitive data.

2.2.2. Iris Recognition

Iris recognition is another strong biometric authentication technology used in IoT and IIoT (Nguyen et al., 2024). It leverages the complex and unique patterns visible within the human iris to confirm users' identities (Islam, 2014; Omolara et al., 2022). People use special iris sensors or cameras to access this technology and can achieve high accuracy and the probability that they will be verified (Vhaduri & Poellabauer, 2019). The distinctive features of iris recognition include its uniqueness, permanence, anti-tampering capabilities, and distinctiveness. The patterns in the iris are highly unique to each individual and remain stable over a person's lifetime, making iris recognition an extremely reliable method for authentication. Additionally, the iris is protected by the cornea, making it less susceptible to damage and tampering compared to other biometric traits. Despite its advantages, iris recognition faces several challenges that can hinder its widespread adoption in IoT and IIoT environments. One major barrier is the hardware requirement; specialized cameras and sensors are needed to capture high-quality iris images, which can be expensive and complex to integrate into existing systems (Lien & Vhaduri, 2023). Lighting conditions can also impact the accuracy of iris recognition, as poor lighting or reflections can affect the quality of the captured images. Furthermore, user adoption can be a challenge, as some users may find the technology intrusive or uncomfortable, which can limit its acceptance (Mamdouh et al., 2021; Tawalbeh et al., 2020). In practical applications, iris recognition can be used in various IoT and IIoT scenarios, such as securing access to critical infrastructure, authenticating users in high-security environments, and controlling access to sensitive data. For example, in an industrial setting, iris recognition can ensure that only authorized personnel can access control systems and machinery, thereby enhancing security and preventing unauthorized access.

2.2.3. Face Recognition

Face recognition is one of the widely used biometric authentication utilized in IoT and IIoT implementations. This method works by capturing facial photographs from cameras and comparing each user's facial pattern and features (Sayed et al., 2023). Advanced facial recognition algorithms and technologies allow users to access their devices and services naturally and conveniently using face recognition (Schroff et al., 2015; Taigman et al., 2014; F. Wang et al., 2017). One of the primary advantages of face recognition is its non-intrusive nature. Users can authenticate themselves without physical contact, simply by looking at a camera, which makes the process seamless and user-friendly. Additionally, face recognition works in various environments, whether indoors or outdoors, under different lighting conditions, thanks to the advancements in image processing and machine learning algorithms. Face recognition technology is also integrated into numerous applications, from unlocking smartphones and accessing secure areas to monitoring attendance in workplaces and securing IoT devices in smart homes and industrial settings. Its ability to provide a hands-free authentication experience makes it particularly appealing in scenarios where convenience and hygiene are paramount, such as in healthcare or public transportation.

However, face recognition is not without its challenges. Accuracy can be affected by factors such as changes in lighting, facial expressions, and occlusions (e.g., glasses or masks). There are also significant privacy concerns, as the technology involves the collection and storage of sensitive biometric data. The potential for misuse or unauthorized access to facial data raises ethical and legal issues that need to be carefully managed (Deb & Jain, 2021; Shao et al., 2022). Moreover, face recognition systems can be vulnerable to spoofing attacks, where attackers use photographs, videos, or even 3D masks to impersonate legitimate users. Ensuring robust anti-spoofing measures, such as liveness detection, is crucial to maintain the integrity of face recognition systems. In the context of IoT and IIoT, face recognition can be employed in various applications to enhance security and user convenience. For instance, in a smart factory, face recognition can be used to control access to sensitive areas, ensuring that only authorized personnel can enter. In smart homes, it can provide a secure and convenient way for residents to unlock doors and control devices.

2.3. Behavioral Authentication Methods

Novel approaches to user verification in IoT and IIoT ecosystems are embodied around behavioral authentication methods (Bezawada et al., 2021; Krawiecka et al., 2023). Several types of behavioral authentication techniques that can be utilized for IoT and IIoT systems need to be considered. They include gesture-based authentication, keystroke dynamics, gait recognition, voice recognition, and activity-based authentication. It is essential to understand that they consider unique patterns, provide in-depth characteristics of a particular individual, and can be used as an assistive concept, minimizing the use of direct traditional authentication (Abuhamad et al., 2021; Liang et al., 2020). This paragraph prepares the ground for identifying and discussing each behavioral authentication type, its principles, major use cases, possible benefits, and deficiencies as part of the rapidly changing set of available connection ecosystems.

2.3.1. Gesture-Based Authentication

Another type of input method is gesture-based authentication, which uses touchscreens as a primary interface to authenticate users in IoT environments by using their gestures. Gesture-based authentication allows users to input their gestures most conveniently and naturally to identify the individual securely (Chao et al., 2023; Kong et al., 2019; Pulfrey & Hossain, 2022; Stylios et al., 2023). Users input their gestures on a specific pattern, like swiping, tapping, or drawing, and the sensors on the touchscreen examine the specific characteristic, such as drawing speed, direction, or pressure, to identify the individual accurately (Mahfouz et al., 2024). The benefit of touchscreen-based gesture authentication is ease and natural use without a need for additional gadgets, and it is compatible with multiple devices (Liu et al., 2017; Stylios et al., 2023). However, some challenges, such as gesture recognition accuracy and the user's natural conditions, need to be addressed effectively (Lien & Vhaduri, 2023; Mamdouh et al., 2021;

Sisinni et al., 2018; Tawalbeh et al., 2020). Nevertheless, gesture-based touchscreen authentication could be a promising approach to securing users while enhancing the usability of IoT and IIoT interfaces with a seamless and natural experience.

2.3.2. Keystroke Dynamics

Keystroke dynamics is a type of behavioral authentication that uses the unique patterns and rhythms of a person's typing to verify their identity in IoT and IIoT environments. The method effectively captures a range of typing characteristics, including keystroke timing, duration, and pressure, to actualize a b(Stylios et al., 2023). The benefits of keystroke dynamics authentication are its continuous nature, unobtrusiveness, and ability to be applied across multiple input devices; however, challenges such as variations in behavior and environmental factors can undermine its effectiveness (Kumar & Agrawal, 2023; Lien & Vhaduri, 2023; Mamdouh et al., 2021)In this regard, keystroke dynamics authentication remains a promising practice for ensuring security and usability in surrounding ecosystems, making the user's interaction with remote systems invisible.

2.3.3. Gait Recognition

Gait recognition is a behavioral biometric method that can be used in IoT and IIoT environments for user verification (Xu et al., 2017). This method analyzes the unique walking patterns and characteristics of individuals to authenticate their identities. Gait recognition systems typically utilize sensors such as accelerometers or gyroscopes embedded in wearable devices or smart infrastructure to capture gait data (Axente et al., 2020; Muaaz & Mayrhofer, 2017). The collected data includes parameters such as stride length, and acceleration patterns, which are then processed using machine learning algorithms to create gait profiles for users (Zou et al., 2020). During authentication, the system compares the user's current gait pattern with their pre-registered profile to verify their identity. Gait recognition offers several advantages as a biometric authentication method on IoT and IIoT environments such as continuous authentication and non-intrusive (Abuhamad et al., 2021; De Marsico & Mecca, 2019; Liang et al., 2020). However, it also presents challenges that need to be addressed for effective implementation such as variability in walking and environmental (Mamdouh et al., 2021; Tawalbeh et al., 2020; C. Wang et al., 2020). Despite these challenges, gait recognition holds promise for enhancing security and usability in IoT and IIoT environments, offering a non-intrusive and continuous authentication method based on users' unique behavioral patterns.

2.3.4. Voice Recognition

Voice recognition could serve as a biometric identification technique in IoT and IIoT systems. It works by recognizing the user's identity based on unique vocal characteristics and patterns of speech (Peng et al., 2017; L. Zhang et al., 2017). This system uses voice recordings from the incorporated microphones on the devices or wearables and examines parameters like pitch, tone, and rhythm of speech (C. Shi et al., 2020). Machine learning techniques analyze this information to create voiceprints or biometric signatures for users, which are compared to stored profiles (L. Zhang et al., 2017). Voice recognition is a highly user-friendly technique providing natural and device-independent usage even in hands-free mode. Nonetheless, it can be subject to inaccuracies due to background noise, various accents and languages spoken, and impersonating misuse attempts (Lien & Vhaduri, 2023; Sengupta et al., 2020; Zhou et al., 2018).

2.3.5. Activity Based Authentication

Activity-based user authentication is a novel approach to user authentication in IoT and IoT environments that uses the user's behavior and context to verify his or her identity and grant easy access to resources. Unlike traditional forms of user authentication that primarily depend on passive credentials, such as passwords or biometrics, activity-based authentication is based on assessing the user's interaction, patterns, and environment to establish trust and provide dynamic user authentication (C. Shi et al., 2017, 2021). This methodology could lead to improved security by integrating contextual factors, including location, time, and user activity, to make an authentication decision (Corallo et al., 2022; Saqib & Moon, 2023. Note that this method is also likely to enhance the user experience by requiring fewer manual actions and autographing decision-making based on the user activity (Almadani et al., 2023; Mahfouz et al., 2024). Moreover, the use of activity-based authentication forms to the user is continually changing, and in real-time, defenders might monitor it to effectively react and adapt if a new login attempt seems suspicious (C. Wang et al., 2020). Otherwise, it is possible to implement several novel algorithms within the use of sensors, tracking the user's behavior (Al-Garadi et al., 2020; Xiao et al., 2018).

2.4. Limitations and Challenges

Although authentication techniques for IoT and IIoT contexts have advanced, a few restrictions and difficulties still exist, hindering their broad acceptance and efficacy (Khanh et al., 2022; Mamdouh et al., 2021; Tawalbeh et al., 2020). One major issue is the existence of security flaws (Ebrahimpour & Babaie, 2024; Sengupta et al., 2020), which make authentication systems vulnerable to exploitation via several strategies, such as spoofing and brute force assaults which could result in data breaches and unauthorized access. Moreover, privacy concerns are suffering from the necessity of robust privacy controls and raise issues about the collection and storage of sensitive biometric data (Tawalbeh et al., 2020). Another reason for usability issues is that some authentication processes can be confusing to users, which could aggravate them and lead to disobedience.

2.4.1. Security Vulnerabilities

The proliferation of IoT and IIoT devices has introduced numerous security vulnerabilities related to user authentication, posing significant challenges to the integrity and confidentiality of connected ecosystems (Ebrahimpour & Babaie, 2024; Sengupta et al., 2020). One of these concerns is the susceptibility of authentication mechanisms to various forms of attacks, including brute force attacks, credential stuffing, and password spraying (Al-Naji & Zagrouba, 2020; Dammak et al., 2019; C. Wang et al., 2020). Weak or default passwords, commonly found in IoT and IIoT devices, provide easy entry points for attackers to gain unauthorized access to devices, networks, or sensitive data (Feng et al., 2024). Additionally, inadequate authentication protocols, such as lack of multi-factor authentication (MFA) or ineffective session management, further exacerbate these vulnerabilities, enabling attackers to bypass authentication controls and compromise user accounts (Ebrahimpour & Babaie, 2024; Sengupta et al., 2020). Insecure transmission of authentication data, susceptibility to man-in-the-middle (MitM) attacks and inadequate access control mechanisms also contribute to the risk landscape, potentially exposing users to identity theft, data breaches, and unauthorized access (Kumar & Agrawal, 2023; Lee, 2020; Sengupta et al., 2020; Sisinni et al., 2018; Tawalbeh et al., 2020).

2.4.2. Privacy Concerns

The widespread adoption of IoT and IIoT technologies has raised significant privacy concerns related to user authentication practices within connected ecosystems (Tawalbeh et al., 2020). One of the primary concerns revolves around the collection and storage of sensitive user authentication data, including biometric information, passwords, and personal identifiers (Lien & Vhaduri, 2023; Yang et al., 2021). In many cases, IoT and IIoT devices collect and process this data without adequate transparency or user consent (Al-Naji & Zagrouba, 2020; Omolara et al., 2022), raising concerns about unauthorized access, data breaches, and potential misuse of personal information. Additionally, the lack of standardized privacy regulations and guidelines for IoT and IIoT authentication practices triggers these concerns, leaving users vulnerable to privacy violations and data exploitation (Ebrahimpour & Babaie, 2024; Lee, 2020; Lien & Vhaduri, 2023; Sengupta et al., 2020). To address these privacy concerns, the implementation of privacy-enhancing technologies should be adapted (Corallo et al., 2022; Ghimire & Rawat, 2022), such as encryption, anonymization, and data minimization techniques, to protect user authentication data from unauthorized access or misuse.

2.4.3. Usability Issues

Usability is very important for users to help them accommodate and use an authentication method (Abuhamad et al., 2021; C. Wang et al., 2020; Yang et al., 2021). The complexity of authentication techniques is one of the main obstacles to usability (Abuhamad et al., 2021; Lien & Vhaduri, 2023), especially for end users who could find it difficult to remember and manage several passwords, PINs, or cryptographic keys across multiple platforms and devices (Saqib & Moon, 2023). Furthermore, frequent authentication interactions are required(Al-Naji & Zagrouba, 2020; Kong et al., 2019; Liang et al., 2020), especially in situations where security requirements are stringent. This can affect the user's productivity and decrease their willingness to accommodate a secure authentication procedure (Khan et al., 2016). Consequently, the design and implementation of user-friendly authentication techniques are required due to the limited capabilities of some IoT devices in terms of their user interface, such as tiny displays or restricted input mechanisms (Omolara et al., 2022; Sisinni et al., 2018). Correspondingly, considering the user-centric authentication systems while designing, emphasis on ease of use, simplicity, and efficiency while upholding strict security assurances must be prioritized to solve these issues(Al-Naji & Zagrouba, 2020; D. Shi et al., 2021; Yang et al., 2021). Designing an authentication process that considers usability measures without sacrificing security could be achieved by utilizing strategies like biometric authentication, single sign-on (SSO) (Ebrahimpour & Babaie, 2024), and contextual authentication (Corallo et al., 2022; Saqib & Moon, 2023).

2.4.4. Implementation Complexity

The implementation of user authentication in IoT and IIoT environments is often complex, presenting challenges for developers and administrators (Sisinni et al., 2018; Tawalbeh et al., 2020). One significant complexity arises from the heterogeneous nature of IoT and IIoT ecosystems (Abu Waraga et al., 2020), where diverse devices, platforms, and protocols coexist, requiring interoperable authentication solutions (Hazra et al., 2021). Integrating authentication mechanisms across different devices and platforms while ensuring compatibility and security adds layers of complexity to the implementation process (Abu Waraga et al., 2020; Hazra et al., 2021). Moreover, resource constraints, such as limited processing power, memory, and energy, further complicate authentication implementation, necessitating lightweight and efficient authentication (Ebrahimpour & Babaie, 2024; Ghimire & Rawat, 2022; Jiang et al., 2018; Xiao et al., 2018). Additionally, the distributed architecture of IoT and IIoT deployments introduces challenges in securely managing user credentials and access control policies across interconnected devices and networks (Dammak et al., 2019; Mohamad Noor & Hassan, 2019; C. Shi et al., 2017).

3. EMERGING TRENDS IN USER AUTHENTICATION TECHNOLOGIES

As the IoT and IIoT ecosystems continue to expand, the need for robust and adaptive user authentication technologies becomes increasingly important (Al-Naji & Zagrouba, 2020; Omolara et al., 2022; Saqib & Moon, 2023). In response to evolving security threats and the growing complexity of connected environments (Ebrahimpour & Babaie, 2024; Sengupta et al., 2020; C. Wang et al., 2020), emerging trends in user authentication technologies are reshaping the landscape of authentication practices (C. Wang et al., 2020). These trends encompass a diverse array of innovative approaches, ranging from continuous authentication mechanisms that monitor user behavior in real-time to behavioral biometrics that analyze unique patterns in user interactions (Abuhamad et al., 2021; Al-Naji & Zagrouba, 2020; Liang et al., 2020). Multi-factor authentication solutions (Ometov et al., 2018), combining multiple authentication factors for enhanced security, are also gaining traction, alongside advancements in contextual authentication (Saqib & Moon, 2023) and passwordless authentication methods (Vhaduri & Poellabauer, 2019). These emerging trends represent the forefront of innovation in user authentication, offering promising solutions to address the challenges of securing IoT and IIoT environments while balancing security, usability, and scalability requirements (Kumar & Agrawal, 2023; Lien & Vhaduri, 2023; Mamdouh et al., 2021; Tawalbeh et al., 2020).

3.1. Implicit and Continuous Authentication

Implicit and continuous authentication represents a transformative approach to user authentication in IoT and IIoT environments, characterized by real-time identity verification without explicit user involvement (Al-Naji & Zagrouba, 2020; Vhaduri & Poellabauer, 2019). Unlike conventional authentication methods that rely on discrete user actions such as entering passwords or providing biometric credentials, implicit and continuous authentication operates seamlessly in the background, continuously monitoring user behavior and interaction patterns to ascertain identity dynamically (Abuhamad et al., 2021; Liang et al., 2020). This innovative approach leverages a multitude of contextual cues, including device usage patterns (Saqib & Moon, 2023), location data (Albayram et al., 2014), biometric indicators (Vhaduri

& Poellabauer, 2019), and behavioral analytics (Bezawada et al., 2021), to establish and maintain user trust levels in real time. By analyzing ongoing users, implicit and continuous authentication systems can promptly detect anomalies and suspicious activities (Ebrahimpour & Babaie, 2024; Sengupta et al., 2020), supporting security posture and mitigating risks associated with unauthorized access (C. Wang et al., 2020). Furthermore, the non-intrusive nature of implicit authentication minimizes user burden and friction typically associated with traditional authentication methods (Khan et al., 2019), thereby enhancing usability and productivity in IoT and IIoT deployments.

3.2. Multi-Modal Authentication

Multi-modal authentication, often referred to as fusion-based authentication, represents a cutting-edge approach to user authentication in IoT and IIoT environments (Kumar & Agrawal, 2023; Stylios et al., 2023; Vhaduri & Poellabauer, 2019). This emerging trend involves combining multiple biometric modalities, such as fingerprint recognition, facial recognition, iris scanning, and voice authentication, to create a comprehensive and robust authentication system (Kuncheva, 2014; Mondal & Bours, 2017). By leveraging the strengths of various biometric identifiers, multi-modal authentication enhances authentication accuracy, reliability, and security (Ometov et al., 2018; Vhaduri & Poellabauer, 2019). Moreover, fusion-based authentication mitigates the limitations of individual biometric modalities, such as susceptibility to spoofing attacks or environmental factors (Kumar & Agrawal, 2023; Lien & Vhaduri, 2023; Mamdouh et al., 2021). The integration of multiple biometric modalities enables more sophisticated and resilient authentication mechanisms capable of adapting to diverse user environments and scenarios (Islam, 2014; Stylios et al., 2023). As organizations prioritize stronger authentication measures to safeguard sensitive data and critical assets in IoT and IIoT deployments, multi-modal authentication emerges as a compelling trend to enhance security while ensuring user convenience and usability.

3.3. Zero-Trust Authentication

Zero-trust authentication is gaining prominence as a revolutionary approach to user authentication in IoT and IIoT environments. This emerging trend challenges the traditional security model by assuming that no user or device can be inherently trusted, regardless of their location or network status (Syed et al., 2022). Zero-trust authentication mandates continuous verification of user identity and device posture before granting access to resources, applications, or sensitive data. By implementing stringent authentication and authorization policies based on dynamic risk assessments (Ragothaman et al., 2023), zero-trust authentication models mitigate the risk of unauthorized access and lateral movement within connected ecosystems (Syed et al., 2022). Moreover, zero-trust authentication aligns with the principles of least privilege (Aboukadri et al., 2024) and micro-segmentation (Syed et al., 2022), ensuring that users and devices only access the resources necessary for their specific roles or tasks. As organizations seek to enhance security posture and mitigate the impact of advanced threats in IoT and IIoT deployments, zero-trust authentication can establish a robust security foundation while enabling secure access to critical resources.

3.4. Blockchain-Based Authentication

Blockchain-based authentication is revolutionizing user authentication in IoT and IIoT environments by leveraging the decentralized and immutable properties of blockchain technology (Almadani et al., 2023). Unlike traditional authentication methods that rely on centralized authorities or intermediaries to verify user identities, blockchain-based authentication operates on a distributed ledger system, where authentication records are securely stored across multiple nodes in a network (Sengupta et al., 2020). This decentralized approach ensures that authentication transactions are transparent, tamper-proof, and resistant to unauthorized modifications or data breaches. Blockchain-based authentication eliminates the need for trust in a single entity by distributing authentication responsibilities among multiple nodes in the network (Al-Garadi et al., 2020; Almadani et al., 2023; Mamdouh et al., 2021). Each authentication event is recorded as a transaction on the blockchain, providing a verifiable and auditable trail of user interactions with connected devices and systems (Almadani et al., 2023; Sengupta et al., 2020). Moreover, cryptographic techniques such as digital signatures and hash functions ensure the integrity and authenticity of authentication records, enhancing security and trust in the authentication process (Feng et al., 2024). One of the key advantages of blockchain-based authentication is its ability to provide secure and privacy-preserving authentication without compromising user data privacy or confidentiality. Since authentication records are encrypted and stored on a distributed ledger, sensitive user information remains protected from unauthorized access or disclosure. As organizations increasingly prioritize security and trust in IoT and IIoT deployments, blockchain-based authentication establishes a secure, decentralized, and transparent authentication framework for connected environments.

3.5. Passwordless Authentication

Passwordless authentication is emerging as a transformative trend. Unlike traditional authentication methods that rely on passwords or PINs, passwordless authentication eliminates the need for users to remember complex passwords, thereby reducing the risk of credential-based attacks such as phishing and brute force attacks (Ebrahimpour & Babaie, 2024; Sengupta et al., 2020). This emerging trend leverages a variety of authentication factors (Almadani et al., 2023; Ometov et al., 2018), including biometrics (Yang et al., 2021), cryptographic keys, and device-based authentication (Mamdouh et al., 2021; C. Wang et al., 2020), to verify user identities without requiring a password. Biometric authentication methods, such as fingerprint recognition (Bezawada et al., 2021), facial recognition (Lien & Vhaduri, 2023; Yang et al., 2021), and iris scanning (Nguyen et al., 2024) offer a convenient and secure way for users to authenticate themselves using their unique physiological traits. Cryptographic keys, such as public-private key pairs, are another key component of passwordless authentication. These keys are generated and stored securely on the user's device or a hardware security module (HSM) (Butun et al., 2020), providing a tamper-resistant mechanism for verifying user identities without transmitting passwords over the network. Device-based authentication methods, such as authentication tokens (Dammak et al., 2019) and digital certificates further enhance the security of passwordless authentication by tying user identities to specific devices or hardware tokens.

4. SECURITY IMPLICATIONS AND THREAT LANDSCAPE

Security implications refer to the potential consequences or impacts that arise from security vulnerabilities, threats, or breaches within a system or environment (Radoglou Grammatikis et al., 2019). These implications can include risks to data confidentiality, integrity, and availability, as well as regulatory compliance, financial loss, reputational damage, and legal liabilities (Lata & Kumar, 2021). Security implications highlight the importance of identifying and mitigating security risks to prevent or minimize potential harm to an organization's operations, assets, and stakeholders. On the other hand, the threat landscape refers to the overall environment of potential cybersecurity threats facing an organization. It encompasses various factors such as the types of threats, their frequency, sophistication, and potential impact (Radoglou Grammatikis et al., 2019). The threat landscape is dynamic and constantly evolving, influenced by factors such as technological advancements, emerging attack techniques, and changes in the cybersecurity landscape.

4.1. Vulnerabilities

In the Vulnerability Analysis, an examination of potential weaknesses inherent in user authentication systems within IoT and IIoT environments is undertaken (Sengupta et al., 2020; C. Wang et al., 2020). Various facets of authentication, including authentication protocols, encryption methods, access control mechanisms, and user credential management practices, are investigated to identify vulnerabilities that could compromise the security and integrity of user authentication processes (Ebrahimpour & Babaie, 2024). Through a comprehensive assessment of authentication protocol vulnerabilities, encryption method vulnerabilities, access control vulnerabilities, and user credential management vulnerabilities, organizations can gain insights into the security posture of their IoT and IIoT environments.

4.2. Threat Analysis

Threat analysis in user authentication within IoT and IIoT environments is pivotal for safeguarding against evolving cybersecurity risks inherent in interconnected systems. As IoT devices proliferate across various domains, ranging from smart homes to industrial facilities, the potential attack surface for malicious actors expands exponentially (Ebrahimpour & Babaie, 2024; C. Wang et al., 2020). Threat analysis involves a systematic examination of potential vulnerabilities and risks that could compromise the integrity and security of user authentication mechanisms (Ebrahimpour & Babaie, 2024; Sengupta et al., 2020). By identifying and assessing these threats, organizations can proactively implement robust security measures to mitigate risks and ensure the resilience of authentication processes. The following list represents the main items in threat analysis:

1. **Identification and Profiling of Threat Actors:** In conducting a comprehensive threat analysis for user authentication in IoT environments, it's imperative first to identify and profile the various threat actors that pose risks to the security of authentication systems (C. Wang et al., 2020).

2. **Assessment of Attack Vectors and Common Threats:** It provides insight into the methods and strategies adversaries employ to compromise user authentication. Unauthorized access attempts are a prevalent threat, with attackers exploiting weak passwords, misconfigured settings, or unpatched vulnerabilities to enter IoT devices or networks (Radoglou Grammatikis et al., 2019; C. Wang et al., 2020).

3. **Evaluation of Emerging Threats:** The proliferation of IoT botnets (Al-Garadi et al., 2020; Boyes et al., 2018) capable of orchestrating large-scale attacks, highlights the need for robust authentication measures to thwart malicious (Butun et al., 2020; Radoglou Grammatikis et al., 2019; Ragothaman et al., 2023; Syed et al., 2022).

4.3. Risk Mitigation

In the domain of user authentication within IoT and IIoT environments, effective risk mitigation strategies and adherence to compliance standards are paramount for ensuring the security and integrity of connected systems (Lee, 2020). Risk mitigation includes identifying, assessing, and prioritizing potential threats and vulnerabilities, followed by the implementation of measures to reduce their likelihood and impact (Al-Naji & Zagrouba, 2020; Ebrahimpour & Babaie, 2024; C. Wang et al., 2020). This includes deploying robust authentication protocols, encryption mechanisms, and access control mechanisms to fortify defenses against unauthorized access, data breaches, and cyberattacks (Ebrahimpour & Babaie, 2024; Sengupta et al., 2020). Additionally, proactive monitoring, threat intelligence sharing, and incident response planning play crucial roles in mitigating risks and minimizing the impact of security incidents (Lee, 2020)..

4.4. Emerging Threats Monitoring and Incident Response

Emerging Threats Monitoring and Incident Response represent critical components of cybersecurity strategies in IoT and IIoT environments. There is a need to focus on the proactive surveillance and rapid response mechanisms necessary to address evolving security threats effectively (Makhdoom et al., 2019; C. Wang et al., 2020). It involves continuous monitoring of emerging threats, vulnerabilities, and attack vectors specific to IoT and IIoT landscapes (Radoglou Grammatikis et al., 2019). By leveraging threat intelligence feeds (Liang et al., 2020), security analysts can stay abreast of emerging trends, tactics, and techniques employed by threat actors targeting connected devices and systems. In parallel, robust incident response protocols are essential for promptly detecting (Ebrahimpour & Babaie, 2024), containing, and mitigating security incidents within IoT and IIoT ecosystems (Feng et al., 2024; Radoglou Grammatikis et al., 2019). This includes establishing clear escalation procedures, incident classification criteria, and responses tailored to the unique characteristics of connected environments (Mamdouh et al., 2021; Sengupta et al., 2020; Tawalbeh et al., 2020).

5. INDUSTRY COMPLIANCE AND REGULATORY CONSIDERATIONS

In navigating the landscape of user authentication in IoT and IIoT environments, industry compliance and regulatory considerations serve as guiding principles, ensuring that organizations adhere to established standards and legal requirements in their authentication practices (Ragothaman et al., 2023). This section presents the regulatory frameworks, standards, and industry guidelines that shape the security posture of authentication mechanisms within connected ecosystems (Ebrahimpour & Babaie, 2024; Mohamad Noor & Hassan, 2019). From stringent data privacy regulations to sector-specific compliance mandates, organizations must navigate a complex web of legal obligations to safeguard sensitive user information and ensure the integrity of their authentication systems (Sengupta et al., 2020).

At the forefront of industry compliance are regulatory frameworks such as the General Data Protection Regulation (GDPR) from the European Commission, the European Telecommunications Standards Institute (ETSI), and the National Institute of Standards and Technologies (NIST), which establish stringent guidelines for data protection, privacy, and security across various sectors (Lata & Kumar, 2021). These frameworks set the foundation for robust authentication practices, requiring organizations to implement comprehensive safeguards to mitigate the risk of unauthorized access and protect user credentials. Table 1 provides an overview of various regulatory frameworks for IoT security, along with brief descriptions, applicability, and key requirements associated with each framework. It can serve as a reference for organizations navigating compliance requirements and implementing security measures for their IoT deployments. One significant aspect is data privacy regulations, such as the GDPR in the European Union and the California Consumer Privacy Act (CCPA) in the United States. These regulations mandate strict protocols for handling personal data, including consent mechanisms, breach notification procedures, and privacy by design principles. Moreover, security compliance requirements, like those outlined in the Health Insurance Portability and Accountability Act (HIPAA) and the National Institute of Standards and Technology (NIST) Cybersecurity Framework, establish standards for safeguarding sensitive information and mitigating cyber threats (Lata & Kumar, 2021; Ragothaman et al., 2023).

Table 1. Various regulatory frameworks for IoT security

Regulatory Framework	Description	Applicability	Key Requirements
General Data Protection Regulation (GDPR, 2016)	Comprehensive data protection law in the EU, regulating the processing of personal data.	Organizations handling personal data of EU residents	Data protection, user consent, breach notification, privacy by design and default
California Consumer Privacy Act (CCPA, 2018)	State-level privacy law in California, granting consumers rights over their personal information.	Organizations operating in California	Consumer data rights, transparency, opt-out mechanisms, prohibition against discrimination
Health Insurance Portability and Accountability Act (HIPAA, 2009)	Federal law in the US establishing privacy and security standards for protected health information.	Healthcare organizations and their business associates	Protected health information (PHI) safeguarding, privacy practices, security controls
National Institute of Standards and Technology: Cybersecurity Framework (NIST, 2024)	Framework for improving cybersecurity across sectors, providing guidelines and best practices.	Organizations seeking to enhance cybersecurity resilience	Risk management, security controls, continuous improvement
European Telecommunications Standards Institute: IoT Security Standards (ETSI, 2020)	Standards addressing security challenges in IoT ecosystems, covering authentication, encryption, etc.	IoT device manufacturers, service providers	Device authentication, secure communication protocols, data encryption
International Organization for Standardization (ISO)	International standards ensuring quality, safety, and efficiency, including information security.	Organizations seeking to establish security management systems	Information security management, risk assessment, security controls, continuous improvement
Federal Information Processing Standards (NIST-FIPS, 2008)	US government standards specifying security requirements for federal agencies and contractors.	US government agencies, contractors	Cryptographic module security, data protection, compliance with federal regulations

6. PRACTICAL RECOMMENDATIONS FOR IMPLEMENTATION

Practical recommendations for implementing robust user authentication in IoT and IIoT environments are crucial for ensuring the security and integrity of connected systems. Organizations should adopt a layered approach to authentication, incorporating multiple factors such as passwords, biometrics, and tokens to enhance security (Lata & Kumar, 2021). Another important consideration is the implementation of access control mechanisms to restrict unauthorized access to sensitive resources and functionalities. Role-based access control (RBAC) and least privilege principles should be employed to ensure that users and devices only have access to the resources necessary for their roles and responsibilities (Ragothaman et al., 2023). Moreover, organizations should invest in employee training and awareness programs to educate users about the importance of strong authentication practices and security hygiene. This includes teaching users how to create and manage secure passwords, recognize phishing attempts, and report suspicious activities (Corallo et al., 2022).

6.1. Layered Authentication Approach

The Layered Authentication Approach involves the implementation of multiple authentication factors to strengthen security measures within IoT and IIoT environments (Ometov et al., 2018). By employing a combination of different authentication methods, such as passwords, biometrics, tokens, and behavioral analytics, organizations can create layers of defense against unauthorized access attempts (Almadani et al., 2023). This approach adds complexity for potential attackers, as they would need to overcome multiple hurdles to gain access to sensitive resources. Additionally, layering authentication methods can provide redundancy and resilience, reducing the likelihood of successful security breaches (Lien & Vhaduri, 2023).

6.2. Access Control Mechanisms

Access control mechanisms play a pivotal role in ensuring the security and integrity of IoT and IIoT environments by regulating user access to resources, devices, and data (Ragothaman et al., 2023). Implementing robust access control mechanisms involves several key components:

1. **Role-Based Access Control (RBAC):** RBAC assigns permissions to users based on their roles within an organization (Radoglou Grammatikis et al., 2019).
2. **Least Privilege Principle:** The least privilege principle restricts user access rights to the minimum level required to perform their tasks (Syed et al., 2022).
3. **Access Policies and Enforcement:** Establishing clear access policies and enforcing them through technical controls ensures compliance with security requirements.
4. **Continuous Monitoring and Auditing:** Continuous monitoring of user access activities and regular auditing of access logs help detect and mitigate security incidents in real time.

6.3. Employee Training and Awareness

Employee training and awareness programs are crucial elements of user authentication in IoT and IIoT environments. These initiatives aim to educate employees on cybersecurity principles, their roles in protecting sensitive information, and best practices for mitigating security risks. By following the culture of security awareness, organizations can enhance the overall resilience of their IoT and IIoT ecosystems (Corallo et al., 2022). One key aspect of employee training is to ensure familiarity with the organization's user authentication policies and procedures (Ragothaman et al., 2023). Phishing awareness is another critical focus area in employee training. Phishing attacks pose significant threats to user authentication in IoT and IIoT environments (Ebrahimpour & Babaie, 2024; Sengupta et al., 2020), making it essential for employees to recognize and report phishing attempts.

7. CASE STUDIES AND REAL-WORLD APPLICATIONS

7.1. Wi-Fi User Authentication Case Study

In response to the escalating concerns surrounding security and user experience within IoT environments, organizations undertook a strategic endeavor to implement Wi-Fi user authentication leveraging IoT devices (C. Shi et al., 2017). Driven by the imperative for fortified security measures and the desire to streamline user authentication processes, the organization embarked on a journey to explore innovative solutions utilizing Wi-Fi signals as a cornerstone of its authentication framework (C. Shi et al., 2021). Figure 2 shows an example of using Wi-Fi signal antenna for user authentication.

Figure 2. Using Wi-Fi signal antenna for user authentication (C. Shi et al., 2017)

The implementation strategy began with an integration of Wi-Fi-enabled IoT devices into the organization's existing infrastructure. This integration process emphasized seamless compatibility and the establishment of robust, secure communication channels to ensure the integrity of data transmission between devices and authentication systems (Jiang et al., 2018). With the IoT devices seamlessly integrated, the organization turned its focus towards the analysis of Wi-Fi signals—a pivotal component of the authentication process (C. Shi et al., 2017). Advanced signal processing techniques were deployed to dissect and interpret the intricate characteristics of Wi-Fi signals (Jiang et al., 2018). Through deep analysis, unique features indicative of user interactions with IoT devices were extracted, laying the groundwork for robust authentication mechanisms. Leveraging the insights from Wi-Fi signal analysis (Jiang et al., 2018), relevant features capturing users' physiological and behavioral traits were carefully extracted (Al-Garadi et al., 2020) and complemented by the deployment of sophisticated machine-learning models (Al-Garadi et al., 2020; Amanullah et al., 2020).

7.2. Smart Home Security

This case study explores the implementation of user authentication in a smart home environment, focusing on enhancing security through advanced biometric methods. The smart home setup includes a variety of IoT devices such as smart locks, security cameras, and automated lighting and heating systems, all interconnected to provide convenience and security for the residents. The smart home system integrates fingerprint recognition technology to secure access to the home and its various IoT devices. Each family member's fingerprint is registered and stored securely in the system. Smart locks on doors and windows are equipped with fingerprint scanners, allowing authorized users to unlock them with a simple touch. Additionally, security cameras with facial recognition capabilities are installed at entry points to verify identities and grant access accordingly.

The implementation faced several challenges, including environmental factors such as dust and oil affecting fingerprint scanner accuracy. Variations in lighting conditions also impacted the performance of facial recognition cameras. Furthermore, there were initial concerns about user acceptance and the learning curve associated with using biometric authentication systems. To address these challenges, the system was enhanced with multi-factor authentication, combining fingerprint recognition with traditional PIN codes for added security.

8. FUTURE DIRECTIONS AND CONCLUDING REMARKS

Looking towards the future of user authentication in the IoT and IIoT landscape, it is evident that ongoing advancements in technology will shape the evolution of security measures. As we move forward, the integration of biometric authentication, behavioral analytics, and AI-driven solutions will become increasingly prevalent, offering enhanced security while ensuring seamless user experiences. Additionally, the rise of decentralized identity frameworks, such as blockchain-based authentication, holds promise for bolstering security and privacy in connected ecosystems. However, alongside technological advancements, it is crucial to address emerging threats and vulnerabilities proactively. Collaborative efforts between industry stakeholders, researchers, and policymakers will be essential in driving innovation and establishing robust regulatory frameworks to safeguard IoT and IIoT environments. In conclusion, the journey towards securing IoT and IIoT systems is dynamic and ongoing, requiring continuous adaptation and collaboration to stay ahead of evolving cyber threats and ensure the integrity of connected ecosystems.

REFERENCES

Aboukadri, S., Ouaddah, A., & Mezrioui, A. (2024). Machine learning in identity and access management systems: Survey and deep dive. *Computers and Security, 139*, 103729. 10.1016/j.cose.2024.103729

Abu Waraga, O., Bettayeb, M., Nasir, Q., & Abu Talib, M. (2020). Design and implementation of automated IoT security testbed. *Computers & Security*, 88, 101648. Advance online publication. 10.1016/j.cose.2019.101648

Abuhamad, M., Abusnaina, A., Nyang, D., & Mohaisen, D. (2021). Sensor-Based Continuous Authentication of Smartphones' Users Using Behavioral Biometrics: A Contemporary Survey. *IEEE Internet of Things Journal*, 8(1), 65–84. 10.1109/JIOT.2020.3020076

Adi, E., Anwar, A., Baig, Z., & Zeadally, S. (2020). Machine learning and data analytics for the IoT. *Neural Computing & Applications*, 32(20), 16205–16233. 10.1007/s00521-020-04874-y

Al-Garadi, M. A., Mohamed, A., Al-Ali, A. K., Du, X., Ali, I., & Guizani, M. (2020). A Survey of Machine and Deep Learning Methods for Internet of Things (IoT) Security. *IEEE Communications Surveys and Tutorials*, 22(3), 1646–1685. 10.1109/COMST.2020.2988293

Al-Naji, F. H., & Zagrouba, R. (2020). A survey on continuous authentication methods in Internet of Things environment. *Computer Communications*, 163(June), 109–133. 10.1016/j.comcom.2020.09.006

Albayram, Y., Khan, M. M. H., Bamis, A., Kentros, S., Nguyen, N., & Jiang, R. (2014). A location-based authentication system leveraging smartphones. *Proceedings - IEEE International Conference on Mobile Data Management, 1*, 83–88. 10.1109/MDM.2014.16

Almadani, M. S., Alotaibi, S., Alsobhi, H., Hussain, O. K., & Hussain, F. K. (2023). Blockchain-based multi-factor authentication: A systematic literature review. *Internet of Things : Engineering Cyber Physical Human Systems*, 23(June), 100844. 10.1016/j.iot.2023.100844

Amanullah, M. A., Habeeb, R. A. A., Nasaruddin, F. H., Gani, A., Ahmed, E., Nainar, A. S. M., Akim, N. M., & Imran, M. (2020). Deep learning and big data technologies for IoT security. *Computer Communications, 151*, 495–517. 10.1016/j.comcom.2020.01.016

Andriotis, P., Tryfonas, T., Oikonomou, G., & Yildiz, C. (2013). A pilot study on the security of pattern screen-lock methods and soft side channel attacks. *WiSec 2013 - Proceedings of the 6th ACM Conference on Security and Privacy in Wireless and Mobile Networks*, 1–6. 10.1145/2462096.2462098

Axente, M. S., Dobre, C., Ciobanu, R. I., & Purnichescu-Purtan, R. (2020). Gait recognition as an authentication method for mobile devices. *Sensors (Basel)*, 20(15), 1–17. 10.3390/s2015411032718088

Bezawada, B., Ray, I., & Ray, I. (2021). Behavioral fingerprinting of Internet-of-Things devices. *Wiley Interdisciplinary Reviews. Data Mining and Knowledge Discovery*, 11(1), 1–15. 10.1002/widm.1337

Bojinov, H., & Boneh, D. (2011). Mobile token-based authentication on a budget. *HotMobile 2011: The 12th Workshop on Mobile Computing Systems and Applications*, 14–19. 10.1145/2184489.2184494

Boyes, H., Hallaq, B., Cunningham, J., & Watson, T. (2018). The industrial internet of things (IIoT): An analysis framework. *Computers in Industry*, 101(June), 1–12. 10.1016/j.compind.2018.04.015

Butun, I., Sari, A., & Österberg, P. (2020). Hardware security of fog end-devices for the internet of things. *Sensors (Basel)*, 20(20), 1–28. 10.3390/s2020572933050165

CCPA. (2018). *California Consumer Privacy Act (CCPA)*. https://oag.ca.gov/privacy/ccpa

Chao, J., Hossain, M. S., & Lancor, L. (2023). Swipe gestures for user authentication in smartphones. *Journal of Information Security and Applications*, 74(March), 103450. 10.1016/j.jisa.2023.103450

Corallo, A., Lazoi, M., Lezzi, M., & Luperto, A. (2022). Cybersecurity awareness in the context of the Industrial Internet of Things: A systematic literature review. *Computers in Industry*, 137, 103614. Advance online publication. 10.1016/j.compind.2022.103614

Dammak, M., Boudia, O. R. M., Messous, M. A., Senouci, S. M., & Gransart, C. (2019). Token-Based Lightweight Authentication to Secure IoT Networks. *2019 16th IEEE Annual Consumer Communications and Networking Conference, CCNC 2019*. 10.1109/CCNC.2019.8651825

De Marsico, M., & Mecca, A. (2019). A survey on gait recognition via wearable sensors. *ACM Computing Surveys*, 52(4), 1–39. Advance online publication. 10.1145/3340293

Deb, D., & Jain, A. K. (2021). Look Locally Infer Globally: A Generalizable Face Anti-Spoofing Approach. *IEEE Transactions on Information Forensics and Security*, 16, 1143–1157. 10.1109/TIFS.2020.3029879

Ebrahimpour, E., & Babaie, S. (2024). Authentication in Internet of Things, protocols, attacks, and open issues: A systematic literature review. *International Journal of Information Security*, 23(3), 1583–1602. Advance online publication. 10.1007/s10207-023-00806-8

ETSI. (2020). *European Telecommunications Standards Institute*. https://www.etsi.org/

Feng, J., Yan, R., Han, G., & Zhang, W. (2024). BDPM: A secure batch dynamic password management scheme in industrial internet environments. *Future Generation Computer Systems, 157*, 193–209. 10.1016/j.future.2024.03.030

GDPR. (2016). *General Data Protection Regulation (GDPR)*. https://gdpr-info.eu/

Ghimire, B., & Rawat, D. B. (2022). Recent Advances on Federated Learning for Cybersecurity and Cybersecurity for Federated Learning for Internet of Things. *IEEE Internet of Things Journal*, 9(11), 8229–8249. 10.1109/JIOT.2022.3150363

Harbach, M., von Zezschwitz, E., Fichtner, A., De Luca, A., & Smith, M. (2016). It's a Hard Lock Life: A Field Study of Smartphone (Un)Locking Behavior and Risk Perception. *SOUPS '14: Proceedings of the Tenth Symposium On Usable Privacy and Security*, 213–230. https://www.usenix.org/conference/soups2014/proceedings/presentation/harbach

Hazra, A., Adhikari, M., Amgoth, T., & Srirama, S. N. (2021). A Comprehensive Survey on Interoperability for IIoT: Taxonomy, Standards, and Future Directions. *ACM Computing Surveys*, 55(1), 1–35. 10.1145/3485130

HIPAA. (2009). *Health Insurance Portability and Accountability Act (HIPAA)*. https://www.hhs.gov/hipaa/index.html

Islam, M. R. (2014). Feature and score fusion based multiple classifier selection for iris recognition. *Computational Intelligence and Neuroscience*, 2014, 1–11. 10.1155/2014/38058525114676

Jiang, H., Cai, C., Ma, X., Yang, Y., & Liu, J. (2018). Smart Home Based on WiFi Sensing: A Survey. *IEEE Access: Practical Innovations, Open Solutions*, 6, 13317–13325. 10.1109/ACCESS.2018.2812887

Khan, H., Hengartner, U., & Vogel, D. (2016). Targeted mimicry attacks on touch input based implicit authentication schemes. *MobiSys 2016 - Proceedings of the 14th Annual International Conference on Mobile Systems, Applications, and Services*, 387–398. 10.1145/2906388.2906404

Khan, H., Hengartner, U., & Vogel, D. (2019). Usability and security perceptions of implicit authentication: Convenient, secure, sometimes annoying. *SOUPS 2015 - Proceedings of the 11th Symposium on Usable Privacy and Security*, 225–239. https://www.usenix.org/conference/soups2015/proceedings/presentation/khan

Khanh, Q. V., Hoai, N. V., Manh, L. D., Le, A. N., & Jeon, G. (2022). Wireless Communication Technologies for IoT in 5G: Vision, Applications, and Challenges. *Wireless Communications and Mobile Computing*, 2022, 1–12. Advance online publication. 10.1155/2022/3229294

Kong, H., Lu, L., Yu, J., Chen, Y., Kong, L., & Li, M. (2019). Fingerpass: Finger gesture-based continuous user authentication for smart homes using commodity wifi. *Proceedings of the International Symposium on Mobile Ad Hoc Networking and Computing (MobiHoc)*, 201–210. 10.1145/3323679.3326518

Krawiecka, K., Birnbach, S., Eberz, S., & Martinovic, I. (2023). BeeHIVE: Behavioral Biometric System Based on Object Interactions in Smart Environments. In *Proceedings of the International Conference on Security and Cryptography* (Vol. 1, Issue 1). Association for Computing Machinery. 10.5220/0012088900003555

Kumar, R., & Agrawal, N. (2023). Analysis of multi-dimensional Industrial IoT (IIoT) data in Edge–Fog–Cloud based architectural frameworks : A survey on current state and research challenges. *Journal of Industrial Information Integration, 35*, 100504. 10.1016/j.jii.2023.100504

Kuncheva, L. I. (2014). Combining Pattern Classifiers: Methods and Algorithms: Second Edition. In *Combining Pattern Classifiers: Methods and Algorithms: Second Edition* (Vol. 9781118315). John Wiley & Sons. 10.1002/9781118914564

Lata, M., & Kumar, V. (2021). Standards and regulatory compliances for IoT security. *International Journal of Service Science, Management, Engineering, and Technology*, 12(5), 133–147. 10.4018/IJSSMET.2021090109

Lee, I. (2020). Internet of Things (IoT) cybersecurity: Literature review and iot cyber risk management. *Future Internet*, 12(9), 157. Advance online publication. 10.3390/fi12090157

Li, Y., Yang, J., Xie, M., Carlson, D., Jang, H. G., & Bian, J. (2015). Comparison of PIN- and pattern-based behavioral biometric authentication on mobile devices. *Proceedings - IEEE Military Communications Conference MILCOM*, 1317–1322. 10.1109/MILCOM.2015.7357627

Liang, Y., Samtani, S., Guo, B., & Yu, Z. (2020). Behavioral Biometrics for Continuous Authentication in the Internet-of-Things Era: An Artificial Intelligence Perspective. *IEEE Internet of Things Journal*, 7(9), 9128–9143. 10.1109/JIOT.2020.3004077

Lien, C. W., & Vhaduri, S. (2023). Challenges and Opportunities of Biometric User Authentication in the Age of IoT: A Survey. *ACM Computing Surveys*, 56(1), 1–37. 10.1145/3603705

Liu, C., Clark, G. D., & Lindqvist, J. (2017). Where usability and security go hand-in-hand: Robust gesture-based authentication for mobile systems. *Conference on Human Factors in Computing Systems - Proceedings*, 374–386. 10.1145/3025453.3025879

Mahfouz, A., Hamdy, A., Eldin, M. A., & Mahmoud, T. M. (2024). B2auth: A contextual fine-grained behavioral biometric authentication framework for real-world deployment. *Pervasive and Mobile Computing, 99*, 101888. 10.1016/j.pmcj.2024.101888

Makhdoom, I., Abolhasan, M., Lipman, J., Liu, R. P., & Ni, W. (2019). Anatomy of Threats to the Internet of Things. *IEEE Communications Surveys and Tutorials*, 21(2), 1636–1675. 10.1109/COMST.2018.2874978

Mamdouh, M., Awad, A. I., Khalaf, A. A. M., & Hamed, H. F. A. (2021). Authentication and Identity Management of IoHT Devices: Achievements, Challenges, and Future Directions. *Computers & Security*, 111, 102491. 10.1016/j.cose.2021.102491

Masud, M., Gaba, G. S., Choudhary, K., Hossain, M. S., Alhamid, M. F., & Muhammad, G. (2022). Lightweight and Anonymity-Preserving User Authentication Scheme for IoT-Based Healthcare. *IEEE Internet of Things Journal*, 9(4), 2649–2656. 10.1109/JIOT.2021.3080461

Mohamad Noor, M., & Hassan, W. H. (2019). Current research on Internet of Things (IoT) security: A survey. *Computer Networks*, 148, 283–294. 10.1016/j.comnet.2018.11.025

Mondal, S., & Bours, P. (2017). A study on continuous authentication using a combination of keystroke and mouse biometrics. *Neurocomputing, 230*, 1–22. 10.1016/j.neucom.2016.11.031

Muaaz, M., & Mayrhofer, R. (2017). Smartphone-Based Gait Recognition: From Authentication to Imitation. *IEEE Transactions on Mobile Computing*, 16(11), 3209–3221. 10.1109/TMC.2017.2686855

Nguyen, K., Proença, H., & Alonso-Fernandez, F. (2024). Deep Learning for Iris Recognition: A Survey. *ACM Computing Surveys*, 56(9), 1–35. Advance online publication. 10.1145/3651306

NIST. (2024). *National Institute of Standards and Technology (Nist)*. https://www.nist.gov/

NIST-FIPS. (2008). *Federal Information Processing Standards*. NIST-FIPS. https://www.nist.gov/itl/fips-general-information

Ometov, A., Bezzateev, S., Mäkitalo, N., Andreev, S., Mikkonen, T., & Koucheryavy, Y. (2018). Multi-factor authentication: A survey. *Cryptography*, 2(1), 1–31. 10.3390/cryptography2010001

Omolara, A. E., Alabdulatif, A., Abiodun, O. I., Alawida, M., Alabdulatif, A., Alshoura, W. H., & Arshad, H. (2022). The internet of things security: A survey encompassing unexplored areas and new insights. *Computers & Security*, 112, 102494. 10.1016/j.cose.2021.102494

Owusu, E., Han, J., Das, S., Perrig, A., & Zhang, J. (2012). ACCessory: Password inference using accelerometers on smartphones. *HotMobile 2012 - 13th Workshop on Mobile Computing Systems and Applications*, 1. 10.1145/2162081.2162095

Peng, G., Zhou, G., Nguyen, D. T., Qi, X., Yang, Q., & Wang, S. (2017). Continuous Authentication With Touch Behavioral Biometrics and Voice on Wearable Glasses. *IEEE Transactions on Human-Machine Systems*, 47(3), 404–416. 10.1109/THMS.2016.2623562

Pulfrey, J., & Hossain, M. S. (2022). Zoom gesture analysis for age-inappropriate internet content filtering. *Expert Systems with Applications*, 199(March), 116869. 10.1016/j.eswa.2022.116869

Radoglou Grammatikis, P. I., Sarigiannidis, P. G., & Moscholios, I. D. (2019). Securing the Internet of Things: Challenges, threats and solutions. *Internet of Things : Engineering Cyber Physical Human Systems*, 5, 41–70. 10.1016/j.iot.2018.11.003

Ragothaman, K., Wang, Y., Rimal, B., & Lawrence, M. (2023). Access Control for IoT: A Survey of Existing Research, Dynamic Policies and Future Directions. *Sensors (Basel)*, 23(4), 1–24. 10.3390/s2304180536850403

Saqib, M., & Moon, A. H. (2023). A Systematic Security Assessment and Review of Internet of Things in the Context of Authentication. *Computers & Security*, 125, 103053. 10.1016/j.cose.2022.103053

Sayed, A., Kinlany, S., Zaki, A., & Mahfouz, A. (2023). VeriFace: Defending against Adversarial Attacks in Face Verification Systems. *Computers, Materials & Continua*, 76(3), 3151–3166. 10.32604/cmc.2023.040256

Schroff, F., Kalenichenko, D., & Philbin, J. (2015). FaceNet: A unified embedding for face recognition and clustering. *Proceedings of the IEEE Computer Society Conference on Computer Vision and Pattern Recognition*, 815–823. 10.1109/CVPR.2015.7298682

Sengupta, J., Ruj, S., & Das Bit, S. (2020). A Comprehensive Survey on Attacks, Security Issues and Blockchain Solutions for IoT and IIoT. *Journal of Network and Computer Applications, 149*, 102481. 10.1016/j.jnca.2019.102481

Shao, R., Perera, P., Yuen, P. C., & Patel, V. M. (2022). Federated Generalized Face Presentation Attack Detection. *IEEE Transactions on Neural Networks and Learning Systems.* Advance online publication. 10.1109/TNNLS.2022.317231635609091

Shi, C., Liu, J., Liu, H., & Chen, Y. (2017). Smart User authentication through actuation of daily activities leveraging wifi-enabled IoT. *Proceedings of the International Symposium on Mobile Ad Hoc Networking and Computing (MobiHoc), Part F1291*, 1–10. 10.1145/3084041.3084061

Shi, C., Liu, J., Liu, H., & Chen, Y. (2021). WiFi-Enabled User Authentication through Deep Learning in Daily Activities. *ACM Transactions on Internet of Things*, 2(2), 1–25. 10.1145/3448738

Shi, C., Wang, Y., Chen, Y., Saxena, N., & Wang, C. (2020). WearID: Low-Effort Wearable-Assisted Authentication of Voice Commands via Cross-Domain Comparison without Training. In *ACM International Conference Proceeding Series* (Vol. 1, Issue 1). Association for Computing Machinery. 10.1145/3427228.3427259

Shi, D., Tao, D., Wang, J., Yao, M., Wang, Z., Chen, H., & Helal, S. (2021). Fine-Grained and Context-Aware Behavioral Biometrics for Pattern Lock on Smartphones. *Proceedings of the ACM on Interactive, Mobile, Wearable and Ubiquitous Technologies*, 5(1), 1–30. 10.1145/3448080

Sisinni, E., Saifullah, A., Han, S., Jennehag, U., & Gidlund, M. (2018). Industrial internet of things: Challenges, opportunities, and directions. *IEEE Transactions on Industrial Informatics*, 14(11), 4724–4734. 10.1109/TII.2018.2852491

Smith, M., & Hans, M. (2004). Sensor-Enhanced Authentication Token for Dynamic Identity Management Sensor-Enhanced Authentication Token for Dynamic Identity Management. *Hp*.

Stylios, I., Chatzis, S., Thanou, O., & Kokolakis, S. (2023). Continuous authentication with feature-level fusion of touch gestures and keystroke dynamics to solve security and usability issues. *Computers & Security*, 132, 103363. 10.1016/j.cose.2023.103363

Syed, N. F., Shah, S. W., Shaghaghi, A., Anwar, A., Baig, Z., & Doss, R. (2022). Zero Trust Architecture (ZTA): A Comprehensive Survey. *IEEE Access: Practical Innovations, Open Solutions*, 10, 57143–57179. 10.1109/ACCESS.2022.3174679

Taigman, Y., Yang, M., Ranzato, M., & Wolf, L. (2014). DeepFace: Closing the gap to human-level performance in face verification. *Proceedings of the IEEE Computer Society Conference on Computer Vision and Pattern Recognition*, 1701–1708. 10.1109/CVPR.2014.220

Tawalbeh, L., Muheidat, F., Tawalbeh, M., & Quwaider, M. (2020). IoT privacy and security: Challenges and solutions. *Applied Sciences (Basel, Switzerland)*, 10(12), 1–17. 10.3390/app10124102

Tolosana, R., Vera-Rodriguez, R., & Fierrez, J. (2020). BioTouchPass: Handwritten Passwords for Touchscreen Biometrics. *IEEE Transactions on Mobile Computing*, 19(7), 1532–1543. 10.1109/TMC.2019.2911506

Vhaduri, S., & Poellabauer, C. (2019). Multi-modal biometric-based implicit authentication of wearable device users. *IEEE Transactions on Information Forensics and Security*, 14(12), 3116–3125. 10.1109/TIFS.2019.2911170

Von Zezschwitz, E., Dunphy, P., & De Luca, A. (2013). Patterns in the wild: A field study of the usability of pattern and PIN-based authentication on mobile devices. *MobileHCI 2013 - Proceedings of the 15th International Conference on Human-Computer Interaction with Mobile Devices and Services*, 261–270. 10.1145/2493190.2493231

Wang, C., Wang, Y., Chen, Y., Liu, H., & Liu, J. (2020). User authentication on mobile devices: Approaches, threats and trends. *Computer Networks*, 170, 107118. 10.1016/j.comnet.2020.107118

Wang, F., Xiang, X., Cheng, J., & Yuille, A. L. (2017). NormFace: L2 hypersphere embedding for face verification. *MM 2017 - Proceedings of the 2017 ACM Multimedia Conference*, 1041–1049. 10.1145/3123266.3123359

Xiao, L., Wan, X., Lu, X., Zhang, Y., & Wu, D. (2018). IoT Security Techniques Based on Machine Learning: How Do IoT Devices Use AI to Enhance Security? *IEEE Signal Processing Magazine*, 35(5), 41–49. 10.1109/MSP.2018.2825478

Xu, W., Shen, Y., Zhang, Y., Bergmann, N., & Hu, W. (2017). Gait-watch: A context-aware authentication system for smart watch based on gait recognition. *Proceedings - 2017 IEEE/ACM 2nd International Conference on Internet-of-Things Design and Implementation, IoTDI 2017 (Part of CPS Week)*, 59–70. 10.1145/3054977.3054991

Yang, W., Wang, S., Sahri, N. M., Karie, N. M., Ahmed, M., & Valli, C. (2021). Biometrics for internet-of-things security: A review. *Sensors (Basel)*, 21(18), 1–26. 10.3390/s2118616334577370

Zaidi, A. Z., Chong, C. Y., Jin, Z., Parthiban, R., & Sadiq, A. S. (2021). Touch-based continuous mobile device authentication: State-of-the-art, challenges and opportunities. *Journal of Network and Computer Applications*, 191(June), 103162. 10.1016/j.jnca.2021.103162

Zhang, J., Li, Z., Zhang, H., Zhang, W., Ling, Z., & Yang, M. (2023). Sensor-based implicit authentication through learning user physiological and behavioral characteristics. *Computer Communications*, 208(March), 244–255. 10.1016/j.comcom.2023.06.016

Zhang, L., Tan, S., & Yang, J. (2017). Hearing Your Voice is Not Enough: An Articulatory gesture based liveness detection for voice authentication. *Proceedings of the ACM Conference on Computer and Communications Security*, 57–71. 10.1145/3133956.3133962

Zhou, M., Wang, Q., Yang, J., Li, Q., Xiao, F., Wang, Z., & Chen, X. (2018). PatternListener: Cracking android pattern lock using acoustic signals. *Proceedings of the ACM Conference on Computer and Communications Security*, 1775–1787. 10.1145/3243734.3243777

Zimmermann, V., & Gerber, N. (2020). The password is dead, long live the password – A laboratory study on user perceptions of authentication schemes. *International Journal of Human Computer Studies*, 133, 26–44. 10.1016/j.ijhcs.2019.08.006

Zou, Q., Wang, Y., Wang, Q., Zhao, Y., & Li, Q. (2020). Deep Learning-Based Gait Recognition Using Smartphones in the Wild. *IEEE Transactions on Information Forensics and Security*, 15, 3197–3212. 10.1109/TIFS.2020.2985628

Chapter 9
Security of Connected Devices:
Challenges and Solutions

Stéphanie Chollet
Laboratoire de Conception et d'Intégration des Systèmes, France

Arthur Desuert
Laboratoire de Conception et d'Intégration des Systèmes, France

David Hély
Laboratoire de Conception et d'Intégration des Systèmes, France

Laurent Pion
Laboratoire de Conception et d'Intégration des Systèmes, France

ABSTRACT

Connected devices have become increasingly prevalent in the daily lives of human users, forming the basis of smart spaces designed to provide valuable services, such as remote control of users' homes or efficient energy usage in large buildings. However, they also pose significant challenges, particularly in terms of security. This chapter aims to clearly define these challenges, focusing on device authentication, data confidentiality, and integrity. It begins by outlining a classical architecture for connecting devices and applications in commercial or industrial smart spaces. Various facets of this framework are explored, emphasizing the security requisites. The authors then delve into several key points of this architecture and explore the associated security needs. Current technologies are introduced, along with proof of concept from recent research work, including the promising physically unclonable function (PUF) technology, which offers a cost-effective hardware primitive for enhancing security in connected devices.

INTRODUCTION

In the landscape of the Internet of Things (IoT) and Industrial Internet of Things (IIoT), the proliferation of connected devices has indeed ushered in a new era of technological interconnectivity. These devices, spanning from smart sensors to intelligent appliances, seamlessly integrate into our daily lives, gathering data and facilitating communication with remote platforms. As this ecosystem expands, it opens up numerous opportunities for pervasive applications (Weiser, 1995), which in turn create envi-

DOI: 10.4018/979-8-3693-3451-5.ch009

ronments that are not only intelligent but truly immersive. By harnessing the potential of these devices, pervasive applications seamlessly merge software systems into the physical world, offering to users intelligent environments characterized by ubiquitous ambient intelligence, seamless integration, and smooth operation (Escoffier et al., 2014).

However, the end user must be able to trust these increasingly intelligent device-based applications to adopt them into their daily lives. Nevertheless, many recent examples have shown that cyberattacks are possible, notably due to the low level of security of some connected objects. Therefore, it is essential, as a developer of such applications, to consider security issues in the development process from the design time, at both the software and hardware levels. An important aspect of security is to ensure the authenticity of connected devices from their manufacturing to their deployment in their runtime environment, and to also ensure the integrity and confidentiality of communications between other devices or with remote platforms.

Today, there is a wide variety of technologies used for integrating connected devices, particularly for IoT and IIoT communication protocols. These technologies vary in their suitability for constrained embedded systems, which may have limitations in terms of energy consumption, bandwidth, and latency. In terms of security, there is also a wide range of hardware and software solutions available. However, achieving a high level of security for connected devices is a challenge that may conflict with constraints such as energy consumption, bandwidth, latency, and user-friendliness. Additionally, securing a connected device inevitably increases its cost due to factors such as manufacturing expenses (e.g., adding specific electronic components), development costs, and maintenance. In general, a compromise must be struck between the level of security and the cost of the object for it to be adopted by users.

The aim of this chapter is to provide an overview of current solutions for securing connected devices. This chapter is organized as follows. After introducing key security concepts such as symmetric and asymmetric cryptography, a study of the main communication protocols currently used in IoT and IIoT applications is conducted, with a particular focus on how security is handled within these protocols. The security of protocols notably relies on the use of secrets. In a third part, we explore how secrets can be managed in a hardware-based manner to ensure their secrecy. Finally, before concluding, we present the results of recent works on lightweight protocols based on PUF for device authentication.

SECURITY BACKGROUND

Symmetric and Asymmetric Cryptography

There are two main categories of cryptographic encryption algorithms: symmetric and asymmetric cryptography algorithms.

In symmetric cryptography, a single key is used to encrypt and decrypt the message. The algorithms in this category have both an encryption function and a decryption function, which utilize this key. Symmetric algorithms consist of a series of linear and non-linear operations between the input data and the key, repeated a certain number of times. Thus, a symmetric key is simply a data vector of a defined size, often expressed in bits. Generating a symmetric key involves creating a vector of random data of the desired size. If the key generation is truly unpredictable, an attacker will have no choice but to test all possible keys in hopes of finding the used key. This constitutes a brute-force attack. By choosing a sufficiently large key size, greater than 128 bits according to the recommendations of renowned organizations like ANSSI[1], the time required to test all possible key combinations exceeds decades or even centuries. The success chances of this attack are then considered negligible.

Symmetric algorithms are known for their performance due to the simple operations they use and the small size of their keys, compared to asymmetric algorithms. This makes them an ideal choice for securing systems with limited resources. A delicate aspect of these algorithms is key distribution. Secure distribution methods must therefore be planned, potentially through a different channel than the standard communication channel. The scope of key usage is also an important characteristic: it can range from a single key for all participants in a communication network to a different key for each pair of participants. The latter solution is much more secure in terms of isolating communications between different participants: in the event of a key theft, only the communication link between a pair of participants is compromised and not the entire system. However, this solution is also much more complex to manage and scale as the number of participants increases, due to the exponential growth in the number of keys.

Some well-known examples of symmetric cryptographic algorithms include the Triple Data Encryption Algorithm (TDEA), standardized by RFC 1851 (Kan et al., 1995), the Advanced Encryption Standard (AES), standardized by NIST (Dworkin et al., 2001), and Chacha20, standardized by RFC 7539 (Nir and Langley, 2015), RFC 7634 (Nir, 2015), and RFC 7905 (Langley et al., 2016).

In asymmetric cryptography, a key has two parts that play distinct roles. One part of the key is named private, while the other part is named public. The private part allows obtaining the public part of the key, but the public part normally does not allow retrieving the private part of a key. With this property, it is possible to publicly distribute the public part of a key without compromising it. To facilitate reading, we will colloquially use the terms private key and public key to respectively refer to the private and public parts of an asymmetric key. Each algorithm in this category also has an encryption function and a decryption function, but these functions do not use the same key. Asymmetric algorithms rely on mathematically challenging problems to solve algorithmically, such as the factorization of large prime numbers or the discrete logarithm problem. An asymmetric key is actually a collection of mathematical parameters that must be carefully chosen because while the mathematical problems mentioned are difficult to solve in general, certain specific cases can be easily solved and thus weaken the security offered.

Asymmetric algorithms are known to be resource-intensive due to the complexity of some of the mathematical operations involved and the size of the keys manipulated, which is larger than the keys used in symmetric algorithms with equivalent security levels. For this reason, these algorithms are rarely used to encrypt entire communications but rather to start them by securely exchanging a session key between participants, meaning a temporary secret, which is then used with a more efficient symmetric encryption algorithm. Key distribution is not a problem in asymmetric cryptography. Each participant can generate their own key and distribute the public part to the other participants. However, another problem arises: knowing a specific public key, it is not possible to definitively identify the holder of the associated private key. Thus, it is possible for an attacker to impersonate a trusted sender of a public key, which constitutes a Man-in-the-Middle attack. To prevent such attacks, a set of standards, infrastructures, and processes have been developed to instill trust in public keys: Public Key Infrastructure (PKI).

Examples of asymmetric algorithms include the RSA algorithm, described by Rivest, Shamir, and Adleman (1978), and Elliptic Curve Cryptography (ECC), suggested from 1985 by both Miller (1985) and Koblitz (1987). The level of security offered by these algorithms depends on the size of the key used.

Certificates and Public Key Infrastructure

Standards for metadata have been developed to link information about the owner of the associated private key to a public key. The most widely used standard currently is the X.509 standard (Boeyen et al., 2008). It defines the format of electronic certificates that bind a public key to the metadata of the associated private key. These certificates are validated by trusted third parties, called Certificate Authorities (CA), through an electronic signature process that also involves asymmetric cryptography.

The Public Key Infrastructure (PKI) is a hierarchical system of certification authorities. A certification authority holds a root certificate, which serves as the basis of trust and is self-signed by the authority. A user must trust a certification authority by recognizing its root certificate as valid. The certification authority then issues certificates based on approved requests, signing these certificates with its private key associated with its root certificate. Each certificate indicates the certifying authority, enabling a user encountering a certificate to reconstruct the certification path, which is the sequence of signatures and certificates up to a root certificate. If the root certificate belongs to a recognized authority by the user and the certification path is correct, then the user can trust the end-entity certificate.

The Public Key Infrastructure also includes key lifecycle management functionalities. Each certificate has a defined validity period specified by a start date and an end date, typically ranging from one to several years depending on the certificate type. This ensures that certificates are periodically renewed. A revocation system also exists, allowing immediate termination of a certificate's validity. Such a system is useful in cases of certificate compromise or malicious use. However, in practice, revocation relies on mechanisms such as the publication of revocation lists, which must be widely distributed to ensure effective revocation.

Asymmetric cryptography and associated Public Key Infrastructures are now widely deployed and used for authentication purposes. However, this type of authentication encounters some limitations when applied to the domain of connected objects, especially constrained devices, for several reasons:

- Some operations in asymmetric cryptography are resource-intensive (CPU time, memory) due to their complexity. For example, the decryption operation of the RSA algorithm involves mathematical operations on very large numbers, represented by several thousand bits. This can affect the performance or lifespan of connected objects.
- Deploying, maintaining, and scaling a Public Key Infrastructure entails significant financial costs that can impact the profitability of a connected solution or even render it unviable.
- A process for certificate renewal must be planned. This may involve renewing the certificate specific to the object as well as the certificates in the trust store that allow the object to authenticate other devices.

SECURITY IN IOT AND IIOT PROTOCOLS

Overview of IoT and IIoT Protocols

In this section, commonly used communication protocols for IoT and IIoT devices are introduced, with a specific focus on their security features, while also addressing energy consumption, bandwidth, and latency constraints.

BLE[2] (***Bluetooth Low Energy***) is a communication protocol defined by the Bluetooth Special Interest Group[3] aimed at complementing the Bluetooth standard by offering reduced energy consumption and limited bandwidth, without replacing it. BLE offers secure pairing mechanisms to establish connections between devices, including passkey pairing, numeric pairing, and button-push pairing. These mechanisms ensure that only authorized devices can communicate with each other. Additionally, BLE utilizes data encryption to protect sensitive information exchanged between devices. Data is encrypted using a shared key established during the secure pairing process, preventing unauthorized interception and reading of data during transit. Concretely, the AES symmetric cipher in CTR mode is used with a 128-bit shared key is generated during the connection process. Furthermore, BLE supports authentication mechanisms to verify the identity of devices prior to connection establishment, thus ensuring that only legitimate devices can communicate together. Data integrity and authentication are guaranteed through Message Authentication Codes (MAC), computed using the AES cipher in CCM mode.

LoRaWAN[4] (***Long Range Area Network***) is a standard of the International Telecommunication Union for low power IoT devices. It enables data transmission over long distances while maintaining low energy consumption thanks to a proprietary technique of spread spectrum modulation, named LoRa. LoRaWAN implements end-to-end encryption to protect sensitive data exchanged between devices and server applications. Data is encrypted with AES cipher before transmission over the network and can only be decrypted by authorized recipients. Additionally, LoRaWAN integrates a mutual authentication mechanism between devices and the network, ensuring that solely authorized devices can access the LoRaWAN network for data exchange. Session keys, used for both data encryption and mutual authentication, are securely managed and periodically renewed to uphold communication security.

Zigbee[5] is a high-level protocol, specified by the Zigbee Alliance, designed for communication among devices equipped with small radio transmitters that require low energy consumption and can tolerate low data rates. Widely used in IoT applications, Zigbee facilitates the creation of robust and scalable mesh networks. Authentication mechanisms are employed by Zigbee to verify the identity of devices before establishing connections, ensuring that only authorized devices can access the network and exchange data. The security of the Zigbee network is ensured by two encryption keys: the network key and the link key, which are respectively used for broadcast and unicast communications. These keys are shared among all devices or between two devices, depending on the case. Devices can acquire these keys through pre-installation or key transport methods. Prior to transmission between devices, data is encrypted using the AES cipher, thwarting potential attackers from intercepting and deciphering the data. Moreover, Zigbee implements key management mechanisms to generate, distribute, and periodically update encryption keys used for securing communications over the network. This approach guarantees the protection of keys and restricts access solely to authorized devices.

CoAP (***Constrained Application Protocol***) (Shelby et al., 2014), developed by the Constrained RESTful Environment (CoRE) working group, is an extension of the IETF's efforts with the 6LoWPAN specification (Thubert et al., 2017), enabling wireless sensor networks to leverage the IPv6 protocol.

CoAP facilitates interaction with these sensors through RESTful web services. Specifically designed for battery-powered, resource constrained devices with low-power microprocessors and limited memory, CoAP optimizes communication for such devices by using the UDP (*User Datagram Protocol*) transport protocol easily supporting low-latency and sporadic connectivity. Security for CoAP can be ensured by DTLS, a secure version of UDP based on TLS (*Transport Layer Security*), providing data encryption and mutual authentication between CoAP clients and servers, ensuring the confidentiality and integrity of communications. CoAP security is also achieved with Pre-Shared Keys (PSK) shared between clients and servers to encrypt data and to guarantee the authenticity of participants.

The **Modbus**[6] protocol is widely used in industrial automation systems for facilitating data exchange between control and monitoring devices. Developed in the 1970s, it has emerged as an industry standard due to its simplicity and reliability. Nevertheless, it lacks inherent advanced security features. The **Secure Modbus** protocol addresses this gap by providing a secure version of the Modbus/TCP protocol with TLS support to enhance communication security in industrial environment. Secure Modbus mandates the use of encryption suites, with AES-128 as the minimum requirement, for encrypting data transmitted over the network. Device authentication is managed through digital certificates, introducing the need of a Public Key Infrastructure (PKI) to provide and verify certificates. Moreover, the certificates must be deployed on all the connected devices. Secure Modbus ensures data integrity through mechanisms such as Message Authentication Codes (MAC).

OPC UA[7] (***Open Platform Communications Unified Architecture***) is a standardized and object-oriented industrial communication protocol designed to enable interoperability among various systems and devices in the field of industrial automation and IoT, notably for real-time data collection, remote monitoring, process control, etc. It provides a unified data model and standardized communication mechanisms to facilitate data exchange between different entities. OPC UA employs classic algorithms (for encryption with AES and RSA, for hashing with HMAC and SHA, and for key exchange with ECDH) to secure communications, along with client and server authentication (via login/password, digital certificates, etc.). Fine-grained access control management is also possible. With its advanced security features, OPC UA provides a safe and reliable means of communicating and sharing data in critical industrial environments.

MQTT[8] (***Message Queuing Telemetry Transport***) is a lightweight protocol based on the publish/subscribe pattern for machine to machine (M2M) and IoT communication. Initially developed by IBM in the 1990's, it was designed to connect with remote locations housing devices with resource constraints or limited network bandwidth. Devices publish messages on specific topics and subscribe to topics to receive relevant messages. This allows asynchronous and decentralized communication. MQTT requires a transport protocol that provides bidirectional connections that do not loose order such as TCP/IP. It is now an open OASIS standard and an ISO recommendation (ISO/IEC 20922). To enhance security, MQTT can rely on TLS to encrypt communications. Additionally, it supports multiple authentication mechanisms, including certificate-based, username-based, and password-based authentication. Several MQTT servers implementation (e.g., Mosquitto[9], HiveMQ[10], Active MQ[11]...) offer access control features to restrict the actions that MQTT clients can perform on the server, such as posting messages on specific topics or subscribing to certain topics.

AMQP[12] (***Advanced Message Queuing Protocol***) is a sophisticated messaging protocol facilitating reliable and asynchronous communication between applications. It employs queues for message storage and supports various data exchange patterns, including point-to-point and publish/subscribe. With built-in features for authentication (with login/password, certificates...) and encryption based on SASL (Zeilenga and Melnikov, 2006) and/or TLS, AMQP ensures efficient and secure communication, relying on a reliable transport layer protocol such as TCP (Eddy, 2022). While AMQP serves specific application areas, other specifications like Streaming Text Oriented Messaging Protocol[13] (STOMP), Extensible Messaging and Presence Protocol[14] (XMPP), or MQTT serve similar purposes. AMQP is often compared to Java Message Service[15] (JMS), which is an API specification defining message producer and consumer implementations. Unlike JMS, AMQP operates as a wire-level protocol specification, describing the data format sent across the network as a stream of bytes. This difference ensures interoperability as different AMQP-compliant software can be deployed on both client and server sides.

DDS[16] (***Data Distribution Service***) is a distributed data communication protocol designed for real-time systems and large-scale applications requiring reliable and efficient data exchange between software components. It provides a means of distributing data asynchronously and in a decentralized manner, enabling robust and dependable communication among various network nodes. DDS employs a publish/subscribe model for data distribution. Data producers publish information on topics, while consumers subscribe to these topics. Data distribution policies can be tailored to meet specific requirements such as ensuring reliability, persistence, message priority, and delivery order. DDS supports network node authentication to ensure that only legitimate nodes can participate in communication, using methods such as digital certificates or username/password pairs. Administrators can define authorization policies to specify user privileges and permissible actions. While the DDS protocol itself does not specify specific encryption algorithms to ensure data and communication integrity, algorithms like AES, RSA, ECC, or the TLS protocol can be utilized within secure DDS solutions to safeguard data in transit, ensure the authenticity of communicating parties, and uphold communication confidentiality. The choice of these security solutions depends on the application and software implementations used.

HTTP (***Hypertext Transfer Protocol***) (Nielsen et al, 1999) is a communication protocol used for data transfer. HTTP follows a request/response model, where clients send requests to servers to request specific resources, and servers respond with data requested. In the realm of IoT, HTTP is utilized for communication between Internet-connected devices and web servers. It enables IoT devices to transfer data to remote servers and receive commands and software updates in return. HTTP is platform-independent, meaning it can be used across a variety of devices and different operating systems, making IoT communications more flexible and scalable. To ensure the confidentiality of data exchanged between IoT devices and servers, it is recommended to use HTTPS (Secure HTTP) (Rescorla, 2018), which employs TLS to encrypt communications. HTTPS utilizes standard encryption algorithms to encrypt data exchanged between the client and server. This ensures that sensitive information such as passwords, payment information, and personal data are protected from interception by unauthorized third parties. Through encryption, HTTPS also ensures communication confidentiality and data integrity by utilizing cryptographic hash functions. HTTPS uses TLS certificates to authenticate the server to the client. Certificates are issued by trusted Certification Authorities (CA) and guarantee that the server the client connects to is legitimate and secure.

Focus on Authentication in TLS

The Transport Layer Security (TLS) protocol (Rescorla, 2018) is specifically engineered to secure communication between two hosts across a computer network. It operates atop a dependable transport protocol, such as the Transmission Control Protocol (TCP) (Eddy, 2022), providing security enhancements to higher-level application protocols. TLS offers a spectrum of host authentication levels, ranging from none to mutual authentication. Once a secure channel is established, TLS ensures the confidentiality and integrity of transmitted data, even in scenarios where a malicious actor gains control over the network. Consequently, communications are shielded from common attack vectors like eavesdropping, tampering, and packet injection. This protocol is standardized by the Internet Engineering Task Force[17] (IETF) and is widely adopted in practice. In terms of authentication, TLS offers three main categories:

- **Certificate-based authentication** employing asymmetric cryptography, such as RSA or ECC algorithms. This method relies on a Public Key Infrastructure (PKI) (Boeyen et al., 2008), which distributes certificates to trusted hosts. During the Handshake Protocol, a host sends its certificate linked to its identity, which is then verified using the PKI. If the certificate is deemed valid, the host is authenticated, and the protocol proceeds. If both hosts require authentication, each must possess a valid certificate. While this method is commonly used for web browsing to authenticate web servers, it presents challenges in IoT scenarios. Firstly, most connected devices have limited resources compared to computers, yet they are required to execute complex cryptographic operations to verify a certificate. Secondly, securely storing the certificate and its secret key long-term is more challenging for connected devices, as they are more susceptible to external threats, particularly physical ones.

- **Pre-Shared Key (PSK) authentication** (Tschofenig and Eronen, 2005). In this approach, a shared long-term secret is pre-installed in both hosts before their initial communication. This shared secret is then utilized to compute temporary secrets as required. Hosts are authenticated based on their possession of this long-term secret. While this method is more lightweight in terms of resource requirements compared to certificate-based authentication, it still necessitates secure storage to safeguard the long-term secret. Additionally, key management may become complex as the number of devices increases, thereby limiting the scalability of this method.

- **Secure Remote Password (SRP) authentication** (Taylor et al., 2007) is another method available for TLS. This approach enables the integration of username and password authentication with the TLS protocol. It was primarily developed to facilitate applications reliant on this form of authentication, such as email services, allowing for interactive prompting of user credentials. However, SRP authentication may not be well-suited for most IoT scenarios, as it would require users to input a password for each new device, which could be impractical and cumbersome. Therefore, we did not include this type of authentication in our study.

Secret Management and Security

The security of many protocols relies on the secure management of secrets, also known as secret keys or cryptographic keys, which are used by these protocols, as stated by Kerckhoffs' principle: the security of a cryptosystem should rely solely on the secrecy of its key. (Shannon, 1949)

To store a secret securely on a connected device, several methods exist. These methods do not offer the same level of security against attacks and have varying deployment costs.

The simplest way to store a secret on a connected device is to save it in the non-volatile memory of the device. Non-volatile memory retains its information even when the circuit is not powered. This type of memory allows information to persist throughout the life of the device and is present on most embedded boards and microcontrollers used as the basis for connected objects, making it a very cost-effective storage medium. However, this type of memory generally lacks any protection against software attacks or external physical attacks (Marchand et al., 2018). Non-volatile memory does not restrict read requests made by the software layer. If an attacker manages to take control of this layer and perform readings of memory at arbitrary addresses, they can likely read the entire contents of the memory. Furthermore, non-volatile memories lack protection against physical attacks. Thus, an attacker with physical access to a connected device can retrieve the contents of its non-volatile memory and analyze this data to extract the secrets used by the device. To mitigate this type of attack, more secure alternatives have been developed.

Firstly, memory isolation mechanisms aim to limit the possibilities of extraction from software attacks. With this type of mechanism, a portion of the non-volatile memory is isolated either by hardware or software means, and the microcontroller operating the connected object alternates between two contexts:

- A conventional context, also known as the Rich Execution Environment (REE), in which basic applications run and have unrestricted access to peripherals and can exchange data with the outside world.
- A secure context, also known as the Trusted Execution Environment (TEE), in which critical security features run and interactions with the outside world are greatly limited to prevent information leakage. From this context, it is possible to access the isolated portion of memory.

The transition from one context to another is carried out through a dedicated procedure that safeguards the isolation of data specific to each context as much as possible. Any attempt by an application to access memory space outside of its context triggers an alert and halts the offending application. This helps to limit the scope of extraction, ideally to the classic context where applications most likely to be compromised run. This type of protection is implemented by most microcontroller manufacturers under various names: TrustZone for ARM or SGX for Intel. However, selecting a microcontroller that offers this option often entails additional cost. Therefore, this technology is used in equipment handling sensitive data, such as bank terminals or application servers. The advantage of this type of protection is its native integration into the microcontroller, but it may be less secure than dedicated hardware components, such as Secure Elements, especially against physical attacks.

A Secure Element is a dedicated coprocessor to securely store secrets and perform cryptographic calculations and operations such as data signing or encryption. It is typically an external hardware component separate from the main microcontroller that must be integrated during the electronic design phase of a connected device. This coprocessor features enhanced protections against a wide range of physical attacks aimed at retrieving an object's secrets, including power consumption analysis (Kocher et al., 1999) or fault attacks (Papadimitriou et al., 2020). Equipped with a series of embedded sensors, a Secure Element can detect physical intrusion attempts and respond accordingly, for example, by wiping internal memory to prevent compromise of stored secrets. A Secure Element is designed with security in mind, adhering to a set of standards such as Common Criteria (CC)[18] and may undergo certification by a qualification body. However, this level of security entails a significant additional cost compared to previous methods. Firstly, there is the cost of acquiring the coprocessor itself, along with the design or modification of the electronic circuitry of the connected device to incorporate this new element. Additionally, consideration must be given to the training of embedded developers who will need to design their applications making effective use of the Secure Element's features. For these reasons, the deployment and use of Secure Elements are typically reserved for highly sensitive environments such as the military domain, sensitive industrial applications such as banking or telemedicine.

Lightweight PUF Authentication Protocol

Upon examining the spectrum of available authentication options, it becomes evident that the current methods may not be ideally suited for all IoT scenarios due to three primary reasons:

- The complexity associated with validating certificate-based authentications, particularly for resource-constrained devices.
- The requirement for a secure long-term storage of secret keys.
- The cost for design and implementation of specific hardware and software components.

These factors pose limitations on the widespread deployment of TLS in IoT solutions featuring low-cost and constrained devices. Nevertheless, given that security remains a crucial requirement for such solutions, there is a pressing need for new authentication options that can effectively address these constraints. In such cases, a promising alternative is the use of Physical Unclonable Function (PUF) technology.

PHYSICAL UNCLONABLE FUNCTIONS

Physical Unclonable Functions (PUF) are physical systems that respond to an input stimulus by producing a unique and characteristic output of the system. Introduced by R. S. Pappu (2001) in 2001 under the name "*Physical one-way functions*", a PUF leverages variations caused by any manufacturing process or physical disorder affecting the majority of physical systems (Rührmair and Holcomb, 2014). At a high level, a PUF can be modeled as a function, as illustrated in Figure 1.

Figure 1. High-level Modeling of a PUF

A PUF operates by receiving an input stimulus known as a challenge, which is then processed by the PUF circuit to generate a unique output known as a response. This response is determined by both the input challenge and the internal fingerprint of the PUF. As a result, each Challenge Response Pair (CRP) produced by the PUF is inherently linked to its specific instance and can be utilized for several use cases in the security domain, including:

- Generating physical randomness for reliable random source usage in cryptographic processes (Holcomb et al., 2009),
- Secure storage of secrets at low cost, compared to current solutions previously presented (Sigl et al., 2018),

- Equipment identification and authentication at low cost (Suh and Devadas, 2007; Maes, 2013). By identification, it means the reliable and repeated production of an identifier over time. By authentication, it means the action of ensuring the identity of a system.

In practice, a PUF is a hardware system that leverages physical disorder to generate a unique fingerprint. Each PUF instance possesses its own distinct fingerprint, even if they are fabricated using the same architecture. These inherent variations occurring during the fabrication process make it exceedingly improbable to reproduce a specific PUF fingerprint, thus ensuring its unclonability property. PUF can be implemented using electronic circuits, facilitating their integration into microcontrollers (Gassend et al., 2002). This fingerprint relies on physical characteristics of the system that are challenging to observe, rendering reproduction of a specific PUF instance exceedingly complex, and thus greatly complicating the cloning process. This is one of the key features of PUF, which motivates their use for securing systems.

PUF designs typically fall into two main categories: weak PUFs and strong PUFs. Weak PUF are capable of accepting only a limited and easily enumerable set of challenges, while strong PUF can accommodate a much larger and non-enumerable range of challenges. The latter category is often preferred for authentication purposes, as protocols commonly require a significant number of CRP. However, some research has indicated the possibility of emulating the behavior of a strong PUF by combining a weak PUF with a cryptographic primitive (Bhargava and Mai, 2014).

Authentication Using the PUF Technology

Most authentication protocols leveraging PUF technology involve the exchange of Challenge Response Pairs (CRP) between hosts, with at least one host incorporating a PUF circuit. These protocols typically unfold in at least two distinct phases:

1. **Registration Phase:** During this phase, a predetermined number of CRP is gathered from the host containing the PUF circuit. This host is often a resource-constrained connected device in IoT scenarios. The collected CRPs are securely stored in a database for subsequent usage.

2. **Authentication Phase:** In this phase, the data obtained during the registration phase is utilized to execute an authentication process. The specific sequence of actions within this phase, as well as the level of authentication achieved (*i.e.*, simple or mutual), vary depending on the protocol in use.

A wide range of authentication protocol designs have been proposed, as documented in various surveys (Delvaux et al., 2015; Lounis and Zulkernine, 2021; Lounis and Zulkernine, 2022). However, many of these protocols are presented as standalone solutions. To the best of our knowledge, there has been limited effort to integrate PUF-based authentication protocols into existing solutions like TLS. However, not every PUF authentication protocol can seamlessly integrate with TLS due to constraints imposed by the standard.

Desuert et al. (2022) propose a lightweight PUF-based authentication protocol integrated with TLS to address the identified limitations. The protocol is incorporated into the device's life cycle, clearly defining the entity responsible for authentication register management and offering a secure procedure for generating new authentication data while the device is in the field. The device, serving as a smart object, can be seamlessly integrated into the end user's environment as part of a pervasive application. The protocol is illustrated in Figure 2.

Figure 2. Lifecycle of a device integrating a PUF

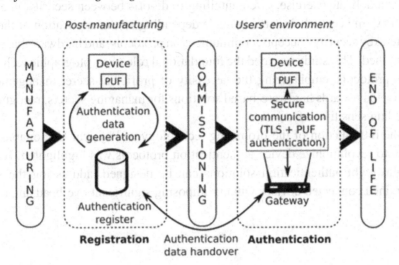

The protocol is composed by three steps:

1. **Registration**: This is the initialization phase where authentication data are collected using the embedded PUF of the device. Upon completion of this step, the device is commissioned and becomes operational in a pervasive environment.

2. **Authentication**: In this phase, the device and the end-user's gateway exchange authentication data previously gathered to achieve mutual authentication in the field.

3. **Secure Refill**: After mutual authentication between the device and the end-user's gateway, a secure channel is established, enabling the gateway to collect new authentication data from the device while in operation in the field.

Considering its capability to gather data about the user's environment or even alter it, authenticating the device as genuine becomes imperative. Using a PUF for authentication presents a cost-effective alternative to methods like memory isolation mechanisms and Secure Elements, as it eliminates the need for additional electronic components. Although the security provided by PUF may not match that of traditional solutions, it nonetheless enables the authentication of connected devices at a more affordable expense.

CONCLUSION

In conclusion, this chapter has examined the challenges and solutions related to securing connected devices in the IoT and IIoT domains. Today, the significant impact of these devices on our daily lives has been acknowledged, alongside the increasing importance of trust and security in their use. However, as our reliance on these intelligent applications grows, so does the imperative for trustworthiness, particularly in the face of emerging cyber threats.

The critical need for security considerations throughout the development lifecycle, from design to deployment, was underscored. This necessitates a multifaceted approach, encompassing both software and hardware levels, to ensure the authenticity, integrity, and confidentiality of connected devices and their communications. While a plethora of technologies and solutions exist, achieving a high level of security remains a delicate exercise, often entailing trade-offs between security, energy consumption, bandwidth, latency, and cost, choices being made depending on the application of the technology.

In this chapter, key security concepts, communication protocols, and hardware-based security mechanisms were examined. This study revealed the foundational role of cryptographic techniques in securing communication protocols, emphasizing the necessity of proficient secret management. Additionally, scrutiny was directed towards hardware-based solutions for managing secrets, recognizing their critical role in safeguarding sensitive information.

Moreover, the introduction of the promising technology of Physical Unclonable Functions (PUF) and its potential to revolutionize device authentication protocols was highlighted. By harnessing PUF technology, lightweight authentication solutions can be designed, addressing the security needs of resource-constrained connected devices without imposing significant overhead and costs.

REFERENCES

Bhargava, M., & Mai, K. (2014). An efficient reliable PUF-based cryptographic key generator in 65nm CMOS. In *Design, Automation & Test in Europe Conference & Exhibition, DATE 2014, Dresden, Germany, March 24-28, 2014*. European Design and Automation Association.

Boeyen, S., Santesson, S., Polk, T., Housley, R., Farrell, S., & Cooper, D. (2008). *Internet X.509 Public Key Infrastructure Certificate and Certificate Revocation List (CRL) Profile*. RFC 5280.

Delvaux, J., Peeters, R., Gu, D., & Verbauwhede, I. (2015). *A Survey on Lightweight Entity Authentication with Strong PUFs*. Academic Press.

Desuert, A., Chollet, S., Pion, L., & Hély, D. (2022). Refillable PUF authentication protocol for constrained devices. *Journal of Ambient Intelligence and Smart Environments*, 14(3), 195–212. 10.3233/AIS-210325

Dworkin, M., Barker, E., Nechvatal, J., Foti, J., Bassham, L., Roback, E., & Dray, J. (2001). *Advanced Encryption Standard*. AES.

Eddy, W. (2022). *Transmission Control Protocol (TCP)*. RFC 9293.

Escoffier, C., Chollet, S., & Lalanda, P. (2014). Lessons Learned in Building Pervasive Platforms. In *11th IEEE Consumer Communications and Networking Conference (CCNC), CCNC 2014*, Las Vegas, NV, USA, January 10-13, 2014. IEEE.

Gassend, B., Clarke, D. E., van Dijk, M., & Devadas, S. (2002). Silicon physical random functions. In *Proceedings of the 9th ACM Conference on Computer and Communications Security, CCS 2002*, Washington, DC, USA, November 18-22, 2002. ACM. 10.1145/586110.586132

Holcomb, D. E., Burleson, W. P., & Fu, K. (2009). Power-Up SRAM State as an Identifying Fingerprint and Source of True Random Numbers. *IEEE Transactions on Computers*, 58(9), 1198–1210. 10.1109/TC.2008.212

Karn, P. R., Simpson, W. A., & Metzger, P. E. (1995). *The ESP Triple DES Transform*. RFC 1851.

Koblitz, N. (1987). Elliptic Curve Cryptosystems. *Mathematics of Computation*, 48(177), 203–209. 10.1090/S0025-5718-1987-0866109-5

Kocher, P. C., Jaffe, J., & Jun, B. (1999). Differential Power Analysis. In *Advances in Cryptology - CRYPTO '99, 19th Annual International Cryptology Conference, Santa Barbara, CA, USA, August 15-19, 1999, Proceedings*. Springer.

Langley, A., Chang, W.-T., Mavrogiannopoulos, N., Strombergson, J., & Josefsson, S. (2016). *ChaCha20-Poly1305 Cipher Suites for Transport Layer Security (TLS)*. RFC 7905.

Lounis, K. & Zulkernine, M. (2021). More Lessons: Analysis of PUF-based Authentication Protocols for IoT. *IACR Cryptology ePrint Archive*, 1509.

Lounis, K., & Zulkernine, M. (2022). Lessons Learned: Analysis of PUF-based Authentication Protocols for IoT. *Digital Threats : Research and Practice*, 4(2), 1–33. 10.1145/3487060

Maes, R. (2013). *Physically Unclonable Functions - Constructions, Properties and Applications*. Springer. 10.1007/978-3-642-41395-7

Marchand, C., Bossuet, L., Mureddu, U., Bochard, N., Cherkaoui, A., & Fischer, V. (2018). Implementation and Characterization of a Physical Unclonable function for IoT: A Case Study with the TERO-PUF. *IEEE Transactions on Computer-Aided Design of Integrated Circuits and Systems*, 37(1), 97–109. 10.1109/TCAD.2017.2702607

Miller, V. S. (1985). Use of Elliptic Curves in Cryptography. In *Advances in Proceedings of Cryptology - CRYPTO '85*. Springer.

Nielsen, H., Mogul, J., Masinter, L. M., Fielding, R. T., Gettys, J., Leach, P. J., & Berners-Lee, T. (1999). *Hypertext Transfer Protocol – HTTP/1.1*. RFC 2616.

Nir, Y. (2015). *ChaCha20, Poly1305, and Their Use in the Internet Key Exchange Protocol (IKE) and IPsec*. RFC 7634.

Nir, Y., & Langley, A. (2015). *ChaCha20 ans Poly1305 for IETF Protocols*. RFC 7539.

Papadimitriou, A., Nomikos, K., Psarakis, M., Aerabi, E., & Hély, D. (2020). You can detect but you cannot hide: Fault Assisted Side Channel Analysis on Protected Software-based Block Ciphers. In *IEEE International Symposium on Defect and Fault Tolerance in VLSI and Nanotechnology Systems, DFT 2020*. IEEE.

Pappu, R. S. (2001). *Physical One-Way Functions*. PhD thesis, Massachusetts Institute of Technology.

Rescorla, E. (2018). *The Transport Layer Security (TLS) Protocol Version 1.3*. RFC 8446.

Rivest, R. L., Shamir, A., & Adleman, L. M. (1978). A Method for Obtaining Digital Signatures and Public-Key Cryptosystems. *Communications of the ACM*, 21(2), 120–126. 10.1145/359340.359342

Rührmair, U., & Holcomb, D. E. (2014). PUFs at a glance. In *Design, Automation & Test in Europe Conference & Exhibition, DATE 2014*. European Design and Automation Association.

Shannon, C. E. (1949). Communication Theory of Secrecy Systems. *The Bell System Technical Journal*, 28(4), 656–715. 10.1002/j.1538-7305.1949.tb00928.x

Shelby, Z., Hartke, K., & Bormann, C. (2014). *The Constrained Application Protocol (CoAP)*. RFC 7252.

Sigl, G., Gross, M., & Pehl, M. (2018). Where Technology Meets Security: Key Storage and Data Separation for System-on-Chips. In *44th IEEE European Solid State Circuits Conference, ESSCIRC 2018*. IEEE. 10.1109/ESSCIRC.2018.8494319

Suh, G. E., & Devadas, S. (2007). Physical Unclonable Functions for Device Authentication and Secret Key Generation. In *Proceedings of the 44th Design Automation Conference, DAC 2007*. IEEE.

Taylor, D., Perrin, T., Wu, T., & Mavrogiannopoulos, N. (2007). *Using the Secure Remote Password (SRP) Protocol for TLS Authentication*. RFC 5054.

Thubert, P., Bormann, C., Toutain, L., & Cragie, R. (2017). *IPv6 over Low-Power Wireless Personal Area Network (6LoWPAN) Routing Header*. RFC 8138.

Tschofenig, H. & Eronen, P. (2005). *Pre-Shared Key Ciphersuites for Transport Layer Security (TLS)*. RFC 4279.

Weiser, M. (1995). The computer for the 21st century. In *Human-computer interaction* (pp. 993–940). Morgan Kaufmann Publishers Inc.

Zeilenga, K. & Melnikov, A. (2006*). Simple Authentication and Security Layer (SASL)*. RFC 4422.

ENDNOTES

1   French National Agency for Security of Information Systems.

2   https://www.bluetooth.com/specifications/

3   https://www.bluetooth.com/learn-about-bluetooth/tech-overview/

4   https://resources.lora-alliance.org/technical-specifications/

5   https://csa-iot.org/all-solutions/zigbee/

6   https://modbus.org/

7   https://reference.opcfoundation.org/

8   https://mqtt.org/mqtt-specification/

9   https://mosquitto.org/

10   https://www.hivemq.com/

11   https://activemq.apache.org/

12   https://www.amqp.org/

13   https://stomp.github.io/

14   https://xmpp.org/fr/

15   https://javaee.github.io/jms-spec/

16   https://www.omg.org/spec/DDS/1.4/About-DDS

17   https://www.ietf.org/

18   https://www.commoncriteriaportal.org/

Chapter 10
Supply Chain Security, Technological Advancements, and Future Trends

Shahad Ammar Al-Tamimi
https://orcid.org/0009-0005-3270-8200
Prince Sumaya University for Technology, Jordan

Qasem Abu Al-Haija
https://orcid.org/0000-0003-2422-0297
Jordan University of Science and Technology, Jordan

ABSTRACT

In the digital era, supply chain security (SCS) is paramount for companies, governments, and consumers. Technological advancements, notably IoT and blockchain, enhance supply chain safety and transparency. Blockchain ensures data integrity and traceability, reducing fraud. IoT devices enable real-time monitoring for proactive risk management. Networked sensors provide asset data for preventive maintenance and route optimization. ML and AI algorithms detect security issues, while UAVs and self-driving vehicles enhance logistics. Automated last-mile delivery mitigates human risk. The chapter explores blockchain's role in SCS, addresses challenges, and discusses future advancements to bolster global resilience.

1. INTRODUCTION

Nowadays, in the SCS scenario, conventional security measures such as cryptographic techniques are inadequate to ensure data integrity in a large arena of developing technology. This constraint significantly hinders the broad use of intelligent technologies in SC operations. This chapter directed to those interested in the field of cybersecurity, especially those interested in SCS. It may also be of interest to technology developers to work on developing technological solutions for SCS.

DOI: 10.4018/979-8-3693-3451-5.ch010

1.1 Background

SCS refers to the procedures and practices used to secure the integrity, confidentiality, and availability of resources, information, and items across the SC (Shamsi et al., 2019). It protects against threats such as counterfeiting, tampering, theft, and unauthorized access as goods and services pass through the SC, including design and delivery. Security measures for the SC began in 2004. Where it begins is with the 9/11 strikes on the United States. The last updates occurred in 2018. Figure 1 depicts the development of SCS throughout time.

Figure 1. Supply Chain History

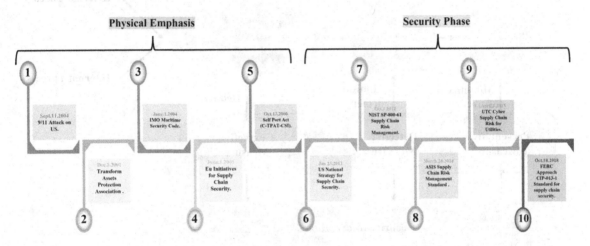

SCS is important for many reasons: Protecting intellectual property requires preserving designs, sensitive data, and trade secrets against theft and unauthorized access. Also, ensuring product integrity entails preventing imitations, tampering, and unauthorized adjustments to assure product quality and safety. Furthermore, maintaining customer confidence involves ongoing dedication to security and reliability (Shamsi et al., 2019). SCS plays an essential role since it involves recognizing risks that may jeopardize the efficacy of the SC network. Trafficking, tampering, and theft are security threats that may result in financial losses, reputational damage, and a lack of demand. Implementing security systems, including ISO standards, reduces security risks, ensures commodity flow, and protects sensitive data across the SC (Kusrini et al., 2021). SCS is a comprehensive strategy that includes organizations, technology, people, and processes for safeguarding networks, systems, devices, services, funds, and resources from attacks and illegal access. It seeks to protect the SC network against vulnerabilities that agents or attackers may exploit directly or indirectly. Security measures include the use of security technology, adherence to established standards, and the engagement of persons responsible for network, system, and resource security (Ismail & Reza, 2022). The SC can be disrupted, businesses and societies may suffer financially, and citizens' health and safety may occasionally be harmed by security incidents brought on by internal and external threats from criminal and terrorist actors. Mostly, preventive actions aim to remove vulnerabilities, which reduces the likelihood that security events will occur. Possible occurrences may be watched for and identified by detective security techniques. Minimizing harm and recovering from it need corrective security measures. Preventive, investigative, and corrective risk mitigation strategies are needed for and/or to generate security information components. An overarching structure for security management and crime prevention in the SC is shown in Figure 2.

Figure 2. Overall General SCS Architecture

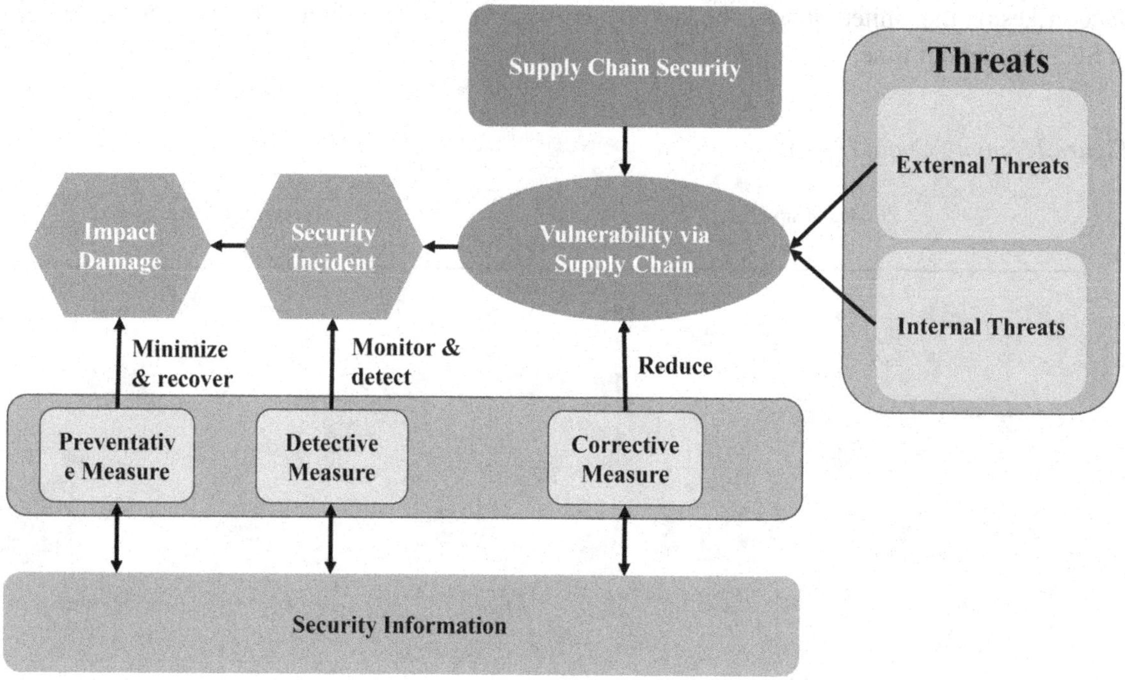

1.2 Motivation

SCS involves protecting commodities, information, and currency across the SC from threats such as theft, fraud, and disruptions. The purpose is to ensure the integrity, confidentiality, availability, and authenticity of commodities and data across the SC. Improving security measures may help organizations decrease risks and secure their SC operations more effectively (Bellal et al., 2023). Also, the SCs integrity can be ensured by monitoring assets and infrastructure to prevent unwanted access or manipulation (Qaqish et al., 2023). SCS is critical since of the growing dependence on digital platforms for product distribution, the need to preserve customer confidence in the face of security concerns, and the hazards presented by unauthorized users and cyber-attacks inside the SC. Maintaining security assures product integrity, transparency, and traceability, which are critical to customer pleasure and corporate success. Implementing strong security measures helps to avoid threats such as MITM attacks, ransomware assaults, and unauthorized intrusions, ensuring the smooth operation of the SC and preserving critical data (Vashisth & Verma, 2023).

1.3 Contribution

The main contributions of this chapter SCS technology review is provided over last seven years. Where all references are related directly to the SCS. Analytical summarization for the most recent trends in SCS, characterizing the various majors SCS applications, including cryptocurrency, the IoT, healthcare, ML, software SCS and SCS network. Moreover, advancement of SCS employing via IoT by evaluating the security of IoT, SCS specialization for optimized IoT security.

1.4 Chapter Organization

Additionally, this chapter includes a discussion on the principles and fundamentals of SCS technology, as well as its secure architecture. It also explores the motivation behind this chapter and provides a summary of its major contributions within Section 1. The subsequent sections of this chapter are structured as follows. Section 2 presents the latest trends within SCS, organized into main categories: Cryptography, the IoT, and healthcare. Software SCS and ML for SCS. Section 3 provides the advancement of SCS via IoT environment. Thus, Section 4 contains a thorough SCS vulnerability, attacks, and open challenges—finally, the concluding chapter of Section 5 includes conclusions and remarks.

In short, the chapter provides a substantial and well-documented background on SCS, integrating a historical perspective with a review of technological advancements and current trends, such as the IoT, blockchain and ML.

2. CURRENT TRENDS VIA SUPPLY CHAIN SECURITY

Current SCS trends emphasize the use of emerging technologies such as blockchain and IoT to improve traceability and transparency, as well as the implementation of robust authentication mechanisms, regulatory compliance, and risk-based approaches to address evolving threats, all to protect the integrity, confidentiality, and availability of SC operations. Furthermore, the current section provides a brief detail about SCS trends via last seven years. Moreover, Table 1, provides overall summary of recent trends over last years.

2.1 Internet of Things (IoT)

The research (Zhang et al., 2019) focuses on how new information technologies such as IoT, cloud computing, and blockchain may improve SCS. It covers security challenges from integrating different technologies, emphasizing the need for appropriate security risk management solutions in SC management systems. Using these technologies, the study intends to increase SC transparency, visibility, accountability, traceability, and dependability. The research (He, 2023) uses fuzzy logic models to link IoT data with blockchain technology to monitor security risks in the power SC. It focuses on encryption and decryption operations using blockchain encryption standards. The study may solve the blockchain and data management security challenges of the SC. In another reference, the research (Jiang et al., 2022) uses security metrics and controls in the SC. It highlights the use of metrics in privacy and security decision-making, especially when monitoring and managing information systems. The project intends to provide a framework consistent with ISA/IEC 62443 standards to improve industrial automation and control systems security levels. Compliance with these measurements and controls is critical to the efficiency and security of supply networks. The research (Santos et al., 2021) provides a grounded theory method to examine emerging trends in SCS in the context of Industry 4.0. It finds flaws in specific efforts and fixes them via sub-categorization to supplement the growing Industry 4.0 concepts. The study aims to enhance reaction and recovery planning in SC, especially for Small and Medium Enterprises (SMEs), by integrating cyber recovery planning with ML and feedback mechanisms. The research (Petar, 2020) focuses on reducing product safety and security concerns in global SC design. It underlines the need to tackle SC difficulties to improve knowledge transfer and maintain long-term SC network sustainability. The results imply that process complexity significantly influences knowledge transfer, emphasizing the need for effective methods and technology to reduce SC complexities and ensure SCS. Also, research (Shah et al., 2023) analyses industrial applications, technology, and SC digitalization themes to improve SC performance. It highlights the value of knowledge management in transforming data into knowledge in SC digitalization. The research (Dutta et al., 2020) examines the use of knowledge management to improve SC digitization, especially about industrial and field applications, technologies, and themes. It highlights the necessity of identifying and managing SC network difficulties such as biases, noise, data anomalies, and cross-organizational information exchange. The study uses knowledge management approaches to improve SC digital performance and generate value for internal and external stakeholders in the SC network. The research (Schniederjans et al., 2020) aims to improve SCS using blockchain technology. They suggest solutions such as blockchain-based systems for safe data integration, security measures to prevent illegal access, and smart contracts for information exchange in global SC. These techniques solve issues with information authenticity, product stewardship, and real-time tracking, resulting in a more secure and dependable SC environment. Moreover, the study (Wang et al., 2019) examines a range of topics related to SCS, such as categorizing security practices, developing threat modeling frameworks for software SC, utilizing unique chip IDs for authentication, implementing dynamic obfuscation on chips to prevent piracy attacks, employing security mechanisms based on web authentication, and exploring the concept of "Supply Chain of Things (SCoT)." This research aims to tackle security weaknesses in contemporary SCs, including issues related to establishing confidence, counterfeiting, physical risks, and information security concerns. The project also examines using technologies such as blockchain, ML, and physically unclonable functions (PUFs) to improve the SCS. The research (Prathyusha et al., 2023) analyzes the influence of developing technologies on SCS, particularly on comprehending how these new technologies affect military SC s from a cybersecurity standpoint. The essay emphasizes the significance of considering technology-specific characteristics, contextual implementation contexts, and cyber risk assessment to facilitate the effective integration of technologies and understand their influence on cyber security.

2.2 Healthcare

The research (Chen et al., 2023) provides a Bayesian Network Model to evaluate the technological and organizational aspects that influence SC resilience and security. It tackles current issues in emergency response and presents a dynamic Bayesian network-based assessment methodology. The report also explores how COVID-19 affects manufacturing and global SC, highlighting the necessity of logistical services, information utilization, and service outsourcing in improving SCS.

2.3 Cryptography Supply Chain Security

The paper (Albulayhi & Abu Al-Haija, 2022) examines the use of Blockchain technology in the SCS environment. It emphasizes using cryptographic techniques for security, minimal privilege principles, vulnerability management, risk reduction, and patch management. The report also cites unique security difficulties in Blockchain technology, including a 51% vulnerability risk, double spending, and worries about private key security, all of which are important to SCS implementations. Furthermore, the report underlines the significance of methodically addressing security vulnerabilities to improve Blockchain applications' security across various industries, including SC management. The main objective of the research (Singla et al., 2023) is to uncover SC vulnerabilities, risks, and security concerns. It underlines the need to conduct a complete security study of SC processes, infrastructures, technologies, and linkages to improve final goods' security. The study examines technological implementation methods, such as encryption and blockchain technology, for achieving high levels of security for goods and processes in the SC. The paper also offers security techniques such as risk assessment frameworks, integrity controls, and blockchain technologies to solve SCS concerns. The research (Hareer, 2024) addresses concerns about the influence of digitalization on supply networks, namely SC resilience, sustainability, and transparency. They discuss the changing nature of supply networks and the necessity for empirical research to identify changes and hazards. The study explains how digital technologies may improve SCS and efficiency, emphasizing the significance of adapting to digital SC networks for better performance and competitiveness.

2.4 Software Supply Chain Security

The research (Ismail et al., 2024) used security qualities, including transparency, validity, and isolation, to improve the security of software SC s. It also assesses existing security methods and frameworks in business, academia, and government to help enhance the overall security posture of software SCs. The study intends to act as a resource and guidance for developing frameworks and improving security in software SCs. Also, the research (Okafor et al., 2022) addressed in the papers aims to improve SCS in the software industry by stressing safe development techniques, dependency scanning, third-party risk management, and compliance with security standards. These techniques seek to reduce cybersecurity risks, maintain software integrity, and address vulnerabilities in the software SC. The study recommends improving security policies, risk management, and compliance methods to protect software SC s from possible risks and assaults. Furthermore, the research (Sun et al., 2024) uses Large Language Models (LLMs) to investigate software SCS problems. It examines the influence of third-party dependencies on software SCs, emphasizing the risks they present. The study shows that advances in NLP, especially in LLMs, might allow for large-scale analysis of SC breakdowns, perhaps automating human analysis chores in the future. Also, the paper (Hammi et al., 2023) examines the security risks and vulnerabilities in the Pre-trained Model (PTM) SC and compares it to standard software SCs. It recommends additional metrics and technologies to improve the dependability and security of the PTM SC. The study emphasizes the need to broaden our understanding of conventional SC management to include Deep Learning (DL) software SCs and the creation of automated audit tools and more empirical investigations to address security risks in model hubs.

2.5 ML for Supply Chain Security

The study (Hassija et al., 2021) utilizes cyber threat intelligence and ML techniques for SCS. The objective is to efficiently forecast and manage cyber hazards by examining threats' origins, categories, trends, and pathways. By using these solutions, the overall cybersecurity of the SC ecosystem is enhanced. Furthermore, the research (Yeboah-Ofori et al., 2021) utilizes the STIX threat model and a discrete probability approach to examine cyber risks within the SC context. The main objective is to evaluate the risks related to cyber-attacks among the many participants in the SC. Also, SCs may improve security and information transmission quality by using blockchain technology. Smart contracts automate, monitor, and secure the SC ecosystem. Blockchain technology improves SCS, highlighting the need for continued research and development to decrease risks. Protecting data flows in the SC requires SCS. According to the study, incident management helps detect, prevent, react to, and mitigate security breaches. It also highlights the diversifying SC dangers, the challenges of organized cybercrime, and the necessity for robust security measures to counteract them (Chang & Chen, 2020; Sobb et al., 2020).

Table 1. Overall CSC Trends Summary

Ref.	Contribution	Approach	Results	Limitations
(Prathyusha et al., 2023)	Integration of new technologies and models for assessing defence SCs.	Utilization of technology-specific frameworks and assessment models.	Lack of comprehensive models meeting all assessment criteria.	Lack of cross-applicability of frameworks across different technologies.
(Sobb et al., 2020)	The study contributes to understanding blockchain applications in the field of SC by exploring research topics and directions for future study.	Utilized a systematic literature review to analyze existing literature on blockchain technology in the context of SC..	Identified emerging research areas such as extended visibility, digitalization, and smart contracts in the SC.	Few studies on blockchain's impact on multi-tier networks and diverse SC actors
(Altaleb et al., 2024)	The research explores the transformative potential of integrating blockchain, IoT, and AI for enhanced transparency and security in global SC.	Methodological involves an exhaustive examination of textual data from academic literature, and case studies related to blockchain, IoT, and AI applications in SC management.	The research aims to discern patterns, trends, and divergences in the adoption and outcomes of these technologies within various SC contexts.	The study may face challenges related to interoperability and compatibility of technologies.
(Qose & Zoltán, 2024)	The research aims to provide findings on the legal issues of SCS within the context of Balkan adoption of 5G network technology.	Authors focused on assessing the vulnerability of 5G network infrastructure, identifying critical components, and evaluating national security requirements and risk management techniques.	The study highlighted the risks associated with suppliers in building and operating 5G networks, emphasizing the complexity of supplier relationships and the reliance on individual suppliers.	The limitations may include challenges in accurately assessing and mitigating cybersecurity risks in 5G networks, especially concerning the involvement of suppliers from third-world countries and potential vulnerabilities.
(Moosavi et al., 2021)	Highlighted gaps in real-world empirical studies on blockchain in SC, suggesting future research opportunities.	Utilized a four-step methodology based on Coalter and Tchangalova's system.	Found that traceability and transparency are the most stated contributions of blockchain in SC management.	Challenges in identifying the most valuable technology integration with blockchain in SC management.

3. ADVANCEMENT OF SUPPLY CHAIN SECURITY VIA IOT ENVIRONMENT

The growth of SCS via IoT settings transforms risk management and operational efficiencies. IoT devices integrated into SC networks provide real-time monitoring and data collecting capabilities, allowing for proactive detection of possible security risks and weaknesses. These sensors provide more insight into the transit items' conditions, such as temperature, humidity, and location, allowing stakeholders to make timely interventions and improve logistical operations. In an increasingly linked world, SC players may strengthen resilience, manage risks, and ensure the integrity of their operations by embracing IoT technology.

3.1 Supply Chain Security and Blockchain

SCS uses blockchain technology to improve transparency, traceability, and trust throughout the SC ecosystem. By providing a decentralized and immutable ledger, blockchain allows for safe transaction recording and tracking, lowering the risks of fraud, counterfeiting, and unauthorized access. Its implementation encourages better stakeholder engagement, enables real-time monitoring of items in transit, and increases SC networks' resilience to potential risks and disruptions. Blockchain and Distributed Ledger Technologies (DLTs) are important in improving SCS by providing transaction transparency and integrity. However, difficulties such as privacy concerns, criminal activity, and limits in user experience restrict the mainstream use of these technologies for SCS. Experts call for government assistance, improved infrastructure, and legislative steps to overcome these obstacles to facilitate blockchain integration, resulting in a more secure and efficient SC ecosystem (Altaleb et al., 2024; Chang & Chen, 2020). Figure 3 depicts a blockchain-based SC system with three layers: SC, blockchain, and IoT. Multi-layered architecture refers to SC systems with several levels that work together as one entity. The SC layer involves several players, including suppliers, manufacturers, distributors, wholesalers, retailers, and consumers, who communicate and transact in the physical flow of the SC. The SC layer coordinates product transportation and associated operations from source to destination. The blockchain layer stores SC transactions as encrypted data blocks, managed by smart contracts and disseminated to all system entities via a shared ledger (Ismail & Reza, 2022). Figure 3 illustrates the general structure of SCS based on blockchain and IoT. Where the figure provides three layers:

Figure 3. The multifaceted structure of SCS is based on blockchain

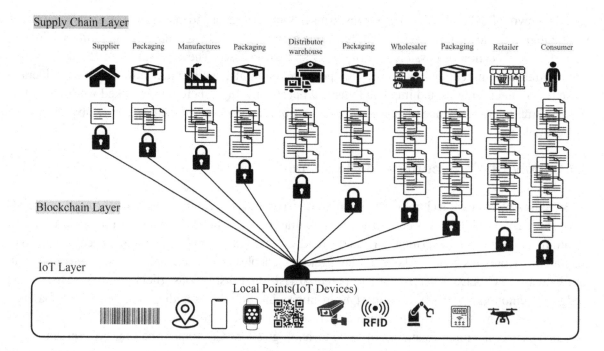

i.   Supply Chain Layer:

The SC involves manufacturing, packaging, and raw material-to-customer transfer. Suppliers, manufacturers, distributors, wholesalers, retailers, and consumer's matter. Businesses and partners trade commodities, data, and services across complicated SCs, confusing actor interactions. Adding partners, resources, and services to a blockchain SC increases risk and security. Security issues include internal and external attacks. The infrastructure of stakeholders or blockchains is threatened by internal computational attacks and external communication threats (Ismail & Reza, 2022). Incorrect coding might increase the software SCs internal attack risk. Exploiting malicious code allows assaults. A SC equipment deployment with faulty parts is another. Compromise software or hardware may have hidden dangers, such as external attacks, including selective forwarding, packet loss, fake information injection, and target SC data exchanges.

ii. Blockchain Layer:

Blockchain safeguards SCs with immutable transactions. Secure and validated data communication between SC parties prevents fraud and mistakes. Blockchain may increase product authenticity, process efficiency, and SCS (Altaleb et al., 2024). Blockchain transactions impact supply networks and product lifecycles. Transactions include processing, packaging, storage, quality control, value-added, and logistics. All parties may view block-level ledger transactions (Epiphaniou et al., 2020). All nodes access the immutable ledger, ensuring openness, reliability, and no third-party interference—public or private blockchain architecture. Private permissioned blockchains are safer and more resource-efficient in smaller SCs. Public permissionless blockchains let anybody join and transact, whereas private blockchains are governed by a trusted organization and restricted to stakeholders. Private blockchains let stakeholders develop and exchange goods. Cryptographic signatures and stakeholder authentication are needed for the network. Consensus allows ledger transaction reading, writing, and validation. SC access to the complete ledger varies to prevent firm data abuse. Blockchain technology improves data integrity and transparency in SCS solutions. Despite the benefits, high prices, poor market acceptance, and interoperability concerns must be addressed. Third-party privacy issues in blockchain-supported SCS must be addressed to enable successful deployment and sensitive data security (Etemadi et al., 2021).

iii. IoT Layer:

The IoT layer in commercial product SCs benefits from worldwide monitoring vital items, but IoT devices' heterogeneity and resource restrictions provide security and privacy problems. The Strong RFID Authentication Protocol (STRAP) addresses flaws in current authentication protocols to increase IoT SCS via reciprocal authentication, key updates, and enhanced performance (Nurgazina et al., 2021). The IoT layer consists of hardware and software components. Hardware refers to wirelessly communicating devices at the network's edge that capture real-time track and trace data. Physical devices include:

- Wireless sensors include temperature, humidity, pressure, gas, motion, and liquid level.
- Robotic devices and drones.
- Wearable devices such as wristbands, smartwatches, and wearable cameras.
- Radio frequency identification (RFID) devices.
- Scanning machines for reading optical labels, such as QR and bar codes.
- Smart weighing devices.
- surveillance cameras.
- Handheld and portable contamination inspection devices.
- GPS trackers.

The association between SCS and blockchain is mutually beneficial, with blockchain technology providing improved SCS. Blockchain improves SCS by making transactions more transparent, immutable, and traceable, lowering the risk of fraud, manipulation, and unauthorized access (Szymonik & Stanisławski, 2022). However, privacy, criminal activity, and user experience concerns might prevent blockchain's complete incorporation into SCS. Overcoming these issues with government backing, infrastructural upgrades, and regulatory frameworks may strengthen the link across SCS and blockchain, resulting in a more robust SCS.

3.2 Security Evaluation of IoT

SCS assesses IoT risk management to reduce SC vulnerabilities. Enterprise security is affected by counterfeit products, foreign dependency, and insufficient security infrastructure. A SC risk assessment system like the FICO credit scoring model might address these challenges and improve national security by addressing SC vulnerabilities more effectively. IoT SCS evaluation assesses SC integration of IoT technology to increase security. IoT devices can track and monitor items quickly, reducing theft and manipulation.

Figure 4. IoT layers architecture

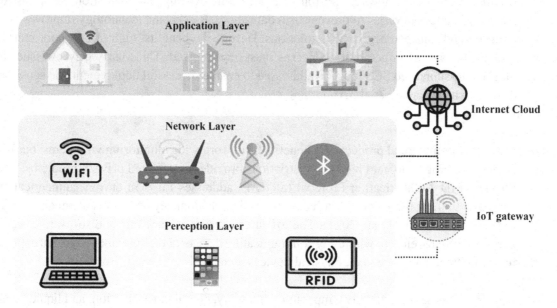

The network layer links IoT nodes and regulates OSI sublayer information transit. It has six sublayers: application, session, transport, network, MAC, and physical. Figure 4 depicts the basic IoT architecture levels (Norris et al., 2020). Code injection, sniffer, cross-site scripting, and phishing may compromise the IoT application layer and the network. The network layer verifies data during transmission and reception. Therefore, packet eavesdropping, masquerading, man-in-the-middle, and denial of service attacks may occur at this layer. Updating or upgrading nodes to the perception layer, which is connected to the real world, gives attackers access to IoT resources. Timing, node capturing, eavesdropping, reply attacks, and node capture are possible with the insecure perception layer (Abu Al-Haija & Zein-Sabatto, 2020; Norris et al., 2020). Increased connectivity presents vulnerabilities that have to be addressed by effective cybersecurity measures to protect private data and prevent unauthorized access. Adopting IoT in SCS requires balancing visibility and cyberattack risks (Epiphaniou et al., 2020; Etemadi et al., 2021). To increase SCS without compromising standards, IoT security assessments emphasize real-time monitoring and affordable security solutions. AI monitoring systems may detect SC abnormalities and security breaches, reducing risk and speeding response. AI-integrated SC management improves threat detection, predictive analytics, and autonomous decision-making, completing SC resilience and security (Norris et al., 2020).

3.3 Supply Chain Security Specialization for Optimized IoT Security and Integration

SCS demands a complete SC network strengthening plan, particularly with integrated and improved IoT security. Integrating IoT devices with robust security standards, including authentication and encryption, reduces risks and ensures data integrity across the SCS. This expertise emphasizes proactive risk control, real-time monitoring, and IoT integration to increase SC transparency, traceability, and security (Szymonik & Stanisławski, 2022).

Figure 5. 14.0 target state for integrating IoT in digital SCs

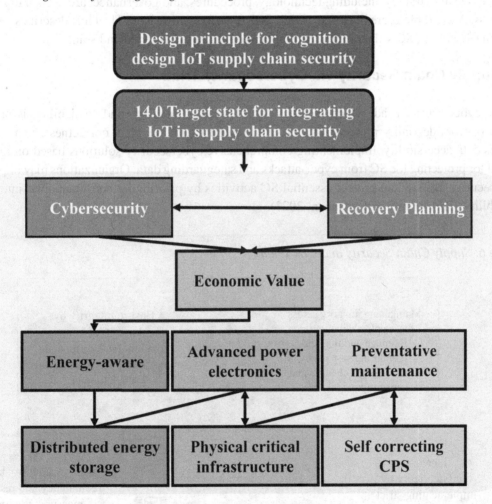

The conceptual model in Figure 5 offers Small and medium-sized companies (SMEs) a summary of the I4.0 goal state for integrating IoT into their digital SCs. This presentation covers smart capability functions at the strategic, business process, and technological levels. This is the second step of creating a self-adapting system using AI/ML and real-time information for predictive cyber risk analytics. This will improve understanding of the opportunities and hazards of edge computing nodes and AI/ML migration to local IoT networks.

4. SUPPLY CHAIN SECURITY AND OPEN CHALLENGES

Nowadays, SCS is a major issue with many unresolved issues. Malicious actors may exploit global SC weaknesses to compromise product and service integrity, confidentiality, and availability. Providing end-to-end visibility and transparency, strong authentication, SC partner trust, minimizing insider threats, and reacting to evolving cybersecurity threats are open problems. Collaboration, creativity, and a comprehensive strategy, including technology, procedures, and governance, are needed to solve these problems. Also, Table 2, are illustrate overall SCS security comparison. The table describes comparison through (SC attack, SC vulnerability, SC application, against CIA tried and solution).

4.1 Supply Chain Security via Cybersecurity Triad

The cybersecurity triad, which includes confidentiality, integrity, and availability, is provided in Figure 6. Confidentiality protects data privacy, integrity provides data correctness, and availability ensures data accessibility. Implementing comprehensive cybersecurity solutions based on this triad is critical for protecting the SC from cyber-attacks and safeguarding data. Organizations may improve their cybersecurity posture and protect essential SC activities by prioritizing confidentiality, integrity, and availability (Türksönmez & Ozcanhan, 2023).

Figure 6. Supply Chain Security and CIA Triad

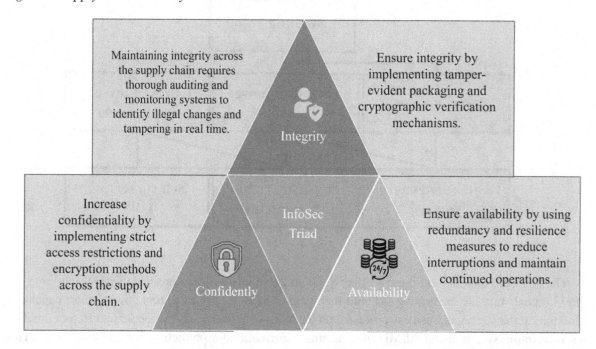

The cybersecurity triad for the SC ensures trusted vendors by avoiding malicious actions that may compromise product security, safeguarding product authenticity against unauthorized alterations or substitutions, and designing products with inherent security features using security engineering best practices. These three pillars protect the SC from threats and vulnerabilities which might compromise product security (Abu Al-Haija et al., 2023).

4.2 Supply Chain Security and Security Applications

Incorporating blockchain, AI, and IoT technologies enhances SCS by providing improved transparency, efficiency, and security measures. Blockchain guarantees the safety and openness of data exchange, AI enhances efficiency and allocation of resources, and IoT enables immediate monitoring capabilities (Chukwu & Simo, 2024). Nevertheless, data tampering and vulnerabilities in IoT devices emphasize the need to implement strong cybersecurity measures. These measures are essential for protecting against possible attacks and maintaining the integrity of the SC network. SCS protects businesses against cyberattacks, data breaches, malware infections, insider threats, and physical theft. Reducing the Bullwhip impact, enhancing visibility, adapting demand changes, and regulating supplier performance improve security. These apps reduce hazards, maintain operations, and safeguard sensitive data, improving SCS (Irfan et al., 2024).

Figure 7. Top Six Applications of Supply Chain Security

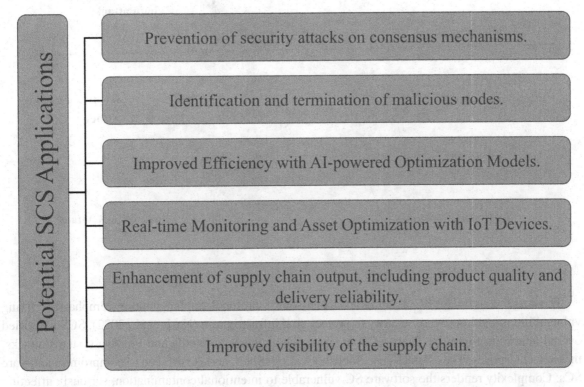

Thus, Figure 7 illustrates the top six applications of SCS. SCS solutions improve data visibility, product traceability, and stakeholder data sharing to solve issues such as inefficient information exchange, lack of transparency, and product provenance. These apps protect against data tampering, counterfeiting, and illegal access, which may harm consumers, corporations, and governments (Lee et al., 2022). In conclusion, SCS applications help to enhance stakeholder trust, transparency, and security. Trust models and networks may help businesses establish more authentic, transparent, and trustworthy SCs. SCS should adapt to address issues, enhance data interchange, and maintain data integrity (Nasir et al., 2024).

4.3 Attacks via Supply Chain Security

SCS attacks may take many forms, including malware infiltration, counterfeit components, and insider threats. These attacks target weaknesses in the SC ecosystem to jeopardize the integrity, confidentiality, and availability of goods and services, resulting in financial losses, reputational harm, and operational disruption for enterprises across sectors. SCS risks include software SC attacks, communication protocol cyber vulnerabilities, and ICS insider threats. These attacks threaten industrial control systems (ICS) and non-ICS protocols, requiring risk assessment and protection.

Figure 8. Attacks Detected by Supply Chain Security

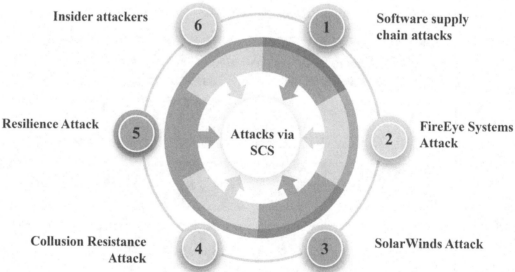

The surge in software SC assaults and open-source protocol implementations emphasizes fixing vulnerabilities and improving security to protect vital infrastructure (Nasir et al., 2022). SCS identified overall attacks in Figure 8. These SCS attacks, such as the SolarWinds and FireEye systems attacks, threaten enterprises. These attacks use Shellshock, Log4Shell, and Heartbleed to compromise software SCs. Complexity renders the software SC vulnerable to intentional contamination, seriously affecting end users and businesses. Integrity, authentication, availability, scalability, and non-repudiation must be addressed in an end-to-end security strategy to reduce cyber threats (Mussa et al., 2023). IoT links smart devices for gathering information and decision-making. IoT is exposed to privacy and security vulnerabilities due to its lack of inherent security. The IoT's dispersed and centralized design is problematic. IoT nodes are vulnerable to cyberattacks (Krichen et al., 2022). Furthermore, the IoT SCS model covers collision resistance and resilience. Defending against collaboration between novel and compromised nodes requires compromising several nodes to leak network keys. To minimize SC disruptions from compromised nodes, resilience emphasizes preventing attackers from physically assaulting nodes to extract protected data. The security architecture uses a secure, distributed design to protect the SC network, prioritizing scalability, memory, bandwidth, energy usage, and node revocation (Hammi & Zeadally, 2023). Also, SCS vulnerabilities via (Alsulami et al., 2022) include fuzzing, video injection, ARP vulnerabilities, wiretap threats, SSDP risks, DoS attacks, SSL/DoS weaknesses, probe vulnerabilities, R2L exploits, and U2R exploits. The SC ecosystem faces different security vulnerabilities in each categorization.

4.4 Supply Chain Security Vulnerabilities Classification

SCS vulnerabilities include threats inside the linked network of companies and stakeholders that disrupt, compromise, or exploit. Unsolved research hurdles include performance, computational overhead, storage restrictions, and blockchain platform selection. Identity-based attacks, data tampering, malware insertion, and other malicious activities also threaten modern SC systems, highlighting the complexity and importance of cybersecurity (Chamekh et al., 2018). Furthermore, SCS vulnerabilities within (Babarinde, 2024) may cause operational interruptions, financial losses, reputational harm, and customer data breaches. A comprehensive cybersecurity solution is needed to handle the complex SC cyber threats. These weaknesses threaten national security. Thus, the research (Wang & Sua, 2023) lists various SCS vulnerabilities. Classify SC, demands on logistical disruptions by origin. Environmental, geopolitical, economic, and technological variables may disrupt supply networks. Complex transactions and chain partner interactions increase fraud vulnerabilities, requiring ML models for detection and risk mitigation. Global competition requires proactive risk mitigation and resilient supply networks to solve shortcomings in SC management.

Table 2. Overall SCS Security Compression.

Ref.	SCS Attack	SCS Vulnerability	SCS Application	Against CIA Tried	Solution
(Nasir et al., 2024)	Collusion Resistance Attack	Resilience Vulnerability	Merkle tree for key management in IoT-based SCs.	Confidentiality and Integrity	Establishes a tree-based architecture to secure SC network
(Mussa et al., 2023)	Phishing, Man-in-the-Middle (MITM) and Malicious Insertion	Identity attacks (Identity Spoofing, Counterfeit Identity, Insider attackers, Brute Force Attack, Account Hijacking)	Blockchain-Based Zero Trust CSCS Integrated with Deep Reinforcement Learning (DRL)	Confidentiality, Integrity and Availability	Implementing a thrustless framework, BC-DRL, SC, which integrates blockchain and DRL to protect SC from threats.
(Krichen et al., 2022)	Business Email Compromise scams as a significant SCS attack.	Vulnerabilities within SC networks were exploited by cyber adversaries to carry out attacks like BEC scams.	Advanced cybersecurity technologies within SCs to enhance resilience against cyber threats.	Cyber adversaries attempted to compromise the CIA of SCC operations through tactics like BEC scams.	The study recommended strengthening cybersecurity education, integrating advanced technologies, and enhancing employee training and awareness programs to address cyber threats within SCs.
(Chamekh et al., 2018)	Sybil attack, Eclipse attack and Majority attack	Tamper-proof data SCS	Supply chain management	Confidentiality, Integrity and Availability	Employ blockchain-based SC management

4.5 Supply Chain Security Case Studies

i. **Blockchain Technology in Pharmaceutical Supply Chain:** Within pharmaceutical industry, collaboration between organizations is essential for drug development programs. However, securely sharing sensitive intellectual property and regulated data poses challenges. Blockchain technology emerges as a solution to verify collaborative contributions and facilitate secure data sharing. By implementing blockchain in the pharmaceutical SC, organizations can ensure data integrity, transparency, and secure sharing of patient-level data post-clinical trials. The adoption of blockchain technology enhances trust among stakeholders, streamlines collaboration processes, and protects intellectual property, setting a precedent for secure data management within industry (Chang & Chen, 2020).

ii. The case study via (Omitola & Wills, 2018), examines the lifecycle stages of an IoT endpoint, focusing on the concept, development, production, deployment, utilisation, support, and retirement phases. It highlights the security challenges posed by malicious insertion vulnerabilities in the IoT, supply chain, using the iPhone SC as a prime example. The study underscores the importance of understanding and mitigating threats in the SC to ensure the security and integrity of IoT devices.

4.6 Open Challenges

SCS has several open concerns that need new solutions to protect global trade and prevent hazards. As SCs grow more complicated, firms face risks from raw material sourcing to product delivery. These challenges include protecting the integrity, confidentiality, and availability of goods and information throughout the SC network, fighting counterfeit products and components, addressing software and hardware SC vulnerabilities, and managing third-party dependencies and outsourcing risks. This section discusses these outstanding problems and possible SCS mitigation techniques.

One of the main issues in SCS is the dynamic nature of risks and threats, which necessitates ongoing monitoring and adaption of security solutions (Todos, 2023). Another problem is the complexity of multinational SCs, which include various stakeholders and partners, making it difficult to maintain uniform security requirements across the chain. Furthermore, as technology and digitalization evolve in SC management, new vulnerabilities must be addressed to protect the SCS and integrity (Todos, 2023), where SCS is hampered by the delayed implementation of blockchain technology owing to a lack of norms for participant agreements, legal protection for security, and evaluation procedures. Trust concerns inside and outside businesses, the lack of electronic business networks, and information systems slow growth. Blockchain implementation in SC management confronts problems such as visibility gaps, lack of transparency, trust and security concerns, and operational challenges for successful integration (Sharma et al., 2023).

Implementing SCS requires assuring the quality and availability of data inputs for AI algorithms, especially in complex and fragmented SCs where data inconsistencies and gaps might hinder AI-driven solutions. When using AI to protect sensitive data, firms must handle data privacy, security, and ethical issues. These hurdles must be overcome to deploy AI-driven industrial SCS strategies that improve security, dependability, and competitiveness in today's dynamic market (Ahmad, 2024). Finally, SCS problems stem from contemporary supply networks' complexity and interconnectedness. Due to various stakeholders, varied technologies, and worldwide supplier networks, securing the SC from inception to retirement is difficult. Effective vulnerability mitigation requires detecting and reacting to SC attacks, securing vital information and systems, and recovering from security breaches. Integrated security measures throughout the SC lifecycle and dynamic threats are key hurdles to improving SCS (Omitola & Wills, 2018).

Through the current chapter comprehensively covers the advancements in SCS technologies, such as blockchain and IoT. It presents a thorough review of the cybersecurity triad (confidentiality, integrity, and availability), which is crucial for protecting SC operations. The inclusion of various models and frameworks, as well as detailed tables and figures, for enhancement understanding of SCS concepts and their applications.

CONCLUSIONS AND REMARKS

Ultimately, SCS technologies emphasize the significance of implementing robust security measures to secure SC activities. SCs which is includes technologies such as blockchain, IoT, ML and cryptography, may improve transparency, traceability, and resistance to cyber-attacks. The emphasis on develop authentication systems and secure architectures is critical for ensuring the integrity and confidentiality of SCs. While, review of recent technological trends in SCS, including blockchain, IoT, ML and Software SCS. Also, comprehensive discussion of the cybersecurity triad in SCS. nevertheless, limited critical analysis of prior literature, focusing more on descriptions rather than in-depth evaluations. Thus, there's lack on practical scenarios and case studies which the illustrate theoretical concepts. furthermore, no enough real-world examples or case studies to support theoretical ideas.

In short, the chapter effectively underscores the requirement for strong authentication approach, secure architectures, and collaborative efforts to enhance SCS. It identifies key areas for improvement, such as addressing vulnerabilities in IoT devices and adopting advanced technologies predictive analytics. For the future, may involves integrating more real-world case studies to demonstrate practical applications of SCS, providing a critical review of existing literature, and emphasizing continuous innovation and adaptation to address evolving cyber threats in the digital economy.

REFERENCES

Abu Al-Haija, Q., Alnabhan, M., Saleh, E., & Al-Omari, M. (2023). *Applications of blockchain technology for improving security in the Internet of Things (IoT).* 10.1016/B978-0-323-99199-5.00003-3

Abu Al-Haija, Q., & Zein-Sabatto, S. (2020). An efficient deep-learning-based detection and classification system for cyber-attacks in IoT communication networks. *Electronics (Basel)*, 9(12), 2152. 10.3390/electronics9122152

Ahmad, N. (2024). Securing Supply Chains: AI-driven Approaches to Risk Mitigation in Manufacturing. 10.13140/RG.2.2.20900.28807

Albulayhi, K., & Abu Al-Haija, Q. (2022). *Security and Privacy Challenges in Blockchain Application.* .10.1201/9781003269281-14

Alsulami, A., Abu Al-Haija, Q., Tayeb, A., & Alqahtani, A. (2022). An Intrusion Detection and Classification System for IoT Traffic with Improved Data Engineering. *Applied Sciences (Basel, Switzerland)*, 12(23), 12336. 10.3390/app122312336

Altaleb, H., Beatrix, F., Azemi, F., & Rajnai, Z. (2024). *5G Evolution and Supply Chain Security in MENA Region: Challenges and Opportunities.* 10.1109/SAMI60510.2024.10432797

Babarinde, T. (2024). Effect of Supply Chain Resilience on USA Cyber Security. 10.13140/RG.2.2.16275.04641

Bellal, S. E., El Islam Bousiouda, S., & Dekhinet, A. (2023). Blockchain and Supply Chain in Algeria: Enhancing Transparency and Security of Operations. *2023 International Conference on Decision Aid Sciences and Applications (DASA)*, 464-468. 10.1109/DASA59624.2023.10286589

Chamekh, M., Hamdi, M., El Asmi, S., & Kim, T.-H. (2018). Secured Distributed IoT Based Supply Chain Architecture. *2018 IEEE 27th International Conference on Enabling Technologies: Infrastructure for Collaborative Enterprises (WETICE)*, 199-202. 10.1109/WETICE.2018.00045

Chang, S. E., & Chen, Y. (2020). When Blockchain Meets Supply Chain: A Systematic Literature Review on Current Development and Potential Applications. *IEEE Access : Practical Innovations, Open Solutions*, 8, 62478–62494. 10.1109/ACCESS.2020.2983601

Chen, J., Dai, H., & Yuan, X. (2023). Bayesian-based assessment of emergency supply chain resilience and security levels. *2023 7th International Conference on Transportation Information and Safety (ICTIS)*, 2013-2021. 10.1109/ICTIS60134.2023.10243912

Chukwu, N., & Simo, S. (2024). Resilient Chain: AI-Enhanced Supply Chain Security and Efficiency Integration. *International Journal of Scientific and Management Research.*, 7(3), 46–65. 10.37502/IJSMR.2024.7306

Dutta, P., Choi, T. M., Somani, S., & Butala, R. (2020). Blockchain technology in supply chain operations: Applications, challenges and research opportunities. *Transportation research part e: Logistics and transportation review, 142*, 102067.

Epiphaniou, G., Pillai, P., Bottarelli, M., Al-Khateeb, H., Hammoudesh, M., & Maple, C. (2020). Electronic regulation of data sharing and processing using smart ledger technologies for supply-chain security. *IEEE Transactions on Engineering Management*, 67(4), 1059–1073. 10.1109/TEM.2020.2965991

Etemadi, N., Van Gelder, P., & Strozzi, F. (2021). An ISM Modeling of Barriers for Blockchain/Distributed Ledger Technology Adoption in Supply Chains towards Cybersecurity. *Sustainability (Basel)*, 13(9), 4672. 10.3390/su13094672

Hammi, B., & Zeadally, S. (2023). Software Supply-Chain Security: Issues and Countermeasures. *Computer*, 56(7), 54–66. Advance online publication. 10.1109/MC.2023.3273491

Hammi, B., Zeadally, S., & Nebhen, J. (2023). Security Threats, Countermeasures, and Challenges of Digital Supply Chains. *ACM Comput. Surv., 55*(14s), Article 316.

Hareer, F. A. (2024). Supply Chain Complexity and Its Impact on Knowledge Transfer: Incorporating Sustainable Supply Chain Practices in Food Supply Chain Networks. *Logistics*, 8(1), 5. 10.3390/logistics8010005

Hassija, Chamola, Gupta, Jain, & Guizani. (2021). A Survey on Supply Chain Security: Application Areas, Security Threats, and Solution Architectures. *IEEE Internet of Things Journal, 8*(8), 6222-6246. .10.1109/JIOT.2020.3025775

He, Z. (2023). Blockchain Security Risk Monitoring of Power Supply Chain Based on Fuzzy Neural Network. *2023 IEEE 2nd International Conference on Electrical Engineering, Big Data and Algorithms (EEBDA)*, 446-451. 10.1109/EEBDA56825.2023.10090552

Irfan, M., Ali, S., Hussain, S. I., Muhammad, Z., & Raza, S. (2024). *Exploring the synergistic effects of blockchain integration with IoT and AI for enhanced transparency and security in global supply chains.* Academic Press.

Ismail, S., Moudoud, H., Dawoud, D., & Reza, H. (2024). Blockchain-Based Zero Trust Supply Chain Security Integrated with Deep Reinforcement Learning. 10.20944/preprints202403.0714.v1

Ismail & Reza. (2022). Security Challenges of Blockchain-Based Supply Chain Systems. *2022 IEEE 13th Annual Ubiquitous Computing, Electronics & Mobile Communication Conference (UEMCON)*, 1-6. .10.1109/UEMCON54665.2022.9965682

Jiang, W., Synovic, N., Sethi, R., Indarapu, A., Hyatt, M., Schorlemmer, T. R., Thiruvathukal, G. K., & Davis, J. C. (2022). An Empirical Study of Artifacts and Security Risks in the Pre-trained Model Supply Chain. In *Proceedings of the 2022 ACM Workshop on Software Supply Chain Offensive Research and Ecosystem Defenses (SCORED'22)*. Association for Computing Machinery. 10.1145/3560835.3564547

Krichen, M., Ammi, M., Mihoub, A., & Abu Al-Haija, Q. (2022). *Short Survey on Using Blockchain Technology in Modern Wireless Networks*. IoT and Smart Grids.

Kusrini, E., Anggarani, I., & Praditya, T. A. (2021). Analysis of Supply Chain Security Management Systems Based on ISO 28001: 2007: Case Study Leather Factory in Indonesia. *2021 IEEE 8th International Conference on Industrial Engineering and Applications (ICIEA)*, 471-477. 10.1109/ICIEA52957.2021.9436705

Lee, K., Romzi, P., Hanaysha, J., Alzoubi, H., & Alshurideh, M. (2022). Investigating the impact of benefits and challenges of IOT adoption on supply chain performance and organizational performance: An empirical study in Malaysia. *Uncertain Supply Chain Management*, 10(2), 537–550. 10.5267/j.uscm.2021.11.009

Moosavi, J., Naeni, L. M., Fathollahi-Fard, A. M., & Fiore, U. (2021). Blockchain in supply chain management: A review, bibliometric, and network analysis. *Environmental Science and Pollution Research International*, 1–15. 10.1007/s11356-021-13094-333638786

Mussa, Younis, Hu, & Abdunabi. (2023). *Analyzing Software Supply Chain Security Risks in Industrial Control System Protocols: An OpenSSF Scorecard Approach.* .10.1109/DSA59317.2023.00044

Nasir, Hassan, Mohd Zaini, & Nordin. (2022). *Blockchain Trust Impact in Agribusiness Supply Chain: A Survey, Challenges, and Directions.* 10.1109/TENSYMP54529.2022.9864418

Nasir, Mohd Zaini, Hassan, & Nordin. (2024). *Blockchain-Based Supply Chain for a Sustainable Digital Society: Security Challenges and Proposed Approach.* 10.1007/978-981-99-9589-9_4

Norris, W., Rodgers, J. B., Blazek, C., Hewage, T., & Kobza, B. (2020). A Market-Oriented Approach to Supply Chain Security. *Security Challenges, 16*(4), 65–81. https://www.jstor.org/stable/26976258

Nurgazina, J., Pakdeetrakulwong, U., Moser, T., & Reiner, G. (2021). Distributed Ledger Technology Applications in Food Supply Chains: A Review of Challenges and Future Research Directions. *Sustainability (Basel)*, 13(8), 4206. 10.3390/su13084206

Okafor, C., Schorlemmer, T. R., Torres-Arias, S., & Davis, J. C. (2022). SoK: Analysis of Software Supply Chain Security by Establishing Secure Design Properties. In *Proceedings of the 2022 ACM Workshop on Software Supply Chain Offensive Research and Ecosystem Defenses (SCORED '22)*. Association for Computing Machinery. 10.1145/3560835.3564556

Omitola, T., & Wills, G. (2018). Towards mapping the security challenges of the Internet of Things (IoT) supply chain. *Procedia Computer Science*, 126, 441–450. 10.1016/j.procs.2018.07.278

Petar, R. (2020). Cyber risk at the edge: Current and future trends on cyber risk analytics and artificial intelligence in the industrial Internet of things and industry 4.0 supply chains. *Cybersecurity*, 3(1), 13. Advance online publication. 10.1186/s42400-020-00052-8

Prathyusha, J. R. V. S. L. P., Jyothi, V. E., Jhansi, V., Chowdary, N. S., Madhuri, A., & Sindhura, S. (2023). Securing the Cyber Supply Chain: A Risk-based Approach to Threat Assessment and Mitigation. *2023 4th International Conference on Electronics and Sustainable Communication Systems (ICESC)*, 508-513. 10.1109/ICESC57686.2023.10193255

Qaqish, E., Aranki, A., Al-Haija, Q. A., & Qusef, A. (2023). Security Comparison of Blockchain and Cloud-based Identity Management: Considering the Scalability Problem. *2023 International Conference on Inventive Computation Technologies (ICICT)*, 1078-1085. 10.1109/ICICT57646.2023.10134231

Qose, S., & Zoltán, R. (2024). Supply Chain in the Context of 5G Technology Security and Legal Aspects. *2024 IEEE 22nd World Symposium on Applied Machine Intelligence and Informatics (SAMI)*, 143-148. 10.1109/SAMI60510.2024.10432844

Santos, H., Oliveira, A., Soares, L., Satis, A., & Santos, A. (2021). Information Security Assessment and Certification within Supply Chains. In *Proceedings of the 16th International Conference on Availability, Reliability and Security (ARES '21)*. Association for Computing Machinery. 10.1145/3465481.3470078

Schniederjans, D. G., Curado, C., & Khalajhedayati, M. (2020). Supply chain digitization trends: An integration of knowledge management. *International Journal of Production Economics*, 220, 107439. 10.1016/j.ijpe.2019.07.012

Shah, K., Sharma, M., & Joshi, S. (2023). Digital Supply Chain Management: A Comprehensive Review Using Cluster Analysis, with Future Directions and Open Challenges. *International Journal of Supply and Operations Management*, 10(3), 337–364.

Shamsi, K., Li, M., Plaks, K., Fazzari, S., Pan, D. Z., & Jin, Y. (2019). *IP Protection and Supply Chain Security through Logic Obfuscation: A Systematic Overview. ACM Trans. Des. Autom. Electron. Syst.,* 24(6), Article 65. 10.1145/3342099

Sharma, Goar, Kuri, & Chowdhary. (2023). *Supply Chain Management Using Blockchain Security Enhancement.* 10.1007/978-981-19-9888-1_15

Singla, T., Anandayuvaraj, D., Kalu, K. G., Schorlemmer, T. R., & Davis, J. C. (2023). An Empirical Study on Using Large Language Models to Analyze Software Supply Chain Security Failures. In *Proceedings of the 2023 Workshop on Software Supply Chain Offensive Research and Ecosystem Defenses (SCORED '23)*. Association for Computing Machinery. 10.1145/3605770.3625214

Sobb, T., Turnbull, B., & Moustafa, N. (2020). Supply Chain 4.0: A Survey of Cyber Security Challenges, Solutions and Future Directions. *Electronics (Basel)*, 9(11), 1864. 10.3390/electronics9111864

Sun, Z., Quan, Z., Yu, S., Zhang, L., & Mao, D. (2024). A Knowledge-driven Framework for Software Supply Chain Security Analysis. In *Proceedings of the 2024 8th International Conference on Control Engineering and Artificial Intelligence (CCEAI '24)*. Association for Computing Machinery. 10.1145/3640824.3640866

Szymonik, A., & Stanisławski, R. (2022). *Supply Chain Security: How to Support Safety and Reduce Risk in Your Supply Chain Process.* Productivity Press.

Todos, I. (2023). *Ensuring the security of the supply chain through the implementation of ISO 28001.* .10.53486/icspm2023.11

Türksönmez, H., & Ozcanhan, M. (2023). Enhancing Security of RFID-Enabled IoT Supply Chain. *Malaysian Journal of Computer Science*, 36(3), 289–307. 10.22452/mjcs.vol36no3.5

Vashisth, M., & Verma, S. K. (2023). State of the Art Different Security Challenges, Solutions on Supply Chain: A Review. *2023 International Conference on Innovative Data Communication Technologies and Application (ICIDCA)*, 427-431. 10.1109/ICIDCA56705.2023.10099966

Wang, H., & Sua, S. (2023). *Enhancing supply chain security with automated machine learning.* 10.21203/rs.3.rs-3317886/v1

Wang, Y., Han, J. H., & Beynon-Davies, P. (2019). Understanding blockchain technology for future supply chains: A systematic literature review and research agenda. *Supply Chain Management*, 24(1), 62–84. 10.1108/SCM-03-2018-0148

Yeboah-Ofori, A., Islam, S., Lee, S. W., Shamszaman, Z. U., Muhammad, K., Altaf, M., & Al-Rakhami, M. S. (2021). Cyber Threat Predictive Analytics for Improving Cyber Supply Chain Security. *IEEE Access : Practical Innovations, Open Solutions*, 9, 94318–94337. 10.1109/ACCESS.2021.3087109

Zhang, H., Nakamura, T., & Sakurai, K. (2019). Security and Trust Issues on Digital Supply Chain. *2019 IEEE Intl Conf on Dependable, Autonomic and Secure Computing, Intl Conf on Pervasive Intelligence and Computing, Intl Conf on Cloud and Big Data Computing, Intl Conf on Cyber Science and Technology Congress (DASC/PiCom/CBDCom/CyberSciTech)*, 338-343. 10.1109/DASC/PiCom/CBDCom/CyberSciTech.2019.00069

Chapter 11
Human Factors in Cybersecurity

Walaa R. Ayyad
Jordan University of Science and technology, Jordan

Qasem Abu Al-Haija
http://orcid.org/0000-0003-2422-0297
Jordan University of Science and Technology, Jordan

Hussein M. K. Al-Masri
Yarmouk University, Jordan & American University of the Middle East, Kuwait

ABSTRACT

Human factors (HFs) play a primary role in cybersecurity. They can either improve the efficiency of security measures or produce susceptibilities that hackers can exploit. Hackers manipulate human error, making an organization's digital content attackable. Employee behavior, decision-making, and communication are all conducive factors that can result in security breaches. In cybersecurity, the human element should be addressed and addressed. Therefore, it's crucial to acknowledge the value of human factors and take integral steps to diminish the associated risks. It is necessary to reduce the hazard of such occurrences to safeguard an organization from data breaches and conserve its reputability and financial security. This protects sensitive data, secures unauthorized access, and prevents malicious performers. This chapter highlights the significance of the human factor in cybersecurity and urges us to take it seriously.

1. INTRODUCTION

In the current digital world, the security of Internet of Things (IoT) devices and their connected networks against cyber intrusions is necessary. These devices include automated home appliances, monitoring equipment, industrial sensors, smart locks, and autonomous vehicles. The risk of cyber threats continues to rise even when devices communicate over a secure network (Al-Bzoor, Ayyad, Alta'ani, & Telecommunications, 2022). While strategies are in place to safeguard IoT systems against cyber threats, new attacks emerge frequently, leaving these appliances vulnerable when connected to unrestricted networks, despite their protection, as shown in Figure 1. The Industrial Internet of Things (IIoT) utilizes IoT in industrial and manufacturing sectors, connecting sensors, actuators, and autonomous instruments to establish an

DOI: 10.4018/979-8-3693-3451-5.ch011

organized system that can predict potential errors and prevent system damage caused by various attacks (Anirudh, Thileeban, & Nallathambi, 2017). Smart machines anticipating system failures play a crucial role in the automated infrastructure and high productivity, lowering maintenance and operational costs.

Much attention is given to physical and technological safeguards like network security and encryption in cyber security. However, the human element is continually disregarded in the cybersecurity chain. Human factors are frequently considered static compared to other dynamic elements, causing a shortage of assurance on their role in the cyber security chain (Hassanzadeh, Modi, & Mulchandani, 2015; Rahman, Rohan, Pal, & Kanthamanon, 2021). Human factors persist as a serious origin of susceptibility. Therefore, it is crucial to value and recognize the importance of human factors in cyber security. This chapter delves into the influential contribution of the human element in cybersecurity by shedding light on how human factors play a vital role in the achievement or deterioration of security principles. A literature review of previous cybersecurity human-centric works is introduced in the next section. Section 3 addresses various types of cyber-attacks. Section 4 discussed that the human element is still involved in cybersecurity by identifying challenges associated with human factors in cyber risks. Finally, Section 5 concludes the work.

Figure 1. IoT applications attacks

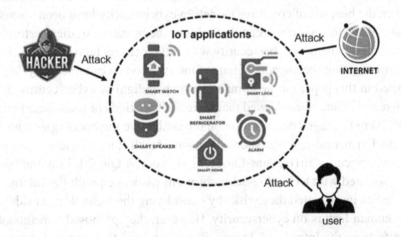

2. RELATED WORK

In (Avlakulovich, Valijonovich, Ismatulloyevich, & Humanities, 2023), the authors investigated the crucial impacts of human factors on cybersecurity. It has been concluded that human intervention is essential to reduce the risks and threats associated with technology advancements. This can be done through collaborations with academia and private institutions. This covers the gap between the human factors and solutions associated with technological advancements, which will eventually foster the ultimate goal of cybersecurity. In (Ayodeji et al., 2023), the researchers performed a review study on the impacts of human factors on cyber security in the control scheme and instruments of the nuclear power plants. They reviewed the recent risks associated with digitalizing the control and instruments of nuclear power plants based on five classifications. A resilient attack control system has been suggested for the nuclear generators, which promotes the cybersecurity associated with this power production facility. In (Buja, Apostolova, Luma, & Januzaj, 2022), the authors proposed cybersecurity standards and a simulated environment focusing on the Industrial Internet of Things (IIOT). This helps protect the sensors involved with the technological and industrial instruments from various threats and common risks. In (Rohan, Funilkul, Pal, & Thapliyal, 2021), the researchers proposed a human-centric method that helps involve people in optimizing cybersecurity solutions against numerous risks and threats. This is done by finding a human-based solution customized to the user's requirements. In (Alsharida, Al-rimy, Al-Emran, & Zainal, 2023), the authors reviewed human intervention in cybersecurity behavior. They stated that the human role can't be ignored even though most current cybersecurity solutions are data-driven. Different models and methodologies have been systematically investigated. Results showed that two theories are the most common in the literature: the protection motivation theory and the theory of planned behavior. Most of the studies were performed at the individual level in the education sector. In (Triplett & Privacy, 2022), the researcher discussed a systematic methodology that identifies human intervention in cybersecurity leadership by considering certain human factors, such as unintentional behavior. Furthermore, ignoring leaders and employees in cybersecurity has been discussed. Also, alternative human factors, such as training, culture, and some infrastructural indicators, have been addressed. Moreover, the benefits of cognitive models in cybersecurity have been discussed in this paper. In (Rahman et al., 2021), the authors stated that most of the literature studies performed so far were on the encryption and mechanisms of cybersecurity with little focus on human factors. However, there is a current trend in investigating the impacts of human intervention on cybersecurity. So, a scoping review has been conducted in this paper on the human-centric paradigm of cybersecurity by reviewing many prestigious conferences. Outcomes showed that there are two kinds of users based on their experience. It was shown that there is a high concentration on the qualitative methodologies with little focus on the theoretical aspects. Furthermore, it was shown that some small standards and scales govern the human factors related to cybersecurity. In (Hughes-Lartey, Li, Botchey, & Qin, 2021), the authors stated that there are many risks associated with technological innovations associated with the Internet of Things. Most of the research studies investigated these risks by considering the technological side with little interest in the Impact of human factors on cybersecurity. However, they proposed a methodology that applied human factors' effects on the Internet of Things. Results showed that human factors can identify 5 out of 7 breaches. In (Nifakos et al., 2021), the researchers studied the common cybersecurity threats within healthcare systems. Further, the function of human factors in strengthening the protection schemes in cybersecurity among healthcare institutions has been discussed. The need to adopt cybersecurity within the healthcare sector in social media has been highlighted in this paper, along with investigating the effects of social engineering in cybersecurity. Also, many cyberattacks have been reported by studying the economic and social effects of disrupting real-life services. In (Maalem Lahcen, Caulkins, Mohapatra, & Kumar, 2020), the authors investigated human factors to understand cybercrimes better. It has been concluded that cyber experts should evaluate the outcomes of recent cybersecurity research studies to get an organized methodology to secure the information technology infrastructure of healthcare industrial institutions. Also, it was recommended that many cyber evaluation indicators should be evaluated in the healthcare industry to promote cybersecurity concerns. In (Alsharif, Mishra, AlShehri, & Engineering, 2022), the authors stated that human factors are crucial in accomplishing cybersecurity goals against various online threats such as password attacks. It was mentioned that human factors are the reason for 39% of these risks. Furthermore, around 95% of the corresponding cyberattacks result from human mistakes. This work focuses on increasing awareness of the objective of promoting cybersecurity. In (Rohan, Funilkul, Pal, & Chutimaskul, 2021), the researchers investigated the important role of human factors in mitigating cyber risks as the technological-based solutions are not fully efficient. Further, the users have been classified into three categories: University level, institutional level, and unspecified level. Seventeen human factors, such as awareness, were identified.

3. FORMS OF CYBER ATTACKS

Any action that aims to change, destroy, or corrupt information is considered a cyber-attack. Network and data are the main targets for cyber-attacks (Kadivar, 2014). In recent years, numerous attacks have been developed. Next are the nearly common cyber-attack types include spear-phishing, ransomware, distributed denial of service (DDoS), port scanning, supply chain, and man in the middle.

3.1 Spear-Phishing

This type is considered the most common kind of digital attack. Attackers send faked legal messages or links, typically through email, to deceive the user into entering personal information without being aware of the consequences of this unauthorized access (Kwak, Lee, Damiano, Vishwanath, & Informatics, 2020). Social engineering and malware-based attacks are the two major kinds of spear-phishing.

3.1.1 Social Engineering

The main targets of social engineering are user's trust and curiosity. Once people feel confident about a faked legitimate source such as a link, email, website, or software, they are easily hacked (Jensen, 2015). Social engineering includes sharing private information with cyber hackers, downloading software that harms your machine, browsing untrusted websites, and fabricating online shopping (Siddiqi, Pak, & Siddiqi, 2022). Social engineering exploits human vulnerabilities instead of spotting the light in digital or technical systems. The huge risk of social engineering creates new and large-scale cyberattacks (Wang, Zhu, & Sun, 2021). For instance, hackers may deceive individuals into sharing personal data such as primary account number, social security nine-digit number, bank account secret code, username, etc (Daniel & Sipper, 2023). Cybercriminals then use all this personal information to hack the victim's organization's network. Usually, cybercriminals prefer social engineering because they access machines, networks, computers, accounts, and emails without the technical effort required to bypass firewalls, antimalware software, and other cyber-attack mechanisms (Breda, Barbosa, & Morais, 2017).

3.1.2 Malware-Based Attack

Malware-based attacks are malicious programs downloaded on the victim's machine. This attack is intended to harm, steal, or change software or a computer system by infecting and exploiting system vulnerabilities (J. Singh & Singh, 2021). Common malware-based attacks include Trojans, viruses, spyware, Ransomware, and adware (Ö. A. Aslan & Samet, 2020). These attacks desire to disrupt a computer system, sneak on a network, or unauthorized access of sensitive information.

3.2 Ransomware

Ransomware is a malware attack that uses malicious software to disrupt a network, application, or computer system (Tandon, Nayyar, & Innovation: Proceedings of ICDMAI 2019). The attached files in a received email, such as Portable Document Format (PDF) or compressed (ZIP), are the most popular forms of Ransomware (P. Singh, Tapaswi, & Gupta, 2020). Opening these files causes severe consequences like rejection of accessing the system, network, or application. As a result, cybercriminals successfully gain full access and control over the attacked system (Ö. Aslan, Aktuğ, Ozkan-Okay, Yilmaz, & Akin, 2023). The most common types of Ransomware are summarized in Figure 2.

Figure 2. Common types of ransomware

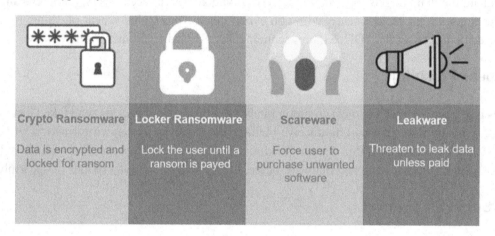

3.3 Distributed Denial of Service

DDoS attacks seek to stop end users from accessing online services by blocking all servers connected to the Internet (Abhishta, van Heeswijk, Junger, Nieuwenhuis, & Joosten, 2020). The danger of a DDoS attack lies when perpetrators have full control and access to the network. Subsequently, they launch much more harmful digital attacks. This leads to difficulty in figuring out the exact source of DDoS attacks (Chang, 2002). Types of DDoS attacks are volume-based protocol and application layer attacks. In volume-based, cybercriminals seek to saturate the bandwidth of the hacked network (Navruzov & Kabulov, 2022). Spoofed packet floods are volume-based attacks like user datagram protocol (UDP) and internet control message protocol (ICMP) floods. Attackers deplete the active server resources in the protocol attack type. Examples of this type are fragmented packets, ping of death, and synchronize (SYN) floods (Obaid, Abeed, & Publications, 2020). The target of an application layer attack is to break the web server using cyberattacks such as low-and-slow attacks (Nebbione & Calzarossa, 2020).

3.4 Port Scanning

This attack discovers potential weaknesses in a network by sending packets to a target port. Analyzing the received packet gives the criminals a big picture of network vulnerabilities. As shown in Figure 3, the major goal of port scanning is to specify open ports in the destitution network by scanning connected devices and sending messages with different port numbers (Nebbione & Calzarossa, 2020). Transmission control protocol (TCP), UDP, and ICMP are usually the ports used in port scanning attacks (Upadhya, Srinivas, & technology, 2020). Depending on the way of performing port scanning, two categories were developed. First, a single source port scan is also called a one-to-many model, where only one node is used to perform scanning. Second, a distributed port scan is called a many-to-one or many-to-many model. Different sources are involved in scanning in this category (Ring, Landes, & Hotho, 2018).

Figure 3. Port scanning attack

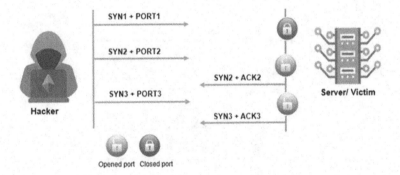

3.5 Supply Chain

In IIoT, a sequence of connections between vendors, machines, equipment, assembly lines, or customers is considered a supply chain (Babaeinesami, Tohidi, Ghasemi, Goodarzian, & Tirkolaee, 2022). This industrial supply series produces hardware or software products or provides customer services. Cyberattacks threaten supply chain components such as routers using hidden malware in installed software (Eggers & Technology, 2021). Based on the attacked element, a supply chain attack is classified into two categories: software supply chain attack and hardware supply chain attack (Ohm, Plate, Sykosch, & Meier, 2020). Software supply chain attacks implant spyware into an application or firmware. In a hardware supply chain attack, physical elements such as equipment and servers are disrupted (Ohm, Sykosch, & Meier, 2020). Cybercriminals in the supply chain exploit voluntaries in the supply series to create denial-of-service.

3.6 Man in the Middle

Man in the middle (MITM) attack is when a criminal involves himself in a communication between two parties, making it appear as a normal transfer of data (Sivasankari & Kamalakkannan, 2022). As shown in Figure 4, attackers eavesdrop on two parties' conversations and then hack and control the whole communication. Consequently, an MITM attack anticipates and edits communicated packets and then sends them back to the sender (Andreica, Bozga, Zinca, & Dobrota, 2020). This allows criminals to manipulate and change private data such as bank account passwords or card numbers. MITM attacks are grouped into residual-based and statistical-based attacks (Guo, Shi, Johansson, & Shi, 2016). Residual-based attacks contradict the residual-based detector techniques. Statistical-based attacks utilize the weak point of a system to keep spying by avoiding the statistical-based detection methods (T.-Y. Zhang & Ye, 2020).

Figure 4. Man in the middle attack

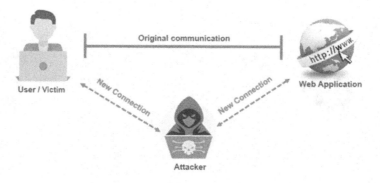

4. ADDRESSING THE HUMAN ELEMENT IN CYBERSECURITY

In the modern digitized world, the paramount concern is on technological measures such as firewalls, cyber-attack detection, encryption, and so on, overlooking the human aspect, which is equally important (Triplett & Privacy, 2022). Humans are essential in information technology security, as they are cybersecurity systems' architects, developers, and managers. Further, the daily use of technology by humans exposes cyber systems to deficiencies and future social engineering attacks (Heartfield, Loukas, & Security, 2018). Neglecting the end-user element generates critical outcomes like data loss, system damage, and service block. It is important to recognize the human element to enhance the principle of cybersecurity. This section emphasizes the significance of understanding the role played by humans in advanced threat protection. The most common challenges of human factors that influence the cybersecurity framework are classified into three groups, as appeared in Figure 5.

Figure 5. Challenges related to cybersecurity

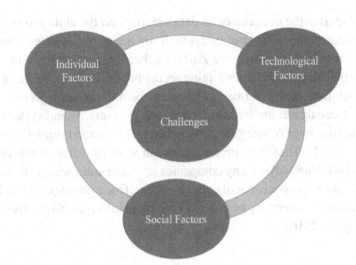

4.1 The Individual Factor

This factor involves everything related to individual characteristics and attributes of a person that reflect behavioral aspects. Personal characteristics include skills, decisions, personality, behaviors, experience, thoughts, ethics, and perspectives (Kumar, Bhatt, & Ganguly, 2022). Realizing and understanding personal factors are important in making enlightened decisions and drawing accurate conclusions. In cyber security, the contribution of individual factors is crucial in protecting sensitive data and devices against cyber-attacks (Kont, 2024). System problems, errors, and malware result from users ignoring security manners. Thus, specifying the exact reasons that influence the security of a system is simple when understanding individual factors (Diesch, Pfaff, Krcmar, & Security, 2020). Table 1 summarizes the different individual factors that challenge the security of a system.

Table 1. Summary of the individual factors

Factor	The Main Impact
Acquaintance and education	Cybersecurity awareness and education gradually minimize cyber threats. Various individuals have distinct requirements for cybersecurity training and interventions.
Age	The risk factor associated with cybersecurity increases with the younger generation. As people age, they become more knowledgeable and aware of cybersecurity matters.
Gender	Males tend to have greater knowledge and awareness regarding cybersecurity matters. Females have a higher level of knowledge and awareness regarding cybersecurity-related matters.
Experience	Previous experience in cybersecurity positively impacts individual awareness of cybersecurity-related issues.
Personality	An individual's personality influences their perception, attitudes, and behavior towards information and cybersecurity.

4.1.1 Acquaintance and Education

Acquaintance recognizes the importance of data security and the ability to behave accordingly. Education comes after acquaintance because individuals are aware of possible cyber-attacks and seek to learn more and more about cybersecurity (de Zafra, Pitcher, Tressler, & Ippolito, 1998). Acquaintance includes recognizing potential threats and adopting secure behavior (Bada, Sasse, & Nurse, 2019). In this informative Age, institutions with informed employees about the recent injection attacks and methods of protecting against these threats are less susceptible to cyber-attacks and system breaches. Educating staff is considered the first stage of safeguarding against malware and keeping confidential information safe (Proctor & Chen, 2015). Therefore, investing time in learning different aspects of cybersecurity in the long run is important. Nowadays, many companies take necessary actions to protect their system by being aware of the negative consequences of cyber breaches. One example of this is hosting free summits to educate individuals on cybersecurity basics and keep them informed about emerging threats (Ögütçü, Testik, & Chouseinoglou, 2016).

4.1.2 Age

Age is a significant factor in cybersecurity when categorizing individuals attributed to distinct life stages and their social, organizational, and environmental contexts (Jones, Collins, Levordashka, Muir, & Joinson, 2019). In the literature, several studies have shown that young persons have more risk factors than older people (Myyry, Siponen, Pahnila, Vartiainen, & Vance, 2009). Since the younger generation frequently uses technology (like social media), they are more susceptible to cyber threats. Further, most young people need more awareness, experience, and education regarding cyber protection and responding to possible digital attacks (Ki-Aries, Faily, & security, 2017). In contrast, older adults have more knowledge and experience in cybersecurity, even though they are usually less in contact with the digital landscape than youth (A. Neupane, Saxena, Maximo, Kana, & security, 2016). The results in (Jones et al., 2019) showed that the Information Security Awareness (ISA) scores for older people are higher than those of young individuals. In sum, educating and providing people of all ages with the necessary knowledge and tools to ensure their online safety is crucial.

4.1.3 Gender

Gender plays a significant role in cybersecurity because males and females have different perspectives on security. Men and women adopt security and react to cyber threats in different ways; thus, it is important to train and educate individuals on security basics (Anwar et al., 2017). Gender differences involve experience, security efficacy, web skills, and social perspectives. According to the findings (Morris, Venkatesh, & Ackerman, 2005), women are more vulnerable to threats due to their lower security efficacy compared to men. Studies suggest that developing gender-specific cybersecurity training can enhance cybersecurity behavior.

4.1.4 Experience

Experience in cybersecurity is obtained over time and positively affects the overall protection of the system. Experience is still the most important attribute in cybersecurity due to individuals' heightened security awareness levels. People cope with cyber threats according to their previous attitudes and perceptions shaped by their experience (Y. Chen, Ramamurthy, & Wen, 2015). Individuals with cyber experience practice security activities in their daily lives. Examples include generating powerful words of identification (ex., Password), regularly updating programs and operating systems, frequently backing up sensitive information, and using updated antivirus versions (Hajny et al., 2021).

4.1.5 Personality

Personality is a crucial factor in cybersecurity due to personality's stable nature throughout an individual's lifetime. Personality-related things include mental processes, behavior, beliefs, thoughts, and attitudes (McBride, Carter, & Warkentin, 2012). Individuals react toward cyber threats based on their attitudes, points of view, and behaviors. Types of individuals' personalities impact how they respond to cyber-attacks. Some people are susceptible to digital attacks, while others are less prone to system breaks because of their stand regarding technical, adherence, and approaches to data security (Pattinson, Butavicius, Parsons, McCormac, & Calic, 2015). In literature, many studies have investigated the Impact of employees' personalities on cybersecurity policies. It is essential to realize individual differences among employees to improve the overall outcomes of the system (Hadlington, 2017).

4.2 The Social Factor

The social factor is a fundamental angle that must be addressed to make the digital era more secure. The social factor is the cultural aspect that impacts a community's security (Gregory, Prifling, Beck, & People, 2009). The evaluation of cybersecurity danger may vary based on the cultural proportions of each country. Social factors are categorized into two groups: geographical and governmental. These two aspects challenge the digital safety of human cultures. Table 2 provides a summary of these two social factors.

Table 2. Summary of social factors

Social Factor	Main Impact
Geographical	The location of centers, devices, users, and servers impacts system security. Each region has unique security practices, perspectives, attitudes, and rules specific to its community.
Governmental	Cybersecurity levels vary among countries and are heavily influenced by infrastructure. The Government and local councils face cybersecurity issues both nationally and internationally.

4.2.1 Geographical Factor

The geographical factor has two dimensions that significantly impact the cybersecurity chain. First is the geographical location of information centers, digital devices, end-users, and servers in a system where different locations impact the achieved level of security. Therefore, understanding the cybersecurity geography is important in keeping a nation's systems secure and on standby to face cybercriminals

(Schmidt, Zöller, & Rosenkranz, 2016). Second, is the geographical location of a national culture with a group of settlements. The national culture of the individuals differs depending on the region in which they settle. The location factor affects their response, contribution, attitudes, and performance (S. Chen et al., 2023). Each region has its practices, perspectives, attitudes, and rules regarding the security of its community. Some countries are more prone to digital attacks than others because of the culture of the people in the region. For instance, rural areas are less aware of cybersecurity due to their simple lifestyle and less educated people. In rural areas, people use less technology due to their dependence on agriculture and farming. In contrast, urban areas are more conscious of cybersecurity due to their daily use of technology (Lusthaus, Bruce, & Phair, 2020).

4.2.2 Governmental Factor

In this technological Age, addressing the Impact of governmental factors on cybersecurity is crucial. When it comes to ensuring cybersecurity, the role of governments cannot be overstated. Without secure and reliable digital connectivity, economies cannot prosper, and societies cannot grow. Thus, it is essential to formulate national cybersecurity defense procedures to resist the dangers individuals and businesses encounter (Conklin & White, 2006). Prominent countries worldwide typically have highly secure systems, while other countries, particularly those with fewer resources, often practice basic security measures. The level of cybersecurity employed in a country is heavily influenced by its infrastructure, as establishing a fully secure country can be quite costly. It's important to truly secure each sector within a country to consider it a fully secure nation.

The Government faces various cybersecurity challenges at both national and international levels. Cybersecurity challenges for local governments are widespread nationwide, with attacks disrupting services, stealing data, blackmail, and other serious criminal activities. Countries are prone to ransomware attacks, where private information is accessed and local authority payments are suspended. Although retrieval is hard, local councils must implement new cybersecurity measures and develop strategies to stop similar crimes from occurring again hereafter (Alawida, Omolara, Abiodun, Al-Rajab, & Sciences, 2022). The loss of services is estimated to have a huge cost, so councils must upgrade their systems across multiple locations and focus more on cybersecurity strategies to prevent future threats. Countries may also face international cybersecurity challenges. As geopolitical tensions continue to rise, there will be strains in intensified collaboration and mastery of security (Burton & Lain, 2020). There is an urgent need to secure digital ad rules and other digital areas to prevent external snooping.

4.3 The Technological Factor

In cybersecurity, it's essential to consider the three fundamental components: people, process, and technology (PPT). These elements together form the PPT framework (see Figure 6), which outlines the methods used to safeguard networks, data, devices, and programs against unauthorized access, damage, or attack. The PPT framework identified four crucial factors: people, structure, tasks, and technology (Poehlmann et al., 2021). The term "technology" refers to the tools and resources individuals use to enhance their work, particularly in the Age of artificial intelligence. The technological aspects of cybersecurity involve secure networks and encryption techniques. As technology advances, so do the tactics and techniques used by cybercriminals. Organizations and persons must keep up with the latest cybersecurity technology and best practices to stay protected (Auyporn, Piromsopa, & Chaiyawat, 2020).

However, more than relying solely on technology is needed, as the human element is also considered a crucial aspect of cybersecurity. It is important to remember that technology alone cannot prevent all cyber threats and that human error and behavior can also put sensitive information at risk. While technological innovations are critical in detecting and mitigating threats, they are only as effective as those who design, implement, and utilize them (Daim et al., 2020).

Figure 6. PPT framework

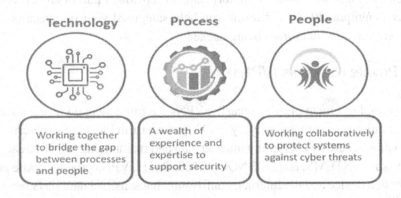

Undoubtedly, technological advancements play a crucial role in identifying and reducing risks. However, we must recognize that they are only a portion of the solution. To effectively tackle the intricate issues of today's world, we must adopt a comprehensive approach that integrates the potential of technology with human knowledge and proficiency. Cybersecurity technologies aim to detect, prevent, and solve security attacks to protect organizations from attackers. Figure 7 depicts common cybersecurity technologies.

Figure 7. Common cybersecurity technologies

4.3.1 Firewall

A firewall is an indispensable component of cybersecurity that no organization can afford to ignore. It acts as a partition between an authenticated local network and an unauthenticated external network like the Internet. With the growing prevalence of cyber threats, it is critical to have a reliable security system in location that can monitor and surveillance entering and leaving network traffic depending on pre-established security regulations (K. Neupane, Haddad, & Chen, 2018). Firewalls protect untrusted access to or from a private network while allowing the necessary communication. These security systems can be implemented in hardware or software form and are a primary part of any cybersecurity technique (Gupta, Naik, & Sengupta, 2017). A firewall can help safeguard your organization against malicious attacks and prevent sensitive data from being hacked.

4.3.2 Virtual Private Networks (VPNs)

VPNs are a pivotal fragment of cybersecurity. VPNs are fundamental for organizations and individuals interested in online security and privacy. VPNs can assist in blocking cybercriminals and keeping sensitive information secure by encrypting internet data and maintaining sensitive data security (Hunko, Ruban, Hvozdetska, SYSTEMS, & TECHNOLOGIES, 2021). VPNs produce a safe and encrypted link between the user of a device and the Internet, confirming that sensitive data stays secure from criminals. VPNs can prohibit attacks, cybercriminals, and other malicious sources from attacking information and accessing sensitive data by establishing a virtual pipe between the user of the device and the Internet (Tambe et al., 2019). Also, VPNs can secure valuable information, such as corporate and Government information. However, VPNs are mostly implemented by distant agents, businesses with several locations, and users who aim to save their privacy while browsing the Internet. VPNs can also be utilized to avoid internet supervision and limited access to websites and services. Further, not all VPNs are equally produced, where VPN designers may keep logs of users' online actions, which can adjust user privacy and security (Z. Zhang, Zhang, Chu, & Li, 2004). Therefore, users need to choose a reputed VPN supplier that doesn't keep logs and has a robust reputation for security and privacy.

4.3.3 Access Control

Access control is an important method of cybersecurity in the IoT ecosystem. It is crucial to prevent unofficial access to sensitive information and systems with the spread of connected devices. Access control is related to regulating and organizing access to resources, including information, services, and devices. It is the fundamental way of implementing security regulations and protecting IoT systems from cyber threats (Ravidas, Lekidis, Paci, Zannone, & Applications, 2019). In IoT ecosystems, access control is mostly challenging because of the diversity of devices and the heterogeneity of communication protocols utilized. Access control techniques must be adaptable enough to harbor numerous devices and communication protocols while confirming that security policies are applied consistently (Qiu et al., 2020). One method of access control in IoT is to implement role-based access control (RBAC). RBAC is a well-determined access control pattern widely used in industrial systems. In RBAC, resource access depends on the end user's role in the system. For instance, a normal user may only have access to a limited number of resources, while an administrator may have full access to all resources (Aftab et al., 2021). RBAC is an appropriate pattern in IoT systems because of the well-established regulations correlating with different types of devices, services, and users. Another model of using access control in IoT is to apply attribute-based access control (ABAC). ABAC is a more adaptable access control method that permits access to resources based on features that characterize the user, device, or service order of access. For example, access to a specific resource may be given only to devices positioned in a certain geographic location or with a confirmed security level (Ameer, Benson, & computing, 2022). ABAC is appropriate to IoT ecosystems because of the variation of devices and communication protocols applied.

4.3.4 Antivirus

Antivirus software is a fundamental aspect of cybersecurity. Antivirus is implemented to predict and remove malicious programs from computer systems and networks. Additionally, antivirus tools are used to prevent numerous cyber-attacks involving viruses, worms, Trojans, and other types of malware (Mukkamala, Sung, & Abraham, 2005). Antivirus mainly scans documents and software for common malicious threats and actions. Once a malicious threat is detected, the antivirus program will isolate or remove the victim document. Furthermore, antivirus software cannot protect against all cyber-attacks, which makes it a trustworthy technique (Jardine, 2020). Useful habits include safe browsing practices, frequent updates of software tools, and applying secondary security methods such as firewalls and intrusion detection systems to guarantee inclusive protection against cyber criminals.

In addition, antivirus software is also a primary practice in the field of Internet of Things (IoT) security. The risk of cyber threats has escalated significantly with the propagation of internet-based devices in homes, workplaces, and industrial sectors. IoT devices' restricted processing power and memory make them weak victims of malware breaches (Silva et al., 2023). Thus, practicing antivirus software helps safeguard these devices by identifying and deleting malicious code. However, traditional antivirus software may not be suitable for IoT devices because of its limited resources.

In some cases, fundamental antivirus software developed specifically for IoT devices may be needed (Dahiya, 2022). Also, other security methods, such as encryption, access control, and network segmentation, should be implemented to maintain inclusive protection against IoT-based attacks. Understanding that IoT security is a sophisticated and quickly progressing field, organizations must keep up-to-date with the recent security evolutions and best implementations to guarantee the safety and probity of their IoT systems (Toma, Boja, Popa, Doinea, & Ciurea, 2021).

4.3.5 Data Loss Prevention (DLP)

DLP is a substantial cybersecurity approach in IoT practice. The danger of information loss and breaches escalates as more devices connect to the Internet. DLP technologies protect confidential data from unauthorized attacks, loss, and breaches (Takebayashi, Tsuda, Hasebe, Masuoka, & Journal, 2010). One of the major challenges in DLP for IoT is the huge number of devices that must be secured. As IoT systems typically include many sensors and other connected devices, it is not easy to monitor them all and guarantee they are all fully protected (Hussain & Hussain, 2021). Organizations apply various DLP strategies and technologies, such as encryption, access controls, and monitoring tools, to overcome this challenge. Encryption, in particular, is crucial for safeguarding sensitive information as this data is forwarded between interconnected devices and stored on servers (Rogowski & Security, 2013). Access controls can also be utilized to specify eligible individuals and devices to access sensitive data and equipment. Moreover, organizations can use monitoring tools to prevent possible security breaches and take immediate action before data loss or theft. Monitoring tools include firewalls, intrusion detection systems, and other security software tools developed to track network traffic and distinguish malicious actions (Charbonneau & Security, 2011).

5. CONCLUSION

Technology advances unprecedentedly in today's information era, presenting new challenges to society. One of the most harmful challenges is the increasing threat of cyber-attacks. Cyber-attacks' danger lies in the high potential of severe damage to critical infrastructure, national security, the economy, and even individuals' security. Thus, cybersecurity is a crucial aspect of modern life, given our dependence on technology to perform daily activities.

One of the key conclusions of our article is that human vulnerabilities play a crucial role in cybersecurity. Attackers frequently exploit human error or inattention to access personal information or take control of systems. Thus, it is important to recognize the human factor in order to manipulate security risks successfully. There are numerous ways in which human susceptibilities can be addressed to perfect cybersecurity. For instance, education and training programs can assist people in learning how to distinguish and prevent common cybercriminals.

Furthermore, strict security protocols and policies minimize the hazard of human error and make it more complicated for cyber offenders to exploit weaknesses. In sum, as technology evolves, it is important to prioritize cybersecurity and take far-reaching actions to address the human element in the cybersecurity chain.

REFERENCES

Abhishta, A., van Heeswijk, W., Junger, M., Nieuwenhuis, L. J., & Joosten, R. (2020). *Why would we get attacked? An analysis of attacker's aims behind DDoS attacks*. Academic Press.

Aftab, M. U., Oluwasanmi, A., Alharbi, A., Sohaib, O., Nie, X., Qin, Z., & Ngo, S. (2021). *Secure and dynamic access control for the Internet of Things (IoT) based traffic system*. Academic Press.

Al-Bzoor, M., Ayyad, W., Alta'ani, O. (2022). *A Survey on Efficient Routing Strategies for The Internet of Underwater Things (IoUT)*. Academic Press.

Alawida, M., Omolara, A. E., Abiodun, O. I., & Al-Rajab, M. (2022). A deeper look into cybersecurity issues in the wake of Covid-19. 10.1016/j.jksuci.2022.08.00337521180

Alsharida, R. A., Al-rimy, B. A. S., Al-Emran, M., & Zainal, A. (2023). *A systematic review of multi perspectives on human cybersecurity behavior*. Academic Press.

Alsharif, M., Mishra, S., AlShehri, M. (2022). *Impact of Human Vulnerabilities on Cybersecurity*. Academic Press.

Ameer, S., Benson, J. (2022). *Hybrid approaches (ABAC and RBAC) toward secure access control in smart home IoT*. Academic Press.

Andreica, G. R., Bozga, L., Zinca, D., & Dobrota, V. (2020). *Denial of service and man-in-the-middle attacks against IoT devices in a GPS-based monitoring software for intelligent transportation systems*. Paper presented at the 2020 19th RoEduNet Conference: Networking in Education and Research (RoEduNet). 10.1109/RoEduNet51892.2020.9324865

Anirudh, M., Thileeban, S. A., & Nallathambi, D. J. (2017). *Use of honeypots for mitigating DoS attacks targeted on IoT networks*. Paper presented at the 2017 International conference on computer, communication and signal processing (ICCCSP). 10.1109/ICCCSP.2017.7944057

Anwar, M., He, W., Ash, I., Yuan, X., Li, L., & Xu, L. (2017). *Gender difference and employees' cybersecurity behaviors*. Academic Press.

Aslan, Ö., Aktuğ, S. S., Ozkan-Okay, M., Yilmaz, A. A., & Akin, E. (2023). *A comprehensive review of cyber security vulnerabilities, threats, attacks, and solutions*. Academic Press.

Aslan, Ö. A., & Samet, R. (2020). *A comprehensive review on malware detection approaches*. Academic Press.

Auyporn, W., Piromsopa, K., & Chaiyawat, T. (2020). Critical factors in cybersecurity for SMEs in technological innovation era. *ISPIM Conference Proceedings*.

Avlakulovich, D. M., Valijonovich, T. O., & Ismatulloyevich, R. (2023). *Understanding of Human Factors and Impact in Cybersecurity*. Academic Press.

Ayodeji, A., Mohamed, M., Li, L., Di Buono, A., Pierce, I., & Ahmed, H. (2023). *Cyber security in the nuclear industry: A closer look at digital control systems, networks and human factors*. Academic Press.

Babaeinesami, A., Tohidi, H., Ghasemi, P., Goodarzian, F., & Tirkolaee, E. (2022). *A closed-loop supply chain configuration considering environmental impacts: a self-adaptive NSGA-II algorithm.* Academic Press.

Bada, M., Sasse, A. M., & Nurse, J. R. J. a. (2019). Cyber security awareness campaigns: Why do they fail to change behaviour? *INTED2017 Proceedings.*

Buja, A., Apostolova, M., Luma, A., & Januzaj, Y. (2022). *Cyber security standards for the industrial internet of things (iiot)–a systematic review.* Paper presented at the 2022 International Congress on Human-Computer Interaction, Optimization and Robotic Applications (HORA). 10.1109/HORA55278.2022.9799870

Burton, J., & Lain, C. (2020). *Desecuritising cybersecurity: towards a societal approach.* Academic Press.

Chang, R. (2002). *Defending against flooding-based distributed denial-of-service attacks: A tutorial.* Academic Press.

Charbonneau, S. (2011). *The role of user-driven security in data loss prevention.* Academic Press.

Chen, S., Hao, M., Ding, F., Jiang, D., Dong, J., Zhang, S. (2023). *Exploring the global geography of cybercrime and its driving forces.* Academic Press.

Chen, Y., Ramamurthy, K., & Wen, K.-W. (2015). *Impacts of comprehensive information security programs on information security culture.* Academic Press.

Conklin, A., & White, G. B. (2006). E-government and cyber security: the role of cyber security exercises. *Proceedings of the 39th Annual Hawaii International Conference on System Sciences (HICSS'06).* 10.1109/HICSS.2006.133

Dahiya, P. (2022). Malware Detection in IoT. In *Internet of Things: Security and Privacy in Cyberspace* (pp. 133-164). Springer. 10.1007/978-981-19-1585-7_7

Daim, T., Lai, K. K., Yalcin, H., Alsoubie, F., & Kumar, V. (2020). *Forecasting technological positioning through technology knowledge redundancy: Patent citation analysis of IoT, cybersecurity, and Blockchain.* Academic Press.

Daniel, C., & Sipper, J. (2023). Hacking Humans. *The Art of Exploiting Psychology in the Digital Age, 10,* 224.

de Zafra, D. E., Pitcher, S. I., Tressler, J. D., & Ippolito, J. (1998). *Information technology security training requirements: A role-and performance-based model.* Academic Press.

Diesch, R., Pfaff, M., & Krcmar, H. (2020). *A comprehensive model of information security factors for decision-makers.* Academic Press.

Eggers, S. (2021). *A novel approach for analyzing the nuclear supply chain cyber-attack surface.* Academic Press.

Gregory, R., Prifling, M., & Beck, R. (2009). *The role of cultural intelligence for the emergence of negotiated culture in IT offshore outsourcing projects.* Academic Press.

Guo, Z., Shi, D., Johansson, K. H., & Shi, L. (2016). *Optimal linear cyber-attack on remote state estimation*. Academic Press.

Gupta, N., Naik, V., & Sengupta, S. (2017). *A firewall for internet of things*. Paper presented at the 2017 9th International Conference on Communication Systems and Networks (COMSNETS). 10.1109/COMSNETS.2017.7945418

Hadlington, L. (2017). *Human factors in cybersecurity; examining the link between Internet addiction, impulsivity, attitudes towards cybersecurity, and risky cybersecurity behaviours*. Academic Press.

Hajny, J., Ricci, S., Piesarskas, E., Levillain, O., Galletta, L., & De Nicola, R. (2021). *Framework, tools and good practices for cybersecurity curricula*. Academic Press.

Hassanzadeh, A., Modi, S., & Mulchandani, S. (2015). *Towards effective security control assignment in the Industrial Internet of Things*. Paper presented at the 2015 IEEE 2nd World Forum on Internet of Things (WF-IoT). 10.1109/WF-IoT.2015.7389155

Heartfield, R., & Loukas, G. (2018). *Detecting semantic social engineering attacks with the weakest link: Implementation and empirical evaluation of a human-as-a-security-sensor framework*. Academic Press.

Hughes-Lartey, K., Li, M., Botchey, F. E., & Qin, Z. J. H. (2021). Human factor, a critical weak point in the information security of an organization's. *Internet of Things : Engineering Cyber Physical Human Systems*, 7(3).33768182

Hunko, M., Ruban, I., & Hvozdetska, K. (2021). *Securing the Internet of Things via VPN technology*. Academic Press.

Hussain, M. E., & Hussain, R. (2021). *Cloud Security as a Service Using Data Loss Prevention: Challenges and Solution*. Paper presented at the International Conference on Internet of Things and Connected Technologies.

Jardine, E. (2020). *The case against commercial antivirus software: Risk homeostasis and information problems in cybersecurity*. Academic Press.

Jensen, L. (2015). *Challenges in maritime cyber-resilience*. Academic Press.

Jones, S. L., Collins, E. I., Levordashka, A., Muir, K., & Joinson, A. (2019). *What is' Cyber Security'? Differential Language of Cyber Security Across the Lifespan*. Paper presented at the Extended Abstracts of the 2019 CHI Conference on Human Factors in Computing Systems. 10.1145/3290607.3312786

Kadivar, M. (2014). *Cyber-attack attributes*. Academic Press.

Ki-Aries, D., & Faily, S. (2017). *Persona-centred information security awareness*. Academic Press.

Kont, K.-R. (2024). *Libraries and cyber security: the importance of the human factor in preventing cyber attacks*. Academic Press.

Kumar, S., Bhatt, R., & Ganguly, D. G. (2022). *Organizational behaviour*. Academic Guru Publishing House.

Kwak, Y., Lee, S., Damiano, A., Vishwanath, A. (2020). *Why do users not report spear phishing emails?* Academic Press.

Lusthaus, J., Bruce, M., & Phair, N. (2020). *Mapping the geography of cybercrime: A review of indices of digital offending by country.* Paper presented at the 2020 IEEE European Symposium on Security and Privacy Workshops (EuroS&PW). 10.1109/EuroSPW51379.2020.00066

Maalem Lahcen, R. A., Caulkins, B., Mohapatra, R., & Kumar, M. (2020). *Review and insight on the behavioral aspects of cybersecurity.* Academic Press.

McBride, M., Carter, L., & Warkentin, M. (2012). *Exploring the role of individual employee characteristics and personality on employee compliance with cybersecurity policies.* Academic Press.

Morris, M. G., Venkatesh, V., & Ackerman, P. (2005). *Gender and age differences in employee decisions about new technology: An extension to the theory of planned behavior.* Academic Press.

Mukkamala, S., Sung, A., & Abraham, A. (2005). Enhancing Computer Security with Smart Technology. *Cyber security challenges: Designing efficient intrusion detection systems and antivirus tools,* 125-163.

Myyry, L., Siponen, M., Pahnila, S., Vartiainen, T., & Vance, A. (2009). *What levels of moral reasoning and values explain adherence to information security rules? An empirical study.* Academic Press.

Navruzov, E., & Kabulov, A. (2022). *Detection and analysis types of DDoS attack.* Paper presented at the 2022 IEEE International IOT, Electronics and Mechatronics Conference (IEMTRONICS). 10.1109/IEMTRONICS55184.2022.9795729

Nebbione, G., & Calzarossa, M. C. (2020). *Security of IoT application layer protocols: Challenges and findings.* Academic Press.

Neupane, A., Saxena, N., Maximo, J. O., Kana, R. (2016). *Neural markers of cybersecurity: An fMRI study of phishing and malware warnings.* Academic Press.

Neupane, K., Haddad, R., & Chen, L. (2018). *Next generation firewall for network security: A survey.* Paper presented at the SoutheastCon 2018. 10.1109/SECON.2018.8478973

Nifakos, S., Chandramouli, K., Nikolaou, C. K., Papachristou, P., Koch, S., Panaousis, E., & Bonacina, S. J. S. (2021). Influence of human factors on cyber security within healthcare organisations. *Systematic Reviews,* 21(15), 5119.34372354

Obaid, H. S., & Abeed, E. (2020). *DoS and DDoS attacks at OSI layers.* Academic Press.

Ögütçü, G., Testik, Ö. M., & Chouseinoglou, O. (2016). *Analysis of personal information security behavior and awareness.* Academic Press.

Ohm, M., Plate, H., Sykosch, A., & Meier, M. (2020). *Backstabber's knife collection: A review of open source software supply chain attacks.* Paper presented at the Detection of Intrusions and Malware, and Vulnerability Assessment: 17th International Conference, DIMVA 2020, Lisbon, Portugal. 10.1007/978-3-030-52683-2_2

Ohm, M., Sykosch, A., & Meier, M. (2020). Towards detection of software supply chain attacks by forensic artifacts. *Proceedings of the 15th international conference on availability, reliability and security.* 10.1145/3407023.3409183

Pattinson, M., Butavicius, M., Parsons, K., McCormac, A., & Calic, D. (2015). *Factors that influence information security behavior: An Australian web-based study.* Paper presented at the Human Aspects of Information Security, Privacy, and Trust: Third International Conference, HAS 2015. 10.1007/978-3-319-20376-8_21

Poehlmann, N., Caramancion, K. M., Tatar, I., Li, Y., Barati, M., Merz, T. J. A. i. S., Networks,, . . . ESCS'20. (2021). The organizational cybersecurity success factors: an exhaustive literature review. 377-395.

Proctor, R. W., & Chen, J. (2015). *The role of human factors/ergonomics in the science of security: decision making and action selection in cyberspace.* Academic Press.

Qiu, J., Tian, Z., Du, C., Zuo, Q., Su, S., & Fang, B. (2020). *A survey on access control in the age of internet of things.* Academic Press.

Rahman, T., Rohan, R., Pal, D., & Kanthamanon, P. (2021). *Human factors in cybersecurity: a scoping review.* Paper presented at the 12th International Conference on Advances in Information Technology. 10.1145/3468784.3468789

Ravidas, S., Lekidis, A., Paci, F., & Zannone, N. (2019). Access control in Internet-of-Things. Academic Press.

Ring, M., Landes, D., & Hotho, A. (2018). *Detection of slow port scans in flow-based network traffic.* Academic Press.

Rogowski, W. (2013). *The right approach to data loss prevention.* Academic Press.

Rohan, R., Funilkul, S., Pal, D., & Chutimaskul, W. (2021). *Understanding of human factors in cybersecurity: A systematic literature review.* Paper presented at the 2021 International Conference on Computational Performance Evaluation (ComPE). 10.1109/ComPE53109.2021.9752358

Rohan, R., Funilkul, S., Pal, D., & Thapliyal, H. (2021). *Humans in the loop: cybersecurity aspects in the consumer IoT context.* Academic Press.

Schmidt, N., Zöller, B., & Rosenkranz, C. (2016). *The clash of cultures in information technology outsourcing relationships: An institutional logics perspective.* Paper presented at the Shared Services and Outsourcing: A Contemporary Outlook: 10th Global Sourcing Workshop 2016, Val d'Isère, France.

Siddiqi, M. A., Pak, W., & Siddiqi, M. A. (2022). *A study on the psychology of social engineering-based cyberattacks and existing countermeasures.* Academic Press.

Silva, S., Lima, S. M. L., Pinheiro, R. P., Abreu, L. M. S., Lima, R. D. T., & Fernandes, S. M. M. (2023). *Antivirus Solution to IoT Malware Detection with Authorial Next-Generation Sandbox.* Academic Press.

Singh, J., & Singh, J. (2021). *A survey on machine learning-based malware detection in executable files.* Academic Press.

Singh, P., Tapaswi, S., & Gupta, S. (2020). Malware detection in pdf and office documents. 10.1080/19393555.2020.1723747

Sivasankari, N., & Kamalakkannan, S. (2022). *Detection and prevention of man-in-the-middle attack in iot network using regression modeling.* Academic Press.

Takebayashi, T., Tsuda, H., Hasebe, T., & Masuoka, R. (2010). *Data loss prevention technologies.* Academic Press.

Tambe, A., Aung, Y. L., Sridharan, R., Ochoa, M., Tippenhauer, N. O., Shabtai, A., & Elovici, Y. (2019). Detection of threats to IoT devices using scalable VPN-forwarded honeypots. *Proceedings of the Ninth ACM Conference on Data and Application Security and Privacy.* 10.1145/3292006.3300024

Tandon, A., & Nayyar, A. (2019). *A comprehensive survey on ransomware attack: A growing havoc cyberthreat.* Academic Press.

Toma, C., Boja, C., Popa, M., Doinea, M., & Ciurea, C. (2021). *Viruses, Exploits, Malware and Security Issues on IoT Devices.* Paper presented at the International Conference on Information Technology and Communications Security.

Triplett, W. (2022). *Addressing human factors in cybersecurity leadership.* Academic Press.

Upadhya, A., & Srinivas, B. (2020). *A Survey on different Port Scanning Methods and the Tools used to perform them.* Academic Press.

Wang, Z., Zhu, H., & Sun, L. (2021). *Social engineering in cybersecurity: Effect mechanisms, human vulnerabilities and attack methods.* Academic Press.

Zhang, T.-Y., & Ye, D. (2020). *False data injection attacks with complete stealthiness in cyber–physical systems: A self-generated approach.* Academic Press.

Zhang, Z., Zhang, Y.-Q., Chu, X., & Li, B. (2004). *An overview of virtual private network (VPN): IP VPN and optical VPN.* Academic Press.

Abbreviations

H.F.s: Human Factors
IoT: Internet of Things
IIoT: Industrial Internet of Things
PDF: Portable Document Format
ZIP: Compressed
DDoS: Distributed Denial of Service
UDP: User Datagram Protocol (UDP)
ICMP: Internet Control Message Protocol
TCP: Transmission Control Protocol
SYN: Synchronize
MITM: Man in the middle attack
ISA: Information Security Awareness
PPT: People Process and Technology
VPN: Virtual Private Networks
RBAC: Role-Based Access Control
ABAC: Attribute-Based Access Control
DLP: Data loss prevention

Chapter 12
Forensic Approaches to Cybersecurity Challenges:
Protecting Digital Landscapes in an Evolving Threat Environment

Akash Bag
https://orcid.org/0000-0001-8820-171X
Amity University, India

Parul Sinha
Amity University, India

ABSTRACT

The growth of internet of things (IoT) devices across industries has brought advances but also revealed security risks and digital forensic challenges. This chapter examines IoT security threats, student under-standing of them and their remedies, and IoT forensic examination issues. The research highlights the need for user training in IoT security, identifies prevalent dangers including malware and DDoS attacks, and highlights mitigation solutions through a synergistic literature analysis and comprehensive survey. It explores IoT forensics, its core processes, its crucial importance, and the many obstacles that hinder digital investigations in the IoT ecosystem. This chapter adds to the body of information on IoT device security, emphasizes user awareness, and highlights the challenges of IoT forensics.

INTRODUCTION

The term "Internet of Things" (IoT) describes a broad network of objects that can compute, perceive their surroundings, link to other objects and networks, and carry out tasks on their own. These devices can interchange data and be integrated with cloud computing platforms for improved data storage and processing efficiency (Assiri & Almagwashi, 2018). They can interact using a variety of wireless pro-tocols, such as Bluetooth, Zigbee, and Wi-Fi. IoT devices are incredibly popular; by 2025, there will be 30.9 billion of them worldwide, up from an expected 19.8 billion in 2023. This growth indicates how IoT technologies are being incorporated into a wider range of industries, including manufacturing, healthcare, urban development, and transportation, indicating how important they are to the advancement of these

DOI: 10.4018/979-8-3693-3451-5.ch012

industries. IoT technology adoption is happening quickly, but not without its problems, chief among them being security and privacy issues (Assiri & Almagwashi, 2018). IoT devices are attractive targets for hostile actors due to the volume of data they generate and handle. Common security concerns include DDoS and virus attacks, unauthorized access, and more advanced methods such as Man in The Middle (MITM) assaults (Priya et al., 2021). Notably, events like the massive DDoS attack launched by the Mirai botnet, the Verkada hack, and the compromise of implant devices at St. Jude Medical have highlighted the serious consequences of these security breaches, which impact not only personal privacy but also the integrity of vital infrastructure and have a substantial negative impact on the economy and society.

The potential extent of disruption that IoT vulnerabilities could create was exemplified by the Mirai botnet attack, which resulted in widespread internet disruptions and substantial financial losses for impacted firms. The incidents above highlight the urgent necessity of implementing strong IoT security protocols and creating effective IoT forensic techniques (Langner, 2011). Addressing and minimizing the fallout from cybercrimes employing IoT technology largely depends on IoT forensics, the field devoted to extracting, analyzing, and preserving digital evidence from IoT devices. However, the heterogeneity of IoT ecosystems and devices, including differences in device capabilities, data formats, and communication protocols, presents the sector with major problems (Alayande et al., 2018). The scattered nature of data across international cloud platforms and the constrained computational capabilities of many Internet of Things (IoT) devices, which provide further challenges in evidence collecting and analysis, further complicate the forensic procedure.

There is a noticeable lack of standardized forensic approaches that can traverse the complex terrain of IoT designs, even though research in IoT security and forensics is rapidly expanding. The vast array of security risks and the general difficulties forensic analysts face are sufficiently identified and described in the literature now in publication. It does not, however, succeed in providing a unified framework or toolbox that can be used consistently over the diverse IoT spectrum (Stoyanova et al., 2020). Research that not only connects the various technological aspects of IoT devices and their operational settings but also tackles the legal and logistical challenges of conducting digital investigations in an increasingly interconnected global digital landscape, is desperately needed. This includes the creation of international cooperation protocols to expedite the investigation of cybercrimes that cross national jurisdictions and the development of sophisticated forensic tools that can effectively gather and analyze evidence from a variety of IoT devices and cloud services.

PROBLEM FORMULATION

Examining the terrain of security risks and forensic difficulties in the Internet of Things (IoT) ecosystem reveals a rich mosaic of research, highlighting the extent and quality of current scholarly involvement with these urgent issues. The identification and mitigation of security dangers inherent to Internet of Things (IoT) devices, as well as a critical analysis of the forensic issues that arise as these technologies become more and more ingrained in daily life, are at the core of this investigation (Janarthanan et al., 2021). The academic conversation takes the form of a thorough analysis of the body of literature, with important references including works by Ratna et al. and Alauddin et al. While these contributions are crucial in helping to map the shapes of IoT security threats across the three layers of the architecture—the network, application, and perception layers—they also draw attention to the growing number of security vulnerabilities that are being exacerbated by the growing number of IoT devices and the ensuing privacy concerns. Despite these observations, there is still a gap in the discussion, especially when it comes to the practical consequences of these kinds of threats (Jindal & Sharma, 2014).

Concurrent with the conversation about security risks, IoT forensics is becoming recognized as an important field of paper. Through the work of academics like Maryam et al. and Geetanjali et al., the story of the fundamental difficulties faced by forensic investigators in IoT environments is revealed. The story highlights a basic contradiction between the multidimensional, layered complexity of IoT ecosystems and traditional forensic investigative tools (Hu et al., 2023). In this instance, the discussion goes beyond just listing obstacles to include the cyberattacks triggered by the increasing pervasiveness of IoT devices in daily life, along with the corresponding forensic obstacles that impede efficient digital investigations. Although significant progress has been achieved in clarifying the dynamics of IoT security and forensics, the discussion highlights an ongoing gap in the academic knowledge of these fields (Tabassum et al., 2019). The need for greater paper is evident and urgent, stemming from the need to develop a more thorough and sophisticated knowledge of IoT forensic investigations. It is imperative to close these knowledge gaps because the number of IoT devices is increasing steadily, which is raising the corresponding security risks and forensic difficulties. As a result, research questions act as a beacon, directing the course of subsequent investigations (Bhattasali et al., 2012). These inquiries include the range of IoT security risks and assaults, people's knowledge and opinions about these risks and how to reduce them, and the complex difficulties facing IoT forensics. As such, this section anchors the investigation inside a framework that is set to unravel the complexity of the Internet of Things ecosystem, not only outlining the current state of scholarly debate but also outlining a path forward for future research attempts. The research questions are as follows:

RQ1: What are the most common IoT security threats and attacks, their mitigation techniques, and their consequences in real-world incidents?

RQ2: What is the level of students' awareness of IoT security threats and their mitigation techniques, and how do they perceive the most effective ways to enhance IoT security?

RQ3: What are the key challenges associated with IoT forensics, and how do they impact the effectiveness of digital investigations in the IoT ecosystem?

METHODOLOGY

The paper encapsulated within the scope of this scholarly pursuit is to dissect and elucidate the multifaceted dimensions of security threats and forensic challenges inherent to the Internet of Things (IoT), employing a methodological framework that straddles both theoretical exposition and empirical inquiry. Anchored in a mixed-method approach, this paper endeavors to traverse the theoretical landscapes and practical terrains of IoT security and forensic analysis, thereby furnishing a panoramic understanding that spans both conceptual and operational paradigms. At the heart of the methodological odyssey is a delineated roadmap comprising a series of objectives meticulously designed to bridge extant knowledge gaps while advancing the frontiers of understanding concerning IoT security threats, their mitigation, and the attendant forensic challenges. A preliminary literature review constitutes the foundational phase of this exploration, aiming to scaffold the theoretical edifice upon which subsequent empirical inquiries are predicated. This initial foray into the academic and technical corpus serves not only to chart the currents of existing knowledge but also to spotlight the interstices that beckon further scholarly engagement.

Complementing the literature review is an empirical investigation, manifesting through a survey targeted at elucidating the awareness, knowledge, and perceptions of students regarding IoT security threats and the gamut of strategies deemed efficacious in fortifying against such vulnerabilities. This bifurcated methodological stance—encompassing both literature review and survey—embodies the essence of a multimethod research strategy, ensuring a holistic apprehension of the subject matter at hand. The literature review, conducted with a nod to Kitchenham's guidelines albeit with adaptations for a less formalized review, unfolds through a sequence of meticulously orchestrated steps. These include the articulation of research questions that guide the scope of the literature search, a comprehensive trawl through relevant databases employing a combination of keywords and Boolean operators to zero in on pertinent literature, and a rigorous process of data extraction and quality assessment predicated on pre-defined inclusion and exclusion criteria. The outcome of this rigorous scholarly exercise is a distilled compendium of academic papers, each subjected to a meticulous quality assessment to ascertain its relevance, validity, and contribution to the overarching research objectives.

Through this intricate tapestry of methodological rigor and scholarly inquiry, the paper aspires to not only augment the corpus of knowledge on IoT security and forensic challenges but also to illuminate the pathways towards enhancing the resilience of IoT ecosystems against the multifarious threats that beleaguers them. In doing so, the paper positions itself as a beacon of insight in the ongoing discourse on securing the burgeoning expanse of IoT technologies against the ever-evolving landscape of cyber threats and vulnerabilities. The papers included in the literature review were specifically selected from publications spanning the years 2016 to 2023. This time frame was chosen to ensure that the information and insights derived are both recent and up-to-date, reflecting the latest developments and scholarly discourse in the fields of IoT security and forensics. The sources for the literature review encompassed a comprehensive search across multiple academic databases and platforms, including IEEE Xplore, ScienceDirect, ResearchGate, and Google Scholar. This broad selection criterion was aimed at capturing a wide range of published and peer-reviewed articles, chapters, and theses relevant to the research questions, particularly focusing on IoT security, IoT attacks, and cloud forensics. Embarking upon a scholarly inquiry into the consciousness and preparedness of Information Technology (IT) students vis-à-vis the security threats plaguing the Internet of Things (IoT) necessitated the meticulous construction and deployment of a survey instrument. To this end, a Google Form was designed and utilized as a pivotal tool for gathering data for a survey. This digital platform facilitated the collection of responses from a diverse cohort of IT students, enabling an assessment of their level of awareness regarding IoT security threats and their mitigation techniques.

THEORETICAL BACKGROUND

The expansive growth of the Internet of Things (IoT) intertwines with a spectrum of advancements enhancing various facets of daily life, yet concurrently unfurls a matrix of security dilemmas and forensic complexities necessitating adept resolutions. At the heart of this discourse lies the recognition of IoT's pivotal role in propelling technological integration across sectors, underlined by an urgent call to fortify these systems against emergent threats (Tabassum et al., 2019). The crux of addressing these challenges is a nuanced comprehension of the security perils inherent to IoT, coupled with the formulation and application of strategic countermeasures, an endeavor critically examined through a methodical survey of existing literature. Security threats to IoT systems manifest in diverse forms, each with unique implications for data privacy, integrity, and the operational viability of devices (Shafiei et al., 2014). Malware and malicious code injection attacks epitomize such threats, targeting the very functionality of IoT devices to compromise data or gain unauthorized control. These incursions not only risk data sanctity but also the physical integrity of critical infrastructure, as evidenced by the notorious Stuxnet attack. Counteracting these threats demands a multi-faceted strategy emphasizing regular security updates, robust authentication protocols, and advanced intrusion detection systems, aiming to fortify the IoT ecosystem against unauthorized access and data breaches (Stoyanova et al., 2020).

Among the array of assaults, False Data Injection (FDI) attacks and Replay attacks distinctly underscore the vulnerabilities in data transmission protocols, posing severe risks to data integrity and system reliability. The mitigation of these threats' hinges on the deployment of encryption and secure communication protocols, supplemented by intrusion detection mechanisms vigilant against unauthorized data manipulation (Assiri & Almagwashi, 2018). Furthermore, the intricacy of cryptanalysis and side-channel attacks reveals the critical need for secure cryptographic practices, ensuring the confidentiality and integrity of data amidst the potential for unauthorized decryption and information leakage. The phenomenon of Distributed Denial of Service (DDoS) attacks, leveraging the vast network of IoT devices, amplifies the urgency for comprehensive network monitoring and stringent access controls to safeguard against service disruptions and data theft. Similarly, the subterfuge of spoofing and Man In The Middle (MITM) attacks necessitates robust authentication and encryption measures to preserve the sanctity of data transmissions within the IoT landscape (Cekerevac et al., 2017).

Conversely, the realm of IoT forensics emerges as a vital frontier in deciphering the digital footprints left by cyber intrusions. Herein, the investigative journey spans the identification, collection, and meticulous analysis of digital evidence, culminating in the articulation of findings within legal frameworks. This forensic odyssey is intricately woven through the tapestry of IoT's architecture, from device-level scrutiny to the exploration of cloud and network interactions, each layer presenting distinct challenges and requiring specialized investigative approaches. The significance of IoT forensics extends beyond the mere reconstruction of cyber incidents; it is instrumental in unveiling vulnerabilities, guiding the fortification of IoT systems against future attacks, and shaping the development of more secure technologies (Hu et al., 2023). Amidst this, the data emanating from IoT ecosystems—spanning devices, networks, and cloud platforms—serves as a cornerstone for forensic analyses, offering insights into system behaviors and potential security lapses. Nevertheless, the endeavor of IoT forensics is fraught with obstacles, from the heterogeneity of devices and data formats to the limitations imposed by device storage and processing capacities (Fardan & Paterson, 2013). These challenges are compounded by the dispersed nature of IoT data across multiple locales and jurisdictions, adding layers of complexity to forensic investigations. The exigency for enhanced technical capabilities, including specialized forensic tools and the requisite training for investigators, stands out as a critical need in navigating the intricacies of IoT forensics (A. Khattab, 2021).

RESULTS

The survey in question is driven by the necessity to evaluate students' awareness of IoT security threats, particularly focusing on those requiring user action for effective mitigation. Its primary aim is to narrow the gap between theoretical knowledge of these threats and the practical steps users can undertake for a secure IoT environment. Divided into sections, the first segment, IoT Familiarity, and Security Concerns, uses responses to the initial questions to shed light on students' understanding of IoT and their security concerns regarding IoT devices. This division is essential for a detailed examination of students' knowledge and their perceptions of IoT security.

IoT Familiarity and Security Concerns

This part of the survey includes answers to the first two questions, offering insights into the students' understanding of IoT (Internet of Things) and their worries about the security of IoT devices.

Q1: Familiarity With the Concept of IoT

The investigation reveals a notable gradation in familiarity with the Internet of Things (IoT) among participants. Conducted with 33 respondents, the chapter identifies a spectrum of awareness levels: a minority of 9.1% (3 individuals) acknowledge no prior knowledge of IoT. In contrast, 30.3% (10 individuals) possess a basic understanding, situating themselves as somewhat familiar with the concept. The survey further distinguishes 33.3% (11 individuals) as moderately acquainted with IoT, while 27.3% (9 individuals) claim a high level of familiarity, asserting they are very familiar with the subject. This distribution underscores a predominant awareness of IoT among the participants, which is paramount for cultivating an informed discourse on related security concerns.

Figure 1. Familiarity with the concept of IoT

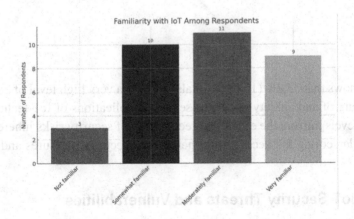

Significantly, the research delineates a methodological approach wherein the three respondents lacking awareness of IoT were excluded from subsequent inquiries, ensuring the analysis remained focused on informed perspectives. This procedural nuance highlights the chapter's commitment to relevance and specificity in evaluating the participants' understanding and concerns regarding IoT security implications.

Q2: Concerns About IoT Device Security

The survey elucidates a prevalent concern among respondents regarding the security of Internet of Things (IoT) devices. A nuanced breakdown of these concerns reveals that 26.7% (8 individuals) are somewhat concerned, suggesting an initial awareness of potential security risks. A further 40% (12 individuals) articulate a moderate level of concern, indicative of a more considered apprehension about the vulnerabilities associated with IoT devices.

Figure 2. Level of Concern Regarding IoT Device Security

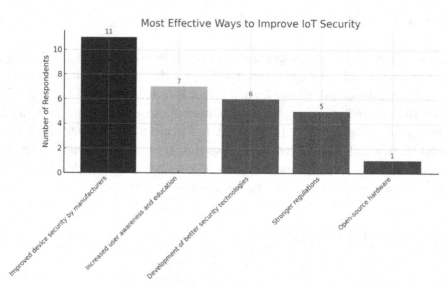

The data also shows that 33.3% (10 individuals) express a very high level of concern, demonstrating a deep understanding of and anxiety about the security implications of IoT technologies. This stratification of concern levels mirrors the escalating recognition of security risks inherent to the proliferation of IoT devices, underscoring the necessity for heightened security measures and awareness within the IoT ecosystem.

Awareness of IoT Security Threats and Vulnerabilities

This survey section delves into how much the participants know about common security weaknesses in IoT (Internet of Things) devices, their understanding of various security threats, and their views on what the biggest security risks are. By looking at the responses to Questions 3, 5, and 6, we get a clearer picture of how well the respondents grasp the security issues that come with IoT technology.

Q3: Awareness of Common IoT Security Vulnerabilities

In the subsequent analysis, the survey targets the participants' comprehension of prevalent security vulnerabilities within the Internet of Things (IoT) domain. A commanding majority, 83.3% (25 of 30 respondents), pinpoint weak or easily guessable passwords as a significant vulnerability, underscoring a critical and widespread concern over basic security practices. The absence of regular updates and patches constitutes the second most recognized issue, identified by 66.7% (20 respondents), highlighting a crucial gap in maintaining the security integrity of IoT devices over time. Additionally, three distinct issues each garner acknowledgment from 53.3% (16 respondents): unsecured remote management access, the absence of encryption for data transmission, and inadequate user authentication and authorization mechanisms. These findings collectively point to a broad awareness among participants of the multifaceted security challenges that IoT ecosystems face. A singular response (3.3%) brings attention to other less commonly cited vulnerabilities, including physical hardware access, the implications of limited user knowledge, challenges posed by abandoned or obsolete hardware, and the risks of shared Wi-Fi networks. This diverse range of identified vulnerabilities illustrates the complexity of the security landscape in IoT contexts, calling for a comprehensive and multi-layered approach to safeguarding devices and data.

Figure 3. Awareness of Common IoT Security Vulnerabilities

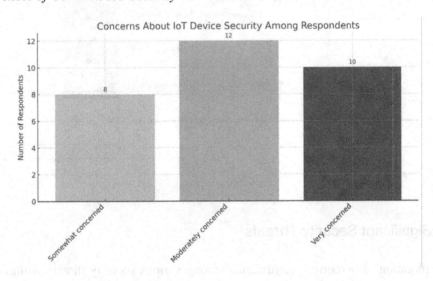

Q5: Familiarity With IoT Threats

The investigation into the familiarity with specific Internet of Things (IoT) security threats among participants yields insightful distinctions across various types of cybersecurity challenges. Man In The Middle (MITM) attacks emerge as the most recognized threat, with 73.3% (22 out of 30 respondents) indicating familiarity. This high level of awareness reflects the prominence of MITM attacks in discussions around digital security vulnerabilities, particularly in intercepting or altering communications. Unauthorized access follows closely, acknowledged by 66.7% (20 respondents), underscoring concerns over the unauthorized exploitation of IoT devices. Distributed Denial of Service (DDoS) and Malware attacks are familiar to 63.3% (19 respondents) and 60% (18 respondents) of the sample, respectively, highlighting awareness of these significant threats that can disrupt services or compromise device integrity. Spoofing attacks, involving the forgery of communications from trusted sources, are recognized by 43.3% (13 respondents). This relatively lower recognition may suggest a nuanced understanding of threat vectors among participants. Additionally, a marginal 3.3% (2 respondents) mention other threats, such as physical attacks on the devices themselves and data misuse, indicating a broader but less commonly acknowledged range of concerns within IoT security. These findings collectively underline a varied but substantial level of awareness among respondents towards the multifarious security challenges facing IoT ecosystems.

Figure 4. Familiarity With Various IoT Security Threats

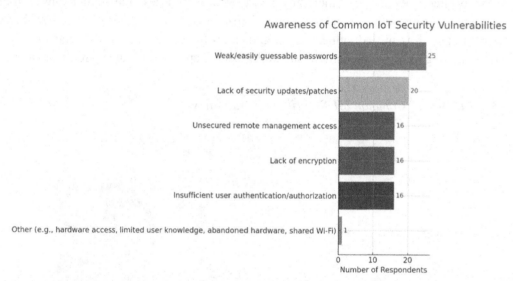

Q6: Most Significant Security Threats

In the exploration of perceived significance among various security threats within the Internet of Things (IoT) environment, unauthorized access stands out as the principal concern, highlighted by 33.3% (10 out of 30 respondents) of the participants. This prioritization underscores the acute awareness of the risks associated with unauthorized entities gaining access to IoT systems, reflecting broader apprehensions about privacy and data integrity. Malware attacks are closely regarded, with 30% (9 respondents) considering them the most substantial threat. This perception aligns with the widespread understanding of malware's capability to disrupt, damage, or gain unauthorized access to devices and networks, signifying its critical threat to the IoT ecosystem.

Figure 5. Most Significant IoT Security Threats According to Respondents

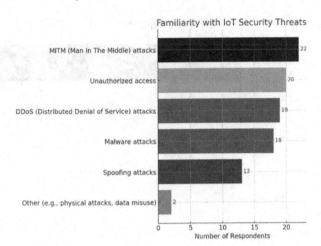

Distributed Denial of Service (DDoS) attacks are identified by 20% (6 respondents) as the most significant threat, illustrating concerns over the ability of such attacks to incapacitate networked services by overwhelming them with traffic. Man in the Middle (MITM) attacks are perceived as the most significant threat by a smaller fraction, 13.3% (4 respondents), indicating a nuanced recognition of the potential for eavesdropping and interception in compromised communication channels. Spoofing attacks, involving the falsification of data to masquerade as a trusted entity, are deemed the least significant, with only one respondent (3.3%) highlighting it as a primary concern. This distribution of concern levels vividly illustrates the diverse landscape of security threats in IoT, with unauthorized access and malware attacks emerging as the foremost anxieties among the participants.

Security Measures, Practices, and Shared Responsibilities

The third part of the survey looks into what people think about having security features already included in IoT (Internet of Things) devices, what they do to keep their devices safe, how important it is to teach users about security, the idea that everyone involved should help protect against threats, and the best methods to make IoT security better.

Q4: Importance of Built-In Security Features

An inquiry into the valuation of inherent security mechanisms within Internet of Things (IoT) devices yields a significant consensus on their criticality. Seventy percent of respondents (21 out of 30) assert these features as "very important," reflecting a strong acknowledgment of the need for fundamental security measures. Additionally, 26.7% (8 respondents) categorize these features as "important," reinforcing the widespread recognition of security's essential role in IoT devices. A solitary respondent regards such features as merely "somewhat important," suggesting a near-universal agreement on the imperative of embedding security within these technologies from the outset.

Figure 6. Perceived Importance of Built-in Security Features in IoT Devices

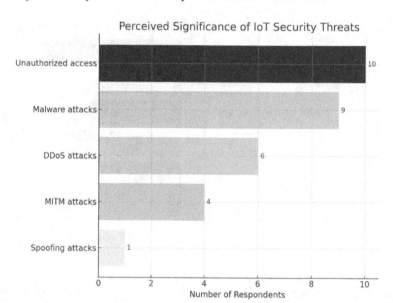

Perceived Significance of IoT Security Threats

Q7: Security Measures Taken by Participants

The survey probes into the security practices employed by participants to safeguard their Internet of Things (IoT) devices. The predominant measure, adopted by 83.3% (25 of 30 respondents), involves altering default passwords, highlighting a fundamental step towards enhancing device security. The practice of regularly updating device firmware, as a means to fortify devices against known vulnerabilities, is undertaken by 63.3% (19 respondents), signifying its importance in maintaining device integrity. Utilization of strong encryption for data transmission is implemented by half of the participants (15 respondents), reflecting awareness of the need to protect data privacy and integrity. Additionally, 40% (12 respondents) disable remote management features to mitigate unauthorized access risks, and 30% (9 respondents) engage in monitoring network traffic to identify anomalous activities, further evidencing proactive security measures. Remarkably, a single respondent underscores the significance of using devices with Internet of Secure Things (IoXT) certification, indicating a preference for standardized security benchmarks. Another individual notes additional precautions, such as decommissioning obsolete devices and adopting secure shell (SSH) access with keys only, pointing towards a comprehensive approach to IoT security.

Figure 7. Measures Taken by Respondents to Secure IoT Devices

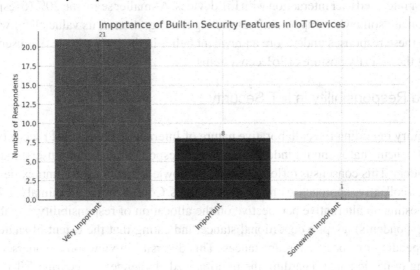

Q8: Importance of User Education

Figure 8. Perceived Importance of User Education in Maintaining IoT Security

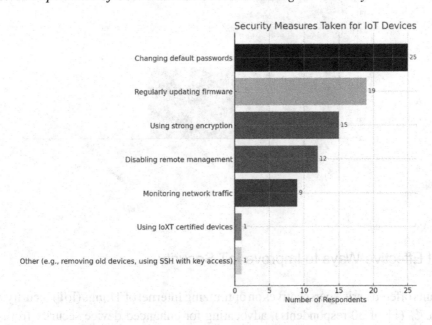

The survey sheds light on the perception of the necessity for user education in bolstering Internet of Things (IoT) security. A majority, 53.3% (16 of 30 respondents), deem it "very important," illustrating a strong consensus on the pivotal role of educating users in mitigating security risks. Another 26.7% (8 respondents) acknowledge its significance by rating it as "important," further underscoring the acknowledged need for informed user interaction with IoT devices. A smaller segment, 20% (6 respondents), views user education as "somewhat important," suggesting a recognition of its value albeit with less urgency. Collectively, these responses underscore a prevalent belief in the integral role that user education plays in enhancing the security posture of IoT ecosystems.

Q9: Shared Responsibility in IoT Security

In the inquiry regarding the collaborative nature of Internet of Things (IoT) security, 60% (18 of 30 respondents) concur that it should indeed be a shared responsibility among users, manufacturers, and service providers. This consensus reflects a broad acknowledgment of the complexities of IoT security, necessitating a collective approach to mitigation strategies. Contrastingly, a minimal 6.7% (2 respondents) dissent, suggesting an alternative perspective on the allocation of responsibility. Notably, a substantial 33.3% (10 respondents) adopt a conditional stance, indicating that the extent of shared responsibility may vary depending on specific circumstances. This diversity in viewpoints underscores the nuanced understanding of participants regarding the multifaceted challenges in securing IoT environments and highlights the majority opinion favoring a collaborative security framework.

Figure 9. Belief in Shared Responsibility for IoT Security

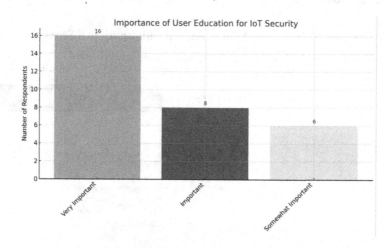

Q10: Most Effective Ways to Improve IoT Security

Participants offered varied perspectives on optimizing Internet of Things (IoT) security, with the largest segment, 36.7% (11 of 30 respondents), advocating for enhanced device security from manufacturers as the paramount approach. This preference underscores the pivotal role of manufacturers in instituting robust security frameworks at the device level. Subsequently, 23.3% (7 respondents) emphasize the importance of amplifying user awareness and education, signaling the critical need for informed user engagement in security practices. The development of advanced security technologies was identified by 20% (6 respondents) as a key measure, pointing towards the necessity for ongoing innovation in security solutions. Stronger regulations garnered support from 16.7% (5 respondents), indicating a recognition of the need for comprehensive legal and regulatory frameworks to ensure device security. Notably, a single respondent advocates for open-source hardware as a potential strategy, suggesting an alternative approach that emphasizes transparency and community involvement in security enhancement. Collectively, these responses highlight a multifaceted approach to improving IoT security, with a significant focus on manufacturer responsibility and user education.

Figure 10. Most Effective Approaches to Improving IoT Security

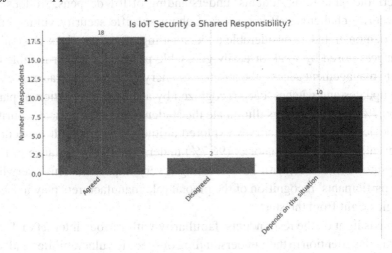

ANALYSIS AND DISCUSSION

This chapter aims to understand the most frequent security problems and attacks on IoT (Internet of Things) devices, the challenges of investigating these issues (IoT forensics), and how aware students are of these security risks and how to deal with them. To find answers, the chapter used a mixed-method approach, combining a review of existing literature and a survey. The literature review helped answer some specific research questions, while the survey targeted a different question. This chapter discusses the main discoveries from both the literature review and the survey.

The survey unveils key insights into students' awareness and perceptions regarding security threats to the Internet of Things (IoT), their grasp of countermeasures, and their views on enhancing IoT security. It emerged that a substantial majority, 90.9% (30 of 33 respondents), possess at least a foundational understanding of IoT. This foundational knowledge is pivotal, forming the groundwork for their awareness of security challenges and potential counteractions within the IoT realm. By focusing on participants with a baseline familiarity with IoT, the survey ensures that the findings accurately reflect the insights of individuals cognizant of IoT and its security implications. A significant proportion of the surveyed cohort, 73.3%, voiced concerns over IoT device security, with delineations of 40% expressing concern and an additional 33.3% indicating substantial concern. This trend underscores a prevalent recognition among students of the inherent security vulnerabilities in IoT devices. Such a level of concern is indicative of a general awareness among the student body of the risks IoT technology may pose, potentially acting as a catalyst for deeper engagement and learning about IoT security measures and best practices. This engagement is crucial for fostering an informed and vigilant user base capable of navigating the complexities of IoT security.

The survey findings delineate a notable trend among participants regarding their familiarity with the Internet of Things (IoT) and their concerns about IoT security. Specifically, 60.6% of respondents have a moderate to high level of familiarity with IoT, a knowledge that correlates with heightened concerns about security, as 73.3% express apprehension regarding the safety of IoT devices. This correlation suggests a discernible pattern: as students' understanding of IoT deepens, so does their awareness of its associated security challenges. When queried about specific security vulnerabilities in IoT (Q3), the respondents demonstrated a considerable understanding of various risks. A significant 83.3% were aware of the dangers posed by weak or easily guessable passwords. Other notable concerns included unsecured remote management access, the absence of encryption for data transmission, and insufficient regular security updates and patches, each recognized by a substantial portion of participants (ranging from 53.3% to 66.7%). These findings illuminate the students' grasp of critical security flaws that could jeopardize IoT devices. Further, the survey explored attitudes towards built-in security features in IoT devices (Q4), revealing that a vast majority (96.7%) underscore the importance of integrating security features directly into IoT devices, with 70% deeming it very important. This overwhelming consensus underscores the participants' recognition of the pivotal role manufacturers play in ensuring the security of IoT technologies right from the start.

The survey sheds light on the respondents' familiarity with various Internet of Things (IoT) security threats, with particular attention to their understanding of specific vulnerabilities and their perceptions of the most pressing threats. Notably, Man In The Middle (MITM) attacks emerged as the most recognized threat, with 73.3% of participants indicating familiarity. This was closely followed by concerns over unauthorized access (66.7%), Distributed Denial of Service (DDoS) attacks (63.3%), malware attacks (60%), and spoofing attacks (43.3%). These findings suggest a significant level of awareness among the respondents regarding a range of security challenges that IoT devices face. Further investigation into the perceived severity of these threats (Q6) revealed that unauthorized access was considered the most significant security challenge by 33.3% of respondents, closely trailed by malware attacks (30%). This ranking underscores the respondents' prioritization of threats that directly compromise the integrity and privacy of IoT systems. DDoS attacks, MITM attacks, and spoofing attacks were also acknowledged but perceived as less critical, highlighting a nuanced understanding of the varying levels of threat posed by different types of security vulnerabilities.

The findings from questions 5 (Q5) and 6 (Q6) of the survey provide insightful perspectives on students' attitudes towards IoT security threats. Specifically, students who are aware of various security threats (Q5) predominantly view unauthorized access and malware attacks (Q6) as the most significant risks. This trend suggests that students are particularly concerned with threats that pose direct risks to their data privacy and the functionality of their devices. Such threats, by compromising data integrity or device operation, resonate more deeply with students' security priorities. Further examination of the survey results, particularly responses to question 7 (Q7), reveals the security practices adopted by students to safeguard their IoT devices. The most prevalent measure, adopted by 83.3% of respondents, involves changing default passwords—a fundamental security practice. This is followed by regularly updating device firmware (63.3%), employing strong encryption for data transmission (50%), disabling remote management features to reduce vulnerabilities (40%), and monitoring network traffic for anomalies

(30%). These practices reflect a pragmatic approach to device security, indicating that students possess a functional understanding of essential security precautions.

The link between awareness of common security vulnerabilities (Q3) and the adoption of protective measures (Q7) underscores a crucial relationship: students who are informed about potential security flaws are more inclined to take proactive steps to mitigate these risks. This includes changing passwords, updating firmware, and utilizing encryption—measures that directly address vulnerabilities. This correlation emphasizes the importance of user education in IoT security. By understanding the risks, users are better positioned to implement effective security strategies, highlighting education's pivotal role in promoting more secure IoT usage. This insight underscores the necessity of not only educating users about the existence of various threats but also guiding them toward practical solutions for enhancing the security of their IoT devices. The survey highlights a strong consensus among respondents on the critical role of user education in IoT security, with a majority (53.3%) emphasizing its very importance. An additional 26.7% regard it as important, and 20% see it as somewhat important. This distribution suggests a widespread belief among students that knowledge and awareness are key to securing IoT devices effectively. This acknowledgment of the necessity for user education underlines the belief that users must be informed and vigilant to navigate the complexities of IoT security.

The comparison between responses to questions 4 (Q4) and 8 (Q8) reveals a cohesive view among participants: both built-in security features and user education are deemed essential for the safeguarding of IoT systems. This dual focus illustrates a nuanced understanding that while technology-based solutions are fundamental, they must be complemented by informed user practices to form a comprehensive security framework. Further insights from question 9 (Q9) show that a significant majority of participants (60%) advocate for a shared responsibility model in IoT security, involving users, manufacturers, and service providers. Meanwhile, 33.3% believe the responsibility varies depending on specific contexts. This perspective underscores the complexity of IoT security, suggesting that effective defense mechanisms require collaboration across different stakeholders. Such a collaborative stance is believed to enhance the resilience of IoT systems against security threats. By linking the importance of technological safeguards and the imperative of user education, alongside advocating for shared responsibility, the findings underscore a multifaceted approach to IoT security. This approach combines technical, educational, and cooperative strategies, reflecting a comprehensive perspective on addressing IoT security challenges. The survey results not only validate students' understanding of the complexities involved in securing IoT devices but also highlight the necessity for concerted efforts among all parties involved to navigate these challenges successfully.

In response to inquiries about the optimal strategies for enhancing Internet of Things (IoT) security (Q10), the participants prioritize enhancements in device security by manufacturers (36.7%) as the foremost approach. This preference is followed by the amplification of user awareness and education (23.3%), the innovation of advanced security technologies (20%), and the implementation of stringent regulations (16.7%). These insights underscore the participants' recognition of IoT security as a multifaceted issue, necessitating a comprehensive and collaborative effort across different fronts. The collective viewpoint, emerging from the survey, is that securing IoT environments should not be the sole responsibility of any single entity. Instead, it requires a synergistic effort involving users, manufacturers, and service providers (Q9). This consensus reflects an understanding that while manufacturers play a critical role in embedding robust security features at the device level, this must be complemented by informed users who are adept at employing these features and adhering to best security practices. Additionally, the evolution of superior security technologies and the establishment of rigorous regulatory frameworks are seen as vital components of a holistic security strategy.

The linkage between a shared responsibility model (Q9) and the identified methods for bolstering IoT security (Q10) underscores the imperative for a cooperative approach among all stakeholders involved in the IoT ecosystem. This approach is deemed essential for addressing the complex challenges that IoT security presents effectively. The participants' responses highlight a comprehensive perspective, emphasizing that enhancing IoT security extends beyond technological fixes to include educational initiatives and policy interventions. This integrated approach is crucial for navigating the intricate landscape of IoT security, ensuring that devices are not only built securely by manufacturers but are also deployed and maintained safely through informed user practices and supportive regulatory environments. The exploration into IoT (Internet of Things) forensics reveals several challenges intrinsic to the nature and structure of IoT devices and ecosystems. These challenges stem from characteristics unique to IoT, including the lack of standardization, limited device capabilities, complex data management, and insufficient technical tools and expertise for forensic analysis.

Firstly, the absence of standardization across the IoT landscape, characterized by a wide variety of devices, operating systems, and communication protocols, significantly complicates the establishment of uniform forensic procedures. This diversity hinders the analysis and mitigation of threats like Man In The Middle (MITM), Spoofing, and Sinkhole attacks, as the disparity in technologies used requires bespoke forensic approaches for each type of device or system. Secondly, the constrained storage and processing power of many IoT devices poses significant limitations. These constraints affect the devices' ability to store logs and records crucial for forensic analysis and impede the deployment of sophisticated forensic tools necessary for investigating complex security breaches such as Eavesdropping, Distributed Denial of Service (DDoS) attacks, and others. Devices with minimal processing capabilities are especially vulnerable, lacking the resources to support the analysis required to trace and counteract attacks. The distributed nature of IoT devices further exacerbates the challenge of locating and identifying relevant data during forensic investigations. The difficulty in tracing data exchanges between myriad devices and sensors, compounded by the vast volumes of data generated, makes it challenging to pinpoint the specific information pertinent to a given security incident. This scenario is further complicated by data fragmentation, which poses additional hurdles in probing threats like Eavesdropping and Sinkhole attacks. Lastly, the limited technical capabilities available for IoT forensics—ranging from a scarcity of specialized forensic tools to a lack of expertise specifically tailored to IoT environments—present significant obstacles. This dearth of resources complicates the investigation and mitigation of a broad spectrum of security threats, including those posed by Malware, Malicious code injection, and advanced cryptanalysis techniques.

In the current digital era, consumers must be informed about cyber security, particularly given the rise in online fraud and cyberattack incidents. Several studies have emphasized the significance of raising awareness of cyber security issues among different populations, such as internet users Umam (2019), adults Rose Sebastian & Babu (2022), college students Senthilkumar & Easwaramoorthy (2017), sea-farers Mrakovic & Vojinović (2020), and non-technical staff in organizations (Hart et al., 2020). These results highlight the necessity of extensive awareness programs to enhance cyber habits and knowledge across these diverse populations. Additionally, studies have demonstrated that interdisciplinary efforts and innovative collaborations can effectively raise awareness of cybersecurity issues (Hall et al., 2022). This implies that consumers' awareness of cyber security dangers and acceptable practices might be improved by implementing novel approaches, such as tabletop games and artistic exhibitions. Furthermore, it has been observed that some groups, such as college students Senthilkumar & Easwaramoorthy (2017) and sailors Mrakovic & Vojinović (2020), lack enough cyber-security knowledge and awareness. This emphasizes the importance of implementing focused educational programs to close specific knowledge gaps and raise these groups' understanding of cyber security. Furthermore, it has been noted that cyber security situational awareness, or CSSA, is an essential and developing subject of study (Tianfield, 2017). To help people and organizations make wise decisions and effectively address cyber security concerns, CSSA strives to deliver timely and pertinent information.

Significant security concerns, such as those related to privacy, access control, secure communication, and safe data storage, have been brought about by the Internet of Things (IoT) (Conti et al., 2017). Because of these difficulties, IoT settings now require strong security protocols and forensic tools. Numerous strategies and solutions have been put out to safeguard IoT systems and components once security and privacy concerns are recognized in IoT systems (Tawalbeh et al., 2020). However to reinforce the IoT environment and improve security, specific methods and instruments must be used when implementing efficient forensic procedures in IoT environments (Arshad et al., 2022). The application of traditional digital forensic tools and methodologies in IoT environments presents obstacles. As a result, new digital forensic tools that are specifically designed for IoT environments must be evaluated and developed (Alazab et al., 2023). In addition, there is a significant risk to security and integrity when digital forensic evidence is collected by IoT devices in IoT environments (Bindrwish et al., 2023). This emphasizes the necessity of taking precautions to guarantee the integrity of digital forensic evidence in IoT environments, such as using blockchain technology (Akhtar & Feng, 2022). To successfully apply control mechanisms and reduce security threats, it is imperative to assess the security of IoT-based smart environments, such as smart homes and smart cities (Karie et al., 2021). Furthermore, worries regarding security and privacy in IoT environments have been highlighted by the dearth of available digital forensics tools and techniques for the sharp rise in IoT devices (Liang et al., 2022). Along with the development of lightweight forensic frameworks capable of expanding the breadth of investigations in IoT environments, there has been an emphasis on the necessity of recognizing and analyzing security and privacy concerns faced by IoT-based environments (Alkhamisi, 2023). There is a lack of methods and strategies for forensic acquisition and analysis for IoT devices, even if the majority of current research focuses on security and privacy for IoT environments (Alabdulsalam et al., 2018). Furthermore, it has been highlighted how important it is to have strong security measures in place to guard against hacking of IoT devices and systems (Zaimy et al., 2023).

CONCLUSION

This chapter intricately explores the interconnections between IoT (Internet of Things) security, user awareness, and forensic challenges, advocating for a holistic approach to dissect and address these complexities. It underscores the pressing need for robust security measures and further research to safeguard IoT systems against significant threats, emphasizing that security is not just a technological issue but also a matter of user awareness. The findings advocate for the incorporation of IoT security education into educational curriculums, suggesting that informed users are crucial in preventing and mitigating security risks. Moreover, the chapter identifies a gap in the current forensic capabilities within the IoT domain, calling for the development of advanced forensic tools and methodologies tailored to the IoT environment. Such advancements are deemed essential for conducting effective digital investigations amidst an increasingly interconnected world. The collaborative effort across various stakeholders—researchers, industry professionals, and users—is highlighted as vital in addressing IoT security threats, enhancing awareness, and overcoming forensic challenges. This cooperative approach is presented as a cornerstone for developing a robust defense mechanism against the evolving landscape of IoT threats. Looking forward, the chapter outlines potential areas for future research to broaden the scope of understanding around IoT security. These include conducting extensive surveys across a wider demographic to gauge the awareness and perceptions of IoT security threats more comprehensively. Additionally, the development of standardized forensic frameworks and tools specific to IoT is proposed as a critical area for future exploration. Finally, the chapter suggests further examination into the collaborative dynamics between users, manufacturers, and service providers, aiming to delineate shared responsibilities and enhance the overall security posture of IoT systems.

REFERENCES

Akhtar, M. S., & Feng, T. (2022). Using Blockchain to Ensure the Integrity of Digital Forensic Evidence in an IoT Environment. *EAI Endorsed Transactions on Creative Technologies*, 9(31), 31. Advance online publication. 10.4108/eai.3-6-2022.174089

Alabdulsalam, S., Schaefer, K., Kechadi, T., & Le-Khac, N.-A. (2018). Internet of Things Forensics – Challenges and a Case Study. In Peterson, G., & Shenoi, S. (Eds.), *Advances in Digital Forensics XIV* (pp. 35–48). Springer International Publishing. 10.1007/978-3-319-99277-8_3

Alayande, A. S., Nwulu, N., & Bakare, A. E. (2018). Modelling and Countermeasures of False Data Injection Attacks Against State Estimation in Power Systems. *2018 International Conference on Computational Techniques, Electronics and Mechanical Systems (CTEMS)*, 129–134. 10.1109/CTEMS.2018.8769295

Alazab, A., Khraisat, A., Singh, S., Alazab, A., Khraisat, A., & Singh, S. (2023). *A Review on the Internet of Things (IoT) Forensics: Challenges, Techniques, and Evaluation of Digital Forensic Tools*. IntechOpen. 10.5772/intechopen.109840

Alkhamisi, K. (2023). An Analysis of Security Attacks on IoT Applications. *International Journal of Information Systems and Computer Technologies*, 2(1). Advance online publication. 10.58325/ijisct.002.01.0053

Arshad, M., Rahman, H., Tariq, J., Riaz, A., & Imran, A., & Ihsan, I. (2022). Digital Forensics Analysis of IoT Nodes using Machine Learning. *Journal of Computing & Biomedical Informatics*, 4. Advance online publication. 10.56979/401/2022/107

Assiri, A., & Almagwashi, H. (2018).. . *IoT Security and Privacy Issues*, 1–5, 1–5. Advance online publication. 10.1109/CAIS.2018.8442002

Bhattasali, T., Chaki, R., & Sanyal, S. (2012). Sleep Deprivation Attack Detection in Wireless Sensor Network. *International Journal of Computer Applications*, 40(15), 19–25. 10.5120/5056-7374

Bindrwish, F. B., Ali, A. N. A., Ghabban, W. H., Alrowwad, A., Fallatah, N. A., Ameerbakhsh, O., & Alfadli, I. M. (2023). Internet of Things for Digital Forensics Application in Saudi Arabia. *Advances in Internet of Things*, 13(1), 1–11. Advance online publication. 10.4236/ait.2023.131001

Cekerevac, Z., Dvorak, Z., Prigoda, L., & Čekerevac, P. (2017). Internet of things and the man-in-the-middle attacks – Security and economic risks. *MEST Journal*, 5(2), 15–5. 10.12709/mest.05.05.02.03

Conti, M., Dehghantanha, A., Franke, K., & Watson, S. (2017). Internet of Things Security and Forensics: Challenges and Opportunities. *Future Generation Computer Systems*, 78, 544–546. Advance online publication. 10.1016/j.future.2017.07.060

Fardan, N. J., & Paterson, K. G. (2013). *Lucky thirteen: Breaking the TLS and DTLS record protocols*. 10.1109/SP.2013.42

Hall, L., Paracha, S., Hagan-Green, G., Ure, C., & Jackman, P. (2022). *Cyber Eyes Wide Open: Creative Collaboration between Artists, Academics & Cyber Security Practitioners*. 10.14236/ewic/HCI2022.15

Hart, S., Margheri, A., Paci, F., & Sassone, V. (2020). Riskio: A Serious Game for Cyber Security Awareness and Education. *Computers & Security*, 95, 101827. 10.1016/j.cose.2020.101827

Hu, P., Gao, W., Li, Y., Wu, M., Hua, F., & Qiao, L. (2023). Detection of False Data Injection Attacks in Smart Grids Based on Expectation Maximization. *Sensors (Basel)*, 23(3), 3. Advance online publication. 10.3390/s2303168336772723

Janarthanan, T., Bagheri, M., & Zargari, S. (2021). IoT Forensics: An Overview of the Current Issues and Challenges. In *Advanced Sciences and Technologies for Security Applications* (pp. 223–254). 10.1007/978-3-030-60425-7_10

Jindal, K., & Sharma, K. (2014).. *Analyzing Spoofing Attacks in Wireless Networks*, 398–402, 398–402. Advance online publication. 10.1109/ACCT.2014.46

Karie, N., Sahri, N., Yang, W., Valli, C., & Kebande, V. (2021). A Review of Security Standards and Frameworks for IoT-Based Smart Environments. *IEEE Access*. 10.1109/ACCESS.2021.3109886

Khattab, A., M. (2021). Comprehensive Study of Attacks and Cryptographic Measures for Internet of Things Devices. *The Journal of Scientific and Engineering Research*, 8, 174–188.

Langner, R. (2011). Stuxnet: Dissecting a Cyberwarfare Weapon. *IEEE Security and Privacy*, 9(3), 49–51. 10.1109/MSP.2011.67

Liang, G., Xin, J., Wang, Q., Ni, X., & Guo, X. (2022). Research on IoT Forensics System Based on Blockchain Technology. *Security and Communication Networks*, 2022, e4490757. 10.1155/2022/4490757

Mrakovic, I., & Vojinović, R. (2020). Evaluation of Montenegrin Seafarer's Awareness of Cyber Security. *Transactions on Maritime Science*, 9(2). Advance online publication. 10.7225/toms.v09.n02.005

Priya, R., Utsav, A., Zabeen, A., & Abhishek, A. (2021). Multiple Security Threats with Its Solution in Internet of Things (IoT). *2021 4th International Conference on Recent Developments in Control, Automation & Power Engineering (RDCAPE)*, 221–223. 10.1109/RDCAPE52977.2021.9633759

Rose Sebastian, S., & Babu, B. (2022). Are we Cyber aware? A cross sectional study on the prevailing Cyber practices among adults from Thiruvalla, Kerala. *International Journal of Community Medicine and Public Health*, 10(1), 235. 10.18203/2394-6040.ijcmph20223550

Senthilkumar, K., & Easwaramoorthy, S. (2017). A Survey on Cyber Security awareness among college students in Tamil Nadu. *IOP Conference Series. Materials Science and Engineering*, 263(4), 042043. 10.1088/1757-899X/263/4/042043

Shafiei, H., Khonsari, A., Derakhshi, H., & Mousavi, P. (2014). Detection and mitigation of sinkhole attacks in wireless sensor networks. *Journal of Computer and System Sciences*, 80(3), 644–653. 10.1016/j.jcss.2013.06.016

Stoyanova, M., Nikoloudakis, Y., Panagiotakis, S., Pallis, E., & Markakis, E. (2020). A Survey on the Internet of Things (IoT) Forensics: Challenges, Approaches and Open Issues. *IEEE Communications Surveys & Tutorials*. 10.1109/COMST.2019.2962586

Tabassum, K., Ibrahim, A., & El Rahman, S. A. (2019). Security Issues and Challenges in IoT. *2019 International Conference on Computer and Information Sciences (ICCIS)*, 1–5. 10.1109/ICCISci.2019.8716460

Tawalbeh, L., Muheidat, F., Tawalbeh, M., & Quwaider, M. (2020). IoT Privacy and Security: Challenges and Solutions. *Applied Sciences (Basel, Switzerland)*, 10(12), 12. Advance online publication. 10.3390/app10124102

Tianfield, H. (2017). Cyber security situational awareness. *2016 IEEE International Conference on Internet of Things (iThings) and IEEE Green Computing and Communications (GreenCom) and IEEE Cyber, Physical and Social Computing (CPSCom) and IEEE Smart Data (SmartData)*, 782–787. 10.1109/iThings-GreenCom-CPSCom-SmartData.2016.165

Umam, M. S. (2019). Orientasi Etika dan Cyber Security Awareness (Studi Kasus pada UMKM di Bantul). *Akmenika: Jurnal Akuntansi Dan Manajemen*, 16(2), 2. Advance online publication. 10.31316/akmenika.v16i2.394

Zaimy, N. A., Zolkipli, M. F., Katuk, N., Zaimy, N. A., Zolkipli, M. F., & Katuk, N. (2023). A review of hacking techniques in IoT systems and future trends of hacking on IoT environment. *World Journal of Advanced Research and Reviews*, 17(2), 2. Advance online publication. 10.30574/wjarr.2023.17.2.0310

ADDITIONAL READING

Alrefaei, F. (2020). The Importance of Security In Cyber-Physical System. *2020 IEEE 6th World Forum on Internet of Things (WF-IoT)*, 1–3. 10.1109/WF-IoT48130.2020.9221155

Bandekar, A., & Javaid, A. Y. (2017). Cyber-attack Mitigation and Impact Analysis for Low-power IoT Devices. *2017 IEEE 7th Annual International Conference on CYBER Technology in Automation, Control, and Intelligent Systems (CYBER)*, 1631–1636. 10.1109/CYBER.2017.8446380

Craggs, B., & Rashid, A. (2017). Smart Cyber-Physical Systems: Beyond Usable Security to Security Ergonomics by Design. *2017 IEEE/ACM 3rd International Workshop on Software Engineering for Smart Cyber-Physical Systems (SEsCPS)*, 22–25. 10.1109/SEsCPS.2017.5

Isbell, R. A., Maple, C., Hallaq, B., & Boyes, H. (2019). Development of a capability maturity model for cyber security in IIoT enabled supply chains. *Living in the Internet of Things (IoT 2019)*, 1–8. 10.1049/cp.2019.0128

Karie, N. M., Sahri, N. M., Yang, W., Valli, C., & Kebande, V. R. (2021). A Review of Security Standards and Frameworks for IoT-Based Smart Environments. *IEEE Access : Practical Innovations, Open Solutions*, 9, 121975–121995. 10.1109/ACCESS.2021.3109886

Kumar, J., & Ramesh, P. R. (2018). Low Cost Energy Efficient Smart Security System with Information Stamping for IoT Networks. *2018 3rd International Conference On Internet of Things: Smart Innovation and Usages (IoT-SIU)*, 1–5. 10.1109/IoT-SIU.2018.8519875

Roukounaki, A., Efremidis, S., Soldatos, J., Neises, J., Walloschke, T., & Kefalakis, N. (2019). Scalable and Configurable End-to-End Collection and Analysis of IoT Security Data: Towards End-to-End Security in IoT Systems. *2019 Global IoT Summit (GIoTS)*, 1–6. 10.1109/GIOTS.2019.8766407

Shukla, M., Johnson, S. D., & Jones, P. (2019). Does the NIS implementation strategy effectively address cyber security risks in the UK? *2019 International Conference on Cyber Security and Protection of Digital Services (Cyber Security)*, 1–11. 10.1109/CyberSecPODS.2019.8884963

KEY TERMS AND DEFINITIONS

DDoS (Distributed Denial of Service) Attack: A cyberattack where multiple compromised computer systems attack a target, such as a server, website, or other network resource, causing a denial of service for users of the targeted resource.

Encryption: The process of converting information or data into a code, especially to prevent unauthorized access. It is critical in securing data transmission in IoT devices to prevent eavesdropping and other forms of cyberattacks.

False Data Injection Attack: A type of cyberattack where an attacker injects or alters data in an IoT system. This can lead to incorrect decisions by the system or its users, potentially causing harm or exploitation.

Internet of Things (IoT): A network of physical objects embedded with sensors, software, and other technologies, aimed at connecting and exchanging data with other devices and systems over the internet. These devices range from ordinary household items to sophisticated industrial tools.

IoT Forensics: The science of extracting, analyzing, and preserving evidence from IoT devices. This field faces unique challenges due to the heterogeneity and limited capabilities of many IoT devices, as well as the distributed nature of IoT networks.

Malware: Malicious software designed to harm, exploit, or otherwise illegally access a computer system or network. In the context of IoT, malware can infect devices to compromise data or enlist the devices in botnets.

Man in the Middle (MITM) Attack: A cyberattack where the attacker secretly intercepts and possibly alters the communication between two parties who believe they are directly communicating with each other.

Spoofing Attack: A malicious attack where a person or program successfully masquerades as another by falsifying data and thereby gaining an illegitimate advantage.

Chapter 13
Cybersecurity Strategies for Smart Grids:
Leveraging Agile IoT and IIoT Integration

Abdullah S. Alshra'a
University of Erlangen-Nuremberg, Germany

Mamdouh Muhammad
https://orcid.org/0009-0009-9685-8880
University of Erlangen-Nuremberg, Germany

Reinhard German
University of Erlangen-Nuremberg, Germany

ABSTRACT

The incorporation of information and communication technologies (ICT) into power grids has brought a new generation in energy management, known as smart grids. This digital transformation has also raised new challenges to cybersecurity. This chapter presents the architecture and cybersecurity interplay within smart grids, highlights the need to secure critical infrastructure, and outlines the security requirements and the importance of availability, integrity, and confidentiality. Also, it discovers potential cyber-threats and vulnerabilities inherent in smart grids and analyzes historical incidents to provide insight into real-world implications. Moreover, the strategies for safeguarding smart grids components, such as supervisory control and data acquisition (SCADA) and industrial control systems (ICS), are discussed, alongside a unified framework to address privacy concerns. Finally, the chapter predicts future trends, identifies pioneering issues, and draws tracks for continuous research and development to strengthen smart grids' resilience against evolving threats.

1. INTRODUCTION

The integration of advanced technologies has given rise to the concept of Smart Grids in the ever-evolving landscape of energy distribution. Smart Grids are a paradigm shift from traditional power grids and represent a sophisticated and interconnected system designed to enhance efficiency, reliability,

DOI: 10.4018/979-8-3693-3451-5.ch013

and sustainability (Alotaibi, Abido, Khalid, & Savkin, 2020). The need for more intelligent, responsive, and adaptive energy management solutions to meet the growing demands of our modern society drives this transformative approach. Smart Grids leverage digital communication, automation, and control technologies to optimize electricity generation, transmission, and consumption. Integrating Information and Communication Technologies (ICT) (Panajotovic, Jankovic, & Odadzic, 2011) into power grids allows for real-time monitoring, data analytics, and seamless communication between various components. This enhanced connectivity enables utilities to make informed decisions, promptly respond to changes in demand, and integrate renewable energy sources efficiently. As demonstrated in Figure 1, Smart grids facilitate a twoway flow of power and information, which means power can flow in multiple directions within the grid, allowing for more efficient use of renewable energy and better management of supply and demand. Additionally, advanced communication and control systems enable real-time monitoring and management of grid operations, improving efficiency, reliability, and resilience.

The need to switch to Smart Grids has become more urgent due to the growing difficulties faced by conventional power grids, such as deteriorating infrastructure, rising energy requirements, and the obligation to decrease carbon emissions. By adopting intelligent technologies, these networks provide better insights into the grid's operations for stakeholders, promoting sustainability and enabling the incorporation of renewable energy sources. Smart Grids comprise several components such as advanced metering infrastructure (AMI), sensors, communication networks, and control systems, which work together to facilitate real-time data exchange, remote monitoring, and automated control (Orlando et al., 2021). These components form the fundamental structure of a more resilient and responsive energy ecosystem. In the context of the Industrial Internet of Things (IIoT) (Boyes, Hallaq, Cunningham, & Watson, 2018), Smart Grids are critical in the convergence of physical and digital systems. The Collaboration between IIoT and Smart Grids enhances overall system intelligence, allowing for predictive maintenance, efficient resource allocation, and improved overall performance. However, increased connectivity also poses new challenges, particularly in cybersecurity. As dependence on interconnected technologies grows, the vulnerabilities of Smart Grids to cyber threats become increasingly apparent. The potential for cyber-attacks targeting critical infrastructure components poses a significant risk to the stability and reliability of these networks. This chapter focuses on exploring the intricacies of securing Smart Grids. It delves into critical aspects such as Smart Grid Network Architecture, Hacking the Smart Grid, Privacy Concerns, and Security Models for Supervisory Control and Data Acquisition (SCADA) (Pliatsios, Sarigiannidis, Lagkas, & Sarigiannidis, 2020), Industrial Control Systems (ICS), and the Smart Grid. This in-depth investigation aims to lighten the cybersecurity challenges and provide viable solutions in the evolving landscape of intelligent energy distribution systems.

Figure 1. Two-Way Flow in Smart Grids

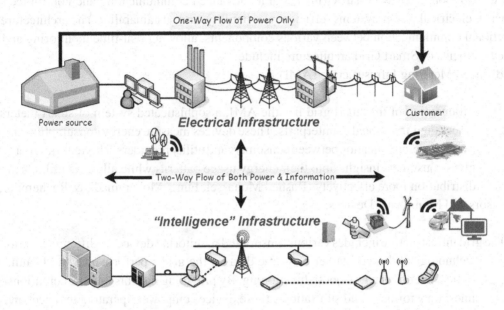

1.1 Overview of the Architecture of Smart Grids

A smart grid is a modernized electricity network that uses advanced technologies to improve energy distribution efficiency, reliability, and sustainability. Unlike traditional grids, Smart Grids use digital communication and real-time data analytics to optimize electricity flow, transforming how power is generated, transmitted, and consumed. Deploying a smart grid involves using cutting-edge technologies such as sensors, smart meters, and communication networks. These components work together to collect and analyze data, enabling utilities to monitor and manage the grid with unprecedented precision (Alotaibi et al., 2020).

Smart Grids help to distribute energy more efficiently by reducing losses during transmission and distribution. This leads to a more reliable and cost-effective energy supply. Additionally, as we move towards more sustainable energy sources like solar, wind, and hydropower, Smart Grids help integrate these intermittent energy sources, ensuring a reliable power supply even when the sun isn't shining, or the wind isn't blowing. Smart Grids also allow consumers to manage energy demand actively, utilizing real-time data and communication to adjust energy usage during peak times. Smart Grids also offer quick fault detection and response capabilities, which enables faster response times when fixing issues, minimizing downtime, and enhancing overall grid reliability. Furthermore, Smart Grids strengthen the resilience of the entire energy infrastructure by adapting and responding to changing conditions, which is crucial in the face of natural disasters or unforeseen events that may disrupt traditional grids. Smart Grids represent a fundamental shift towards a more sustainable, resilient, and efficient energy future, paving the way for a smarter, greener world (Moreno Escobar, Morales Matamoros, Tejeida Padilla, Lina Reyes, & Quintana Espinosa, 2021).

The advent of Smart Grid technology represents a significant leap forward in the modernization of power distribution systems. Smart Grids integrate advanced communication and control technologies to enhance electrical power systems' efficiency, reliability, and sustainability. The architecture enables bidirectional communication between various components, allowing real-time monitoring and control. The key elements of Smart Grid architecture include:

1. Advanced Metering Infrastructure (AMI):

   At the foundation of the smart grid lies the AMI, a sophisticated system of smart meters that replaces their traditional counterparts. These devices measure energy consumption and enable a two-way communication between consumers and utility providers. This real-time data exchange gives consumers insights into their energy usage patterns while allowing utilities to optimize distribution more effectively (Rashed Mohassel, Fung, Mohammadi, & Raahemifar, 2014).

2. Sensors and Monitoring Devices:

   The grid infrastructure includes various sensors and monitoring devices at different locations. These technological devices gather real-time data on the grid's performance and health, which is critical in ensuring its smooth functioning. By providing insights into the conditions of power lines, transformers, and substations, these devices empower operators to detect and respond quickly to faults, which helps to reduce downtime and makes the grid more reliable overall (Gungor, Lu, & Hancke, 2010).

3. Communication Networks:

   A strong communication network plays a crucial role in connecting the different components of the smart grid. These networks guarantee smooth data transmission by incorporating advanced technologies such as fiber optics and wireless communication. This connectivity allows for quick and efficient responses to changes in demand, helps manage the grid effectively, and supports integrating renewable energy sources (Abrahamsen, Ai, & Cheffena, 2021).

4. Control Systems:

   At the heart of the smart grid architecture lie advanced control systems that enable operators to manage and optimize grid operations from remote locations efficiently. These systems offer tools to balance supply and demand effectively, integrate renewable energy sources, and respond to unforeseen events. The control systems enhance the overall efficiency and adaptability of the grid (Mahela et al., 2020).

In other words, the smart grid is an interconnected system comprising three crucial layers that operate together to ensure its smooth functioning. The Infrastructure Layer comprises physical components such as power lines, substations, and transformers. These are equipped with smart sensors that collect real-time data to help the grid function seamlessly. The Communication Layer plays a significant role in facilitating data exchange between different components using advanced technologies, which makes the grid more responsive and adaptable. To enable various devices to communicate with each other, it is crucial to have standardized communication protocols within a network. Protocols like DNP3 (Distributed Network Protocol), Modbus, and IEC 104 facilitate consistent and seamless communication between devices, regardless of the manufacturer. Standardization is an essential aspect of Smart Grids as it allows the integration of various technologies in a cohesive manner. Finally, at the top of the architecture, the

Application Layer hosts software and algorithms that analyze the collected data. This layer includes energy management systems, demand response applications, and other intelligent tools that contribute significantly to the overall efficiency and resilience of the smart grid.

It is worth mentioning that the National Institute of Standards and Technology (NIST) has designed a Smart Grids Conceptual Model and an architecture framework that are widely recognized for their ability to integrate advanced technologies into the power grid infrastructure. The Model provides a systematic approach for stakeholders to design, develop, and deploy Smart Grid technologies and systems. It emphasizes interoperability, standardization, and compatibility among various components and systems within the Smart Gridsecosystem. The conceptual model consists of multiple layers, each representing various aspects of the Smart Grids architecture (Greer et al., 2014; Gopstein et al., 2021).

1. **The Common Services Layer** contains foundational services to support the operation of the Smart Grids, such as security, communication, and network management.
2. **The Grid Domain Layer** defines the various domains within the Smart Grid, including the generation, transmission, distribution, and consumption of electricity, in addition to focusing on domain-specific functions and services.
3. **The Information Domain Layer** manages and exchanges information within the Smart Grids and includes data management, analytics, and decision support systems to enable efficient grid operations.
4. **The Communication Layer** addresses the communication infrastructure required to facilitate real-time data exchange and control signals among grid components, devices, and systems.
5. **The Functional Layers** represent specific functionalities or capabilities of the Smart Grid, such as demand response, grid management, asset management, and customer energy management.

1.2 Interplaying Cybersecurity of Smart Grids With IoT/IIoT

In Smart Grids, the synergy between cybersecurity and the broader fields of IoT, and IIoT environments is pivotal in understanding and addressing current cybersecurity challenges effectively. In the following, there are detailed points of this relationship:

- **Interconnected Ecosystems**: Smart Grids, IoT, and IIoT environments are interconnected systems where devices, sensors, and systems work together to optimize operations and improve efficiency. In Smart Grids, IoT devices such as smart meters and sensors gather data on energy usage and grid performance, while IIoT devices monitor and manage industrial processes. However, this interconnectivity can also bring potential vulnerabilities, as malicious actors can exploit any weak link in the system.
- **Common Architecture and Technologies**: These domains often share similar architectural principles and technological foundations. For instance, they depend on sensors, actuators, communication protocols (such as MQTT, and CoAP), and cloud-based platforms for data collection, processing, and analysis. Consequently, cybersecurity strategies developed for one field can be adapted and applied to the others, leveraging common security controls and protocols (Naik, 2017).
- **Shared Security Challenges**: The convergence of Smart Grids with IoT and IIoT environments boosts shared security challenges. These include unauthorized ac cess, data breaches, ransomware attacks, and supply chain vulnerabilities. Compromises in IoT or IIoT devices can provide entry points for attackers to infiltrate smart grid systems, potentially disrupting energy distribution, industrial operations, and critical infrastructure (Gebremichael et al., 2020).

- **Cross-Domain Interactions**: As Smart Grids technologies integrate with IoT and IIoT devices in homes, buildings, and industrial facilities, cross-domain interactions become more prevalent. Cyberattacks targeting IoT devices or ICS can have cascading effects on Smart Grids operations, leading to service disruptions, financial losses, and compromises to public safety. For instance, a cyberattack on HVAC systems in a building could indirectly impact the performance of smart gridconnected devices (Sabou et al., 2020).
- **Complexity and Scale**: Managing cybersecurity in interconnected smart grid, IoT, and IIoT environments requires addressing these systems' inherent complexity and scale. Organizations must steer diverse networks, protocols, and device types while ensuring interoperability, resilience, and regulatory compliance. This complexity demands robust security measures, continuous monitoring, and proactive threat detection to mitigate evolving cyber threats effectively (Shahinzadeh, Moradi, Gharehpetian, Nafisi, & Abedi, 2019).
- **Opportunities for Synergy**: Despite the challenges, the convergence of cybersecurity efforts across Smart Grids, IoT, and IIoT environments presents opportunities for synergy and collaboration. Sharing best practices, threat intelligence, and standardized security frameworks can enhance overall resilience and response capabilities. Collaborative efforts among stakeholders, including energy providers, IoT manufacturers, regulators, and cybersecurity professionals, are crucial for developing adaptive security strategies and safeguarding critical infrastructure effectively (Hazra, Adhikari, Amgoth, & Srirama, 2021). Understanding the complex relationship between cybersecurity in Smart Grids and IoT/IIoT environments is essential for comprehensively addressing emerging threats and vulnerabilities. By recognizing common challenges, leveraging synergies, and fostering collaboration, stakeholders can collectively enhance cybersecurity resilience and ensure the integrity and reliability of interconnected digital ecosystems.

2. SECURING THE SMART GRID

In the digital world, Smart Grids have become crucial to our energy infrastructure. Therefore, it is crucial to ensure their security. Penetration of Smart Grids goes beyond a mere data breach, which threatens our society's energy resilience. Then, it is necessary to analyze the fundamental security requirements and objectives for Smart Grids and highlight the pillars that strengthen these essential systems.

2.1 Availability

One of the most critical factors for Smart Grids is their availability to function effectively. An attack on their availability can cause severe consequences to power distribution, leading to significant economic and social impacts. To prevent such threats, Smart Grids must employ measures such as redundancy, backup systems, and robust disaster recovery plans. Ensuring a continuous and reliable power supply should remain a foundational security objective (Timčenko, Rakas, Kabović, & Kabović, 2023).

One potential scenario for a smart grid availability compromise involves a cyber attack on the communication infrastructure connecting various components of Smart Grids, which may disrupt crucial services. Suppose a hacker would gain unauthorized access to the communication network that links smart meters, sensors, and other devices within the smart grid. In this scenario, the attacker would disrupt the communication flow, which would cause a breakdown in the coordination and information exchange between different components of the smart grid. This attack scenario could significantly impact the availability of the smart grid's operation (Mirzaee, Shojafar, Cruickshank, & Tafazolli, 2022), as follows:

- Meter Data Manipulation: The attacker alters smart meter data, resulting in inaccurate readings. This can cause billing errors and financial losses for consumers and utility providers.
- Disruption of Control Signals: The attacker interferes with the communication of control signals between substations, affecting the ability to balance the load and manage power distribution efficiently.
- Isolation of Substations: The attacker disrupts communication to certain substations, leading to partial or complete blackouts in specific areas.
- Delayed Response to Outages: Tampering with the communication infrastructure can delay the identification and response to power outages, causing prolonged service restoration times.

On the one hand, inaccurate meter readings can lead to financial losses for utility providers. The costs associated with resolving these issues can be substantial. Moreover, a compromised communication network can cause power outages that can impact businesses, households, and critical infrastructure on a local or larger scale. On the other hand, to mitigate such risks, cybersecurity teams implement robust encryption and authentication measures to secure communication channels. They also employ advanced intrusion detection systems to identify and respond to unauthorized access attempts quickly. These mitigation strategies are critical to ensuring the safety and security of utility providers' information and infrastructure. Redundancy and resilience features should be integrated into the smart grid design to maintain operation during communication disruptions (Qadir & Quadri, 2016; Mirzaee et al., 2022).

2.2 Integrity

Ensuring that the data in a smart grid remains accurate and reliable is of utmost importance. Any unauthorized changes or data manipulation can result in erroneous decisions and operational disruptions. In a smart grid, various devices, such as smart meters, continuously collect and transmit data about energy consumption. This data is crucial for utilities to monitor and manage the grid efficiently. An example of integrity compromise in Smart Grids could be a cyber attack that manipulates or alters data within the grid. This could lead to inaccurate information and disrupt the system's normal functioning (Timčenko et al., 2023; An, Zhang, Yang, & Zhang, 2022). In this scenario, a malicious actor gains unauthorized access to the smart grid's communication network. Thus, the attacker manipulates smart meter readings to misreport lower energy consumption. This data compromise can have serious consequences as follows:

- Fraudulent Billing: Consumers may be billed less than their actual energy usage due to manipulated meter readings. This can lead to financial losses for the utility company and potentially higher costs for honest consumers.
- Overloading the Grid: If the data is manipulated to understate the actual energy demand, the utility might need to allocate more resources to meet the actual energy needs. This, in turn, can cause grid overloading, leading to disruptions, blackouts, or other operational issues.

- Misleading Analytics: Grid operators require accurate data to plan and make decisions. Compromised data integrity can mislead analytics and forecasting tools, making it challenging to anticipate and address issues such as peak demand or grid imbalances.
- Compromised Grid Stability: Inaccurate data can impact grid stability by causing improper load balancing and inadequate response to grid disturbances, increasing the risk of cascading failures and system instability.

To maintain the security of the data transmitted through the smart grid infrastructure, it is important to implement robust security measures such as access controls, encryption, and intrusion detection systems. Regular security audits and updates to address vulnerabilities are also essential to ensure the system's integrity. It is recommended to use cryptographic techniques, digital signatures, and data validation protocols to uphold the authenticity and accuracy of the data (Yee & Zolkipli, 2021; An et al., 2022).

2.3 Confidentiality

It is crucial to protect against cyber threats to maintain consumer privacy and the grid's operational security. Sensitive data in Smart Grids must be kept confidential. In a smart grid system, advanced meters are installed at consumers' premises to monitor energy consumption in real-time. These meters collect detailed information about energy usage patterns, allowing utility companies to optimize grid performance and offer tailored services. However, if confidentiality is compromised, this data can be misused (Jha, 2023).

Once the adversary obtains unauthorized access to the smart grid system, either through exploiting communication infrastructure vulnerabilities or infiltrating the utility company's network. The attacker intercepts the communication between the smart meters and the utility company's central server. This could be done by eavesdropping on wireless communication channels or compromising the encryption used to secure the data. These compromised data contain sensitive information about individual households (called Consumer Privacy Breach), such as when they are typically at home, their energy consumption routines, and even specific appliance usage. This information can be manipulated for malicious purposes, such as targeting homes during periods of low occupancy for theft or conducting unauthorized surveillance (Mirzaee et al., 2022).

In more dangerous cases, the Economic Espionage concept appears when the confidential data collected is valuable to competitors or other entities interested in economic spying. Knowledge of energy consumption patterns in a region could reveal insights into industrial activities, business operations, and even research and development activities. The consequences lead to violating and compromising the individual's privacy, such as making his daily routines and habits accessible to unauthorized parties. Moreover, unauthorized access poses a risk to the overall security of the energy infrastructure, potentially leading to further disruptions or attacks. Also, businesses and individuals may suffer economic losses due to theft, unauthorized access, or misuse of sensitive information. Therefore, Securing the confidentiality of sensitive data within Smart Grids is crucial to prevent unauthorized access. Both personal and operational data need to be protected from cyber threats to maintain consumer privacy and ensure the operational security of the grid. Encryption algorithms and secure communication protocols are essential in preserving the confidentiality of data transmitted across the smart grid network (Jha, 2023).

Authentication and confidentiality are closely interconnected elements within the smart grid systems, representing vital parts of a comprehensive cybersecurity approach. Authentication, the process of verifying the legitimacy and authorization of users, devices, or systems, is pivotal in the cybersecurity context for Smart Grids. It ensures that only authorized entities, such as utility operators, smart meters, or control systems, can access and engage with the grid infrastructure. Authentication safeguards smart grid systems, ensuring only authorized entities can access critical components. Multi-factor authentication, digital certificates, and secure key management are essential tools to prevent unauthorized access attempts. Strict authentication measures strengthen the overall security posture, reducing the risk of malicious actors infiltrating the smart grid infrastructure (Gunduz & Das, 2020).

It is important to mention that all authentication, authorization, and confidentiality functions are interactively incorporated to strengthen the security of smart grid systems. While authentication establishes identity, authorization delineates the privileges and actions allowed for each authenticated entity. Implementing robust authorization mechanisms ensures that only authorized personnel can execute specific commands or access sensitive information. Fine-grained access controls and regular reviews of authorization policies are crucial to maintaining a secure and well-regulated smart grid environment. Authorization, closely aligned with authentication, determines the level of access granted to authenticated entities. Once the legitimacy of a user or device is established, authorization steps in to define the scope of permissible actions within the smart grid infrastructure. This critical control layer ensures that only authorized entities can manipulate, retrieve, or interact with specific system components. By tracing access privileges, authorization acts as a guardian, preventing unauthorized users from tampering with critical infrastructure elements (Samonas & Coss, 2014).

3. EXPLORING POTENTIAL CYBER THREATS AND VULNERABILITIES IN SMART GRIDS

As Smart Grids consistently evolve and integrate advanced technologies, the Digital Landscape might introduce new possibilities but heightened risks. Therefore, it is essential to understand the potential cyber threats and vulnerabilities related to Smart Grids to strengthen the resilience of these critical systems. For example, the interconnection of smart grids has led to numerous cyber attacks. One of the primary concerns is the prospect of malicious actors gaining unauthorized access to the grid's control systems. Cyber attackers may exploit software or hardware components vulnerabilities, aiming to disrupt operations, manipulate data, or even compromise the overall integrity of the energy infrastructure. Another example comes from the fact that smart grid devices are often

distributed across vast geographical areas and are susceptible to remote exploitation. Malicious actors may exploit shortcomings in communication networks or unsecured endpoints, allowing unauthorized access to critical components. This is known as Remote Exploitation which can lead to unauthorized control over grid operations, potentially causing widespread outages or manipulating energy distribution. Moreover, internal actors, such as disgruntled employees or contractors, who have access to the smart grid infrastructure pose a significant hazard. Insider Threats may apply deliberate sabotage, unauthorized data access, or the introduction of malicious software. So, adequate security measures must be implemented to monitor and mitigate the risks associated with insider threats, including robust access controls and persistent monitoring systems (Gunduz & Das, 2020).

In the same context, the Denial of Service attacks overwhelm system resources or disrupt communication channels to paralyze the functionality of Smart Grids. These attacks may be directed to flood communication networks or overload grid components, leading to service disruptions, degraded performance, or a complete shutdown of grid operations. Also, the Lack of Standardization appears with the absence of standardized security protocols for different smart grid components and vendors and hence will create further vulnerabilities. In other words, inconsistencies in the security measures present new shortcomings within the system, which make it easier for attackers to exploit gaps in protection. Establishing industry-wide standards and ensuring compliance with best practices are necessary to mitigate this vulnerability (Huseinović, Mrdović, Bicakci, & Uludag, 2020).

While Smart Grids depend on data exchange, a significant issue appears with the Inadequate Encryption Practices for communication channels which uncovers sensitive information to interception and manipulation. Therefore, robust encryption practices, both in transit and at rest, is essential to safeguard against unauthorized access and tampering of critical data (Syed, Refaat, & Bouhali, 2020). Furthermore, Multiple Smart Grids contain Legacy Systems and equipment that may lack updated security features. These older components usually have vulnerabilities that have become known to attackers over time. Integrating security patches, conducting regular risk assessments, and, when feasible, upgrading outdated systems are important steps in mitigating risks associated with legacy equipment (Asghar, Dán, Miorandi, & Chlamtac, 2017).

Exploring the potential cyber threats and vulnerabilities in Smart Grids is an essential aspect of ensuring the resilience and security of our energy infrastructure. As Smart Grids become more integral to our daily lives, a proactive and multi-faceted approach to cybersecurity, including continuous monitoring, threat intelligence sharing, and collaboration between industry stakeholders, is imperative to stay ahead of evolving cyber threats and strengthen the robustness of smart grid systems.

3.1 Impact of Cyber Threats and Vulnerabilities on Smart Grid Infrastructure

Understanding the impact of these threats is essential for developing effective strategies to mitigate risks and harden the resilience of smart grid infrastructure. In Smart Grids, the potential cyber threats and system vulnerabilities raise significant risks against the integrity, reliability, and overall functionality of critical energy systems. as follows:

- One of the consequences of cyber attacks on the smart grid is the Operational Disruption, especially when a successful breach occurs to the smart grid's defenses. This breach leads to operational disruptions. When the attacker obtains unauthorized access or manipulates control systems, a possible disruption of power distribution causes widespread outages affecting both residential and industrial consumers. The loss of operational control can have severe effects, influencing the stability and reliability of the entire energy grid (Nafees, Saxena, Cardenas, Grijalva, & Burnap, 2023).
- Another severe influence might appear with the Data Manipulation and Falsification, where the attack could target the integrity of smart grid data. Manipulating data, such as changing consumption records or falsifying system health, can lead to false decision-making. This can result in inefficient energy distribution, financial losses for utilities, and a breakdown in the trust consumers place in the accuracy of their energy usage information (Farokhi, 2020).

- Usually, Cyber threats target Smart Grids to compromise the confidentiality of consumer data and raise privacy concerns known as the Compromised Consumer Privacy (Asghar et al., 2017). Thus, many actions would lead to serious privacy implications for consumers Unauthorized access to personal information, consumption patterns, and even location data. The weakening of consumer trust due to privacy breaches can hinder the widespread adoption of smart grid technologies (Butun, Lekidis, & dos Santos, 2020).

- The Financial Impact of cyber threats on smart grid infrastructure has two aspects (Gunduz & Das, 2020). Firstly, the costs associated with mitigating and recovering from a cyber-attack can be significant. Secondly, disruptions to energy distribution and compromised data integrity may result in financial losses for utilities, impacting their ability to provide reliable services and invest in the continuous improvement of the grid (Judge, Khan, Manzoor, & Khattak, 2022).

- Once a successful cyber-attack on a smart grid occurs, the Loss of Public Confidence (Bugden & Stedman, 2021): will be the assured result and corrupt the reliability and security of the energy infrastructure. Consumers and businesses depend on the uninterrupted availability of electricity for their daily operations, and any compromise leads to a loss of trust. Repairing public confidence after a cyber incident can be a problematic and time-consuming process.

- Operational disruptions and manipulations of smart grid systems might pose Safety Concerns. For instance, critical infrastructures such as hospitals, emergency services, and essential facilities depend on a stable and reliable energy supply. Cyberattacks compromise the availability and reliability of the smart grid and can jeopardize the safety of individuals relying on these services.

- The energy infrastructure plays a crucial role in the smooth functioning of a nation. If cybercriminals successfully attack Smart Grids, this has serious National Security Implications. A compromised energy grid can be a part of a bigger cyber campaign targeting a country's critical infrastructure. Also, This can lead to economic instability and potentially threaten national security (Gunduz & Das, 2020).

The impact of cyber threats and vulnerabilities on smart grid infrastructure is multifaceted and extends beyond technical disruptions. It includes financial, societal, and even national security aspects. Addressing these challenges requires a comprehensive and collaborative approach, involving stakeholders from government, industry, and cybersecurity experts to develop and implement robust security measures that safeguard the integrity and reliability of smart grid systems.

3.2 Unveiling Vulnerabilities in Smart Grids

Although cyber attackers employ increasingly sophisticated methods to identify targets, the security landscape of Smart Grids is constantly evolving. The attackers usually utilize various attack tools and vectors to implement multiple attack methods. Therefore, security experts must understand the complexities of malicious actors in navigating the smart grid environment and highlight the need for robust defenses to mitigate potential threats to the energy system.

In the beginning, identifying targets in the targeted Smart Grids is a detailed process driven by an understanding of the system's architecture and vulnerabilities. Attackers often concentrate on critical components such as SCADA systems, AMI infrastructure, and communication networks. These elements house valuable data and control mechanisms, making them main targets for adversaries aiming for financial gains, system disruption, or unauthorized access. The reconnaissance phase involves mapping out the infrastructure, identifying weak points, and assessing potential entry points. Therefore, smart grid operators Penetration Testing Strategies enhance the resilience of their infrastructure by proactively identifying and addressing vulnerabilities in critical components (Aleem, Hussain, & Ustun, 2020). Penetration testing or pen testing is a proactive cybersecurity technique where authorized simulated attacks are launched against an organization's IT infrastructure to identify vulnerabilities. By simulating real-world attack scenarios, penetration testing allows organizations to assess their security situation, detect drawbacks, and prioritize remediation efforts to strengthen their defenses against malicious intrusions. The ultimate goal is to enhance overall security resilience and minimize the risk of successful cyberattacks.

In general, there are many attack tools available to malicious actors in the smart grid landscape, ranging from traditional malware to sophisticated exploitation frameworks mentioned in the following list:

1. **Malware** refers to any type of malicious software that is designed to gain unauthorized access to computer systems or networks and disrupt or damage them. A well-known example of malware is Stuxnet (Matrosov, Rodionov, Harley, & Malcho, 2010), a worm that targeted SCADA systems, including those in Smart Grids, to sabotage industrial processes.

2. **Packet sniffers** are tools that intercept and log traffic passing over a network. Attackers can use them to capture sensitive information like login credentials or proprietary data. For instance, Wireshark is a popular packet analyzer tool normally used for network troubleshooting and analysis. However, it can also be misused for malicious purposes (Pourmirza & Srivastava, 2020).

3. **Remote Access Trojans (RATs)** are malware that provides attackers with unauthorized access to a victim's system, allowing them to control it remotely. DarkComet is a well-known RAT used to gain remote access to a computer system and perform various malicious activities, including data stealing and system manipulation (Farinholt, Rezaeirad, McCoy, & Levchenko, 2020).

4. **Password Crackers** are tools designed to recover passwords from stored or transmitted data. Attackers can use them to gain unauthorized access to systems or accounts. John the Ripper is a widely-used password-cracking tool that can crack various types of passwords through brute-force and dictionary attacks (Marchetti & Bodily, 2022).

5. **DDoS Tools** flood targeted systems or networks with overwhelming traffic, causing them to become unavailable to legitimate users. LOIC (Low Orbit Ion Cannon) is a tool that allows users to launch DDoS attacks by flooding target websites or networks with HTTP or UDP packets (Yuliadi, Hamdani, Fitriana, Oper, et al., 2023).

6. **Social engineering** kits are sets of tools and resources used to manipulate individuals into divulging confidential information or performing actions that compromise security. Social engineering toolkits like SET (Social Engineering Toolkit) automate the creation of phishing attacks, spoofing websites, and generating malicious payloads (Priyadarshini, Kumar, Sharma, Singh, & Satapathy, 2021).

7. **Exploitation Frameworks** are comprehensive tools and resources used to discover, exploit, and control computer systems or networks vulnerabilities. Metasploit is a widely used framework for developing and executing exploit code against remote targets (Raj & Walia, 2020).

The aforementioned tools and numerous others, when exploited by malicious players, represent significant threats to the security and stability of smart grid systems, highlighting the importance of robust cybersecurity measures and proactive defense strategies. Exploiting vulnerabilities in communication networks allows attackers to intercept and manipulate data flows, posing a serious risk to the confidentiality and integrity of information. Weakly protected remote devices or endpoints become entry points for attackers, enabling them to infiltrate the smart grid infrastructure from a distance. Collaborating with internal entities or manipulating personnel provides attackers with insider access, facilitating more covert and targeted attacks. Malicious actors continuously strive to exploit vulnerabilities in communication channels and remote access points, which pose significant risks to the integrity and confidentiality of sensitive data. However, organizations can strengthen their defenses by integrating advanced encryption and authentication mechanisms and effectively mitigate these threats.

Apart from the attacker side, the integration of advanced encryption and authentication mechanisms can mitigate the risks associated with unsecured communication channels and remote exploitation in several ways (Chowdhury, 2020; Chaudhry, Nebhan, Yahya, & Al-Turjman, 2021):

1. **Data Confidentiality**: Encryption ensures that data transmitted over communication channels remains confidential and unreachable to unauthorized parties. Even if intercepted, encrypted data appears as absurd characters, making it unreadable without the decryption key.

2. **Data Integrity**: Encryption mechanisms also provide data integrity by protecting against tampering or unauthorized modification during transmission. Any attempt to alter encrypted data without proper decryption results in corruption, alerting both parties to potential tampering.

3. **Authentication**: Advanced authentication mechanisms, such as multi-factor authentication (MFA) or biometric authentication, verify the identity of users or devices accessing the system. This prevents unauthorized access and reduces the risk of remote exploitation by ensuring that only legitimate users or devices can interact with sensitive resources.

4. **Secure Communication Channels**: Implementing secure communication protocols such as Transport Layer Security (TLS) or Virtual Private Networks (VPNs) establishes encrypted tunnels for data transmission. This prevents eavesdropping and man-in-the-middle attacks, safeguarding sensitive information exchanged between endpoints.

5. **End-to-end Encryption**: By using end-to-end encryption, data stays encrypted throughout its entire transmission from source to recipient, including intermediary points. This ensures that even if communication channels or network infrastructure are compromised, the data remains protected from unauthorized access or interception.

6. **Access Controls**: Encryption and authentication mechanisms can be completed with access controls to enforce granular permissions and restrict unauthorized actions or resource access. Role-based access control (RBAC) and least privilege principles help limit the attack surface and mitigate the impact of potential exploitation (Fragkos, Johnson, & Tsiropoulou, 2022).

7. **Compliance Requirements**: Integration of advanced encryption and authentication mechanisms also allows organizations to meet regulatory compliance requirements, such as GDPR, HIPAA, or NERC CIP standards, which require the protec tion of sensitive data and implementation of robust security measures (Marotta & Madnick, 2021).

Overall, the integration of advanced encryption and authentication mechanisms has an essential role in mitigating the risks associated with unsecured communication channels and remote exploitation by ensuring data confidentiality, integrity, and authenticity throughout the communication process. To safeguard Smart Grids against evolving cyber threats, it is essential to adopt a multi-faceted cybersecurity approach. This approach should include proactive vulnerability assessments, robust encryption protocols, and resilient incident response mechanisms.

3.3 Historical Incidents of Smart Grid Security Breaches

Smart Grids play a crucial role in powering modern societies, but they are also highly vulnerable to cyber threats. To understand the importance of cybersecurity in Smart Grids, the following shows real-world examples of security breaches that have occurred in the past.

In 2015 and 2016, One such incident took place in Ukraine when the country's power grid infrastructure was targeted by cyberattacks (Case, 2016). The attackers successfully compromised SCADA systems, causing widespread power outages affecting hundreds of thousands of people. The use of sophisticated malware to manipulate grid operations remotely demonstrated the vulnerability of interconnected smart grid components to targeted cyber intrusions. This highlights the need for robust security measures, such as regular security audits and intrusion detection systems.

Another cyberattack targeting Ukraine's energy infrastructure occurred in 2017, demonstrating the persistent threat landscape. The attackers leveraged spear-phishing techniques to compromise the systems of key energy organizations. Although the attack did not cause immediate disruptions, it illustrated the potential for adversaries to infiltrate critical components of a smart grid's communication infrastructure. Regular employee training on phishing awareness and implementing advanced threat detection systems are critical to mitigating risks associated with sophisticated cyberattacks.

Similarly, in October 2022, Russian state-sponsored hackers targeted a Ukrainian energy facility in a sophisticated cyber attack last October, causing a temporary power outage. The infamous group Sandworm utilized a previously unseen technique to breach ICS and operational technology (OT), according to cybersecurity firm Mandiant. The incident marks the first public case of a cyberattack-induced power outage during the conflict. It highlights the heightened cyber threats critical infrastructure faces during times of conflict (Izycki & Vianna, 2021).

In 2018, the Puerto Rico Electric Power Authority (PREPA) suffered a data breach that exposed sensitive customer information (Paganini, 2018). The attackers used phishing techniques to gain unauthorized access to PREPA's systems, highlighting the human factor as a potential weak link in smart grid security. This incident underscores the importance of securing customer data within Smart Grids by implementing stringent access controls and strengthening cybersecurity awareness among personnel. In 2019, a report revealed a cyber espionage campaign targeting critical infrastructure, including Smart Grids. The attackers utilized malware to compromise ICS. This incident illustrated the geopolitical nature of cyber threats to Smart Grids and the importance of international cooperation in addressing and mitigating such risks.

In May 2023, Denmark's critical energy infrastructure suffered a highly sophisticated cyber attack, which indicated a significant escalation in cyber warfare tactics (SektorCERT, 2023). The attackers targeted the Danish energy sector, which includes 22 key companies, in a multi-faceted cyber operation. The attack was highly complex, not only in terms of its execution but also in its strategic planning and exploitation of specific vulnerabilities. The attacker used undisclosed vulnerabilities, known as zero-day exploits, highlighting their advanced technical knowledge and resources. They employed spear phishing and social engineering techniques to bypass standard security measures. Once inside the network, the attackers took a stealthy approach, gradually escalating privileges and gaining access to critical systems.

The aforementioned examples highlight the various cyber threats and vulnerabilities that Smart Grids face. A comprehensive and adaptive cybersecurity approach is crucial, encompassing technological solutions, employee training, threat intelligence sharing, and international collaboration. As Smart

Grids continue to evolve, the lessons learned from these historical breaches serve as valuable guides in strengthening the security posture of these critical infrastructures.

4. SAFEGUARDING SCADA, ICS, AND SMART GRIDS

4.1 Privacy Concerns With the Smart Grid

Despite the existing benefits of Smart Grids, there are growing concerns about the privacy implications of Smart Grids. Smart Grids are equipped with advanced sensors, meters, and communication systems to collect and analyze vast amounts of data. This data includes personal information such as household energy usage, appliance usage patterns, and behavioral patterns. This detailed information can expose secret details about a person's daily life such as when they are at home, what appliances they use, and at what times. Since Smart Grids are vulnerable to cyber-attacks, hackers might illegally breach the collected data to expose susceptible personal information, compromise the privacy of individuals, identity theft, fraud, and other cybercrimes. Another concern is the need for more individual control over their data, especially for energy companies that have access to real-time data on an individual's energy usage. This data is used for various purposes, such as optimizing energy distribution and pricing. However, this introduces questions about who owns this data and how it can be used. In addition, individuals mostly do not have control over how their data is collected, stored, and shared, violating their privacy rights. Moreover, using data analytics in Smart Grids may create profiles and potentially lead to discriminatory practices. For example, by analyzing energy usage patterns, companies can determine a person's income level, lifestyle, and even health conditions. This information can target specific groups for marketing purposes or deny access to certain services based on their energy usage.

The implementation of Smart Grids also raises concerns about government oversight. Since governments have the authority to access and monitor energy data, there is a potential for the abuse of power. This can violate individuals' privacy rights and affect their freedom of expression and association. Consequently, there is a need for obvious regulations and policies to govern the collection, storage, and use of data in Smart Grids. These regulations should ensure that individuals have control over their data and that it is only used for legitimate purposes.

Companies should also be transparent about their data collection and usage practices and provide individuals with options to opt out of data collection. Besides, Smart Grids should be designed with privacy in mind, enforcing strong security measures to prevent data violations and anonymizing data to protect individual identities. Companies should also restrict the amount of data collected to only what is necessary and delete when no longer needed. Similarly, individuals should be educated about privacy's implications and rights. This includes understanding the data being collected and used. Also, Individuals should have the privilege to access and correct their data and be notified in case of a data breach. Based on the above discussion, the following points summarize the privacy concerns (Moreno Escobar et al., 2021; Ghelani, 2022; Gough et al., 2021):

1. **Data Proliferation**: Clear understanding and management of the extended amount of data generated.
2. **Granular Consumer Profiling**: Detailed profiling of consumers raises concerns about privacy invasion.
3. **Regulatory Frameworks for Privacy Protection**: Establishing clear rules and regulations to safeguard privacy in smart grid operations.

4. **Informed Consent and Transparency**: Ensuring users are well-informed and transparent about how their data is collected and utilized.

5. **Anonymization and De-Identification Techniques**: Employing methods to anonymize and de-identify data to protect individual identities.

6. **Cybersecurity Measures for Data Protection**: Implementing robust security measures to prevent unauthorized access to sensitive data.

7. **Ongoing Ethical Discussions**: Continuous examination and debate on the ethical implications of smart grid technology.

8. **Public Awareness and Education**: Raising awareness and educating the public about privacy risks and best practices in smart grid usage.

As long as companies, organizations, and governments strive to have a more efficient and sustainable energy future using Smart Grids, the privacy concerns, and their influences must be considerable and find the right balance between leveraging the power of data and safeguarding individual privacy. This requires ongoing collaboration among stakeholders, the establishment of robust regulatory frameworks, and a commitment to ethical considerations. Corporations must also persist in evolving ethical standards around privacy concerns to ensure that innovation is integrated harmoniously with respect for individual rights.

4.2 The Unified Framework of SCADA, ICS, and Smart Grids

First, SCADA is a system of hardware and software components that allows industrial organizations to control and monitor diverse operations, such as manufacturing, infrastructure, and facility-based processes. SCADA systems are typically employed in energy, water treatment, and manufacturing industries. For Data Acquisition, SCADA systems collect real-time data from appliances such as sensors, meters, and other devices in the field and transmit this data to a central location (.i.e., Servers) for monitoring and control. This data could contain information about temperature, pressure, flow rates, and other relevant parameters. Subsequently, the collected data is transmitted to a central computer system through communication networks, often utilizing protocols like Modbus or DNP3. Meanwhile, Central Monitoring and Control operators employ SCADA software at the central location to visualize and analyze the data in real-time and then, if needed, send control commands back to the appliances to adjust processes or operations (Shrestha, Johansen, Noll, & Roverso, 2020).

Likewise, ICS is a more general term containing the whole infrastructure and is crucial for managing complex industrial processes efficiently. ICS controls and operates industrial processes, in addition to the SCADA system, but it extends to cover other control systems like distributed control systems (DCS) and programmed logic controllers (PLCs). Both are used to automate processes in various industries such as manufacturing, energy, and transportation. On the one hand, DCS systems are typically used for centralized control of large-scale industrial processes and managing complex operations, for instance, oil refining, with interconnected control units for real-time monitoring and advanced control algorithms (Manoj, 2021). PLCs, on the other hand, are specialized computers for discrete control tasks in manufacturing, offering flexibility and modularity for machinery automation.

In other words, the ICS systems employ specialized control devices as PLCs to execute control logic. These devices receive input from sensors, process the information, and generate output signals to control actuators and other devices in the field. DCS and PLCs have essential roles in improving efficiency and safety across various industrial applications. In dependence on SCADA and ICS, Smart Grids enhance the optimization of electricity generation, distribution, and consumption by utilizing digital technology, bidirectional communication, and automation. This enables a dynamic exchange of information and energy, facilitating more efficient, sustainable, and dependable energy administration (Siniosoglou, Radoglou-Grammatikis, Efstathopoulos, Fouliras, & Sarigiannidis, 2021; Manoj, 2021).

4.3 Security Landscape for SCADA, ICS, and Smart Grids

The security landscape for SCADA, ICS, and the evolving smart grid infrastructure requires a rugged defense strategy against an ever-expanding array of cyber threats. multiple models present the practical implementation of security standards, advanced measures, and adaptation to the unique requirements of Smart Grids.

For instance, as shown in Figure 2, Defense-in-Depth (DiD) (Mughal, 2018) adopts an approach to layering security mechanisms at different levels of the infrastructure. It contains not only firewalls and IDSs but also physical security measures, employee training, and regular audits to create a comprehensive defense strategy.

Zero Trust Model (Stafford, 2020), another model example, asserts that no entity should be inherently trusted, regardless of its position within the network. Therefore, it is important to continuously verify identity and rigid access controls from the core principles, minimizing the attack surface and ensuring a more resilient security posture.

Similarly, the Purdue Model (Williams, 1994), developed for ICS environments, organizes the control network into hierarchical levels, ranging from Level 0 (sensors and actuators) to Level 5 (business systems). This segmentation facilitates a structured security approach, allowing for tailored security measures in each zone and reducing the risk of lateral movement by attackers.

Figure 2. Fi Defense in Depth Security Layered Concept

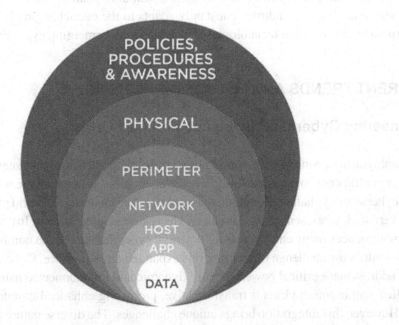

Other existing models for Smart Grids can also be adapted, in addition to the previous models. To incorporate Edge Computing Security (Xiao et al., 2019), Smart Grids can leverage edge computing to process data closer to the source, which reduces latency and enhances efficiency. Security models must adapt to secure edge devices, gateways, and communication channels. In this context, implementing edge-centric security measures, such as edge firewalls and secure gateways, becomes imperative. Smart Grids are different from traditional grids in that they exhibit dynamic and evolving characteristics. To ensure a proactive defense against emerging cyber threats, security models must incorporate Dynamic Risk Assessment mechanisms that continuously evaluate the threat landscape and adapt responses based on real-time risk evaluations. Additionally, as Smart Grids collect more granular data, privacy concerns increase. To address this, security models should incorporate Privacy-Preserving Techniques (Boulemtafes, Derhab, & Challal, 2020) like differential privacy and homomorphic encryption. These mechanisms enable utilities to glean valuable insights from data while safeguarding the anonymity of individual consumers.

Moreover, some security models rely on incorporating advanced security measures such as integrating machine learning and artificial intelligence to enhance their threat detection capabilities. By analyzing patterns, detecting anomalies, and learning from past data, these technologies can help identify potential cyber threats within the smart grid infrastructure more accurately and quickly (Ali & Choi, 2020). In addition, blockchain technology plays a vital role in ensuring the integrity and immutability of critical data within Smart Grids. By creating a tamper-resistant and decentralized ledger, blockchain minimizes the risk of data manipulation and ensures that all data recorded is secure and transparent. To address the evolving cyber threats, security models must implement advanced encryption protocols such as post-quantum cryptography. This technology addresses the potential threat posed by quantum computing to traditional encryption methods safeguards communication channels and protects sensitive data from emerging cryptographic vulnerabilities. As the smart grid ecosystem evolves, bringing a proactive and multidimensional strategy to cybersecurity is essential to guarantee the reliability and resilience of essential services. Thus, the industry constantly adapts to the ever-changing landscape of Smart Grids and incorporates cutting-edge technologies to defend against emerging cyber-attacks.

5. CURRENT TRENDS AND FUTURE DIRECTIONS

5.1 Pioneering Cybersecurity Issues in Smart Grids

The deployment of Smart Grids within power system infrastructure indicates a revolutionary movement towards efficiency and sustainability. However, as these systems merge with the IoT and IIoT, the complex cybersecurity challenges extend. For example, The modern smart grid is a complex network that connects various devices, sensors, and systems. The seamless integration of IoT and IIoT devices into this ecosystem introduces many entry points for potential cyber threats. As the number of connected devices increases, so does the challenge of securing this expanded attack surface. Cybersecurity strategies must evolve to address these critical power systems' dynamic and interconnected nature. The convergence of IoT and IIoT within Smart Grids is transformative, promising enhanced monitoring, control, and data insights. However, this integration brings unique challenges. The diverse nature of devices, each with its vulnerabilities, necessitates comprehensive security protocols. Ensuring the secure integration of these technologies is critical to preventing unauthorized access and potential exploitation of the smart grid infrastructure (Tufail, Parvez, Batool, & Sarwat, 2021).

Furthermore, the massive amounts of data yielded by smart grid devices, such as IoT sensors and IIoT components, emphasize the significance of robust data privacy measures. The potential compromise of sensitive information, ranging from energy consumption patterns to grid operational parameters, raises significant concerns. Thus, employing stringent data encryption techniques and implementing access controls are vital to safeguarding individual privacy and maintaining the confidentiality of critical operational data. Likewise, The increasing reliance on remote monitoring and control facilitated by IoT and IIoT integration boosts the risk of remote exploitation. The adversary exploits vulnerabilities in communication protocols, gaining unauthorized access and manipulating smart grid components from a distance. As a sequence, the system must establish secure communication channels, implement robust authentication mechanisms, and deploy IDSs become essential to mitigate the risks associated with remote exploitation (Faquir, Chouliaras, Sofia, Olga, & Maglaras, 2021).

On the other side, the attendance of IoT and IIoT devices for supply chains and their global nature introduces an additional layer of complexity to smart grid cybersecurity. In addition, Using components from diverse manufacturers raises the probability of vulnerabilities within the supply chain. The existence of a compromised device through the supply chain could act as a vulnerable entry point, penetrating and compromising the integrity of the smart grid infrastructure. Besides, The rapid evolution of IoT and IIoT technologies might surpass the developed security measures, hence leaving systems vulnerable to unknown threats. Also, the zero-day exploits pose a permanent challenge to the security of Smart Grids. To encounter such problems, it is compulsory to establish agile patch management strategies, facilitate collaboration with manufacturers to address vulnerabilities immediately and implement persistent monitoring (Faquir et al., 2021).

Relying on the digitization of power systems presents the possibility for insider threats, whether intentional or unintentional. Employees or contractors with access to IoT or IIoT devices may introduce a risk to the integrity of critical infrastructure. To detect and mitigate insider threats ideally, organizations must implement comprehensive user access controls, continuous monitoring, and user behavior analytics, which are essential. Likewise, APTs represent sophisticated and prolonged cyber-attacks that target specific entities, often with a strategic objective. Smart Grids, with their complex connectivity and vital role in infrastructure, are attractive targets for APTs. Developing advanced threat detection capabilities, threat intelligence sharing, and implementing proactive defense mechanisms are essential to enhance resilience against APTs in critical power system infrastructure (Gönen, Sayan, Yılmaz, Üstünsoy, & Karacayılmaz, 2020).

5.2 Future Directions

The field of cybersecurity in Smart Grids is poised for significant advancements to address the ever-evolving cyber threats and ensure the resilience of critical energy infrastructure. The future directions shape cybersecurity strategies in Smart Grids by considering advanced threat detection, secure-by-design principles, resilience planning, enhanced authentication, IoT integration security, regulatory compliance, and collaborative initiatives. All these directions aim to strengthen smart grid defenses, mitigate risks, and foster a proactive approach to cybersecurity in an increasingly interconnected digital landscape.

One of the key future cybersecurity efforts in Smart Grids will be to develop advanced threat detection and response capabilities. As cyber threats continuously evolve in sophistication and complexity, this will include implementing machine learning, artificial intelligence, and behavioral analytics to identify and mitigate emerging threats in real-time proactively. Smart grid infrastructure requires cybersecurity measures to be integrated into the design and development process. Adopting secure-by-design principles ensures that cybersecurity considerations are embedded throughout the entire lifecycle of smart grid systems, from initial conception to deployment and operation (Shi et al., 2020; Omitaomu & Niu, 2021; Gunduz & Das, 2020).

To resist and recover from potential cyber-attacks, future cybersecurity strategies for Smart Grids will prioritize resilience and continuity planning. This involves the implementation of robust backup and recovery mechanisms, as well as the development of contingency plans to maintain essential services during disruptions (Choi et al., 2021).

Strengthening authentication and access control mechanisms is essential to mitigate insider threats and unauthorized access to critical smart grid assets. This includes adopting multi-factor authentication, biometric authentication, and role-based access control to ensure that sensitive systems and data can only be accessed by authorized personnel (Hamlyn et al., 2008; Tolba & Al-Makhadmeh, 2021). As IoT and IIoT devices become increasingly integrated into Smart Grids, cybersecurity efforts must focus on securing these interconnected systems. This will involve implementing robust security protocols, encryption mechanisms, and device authentication to protect against IoT-based attacks and ensure data integrity between devices and systems (Hussain, Samara, Ullah, & Khan, 2021).

Compliance with regulatory requirements and industry standards will remain a priority for smart grid cybersecurity. It will be essential to stay up-to-date with evolving regulations, such as NERC CIP standards, and adhere to best practices outlined by international cybersecurity frameworks to ensure the resilience and security of smart grid infrastructure (Pavleska, Aranha, Masi, & Sellitto, 2020). Correspondingly, Collaboration among industry stakeholders, government agencies, research institutions, and cybersecurity experts will also be crucial for addressing emerging threats and vulnerabilities in Smart Grids. Future efforts will emphasize the importance of information sharing, threat intelligence collaboration, and joint research initiatives to enhance overall cybersecurity resilience and response capabilities.

5.3 Conclusion

In conclusion, stakeholders can better prepare for the evolving cybersecurity landscape and ensure the integrity, reliability, and security of smart grid systems in the face of emerging cyber threats By focusing on these future directions. Apart from the above, this chapter demonstrates various aspects of cybersecurity in Smart Grids, addressing both foundational concepts and advanced topics. The beginning provides an overview of the smart grid network architecture and emphasizes its complexity and the interplay between cybersecurity and emerging technologies such as IoT/IIoT. The subsequent sections concentrate on securing the smart grid infrastructure by outlining security requirements and objectives, including availability, integrity, and confidentiality considerations. Next, the chapter considers exploring potential cyber threats and vulnerabilities in Smart Grids, highlights examining their impact on infrastructure, and offers historical security breach incidents. Furthermore, the chapter reveals some privacy concerns related to data collection and analysis within the smart grid ecosystem, navigating the ethical landscape associated with these practices. Additionally, security models for SCADA, ICS, and Smart Grids are discussed, underlining the complexity of mitigating cyber threats in these interconnected systems. Finally, the chapter abstracts state-of-the-art cybersecurity issues and future directions, emphasizing the need for continuous adaptation and innovation to address evolving threats effectively.

REFERENCES

Abrahamsen, F. E., Ai, Y., & Cheffena, M. (2021). Communication technologies for smart grid: A comprehensive survey. *Sensors (Basel)*, 21(23), 8087. 10.3390/s2123808734884092

Aleem, S. A., Hussain, S. S., & Ustun, T. S. (2020). A review of strategies to increase pv penetration level in smart grids. *Energies*, 13(3), 636. 10.3390/en13030636

Ali, S. S., & Choi, B. J. (2020). State-of-the-art artificial intelligence techniques for distributed smart grids: A review. *Electronics (Basel)*, 9(6), 1030. 10.3390/electronics9061030

Alotaibi, I., Abido, M. A., Khalid, M., & Savkin, A. V. (2020). A comprehensive review of recent advances in smart grids: A sustainable future with renewable energy resources. *Energies*, 13(23), 6269. 10.3390/en13236269

An, D., Zhang, F., Yang, Q., & Zhang, C. (2022). Data integrity attack in dynamic state estimation of smart grid: Attack model and countermeasures. *IEEE Transactions on Automation Science and Engineering*, 19(3), 1631–1644. 10.1109/TASE.2022.3149764

Asghar, M. R., Dán, G., Miorandi, D., & Chlamtac, I. (2017). Smart meter data privacy: A survey. *IEEE Communications Surveys and Tutorials*, 19(4), 2820–2835. 10.1109/COMST.2017.2720195

Boulemtafes, A., Derhab, A., & Challal, Y. (2020). A review of privacy-preserving techniques for deep learning. *Neurocomputing*, 384, 21–45. 10.1016/j.neucom.2019.11.041

Boyes, H., Hallaq, B., Cunningham, J., & Watson, T. (2018). The industrial internet of things (iiot): An analysis framework. *Computers in Industry*, 101, 1–12. 10.1016/j.compind.2018.04.015

Bugden, D., & Stedman, R. (2021). *Unfulfilled promise: social acceptance of the smart grid.* https://iopscience.iop.org/article/10.1088/ 1748-9326/abd81c/ampdf

Butun, I., Lekidis, A., & dos Santos, D. R. (2020). Security and privacy in smart grids: Challenges, current solutions and future opportunities. *ICISSP*, 10. 10.5220/0009187307330741

Case, D. U. (2016). Analysis of the cyber attack on the ukrainian power grid. *Electricity Information Sharing and Analysis Center (E-ISAC), 388*(1-29), 3.

Chaudhry, S. A., Nebhan, J., Yahya, K., & Al-Turjman, F. (2021). A privacy enhanced authentication scheme for securing smart grid infrastructure. *IEEE Transactions on Industrial Informatics*, 18(7), 5000–5006. 10.1109/TII.2021.3119685

Choi, T., Ko, R. K., Saha, T., Scarsbrook, J., Koay, A. M., Wang, S., … St Clair, C. (2021). Plan2defend: Ai planning for cybersecurity in smart grids. *2021 IEEE PES Innovative Smart Grid Technologies-Asia (ISGT Asia)*, 1–5.

Chowdhury, N. (2020). A survey of cryptography-based authentication for smart grid communication. In *Computer security: Esorics 2020 international workshops, cybericps, secpre, and adiot, guildford, uk, september 14–18, 2020, revised selected papers 6* (pp. 52–66). 10.1007/978-3-030-64330-0_4

Faquir, D., Chouliaras, N., Sofia, V., Olga, K., & Maglaras, L. (2021). Cybersecurity in smart grids, challenges and solutions. *AIMS Electronics and Electrical Engineering*, 5(1), 24–37.

Farinholt, B., Rezaeirad, M., McCoy, D., & Levchenko, K. (2020). Dark matter: uncovering the darkcomet rat ecosystem. In *Proceedings of the web conference 2020* (pp. 2109–2120). 10.1145/3366423.3380277

Farokhi, F. (2020). Review of results on smart-meter privacy by data manipulation, demand shaping, and load scheduling. *IET Smart Grid*, 3(5), 605–613. 10.1049/iet-stg.2020.0129

Fragkos, G., Johnson, J., & Tsiropoulou, E. E. (2022). Dynamic role-based access control policy for smart grid applications: An offline deep reinforcement learning approach. *IEEE Transactions on Human-Machine Systems*, 52(4), 761–773. 10.1109/THMS.2022.3163185

Gebremichael, T., Ledwaba, L. P., Eldefrawy, M. H., Hancke, G. P., Pereira, N., Gidlund, M., & Akerberg, J. (2020). Security and privacy in the industrial internet of things: Current standards and future challenges. *IEEE Access : Practical Innovations, Open Solutions*, 8, 152351–152366. 10.1109/ACCESS.2020.3016937

Ghelani, D. (2022). Cyber security in smart grids, threats, and possible solutions. *Authorea Preprints*. 10.22541/au.166385207.71655799/v1

Gönen, S., Sayan, H. H., Yılmaz, E. N., Üstünsoy, F., & Karacayılmaz, G. (2020). False data injection attacks and the insider threat in smart systems. *Computers & Security*, 97, 101955. 10.1016/j.cose.2020.101955

Gopstein, A., Nguyen, C., O'Fallon, C., Hastings, N., & Wollman, D. (2021). *Nist framework and roadmap for smart grid interoperability standards, release 4.0*. Department of Commerce. National Institute of Standards and Technology. 10.6028/NIST.SP.1108r4

Gough, M. B., Santos, S. F., AlSkaif, T., Javadi, M. S., Castro, R., & Catalão, J. P. (2021). Preserving privacy of smart meter data in a smart grid environment. *IEEE Transactions on Industrial Informatics*, 18(1), 707–718. 10.1109/TII.2021.3074915

Greer, C., Wollman, D. A., Prochaska, D., Boynton, P. A., Mazer, J. A., & Nguyen, C. (2014). *Nist framework and roadmap for smart grid interoperability standards, release 3.0*. Academic Press.

Gunduz, M. Z., & Das, R. (2020). Cyber-security on smart grid: Threats and potential solutions. *Computer Networks*, 169, 107094. 10.1016/j.comnet.2019.107094

Gungor, V. C., Lu, B., & Hancke, G. P. (2010). Opportunities and challenges of wireless sensor networks in smart grid. *IEEE Transactions on Industrial Electronics*, 57(10), 3557–3564. 10.1109/TIE.2009.2039455

Hamlyn, A., Cheung, H., Mander, T., Wang, L., Yang, C., & Cheung, R. (2008). *Computer network security management and authentication of smart grids operations. 2008 IEEE power and energy society general meetingconversion and delivery of electrical energy in the 21st century*.

Hazra, A., Adhikari, M., Amgoth, T., & Srirama, S. N. (2021). A comprehensive survey on interoperability for iiot: Taxonomy, standards, and future directions. *ACM Computing Surveys*, 55(1), 1–35. 10.1145/3485130

Huseinović, A., Mrdović, S., Bicakci, K., & Uludag, S. (2020). A survey of denial-of-service attacks and solutions in the smart grid. *IEEE Access : Practical Innovations, Open Solutions*, 8, 177447–177470. 10.1109/ACCESS.2020.3026923

Hussain, I., Samara, G., Ullah, I., & Khan, N. (2021). Encryption for end-user privacy: a cyber-secure smart energy management system. In *2021 22nd international arab conference on information technology (acit)* (pp. 1–6). 10.1109/ACIT53391.2021.9677341

Izycki, E., & Vianna, E. W. (2021). Critical infrastructure: A battlefield for cyber warfare? In *Iccws 2021 16th international conference on cyber warfare and security* (p. 454). Academic Press.

Jha, R. K. (2023). Cybersecurity and confidentiality in smart grid for enhancing sustainability and reliability. *Recent Research Reviews Journal*, 2(2), 215–241. 10.36548/rrrj.2023.2.001

Judge, M. A., Khan, A., Manzoor, A., & Khattak, H. A. (2022). Overview of smart grid implementation: Frameworks, impact, performance and challenges. *Journal of Energy Storage*, 49, 104056. 10.1016/j.est.2022.104056

Mahela, O. P., Khosravy, M., Gupta, N., Khan, B., Alhelou, H. H., Mahla, R., & Siano, P. (2020). Comprehensive overview of multi-agent systems for controlling smart grids. *CSEE Journal of Power and Energy Systems*, 8(1), 115–131.

Manoj, K. (2021). *Power system automation: Build secure power system scada & smart grids*. Notion Press.

Marchetti, K., & Bodily, P. (2022). *John the ripper: An examination and analysis of the popular hash cracking algorithm. 2022 intermountain engineering, technology and computing (ietc)*.

Marotta, A., & Madnick, S. (2021). Convergence and divergence of regulatory compliance and cybersecurity. *Issues in Information Systems*, 22(1).

Matrosov, A., Rodionov, E., Harley, D., & Malcho, J. (2010, September). Stuxnet under the microscope. *ESET*, LLC, 6.

Mirzaee, P. H., Shojafar, M., Cruickshank, H., & Tafazolli, R. (2022). Smart grid security and privacy: From conventional to machine learning issues (threats and countermeasures). *IEEE Access : Practical Innovations, Open Solutions*, 10, 52922–52954. 10.1109/ACCESS.2022.3174259

Moreno Escobar, J. J., Morales Matamoros, O., Tejeida Padilla, R., Lina Reyes, I., & Quintana Espinosa, H. (2021). A comprehensive review on smart grids: Challenges and opportunities. *Sensors (Basel)*, 21(21), 6978. 10.3390/s2121697834770285

Mughal, A. A. (2018). The art of cybersecurity: Defense in depth strategy for robust protection. *International Journal of Intelligent Automation and Computing, 1*(1), 1–20.

Nafees, M. N., Saxena, N., Cardenas, A., Grijalva, S., & Burnap, P. (2023). Smart grid cyber-physical situational awareness of complex operational technology attacks: A review. *ACM Computing Surveys*, 55(10), 1–36. 10.1145/3565570

Naik, N. (2017). *Choice of effective messaging protocols for iot systems: Mqtt, coap, amqp and http. 2017 IEEE international systems engineering symposium (isse)*.

Omitaomu, O. A., & Niu, H. (2021). Artificial intelligence techniques in smart grid: A survey. *Smart Cities*, 4(2), 548–568. 10.3390/smartcities4020029

Orlando, M., Estebsari, A., Pons, E., Pau, M., Quer, S., Poncino, M., Bottaccioli, L., & Patti, E. (2021). A smart meter infrastructure for smart grid iot applications. *IEEE Internet of Things Journal*, 9(14), 12529–12541. 10.1109/JIOT.2021.3137596

Paganini, P. (2018). *Puerto rico electric power authority (prepa) hacked over the weekend.*https://www.cyberdefensemagazine.com/puerto-rico

Panajotovic, B., Jankovic, M., & Odadzic, B. (2011). Ict and smart grid. In *2011 10th international conference on telecommunication in modern satellite cable and broadcasting services (telsiks)* (Vol. 1, pp. 118–121). 10.1109/TELSKS.2011.6112018

Pavleska, T., Aranha, H., Masi, M., & Sellitto, G. P. (2020). Drafting a cybersecurity framework profile for smart grids in eu: a goal-based methodology. In *Dependable computing-edcc 2020 workshops: Ai4rails, dreams, dsogri, serene 2020, munich, germany, september 7, 2020, proceedings 16* (pp. 143–155). Academic Press.

Pliatsios, D., Sarigiannidis, P., Lagkas, T., & Sarigiannidis, A. G. (2020). A survey on scada systems: Secure protocols, incidents, threats and tactics. *IEEE Communications Surveys and Tutorials*, 22(3), 1942–1976. 10.1109/COMST.2020.2987688

Pourmirza, Z., & Srivastava, A. (2020). Cybersecurity analysis for the communication protocol in smart grids. In *2020 IEEE 8th international conference on smart energy grid engineering (sege)* (pp. 58–63). IEEE.

Priyadarshini, I., Kumar, R., Sharma, R., Singh, P. K., & Satapathy, S. C. (2021). Identifying cyber insecurities in trustworthy space and energy sector for smart grids. *Computers & Electrical Engineering*, 93, 107204. 10.1016/j.compeleceng.2021.107204

Qadir, S., & Quadri, S. M. K. (2016). Information availability: An insight into the most important attribute of information security. *Journal of Information Security*, 7(3), 185–194. 10.4236/jis.2016.73014

Raj, S., & Walia, N. K. (2020). *A study on metasploit framework: A pen-testing tool. 2020 international conference on computational performance evaluation (compe).*

Rashed Mohassel, R., Fung, A., Mohammadi, F., & Raahemifar, K. (2014). A survey on advanced metering infrastructure. *International Journal of Electrical Power & Energy Systems*, 63, 473–484. 10.1016/j.ijepes.2014.06.025

Sabou, M., Biffl, S., Einfalt, A., Krammer, L., Kastner, W., & Ekaputra, F. J. (2020). Semantics for cyber-physical systems: A cross-domain perspective. *Semantic Web*, 11(1), 115–124. 10.3233/SW-190381

Samonas, S., & Coss, D. (2014). The cia strikes back: Redefining confidentiality, integrity and availability in security. *Journal of Information System Security*, 10(3).

Sektor, C. E. R. T. (2023). *The attack against danish, critical infrastructure.*https://sektorcert.dk/wp-content/uploads/ 2023/11/SektorCERT-The-attack-against-Danish-critical-infrastructure-TLP-CLEAR.pdf

Shi, Z., Yao, W., Li, Z., Zeng, L., Zhao, Y., Zhang, R., Tang, Y., & Wen, J. (2020). Artificial intelligence techniques for stability analysis and control in smart grids: Methodologies, applications, challenges and future directions. *Applied Energy*, 278, 115733. 10.1016/j.apenergy.2020.115733

Shrestha, M., Johansen, C., Noll, J., & Roverso, D. (2020). A methodology for security classification applied to smart grid infrastructures. *International Journal of Critical Infrastructure Protection*, 28, 100342. 10.1016/j.ijcip.2020.100342

Siniosoglou, I., Radoglou-Grammatikis, P., Efstathopoulos, G., Fouliras, P., & Sarigiannidis, P. (2021). A unified deep learning anomaly detection and classification approach for smart grid environments. *IEEE Transactions on Network and Service Management*, 18(2), 1137–1151. 10.1109/TNSM.2021.3078381

Stafford, V. (2020). Zero trust architecture. *NIST Special Publication, 800*, 207.

Syed, D., Refaat, S. S., & Bouhali, O. (2020). Privacy preservation of data-driven models in smart grids using homomorphic encryption. *Information (Basel)*, 11(7), 357. 10.3390/info11070357

Timčenko, V., Rakas, S. B., Kabović, M., & Kabović, A. (2023). Digitalization in power energy sector: Principles of cybersecurity. In *2023 30th international conference on systems, signals and image processing (iwssip)* (pp. 1–5). Academic Press.

Tolba, A., & Al-Makhadmeh, Z. (2021). A cybersecurity user authentication approach for securing smart grid communications. *Sustainable Energy Technologies and Assessments*, 46, 101284. 10.1016/j.seta.2021.101284

Tufail, S., Parvez, I., Batool, S., & Sarwat, A. (2021). A survey on cybersecurity challenges, detection, and mitigation techniques for the smart grid. *Energies*, 14(18), 5894. 10.3390/en14185894

Williams, T. J. (1994). The purdue enterprise reference architecture. *Computers in Industry*, 24(2-3), 141–158. 10.1016/0166-3615(94)90017-5

Xiao, Y., Jia, Y., Liu, C., Cheng, X., Yu, J., & Lv, W. (2019). Edge computing security: State of the art and challenges. *Proceedings of the IEEE*, 107(8), 1608–1631. 10.1109/JPROC.2019.2918437

Yee, C. K., & Zolkipli, M. F. (2021). Review on confidentiality, integrity and availability in information security. *Journal of ICT in Education*, 8(2), 34–42. 10.37134/jictie.vol8.2.4.2021

Yuliadi, Y., Hamdani, F., Fitriana, Y. B., & Oper, N. (2023). Analisis keamanan website terhadap serangan ddos menggunakan metode national institute of standards and technology (nist). *KLIK: Kajian Ilmiah Informatika dan Komputer, 3*(6), 1296–1302.

Chapter 14
ZTA–DEVSECOPS:
Strategies Towards Network Zero Trust Architecture and DevSecops in Cybersecurity and IIoT Environments

Ajay B. Gadicha
P.R. Pote Patil College of Engineering and Management, India

Vijay B. Gadicha
P.R. Pote Patil College of Engineering and Management, India

Mohammad Zuhair
P.R. Pote Patil College of Engineering and Management, India

Vishal A. Ingole
http://orcid.org/0009-0004-2061-9879
P.R. Pote Patil College of Engineering and Management, India

Sachin S. Saraf
P.R. Pote Patil College of Engineering and Management, India

ABSTRACT

In today's dynamic and interconnected digital landscape, traditional cybersecurity approaches are proving insufficient against evolving threats. This chapter explores emerging technologies that are driving smart and agile cybersecurity solutions. The authors examine how these innovations are reshaping security practices to adapt to modern challenges efficiently and effectively.

DOI: 10.4018/979-8-3693-3451-5.ch014

1. INTRODUCTION

In the world of escalating cyber threats and sophisticated attack vectors, organizations are increasingly turning to innovative strategies such as Network Zero Trust Architecture (ZTA) and DevSecOps to fortify their cybersecurity defenses. This introduction sets the stage for understanding the significance of these strategies and their implementation within modern cybersecurity frameworks.

Network Zero Trust Architecture (ZTA) represents a paradigm shift from traditional perimeter-based security models to a more dynamic and adaptive approach. The core tenet of ZTA is to never trust any entity, whether inside or outside the network perimeter, by default. This approach challenges the conventional notion of implicit trust granted to users and devices once they gain access to the network. Instead, ZTA advocates continuous verification and strict access controls based on user identity, device posture, and contextual factors.

Key strategies within Network ZTA include micro-segmentation, continuous authentication, and endpoint security. Micro-segmentation involves dividing the network into granular segments and enforcing stringent access controls between them, minimizing the lateral movement of attackers in case of a breach. Continuous authentication leverages behavioral analytics and contextual information to continuously verify the identity of users and devices throughout their interaction with network resources. Endpoint security, on the other hand, focuses on bolstering the security posture of individual devices, ensuring they adhere to security policies and are protected against potential threats.

DevSecOps, an amalgamation of Development (Dev), Operations (Ops), and Security (Sec), embodies the integration of security practices throughout the software development lifecycle (SDLC). Unlike traditional approaches where security is often retrofitted as an afterthought, DevSecOps advocates for embedding security into every stage of the development procIn ess. By integrating security automation, shift-left practices, and continuous monitoring and feedback loops, DevSecOps enables organizations to deliver secure and reliable software at a rapid pace.

The convergence of Network Zero Trust Architecture (ZTA) and DevSecOps presents a holistic approach to cybersecurity, addressing both network-level security and application security within a unified framework. This integration fosters a culture of collaboration and shared responsibility among development, operations, and security teams, driving continuous improvement and resilience against evolving cyber threats.

1.1 Zero Trust and IoT Environment

The Industrial Revolution, benefiting from advancements within artificial intelligence, 5G, the Internet of Things, and blockchain technology has introduced a massive surge in technology inclusion, expansion, innovation, and research. Such paradigm shifts have highlighted the need for machine-to-machine and machine-to-human interactions where a huge amount of data transfer occurs during the process of communication devices setting up an Internet of Things network (Rose et al., 2020). Alongside the need to transfer data at high speeds with low latency, the security of such systems is crucial due to applications dealing with sensitive user data or critical national infrastructure (Evan & Barth, 2017).

These types of massive communication handling require fool-proof security because whether the data come from home users or the data are being dealt with by any commercial company, such as smart industries or smart grid stations, a security breach can risk multiple human lives or the unavailability of resources offered by critical cyber-physical systems (Evan & Barth, 2017). Smart grids have long been a crucial component of energy networks, incorporating a variety of instruments, such as IoT devices, sensors and linked gadgets, that monitor and analyse the physical processes. It has aided in the optimization of energy production, distribution, consumption, and storage. In 2007, the sophisticated attack on Iran's nuclear power plant disturbed the distribution and development of the country's nuclear energy resources (NIST, 2019; Winckless & MacDonald, 2021). Hence, security is the most crucial aspect of these cyber-physical systems nowadays. With the increase in the number of technologies coming out, the security risks associated with them are also increasing exponentially. It is impossible for security systems to achieve 100% efficiency, and even military-grade technologies are somewhat vulnerable when they are attached to the Internet (Allan, 2021; Matthias, 2015; Seals, 2022).

Hackers have several ways to compromise systems if traditional boundary security measures are deployed. Detecting an intrusion in such a setup becomes increasingly challenging if an attacker successfully breaches that parameter layer of defence. In contrast to these trust-based systems, authentication provides a way to present the credentials that the user or machine is the legitimate user of the network. The traditional authentication and authorization system might not be directly deployed in the IoT network because of resource limitations and the dynamic nature of the network. The network requires a dynamic policy-based system that enforces policies in real-time considering the user's constraints as well as the dynamic nature of the network (Columbus, 2022).

Within this setup, a zero-trust (ZT) model applies some kind of policy decision to authorize every action of a user or device. Every attempt to access data or resources is verified by the organization, hence common modern attacks make it very difficult for intruders to impersonate or masquerade as an authenticated device or authorized user. ZT promotes a host-based monitoring approach where every host or owner device gets to set the criteria required to access it. Fine-grained data access control allows the host to dictate the intended audience and makes sure that the data cannot be accessed by any undesired user. Hence, ZT opens up new ways for security-enabled collaboration opportunities between organizations. On the implementation side, only regular updates of new technologies and methodologies with the pace of research and innovation, such as ZT, ABAC, and blockchain, can support a system to become less vulnerable against intruder attacks.

With the changing environment of networks and the new ways of communication among devices, a lot of effort is required to manage network security in real-time in a dynamic environment. The best practices of cybersecurity are becoming obsolete with the passage of time and new approaches are coming into the realization stage with every passing day. The issues associated with network security are no longer general, and the same policy and standards for each network cannot be replicated for every network. Therefore, aggressive encounter measures are required that not only support the network as a gatekeeper but also secure the system from malicious activities (Winckless & Olyaei, 2022). Access and authentication policies should be uniform at one end but must also be dynamic to reduce the vulnerabilities within the network in real-time. The Internet of Things deals with machine–machine and machine–human interactions over the Internet and blockchain is a distributed ledger primarily available for tamper-proof, hack-proof, and immutable recording of transactions into the ledger (Alevizos et al., 2022). The combination of the IoT and blockchain-based networks somehow sorts out the problems associated with the domain. Similarly, access control generally implemented through MAC address, IP, and other tags is not sufficient. A modern and evolved approach is required to deal with network security (Palmo et al., 2022). In this paper, we have introduced a method to make security as efficient as possible compared to conventional ways. We proposed a system that ensures the security of IoT devices and users through the use of emerging concepts of zero-trust architecture, attribute-based access control, blockchain, and IPFS. The system will be used to sustain a network and communication as efficiently as possible to reduce real-time attacks through the implementation of real-time monitoring, dynamic policy generation mechanisms, and interminable monitoring of the various aspects of network security and communication.

1.2 Zero Trust Architecture

The issue of information security has become increasingly difficult as information technology has continued to advance and find practical applications since the inception of the digital age. The prevalence and intensity of attacks related to cyber-security on networks has risen significantly in recent years. Even medium-sized business data centers can experience more than 1 million security attacks each day. These attacks can be carried out by a variety of opponents, from solitary hackers to organized cyber-gangs. Their goals may include compromising essential network resources that include software-defined networks or Domain Name Servers, potentially jeopardizing their integrity and functionality (Rose et al., 2020). As telecommuting and digital transformation gain traction, traditional company boundaries have diminished, removing digital boundaries entirely. As a result, the growing need for remote access has outpaced the capabilities offered by conventional perimeter safety measures. As a result of this trend, various businesses have been forced to reconsider their approach to network security. As a result, a concept known as Zero Trust Architecture has arisen, concentrating on resource security rather than just on perimeters of network. The security posture of a resource is no longer primarily governed by its network location under this approach (Evan & Barth, 2017).

Zero Trust Architecture research is now in its early stages, with a primary focus on the framework itself, access control, algorithms of trust evaluation, and identity authentication. These are the primary study domains within the Zero Trust field. Hence, the goal of this research is to provide a complete overview of the current research state in Zero Trust Architecture development, with a focus on four major topics. It covers the primary obstacles encountered in each discipline and investigates potential pathways for future study to successfully address these issues. Figure 1 depicts the work flow of the research article emphasizing the interconnections and relationships among different aspects of the conducted analysis.

Network Zero Trust Architecture (ZTA) represents a paradigm shift from traditional perimeter-based security models towards a more rigorous and dynamic security posture. The fundamental premise of ZTA revolves around the principle of "never trust, always verify." In essence, ZTA challenges the default assumption of trust once an entity gains access to the network, advocating for continuous verification of user identity, device integrity, and contextual factors before granting access to resources.

Key principles of Network ZTA include micro-segmentation, least privilege access, continuous authentication, and strict access controls based on user behavior and attributes. By implementing micro-segmentation, organizations compartmentalize their network into smaller, manageable segments, limiting lateral movement in case of a breach and reducing the attack surface. Continuous authentication mechanisms continuously verify the legitimacy of users and devices based on real-time contextual data, ensuring that access privileges remain aligned with current security postures.

Figure 1. Emerging Zero Trust Security Parameters

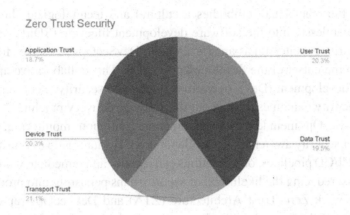

1.3 How It Works

Execution of this framework combines advanced technologies such as risk based multi-factor authentication, identity protection, next-generation endpoint security, and robust cloud workload technology to verify a user or systems identity, consideration of access at that moment in time, and the maintenance of system security. Zero Trust also requires consideration of encryption of data, securing email, and verifying the hygiene of assets and endpoints before they connect to applications.

Zero Trust is a significant departure from traditional network security which followed the "trust but verify" method. The traditional approach automatically trusted users and endpoints within the organization's perimeter, putting the organization at risk from malicious internal actors and legitimate credentials taken over by malicious actors, allowing unauthorized and compromised accounts wide-reaching access once inside.

Figure 2. Classical Approach vs. ZTA (Winckless & MacDonald, 2021)

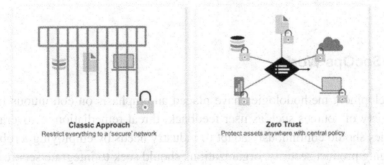

1.4 DevSecOps

DevSecOps, on the other hand, embodies a cultural and technological shift towards integrating security practices seamlessly into the software development lifecycle (SDLC). Unlike traditional approaches where security is bolted on as an afterthought, DevSecOps advocates for embedding security considerations from the outset of the development process. This collaborative approach fosters closer alignment between development (Dev), operations (Ops), and security (Sec) teams, promoting shared responsibility for security outcomes throughout the software delivery pipeline.

Key tenets of DevSecOps include security automation, continuous monitoring, shift-left security, and fostering a culture of security awareness and collaboration. By automating security testing and compliance checks within CI/CD pipelines, organizations can identify and remediate vulnerabilities early in the development process, reducing the likelihood of security gaps persisting into production environments.

In summary, Network Zero Trust Architecture (ZTA) and DevSecOps represent complementary strategies aimed at strengthening cybersecurity postures and adapting to the evolving threat landscape. By embracing the principles of ZTA to enforce strict access controls and continuous verification, and integrating DevSecOps practices to embed security throughout the development lifecycle, organizations can proactively mitigate risks, improve incident response capabilities, and foster a security-first mindset across the enterprise.

Figure 3. Overview of DevSecOps

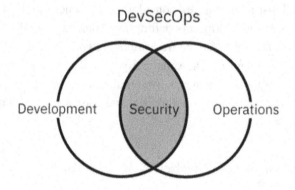

1.5 How DevSecOps Works

Modern development methodologies have placed an emphasis on continuous feedback which can stem from a variety of sources such as user feedback, threat remediation, or overall feature improvements. Companies should continuously adapt to industry needs by employing a robust planning methodology. Regarding product security, organizations should seek to integrate secure planning steps into the DevSecOps planning process. Whether it be the output from activities such as threat modeling or establishing organizational policies for security-focused requirements/user stories. Note that any tools mentioned here are simply suggestions. Each organization should determine which may be appropriate to fulfill the DevSecOps strategy.

Code

The coding phase arguably requires the highest level of scrutiny in the DevSecOps methodology. Developers should constantly be trained on secure coding practices while simultaneously implementing a variety of tools to aid in identifying vulnerabilities early and often. It is imperative that organizations create a baseline for development strategies such as branching, pre-commit rules, and style guides. It is worth mentioning that opportunities for improving secure coding can also aid in improving the quality and consistency of code being developed.

Table 1.

Challenges	Opportunities	Tools
Insecure Coding Practices	Static Application Security Testing (SAST)	GrammaTech/Checkmarx
Inconsistent Coding Convention	Coding Style/Quality Scanners	SonarQube/PMD/checkstyle
Coding Quality	Repository Policies	GitHub/SVN/Perforce

Build

Once code is committed to a shared repository, a variety of quick functional unit tests are often performed. Integrating security into this step allows developers to analyze the source code from a Software Composition Analysis (SCA) perspective. Often developers tend to leverage third-party libraries solely on their functional benefit without considering the potential security implications. Developers that understand dependencies as they are being introduced into a project can be more aware of the potential security risks as well as license violations that impact the organization.

Table 2.

Challenges	Opportunities	Tools
Limited Understanding of Third-Party Usage/Vulnerabilities	Software Composition Analysis (SCA)	CAST/DependencyTrack
Open-Source License Non-Compliance	Secrets Scanning	TruffleHog/Gitsecrets
Insecure Code Being Bundled Into Builds	Quality Gates/Policy Enforcement	Yocto Project/Buildrood/GNU

Test

Historically regression testing has been a tedious manual process that requires manual interaction to confirm baseline functionality. With the growing popularity of Infrastructure-as-Code (IaC) solutions, extensive acceptance/validation testing can be performed in parallel with Dynamic Application Security Testing (DAST). In addition to the extensive unit test cases that will likely be performed on an application, organizations should be diligent about creating security-focused unit test cases that aim to identify low-level security vulnerabilities that might have been introduced. Note that unit testing IoT devices is not a trivial task and ample time should be allocated to ensure these test cases can be designed and implemented properly.

Table 3.

Challenges	Opportunities	Tools
Testing Coverage for Secure Vulnerabilities	Dynamic Application Security Testing (DAST)	C/ C++ Test Framework/ OWASP ZAP/ LibFuzzer
Automated Testing Framework	Functional Unit Testing	Vector Software/ Tessy/ Parasoft
Manual Testing Latency	Infrastructure-as-Code (IaC)	Terraform/ Ansible/ Chef

DevOpsSec in IIoT Enviroment

DevSecOps integrates security into the DevOps lifecycle, including security considerations not as an afterthought but as a fundamental aspect of the development process. The security-first approach encourages a collaborative effort between development, operations, and security teams.

When security tools and practices are included at the beginning of the process, they enable the identification and mitigation of vulnerabilities at the earliest possible stage. This can significantly reduce the risk of security breaches. Continuous IoT security testing, threat modeling, and automated security checks become part of the continuous integration and DevOps deployment pipeline. This can then ensure continuous security assessment.

DevOpsSec is a set of practices that integrates security into the DevOps process, ensuring that security measures are implemented throughout the development and deployment lifecycle. In the context of IIoT environments, where critical infrastructure and sensitive data are at stake, DevOpsSec becomes even more important. By incorporating security into every stage of the IIoT development process, organizations can proactively identify and mitigate potential security risks, ensuring the integrity and confidentiality of their data.

One of the key principles of DevOpsSec in IIoT environments is automation. By automating security processes such as vulnerability scanning, code analysis, and compliance checks, organizations can identify and address security issues in real-time, reducing the risk of cyber attacks. Automation also enables organizations to respond quickly to security incidents, minimizing the impact on their operations and reputation.

Another important aspect of DevOpsSec in IIoT environments is collaboration. By bringing together development, operations, and security teams, organizations can create a culture of shared responsibility for security. This collaboration ensures that security considerations are integrated into every aspect of the IIoT development process, from design to deployment. By working together, teams can identify and address security issues early on, reducing the likelihood of security breaches.

Furthermore, continuous monitoring is essential for ensuring the security of IIoT environments. By monitoring the performance and behavior of devices, sensors, and networks in real-time, organizations can detect and respond to security threats before they escalate. Continuous monitoring also enables organizations to identify vulnerabilities and weaknesses in their IIoT infrastructure, allowing them to take proactive measures to strengthen their security posture.

2. LITERATURE SURVEY

Winckless and MacDonald (2021) proposed the concept of a zero-trust architecture model and a method to implement it in a practical environment and innovatively proposed a zero trust architecture based on "Data Acquisition Network" (DAN) in the paper. DAN helps to extract network data to the management center and then realizes inspection and analysis of it in real time, thus realizing the concept of zero trust, but this is also accompanied by problems of higher network complexity and increased user communication delay.

Ferrill (2022) proposed a zero trust method based on transport access control. This method is based on steganography and overwriting, and the authentication token is embedded in the TCP request packet and the first authentication packet. Thus realizing the concept of zero trust, this approach increases the security of enterprises in cloud computing environments and prevents unwanted fingerprinting of protected resources; this approach provides protection at layer 3/4 but not at layer 7.

Subsequently, in 2022, Seals (2022) summarized the existing basic zero trust architecture schemes and proposed the basic logical components of the zero trust architecture. In addition, the author paid more attention to the implementation of the zero trust architecture, considering the realization of ZTA. Rather than a massive replacement of infrastructure or processes, it is a process that proposes specific steps to apply ZTA to a perimeter-based architecture network.

Allan (2021) proposed a secure medical image sharing system based on the principle of zero trust and blockchain technology. The system combines zero trust with blockchain. The blockchain is used to protect sensitive information. Comprehensive protection of medical data, but this also increases the complexity of the system and needs to be studied in terms of efficiency.

Matthias (2015) proposed a zero trust network security model in a containerized environment, which solved how to implement zero trust for "east-west" traffic between microservices in a containerized environment, using Kubernetes and Istio service mesh to build. A zero trust model in containerized environments reduces data leakage in containerized environments, but this model does not implement behavioral analysis and data leakage detection.

Columbus (2022) proposed an artificial intelligence-based zero trust architecture (i-ZTA), which uses artificial intelligence for intelligent detection, evaluation, and decision-making, which can improve the efficiency of ZTA components in processing big data. The architecture combines artificial intelligence with PEP and PDP in the traditional zero trust architecture. The former uses reinforcement learning with the goal of maximizing guaranteed scores, while the latter uses joint learning to provide users with context-aware scores.

Valero et al. (2022) proposed a zero trust approach based on BLP and BIBA models, which conducts comprehensive trust scores for system components such as users, terminals, channels, files, and applications, and requires confidentiality and integrity, setting different weights to achieve better confidentiality and integrity protection of objects, but does not consider the initial trust value granting method of users, terminals, environments, objects, and other entities, and cannot effectively avoid human-factor errors in initial trust. The assignment, as well as the completeness and rationality of the list weight assignment, is for further study.

Alevizos et al. (2022) proposed an advanced zero trust architecture that leverages generalized attribute relation extraction to automate fine-grained access control to achieve low-cost fine-grained access control, performance, scalability, and security for real enterprise networks. The evaluation is for future work.

Chen et al. (2020) presented a safe medical image allocation platform based on ZT concepts and technology of blockchain. This technology provides the complete security of sensitive medical data. The technology improves information security by utilizing blockchain. However, it is critical to examine the possible complexity and efficiency consequences of combining these technologies, and additional research is needed in this field. Zhang et al. (2021) suggested a ZT strategy based on the BIBa and BLP models. This method does thorough trust assessments for numerous system components. It emphasizes the importance of confidentiality and integrity and assigns different weights to achieve greater security. It does not, however, address the initial trust value assignment for entities such as users, terminals, environments, and objects, which could lead to human errors. Furthermore, the completeness and logic of the weight assignment list need to be investigated further. Dayna et al. suggested a ZT model specifically intended for cloud data centre networks in a separate study (Rapuzzi & Repetto, 2018) for the creation of trust; their model blends identity management, packet-based authentication, and automated threat response. It controls the model's eight different network trust levels dynamically.

Traditional network security measures that focus on basics a border between trustworthy and local networks are no longer viable, as cloud apps and IoT networks have become more commonly used. ZT architecture has emerged to meet the need for secure and intelligent access management in the absence of trusted networks or devices. To fulfil the particular security requirements of respective networks, researchers devised and implemented numerous variants of ZTA. Pedro Assuncao proposed a ZT architecture in Mehraj and Banday (2020) that eliminates unchanged credentials, uses multifaceted verification, and keeps a proper record of devices and network congestion. In the meantime, Hunker and Probst (2011) proposed a context-based ZT architecture access control system to address security issues in a heterogeneous Moodle application. This framework employs the Zero Trust concept to offer access control for the e-Learning platform Moodle, demonstrating positive webserver performance gains. However, additional tests are required to evaluate the Zero Trust model's non-functional performance.

The ZT security framework that features continual verification of identity and minimal power distribution, is capable of meeting the safety control needs of various contemporary networked devices. A proposed system for access control and permission relies on the ZT security architecture. Individual identities and confidence from users are derived based on behavior of users. The system utilizes real-time hierarchy oversight across many settings to effectively accomplish flexible and precise control of access and authentication.

2.1 Comparative Analysis of Zero Trust Analysis

Zero Trust is a collection of established and new technologies, rather than a single, rigid design. It is critical to compare various technologies in order to identify which aspects have the greatest or worst fit. Table 2 represents the comparison between different approaches of ZT network based upon some significant parameters. Outdated designs can be changed with more effective ones as opponents progress. The model's operational requirement takes precedence above its economic efficiency. Furthermore, writers have provided useful insights into how the majority of articles have primarily contributed to the framework design and strategy of ZT networks (U.S. Institute of Peace, 2021). Such comparative metrics highlight the common key requirements identified across various cloud network implementations. Beneficiary node cooperation as a distinct group is crucial for network security in an unstable computer network environment. Given the critical necessity of resource security in cloud networks, determining the reliability of requests must rely on past data. Using different rules and standardized methods for the implementing restrictions of access for people in a fragmented network is not a novel approach. Creating a network's restricted visibility buffer zone serves as the main network's outer layer (Zetter, 2010).

3. CHALLENGE AND FUTURE TRENDS

Today, the basic ZTAs have been determined, but how to make various technologies meet the standard of ZTA is still a difficult problem. At present, the access control, identity authentication, and trust assessment in ZTA are still in the preliminary research stage. In the future, how to use these technologies to enhance the security protection capability and practicability of ZTA is still a hot topic worthy of research. After proposing a new ZTA, how to apply it to the real enterprise network environment is also a challenging research topic.

In identity authentication, because single-factor authentication has only one unique factor for identity authentication, once the unique password or biometrics is stolen, it will collapse completely, while multifactor authentication can improve the defects of single-factor and greatly reduce the threat of network attacks. Because even if the attacker intercepts the password information, the difficulty of obtaining the authorization of the second or third factor is greatly increased. However, the incomplete authentication information is not enough to access. Continuous authentication changes the way that visitors can access system information for a long time after one-time authentication in the initial stage. It continuously grants user resource access rights before and during the session, reducing the security risks caused by attackers in the middle of the session, to enhance the security of the system. From single-factor authentication to two-factor and multifactor authentication, from one-time authentication to continuous authentication, security continues to improve.

In the future, multifactor authentication methods and continuous authentication methods will be widely used in zero trust architectures because of their better security. Whether based on certificates, encrypted authentication protocols, or non encrypted protocols, different protocols have trade-offs between security and resource consumption. It aims to reduce resource consumption as much as possible in the authentication process under the premise of ensuring the security of the zero-trust system, which is also the direction of the identity authentication part of the future zero trust architecture.

3.1 IIoT Gaining Momentum in Security

IIoT adoption is real, pays off, and helps manufacturers stay (digitally) relevantAlthough we see signs that IIoT adoption has been slower than expected, it is nevertheless real and becoming more widespread . With digital manufacturing expected to capture a significant share of the overall IoT market by 2025, it is clear that there are big gain to be made

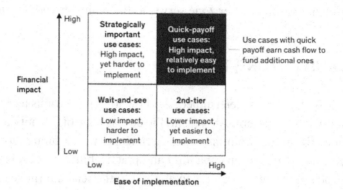

4. IMPLEMENTATION

Creating pseudocode for implementing security practices within a DevSecOps pipeline involves outlining steps and considerations for integrating security checks and controls into the software development lifecycle. Below is an example of pseudocode illustrating key components of DevSecOps:

```
// Define a DevSecOps pipeline pseudocode


function devSecOpsPipeline() {


try {


// Stage 1: Code Development


codeDevelopment();


// Stage 2: Security Checks


securityChecks();


// Stage 3: Build and Test
```

```
    buildAndTest();

    // Stage 4: Security Scans

    securityScans();

    // Stage 5: Deployment

    deploy();

    // Stage 6: Monitoring and Feedback

    monitorAndFeedback();

    } catch (error) {

    handlePipelineFailure(error);

    }

    }


    function codeDevelopment() {

    // Developers write and commit code changes

    // Code is reviewed and approved before merging

    }
```

```
function securityChecks() {

    // Static Application Security Testing (SAST)

    runSAST();

    // Dynamic Application Security Testing (DAST)

    runDAST();

    // Software Composition Analysis (SCA)

    runSCA();

    // Container Security Scans

    runContainerSecurityScans();

}

function buildAndTest() {

    // Continuous Integration (CI) - Build process

    runBuild();

    // Automated Unit and Integration Tests

    runTests();
```

```
}


function securityScans() {


// Vulnerability Assessment


assessVulnerabilities();


// Compliance Checks


performComplianceChecks();


}


function deploy() {


// Continuous Deployment (CD)


deployToStaging();


deployToProduction();

}


function monitorAndFeedback() {


// Continuous Monitoring


startMonitoring();
```

```
// Provide security feedback to developers

provideSecurityFeedback();

}

function handlePipelineFailure(error) {

// Handle pipeline failure gracefully

logError(error);

notifyTeam();

}
```

5. CONCLUSION

Promoting a Network Zero Trust Architecture and implementing DevSecOps are crucial strategies in modern cybersecurity, driven by the need to adapt to evolving threats and secure dynamic IT environments effectively. Network Zero Trust Architecture rejects the traditional perimeter-based security model, focusing instead on strict access controls, continuous verification, and least privilege principles. By adopting this approach, organizations can minimize the attack surface and mitigate the risks posed by insider threats and advanced external attacks. Zero Trust ensures that every access attempt is rigorously authenticated and authorized based on contextual factors like user identity, device health, and behavior, enhancing overall network security posture.

Similarly, embracing DevSecOps practices integrates security seamlessly into the software development lifecycle, emphasizing collaboration, automation, and early security involvement. This strategy enhances the security posture of applications and infrastructure by embedding security controls at every stage, from code development and testing to deployment and monitoring. DevSecOps enables organizations to identify and remediate security vulnerabilities rapidly, reducing the time to detect and respond to threats. By fostering a culture of shared responsibility and continuous improvement, DevSecOps promotes innovation while maintaining a robust security framework. Together, Network Zero Trust Architecture and DevSecOps represent proactive and holistic cybersecurity strategies that prioritize prevention, detection, and response in an increasingly complex threat landscape.

In response to the escalating internal threat incidents, the concept of a trusted internal network within the scope of a traditional network perimeter can no longer be regarded as secure. Consequently, the zero trust paradigm has emerged, aiming to eradicate the reliance on implicit trust in networks and systems. This paper conducted a survey on the theory and application of zero trust security, organizing and summarizing the fundamental theories and architectural frameworks, as well as the application of zero trust in cloud computing and the IoT. Diverging from other survey articles that primarily focus on the detailed implementation aspects of zero trust, this paper attempts to analyze the essence of zero trust from a more fundamental perspective, i.e., what trust means within the context of zero trust. The review of the literature reveals that zero trust fundamentally entails a continuous suspicion of the trustworthiness of implicit trust. In other words, the formerly implicit trust can no longer be deemed reliable, necessitating the transformation of implicit trust into explicit trust through technological means or verification mechanisms. Consequently, this paper proposes a novel concept, namely the "trustbase", serving as the foundation of explicit and implicit trust. When both explicit and implicit trust fails simultaneously, the trustbase can serve as a substitute for trust to fulfill the minimal security requirements. Furthermore, this paper examines the future research trends and challenges of zero trust from the perspective of trust. The results indicate that both the theoretical concepts and technical aspects of zero trust revolve around the fundamental questions of how to establish trust and how to verify trust. Thus, this paper presents several research aspects within zero trust security and provides reference research ideas and methods, aiming to assist readers in identifying intriguing and challenging research topics. The intention is for the content of this paper to facilitate beginners in zero trust research to attain the essential knowledge required for studying zero trust, as well as provide dependable references for conducting related research.

REFERENCES

Alevizos, L., Ta, V. T., & Hashem Eiza, M. (2022). Augmenting zero trust architecture to endpoints using blockchain: A state-of-the-art review. *Security and Privacy*, 5(1), 191. 10.1002/spy2.191

Allan, A. (2021). *Shift Focus From MFA to Continous Adaptive Trust*. Available: www.gartner.com

Arshad, J., Azad, M. A., Mahmoud Abdellatif, M., Ur Rehman, M. H., & Salah, K. (2019). COLIDE: A collaborative intrusion detection framework for Internet of Things. *IET Networks*, 8(1), 3–14. 10.1049/iet-net.2018.5036

Chen, Z., Yan, L., Lü, Z., Zhang, Y., Guo, Y., Liu, W., & Xuan, J. (2020). Research on zero-trust security protection technology of power IoT based on blockchain. *Proceedings of the 5th International Conference on Computer Science and Information Engineering (ICCSIE 2020)*.

Columbus, L. (2022). *Why the future of APIs must include zero trust*. VentureBeat. Available: https://venturebeat.com/2022/08/01/why-the-future-of-apis-must-includezero-trust/

Evan, G., & Barth, D. (2017). *Zero Trust Networks: Building Secure Systems in Untrusted Networks*. O'Reilly.

Ferrill, P. (2022). What Is Zero Trust Architecture? *The New Stack*. Available: https://thenewstack.io/what-is-zero-trust-architecture/

Hunker, J., & Probst, C. W. (2011). Insiders and Insider Threats-An Overview of Definitions and Mitigation Techniques. *J. Wirel. Mob. Netw. Ubiquitous Comput. Dependable Appl.*, 2, 4–27. Available online: https://www.trellix.com/en-us/security-awareness/ransomware/what-is-stuxnet.html

Li, S., Iqbal, M., & Saxena, N. (2022). Future industry internet of things with zero-trust security. *Information Systems Frontiers*, 1–14. 10.1007/s10796-021-10199-5

Matthias. (2015). *Using 'fwknop' on OpenWRT*. Academic Press.

Mehraj, S., & Banday, M. T. (2020). Establishing a zero trust strategy in cloud computing environment. *Proceedings of the 2020 International Conference on Computer Communication and Informatics (ICCCI)*. 10.1109/ICCCI48352.2020.9104214

NIST. (2019). *Developing Cyber Resilient Systems A Systems Security Engineering Approach SP800-160*. NIST. 10.6028/NIST.SP.800-160v2

Palmo, Y., Tanimoto, S., Sato, H., & Kanai, A. (2022). Optimal Federation Method for Embedding Internet of Things in Software-Defined Perimeter. *IEEE Consumer Electronics Magazine*, 12(5), 68–75. 10.1109/MCE.2022.3207862

Rapuzzi, R., & Repetto, M. (2018). Building situational awareness for network threats in fog/edge computing: Emerging paradigms beyond the security perimeter model. *Future Generation Computer Systems*, 85, 235–249. 10.1016/j.future.2018.04.007

Razzaq, M. A., Gill, S. H., Qureshi, M. A., & Ullah, S. (2020). Security issues in the Internet of Things (IoT): A comprehensive study. *Mechanical Systems and Signal Processing*, 136, 106436.

Rose, Borchert, Mitchell, & Connelly. (2020). *Zero Trust Architecture: NIST SP 800-207*. 10.6028/NIST.SP.800-207

Seals, T. (2022). *Zero-Trust For All: A Practical Guide.* Available: https://docs.microsoft.com/en-us/azure/active-directory/conditional-access/overview

U.S. Institute of Peace. (2021). *Israeli Sabotage of Iran's Nuclear Program.* Available online: https://iranprimer.usip.org/blog/2021/apr/12/israeli-sabotage-iran%E2%80%99s-nuclear-program (accessed on 12 April 2021).

Valero, J. M. J., Sánchez, P. M. S., Lekidis, A., Hidalgo, J. F., Pérez, M. G., Siddiqui, M. S., Celdrán, A. H., & Pérez, G. M. (2022). Design of a Security and Trust Framework for 5G Multi-domain Scenarios. *Journal of Network and Systems Management*, 30(1), 7. 10.1007/s10922-021-09623-7

Winckless, C., & MacDonald, N. (2021). *Quick Answer: How to Explain Zero Trust Technology to Executives.* Available: www.gartner.com

Winckless, C., & Olyaei, S. (2022). *How to Decipher Zero Trust for Your Business.* Available: www.gartner.com

Zetter, K. (2010). *Inside the Cunning, Unprecedented Hack of Ukraine's Power Grid.* Available online: https://www.wired.com/2016/03/inside-cunning-unprecedented-hack-ukraines-power-grid/

Zhang, X., Chen, L., Fan, J., Wang, X., & Wang, Q. (2021). Power IoT security protection architecture based on zero trust framework. *Proceedings of the 2021 IEEE 5th International Conference on Cryptography, Security and Privacy (CSP).*

Chapter 15
Securing Wireless MIMO Systems:
Computational Insights

Khadiga Eltira
University of Benghazi, Libya

Abdelhamid Younis
(iD) https://orcid.org/0000-0002-2499-8536
University of Benghazi, Libya

Raed Mesleh
(iD) https://orcid.org/0000-0001-6838-2816
German Jordanian University, Jordan

ABSTRACT

This chapter proposes computationally secure physical layer wireless communication for multiple–input multiple–output (MIMO) systems. The algorithm presented is applicable across various MIMO configurations and resistant to attacks. It relies on accurate knowledge of wireless channel characteristics and channel reciprocity. Both transmitter and legitimate receiver generate a permutation vector based on channel fading paths to create the security key. The vast number of potential combinations makes decryption nearly infeasible. Additionally, secrecy rate analysis is introduced, considering space modulation techniques (SMTs) and spatial multiplexing (SMX) MIMO approaches, evaluating mutual information and average bit error rate (ABER) at both ends. Various SMTs schemes including space shift keying (SSK), spatial modulation (SM), and quadrature spatial modulation (QSM) are examined to validate the derived formulations.

INTRODUCTION

In recent years, the burgeoning growth of decentralized networks and advanced communication systems, including 5G and beyond, has sparked considerable interest in wireless physical layer security (PLS) (Jorswieck, Wolf, & Gerbracht, 2010; Annamalai, Olaluwe, & Adebola, 2014). PLS offers a distinctive approach to safeguarding communication channels from potential threats without the need

DOI: 10.4018/979-8-3693-3451-5.ch015

for additional upper-layer security measures. It capitalizes on the inherent unpredictability of wireless channel variations between transmitters and legitimate receivers, ensuring secure communication with minimal computational complexity (Yener & Ulukus, 2015; Hyadi, Rezki, & Alouini, 2016).

Amidst the evolution of telecommunications systems, the prominence of PLS as a robust framework is increasingly evident. Here, data confidentiality is assured by leveraging the intrinsic physical layer characteristics of the network. Previous research on PLS has primarily focused on information theoretic aspects, aiming to enhance secrecy measures such as secrecy capacity and outage probability (Hyadi et al., 2016; Noura, Melki, & Chehab, 2021 ; Yungaicela-Naula, Vargas-Rosales, Perez-D ́ ́ıaz, & Zareei, 2022 ; Parkouk, Torabi, & Shokrollahi, 2022; Y. Wang et al., 2021; Mukherjee, Fakoorian, Huang, & Swindlehurst, 2014; Nguyen, Lin, Cheng, Hwang, & Lin, 2021; N. Yang et al., 2015; Yerrapragada, Eisman, & Kelley, 2021). Additionally, several studies have examined the behavior of fluctuating fading channels, delving into parameters such as average bit error rate (ABER) and signal-to-noise-ratio (SNR) for both legitimate receivers and potential eavesdroppers (Wu, Xiao, & Yang, 2020; Bloch, 2016; Lin, Lai, Lin, & Su, 2013).

Commonly employed security algorithms, like the Advanced Encryption Standard (AES) (Biryukov & Khovratovich, 2009), theoretically present a zero-secrecy rate scenario, implying that eavesdroppers could potentially recover transmitted data through brute-force methods. However, the inherent computational complexity of AES renders it computationally secure against such attacks. To illustrate, even with access to the world's fastest reported supercomputer, capable of processing at a rate of (1.102×10^{18}) floatingpoint operations per second (FLOPS) (In Data, n.d.; TOP500, n.d.; RankRed, n.d.), the time required for a brute-force decryption attempt would be staggering. Decrypting an AES-128 encryption key would take approximately 9.79×1020 years, and for an AES-256 bit key, the estimate rises to nearly 3.33×10^{51} years. This assumes an optimistic scenario where the supercomputer can attempt encryption keys at its maximum processing speed.

This chapter presents a robust and secure physical layer technique for multiple–input multiple–output (MIMO) wireless communication systems. The proposed algorithm achieves a secrecy rate of zero, implying that, theoretically, even an eavesdropper with advanced computational abilities and complete knowledge of the transmission protocol may struggle to decipher the transmitted message. The study demonstrates that, despite employing the world's fastest supercomputer, the computational time required is exceptionally long, making detection nearly unfeasible, especially in large MIMO configurations. The methodology proposed here relies on the unpredictability of the physical channel in a time division duplex (TDD) MIMO system and leverages channel reciprocity to devise a secure encryption solution. Additionally, it is assumed that channel estimation occurs at each coherence time, typically ranging from nano to microseconds in wireless systems.

MIMO technology, which involves deploying multiple antennas at both the transmitting and receiving ends, has been pivotal in the development of 4G and 5G wireless standards and is expected to continue influencing the forthcoming 6G standard (S. Chen, Sun, Xu, Su, & Cai, 2020). In recent years, there has been a surge of research interest in developing PLS algorithms for MIMO systems (Yin, Yang, & Jiao, 2020; Oggier & Hassibi, 2011; J. Liu, Zhang, Zhang, Wang, & Sun, 2021).

Researchers in Oggier & Hassibi, (2011) investigated the secrecy capacity of MIMO wiretap channels. Most existing approaches capitalize on the multitude of antennas available to disrupt the eavesdropper's connection while enhancing the performance of the legitimate receiver (X. Chen, Ng, Gerstacker, & Chen, 2016). Among these techniques, spatial modulation (SM) (Mesleh, Haas, Ahn, & Yun, 2006) has been frequently considered due to its inherent advantages (L. Wang, Bashar, Wei, & Li, 2015; C. Liu, Yang, & Wang, 2017; L. Yu, Fan, & Han, 2019).

Numerous PLS MIMO algorithms have been developed in various studies, employing approaches such as precoding, beamforming, and artificial noise, while considering full knowledge of the channel statistics of both the legitimate receivers and eavesdroppers (Shu, Wang, Chen, Wu, & Wang, 2018; Xia, Lin, Liu, Shu, & Hanzo, 2020 ; Y. Yang & Guizani, 2018).

The proposed secure computational scheme for PLS demonstrates its versatility and applicability across various MIMO systems. In this communication scenario, we envision a transmitter engaged in communication with a legitimate receiver, while an eavesdropper attempts to intercept and retrieve the transmitted message. Notably, the system relies on the transmitter and legitimate receiver possessing knowledge of the channel statistics between them, facilitated by channel reciprocity, while remaining unaware of the channel characteristics between the transmitter and eavesdropper. The transmitter exploits this shared channel statistics to compute the power associated with each transmit antenna. These computed channel power values are subsequently sorted, and the corresponding antenna indices form a permutation vector. This vector is then utilized to shuffle the rows of the constellation matrix, associating data bits with transmit antenna vectors. The legitimate receiver, equipped with an identical permutation vector, adjusts the constellation matrix accordingly.

However, the eavesdropper operates without constraints regarding resources such as SNR, communication protocol, and other system variables. Despite this advantage, the eavesdropper remains unaware of the channel statistics governing the connection between the transmitter and legitimate receiver, preventing her from correctly updating the constellation matrix. Our results highlight the legitimate receiver's ability to successfully decode data bits across various MIMO approaches, specifically spatial multiplexing (SMX), space shift keying (SSK), SM, and quadrature spatial modulation (QSM) (Mesleh & Alhassi, 2018; Eltira, Younis, & Mesleh, 2023). Interestingly, the eavesdropper's ABER ranges from 0.35 to 0.5 for various space modulation techniques (SMTs) configurations considered. Additionally, our analysis indicates that the eavesdropper would require a significantly long time to successfully decipher the transmitted message. For example, with computational resources comparable to the aforementioned supercomputer, the eavesdropper would demand a mere 8 milliseconds to decrypt a MIMO system featuring 16 transmit antennas. However, this decryption time increases exponentially, reaching an astounding 2.48×10^{13} years for systems equipped with 32 antennas. The computational requirements become even more formidable for larger configurations.

To enhance privacy and mitigate possible man-in-the-middle (MiTM) attacks, the PLS strategy, in conjunction with robust authentication techniques, can be advantageous (Das, Basu, & Karmakar, 2022). However, delving into extensive detail on integrating this combination and conducting a thorough evaluation and verification extends beyond the scope of this current work. We acknowledge the significance of this subject and intend to delve deeper into it in our future research, providing a more comprehensive and practical perspective on wireless communication security.

SYSTEM MODEL

Consider a wiretap MIMO system comprising a transmitter, a legitimate receiver, and an eavesdropper endeavoring to intercept the transmitted signal. Each party possesses multiple antennas: the transmitter has N_t antennas, the legitimate receiver has N_r antennas, and the passive eavesdropper has N_e receive antennas. At each time instant, the transmitter conveys η information bits through MIMO channels **H** and **G**, representing the channels between the transmitter and legitimate receiver $(N_r \times N_t)$ and between the transmitter and eavesdropper $(N_e \times N_t)$, respectively. Both channels exhibit independent and identically distributed (i.i.d.) Gaussian distribution entries. Consequently, the received signal at both the legitimate and eavesdropper receivers can be expressed as:

$$\mathbf{y}_b = \mathbf{H}x + \mathbf{n}_b ; \tag{1}$$

$$\mathbf{y}_e = \mathbf{G}x + \mathbf{n}_e ; \tag{2}$$

Here, $\mathbf{y}_b$ and $\mathbf{y}_e$ denote the received signal at the legitimate and eavesdropper receivers, respectively. $\mathbf{n}_b$ represents $N_r \times 1$ additive white Gaussian noise (AWGN) at the legitimate terminal with zero mean and variance $\sigma_{n_b}^2$, while ne represents $N_e \times 1$ AWGN at the eavesdropper terminal with zero mean and variance $\sigma_{n_e}^2$. Assuming the transmitted power is normalized to unity, the received SNR at the legitimate terminal is $SNR_b = 1/\sigma_{n_b}^2$, and at the eavesdropper is $SNR_e = 1/\sigma_{n_e}^2$. Finally, $x = \begin{bmatrix} x_1 & ;\ldots; & x_i & ;\ldots; & x_{N_t} \end{bmatrix}$ represents the $N_t \times 1$ transmitted vector, where x_i is a signal symbol drawn from an $M \times 1$ signal constellation matrix X, with M denoting the modulation order and $i \in 1 : N_t$.

The incoming information bits are modulated depending on the approach used at the transmitter terminal. This chapter specifically focuses on SMX and SMTs techniques, particularly QSM, SM, and SSK.

In this chapter, we will provide a brief overview of the suggested MIMO approaches:

- SSK: This fundamental SMTs solely utilizes spatial symbols to transfer messages. Thus, at each time instant, a single antenna will be active for transmitting data without considering regular modulation. Consequently, the spectral efficiency of the SSK system is determined by $\eta = \log_2(N_t)$ bits/s/Hz.
- SM: In this approach, a modulated carrier is sent from the active antenna in the SSK system, resulting in spatial modulation. When transmitting data, both the signal symbol and spatial symbol are employed, with the spectral efficiency determined by $\eta = \log_2(M) + \log_2(N_t)$ bits/s/Hz.
- QSM: This technique divides the modulated symbol into imaginary and real components, which are then simultaneously sent from two different active antennas. Consequently, the spectral efficiency of this approach is given by $\eta = 2\log_2(N_t) + \log_2(M)$ bits/s/Hz.
- SMX: In SMX, all available transmit antennas are activated, each transmitting an individual modulated symbol. Consequently, the spectral efficiency is $\eta = N_t \log_2(M)$ bits/s/Hz.

For SMTs systems, the received signals at the legitimate and eavesdropper receivers (1) and (2) can be reformulated as follows:

$$\mathbf{y}_b = \mathcal{H}_{\ell_b} x_i + \mathbf{n}_b ; \tag{3}$$

$$\mathbf{y}_e = \mathcal{G}_{\ell_e} x_i + \mathbf{n}_e ; \tag{4}$$

Here, $\mathscr{H}_{\ell_b}$ represents the ℓ_b^{th} legitimate spatial symbol drawn from the Hspatial constellation matrix, and x_i denotes the ith signal symbol drawn from the signal constellation matrixX. Similarly, $\mathscr{G}_{\ell_e}$ denotes the ℓ_e^{th} eavesdropper spatial symbol drawn from the corresponding Gspatial constellation matrix.

Assuming both the legitimate and eavesdropper terminals employ maximum–likelihood (ML) receivers to retrieve the transmitted symbols, the respective expressions for SMX are given as:

$$\left[\widehat{x}_b\right] = \underset{\widehat{x}_b \in \mathcal{X}}{\arg\min} \left\| \mathbf{y}_b - \mathbf{H}x_i \right\|_F^2 ; \tag{5}$$

$$\left[\widehat{x}_e\right] = \underset{\widehat{x}_e \in \mathcal{X}}{\arg\min} \left\| \mathbf{y}_e - \mathbf{G}x_i \right\|_F^2 ; \tag{6}$$

where $\widehat{x}_b$ and $\widehat{x}_e$ represent the estimated transmit vector at legitimate and eavesdropper terminal respectively, and $\| . \|_F$ denotes the Frobenius norm. For SMTs systems, the expressions are given as:

$$\left[\widehat{x}_{i_b}, \widehat{\mathscr{H}}_{\ell_b}\right] = \arg \underset{\widehat{x}_i \in \mathcal{X}, \widehat{\mathscr{H}}_\ell \in \mathscr{H}}{\min} \left\| \mathbf{y}_b - \mathscr{H}_{\ell_b}x_i \right\|_F^2 ; \tag{7}$$

$$\left[\widehat{x}_{i_e}, \widehat{\mathscr{G}}_{\ell_e}\right] = \arg \underset{\widehat{x}_i \in \mathcal{X}, \widehat{\mathscr{G}}_\ell \in \mathscr{G}}{\min} \left\| \mathbf{y}_e - \mathscr{G}_{\ell_e}x_i \right\|_F^2 ; \tag{8}$$

Here, $\widehat{x}_{i_b}$ and $\widehat{x}_{i_e}$ are the estimated signal symbols, and , $\widehat{\mathscr{H}}_{\ell_b}$ and $\widehat{\mathscr{G}}_{\ell_e}$ are the estimated spatial symbols at the legitimate and eavesdropper receivers, respectively.

The proposed PLS algorithm is applied to the constellation matrix before the generation of the transmitted vector. It is assumed that both the transmitter, eavesdropper, and the legitimate receiver have complete knowledge of the statistical properties of the channel matrix. This knowledge can be obtained through means such as reciprocity, as observed in TDD systems (D. Liu, Ma, Shao, Shen, & Tang, 2015), or through a secure feedback link. This assumption is widely accepted and facilitates various transmitter-side strategies, including precoding, beamforming, adaptive modulation, adaptive coding, and power allocation (Rosenzweig, Steinberg, & Shamai, 2005 ; H. Yu et al., 2019; Mukherjee, 2020).

THE PROPOSED COMPUTATIONAL PHYSICAL LAYER ALGORITHM

This section describes the proposed PLS algorithm in detail. To begin with, it is assumed that the channel state information (CSI) at the transmitter, and legitimate receiver are fully known. At first, the transmitter and legitimate receiver calculate the power of each channel path $\mathbf{h}_i$ as following $p_i = \mathbf{h}_i^H \mathbf{h}_i$, where $(.)^H$ denotes Hermition operator, and arrange the resulting powers in either descending or ascending order as vector $P = \left[p_1, ..., p_i, ..., p_{N_t}\right]$, and the sorted power is labeled as $\mathbf{S} = \left[s_1, ..., s_i, ..., s_{N_t}\right]$, if the power vector is arranged in ascending then s_1 represents the index pertains to the path have lowest power, while if arranged in descending order then s_1 represents the index pertains to the path with highest power.

Thereafter, the produced vector **S** acts as a permutation vector, shuffling the rows of the constellation matrix Cthat contains all possible transmitted vectors.

To elucidate this premise, suppose the following example: Assume (2×4) MIMO channel matrix between the transmitter and legitimate receiver, consider the transmitter uses SM technique with binary phase shift keying (BPSK) modulation. Therefore, $\eta = \log_2(N_t M) = 3$ bps/Hz (Mesleh, Engelken, Sinanovic, & Haas, 2008), the resulting constellation matrix with $(N_t \times 2^n)$ is given by;

$$\mathscr{C} = \begin{bmatrix} 1 & 0 & 0 & 0 & -1 & 0 & 0 & 0 \\ 0 & 1 & 0 & 0 & 0 & -1 & 0 & 0 \\ 0 & 0 & 1 & 0 & 0 & 0 & -1 & 0 \\ 0 & 0 & 0 & 1 & 0 & 0 & 0 & -1 \end{bmatrix}; \tag{9}$$

and consider at specific instant, the MIMO channel entries are as following;

$$\mathscr{H} = \begin{bmatrix} -0.0878 + 0.3457i & 0.9963 + 0.5140i & 0.4748 + 0.2078i & 0.5072 + 0.6282i \\ 1.0534 + 0.7316i & 1.0021 - 0.2146i & -0.8538 - 0.5567i & 1.1528 - 0.8111i \end{bmatrix};$$

according to the concept mentioned above, the power of channel entries is obtained as $P = [$ 1.7721, 2.3071, 1.3076, 2.6386]. Therefore, if the power vector entries are arranged in descending order the appropriate sorted indices are **S** = [4, 2, 1, 3]. Accordingly, the constellation matrix for transmitter and legitimate receiver in (9) is then ordered as;

$$\mathscr{C} = \begin{bmatrix} 0 & 0 & 0 & 1 & 0 & 0 & 0 & -1 \\ 0 & 1 & 0 & 0 & 0 & -1 & 0 & 0 \\ 1 & 0 & 0 & 0 & -1 & 0 & 0 & 0 \\ 0 & 0 & 1 & 0 & 0 & 0 & -1 & 0 \end{bmatrix}; \tag{10}$$

Furthermore, the constellation matrix is not constant and changes with channel characteristics at each instant.

Assuming that, eavesdropper understands the permutation procedure, and generates her constellation matrix using her channel matrix G, thus similarly assume at same specific instant, the MIMO channel entries are as following.

$$\mathscr{G} = \begin{bmatrix} -0.7558 - 0.0723i & -2.0819 + 0.2257i & 0.2299 - 0.6116i & 0.9689 - 0.1166i \\ -0.5724 - 0.1707i & 1.0171 + 0.2212i & -0.5338 - 0.0212i & -1.2102 + 0.4439i \end{bmatrix};$$

therefore $P_g = [0.9333, 5.4688, 0.7123, 2.6141]$, and if the power vector entries are arranged in descending order the appropriate sorted indices are $\mathbf{S}_g = [2, 4, 1, 3]$. Consequently, the constellation matrix for transmitter and eavesdropper receiver is given as;

$$\mathscr{C}_g = \begin{bmatrix} 0 & 1 & 0 & 0 & 0 & -1 & 0 & 0 \\ 0 & 0 & 0 & 1 & 0 & 0 & 0 & -1 \\ 1 & 0 & 0 & 0 & -1 & 0 & 0 & 0 \\ 0 & 0 & 1 & 0 & 0 & 0 & -1 & 0 \end{bmatrix}; \tag{11}$$

Eavesdroppers require to have an in-depth knowledge of the channel matrix between the transmitter and legitimate receiver in order to comprehend the accurate messages. Every time a channel update occurs, the permutation vector varies due to various factors including coherence time, which introduces a degree of unpredictability to enhance data security.

A visual representation of the proposed security algorithm is summarized in Fig. 1.

Figure 1. The Proposed Secure MIMO Algorithm

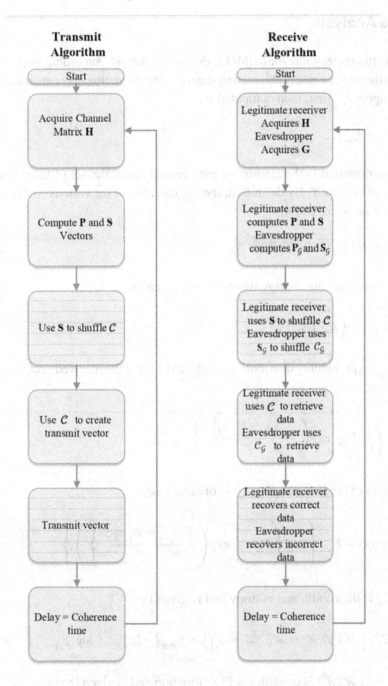

PERFORMANCE ANALYSIS

Secrecy Rate Analysis

In this section the secrecy rate for MIMO is derived in details. According to (J.-S. Chen, Yang, Yao, & Hwang, 2021) the secrecy rate is obtained by determining the mutual information at legitimate receiver I_{Bob} and Eavesdropper I_{Eve} first, then computed as;

$$I_{SR} = \max\{0 \ ; I_{Bob} - I_{Eve}\} \ ; \tag{12}$$

The mutual information is the amount of data gained about the set of transmitted vectors X after receiving the set of vectors Y. By definition, the I_{Bob} calculation for various SMTs can be computed as (Biryukov & Khovratovich, 2009);

$$I_{Bob}^{SMTs}(\mathscr{H}, \mathscr{X}; \mathscr{Y}_b) = H(\mathscr{Y}_b) - H(\mathscr{X}, \mathscr{H} | \mathscr{Y}_b). \tag{13}$$

Here, $H(\cdot)$ represents the entropy function, and given as;

$$H(\mathscr{Y}_b) = -E_{\mathscr{Y}_b}\left\{\log_2\left(p_{\mathscr{Y}_b}(\mathbf{y}_b)\right)\right\} ; \tag{14}$$

where $p_{\mathscr{Y}_b}(\mathbf{y}_b)$ is probability distribution function (PDF) of the received vector at legitimate receiver, and it is defined as;

$$P_{\mathscr{Y}_b}(\mathbf{y}_b) = E_{\mathscr{H}, \mathscr{X}}\left\{\frac{1}{(\pi\sigma_{n_b}^2)^{N_r}}\exp\left(-\frac{\|y_b - \mathscr{H}_{\ell_b}x_i\|_F^2}{\sigma_{n_b}^2}\right)\right\}. \tag{15}$$

By substituting (15) in (14), the $H(\mathscr{Y}_b)$ is obtained as;

$$H(\mathscr{Y}_b) = N_r\log_2(\pi) - E_{\mathscr{Y}_b}\left\{\log_2\left(E_{\mathscr{H}, \mathscr{X}}\left\{\exp\left(-\frac{\|y_b - \mathscr{H}_{\ell_b}x_i\|_F^2}{\sigma_{n_b}^2}\right)\right\}\right)\right\}. \tag{16}$$

$H(\mathscr{X}, \mathscr{H} | \mathscr{Y}_b)$ is the conditional entropy and is given by;

$$H(\mathscr{X}, \mathscr{H} | \mathscr{Y}_b) = E_{\mathscr{H}, \mathscr{X}}\left\{H\left(\mathscr{Y} | \mathscr{H} = \mathscr{H}_{\ell_b}, \mathscr{X} = x_i\right)\right\} = E_{\mathscr{H}, \mathscr{X}}\left\{-E_{(\mathscr{Y}|\mathscr{H}, \mathscr{X})}\left\{\log_2 p_{(\mathscr{Y}|\mathscr{H}, \mathscr{X})}(y_b | \mathscr{H}, \mathscr{X})\right\}\right\} ; \tag{17}$$

where $p_{(\mathscr{Y}|\mathscr{H}, \mathscr{X})}(y_b | \mathscr{H}, \mathscr{X})$ is conditional PDF function and is given by;

$$P_{\mathscr{Y}_b}(\mathbf{y}_b) = \frac{1}{(\pi\sigma_{n_b}^2)^{N_r}}\exp\left(-\frac{\|\mathbf{y}_b - \mathscr{H}_{\ell_b}x_i\|_F^2}{\sigma_{n_b}^2}\right) ; \tag{18}$$

Substituting (18) in (17) resulting in;

$$H\left(\mathcal{X},\mathcal{H}\vert\mathcal{Y}_b\right) = N_r\log_2\left(\pi\sigma_{n_b}^2\exp(1)\right). \tag{19}$$

Plugging (16) and (19) in (13) resulting;

$$I_{Bob}^{SMTs}\left(\mathcal{H},\mathcal{X};\mathcal{Y}_b\right) = -N_r\log_2\left(\exp\left(1\right)\right) - E_{\mathcal{Y}_b}\left\{\log_2\left(E_{\mathcal{H},\mathcal{X}}\left\{\exp\left(-\frac{\Vert y_b - \mathcal{H}_e x\Vert_F^2}{\sigma_{n_b}^2}\right)\right\}\right)\right\}. \tag{20}$$

Similarly, the mutual information at eavesdropper for the SMTs system is given as;

$$I_{Eve}^{SMTs}\left(\mathcal{G},\mathcal{X};\mathcal{Y}_e\right) = -N_e\log_2\left(\exp\left(1\right)\right) - E_{\mathcal{Y}_e}\left\{\log_2\left(E_{\mathcal{G},\mathcal{X}}\left\{\exp\left(-\frac{\Vert y_e - \mathcal{G}_e x\Vert_F^2}{\sigma_{n_e}^2}\right)\right\}\right)\right\}. \tag{21}$$

By the same manner the mutual information at legitimate receiver in the case of SMX is represented as;

$$I_{Bob}^{SMX}\left(\mathcal{X};\mathcal{Y}_b\right) = -N_r\log_2\left(\exp\left(1\right)\right) - E_{\mathcal{Y}_b}\left\{\log_2\left(E_{\mathbf{H}}\left\{\exp\left(-\frac{\Vert y_b - \mathbf{H}x\Vert_F^2}{\sigma_{n_b}^2}\right)\right\}\right)\right\}. \tag{22}$$

Similarly, the eavesdropper mutual information for the SMX system can be written as follows;

$$I_{Eve}^{SMX}\left(\mathcal{X};\mathcal{Y}_e\right) = -N_e\log_2\left(\exp\left(1\right)\right) - E_{\mathcal{Y}_e}\left\{\log_2\left(E_{\mathcal{G},\mathcal{X}}\left\{\exp\left(-\frac{\Vert y_e - \mathbf{G}x\Vert_F^2}{\sigma_{n_e}^2}\right)\right\}\right)\right\}. \tag{23}$$

Legitimate terminal and eavesdropper mutual information calculations produced identical results, suggesting that, given sufficient time and computing capacity, a skilled eavesdropper could possibly to obtain sent data. As a result, the secrecy rate in (12) becomes zero for the suggested system. However, eavesdropper would have to utilize a brute-force algorithm to try out every possible permutation of vectors. The amount of combinations is enormous, particularly when dealing with a significant number of transmit antennas. For instant, Table. I shows the time required for an eavesdropper to decipher the information that was sent, even when equipped with a powerful supercomputer boasting processing capabilities of 442 petaflops.

The table also includes the time required to decrypt AES (128 bits), AES (256 bits) (Biryukov & Khovratovich, 2009), data encryption standard (DES) (56 bits) (Diffie & Hellman, 2022), and DES (168 bits) for comparison. According to the data in the table, decrypting DES with 56 bits takes around 4 milliseconds, but breaking the proposed algorithm with $N_t = 16$ antennas needs about 780 microseconds. However, when the number of transmit antennas rises, the possible combinations increase even more, almost eliminating eavesdropper ability to decipher the transmitted data. For example, with $N_t = 32$ antennas, eavesdropper would require approximately 2.366×10^8 years to attempt all permutation vectors exhaustively, making it an insurmountable challenge. Moreover, the process of generating the permutation vectors is straightforward and involves organizing the results and channel powers. This contrasts with AES, which generates the security key using a large amount of processing power. Furthermore, because the wireless channel is inherently random, channel estimation is necessary at every coherence time, which is typically in the range of nano to microseconds (Zahedi et al., 2016). As a result, a new permutation vector is generated, adding an extra layer of security and complexity to eavesdropper decryption efforts. Because sorting algorithms and fundamental mathematical computations are used, sorting channel path power and rearranging the constellation matrix usually incur low computer overhead. Technical development have further improved the efficiency of these processes, resulting in minimal impact on modern communication systems. The proposed solution keeps the computational requirements of the system-on-a-chip (SoC) devices acceptable even with possible limits in their computational capacity. As well, the scheme's ability to impose a substantial computational burden on potential attackers, such as eavesdropper, fortifies its security, even in resource-constrained environments and in the face of artificial intelligence (AI) and machine learning algorithms.

TABLE 1. The count of potential combinations for the AES, DES, and the proposed PLS algorithm, coupled with the time needed to decrypt the security key on the most powerful supercomputer known to date, which boasts an astonishing processing capability of 1.102×10^{18} flops (In Data, n.d.; TOP500, n.d.; RankRed, n.d.).

System	System Number of Possible Combinations	Approximate Required time to decrypt using 1.102×10^{18} FLOPS
AES(128 bits)	$2128 = 3.4 \times 10^{38}$	$\approx 10^{12.54} \approx 3.4303$ trillion years
DES (56 bits)	$256 = 7.2 \times 10^{16}$	$\approx 10^{2.09} \approx 122.537$ years.
AES(256 bits)	$2256 = 1.1510^{77}$	$\approx 10^{54.27} \approx 1.8528$ quattuordecillion years
DES (168 bits)	$2128 = 3.7410^{50}$	$\approx 10^{9.46} \approx 2.8792$ billion years
Proposed (8 Antennas)	$(8 - 1)! = 5040$	$\approx 10^{-5.22} \approx 5.9512$ microseconds
Proposed (16 Antennas)	$(16 - 1)!= 1.307710^{-12}$	$\approx 10^{0.1} \approx 1.2623$ years
Proposed (32 Antennas)	$(32 - 1)! = 8.221033$	$\approx 10^{3.18} \approx 1.4993$ million years
Proposed (64 Antennas)	$(64 - 1)!= 1.9826 \times 10^{87}$	$\approx 10^{9.81} \approx 6.4681$ billion years
Proposed(128 Antennas)	$(128 - 1)! = 3.012710^{213}$	$\approx 10^{12.78} \approx 6.0385$ trillion years

NUMERICAL EVALUATION

This section verifies the robustness of the suggested algorithm and the accuracy of the derived formulas through Monte Carlo simulation. Thus, a numerical assessment of the proposed algorithm for various MIMO techniques, including SMX, SM, SSK and QSM with various system configurations are evaluated. The evaluation is performed over a Rayleigh fading channel and considering full CSI knowledge at three terminals. The assessment includes the ABER at legitimate and eavesdropper receiver, as well as the secrecy rate.

ABER Results

The ABER performance of the proposed algorithm for SM, SSK and QSM at legitimate and eavesdropper receivers is illustrated in Fig. 2. The results reveal that the legitimate receiver can retrieve the transmitted bits successfully, however, the eavesdropper struggles to obtain the proper data bits. As was mentioned in the section above, retrieve the accurate data at eavesdropper receiver requires knowledge of the right permutation vector, which can be difficult, particularly for larger systems with $\eta \geq 6$ bits/s/Hz. Thus, clearly it can be seen that the ABER at eavesdropper remains extend from $0.53 \rightarrow 0.55$.

The impact of adding more transmit antennas on the error rate of (SM) is illustrated in Fig. 3 for the proposed algorithm. The error rate performance at the intended receiver deteriorates as the number of transmit antennas increases, which could be seen as a consequence of the increased complexity. Furthermore, as demonstrated by the earlier results, it is evident that for an eavesdropper receiver, the error rate roughly ranges from 0.5 to 0.52 as the eavesdropper is unable to intercept the right data, irrespective of the number of transmit antennas.

Fig. 4 shows the impact of increasing the number of eavesdropper antennas in ABER performance at eavesdropper receiver. As previously concluded, irrespective of the number of received antennas at the eavesdropper terminal, the ABER performance does not surpass 0.36 error rate.

Figure 2. The ABER performance analysis is conducted for both a legitimate receiver and an eaves-dropper, with assuming different SMTs schemes, SM, QSM and SSK, considering $\eta = 8, N_r = 4, N_e = 4$ and $M = 4$ for SM and QSM

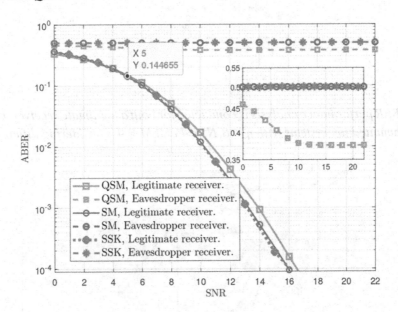

Figure 3. The ABER performance analysis is conducted for both a legitimate receiver and an eavesdropper in SM, with assuming different spectral efficiency, η = 5, 6, 7 and 8 considering $N_r = N_e = 4$ and M = 4

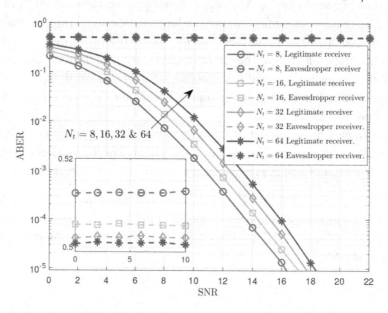

Figure 4. The ABER performance analysis is conducted for both a legitimate receiver and an eavesdropper in QSM communication systems with η = 8, N_r = 4 and M = 4, considering different N_e = 2, 4, & 8

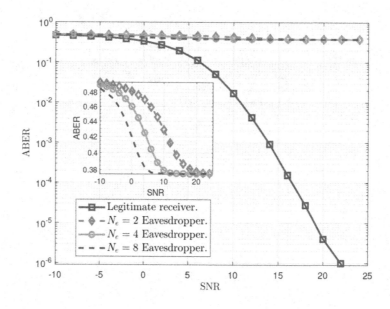

Secrecy Rate

In Fig. 5 the mutual information at legitimate receiver, eavesdropper with secrecy rate is illustrated with assuming QSM technique which have following configuration: $N_t = 16, 8, N_r = N_e = 4$. Clearly, the secrecy rate is zero, given that the number of information bits at both terminals are equal. However, the information received at the eavesdropper's terminal is inaccurate, as indicated by the previously described ABER findings. Furthermore, it is evident that the system's secrecy rate is unaffected by an increase in the number of transmit antennas.

Similar notes can be observed in Figs. 6 and 7. It is noteworthy that, in both results the secrecy rate is zero.

Figure 5. The secrecy rate performance in QSM, with assuming $N_r = N_e = 4, M = 4$ and different $N_t = 8$ and 16

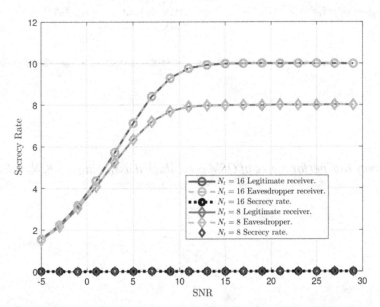

In Fig. 6 the comparison between the mutual information at legitimate, eavesdropper receiver and secrecy rate for SMX, SM and QSM are performed with the same number of information bits $\eta = 8$, and assuming $N_t = N_r = 4$. Similar trends are observed in this result, regardless of the considered configuration the secrecy rate remains zeros.

In Fig 7, the result shows the performance of QSM when different numbers of receive antennas are considered at the eavesdropper terminal, specifically $N_e = 2, 4$ and 8. With an assumption of $\eta = 8$ and at the legitimate receiver $N_r = 4$, it can be observed that for $N_e = 4$ and 8, the secrecy rate is zero, while for $N_e = 2$, the secrecy rate reaches 2.5 bits/Hz at around 6 dB, then decreases and eventually becomes zero.

Figure 6. The secrecy rate performance comparison between SMX, SM and QSM is conducted assuming $\eta = 8, N_r = N_e = 4$ and $M = 4$

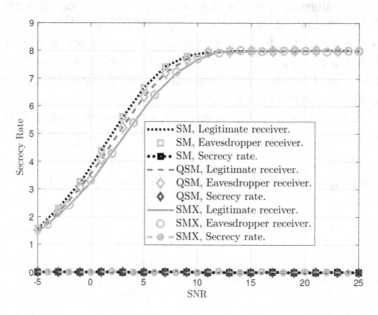

Figure 7. The secrecy rate performance of QSM is conducted assuming $\eta = 8, N_r = 4, M = 4$ and different $N_e = 2, 4$ & 8

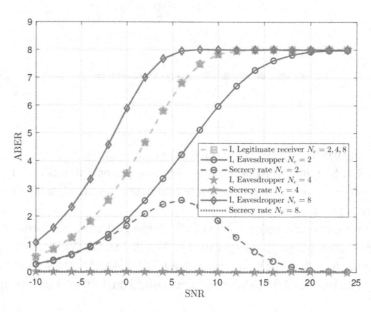

From the obtained results, it is clear that even with complete understanding of the communication channel, the eavesdropper is unable to capture accurate data bits due to the high level of secrecy and encryption involved. Thus, the eavesdropper receiver requires access to transmitter and legitimate receiver channel information to create an accurate constellation matrix for data retrieval. Eavesdropper can attempt all possible mapping table combinations, but bigger MIMO configurations make this effort more complex. Furthermore, this must be completed within the channel's coherence time.

In summary, the results presented in this study underline the resilience and computational security provided by our proposed PLS algorithm across various MIMO communication configurations. The consistent pattern of the eavesdropper's inability to intercept accurate data, even when she is presumed to be knowledgeable about the communication protocol, underscores the efficacy of our security mechanism. While the approach is grounded in Monte Carlo simulations and practical considerations, it is also rooted in established cryptographic assumptions that underpin the computational security framework. These cryptographic principles include the assumption that certain computational problems are computationally infeasible to solve within a reasonable time frame.

It is important to highlight that this increased security doesn't solely depend on the secrecy of the permutation vector but also influences the inherent complexity of decoding within large MIMO systems. The possible vector permutations grow exponentially with an increase in the number of transmit antennas N_t. Eavesdropper will never be able to decode in a time frames that makes sense due to the exponential growth in size. Our algorithm introducing an additional degree of security by utilizing the intricate computational features of MIMO systems in addition to channel statistics. As well, the changing channel statistics over time provide an extra level of security, making it extremely challenging for eavesdropper to reliably decode the signal. Even if, by chance, she manages to obtain a permutation vector at a specific moment, she must contend with the ever-changing statistics over time. These rapid variations take place within milliseconds in the lengthiest scenarios, adding an extra formidable dimension of security to the system, thereby ensuring the protection of transmitted data.

CONCLUSION

In this chapter, we've introduced an innovative computational PLS algorithm tailored for diverse MIMO communication setups. Our approach capitalizes on channel statistics between a transmitter and a legitimate receiver at both ends of the communication link to manipulate a key mapping table. This involves computing the power for each communication path, sorting these powers, and leveraging the sorting indices to permute rows within the constellation matrix. In our analysis, we assume that the eavesdropper possesses complete awareness of the communication protocol and isn't restricted by received SNR or other system parameters. However, a significant constraint for the eavesdropper lies in the lack of access to critical channel statistics between the transmitter and the legitimate receiver, thereby hindering her ability to generate a precise permutation vector. Regardless of the specific MIMO technique used or system setup, our results consistently demonstrate the eavesdropper's inability to correctly decipher the data, as evidenced by the ABER.

It's worth noting that even with a powerful supercomputer, the eavesdropper theoretically attempting every possible permutation using brute-force techniques would still yield no secrecy rate, as she could potentially gain the same mutual knowledge as the legitimate receiver. However, a major challenge highlighted by our analysis is that the eavesdropper would require an impractically long time to exhaustively attempt every possible combination, especially in scenarios with massive MIMO configurations. Consequently, intercepting data becomes nearly impossible. Looking ahead, future research should focus on assessing how effectively our algorithm can adapt to real-world scenarios and devising strategies to effectively tackle practical challenges. Our findings underscore the robustness and computational security that our approach provides, making it a promising solution for secure communication in MIMO systems. Furthermore, we'll delve into issues like cross-layer attacks and adaptive coherence time in our discussions.

REFERENCES

Annamalai, A., Olaluwe, A., & Adebola, E. (2014). Analyzing the ergodic secrecy rates of cooperative amplify-and-forward relay networks over generalized fading channels. In *Emerging Trends in ICT Security* (pp. 227–243). Morgan Kaufmann. 10.1016/B978-0-12-411474-6.00014-1

Biryukov, A., & Khovratovich, D. (2009). Related-key cryptanalysis of the full AES-192 and AES-256. *Advances in Cryptology–ASIACRYPT 2009: 15th International Conference on the Theory and Application of Cryptology and Information Security, Tokyo, Japan, December 6-10, 2009 Proceedings*, 15, 1–18.

Bloch, M. R. (2016). Covert communication over noisy channels: A resolvability perspective. *IEEE Transactions on Information Theory*, 62(5), 2334–2354. 10.1109/TIT.2016.2530089

Chen, J. S., Yang, C. Y., Yao, J. F. J., & Hwang, M. H. (2021, September). Secrecy Rate Analysis in The Cooperative Communication System. In *2021 IEEE International Conference on Consumer Electronics-Taiwan (ICCE-TW)* (pp. 1-2). IEEE. 10.1109/ICCE-TW52618.2021.9603208

Chen, S., Sun, S., Xu, G., Su, X., & Cai, Y. (2020). Beam-space multiplexing: Practice, theory, and trends, from 4G TD-LTE, 5G, to 6G and beyond. *IEEE Wireless Communications*, 27(2), 162–172. 10.1109/MWC.001.1900307

Chen, X., Ng, D. W. K., Gerstacker, W. H., & Chen, H. H. (2016). A survey on multiple-antenna techniques for physical layer security. *IEEE Communications Surveys and Tutorials*, 19(2), 1027–1053. 10.1109/COMST.2016.2633387

Das, K., Basu, R., & Karmakar, R. (2022, October). Man-in-the-middle attack detection using ensemble learning. In *2022 13th International Conference on Computing Communication and Networking Technologies (ICCCNT)* (pp. 1-6). IEEE. 10.1109/ICCCNT54827.2022.9984365

Diffie, W., & Hellman, M. E. (2022). Exhaustive cryptanalysis of the NBS data encryption standard. In *Democratizing Cryptography: The Work of Whitfield Diffie and Martin Hellman* (pp. 391-414). Academic Press.

Eltira, K., Younis, A., & Mesleh, R. (2023). Impact of channel imperfections on variant SMTs MIMO systems over revised Nakagami-m channel model. *AEÜ. International Journal of Electronics and Communications*, 170, 154799. 10.1016/j.aeue.2023.154799

Hyadi, A., Rezki, Z., & Alouini, M. S. (2016). An overview of physical layer security in wireless communication systems with CSIT uncertainty. *IEEE Access : Practical Innovations, Open Solutions*, 4, 6121–6132. 10.1109/ACCESS.2016.2612585

In Data. (n.d.). *Computational capacity of the fastest supercomputers*. Retrieved from https://ourworldindata.org/grapher/supercomputer-power-flops

Jorswieck, E. A., Wolf, A., & Gerbracht, S. (2010). Secrecy on the physical layer in wireless networks. *Trends in Telecommunications Technologies*, 413-435.

Lin, P. H., Lai, S. H., Lin, S. C., & Su, H. J. (2013). On secrecy rate of the generalized artificial-noise assisted secure beamforming for wiretap channels. *IEEE Journal on Selected Areas in Communications*, 31(9), 1728–1740. 10.1109/JSAC.2013.130907

Liu, C., Yang, L. L., & Wang, W. (2017). Secure spatial modulation with a full-duplex receiver. *IEEE Wireless Communications Letters*, 6(6), 838–841. 10.1109/LWC.2017.2748591

Liu, D., Ma, W., Shao, S., Shen, Y., & Tang, Y. (2015). Performance analysis of TDD reciprocity calibration for massive MU-MIMO systems with ZF beamforming. *IEEE Communications Letters*, 20(1), 113–116. 10.1109/LCOMM.2015.2499283

Liu, J., Zhang, J., Zhang, Q., Wang, J., & Sun, X. (2021). Secrecy rate analysis for reconfigurable intelligent surface-assisted MIMO communications with statistical CSI. *China Communications*, 18(3), 52–62. 10.23919/JCC.2021.03.005

Mesleh, R., & Alhassi, A. (2018). *Space modulation techniques*. John Wiley & Sons. 10.1002/9781119375692

Mesleh, R., Engelken, S., Sinanovic, S., & Haas, H. (2008, August). Analytical SER calculation of spatial modulation. In *2008 IEEE 10th International Symposium on Spread Spectrum Techniques and Applications* (pp. 272-276). IEEE. 10.1109/ISSSTA.2008.55

Mesleh, R., Haas, H., Ahn, C. W., & Yun, S. (2006, October). Spatial modulation-a new low complexity spectral efficiency enhancing technique. In *2006 First International Conference on Communications and Networking in China* (pp. 1-5). IEEE. 10.1109/CHINACOM.2006.344658

Mukherjee, A. (2020). Energy-Efficient Beam Management in Millimeter-Wave Shared Spectrum. *IEEE Wireless Communications*, 27(5), 38–43. 10.1109/MWC.001.2000037

Mukherjee, A., Fakoorian, S. A. A., Huang, J., & Swindlehurst, A. L. (2014). Principles of physical layer security in multiuser wireless networks: A survey. *IEEE Communications Surveys and Tutorials*, 16(3), 1550–1573. 10.1109/SURV.2014.012314.00178

Nguyen, V. L., Lin, P. C., Cheng, B. C., Hwang, R. H., & Lin, Y. D. (2021). Security and privacy for 6G: A survey on prospective technologies and challenges. *IEEE Communications Surveys and Tutorials*, 23(4), 2384–2428. 10.1109/COMST.2021.3108618

Noura, H. N., Melki, R., & Chehab, A. (2021). Efficient data confidentiality scheme for 5g wireless NOMA communications. *Journal of Information Security and Applications*, 58, 102781. 10.1016/j.jisa.2021.102781

Oggier, F., & Hassibi, B. (2011). The secrecy capacity of the MIMO wiretap channel. *IEEE Transactions on Information Theory*, 57(8), 4961–4972. 10.1109/TIT.2011.2158487

Parkouk, S., Torabi, M., & Shokrollahi, S. (2022). Secrecy performance analysis of amplify-and-forward relay cooperative networks with simultaneous wireless information and power transfer. *Computer Communications*, 193, 365–377. 10.1016/j.comcom.2022.07.020

RankRed. (n.d.). *17 fastest supercomputers in the world — in 2024*. Retrieved from https://www.rankred.com/fastest-supercomputers-in-the-world/

Rosenzweig, A., Steinberg, Y., & Shamai, S. (2005). On channels with partial channel state information at the transmitter. *IEEE Transactions on Information Theory*, 51(5), 1817–1830. 10.1109/TIT.2005.846422

Shu, F., Wang, Z., Chen, R., Wu, Y., & Wang, J. (2018). Two high-performance schemes of transmit antenna selection for secure spatial modulation. *IEEE Transactions on Vehicular Technology*, 67(9), 8969–8973. 10.1109/TVT.2018.2844401

TOP500. (n.d.). Retrieved from https://www.top500.org/lists/top500/2022/06/

Wang, L., Bashar, S., Wei, Y., & Li, R. (2015). Secrecy enhancement analysis against unknown eavesdropping in spatial modulation. *IEEE Communications Letters*, 19(8), 1351–1354. 10.1109/LCOMM.2015.2440353

Wang, Y., Gou, G., Liu, C., Cui, M., Li, Z., & Xiong, G. (2021). Survey of security supervision on blockchain from the perspective of technology. *Journal of Information Security and Applications*, 60, 102859. 10.1016/j.jisa.2021.102859

Wu, C., Xiao, Y., & Yang, P. (2020). Covert information embedded spatial modulation. *IEEE Communications Letters*, 24(11), 2426–2430. 10.1109/LCOMM.2020.3008430

Xia, G., Lin, Y., Liu, T., Shu, F., & Hanzo, L. (2020). Transmit antenna selection and beamformer design for secure spatial modulation with rough CSI of eve. *IEEE Transactions on Wireless Communications*, 19(7), 4643–4656. 10.1109/TWC.2020.2985968

Yang, N., Wang, L., Geraci, G., Elkashlan, M., Yuan, J., & Di Renzo, M. (2015). Safeguarding 5G wireless communication networks using physical layer security. *IEEE Communications Magazine*, 53(4), 20–27. 10.1109/MCOM.2015.7081071

Yang, Y., & Guizani, M. (2018). Mapping-varied spatial modulation for physical layer security: Transmission strategy and secrecy rate. *IEEE Journal on Selected Areas in Communications*, 36(4), 877–889. 10.1109/JSAC.2018.2824598

Yener, A., & Ulukus, S. (2015). Wireless physical-layer security: Lessons learned from information theory. *Proceedings of the IEEE*, 103(10), 1814–1825. 10.1109/JPROC.2015.2459592

Yerrapragada, A. K., Eisman, T., & Kelley, B. (2021). Physical layer security for beyond 5G: Ultra secure low latency communications. *IEEE Open Journal of the Communications Society*, 2, 2232–2242. 10.1109/OJCOMS.2021.3105185

Yin, M., Yang, Y., & Jiao, B. (2020). Security-oriented trellis code design for spatial modulation. *IEEE Transactions on Wireless Communications*, 20(3), 1875–1888. 10.1109/TWC.2020.3037146

Yu, H., Duan, W., Zhang, G., Ji, Y., Zhu, X., & Choi, J. (2019). A near optimal power allocation scheme for cooperative relay networking with NOMA. *China Communications*, 16(3), 122–131.

Yu, L., Fan, P., & Han, Z. (2019). Maximizing spectral efficiency for scma systems with codebooks based on star-qam signaling constellations. *IEEE Wireless Communications Letters*, 8(4), 1163–1166. 10.1109/LWC.2019.2909913

Yungaicela-Naula, N. M., Vargas-Rosales, C., Pérez-Díaz, J. A., & Zareei, M. (2022). Towards security automation in software defined networks. *Computer Communications*, 183, 64–82. 10.1016/j.comcom.2021.11.014

Zahedi, Y., Ngah, R., Nunoo, S., Mokayef, M., Alavi, S. E., & Amiri, I. S. (2016). Experimental measurement and statistical analysis of the RMS delay spread in time-varying ultra-wideband communication channel. *Measurement*, 89, 179–188. 10.1016/j.measurement.2016.04.009

Compilation of References

Abbasi, F., Naderan, M., & Alavi, S. E. (2021). Anomaly detection in the Internet of Things using feature selection and classification based on Logistic Regression and Artificial Neural Networks on N-BaIoT dataset. *Proceedings of 2021 5th International Conference on Internet of Things and Applications, IoT 2021*. 10.1109/IoT52625.2021.9469605

Abbas, M. M., & Merad-Boudia, O. R. (2022). *On ensuring data integrity in data aggregation protocols in iot environments*. IEEE. 10.1109/ICAEE53772.2022.9962093

Abhishta, A., van Heeswijk, W., Junger, M., Nieuwenhuis, L. J., & Joosten, R. (2020). *Why would we get attacked? An analysis of attacker's aims behind DDoS attacks*. Academic Press.

Aboukadri, S., Ouaddah, A., & Mezrioui, A. (2024). Machine learning in identity and access management systems: Survey and deep dive. *Computers and Security, 139*, 103729. 10.1016/j.cose.2024.103729

Abrahamsen, F. E., Ai, Y., & Cheffena, M. (2021). Communication technologies for smart grid: A comprehensive survey. *Sensors (Basel), 21*(23), 8087. 10.3390/s2123808734884092

Abroshan, H. (2021). Using symmetric and asymmetric cryptography algorithms, a hybrid encryption solution to improve cloud computing security. *International Journal of Advanced Computer Science and Applications, 12*, 31–37.

Abroshan, H. (2021). A hybrid encryption solution to improve cloud computing security using symmetric and asymmetric cryptography algorithms. *International Journal of Advanced Computer Science and Applications, 12*(6), 31–37. 10.14569/IJACSA.2021.0120604

Abu Al-Haija, Q., Alnabhan, M., Saleh, E., & Al-Omari, M. (2023). *Applications of blockchain technology for improving security in the Internet of Things (IoT)*. 10.1016/B978-0-323-99199-5.00003-3

Abu Al-Haija, Q., Alohaly, M., & Odeh, A. (2023). A lightweight double-stage scheme to identify malicious DNS over HTTPS traffic using a hybrid learning approach. *Sensors (Basel), 23*(7), 3489. 10.3390/s2307348937050549

Abu Al-Haija, Q., Odeh, A., & Qattous, H. (2022). PDF malware detection based on optimizable decision trees. *Electronics (Basel), 11*(19), 3142. 10.3390/electronics11193142

Abu Al-Haija, Q., & Zein-Sabatto, S. (2020). An efficient deep-learning-based detection and classification system for cyber-attacks in IoT communication networks. *Electronics (Basel), 9*(12), 2152. 10.3390/electronics9122152

Abu Taleb, A., Abu Al-Haija, Q., & Odeh, A. (2023). Efficient Mobile Sink Routing in Wireless Sensor Networks Using Bipartite Graphs. *Future Internet, 15*(5), 182. 10.3390/fi15050182

Abu Waraga, O., Bettayeb, M., Nasir, Q., & Abu Talib, M. (2020). Design and implementation of automated IoT security testbed. *Computers & Security, 88*, 101648. Advance online publication. 10.1016/j.cose.2019.101648

Abuhamad, M., Abusnaina, A., Nyang, D., & Mohaisen, D. (2021). Sensor-Based Continuous Authentication of Smartphones' Users Using Behavioral Biometrics: A Contemporary Survey. *IEEE Internet of Things Journal, 8*(1), 65–84. 10.1109/JIOT.2020.3020076

Achmadi, D., Suryanto, Y., & Ramli, K. (2018). *On developing information security management system (isms) framework for iso 27001-based data center. 2018 international workshop on big data and information security (iwbis).*

Adi, E., Anwar, A., Baig, Z., & Zeadally, S. (2020). Machine learning and data analytics for the IoT. *Neural Computing & Applications*, 32(20), 16205–16233. 10.1007/s00521-020-04874-y

Aftab, M. U., Oluwasanmi, A., Alharbi, A., Sohaib, O., Nie, X., Qin, Z., & Ngo, S. (2021). *Secure and dynamic access control for the Internet of Things (IoT) based traffic system.* Academic Press.

Ahmad, J., Li, F., & Luo, B. (2022). *Iotprivcomp: A measurement study of privacy compliance in iot apps.* Paper presented at the European Symposium on Research in Computer Security. 10.1007/978-3-031-17146-8_29

Ahmad, N. (2024). Securing Supply Chains: AI-driven Approaches to Risk Mitigation in Manufacturing. 10.13140/RG.2.2.20900.28807

Akhtar, M. S., & Feng, T. (2022). Using Blockchain to Ensure the Integrity of Digital Forensic Evidence in an IoT Environment. *EAI Endorsed Transactions on Creative Technologies*, 9(31), 31. Advance online publication. 10.4108/eai.3-6-2022.174089

Al Hayajneh, A., Bhuiyan, M. Z. A., & McAndrew, I. (2020). Improving Internet of Things (IoT) security with software-defined networking (SDN). *Computers*, 9(1), 1–14. 10.3390/computers9010008

Alabdulsalam, S., Schaefer, K., Kechadi, T., & Le-Khac, N.-A. (2018). Internet of Things Forensics – Challenges and a Case Study. In Peterson, G., & Shenoi, S. (Eds.), *Advances in Digital Forensics XIV* (pp. 35–48). Springer International Publishing. 10.1007/978-3-319-99277-8_3

Alagappan, A., Andrews, L. J. B., & Venkatachary, S. K. (2022, December 23). D, S., & Raj, R. A. (2022). Cybersecurity risks mitigation in the internet of things. *International Journal for Research in Applied Science and Engineering Technology*, 1–6. Advance online publication. 10.1109/CISCT55310.2022.10046549

Alawida, M., Omolara, A. E., Abiodun, O. I., & Al-Rajab, M. (2022). A deeper look into cybersecurity issues in the wake of Covid-19. 10.1016/j.jksuci.2022.08.00337521180

Alayande, A. S., Nwulu, N., & Bakare, A. E. (2018). Modelling and Countermeasures of False Data Injection Attacks Against State Estimation in Power Systems. *2018 International Conference on Computational Techniques, Electronics and Mechanical Systems (CTEMS)*, 129–134. 10.1109/CTEMS.2018.8769295

Alazab, A., Khraisat, A., Singh, S., Alazab, A., Khraisat, A., & Singh, S. (2023). *A Review on the Internet of Things (IoT) Forensics: Challenges, Techniques, and Evaluation of Digital Forensic Tools.* IntechOpen. 10.5772/intechopen.109840

Albayram, Y., Khan, M. M. H., Bamis, A., Kentros, S., Nguyen, N., & Jiang, R. (2014). A location-based authentication system leveraging smartphones. *Proceedings - IEEE International Conference on Mobile Data Management, 1*, 83–88. 10.1109/MDM.2014.16

Albouq, S. S., Abi Sen, A. A., Almashf, N., Yamin, M., & Alshanqiti, A. (2022). A survey of interoperability challenges and solutions for dealing with them in iot environment. *IEEE Access : Practical Innovations, Open Solutions*, 10, 36416–36428. 10.1109/ACCESS.2022.3162219

Albulayhi, K., & Abu Al-Haija, Q. (2022). *Security and Privacy Challenges in Blockchain Application.* .10.1201/9781003269281-14

Al-Bzoor, M., Ayyad, W., Alta'ani, O. (2022). *A Survey on Efficient Routing Strategies for The Internet of Underwater Things (IoUT).* Academic Press.

Aldaej, A., Ahanger, T. A., & Ullah, I. (2023). Deep learning-inspired IOT-IDS mechanism for edge computing environments. *Sensors (Basel)*, 23(24), 9869. 10.3390/s2324986938139716

Al-Duwairi, B., Al-Kahla, W., AlRefai, M. A., Abdelqader, Y., Rawash, A., & Fahmawi, R. (2020). SIEM-based detection and mitigation of IoT-botnet DDoS attacks. *Iranian Journal of Electrical and Computer Engineering*, 10(2), 2182–2191. 10.11591/ijece.v10i2.pp2182-2191

Aleem, S. A., Hussain, S. S., & Ustun, T. S. (2020). A review of strategies to increase pv penetration level in smart grids. *Energies*, 13(3), 636. 10.3390/en13030636

Alevizos, L., Ta, V. T., & Hashem Eiza, M. (2022). Augmenting zero trust architecture to endpoints using blockchain: A state-of-the-art review. *Security and Privacy*, 5(1), 191. 10.1002/spy2.191

Al-Garadi, M. A., Mohamed, A., Al-Ali, A. K., Du, X., Ali, I., & Guizani, M. (2020). A Survey of Machine and Deep Learning Methods for Internet of Things (IoT) Security. *IEEE Communications Surveys and Tutorials*, 22(3), 1646–1685. 10.1109/COMST.2020.2988293

Alhalafi, N., & Veeraraghavan, P. (2019). *Privacy and Security Challenges and Solutions in IOT: A review.* Paper presented at the IOP conference series: Earth and environmental science. 10.1088/1755-1315/322/1/012013

Alhassan, A.-B., Mahama, A.-H., & Alhassan, S. (2022). *Residue architecture enhanced audio data encryption scheme using the rivest, shamir, adleman algorithm.* The Research Institute of Advanced Engineering Technology.

Al-Hawawreh, M., Alazab, M., Ferrag, M. A., & Hossain, M. S. (2024, March). Securing the Industrial Internet of Things against ransomware attacks: A comprehensive analysis of the emerging threat landscape and detection mechanisms. *Journal of Network and Computer Applications*, 223, 103809. 10.1016/j.jnca.2023.103809

Ali, S. S., & Choi, B. J. (2020). State-of-the-art artificial intelligence techniques for distributed smart grids: A review. *Electronics (Basel)*, 9(6), 1030. 10.3390/electronics9061030

Ali, S., Li, Q., & Yousafzai, A. (2024). Blockchain and federated learning-based intrusion detection approaches for edge-enabled industrial iot networks: A survey. *Ad Hoc Networks*, 152, 103320. 10.1016/j.adhoc.2023.103320

Al-Kasassbeh, M., Almseidin, M., Alrfou, K., & Kovacs, S. (2020). Detection of IoT-botnet attacks using fuzzy rule interpolation. *Journal of Intelligent & Fuzzy Systems*, 39(1), 421–431. 10.3233/JIFS-191432

Alkhamisi, K. (2023). An Analysis of Security Attacks on IoT Applications. *International Journal of Information Systems and Computer Technologies*, 2(1). Advance online publication. 10.58325/ijisct.002.01.0053

Allan, A. (2021). *Shift Focus From MFA to Continous Adaptive Trust.* Available: www.gartner.com

Allegue, S., Rhahla, M., & Abdellatif, T. (2020). *Toward gdpr compliance in iot systems.* Springer. 10.1007/978-3-030-45989-5_11

Almadani, M. S., Alotaibi, S., Alsobhi, H., Hussain, O. K., & Hussain, F. K. (2023). Blockchain-based multi-factor authentication: A systematic literature review. *Internet of Things : Engineering Cyber Physical Human Systems*, 23(June), 100844. 10.1016/j.iot.2023.100844

Almalki, L. S., Alnahdi, A. K., & Albalawi, T. F. (2023). The roles of stakeholders in internet of things: A theoretical framework. In *2023 1st international conference on advanced innovations in smart cities (icaisc)* (pp. 1–6). IEEE.

Alnahdi, A., & Albalawi, T. (2023). Role-driven clustering of stakeholders: A study of iot security improvement. *Sensors (Basel)*, 23(12), 5578. Advance online publication. 10.3390/s2312557837420743

Al-Naji, F. H., & Zagrouba, R. (2020). A survey on continuous authentication methods in Internet of Things environment. *Computer Communications*, 163(June), 109–133. 10.1016/j.comcom.2020.09.006

Alotaibi, I., Abido, M. A., Khalid, M., & Savkin, A. V. (2020). A comprehensive review of recent advances in smart grids: A sustainable future with renewable energy resources. *Energies*, 13(23), 6269. 10.3390/en13236269

Alrashdi, I., Alqazzaz, A., Aloufi, E., Alharthi, R., Zohdy, M., & Ming, H. (2019). AD-IoT: Anomaly detection of IoT cyberattacks in the smart city using machine learning. *2019 IEEE 9th Annual Computing and Communication Workshop and Conference, CCWC 2019*, 305–310. 10.1109/CCWC.2019.8666450

Al-Shabi, M. A. (2019). A survey on symmetric and asymmetric cryptography algorithms in information security. *International Journal of Scientific and Research Publications*, 9(3), 576–589. 10.29322/IJSRP.9.03.2019.p8779

Alsharida, R. A., Al-rimy, B. A. S., Al-Emran, M., & Zainal, A. (2023). *A systematic review of multi perspectives on human cybersecurity behavior.* Academic Press.

Alsharif, M., Mishra, S., AlShehri, M. (2022). *Impact of Human Vulnerabilities on Cybersecurity.* Academic Press.

Alshowkan, M., Elleithy, K., Odeh, A., & Abdelfattah, E. (2013). *A new algorithm for three-party Quantum key distribution.* Paper presented at the Third International Conference on Innovative Computing Technology (INTECH 2013). 10.1109/INTECH.2013.6653692

Alshra'a, A. S., & Seitz, J. (2021). Towards applying ipsec between edge switches and end users to counter ddos attacks in sdns. In *2021 IEEE 23rd int conf on high performance computing & communications; 7th int conf on data science & systems; 19th int conf on smart city; 7th int conf on dependability in sensor, cloud & big data systems & application (hpcc/dss/smartcity/dependsys)* (pp. 1545–1551). 10.1109/HPCC-DSS-SmartCity-DependSys53884.2021.00229

Alsulami, A., Abu Al-Haija, Q., Tayeb, A., & Alqahtani, A. (2022). An Intrusion Detection and Classification System for IoT Traffic with Improved Data Engineering. *Applied Sciences (Basel, Switzerland)*, 12(23), 12336. 10.3390/app122312336

Altaleb, H., Beatrix, F., Azemi, F., & Rajnai, Z. (2024). *5G Evolution and Supply Chain Security in MENA Region: Challenges and Opportunities.* 10.1109/SAMI60510.2024.10432797

Amanullah, M. A., Habeeb, R. A. A., Nasaruddin, F. H., Gani, A., Ahmed, E., Nainar, A. S. M., Akim, N. M., & Imran, M. (2020). Deep learning and big data technologies for IoT security. *Computer Communications, 151*, 495–517. 10.1016/j.comcom.2020.01.016

Ameer, S., Benson, J. (2022). *Hybrid approaches (ABAC and RBAC) toward secure access control in smart home IoT.* Academic Press.

An, D., Zhang, F., Yang, Q., & Zhang, C. (2022). Data integrity attack in dynamic state estimation of smart grid: Attack model and countermeasures. *IEEE Transactions on Automation Science and Engineering*, 19(3), 1631–1644. 10.1109/TASE.2022.3149764

Andreica, G. R., Bozga, L., Zinca, D., & Dobrota, V. (2020). *Denial of service and man-in-the-middle attacks against IoT devices in a GPS-based monitoring software for intelligent transportation systems.* Paper presented at the 2020 19th RoEduNet Conference: Networking in Education and Research (RoEduNet). 10.1109/RoEduNet51892.2020.9324865

Andriotis, P., Tryfonas, T., Oikonomou, G., & Yildiz, C. (2013). A pilot study on the security of pattern screen-lock methods and soft side channel attacks. *WiSec 2013 - Proceedings of the 6th ACM Conference on Security and Privacy in Wireless and Mobile Networks*, 1–6. 10.1145/2462096.2462098

Angrishi, K. (2017). *Turning Internet of Things (IoT) into the Internet of Vulnerabilities (IoV) : IoT Botnets.* Academic Press.

Anirudh, M., Thileeban, S. A., & Nallathambi, D. J. (2017). *Use of honeypots for mitigating DoS attacks targeted on IoT networks.* Paper presented at the 2017 International conference on computer, communication and signal processing (ICCCSP). 10.1109/ICCCSP.2017.7944057

Annamalai, A., Olaluwe, A., & Adebola, E. (2014). Analyzing the ergodic secrecy rates of cooperative amplify-and-forward relay networks over generalized fading channels. In *Emerging Trends in ICT Security* (pp. 227–243). Morgan Kaufmann. 10.1016/B978-0-12-411474-6.00014-1

Anwar, M., He, W., Ash, I., Yuan, X., Li, L., & Xu, L. (2017). *Gender difference and employees' cybersecurity behaviors.* Academic Press.

Anwar, M. R., Apriani, D., & Adianita, I. R. (2021). Hash Algorithm In Verification Of Certificate Data Integrity And Security. *Aptisi Transactions on Technopreneurship*, 3(2), 181–188. 10.34306/att.v3i2.212

Arshad, J., Azad, M. A., Abdellatif, M. M., Ur Rehman, M. H., & Salah, K. (2019). COLIDE: A collaborative intrusion detection framework for the Internet of Things. *IET Networks*, 8(1), 3–14. 10.1049/iet-net.2018.5036

Arshad, M., Rahman, H., Tariq, J., Riaz, A., & Imran, A., & Ihsan, I. (2022). Digital Forensics Analysis of IoT Nodes using Machine Learning. *Journal of Computing & Biomedical Informatics*, 4. Advance online publication. 10.56979/401/2022/107

Asghar, M. R., Dán, G., Miorandi, D., & Chlamtac, I. (2017). Smart meter data privacy: A survey. *IEEE Communications Surveys and Tutorials*, 19(4), 2820–2835. 10.1109/COMST.2017.2720195

Ashraf, J., Moustafa, N., Bukhshi, A. D., & Javed, A. (2021). Intrusion Detection System for SDN-enabled IoT Networks using Machine Learning Techniques. *Proceedings - IEEE International Enterprise Distributed Object Computing Workshop, EDOCW*, 46–52. 10.1109/EDOCW52865.2021.00031

Ashton, K. (2009). That 'Internet of things' thing. *RFID Journal*, 22(7), 97–114.

Aslan, Ö. A., & Samet, R. (2020). *A comprehensive review on malware detection approaches.* Academic Press.

Aslan, Ö., Aktuğ, S. S., Ozkan-Okay, M., Yilmaz, A. A., & Akin, E. (2023). *A comprehensive review of cyber security vulnerabilities, threats, attacks, and solutions.* Academic Press.

Assiri, A., & Almagwashi, H. (2018). . . *IoT Security and Privacy Issues*, 1–5, 1–5. Advance online publication. 10.1109/CAIS.2018.8442002

Auyporn, W., Piromsopa, K., & Chaiyawat, T. (2020). Critical factors in cybersecurity for SMEs in technological innovation era. *ISPIM Conference Proceedings*.

Avesani, P., McPherson, B., Hayashi, S., Caiafa, C. F., Henschel, R., Garyfallidis, E., & Olivetti, E. (2019). The open diffusion data derivatives, brain data upcycling via integrated publishing of derivatives and reproducible open cloud services. *Scientific Data*, 6(1), 69. 10.1038/s41597-019-0073-y31123325

Avlakulovich, D. M., Valijonovich, T. O., & Ismatulloyevich, R. (2023). *Understanding of Human Factors and Impact in Cybersecurity.* Academic Press.

Axente, M. S., Dobre, C., Ciobanu, R. I., & Purnichescu-Purtan, R. (2020). Gait recognition as an authentication method for mobile devices. *Sensors (Basel)*, 20(15), 1–17. 10.3390/s2015411032718088

Ayodeji, A., Mohamed, M., Li, L., Di Buono, A., Pierce, I., & Ahmed, H. (2023). *Cyber security in the nuclear industry: A closer look at digital control systems, networks and human factors.* Academic Press.

Babaeinesami, A., Tohidi, H., Ghasemi, P., Goodarzian, F., & Tirkolaee, E. (2022). *A closed-loop supply chain configuration considering environmental impacts: a self-adaptive NSGA-II algorithm.* Academic Press.

Babarinde, T. (2024). Effect of Supply Chain Resilience on USA Cyber Security. 10.13140/RG.2.2.16275.04641

Baca, D., & Carlsson, B. (2011). Agile development with security engineering activities. *Proceedings - International Conference on Software Engineering.* 10.1145/1987875.1987900

Bada, M., Sasse, A. M., & Nurse, J. R. J. a. (2019). Cyber security awareness campaigns: Why do they fail to change behaviour? *INTED2017 Proceedings.*

Bagui, S., Wang, X., & Bagui, S. (2021). Machine Learning Based Intrusion Detection for IoT Botnet. *International Journal of Machine Learning and Computing*, 11(6), 399–406. 10.18178/ijmlc.2021.11.6.1068

Bahsi, H., Nomm, S., & La Torre, F. B. (2018). Dimensionality Reduction for Machine Learning Based IoT Botnet Detection. *2018 15th International Conference on Control, Automation, Robotics and Vision, ICARCV 2018*, 1857–1862. 10.1109/ICARCV.2018.8581205

Baik, J. S. (2020). Data privacy against innovation or against discrimination?: The case of the california consumer privacy act (ccpa). *Telematics and Informatics*, 52, 52. 10.1016/j.tele.2020.101431

Baloyi, N., & Kotzé, P. (2020). *Data privacy compliance benefits for organisations–A cyber-physical systems and internet of things study.* Paper presented at the Information and Cyber Security: 18th International Conference, ISSA 2019, Johannesburg, South Africa. 10.1007/978-3-030-43276-8_12

Barati, M., Petri, I., & Rana, O. F. (2019). *Developing GDPR compliant user data policies for internet of things.* Paper presented at the 12th IEEE/ACM International conference on utility and cloud computing. 10.1145/3344341.3368812

Barati, M., Rana, O., Petri, I., & Theodorakopoulos, G. (2020). GDPR compliance verification in Internet of Things. *IEEE Access : Practical Innovations, Open Solutions*, 8, 119697–119709. 10.1109/ACCESS.2020.3005509

Barrera, D., Bellman, C., & van Oorschot, P. C. (2022). Security best practices: A critical analysis using iot as a case study. *ACM Transactions on Privacy and Security.* 10.1145/3563392

Bartsch, S. (2011). Practitioners' perspectives on security in agile development. *Proceedings of the 2011 6th International Conference on Availability, Reliability and Security, ARES 2011.* 10.1109/ARES.2011.82

Bastos, G., Meira, W., Marzano, A., Fonseca, O., Fazzion, E., Hoepers, C., Steding-Jessen, K., Marcelo, C. H. P. C., Cunha, I., & Guedes, D. (2019). Identifying and Characterizing Bashlite and Mirai CC Servers. *Proceedings - IEEE Symposium on Computers and Communications,* 1–6. 10.1109/ISCC47284.2019.8969728

Bell, L., Brunton-Spall, M., Smith, R., & Bird, J. (n.d.). *Agile Application Security: Enabling Security in a Continuous Delivery Pipeline.* O'Reilly Media, Inc. https://www.oreilly.com/library/view/agile-application-security/9781491938836/

Bellal, S. E., El Islam Bousiouda, S., & Dekhinet, A. (2023). Blockchain and Supply Chain in Algeria: Enhancing Transparency and Security of Operations. *2023 International Conference on Decision Aid Sciences and Applications (DASA),* 464-468. 10.1109/DASA59624.2023.10286589

Ben Said, N., Biondi, F., Bontchev, V., Decourbe, O., Given-Wilson, T., Legay, A., & Quilbeuf, J. (2018). Detection of Mirai by Syntactic and Behavioral Analysis. *Proceedings - International Symposium on Software Reliability Engineering, ISSRE,* 224–235. https://doi.org/10.1109/ISSRE.2018.00032

Bennett, C. H., Bessette, F., Brassard, G., Salvail, L., & Smolin, J. (1992). Experimental quantum cryptography. *Journal of Cryptology*, 5(1), 3–28. 10.1007/BF00191318

Bezawada, B., Ray, I., & Ray, I. (2021). Behavioral fingerprinting of Internet-of-Things devices. *Wiley Interdisciplinary Reviews. Data Mining and Knowledge Discovery*, 11(1), 1–15. 10.1002/widm.1337

Bhardwaj, K., Miranda, J. C., & Gavrilovska, A. (2018). Towards {IoT-DDoS} Prevention Using Edge Computing. *USENIX workshop on hot topics in edge computing (HotEdge 18).*

Bhardwaj, A., Alshehri, M. D., Kaushik, K., Alyamani, H. J., & Kumar, M. (2022, March). Secure framework against cyber attacks on cyber-physical robotic systems. *Journal of Electronic Imaging*, 31(06). Advance online publication. 10.1117/1.JEI.31.6.061802

Bhardwaj, A., Bharany, S., Abulfaraj, A. W., Osman Ibrahim, A., & Nagmeldin, W. (2024, March). Fortifying home IoT security: A framework for comprehensive examination of vulnerabilities and intrusion detection strategies for smart cities. *Egyptian Informatics Journal*, 25, 100443. 10.1016/j.eij.2024.100443

Bhardwaj, A., Kaushik, K., Bharany, S., Elnaggar, M. F., Mossad, M. I., & Kamel, S. (2022, September). Comparison of IoT Communication Protocols Using Anomaly Detection with Security Assessments of Smart Devices. *Processes (Basel, Switzerland)*, 10(10), 1952. 10.3390/pr10101952

Bhardwaj, A., Kaushik, K., Bharany, S., & Kim, S. K. (2023, December). Forensic analysis and security assessment of IoT camera firmware for smart homes. *Egyptian Informatics Journal*, 24(4), 100409–100409. 10.1016/j.eij.2023.100409

Bhardwaj, A., Kaushik, K., Bharany, S., Rehman, A. U., Hu, Y.-C., Eldin, E. T., & Ghamry, N. A. (2022, November). IIoT: Traffic Data Flow Analysis and Modeling Experiment for Smart IoT Devices. *Sustainability (Basel)*, 14(21), 14645. 10.3390/su142114645

Bhardwaj, A., Kaushik, K., Dagar, V., & Kumar, M. (2023, August). Framework to measure and reduce the threat surface area for smart home devices. *Advances in Computational Intelligence*, 3(4), 16. Advance online publication. 10.1007/s43674-023-00062-2

Bhardwaj, A., Kumar, M., Stephan, T., Shankar, A., Ghalib, M. R., & Abujar, S. (2021, October). IAF: IoT Attack Framework and Unique Taxonomy. *Journal of Circuits, Systems, and Computers*, 31(02), 2250029. Advance online publication. 10.1142/S0218126622500293

Bhardwaj, A., Vishnoi, A., Bharany, S., Abdelmaboud, A., Ibrahim, A. O., Mamoun, M., & Nagmeldin, W. (2023, December). Framework to perform taint analysis and security assessment of IoT devices in smart cities. *PeerJ. Computer Science*, 9, e1771. 10.7717/peerj-cs.177138192478

Bhardwaj, F., Al-Turjman, F., Kumar, M., Stephan, T., & Mostarda, L. (2020). Capturing-the-Invisible (CTI): Behavior-Based Attacks Recognition in IoT-Oriented Industrial Control Systems. *IEEE Access : Practical Innovations, Open Solutions*, 8, 104956–104966. 10.1109/ACCESS.2020.2998983

Bhargava, M., & Mai, K. (2014). An efficient reliable PUF-based cryptographic key generator in 65nm CMOS. In *Design, Automation & Test in Europe Conference & Exhibition, DATE 2014, Dresden, Germany, March 24-28, 2014.* European Design and Automation Association.

Bhattasali, T., Chaki, R., & Sanyal, S. (2012). Sleep Deprivation Attack Detection in Wireless Sensor Network. *International Journal of Computer Applications*, 40(15), 19–25. 10.5120/5056-7374

Bilal, D., Rehman, A.-U., & Ali, R. (2018). Internet of Things (IoT) Protocols: A Brief Exploration of MQTT and CoAP. *International Journal of Computer Applications*, 179(27), 9–14. 10.5120/ijca2018916438

Bindrwish, F. B., Ali, A. N. A., Ghabban, W. H., Alrowwad, A., Fallatah, N. A., Ameerbakhsh, O., & Alfadli, I. M. (2023). Internet of Things for Digital Forensics Application in Saudi Arabia. *Advances in Internet of Things*, 13(1), 1–11. Advance online publication. 10.4236/ait.2023.131001

Birkel, H. S., & Hartmann, E. (2020). Internet of things–the future of managing supply chain risks. *Supply Chain Management*, 25(5), 535–548. 10.1108/SCM-09-2019-0356

Biryukov, A., & Khovratovich, D. (2009). Related-key cryptanalysis of the full AES-192 and AES-256. *Advances in Cryptology–ASIACRYPT 2009: 15th International Conference on the Theory and Application of Cryptology and Information Security, Tokyo, Japan, December 6-10, 2009 Proceedings*, 15, 1–18.

Bloch, M. R. (2016). Covert communication over noisy channels: A resolvability perspective. *IEEE Transactions on Information Theory*, 62(5), 2334–2354. 10.1109/TIT.2016.2530089

Boeyen, S., Santesson, S., Polk, T., Housley, R., Farrell, S., & Cooper, D. (2008). *Internet X.509 Public Key Infrastructure Certificate and Certificate Revocation List (CRL) Profile*. RFC 5280.

Bojinov, H., & Boneh, D. (2011). Mobile token-based authentication on a budget. *HotMobile 2011: The 12th Workshop on Mobile Computing Systems and Applications*, 14–19. 10.1145/2184489.2184494

Borangiu, T., Trentesaux, D., Thomas, A., Leitão, P., & Barata, J. (2019). *Digital transformation of manufacturing through cloud services and resource virtualization* (Vol. 108). Elsevier.

Boulemtafes, A., Derhab, A., & Challal, Y. (2020). A review of privacy-preserving techniques for deep learning. *Neurocomputing*, 384, 21–45. 10.1016/j.neucom.2019.11.041

Boyes, H., Hallaq, B., Cunningham, J., & Watson, T. (2018). The industrial internet of things (IIoT): An analysis framework. *Computers in Industry*, 101(June), 1–12. 10.1016/j.compind.2018.04.015

Breitenbacher, D., Homoliak, I., Aung, Y. L., & Tippenhauer, N. O. (2019). *HADES-IoT : A Practical Host-Based Anomaly Detection System for IoT Devices*. Academic Press.

Bugden, D., & Stedman, R. (2021). *Unfulfilled promise: social acceptance of the smart grid*.https://iopscience.iop.org/article/10.1088/ 1748-9326/abd81c/ampdf

Buja, A., Apostolova, M., Luma, A., & Januzaj, Y. (2022). *Cyber security standards for the industrial internet of things (iiot)–a systematic review*. Paper presented at the 2022 International Congress on Human-Computer Interaction, Optimization and Robotic Applications (HORA). 10.1109/HORA55278.2022.9799870

Burton, J., & Lain, C. (2020). *Desecuritising cybersecurity: towards a societal approach*. Academic Press.

Butt, M. A., Ajmal, Z., Khan, Z. I., Idrees, M., & Javed, Y. (2022, July). An In-Depth Survey of Bypassing Buffer Overflow Mitigation Techniques. *Applied Sciences (Basel, Switzerland)*, 12(13), 6702. 10.3390/app12136702

Butun, I., Lekidis, A., & dos Santos, D. R. (2020). Security and privacy in smart grids: Challenges, current solutions and future opportunities. *ICISSP*, 10. 10.5220/0009187307330741

Butun, I., Sari, A., & Österberg, P. (2020). Hardware security of fog end-devices for the internet of things. *Sensors (Basel)*, 20(20), 1–28. 10.3390/s2020572933050165

Case, D. U. (2016). Analysis of the cyber attack on the ukrainian power grid. *Electricity Information Sharing and Analysis Center (E-ISAC), 388*(1-29), 3.

CCPA. (2018). *California Consumer Privacy Act (CCPA)*. https://oag.ca.gov/privacy/ccpa

Cekerevac, Z., Dvorak, Z., Prigoda, L., & Čekerevac, P. (2017). Internet of things and the man-in-the-middle attacks – Security and economic risks. *MEST Journal*, 5(2), 15–5. 10.12709/mest.05.05.02.03

Çelik, Ö. (2018). A Research on Machine Learning Methods and Its Applications. *Journal of Educational Technology and Online Learning*, 1(3), 25–40. 10.31681/jetol.457046

Ceron, J. M., Steding-Jessen, K., Hoepers, C., Granville, L. Z., & Margi, C. B. (2019). Improving IoT botnet investigation using an adaptive network layer. *Sensors (Basel)*, 19(3), 1–16. 10.3390/s1903072730754667

Chamekh, M., Hamdi, M., El Asmi, S., & Kim, T.-H. (2018). Secured Distributed IoT Based Supply Chain Architecture. *2018 IEEE 27th International Conference on Enabling Technologies: Infrastructure for Collaborative Enterprises (WETICE)*, 199-202. 10.1109/WETICE.2018.00045

Chang, R. (2002). *Defending against flooding-based distributed denial-of-service attacks: A tutorial*. Academic Press.

Chang, S. E., & Chen, Y. (2020). When Blockchain Meets Supply Chain: A Systematic Literature Review on Current Development and Potential Applications. *IEEE Access: Practical Innovations, Open Solutions*, 8, 62478–62494. 10.1109/ACCESS.2020.2983601

Chang, V., Golightly, L., Modesti, P., Xu, Q. A., Doan, L. M. T., Hall, K., Boddu, S., & Kobusińska, A. (2022). A Survey on Intrusion Detection Systems for Fog and Cloud Computing. *Future Internet*, 14(3), 89. Advance online publication. 10.3390/fi14030089

Chao, J., Hossain, M. S., & Lancor, L. (2023). Swipe gestures for user authentication in smartphones. *Journal of Information Security and Applications*, 74(March), 103450. 10.1016/j.jisa.2023.103450

Charbonneau, S. (2011). *The role of user-driven security in data loss prevention*. Academic Press.

Chatziamanetoglou, D., & Rantos, K. (2024). Cyber threat intelligence on blockchain: A systematic literature review. *Computers*, 13(3), 60. 10.3390/computers13030060

Chaudhry, S. A., Nebhan, J., Yahya, K., & Al-Turjman, F. (2021). A privacy enhanced authentication scheme for securing smart grid infrastructure. *IEEE Transactions on Industrial Informatics*, 18(7), 5000–5006. 10.1109/TII.2021.3119685

Chaudhuri, A. (2016). Internet of things data protection and privacy in the era of the General Data Protection Regulation. *Journal of Data Protection & Privacy*, 1(1), 64–75.

Chen, J., Dai, H., & Yuan, X. (2023). Bayesian-based assessment of emergency supply chain resilience and security levels. *2023 7th International Conference on Transportation Information and Safety (ICTIS)*, 2013-2021. 10.1109/ICTIS60134.2023.10243912

Chen, S., Hao, M., Ding, F., Jiang, D., Dong, J., Zhang, S. (2023). *Exploring the global geography of cybercrime and its driving forces*. Academic Press.

Chen, Y., Ramamurthy, K., & Wen, K.-W. (2015). *Impacts of comprehensive information security programs on information security culture*. Academic Press.

Chen, J. S., Yang, C. Y., Yao, J. F. J., & Hwang, M. H. (2021, September). Secrecy Rate Analysis in The Cooperative Communication System. In *2021 IEEE International Conference on Consumer Electronics-Taiwan (ICCE-TW)* (pp. 1-2). IEEE. 10.1109/ICCE-TW52618.2021.9603208

Chen, M., Wan, J., & Li, F. (2012). Machine-to-machine communications: Architectures, standards, and applications. *KSII Transactions on Internet and Information Systems*, 6(2), 480–497. 10.3837/tiis.2012.02.002

Chen, S., Sun, S., Xu, G., Su, X., & Cai, Y. (2020). Beam-space multiplexing: Practice, theory, and trends, from 4G TD-LTE, 5G, to 6G and beyond. *IEEE Wireless Communications*, 27(2), 162–172. 10.1109/MWC.001.1900307

Chen, X., Ng, D. W. K., Gerstacker, W. H., & Chen, H. H. (2016). A survey on multiple-antenna techniques for physical layer security. *IEEE Communications Surveys and Tutorials*, 19(2), 1027–1053. 10.1109/COMST.2016.2633387

Chen, Z., Yan, L., Lü, Z., Zhang, Y., Guo, Y., Liu, W., & Xuan, J. (2020). Research on zero-trust security protection technology of power IoT based on blockchain. *Proceedings of the 5th International Conference on Computer Science and Information Engineering (ICCSIE 2020)*.

Chitralekha, G., & Roogi, J. M. (2021). A Quick Review of ML Algorithms. *Proceedings of the 6th International Conference on Communication and Electronics Systems, ICCES 2021*. 10.1109/ICCES51350.2021.9488982

Choi, T., Ko, R. K., Saha, T., Scarsbrook, J., Koay, A. M., Wang, S., … St Clair, C. (2021). Plan2defend: Ai planning for cybersecurity in smart grids. *2021 IEEE PES Innovative Smart Grid Technologies-Asia (ISGT Asia)*, 1–5.

Chowdhury, N. (2020). A survey of cryptography-based authentication for smart grid communication. In *Computer security: Esorics 2020 international workshops, cybericps, secpre, and adiot, guildford, uk, september 14–18, 2020, revised selected papers 6* (pp. 52–66). 10.1007/978-3-030-64330-0_4

Chukwu, N., & Simo, S. (2024). Resilient Chain: AI-Enhanced Supply Chain Security and Efficiency Integration. *International Journal of Scientific and Management Research.*, 7(3), 46–65. 10.37502/IJSMR.2024.7306

Columbus, L. (2022). *Why the future of APIs must include zero trust*. VentureBeat. Available: https://venturebeat.com/2022/08/01/why-the-future-of-apis-must-includezero-trust/

Computers. (n.d.). *Efficient, Lightweight Cyber Intrusion Detection System for IoT Ecosystems Using MI2G Algorithm*. https://www.mdpi.com/2073-431X/11/10/142/review_report

Conklin, A., & White, G. B. (2006). E-government and cyber security: the role of cyber security exercises. *Proceedings of the 39th Annual Hawaii International Conference on System Sciences (HICSS'06)*. 10.1109/HICSS.2006.133

Conti, M., Dehghantanha, A., Franke, K., & Watson, S. (2017). Internet of Things Security and Forensics: Challenges and Opportunities. *Future Generation Computer Systems*, 78, 544–546. Advance online publication. 10.1016/j.future.2017.07.060

Corallo, A., Lazoi, M., Lezzi, M., & Luperto, A. (2022). Cybersecurity awareness in the context of the Industrial Internet of Things: A systematic literature review. *Computers in Industry*, 137, 103614. Advance online publication. 10.1016/j.compind.2022.103614

Cui, P., Guin, U., Skjellum, A., & Umphress, D. (2019). Blockchain in IoT: Current Trends, Challenges, and Future Roadmap. *Journal of Hardware and Systems Security*, 3(4), 338–364. 10.1007/s41635-019-00079-5

Dahiya, P. (2022). Malware Detection in IoT. In *Internet of Things: Security and Privacy in Cyberspace* (pp. 133-164). Springer. 10.1007/978-981-19-1585-7_7

Dai, H.-N., Zheng, Z., & Zhang, Y. (2019). Blockchain for Internet of things: A survey. *IEEE Internet of Things Journal*, 6(5), 8076–8094. 10.1109/JIOT.2019.2920987

Daim, T., Lai, K. K., Yalcin, H., Alsoubie, F., & Kumar, V. (2020). *Forecasting technological positioning through technology knowledge redundancy: Patent citation analysis of IoT, cybersecurity, and Blockchain*. Academic Press.

Dalal, K. R. (2020). Analyzing the Role of Supervised and Unsupervised Machine Learning in IoT. *Proceedings of the International Conference on Electronics and Sustainable Communication Systems, ICESC 2020, Icesc*, 75–79. 10.1109/ICESC48915.2020.9155761

Dammak, M., Boudia, O. R. M., Messous, M. A., Senouci, S. M., & Gransart, C. (2019). Token-Based Lightweight Authentication to Secure IoT Networks. *2019 16th IEEE Annual Consumer Communications and Networking Conference, CCNC 2019*. 10.1109/CCNC.2019.8651825

Daneva, M., & Wang, C. (2018). Security requirements engineering in the agile era: How does it work in practice? *Proceedings - 2018 1st International Workshop on Quality Requirements in Agile Projects, QuaRAP 2018*. 10.1109/QuaRAP.2018.00008

Daniel, C., & Sipper, J. (2023). Hacking Humans. *The Art of Exploiting Psychology in the Digital Age*, 10, 224.

Das, K., Basu, R., & Karmakar, R. (2022, October). Man-in-the-middle attack detection using ensemble learning. In *2022 13th International Conference on Computing Communication and Networking Technologies (ICCCNT)* (pp. 1-6). IEEE. 10.1109/ICCCNT54827.2022.9984365

De Marsico, M., & Mecca, A. (2019). A survey on gait recognition via wearable sensors. *ACM Computing Surveys*, 52(4), 1–39. Advance online publication. 10.1145/3340293

De Neira, A. B., Araujo, A. M., & Nogueira, M. (2020). Early botnet detection for the Internet and the Internet of Things by autonomous machine learning. *Proceedings - 2020 16th International Conference on Mobility, Sensing, and Networking, MSN 2020*, 516–523. 10.1109/MSN50589.2020.00087

de Zafra, D. E., Pitcher, S. I., Tressler, J. D., & Ippolito, J. (1998). *Information technology security training requirements: A role-and performance-based model*. Academic Press.

Deb, D., & Jain, A. K. (2021). Look Locally Infer Globally: A Generalizable Face Anti-Spoofing Approach. *IEEE Transactions on Information Forensics and Security*, 16, 1143–1157. 10.1109/TIFS.2020.3029879

Delvaux, J., Peeters, R., Gu, D., & Verbauwhede, I. (2015). *A Survey on Lightweight Entity Authentication with Strong PUFs*. Academic Press.

Desai, M. G., Shi, Y., & Suo, K. (2020). IoT Bonet and Network Intrusion Detection using Dimensionality Reduction and Supervised Machine Learning. *2020 11th IEEE Annual Ubiquitous Computing, Electronics and Mobile Communication Conference, UEMCON 2020*, 316–322. 10.1109/UEMCON51285.2020.9298146

Desai, M. G., Shi, Y., & Suo, K. (2021). *A Hybrid Approach for IoT Botnet Attack Detection*. 10.1109/IEMCON53756.2021.9623102

Desuert, A., Chollet, S., Pion, L., & Hély, D. (2022). Refillable PUF authentication protocol for constrained devices. *Journal of Ambient Intelligence and Smart Environments*, 14(3), 195–212. 10.3233/AIS-210325

Dhanda, S. S., Singh, B., & Jindal, P. (2020). Lightweight cryptography: A solution to secure IoT. *Wireless Personal Communications*, 112(3), 1947–1980. 10.1007/s11277-020-07134-3

Dhirani, L. L., Armstrong, E., & Newe, T. (2021). Industrial iot, cyber threats, and standards landscape: Evaluation and roadmap. *Sensors (Basel)*, 21(11), 3901. 10.3390/s2111390134198727

Dhir, S., & Kumar, Y. (2020). Study of machine and deep learning classifications in cyber-physical systems. *Proceedings of the 3rd International Conference on Smart Systems and Inventive Technology, ICSSIT 2020, Icssit*, 333–338. 10.1109/ICSSIT48917.2020.9214237

Dibaei, M., & Ghaffari, A. (2017). Tsis: A trust-based scheme for increasing security in wireless sensor networks. *Majlesi Journal of Electrical Engineering*, 11(4), 45–52.

Dibaei, M., Zheng, X., Jiang, K., Abbas, R., Liu, S., Zhang, Y., Xiang, Y., & Yu, S. (2020). Attacks and defences on intelligent connected vehicles: A survey. *Digital Communications and Networks*, 6(4), 399–421. 10.1016/j.dcan.2020.04.007

Diesch, R., Pfaff, M., & Krcmar, H. (2020). *A comprehensive model of information security factors for decision-makers*. Academic Press.

Diffie, W., & Hellman, M. E. (2022). Exhaustive cryptanalysis of the NBS data encryption standard. In *Democratizing Cryptography: The Work of Whitfield Diffie and Martin Hellman* (pp. 391-414). Academic Press.

Doshi, R., Apthorpe, N., & Feamster, N. (2018). Machine learning DDoS detection for consumer Internet of Things devices. *Proceedings - 2018 IEEE Symposium on Security and Privacy Workshops, SPW 2018, MI*, 29–35. 10.1109/SPW.2018.00013

Dowling, S., Schukat, M., & Melvin, H. (2017). A ZigBee honeypot to assess IoT cyberattack behavior. *2017 28th Irish Signals and Systems Conference, ISSC 2017*. 10.1109/ISSC.2017.7983603

Dulac-Arnold, G., Mankowitz, D., & Hester, T. 2019. Challenges of real-world reinforcement learning. *arXiv preprint arXiv:1904.12901*.

Duo, W., Zhou, M., & Abusorrah, A. (2022). A survey of cyber attacks on cyber physical systems: Recent advances and challenges. *IEEE/CAA Journal of Automatica Sinica, 9*(5), 784–800.

Dutta, P., Choi, T. M., Somani, S., & Butala, R. (2020). Blockchain technology in supply chain operations: Applications, challenges and research opportunities. *Transportation research part e: Logistics and transportation review, 142*, 102067.

Dworkin, M., Barker, E., Nechvatal, J., Foti, J., Bassham, L., Roback, E., & Dray, J. (2001). *Advanced Encryption Standard*. AES.

Dwyer, O. P., Marnerides, A. K., Giotsas, V., & Mursch, T. (2019). Profiling IoT-based botnet traffic using DNS. *2019 IEEE Global Communications Conference, GLOBECOM 2019 - Proceedings*. 10.1109/GLOBECOM38437.2019.9014300

Ebrahimpour, E., & Babaie, S. (2024). Authentication in Internet of Things, protocols, attacks, and open issues: A systematic literature review. *International Journal of Information Security*, 23(3), 1583–1602. Advance online publication. 10.1007/s10207-023-00806-8

Eddy, W. (2022). *Transmission Control Protocol (TCP)*. RFC 9293.

Eggers, S. (2021). *A novel approach for analyzing the nuclear supply chain cyber-attack surface*. Academic Press.

El Ghazi, A., & Moulay Rachid, A. (2020). Machine learning and data mining methods for hybrid IoT intrusion detection. *Proceedings of 2020 5th International Conference on Cloud Computing and Artificial Intelligence: Technologies and Applications, CloudTech 2020*. https://doi.org/10.1109/CloudTech49835.2020.9365895

Eltira, K., Younis, A., & Mesleh, R. (2023). Impact of channel imperfections on variant SMTs MIMO systems over revised Nakagami-m channel model. *AEÜ. International Journal of Electronics and Communications*, 170, 154799. 10.1016/j.aeue.2023.154799

Epiphaniou, G., Pillai, P., Bottarelli, M., Al-Khateeb, H., Hammoudesh, M., & Maple, C. (2020). Electronic regulation of data sharing and processing using smart ledger technologies for supply-chain security. *IEEE Transactions on Engineering Management*, 67(4), 1059–1073. 10.1109/TEM.2020.2965991

Erwin, B. (2021). The Groundbreaking 2015 Jeep Hack Changed Automotive Cybersecurity. Fractional CISO - Virtual CISO. https://fractionalciso.com/the-groundbreaking-2015-jeep-hack-changed-automotive-cybersecurity/

Escoffier, C., Chollet, S., & Lalanda, P. (2014). Lessons Learned in Building Pervasive Platforms. In *11th IEEE Consumer Communications and Networking Conference (CCNC), CCNC 2014,* Las Vegas, NV, USA, January 10-13, 2014. IEEE.

Estalenx, A., & Gañán, C. H. (2021). *NURSE : eNd-UseR IoT malware detection tool for Smart homEs.* Academic Press.

Etemadi, N., Van Gelder, P., & Strozzi, F. (2021). An ISM Modeling of Barriers for Blockchain/Distributed Ledger Technology Adoption in Supply Chains towards Cybersecurity. *Sustainability (Basel),* 13(9), 4672. 10.3390/su13094672

ETSI. (2020). *European Telecommunications Standards Institute.* https://www.etsi.org/

Evan, G., & Barth, D. (2017). *Zero Trust Networks: Building Secure Systems in Untrusted Networks.* O'Reilly.

Falco, G., Li, C., Fedorov, P., Caldera, C., Arora, R., & Jackson, K. (2019). NeuroMesh: IoT security enabled by a blockchain-powered botnet vaccine. *ACM International Conference Proceeding Series, Part F1481,* 1–6. 10.1145/3312614.3312615

Faquir, D., Chouliaras, N., Sofia, V., Olga, K., & Maglaras, L. (2021). Cybersecurity in smart grids, challenges and solutions. *AIMS Electronics and Electrical Engineering,* 5(1), 24–37.

Fardan, N. J., & Paterson, K. G. (2013). *Lucky thirteen: Breaking the TLS and DTLS record protocols.* 10.1109/SP.2013.42

Farinholt, B., Rezaeirad, M., McCoy, D., & Levchenko, K. (2020). Dark matter: uncovering the darkcomet rat ecosystem. In *Proceedings of the web conference 2020* (pp. 2109–2120). 10.1145/3366423.3380277

Farokhi, F. (2020). Review of results on smart-meter privacy by data manipulation, demand shaping, and load scheduling. *IET Smart Grid,* 3(5), 605–613. 10.1049/iet-stg.2020.0129

Feng, J., Yan, R., Han, G., & Zhang, W. (2024). BDPM: A secure batch dynamic password management scheme in industrial internet environments. *Future Generation Computer Systems, 157,* 193–209. 10.1016/j.future.2024.03.030

Ferrill, P. (2022). What Is Zero Trust Architecture? *The New Stack.* Available: https://thenewstack.io/what-is-zero-trust-architecture/

Fomichev, V., Bobrovskiy, D., Koreneva, A., Nabiev, T., & Zadorozhny, D. (2022). Data integrity algorithm based on additive generators and hash function. *Journal of Computer Virology and Hacking Techniques,* 18(1), 31–41. 10.1007/s11416-021-00405-y

Fragkos, G., Johnson, J., & Tsiropoulou, E. E. (2022). Dynamic role-based access control policy for smart grid applications: An offline deep reinforcement learning approach. *IEEE Transactions on Human-Machine Systems,* 52(4), 761–773. 10.1109/THMS.2022.3163185

Frank, C., Nance, C., Jarocki, S., Pauli, W. E., & Madison, S. D. (2017). Protecting IoT from Mirai botnets; IoT device hardening. *Proceedings of the Conference on Information Systems Applied Research ISSN, 2167,* 1508.

Galaitsi, S., Trump, B. D., & Linkov, I. (2020). Governance for the internet of things: Striving toward resilience. *Modeling and Design of Secure Internet of Things,* 371–381.

Garah, A., Mbarek, N., & Kirgizov, S. (2022). *An architecture for confidentiality self-management in the internet of things.* Academic Press.

Gassend, B., Clarke, D. E., van Dijk, M., & Devadas, S. (2002). Silicon physical random functions. In *Proceedings of the 9th ACM Conference on Computer and Communications Security, CCS 2002,* Washington, DC, USA, November 18-22, 2002. ACM. 10.1145/586110.586132

GDPR. (2016). *General Data Protection Regulation (GDPR).* https://gdpr-info.eu/

Gebremichael, T., Ledwaba, L. P., Eldefrawy, M. H., Hancke, G. P., Pereira, N., Gidlund, M., & Akerberg, J. (2020). Security and privacy in the industrial internet of things: Current standards and future challenges. *IEEE Access : Practical Innovations, Open Solutions*, 8, 152351–152366. 10.1109/ACCESS.2020.3016937

Ghani, I., Azham, Z., & Jeong, S. R. (2014). Integrating software security into the agile-Scrum method. *KSII Transactions on Internet and Information Systems*, 8(2), 646–663. Advance online publication. 10.3837/tiis.2014.02.019

Gharami, S., Prabadevi, B., & Bhimnath, A. (2019). Semantic analysis - Internet of things, the study of past, present, and future of IoT. *Electronic Government*, 15(2), 144–165. 10.1504/EG.2019.098668

Ghassabi, K., & Pahlevani, P. (2024). DEDUCT: A Secure Deduplication of Textual Data in Cloud Environments. *IEEE Access : Practical Innovations, Open Solutions*, 12, 70743–70758. 10.1109/ACCESS.2024.3402544

Ghelani, D. (2022). Cyber security in smart grids, threats, and possible solutions. *Authorea Preprints*. 10.22541/au.166385207.71655799/v1

Ghimire, B., & Rawat, D. B. (2022). Recent Advances on Federated Learning for Cybersecurity and Cybersecurity for Federated Learning for Internet of Things. *IEEE Internet of Things Journal*, 9(11), 8229–8249. 10.1109/JIOT.2022.3150363

Ghorbani, H., Mohammadzadeh, M. S., & Ahmadzadegan, M. H. (2020, April). DDoS Attacks on the IoT Network with the Emergence of 5G. In *2020 International Conference on Technology and Entrepreneurship-Virtual (ICTE-V)* (pp. 1-5). IEEE. 10.1109/ICTE-V50708.2020.9113779

Giachoudis, N., Damiris, G. P., Theodoridis, G., & Spathoulas, G. (2019). Collaborative agent-based detection of DDoS IoT botnets. *Proceedings - 15th Annual International Conference on Distributed Computing in Sensor Systems, DCOSS 2019*, 205–211. 10.1109/DCOSS.2019.00055

Gillis, A. (n.d.). What is IIoT (Industrial Internet of Things)? Definition from TechTarget.com. IoT Agenda. https://www.techtarget.com/iotagenda/definition/Industrial-Internet-of-Things-IIoT

Goldreich, O. (2019). On the foundations of cryptography. In *Providing sound foundations for cryptography: on the work of Shafi Goldwasser and Silvio Micali* (pp. 411-496). Academic Press.

Goldreich, O. 2019. On the foundations of cryptography. *Providing sound foundations for cryptography: on the work of Shafi Goldwasser and Silvio Micali*. Academic Press.

Golomb, T., Mirsky, Y., & Elovici, Y. (2018). *CIoTA: Collaborative Anomaly Detection via Blockchain*. 10.14722/diss.2018.23003

Gomathi, R. M., Krishna, G. H. S., Brumancia, E., & Dhas, Y. M. (2018). A Survey on IoT Technologies, Evolution and Architecture. *2nd International Conference on Computer, Communication, and Signal Processing: Special Focus on Technology and Innovation for Smart Environment, ICCCSP 2018, Icccsp*, 1–5. 10.1109/ICCCSP.2018.8452820

Gönen, S., Sayan, H. H., Yılmaz, E. N., Üstünsoy, F., & Karacayılmaz, G. (2020). False data injection attacks and the insider threat in smart systems. *Computers & Security*, 97, 101955. 10.1016/j.cose.2020.101955

Gopstein, A., Nguyen, C., O'Fallon, C., Hastings, N., & Wollman, D. (2021). *Nist framework and roadmap for smart grid interoperability standards, release 4.0*. Department of Commerce. National Institute of Standards and Technology. 10.6028/NIST.SP.1108r4

Goudarzi, A., Ghayoor, F., Waseem, M., Fahad, S., & Traore, I. (2022). A survey on IOT-enabled smart grids: Emerging, applications, challenges, and outlook. *Energies*, 15(19), 6984. 10.3390/en15196984

Gough, M. B., Santos, S. F., AlSkaif, T., Javadi, M. S., Castro, R., & Catalão, J. P. (2021). Preserving privacy of smart meter data in a smart grid environment. *IEEE Transactions on Industrial Informatics*, 18(1), 707–718. 10.1109/TII.2021.3074915

Greer, C., Wollman, D. A., Prochaska, D., Boynton, P. A., Mazer, J. A., & Nguyen, C. (2014). *Nist framework and roadmap for smart grid interoperability standards, release 3.0*. Academic Press.

Gregory, R., Prifling, M., & Beck, R. (2009). *The role of cultural intelligence for the emergence of negotiated culture in IT offshore outsourcing projects*. Academic Press.

Grover, A., & Berghel, H. (2011). A Survey of RFID Deployment and Security Issues. *Journal of Information Processing Systems*, 7(4), 561–580. 10.3745/JIPS.2011.7.4.561

Guarnizo, J., Tambe, A., Bhunia, S. S., Ochoa, M., Tippenhauer, N. O., Shabtai, A., & Elovici, Y. (2017). SIPHON: Towards scalable high-interaction physical honeypots. *CPSS 2017 - Proceedings of the 3rd ACM Workshop on Cyber-Physical System Security, Co-Located with ASIA CCS 2017*, 57–68. 10.1145/3055186.3055192

Gunduz, M. Z., & Das, R. (2020). Cyber-security on smart grid: Threats and potential solutions. *Computer Networks*, 169, 107094. 10.1016/j.comnet.2019.107094

Gungor, V. C., Lu, B., & Hancke, G. P. (2010). Opportunities and challenges of wireless sensor networks in smart grid. *IEEE Transactions on Industrial Electronics*, 57(10), 3557–3564. 10.1109/TIE.2009.2039455

Guo, Z., Shi, D., Johansson, K. H., & Shi, L. (2016). *Optimal linear cyber-attack on remote state estimation*. Academic Press.

Gupta, N., Naik, V., & Sengupta, S. (2017). *A firewall for internet of things*. Paper presented at the 2017 9th International Conference on Communication Systems and Networks (COMSNETS). 10.1109/COMSNETS.2017.7945418

Gurulakshmi, K., & Nesarani, A. (2018). Machine Learning_algorithm_prespective.pdf. *2018 2nd International Conference on Trends in Electronics and Informatics (ICOEI)*, 1052–1057.

Gyamfi, E., & Jurcut, A. (2022). Intrusion detection in Internet of Things systems: A review on Design Approaches Leveraging Multi-Access Edge Computing, machine learning, and datasets. *Sensors (Basel)*, 22(10), 3744. 10.3390/s2210374435632153

H., Z., A., H., & M., M. (2015). Internet of Things (IoT): Definitions, Challenges, and Recent Research Directions. *International Journal of Computer Applications*, 128(1), 37–47. 10.5120/ijca2015906430

Habibi, J., Midi, D., Mudgerikar, A., & Bertino, E. (2017). Heimdall: Mitigating the Internet of Insecure Things. *IEEE Internet of Things Journal*, 4(4), 968–978. 10.1109/JIOT.2017.2704093

Hadlington, L. (2017). *Human factors in cybersecurity; examining the link between Internet addiction, impulsivity, attitudes towards cybersecurity, and risky cybersecurity behaviours*. Academic Press.

Hajny, J., Ricci, S., Piesarskas, E., Levillain, O., Galletta, L., & De Nicola, R. (2021). *Framework, tools and good practices for cybersecurity curricula*. Academic Press.

Hakim, M. A., Aksu, H., Uluagac, A. S., & Akkaya, K. (2018). U-PoT: A Honeypot Framework for UPnP-Based IoT Devices. *2018 IEEE 37th International Performance Computing and Communications Conference, IPCCC 2018*. 10.1109/PCCC.2018.8711321

Hall, L., Paracha, S., Hagan-Green, G., Ure, C., & Jackman, P. (2022). *Cyber Eyes Wide Open: Creative Collaboration between Artists, Academics & Cyber Security Practitioners*. 10.14236/ewic/HCI2022.15

Hamdani, R. E., Mustapha, M., Amariles, D. R., Troussel, A., & Meeùs, S., & Krasnashchok, K. (2021). A combined rule-based and machine learning approach for automated gdpr compliance checking. In *Proceedings of the eighteenth international conference on artificial intelligence and law* (pp. 40–49). Academic Press.

Hamlyn, A., Cheung, H., Mander, T., Wang, L., Yang, C., & Cheung, R. (2008). *Computer network security management and authentication of smart grids operations. 2008 IEEE power and energy society general meetingconversion and delivery of electrical energy in the 21st century.*

Hammad, B. T., Sagheer, A. M., Ahmed, I. T., & Jamil, N. (2020). A comparative review on symmetric and asymmetric DNA-based cryptography. *Bulletin of Electrical Engineering and Informatics*, 9(6), 2484–2491. 10.11591/eei.v9i6.2470

Hammi, B., Zeadally, S., & Nebhen, J. (2023). Security Threats, Countermeasures, and Challenges of Digital Supply Chains. *ACM Comput. Surv., 55*(14s), Article 316.

Hammi, B., & Zeadally, S. (2023). Software Supply-Chain Security: Issues and Countermeasures. *Computer*, 56(7), 54–66. Advance online publication. 10.1109/MC.2023.3273491

Hamza, A., Gharakheili, H. H., & Sivaraman, V. (2018). Combining MUD policies with SDN for IoT intrusion detection. *IoT S and P 2018 - Proceedings of the 2018 Workshop on IoT Security and Privacy, Part of SIGCOMM 2018*, 1–7. 10.1145/3229565.3229571

Harbach, M., von Zezschwitz, E., Fichtner, A., De Luca, A., & Smith, M. (2016). It's a Hard Lock Life: A Field Study of Smartphone (Un)Locking Behavior and Risk Perception. *SOUPS '14: Proceedings of the Tenth Symposium On Usable Privacy and Security*, 213–230. https://www.usenix.org/conference/soups2014/proceedings/presentation/harbach

Hareer, F. A. (2024). Supply Chain Complexity and Its Impact on Knowledge Transfer: Incorporating Sustainable Supply Chain Practices in Food Supply Chain Networks. *Logistics*, 8(1), 5. 10.3390/logistics8010005

Hart, S., Margheri, A., Paci, F., & Sassone, V. (2020). Riskio: A Serious Game for Cyber Security Awareness and Education. *Computers & Security*, 95, 101827. 10.1016/j.cose.2020.101827

Haseeb, J., Mansoori, M., Al-Sahaf, H., & Welch, I. (2020). IoT attacks: Features identification and clustering. *Proceedings - 2020 IEEE 19th International Conference on Trust, Security and Privacy in Computing and Communications, TrustCom 2020*, 353–360. 10.1109/TrustCom50675.2020.00056

Hassanzadeh, A., Modi, S., & Mulchandani, S. (2015). *Towards effective security control assignment in the Industrial Internet of Things.* Paper presented at the 2015 IEEE 2nd World Forum on Internet of Things (WF-IoT). 10.1109/WF-IoT.2015.7389155

Hassija, Chamola, Gupta, Jain, & Guizani. (2021). A Survey on Supply Chain Security: Application Areas, Security Threats, and Solution Architectures. *IEEE Internet of Things Journal, 8*(8), 6222-6246. .10.1109/JIOT.2020.3025775

Hazra, A., Adhikari, M., Amgoth, T., & Srirama, S. N. (2021). A Comprehensive Survey on Interoperability for IIoT: Taxonomy, Standards, and Future Directions. *ACM Computing Surveys*, 55(1), 1–35. 10.1145/3485130

He, Z. (2023). Blockchain Security Risk Monitoring of Power Supply Chain Based on Fuzzy Neural Network. *2023 IEEE 2nd International Conference on Electrical Engineering, Big Data and Algorithms (EEBDA)*, 446-451. 10.1109/EEBDA56825.2023.10090552

Heartfield, R., & Loukas, G. (2018). *Detecting semantic social engineering attacks with the weakest link: Implementation and empirical evaluation of a human-as-a-security-sensor framework.* Academic Press.

Hegde, M., Kepnang, G., Al Mazroei, M., Chavis, J. S., & Watkins, L. (2020). Identification of Botnet Activity in IoT Network Traffic Using Machine Learning. *2020 International Conference on Intelligent Data Science Technologies and Applications, IDSTA 2020, 1*, 21–27. 10.1109/IDSTA50958.2020.9264143

He, Y., Zamani, E. D., Lloyd, S., & Luo, C. (2022). Agile incident response (AIR): Improving the incident response process in healthcare. *International Journal of Information Management*, 62, 102435. Advance online publication. 10.1016/j.ijinfomgt.2021.102435

HIPAA. (2009). *Health Insurance Portability and Accountability Act (HIPAA)*. https://www.hhs.gov/hipaa/index.html

Holcomb, D. E., Burleson, W. P., & Fu, K. (2009). Power-Up SRAM State as an Identifying Fingerprint and Source of True Random Numbers. *IEEE Transactions on Computers*, 58(9), 1198–1210. 10.1109/TC.2008.212

Hossayni, H., Khan, I., & Crespi, N. (2021). Privacy-preserving sharing of industrial maintenance reports in industry 4.0. In *2021 IEEE fourth international conference on artificial intelligence and knowledge engineering (aike)* (pp. 17–24). IEEE.

Howell, J. (2024). *An Overview of Integer Overflow Attacks*. 101 Blockchains. https://101blockchains.com/integer-overflow-attacks/

Hromada, D., Costa, R. L. C., Santos, L., & Rabadão, C. (2023). Security aspects of the internet of things. In *Research anthology on convergence of blockchain, internet of things, and security* (pp. 67–87). IGI Global.

Hsiao, S., Mattox, S., Park, T., Selvaraj, S., & Tam, A. (2017). *BotRevealer: Behavioral Detection of Botnets based on Botnet Life-cycle*. IS e C Ure.

Huertas Celdrán, A., Miguel Sánchez Sánchez, P., von der Assen, J., Schenk, T., Bovet, G., Martínez Pérez, G., & Stiller, B. (2024). RL and Fingerprinting to Select Moving Target Defense Mechanisms for Zero-Day Attacks in IoT. *IEEE Transactions on Information Forensics and Security*, 19, 5520–5529. 10.1109/TIFS.2024.3402055

Hughes-Lartey, K., Li, M., Botchey, F. E., & Qin, Z. J. H. (2021). Human factor, a critical weak point in the information security of an organization's. *Internet of Things : Engineering Cyber Physical Human Systems*, 7(3).33768182

Hunker, J., & Probst, C. W. (2011). Insiders and Insider Threats-An Overview of Definitions and Mitigation Techniques. *J. Wirel. Mob. Netw. Ubiquitous Comput. Dependable Appl.*, 2, 4–27. Available online: https://www.trellix.com/en-us/security-awareness/ransomware/what-is-stuxnet.html

Hunko, M., Ruban, I., & Hvozdetska, K. (2021). *Securing the Internet of Things via VPN technology*. Academic Press.

Huong, T. T., Bac, T. P., Long, D. M., Thang, B. D., Binh, N. T., Luong, T. D., & Phuc, T. K. (2021). Lockedge: Low-complexity cyberattack detection in IoT edge computing. *IEEE Access : Practical Innovations, Open Solutions*, 9, 29696–29710. 10.1109/ACCESS.2021.3058528

Hu, P., Gao, W., Li, Y., Wu, M., Hua, F., & Qiao, L. (2023). Detection of False Data Injection Attacks in Smart Grids Based on Expectation Maximization. *Sensors (Basel)*, 23(3), 3. Advance online publication. 10.3390/s2303168336772723

Huseinović, A., Mrdović, S., Bicakci, K., & Uludag, S. (2020). A survey of denial-of-service attacks and solutions in the smart grid. *IEEE Access : Practical Innovations, Open Solutions*, 8, 177447–177470. 10.1109/ACCESS.2020.3026923

Hussain, F., Abbas, S. G., Husnain, M., Fayyaz, U. U., Shahzad, F., & Shah, G. A. (2020). IoT DoS and DDoS Attack Detection using ResNet. *Proceedings - 2020 23rd IEEE International Multi-Topic Conference, INMIC 2020*. 10.1109/INMIC50486.2020.9318216

Hussain, I., Samara, G., Ullah, I., & Khan, N. (2021). Encryption for end-user privacy: a cyber-secure smart energy management system. In *2021 22nd international arab conference on information technology (acit)* (pp. 1–6). 10.1109/ACIT53391.2021.9677341

Hussain, M. E., & Hussain, R. (2021). *Cloud Security as a Service Using Data Loss Prevention: Challenges and Solution.* Paper presented at the International Conference on Internet of Things and Connected Technologies.

Hussain, F., Abbas, S. G., Pires, I. M., Tanveer, S., Fayyaz, U. U., Garcia, N. M., Shah, G. A., & Shahzad, F. (2021). A Two-Fold Machine Learning Approach to Prevent and Detect IoT Botnet Attacks. *IEEE Access : Practical Innovations, Open Solutions*, 9, 163412–163430. 10.1109/ACCESS.2021.3131014

Hussein, A. R. H. (2019). Internet of Things (IoT): Research challenges and future applications. *International Journal of Advanced Computer Science and Applications*, 10(6), 77–82. 10.14569/IJACSA.2019.0100611

Hyadi, A., Rezki, Z., & Alouini, M. S. (2016). An overview of physical layer security in wireless communication systems with CSIT uncertainty. *IEEE Access : Practical Innovations, Open Solutions*, 4, 6121–6132. 10.1109/ACCESS.2016.2612585

IBM. (2023). Cost of a Data Breach 2023. IBM. https://www.ibm.com/reports/data-breach

Ibrahim, A., Sadeghi, A. R., & Tsudik, G. (2019). US-AID: Unattended scalable attestation of IoT devices. *Proceedings of the IEEE Symposium on Reliable Distributed Systems, 2019-Octob*, 21–30. 10.1109/SRDS.2018.00013

In Data. (n.d.). *Computational capacity of the fastest supercomputers.* Retrieved from https://ourworldindata.org/grapher/supercomputer-power-flops

Injadat, M. N., Moubayed, A., & Shami, A. (2020). Detecting Botnet Attacks in IoT Environments: An Optimized Machine Learning Approach. *Proceedings of the International Conference on Microelectronics, ICM, 2020-Decem*. 10.1109/ICM50269.2020.9331794

Irfan, M., Ali, S., Hussain, S. I., Muhammad, Z., & Raza, S. (2024). *Exploring the synergistic effects of blockchain integration with IoT and AI for enhanced transparency and security in global supply chains.* Academic Press.

Islam, M. R. (2014). Feature and score fusion based multiple classifier selection for iris recognition. *Computational Intelligence and Neuroscience*, 2014, 1–11. 10.1155/2014/38058525114676

Ismail & Reza. (2022). Security Challenges of Blockchain-Based Supply Chain Systems. *2022 IEEE 13th Annual Ubiquitous Computing, Electronics & Mobile Communication Conference (UEMCON)*, 1-6..10.1109/UEMCON54665.2022.9965682

Ismail, S., Moudoud, H., Dawoud, D., & Reza, H. (2024). Blockchain-Based Zero Trust Supply Chain Security Integrated with Deep Reinforcement Learning. 10.20944/preprints202403.0714.v1

Ivanchenko, N. S., Lepeshkina, D., Kulguskina, M., & Giniyatullin, A. (2022). Internet of things and compliance control. *Vestnik Rossijskoj akademii estestvennyh nauk.* 10.52531/1682-1696-2022-22-2-116-122

Izycki, E., & Vianna, E. W. (2021). Critical infrastructure: A battlefield for cyber warfare? In *Iccws 2021 16th international conference on cyber warfare and security* (p. 454). Academic Press.

Jabangwe, R., Kuusinen, K., Riisom, K. R., Hubel, M. S., Alradhi, H. M., & Nielsen, N. B. (2019). Challenges and Solutions for Addressing Software Security in Agile Software Development. *International Journal of Systems and Software Security and Protection*, 9(1), 1–17. Advance online publication. 10.4018/IJSSSP.2018010101

Jahwar, A. F., & Ameen, S. Y. (2021). A Review of Cybersecurity based on Machine Learning and Deep Learning Algorithms. *Journal of Soft Computing and Data Mining*, 2(2), 14–25. 10.30880/jscdm.2021.02.02.002

Janarthanan, T., Bagheri, M., & Zargari, S. (2021). IoT Forensics: An Overview of the Current Issues and Challenges. In *Advanced Sciences and Technologies for Security Applications* (pp. 223–254). 10.1007/978-3-030-60425-7_10

Jardine, E. (2020). *The case against commercial antivirus software: Risk homeostasis and information problems in cybersecurity*. Academic Press.

Jatoth, C., Gangadharan, G., Fiore, U., & Buyya, R. (2019). SELCLOUD: A hybrid multi-criteria decision-making model for selection of cloud services. *Soft Computing*, 23(13), 4701–4715. 10.1007/s00500-018-3120-2

Jensen, L. (2015). *Challenges in maritime cyber-resilience*. Academic Press.

Jha, R. K. (2023). Cybersecurity and confidentiality in smart grid for enhancing sustainability and reliability. *Recent Research Reviews Journal*, 2(2), 215–241. 10.36548/rrrj.2023.2.001

Jiang, H., Cai, C., Ma, X., Yang, Y., & Liu, J. (2018). Smart Home Based on WiFi Sensing: A Survey. *IEEE Access : Practical Innovations, Open Solutions*, 6, 13317–13325. 10.1109/ACCESS.2018.2812887

Jiang, W., Synovic, N., Sethi, R., Indarapu, A., Hyatt, M., Schorlemmer, T. R., Thiruvathukal, G. K., & Davis, J. C. (2022). An Empirical Study of Artifacts and Security Risks in the Pre-trained Model Supply Chain. In *Proceedings of the 2022 ACM Workshop on Software Supply Chain Offensive Research and Ecosystem Defenses (SCORED'22)*. Association for Computing Machinery. 10.1145/3560835.3564547

Jindal, K., & Sharma, K. (2014)... *Analyzing Spoofing Attacks in Wireless Networks*, 398–402, 398–402. Advance online publication. 10.1109/ACCT.2014.46

Jin, H., Li, Z., Zou, D., & Yuan, B. (2021). DSEOM: A Framework for Dynamic Security Evaluation and Optimization of MTD in Container-Based Cloud. *IEEE Transactions on Dependable and Secure Computing*, 18(3), 1. Advance online publication. 10.1109/TDSC.2019.2916666

Job, D., & Paul, V. (2022). Challenges, security mechanisms, and research areas in iot and iiot. *Internet of things and its applications*, 523–538.

Jones, S. L., Collins, E. I., Levordashka, A., Muir, K., & Joinson, A. (2019). *What is' Cyber Security'? Differential Language of Cyber Security Across the Lifespan*. Paper presented at the Extended Abstracts of the 2019 CHI Conference on Human Factors in Computing Systems. 10.1145/3290607.3312786

Jorswieck, E. A., Wolf, A., & Gerbracht, S. (2010). Secrecy on the physical layer in wireless networks. *Trends in Telecommunications Technologies*, 413-435.

Judge, M. A., Khan, A., Manzoor, A., & Khattak, H. A. (2022). Overview of smart grid implementation: Frameworks, impact, performance and challenges. *Journal of Energy Storage*, 49, 104056. 10.1016/j.est.2022.104056

Juels, A. (2006). RFID security and privacy: A research survey. *IEEE Journal on Selected Areas in Communications*, 24(2), 381–394. 10.1109/JSAC.2005.861395

Kadivar, M. (2014). *Cyber-attack attributes*. Academic Press.

Kagombe, G. G., Mwangi, R. W., & Wafula, J. M. (2021). Achieving Standard Software Security in Agile Developments. *ACM International Conference Proceeding Series*. https://doi.org/10.1145/3484399.3484403

Kang, J. J., Dibaei, M., Luo, G., Yang, W., & Zheng, X. (2020). A privacypreserving data inference framework for internet of health things networks. In *2020 IEEE 19th international conference on trust, security and privacy in computing and communications (trustcom)* (pp. 1209–1214). IEEE.

Kang, J. J., Dibaei, M., Luo, G., Yang, W., Haskell-Dowland, P., & Zheng, X. (2021). An energy-efficient and secure data inference framework for internet of health things: A pilot study. *Sensors (Basel)*, 21(1), 312. 10.3390/s2101031233466416

Karaca, K. N., & Cetin, A. (2021). Botnet Attack Detection Using Convolutional Neural Networks in the IoT Environment. *2021 International Conference on Innovations in Intelligent Systems and Applications, INISTA 2021 - Proceedings*. 10.1109/INISTA52262.2021.9548445

Karatas, G., & Akbulut, A. (2018). Survey on access control mechanisms in cloud computing. *Journal of Cyber Security and Mobility*, 1–36.

Karie, N., Sahri, N., Yang, W., Valli, C., & Kebande, V. (2021). A Review of Security Standards and Frameworks for IoT-Based Smart Environments. *IEEE Access*. 10.1109/ACCESS.2021.3109886

Karim, A., Salleh, R., Shiraz, M., Shah, S. A. A., Awan, I., & Anuar, N. B. (2014). Botnet detection techniques: Review, future trends, and issues. *Journal of Zhejiang University: Science C*, 15(11), 943–983. 10.1631/jzus.C1300242

Karn, P. R., Simpson, W. A., & Metzger, P. E. (1995). *The ESP Triple DES Transform*. RFC 1851.

Kasse, J. P., Xu, L., Devrieze, P., & Bai, Y. (2019). Verifying for compliance to data constraints in collaborative business processes. In *Collaborative networks and digital transformation: 20th IFIP WG 5.5 working conference on virtual enterprises, pro-ve 2019, Turin, Italy, september 23–25, 2019, proceedings 20* (pp. 259–270). 10.1007/978-3-030-28464-0_23

Keshta, I., & Odeh, A. (2021). Security and privacy of electronic health records: Concerns and challenges. *Egyptian Informatics Journal*, 22(2), 177–183. 10.1016/j.eij.2020.07.003

Khaim, R., Naz, S., Abbas, F., Iqbal, N., & Hamayun, M. (2016). A Review of Security Integration Technique in Agile Software Development. *International Journal of Software Engineering and Its Applications*, 7(3), 49–68. Advance online publication. 10.5121/ijsea.2016.7304

Khaing, M. S., Thant, Y. M., Tun, T., Htwe, C. S., & Thwin, M. M. S. (2020). IoT Botnet Detection Mechanism Based on UDP Protocol. *2020 IEEE Conference on Computer Applications, ICCA 2020*. 10.1109/ICCA49400.2020.9022832

Khan, H., Hengartner, U., & Vogel, D. (2016). Targeted mimicry attacks on touch input based implicit authentication schemes. *MobiSys 2016 - Proceedings of the 14th Annual International Conference on Mobile Systems, Applications, and Services*, 387–398. 10.1145/2906388.2906404

Khan, H., Hengartner, U., & Vogel, D. (2019). Usability and security perceptions of implicit authentication: Convenient, secure, sometimes annoying. *SOUPS 2015 - Proceedings of the 11th Symposium on Usable Privacy and Security*, 225–239. https://www.usenix.org/conference/soups2015/proceedings/presentation/khan

Khanh, Q. V., Hoai, N. V., Manh, L. D., Le, A. N., & Jeon, G. (2022). Wireless Communication Technologies for IoT in 5G: Vision, Applications, and Challenges. *Wireless Communications and Mobile Computing*, 2022, 1–12. Advance online publication. 10.1155/2022/3229294

Khan, J. A. (2024). Role-based access control (rbac) and attribute-based access control (abac). In *Improving security, privacy, and trust in cloud computing* (pp. 113–126). IGI Global. 10.4018/979-8-3693-1431-9.ch005

Khan, R., McLaughlin, K., Laverty, D., & Sezer, S. (2017). *Stride-based threat modeling for cyber-physical systems*. *2017 IEEE pes innovative smart grid technologies conference Europe (isgt-europe)*.

Khattab, A., M. (2021). Comprehensive Study of Attacks and Cryptographic Measures for Internet of Things Devices. *The Journal of Scientific and Engineering Research*, 8, 174–188.

Ki-Aries, D., & Faily, S. (2017). *Persona-centred information security awareness*. Academic Press.

Kim, T. H., & Reeves, D. (2020). A survey of domain name system vulnerabilities and attacks. *Journal of Surveillance, Security, and Safety*, 34–60. https://doi.org/10.20517/jsss.2020.14

Kim, J., Park, J., & Lee, J.-H. (2023). *Analysis of recent iiot security technology trends in a smart factory environment. 2023 international conference on artificial intelligence in information and communication (icaiic).*

Kim, K. H., Kim, K., & Kim, H. K. (2022). Stride-based threat modeling and dread evaluation for the distributed control system in the oil refinery. *ETRI Journal*, 44(6), 991–1003. 10.4218/etrij.2021-0181

Kim, Y. E., Kim, M. G., & Kim, H. (2022). Detecting IoT Botnet in 5G Core Network Using Machine Learning. *Computers, Materials & Continua*, 72(3), 4467–4488. 10.32604/cmc.2022.026581

Koblitz, N. (1987). Elliptic Curve Cryptosystems. *Mathematics of Computation*, 48(177), 203–209. 10.1090/S0025-5718-1987-0866109-5

Kocher, P. C., Jaffe, J., & Jun, B. (1999). Differential Power Analysis. In *Advances in Cryptology - CRYPTO '99, 19th Annual International Cryptology Conference, Santa Barbara, CA, USA, August 15-19, 1999, Proceedings*. Springer.

Kokoris Kogias, E., Malkhi, D., & Spiegelman, A. (2020). Asynchronous Distributed Key Generation for Computationally-Secure Randomness, Consensus, and Threshold Signatures. *Proceedings of the 2020 ACM SIGSAC Conference on Computer and Communications Security*, 1751-1767. 10.1145/3372297.3423364

Kong, H., Lu, L., Yu, J., Chen, Y., Kong, L., & Li, M. (2019). Fingerpass: Finger gesture-based continuous user authentication for smart homes using commodity wifi. *Proceedings of the International Symposium on Mobile Ad Hoc Networking and Computing (MobiHoc)*, 201–210. 10.1145/3323679.3326518

Kont, K.-R. (2024). *Libraries and cyber security: the importance of the human factor in preventing cyber attacks*. Academic Press.

Koroniotis, N., Moustafa, N., Sitnikova, E., & Turnbull, B. (2019). Towards the development of realistic botnet dataset in the Internet of Things for network forensic analytics: Bot-IoT dataset. *Future Generation Computer Systems*, 100, 779–796. 10.1016/j.future.2019.05.041

Krawiecka, K., Birnbach, S., Eberz, S., & Martinovic, I. (2023). BeeHIVE: Behavioral Biometric System Based on Object Interactions in Smart Environments. In *Proceedings of the International Conference on Security and Cryptography* (Vol. 1, Issue 1). Association for Computing Machinery. 10.5220/0012088900003555

Krichen, M., Ammi, M., Mihoub, A., & Abu Al-Haija, Q. (2022). *Short Survey on Using Blockchain Technology in Modern Wireless Networks*. IoT and Smart Grids.

Kulkarni, A. A., Mishra, P. K., Tripathy, B. K., & Panda, M. (2018). A Security Survey on Internet of Things. *International Journal on Computer Science and Engineering*, 6(6), 1227–1233. 10.26438/ijcse/v6i6.12271233

Kumar, A., & Lim, T. J. (2019). EDIMA: Early Detection of IoT Malware Network Activity Using Machine Learning Techniques. *IEEE 5th World Forum on Internet of Things, WF-IoT 2019 - Conference Proceedings*, 289–294. 10.1109/WF-IoT.2019.8767194

Kumar, R., & Agrawal, N. (2023). Analysis of multi-dimensional Industrial IoT (IIoT) data in Edge–Fog–Cloud based architectural frameworks : A survey on current state and research challenges. *Journal of Industrial Information Integration*, 35, 100504. 10.1016/j.jii.2023.100504

Kumar, S., Bhatt, R., & Ganguly, D. G. (2022). *Organizational behaviour*. Academic Guru Publishing House.

Kumar, S., & Jolly, A. (2019). Secure software development by integrating security activities with agile activities. *International Journal of Advanced Science and Technology*, 28(15).

Kuncheva, L. I. (2014). Combining Pattern Classifiers: Methods and Algorithms: Second Edition. In *Combining Pattern Classifiers: Methods and Algorithms: Second Edition* (Vol. 9781118315). John Wiley & Sons. 10.1002/9781118914564

Kusrini, E., Anggarani, I., & Praditya, T. A. (2021). Analysis of Supply Chain Security Management Systems Based on ISO 28001: 2007: Case Study Leather Factory in Indonesia. *2021 IEEE 8th International Conference on Industrial Engineering and Applications (ICIEA)*, 471-477. 10.1109/ICIEA52957.2021.9436705

Kuznetsov, A., Oleshko, I., Tymchenko, V., Lisitsky, K., Rodinko, M., & Kolhatin, A. (2021). Performance analysis of cryptographic hash functions suitable for use in blockchain. *International Journal of Computer Network & Information Security*, 13(2), 1–15. 10.5815/ijcnis.2021.02.01

Kwak, Y., Lee, S., Damiano, A., Vishwanath, A. (2020). *Why do users not report spear phishing emails?* Academic Press.

Langley, A., Chang, W.-T., Mavrogiannopoulos, N., Strombergson, J., & Josefsson, S. (2016). *ChaCha20-Poly1305 Cipher Suites for Transport Layer Security (TLS)*. RFC 7905.

Langner, R. (2011). Stuxnet: Dissecting a Cyberwarfare Weapon. *IEEE Security and Privacy*, 9(3), 49–51. 10.1109/MSP.2011.67

Lata, M., & Kumar, V. (2021). Standards and regulatory compliances for IoT security. *International Journal of Service Science, Management, Engineering, and Technology*, 12(5), 133–147. 10.4018/IJSSMET.2021090109

Lee, S., Abdullah, A., Jhanjhi, N. Z., & Kok, S. H. (2021). Honeypot Coupled Machine Learning Model for Botnet Detection and Classification in IoT Smart Factory – An Investigation. *MATEC Web of Conferences, 335*, 04003. 10.1051/matecconf/202133504003

Lee, I. (2020). Internet of Things (IoT) cybersecurity: Literature review and iot cyber risk management. *Future Internet*, 12(9), 157. Advance online publication. 10.3390/fi12090157

Lee, K., Romzi, P., Hanaysha, J., Alzoubi, H., & Alshurideh, M. (2022). Investigating the impact of benefits and challenges of IOT adoption on supply chain performance and organizational performance: An empirical study in Malaysia. *Uncertain Supply Chain Management*, 10(2), 537–550. 10.5267/j.uscm.2021.11.009

Lefoane, M., Ghafir, I., Kabir, S., & Awan, I. U. (2022). Unsupervised learning for feature selection: A proposed solution for botnet detection in 5g networks. *IEEE Transactions on Industrial Informatics*, 19(1), 921–929. 10.1109/TII.2022.3192044

Le, H. V., & Ngo, Q. D. (2020). V-Sandbox for Dynamic Analysis IoT Botnet. *IEEE Access : Practical Innovations, Open Solutions*, 8, 145768–145786. 10.1109/ACCESS.2020.3014891

Lekssays, A., Landa, L., Carminati, B., & Ferrari, E. (2021). PAutoBotCatcher: A blockchain-based privacy-preserving botnet detector for the Internet of Things. *Computer Networks*, 200, 108512. Advance online publication. 10.1016/j.comnet.2021.108512

Li, Y., Yang, J., Xie, M., Carlson, D., Jang, H. G., & Bian, J. (2015). Comparison of PIN- and pattern-based behavioral biometric authentication on mobile devices. *Proceedings - IEEE Military Communications Conference MILCOM*, 1317–1322. 10.1109/MILCOM.2015.7357627

Liang, G., Xin, J., Wang, Q., Ni, X., & Guo, X. (2022). Research on IoT Forensics System Based on Blockchain Technology. *Security and Communication Networks*, 2022, e4490757. 10.1155/2022/4490757

Liang, X., & Znati, T. (2019). A long short-term memory-enabled framework for DDoS detection. *2019 IEEE Global Communications Conference, GLOBECOM 2019 - Proceedings*. 10.1109/GLOBECOM38437.2019.9013450

Liang, Y., Samtani, S., Guo, B., & Yu, Z. (2020). Behavioral Biometrics for Continuous Authentication in the Internet-of-Things Era: An Artificial Intelligence Perspective. *IEEE Internet of Things Journal*, 7(9), 9128–9143. 10.1109/JIOT.2020.3004077

Lien, C. W., & Vhaduri, S. (2023). Challenges and Opportunities of Biometric User Authentication in the Age of IoT: A Survey. *ACM Computing Surveys*, 56(1), 1–37. 10.1145/3603705

Lindmeier, A., & Mühling, A. (2020). *Keeping secrets: K-12 students' understanding of cryptography*. Paper presented at the 15th Workshop on Primary and Secondary Computing Education. 10.1145/3421590.3421630

Lin, P. H., Lai, S. H., Lin, S. C., & Su, H. J. (2013). On secrecy rate of the generalized artificial-noise assisted secure beamforming for wiretap channels. *IEEE Journal on Selected Areas in Communications*, 31(9), 1728–1740. 10.1109/JSAC.2013.130907

Li, S., Iqbal, M., & Saxena, N. (2022). Future industry internet of things with zero-trust security. *Information Systems Frontiers*, 1–14. 10.1007/s10796-021-10199-5

Litvinov, E., Llumiguano, H., Santofimia, M. J., Del Toro, X., Villanueva, F. J., & Rocha, P. (2023). Code integrity and confidentiality: An active data approach for active and healthy ageing. *Sensors (Basel)*, 23(10), 4794. 10.3390/s2310479437430708

Liu, C., Clark, G. D., & Lindqvist, J. (2017). Where usability and security go hand-in-hand: Robust gesture-based authentication for mobile systems. *Conference on Human Factors in Computing Systems - Proceedings*, 374–386. 10.1145/3025453.3025879

Liu, C., Yang, L. L., & Wang, W. (2017). Secure spatial modulation with a full-duplex receiver. *IEEE Wireless Communications Letters*, 6(6), 838–841. 10.1109/LWC.2017.2748591

Liu, D., Ma, W., Shao, S., Shen, Y., & Tang, Y. (2015). Performance analysis of TDD reciprocity calibration for massive MU-MIMO systems with ZF beamforming. *IEEE Communications Letters*, 20(1), 113–116. 10.1109/LCOMM.2015.2499283

Liu, J., Liu, S., & Zhang, S. (2019). Detection of IoT botnet based on deep learning. *Chinese Control Conference, CCC*, 8381–8385. 10.23919/ChiCC.2019.8866088

Liu, J., Zhang, J., Zhang, Q., Wang, J., & Sun, X. (2021). Secrecy rate analysis for reconfigurable intelligent surface-assisted MIMO communications with statistical CSI. *China Communications*, 18(3), 52–62. 10.23919/JCC.2021.03.005

Liu, S., Dibaei, M., Tai, Y., Chen, C., Zhang, J., & Xiang, Y. (2019). Cyber vulnerability intelligence for internet of things binary. *IEEE Transactions on Industrial Informatics*, 16(3), 2154–2163. 10.1109/TII.2019.2942800

Liu, Z., Thapa, N., Shaver, A., Roy, K., Yuan, X., & Khorsandroo, S. (2020). Anomaly detection on Iot network intrusion using machine learning. *2020 International Conference on Artificial Intelligence, Big Data, Computing and Data Communication Systems, IcABCD 2020 - Proceedings*, 3–7. 10.1109/icABCD49160.2020.9183842

Locke, D. (2010). Mq telemetry transport (mqtt) v3. 1 protocol specification. *IBM DeveloperWorks Technical Library, 15*.

López, L., Burgués, X., Martínez-Fernández, S., Vollmer, A. M., Behutiye, W., Karhapää, P., Franch, X., Rodríguez, P., & Oivo, M. (2022). Quality measurement in agile and rapid software development: A systematic mapping. *Journal of Systems and Software*, 186, 111187. Advance online publication. 10.1016/j.jss.2021.111187

Loukil, F., Ghedira-Guegan, C., Boukadi, K., & Benharkat, A. N. (2018). *Towards an end-to-end IoT data privacy-preserving framework using blockchain technology.* Paper presented at the Web Information Systems Engineering–WISE 2018: 19th International Conference, Dubai, United Arab Emirates. 10.1007/978-3-030-02922-7_5

Lounis, K. & Zulkernine, M. (2021). More Lessons: Analysis of PUF-based Authentication Protocols for IoT. *IACR Cryptology ePrint Archive*, 1509.

Lounis, K., & Zulkernine, M. (2022). Lessons Learned: Analysis of PUF-based Authentication Protocols for IoT. *Digital Threats : Research and Practice*, 4(2), 1–33. 10.1145/3487060

Lusthaus, J., Bruce, M., & Phair, N. (2020). *Mapping the geography of cybercrime: A review of indices of digital offending by country.* Paper presented at the 2020 IEEE European Symposium on Security and Privacy Workshops (EuroS&PW). 10.1109/EuroSPW51379.2020.00066

Lysenko, S., Bobrovnikova, K., Savenko, O., & Shchuka, R. (2020). Technique for cyberattack detection based on DNS traffic analysis. *CEUR Workshop Proceedings*, 2732, 171–182.

Maalem Lahcen, R. A., Caulkins, B., Mohapatra, R., & Kumar, M. (2020). *Review and insight on the behavioral aspects of cybersecurity.* Academic Press.

Maes, R. (2013). *Physically Unclonable Functions - Constructions, Properties and Applications.* Springer. 10.1007/978-3-642-41395-7

Mahela, O. P., Khosravy, M., Gupta, N., Khan, B., Alhelou, H. H., Mahla, R., & Siano, P. (2020). Comprehensive overview of multi-agent systems for controlling smart grids. *CSEE Journal of Power and Energy Systems*, 8(1), 115–131.

Mahfouz, A., Hamdy, A., Eldin, M. A., & Mahmoud, T. M. (2024). B2auth: A contextual fine-grained behavioral biometric authentication framework for real-world deployment. *Pervasive and Mobile Computing, 99*, 101888. 10.1016/j.pmcj.2024.101888

Mahmoud, Q. H., & Ullah, I. (2020). A two-level flow-based anomalous activity detection system for IoT networks. *Electronics (Basel)*, 9(3), 530. Advance online publication. 10.3390/electronics9030530

Majumder, A., Goswami, J., Ghosh, S., Shrivastawa, R., Mohanty, S. P., & Bhattacharyya, B. K. (2017). Pay-Cloak: A Biometric Back Cover for Smartphone with Tokenization Principle for Cashless Payment. *IEEE Consumer Electronics Magazine*, 6(2), 78–88. 10.1109/MCE.2016.2640739

Makhdoom, I., Abolhasan, M., Lipman, J., Liu, R. P., & Ni, W. (2019). Anatomy of Threats to the Internet of Things. *IEEE Communications Surveys and Tutorials*, 21(2), 1636–1675. 10.1109/COMST.2018.2874978

Malatji, M. (2023). *Management of enterprise cyber security: A review of iso/iec 27001: 2022. 2023 international conference on cyber management and engineering (cymaen).*

Mamdouh, M., Awad, A. I., Khalaf, A. A. M., & Hamed, H. F. A. (2021). Authentication and Identity Management of IoHT Devices: Achievements, Challenges, and Future Directions. *Computers & Security*, 111, 102491. 10.1016/j.cose.2021.102491

Manoj, K. (2021). *Power system automation: Build secure power system scada & smart grids.* Notion Press.

Marchand, C., Bossuet, L., Mureddu, U., Bochard, N., Cherkaoui, A., & Fischer, V. (2018). Implementation and Characterization of a Physical Unclonable function for IoT: A Case Study with the TERO-PUF. *IEEE Transactions on Computer-Aided Design of Integrated Circuits and Systems*, 37(1), 97–109. 10.1109/TCAD.2017.2702607

Marchetti, K., & Bodily, P. (2022). *John the ripper: An examination and analysis of the popular hash cracking algorithm. 2022 intermountain engineering, technology and computing (ietc)*.

Marinos, L., & Lourenço, M. (2018). ENISA Threat Landscape Report 2018 15 Top Cyberthreats and Trends. In *European Union Agency For Network and Information Security*. Issue January., 10.2824/622757

Marotta, A., & Madnick, S. (2021). Convergence and divergence of regulatory compliance and cybersecurity. *Issues in Information Systems*, 22(1).

Marquardson, J., & Elnoshokaty, A. (2020). Skills, certifications, or degrees: What companies demand for entry-level cybersecurity jobs. *Information Systems Education Journal*, 18(1), 22–28.

Martin, K. (2020). *Cryptography: The key to digital security, how it works, and why it matters*. WW Norton & Company.

Masud, M., Gaba, G. S., Choudhary, K., Hossain, M. S., Alhamid, M. F., & Muhammad, G. (2022). Lightweight and Anonymity-Preserving User Authentication Scheme for IoT-Based Healthcare. *IEEE Internet of Things Journal*, 9(4), 2649–2656. 10.1109/JIOT.2021.3080461

Matrosov, A., Rodionov, E., Harley, D., & Malcho, J. (2010, September). Stuxnet under the microscope. *ESET*, LLC, 6.

Matthias. (2015). *Using 'fwknop' on OpenWRT*. Academic Press.

McBride, M., Carter, L., & Warkentin, M. (2012). *Exploring the role of individual employee characteristics and personality on employee compliance with cybersecurity policies*. Academic Press.

McDermott, C. D., Majdani, F., & Petrovski, A. V. (2018). Botnet Detection in the Internet of Things using Deep Learning Approaches. *Proceedings of the International Joint Conference on Neural Networks, 2018-July*. 10.1109/IJCNN.2018.8489489

Mehraj, S., & Banday, M. T. (2020). Establishing a zero trust strategy in cloud computing environment. *Proceedings of the 2020 International Conference on Computer Communication and Informatics (ICCCI)*. 10.1109/ICCCI48352.2020.9104214

Meidan, Y., Bohadana, M., Mathov, Y., Mirsky, Y., Shabtai, A., Breitenbacher, D., & Elovici, Y. (2018). N-BaIoT-Network-based detection of IoT botnet attacks using deep autoencoders. *IEEE Pervasive Computing*, 17(3), 12–22. 10.1109/MPRV.2018.03367731

Memos, V. (2020). *AI-Powered Honeypots for Enhanced IoT Botnet Detection*. Academic Press.

Merkow, M. S. (2021). *Practical Security for Agile and DevOps*. 10.1201/9781003265566

Mesleh, R., Engelken, S., Sinanovic, S., & Haas, H. (2008, August). Analytical SER calculation of spatial modulation. In *2008 IEEE 10th International Symposium on Spread Spectrum Techniques and Applications* (pp. 272-276). IEEE. 10.1109/ISSSTA.2008.55

Mesleh, R., & Alhassi, A. (2018). *Space modulation techniques*. John Wiley & Sons. 10.1002/9781119375692

Mesleh, R., Haas, H., Ahn, C. W., & Yun, S. (2006, October). Spatial modulation-a new low complexity spectral efficiency enhancing technique. In *2006 First International Conference on Communications and Networking in China* (pp. 1-5). IEEE. 10.1109/CHINACOM.2006.344658

Mihelič, A., Vrhovec, S., & Hovelja, T. (2023). Agile Development of Secure Software for Small and Medium-Sized Enterprises. *Sustainability (Basel)*, 15(1), 801. Advance online publication. 10.3390/su15010801

Miller, V. S. (1985). Use of Elliptic Curves in Cryptography. In *Advances in Proceedings of Cryptology - CRYPTO '85*. Springer.

Miller, B., Alabama, N., & College, C. (2020). a Multi-Layer Approach To Detecting and Preventing IoT-Based Botnet Attacks. *Issues in Information Systems*, 21(3), 168–178. 10.48009/3_iis_2020_168-178

Mirzaee, P. H., Shojafar, M., Cruickshank, H., & Tafazolli, R. (2022). Smart grid security and privacy: From conventional to machine learning issues (threats and countermeasures). *IEEE Access : Practical Innovations, Open Solutions*, 10, 52922–52954. 10.1109/ACCESS.2022.3174259

Mittelbach, A., & Fischlin, M. (2021). *The theory of hash functions and random oracles. An Approach to Modern Cryptography*. Springer Nature. 10.1007/978-3-030-63287-8

Mnasri, S. (2022). *A new secure architecture for the access control of resources in iot networks. 2022 international conference on emerging trends in computing and engineering applications (etcea)*. IEEE.

Mohamad Noor, M., & Hassan, W. H. (2019). Current research on Internet of Things (IoT) security: A survey. *Computer Networks*, 148, 283–294. 10.1016/j.comnet.2018.11.025

Mondal, S., & Bours, P. (2017). A study on continuous authentication using a combination of keystroke and mouse biometrics. *Neurocomputing, 230*, 1–22. 10.1016/j.neucom.2016.11.031

Moore, W., & Frye, S. (2020). Review of hipaa, part 2: Limitations, rights, violations, and role for the imaging technologist. *Journal of Nuclear Medicine Technology*, 48(1), 17–23. 10.2967/jnmt.119.22782731604900

Moosavi, J., Naeni, L. M., Fathollahi-Fard, A. M., & Fiore, U. (2021). Blockchain in supply chain management: A review, bibliometric, and network analysis. *Environmental Science and Pollution Research International*, 1–15. 10.1007/s11356-021-13094-333638786

Moreno Escobar, J. J., Morales Matamoros, O., Tejeida Padilla, R., Lina Reyes, I., & Quintana Espinosa, H. (2021). A comprehensive review on smart grids: Challenges and opportunities. *Sensors (Basel)*, 21(21), 6978. 10.3390/s2121697834770285

Morris, M. G., Venkatesh, V., & Ackerman, P. (2005). *Gender and age differences in employee decisions about new technology: An extension to the theory of planned behavior*. Academic Press.

Moudoud, H., Khoukhi, L., & Cherkaoui, S. (2020). Prediction and detection of fdia and DDoS attacks in 5g enabled iot. *IEEE Network*, 35(2), 194–201. 10.1109/MNET.011.2000449

Moustafa, N., Turnbull, B., & Choo, K. K. R. (2019). An ensemble intrusion detection technique based on proposed statistical flow features for protecting network traffic of the Internet of Things. *IEEE Internet of Things Journal*, 6(3), 4815–4830. 10.1109/JIOT.2018.2871719

Moyon, F., Almeida, P., Riofrio, D., Mendez, D., & Kalinowski, M. (2020). Security Compliance in Agile Software Development: A Systematic Mapping Study. *Proceedings - 46th Euromicro Conference on Software Engineering and Advanced Applications, SEAA 2020*. 10.1109/SEAA51224.2020.00073

Moyón, F., Méndez, D., Beckers, K., & Klepper, S. (2020). How to Integrate Security Compliance Requirements with Agile Software Engineering at Scale? Lecture Notes in Computer Science (Including Subseries Lecture Notes in Artificial Intelligence and Lecture Notes in Bioinformatics), 12562 LNCS. 10.1007/978-3-030-64148-1_5

Mrakovic, I., & Vojinović, R. (2020). Evaluation of Montenegrin Seafarer's Awareness of Cyber Security. *Transactions on Maritime Science*, 9(2). Advance online publication. 10.7225/toms.v09.n02.005

Muaaz, M., & Mayrhofer, R. (2017). Smartphone-Based Gait Recognition: From Authentication to Imitation. *IEEE Transactions on Mobile Computing*, 16(11), 3209–3221. 10.1109/TMC.2017.2686855

Mudgerikar, A., Sharma, P., & Bertino, E. (2020). Edge-Based Intrusion Detection for IoT Devices. *ACM Transactions on Management Information Systems*, 11(4), 1–21. Advance online publication. 10.1145/3382159

Mughal, A. A. (2018). The art of cybersecurity: Defense in depth strategy for robust protection. *International Journal of Intelligent Automation and Computing, 1*(1), 1–20.

Mukherjee, A. (2020). Energy-Efficient Beam Management in Millimeter-Wave Shared Spectrum. *IEEE Wireless Communications*, 27(5), 38–43. 10.1109/MWC.001.2000037

Mukherjee, A., Fakoorian, S. A. A., Huang, J., & Swindlehurst, A. L. (2014). Principles of physical layer security in multiuser wireless networks: A survey. *IEEE Communications Surveys and Tutorials*, 16(3), 1550–1573. 10.1109/SURV.2014.012314.00178

Mukkamala, S., Sung, A., & Abraham, A. (2005). Enhancing Computer Security with Smart Technology. *Cyber security challenges: Designing efficient intrusion detection systems and antivirus tools,* 125-163.

Mussa, Younis, Hu, & Abdunabi. (2023). *Analyzing Software Supply Chain Security Risks in Industrial Control System Protocols: An OpenSSF Scorecard Approach.* .10.1109/DSA59317.2023.00044

Myridakis, D., Myridakis, P., & Kakarountas, A. (2020). Intrusion Detection and Botnet Prevention Circuit for IoT Devices. *SEEDA-CECNSM 2020 - 5th South-East Europe Design Automation, Computer Engineering, Computer Networks, and Social Media Conference*, 2020–2023. 10.1109/SEEDA-CECNSM49515.2020.9221789

Myridakis, D., Myridakis, P., & Kakarountas, A. (2021). A power dissipation monitoring circuit for intrusion detection and botnet prevention on IoT devices. *Computation (Basel, Switzerland)*, 9(2), 1–11. 10.3390/computation9020019

Myyry, L., Siponen, M., Pahnila, S., Vartiainen, T., & Vance, A. (2009). *What levels of moral reasoning and values explain adherence to information security rules? An empirical study.* Academic Press.

Nafees, M. N., Saxena, N., Cardenas, A., Grijalva, S., & Burnap, P. (2023). Smart grid cyber-physical situational awareness of complex operational technology attacks: A review. *ACM Computing Surveys*, 55(10), 1–36. 10.1145/3565570

Nägele, S., Korn, L., & Matthes, F. (2023). Adoption of Information Security Practices in Large-Scale Agile Software Development: A Case Study in the Finance Industry. *ACM International Conference Proceeding Series*. 10.1145/3600160.3600170

Naik, N. (2017). *Choice of effective messaging protocols for iot systems: Mqtt, coap, amqp and http. 2017 IEEE international systems engineering symposium (isse).*

Namrita Gummadi, A., Napier, J. C., & Abdallah, M. (2024). XAI-IoT: An Explainable AI Framework for Enhancing Anomaly Detection in IoT Systems. *IEEE Access : Practical Innovations, Open Solutions*, 12, 71024–71054. 10.1109/ACCESS.2024.3402446

Nasir, Hassan, Mohd Zaini, & Nordin. (2022). *Blockchain Trust Impact in Agribusiness Supply Chain: A Survey, Challenges, and Directions.* 10.1109/TENSYMP54529.2022.9864418

Nasir, Mohd Zaini, Hassan, & Nordin. (2024). *Blockchain-Based Supply Chain for a Sustainable Digital Society: Security Challenges and Proposed Approach.* 10.1007/978-981-99-9589-9_4

Naveed, K., Wu, H., & Abusaq, A. (2020). Dytokinesis: A Cytokinesis-Inspired Anomaly Detection Technique for IoT Devices. *Proceedings - Conference on Local Computer Networks, LCN*, 2020-Novem, 373–376. 10.1109/LCN48667.2020.9314856

Naveed, K., & Wu, H. (2020). Poster: A Semi-Supervised Framework to Detect Botnets in IoT Devices. *IFIP Networking 2020 Conference and WorkshopsNetworking*, 2020, 649–651.

Navruzov, E., & Kabulov, A. (2022). *Detection and analysis types of DDoS attack*. Paper presented at the 2022 IEEE International IOT, Electronics and Mechatronics Conference (IEMTRONICS). 10.1109/IEMTRONICS55184.2022.9795729

Nazir, A., He, J., Zhu, N., Wajahat, A., Ullah, F., Qureshi, S., Ma, X., & Pathan, M. S. (2024). Collaborative threat intelligence: Enhancing iot security through blockchain and machine learning integration. *Journal of King Saud University. Computer and Information Sciences*, 36(2), 101939. 10.1016/j.jksuci.2024.101939

Nebbione, G., & Calzarossa, M. C. (2020). *Security of IoT application layer protocols: Challenges and findings*. Academic Press.

Neirotti, P., De Marco, A., Cagliano, A. C., Mangano, G., & Scorrano, F. (2014). Current trends in Smart City initiatives: Some stylised facts. *Cities (London, England)*, 38, 25–36. 10.1016/j.cities.2013.12.010

Neupane, A., Saxena, N., Maximo, J. O., Kana, R. (2016). *Neural markers of cybersecurity: An fMRI study of phishing and malware warnings*. Academic Press.

Neupane, K., Haddad, R., & Chen, L. (2018). *Next generation firewall for network security: A survey*. Paper presented at the SoutheastCon 2018. 10.1109/SECON.2018.8478973

Ngo, Q. D., Nguyen, H. T., Tran, H. A., & Nguyen, D. H. (2021). IoT Botnet detection is based on the integration of static and dynamic vector features. *ICCE 2020 - 2020 IEEE 8th International Conference on Communications and Electronics*, 540–545. 10.1109/ICCE48956.2021.9352145

Ngo, Q. D., Nguyen, H. T., Nguyen, V. D., Dinh, C. M., Phung, A. T., & Bui, Q. T. (2021). Adversarial Attack and Defense on Graph-based IoT Botnet Detection Approach. *3rd International Conference on Electrical, Communication and Computer Engineering, ICECCE 2021*, 12–13. 10.1109/ICECCE52056.2021.9514255

Ngo, Q. D., Nguyen, H. T., Tran, H. A., Pham, N. A., & Dang, X. H. (2021). Toward an approach using graph-theoretic for IoT botnet detection. *ACM International Conference Proceeding Series, 1*. 10.1145/3468691.3468714

Nguyen, H. T., Ngo, Q. D., & Le, V. H. (2018). IoT Botnet Detection Approach Based on PSI graph and DGCNN classifier. *2018 IEEE International Conference on Information Communication and Signal Processing, ICICSP 2018, Icsp*, 118–122. 10.1109/ICICSP.2018.8549713

Nguyen, K., Proença, H., & Alonso-Fernandez, F. (2024). Deep Learning for Iris Recognition: A Survey. *ACM Computing Surveys*, 56(9), 1–35. Advance online publication. 10.1145/3651306

Nguyen, V. L., Lin, P. C., Cheng, B. C., Hwang, R. H., & Lin, Y. D. (2021). Security and privacy for 6G: A survey on prospective technologies and challenges. *IEEE Communications Surveys and Tutorials*, 23(4), 2384–2428. 10.1109/COMST.2021.3108618

Nielsen, H., Mogul, J., Masinter, L. M., Fielding, R. T., Gettys, J., Leach, P. J., & Berners-Lee, T. (1999). *Hypertext Transfer Protocol – HTTP/1.1*. RFC 2616.

Nifakos, S., Chandramouli, K., Nikolaou, C. K., Papachristou, P., Koch, S., Panaousis, E., & Bonacina, S. J. S. (2021). Influence of human factors on cyber security within healthcare organisations. *Systematic Reviews*, 21(15), 5119.34372354

Nir, Y. (2015). *ChaCha20, Poly1305, and Their Use in the Internet Key Exchange Protocol (IKE) and IPsec*. RFC 7634.

Nir, Y., & Langley, A. (2015). *ChaCha20 ans Poly1305 for IETF Protocols*. RFC 7539.

NIST. (2019). *Developing Cyber Resilient Systems A Systems Security Engineering Approach SP800-160*. NIST. 10.6028/NIST.SP.800-160v2

NIST. (2024). *National Institute of Standards and Technology (Nist)*. https://www.nist.gov/

NIST-FIPS. (2008). *Federal Information Processing Standards.* NIST-FIPS. https://www.nist.gov/itl/fips-general -information

Norris, W., Rodgers, J. B., Blazek, C., Hewage, T., & Kobza, B. (2020). A Market-Oriented Approach to Supply Chain Security. *Security Challenges, 16*(4), 65–81. https://www.jstor.org/stable/26976258

Noura, H. N., Melki, R., & Chehab, A. (2021). Efficient data confidentiality scheme for 5g wireless NOMA communications. *Journal of Information Security and Applications*, 58, 102781. 10.1016/j.jisa.2021.102781

Nozari, H., & Ghahremani Nahr, J. (2022). The Impact of Blockchain Technology and The Internet of Things on the Agile and Sustainable Supply Chain. *International Journal of Innovation in Engineering*, 2(2), 33–41. Advance online publication. 10.59615/ijie.2.2.33

Nurgazina, J., Pakdeetrakulwong, U., Moser, T., & Reiner, G. (2021). Distributed Ledger Technology Applications in Food Supply Chains: A Review of Challenges and Future Research Directions. *Sustainability (Basel)*, 13(8), 4206. 10.3390/su13084206

Obaid, H. S., & Abeed, E. (2020). *DoS and DDoS attacks at OSI layers.* Academic Press.

Odeh, A., Elleithy, K., Alshowkan, M., & Abdelfattah, E. (2013). *Quantum key distribution by using public key algorithm (RSA).* Paper presented at the Third International Conference on Innovative Computing Technology (INTECH 2013). 10.1109/INTECH.2013.6653697

Odeh, A., Keshta, I. & Abdelfattah, E. (2020). *Efficient detection of phishing websites using multilayer perceptron.* Academic Press.

Odeh, A. (2020). Taxonomy of Cluster-Based Target Tracking System in Wireless Sensor Networks. *International Journal of Sensors, Wireless Communications and Control*, 10(5), 649–658. 10.2174/2210327910999200606230150

Oggier, F., & Hassibi, B. (2011). The secrecy capacity of the MIMO wiretap channel. *IEEE Transactions on Information Theory*, 57(8), 4961–4972. 10.1109/TIT.2011.2158487

Öğütçü, G., Testik, Ö. M., & Chouseinoglou, O. (2016). *Analysis of personal information security behavior and awareness.* Academic Press.

Ohm, M., Plate, H., Sykosch, A., & Meier, M. (2020). *Backstabber's knife collection: A review of open source software supply chain attacks.* Paper presented at the Detection of Intrusions and Malware, and Vulnerability Assessment: 17th International Conference, DIMVA 2020, Lisbon, Portugal. 10.1007/978-3-030-52683-2_2

Ohm, M., Sykosch, A., & Meier, M. (2020). Towards detection of software supply chain attacks by forensic artifacts. *Proceedings of the 15th international conference on availability, reliability and security.* 10.1145/3407023.3409183

Okafor, C., Schorlemmer, T. R., Torres-Arias, S., & Davis, J. C. (2022). SoK: Analysis of Software Supply Chain Security by Establishing Secure Design Properties. In *Proceedings of the 2022 ACM Workshop on Software Supply Chain Offensive Research and Ecosystem Defenses (SCORED'22).* Association for Computing Machinery. 10.1145/3560835.3564556

Ometov, A., Bezzateev, S., Mäkitalo, N., Andreev, S., Mikkonen, T., & Koucheryavy, Y. (2018). Multi-factor authentication: A survey. *Cryptography*, 2(1), 1–31. 10.3390/cryptography2010001

Omitaomu, O. A., & Niu, H. (2021). Artificial intelligence techniques in smart grid: A survey. *Smart Cities*, 4(2), 548–568. 10.3390/smartcities4020029

Omitola, T., & Wills, G. (2018). Towards mapping the security challenges of the Internet of Things (IoT) supply chain. *Procedia Computer Science*, 126, 441–450. 10.1016/j.procs.2018.07.278

Omolara, A. E., Alabdulatif, A., Abiodun, O. I., Alawida, M., Alabdulatif, A., Alshoura, W. H., & Arshad, H. (2022). The internet of things security: A survey encompassing unexplored areas and new insights. *Computers & Security*, 112, 102494. 10.1016/j.cose.2021.102494

Onyebueke, A. E., Emmanuel, S., Mu'awuya Dalhatu, A. S. A., Mazadu, L. E. I. J., Ifeanyi, O. C., & Eyitayo, A. (2023). *Data privacy and compliance in cloud-based iot systems: A security assessment.* Paper presented at the African-European Regional Governance & Development Conference.

Or, E. (2009). *Security Development Lifecycle for Agile Development.* Development. https://www.blackhat.com/presentations/bh-dc-10/Sullivan_Bryan/BlackHat-DC-2010-Sullivan-SDL-Agile-wp.pdf

Oracle. (2022). What is the Internet of Things (IoT)? https://www.oracle.com/in/internet-of-things/what-is-iot

Orlando, M., Estebsari, A., Pons, E., Pau, M., Quer, S., Poncino, M., Bottaccioli, L., & Patti, E. (2021). A smart meter infrastructure for smart grid iot applications. *IEEE Internet of Things Journal*, 9(14), 12529–12541. 10.1109/JIOT.2021.3137596

Ott, D., & Peikert, C. (2019). Identifying research challenges in post quantum cryptography migration and cryptographic agility. *arXiv preprint arXiv:1909.07353.*

Owusu, E., Han, J., Das, S., Perrig, A., & Zhang, J. (2012). ACCessory: Password inference using accelerometers on smartphones. *HotMobile 2012 - 13th Workshop on Mobile Computing Systems and Applications*, 1. 10.1145/2162081.2162095

Oyetoyan, T. D., Jaatun, M. G., & Cruzes, D. S. (2017). A Lightweight Measurement of Software Security Skills, Usage and Training Needs in Agile Teams. *International Journal of Secure Software Engineering*, 8(1), 1–27. Advance online publication. 10.4018/IJSSE.2017010101

Ozcelik, M., Chalabianloo, N., & Gur, G. (2017). Software-Defined Edge Defense Against IoT-Based DDoS. *IEEE CIT 2017 - 17th IEEE International Conference on Computer and Information Technology*, 308–313. 10.1109/CIT.2017.61

Paganini, P. (2018). *Puerto rico electric power authority (prepa) hacked over the weekend.*https://www.cyberdefensemagazine.com/puerto-rico

Palagashvili, L., & Suarez, P. (2020). *Technology startups and industry-specific regulations.* Fraser Institute.

Palmo, Y., Tanimoto, S., Sato, H., & Kanai, A. (2022). Optimal Federation Method for Embedding Internet of Things in Software-Defined Perimeter. *IEEE Consumer Electronics Magazine*, 12(5), 68–75. 10.1109/MCE.2022.3207862

Panajotovic, B., Jankovic, M., & Odadzic, B. (2011). Ict and smart grid. In *2011 10th international conference on telecommunication in modern satellite cable and broadcasting services (telsiks)* (Vol. 1, pp. 118–121). 10.1109/TELSKS.2011.6112018

Panda, M., Mousa, A. A. A., & Hassanien, A. E. (2021). Developing an Efficient Feature Engineering and Machine Learning Model for Detecting IoT-Botnet Cyber Attacks. *IEEE Access : Practical Innovations, Open Solutions*, 9, 91038–91052. 10.1109/ACCESS.2021.3092054

Paolini, A., Scardaci, D., Liampotis, N., Spinoso, V., Grenier, B., & Chen, Y. (2020). Authentication, authorization, and accounting. *Towards Interoperable Research Infrastructures for Environmental and Earth Sciences: A Reference Model Guided Approach for Common Challenges*, 247–271.

Papadimitriou, A., Nomikos, K., Psarakis, M., Aerabi, E., & Hély, D. (2020). You can detect but you cannot hide: Fault Assisted Side Channel Analysis on Protected Software-based Block Ciphers. In *IEEE International Symposium on Defect and Fault Tolerance in VLSI and Nanotechnology Systems, DFT 2020.* IEEE.

Pappu, R. S. (2001). *Physical One-Way Functions*. PhD thesis, Massachusetts Institute of Technology.

Parkouk, S., Torabi, M., & Shokrollahi, S. (2022). Secrecy performance analysis of amplify-and-forward relay cooperative networks with simultaneous wireless information and power transfer. *Computer Communications*, 193, 365–377. 10.1016/j.comcom.2022.07.020

Pasquier, T., Singh, J., Powles, J., Eyers, D., Seltzer, M., & Bacon, J. (2018). Data provenance to audit compliance with privacy policy in the Internet of Things. *Personal and Ubiquitous Computing*, 22(2), 333–344. 10.1007/s00779-017-1067-4

Pathak, A. K., Saguna, S., Mitra, K., & Åhlund, C. (2021). Anomaly detection using machine learning to discover sensor tampering in iot systems. In *ICC 2021-IEEE international conference on communications* (pp. 1–6). 10.1109/ICC42927.2021.9500825

Pattinson, M., Butavicius, M., Parsons, K., McCormac, A., & Calic, D. (2015). *Factors that influence information security behavior: An Australian web-based study*. Paper presented at the Human Aspects of Information Security, Privacy, and Trust: Third International Conference, HAS 2015. 10.1007/978-3-319-20376-8_21

Pavleska, T., Aranha, H., Masi, M., & Sellitto, G. P. (2020). Drafting a cybersecurity framework profile for smart grids in eu: a goal-based methodology. In *Dependable computing-edcc 2020 workshops: Ai4rails, dreams, dsogri, serene 2020, munich, germany, september 7, 2020, proceedings 16* (pp. 143–155). Academic Press.

Peng, G., Zhou, G., Nguyen, D. T., Qi, X., Yang, Q., & Wang, S. (2017). Continuous Authentication With Touch Behavioral Biometrics and Voice on Wearable Glasses. *IEEE Transactions on Human-Machine Systems*, 47(3), 404–416. 10.1109/THMS.2016.2623562

Petar, R. (2020). Cyber risk at the edge: Current and future trends on cyber risk analytics and artificial intelligence in the industrial Internet of things and industry 4.0 supply chains. *Cybersecurity*, 3(1), 13. Advance online publication. 10.1186/s42400-020-00052-8

Peyman, M., Copado, P. J., Tordecilla, R. D., Martins, L. D. C., Xhafa, F., & Juan, A. A. (2021). Edge computing and iot analytics for agile optimization in intelligent transportation systems. *Energies*, 14(19), 6309. Advance online publication. 10.3390/en14196309

Phelps, R. P. (2022). *On security best practices, systematic analysis of security advice, and internet of things devices*. Carleton University., 10.22215/etd/2022-15268

Pliatsios, D., Sarigiannidis, P., Lagkas, T., & Sarigiannidis, A. G. (2020). A survey on scada systems: Secure protocols, incidents, threats and tactics. *IEEE Communications Surveys and Tutorials*, 22(3), 1942–1976. 10.1109/COMST.2020.2987688

Poehlmann, N., Caramancion, K. M., Tatar, I., Li, Y., Barati, M., Merz, T. J. A. i. S., Networks,, . . . ESCS'20. (2021). The organizational cybersecurity success factors: an exhaustive literature review. 377-395.

Popescu, T. M., Popescu, A., & Prostean, G. (2021). Leaders' perspectives on iot security risk management strategies in surveyed organizations relative to iotsrm2. *Applied Sciences (Basel, Switzerland)*, 11(19), 9206. Advance online publication. 10.3390/app11199206

Popoola, S. I., Adebisi, B., Ande, R., Hammoudeh, M., & Atayero, A. A. (2021). Memory-efficient deep learning for botnet attack detection in IoT networks. *Electronics (Basel)*, 10(9), 4944–4956. 10.3390/electronics10091104

Portmann, C., & Renner, R. (2022). Security in quantum cryptography. *Reviews of Modern Physics*, 94(2), 025008. 10.1103/RevModPhys.94.025008

Pourmirza, Z., & Srivastava, A. (2020). Cybersecurity analysis for the communication protocol in smart grids. In *2020 IEEE 8th international conference on smart energy grid engineering (sege)* (pp. 58–63). IEEE.

Prathyusha, J. R. V. S. L. P., Jyothi, V. E., Jhansi, V., Chowdary, N. S., Madhuri, A., & Sindhura, S. (2023). Securing the Cyber Supply Chain: A Risk-based Approach to Threat Assessment and Mitigation. *2023 4th International Conference on Electronics and Sustainable Communication Systems (ICESC),* 508-513. 10.1109/ICESC57686.2023.10193255

Priya, R., Utsav, A., Zabeen, A., & Abhishek, A. (2021). Multiple Security Threats with Its Solution in Internet of Things (IoT). *2021 4th International Conference on Recent Developments in Control, Automation & Power Engineering (RDCAPE),* 221–223. 10.1109/RDCAPE52977.2021.9633759

Priyadarshini, I., Kumar, R., Sharma, R., Singh, P. K., & Satapathy, S. C. (2021). Identifying cyber insecurities in trustworthy space and energy sector for smart grids. *Computers & Electrical Engineering,* 93, 107204. 10.1016/j.compeleceng.2021.107204

Proctor, R. W., & Chen, J. (2015). *The role of human factors/ergonomics in the science of security: decision making and action selection in cyberspace.* Academic Press.

Prokofiev, A. O., Smirnova, Y. S., & Surov, V. A. (2018). A method to detect Internet of Things botnets. *Proceedings of the 2018 IEEE Conference of Russian Young Researchers in Electrical and Electronic Engineering, ElConRus 2018,* 2018-Janua, 105–108. https://doi.org/10.1109/EIConRus.2018.8317041

Pulfrey, J., & Hossain, M. S. (2022). Zoom gesture analysis for age-inappropriate internet content filtering. *Expert Systems with Applications,* 199(March), 116869. 10.1016/j.eswa.2022.116869

Putman, C. G. J., Abhishta, & Nieuwenhuis, L. J. (2018). Business model of a botnet. *2018 26th Euromicro International Conference on Parallel, Distributed and Network-Based Processing (PDP).* https://doi.org/10.1109/pdp2018.2018.0007

Qadir, S., & Quadri, S. M. K. (2016). Information availability: An insight into the most important attribute of information security. *Journal of Information Security,* 7(3), 185–194. 10.4236/jis.2016.73014

Qaqish, E., Aranki, A., Al-Haija, Q. A., & Qusef, A. (2023). Security Comparison of Blockchain and Cloud-based Identity Management: Considering the Scalability Problem. *2023 International Conference on Inventive Computation Technologies (ICICT),* 1078-1085. 10.1109/ICICT57646.2023.10134231

Qishun, Z. (2023). Enhancing reliability of iot adoption in e-government: A conceptual framework. *Journal of DigitainabilityRealism & Mastery,* 2(05), 38–44.

Qiu, J., Tian, Z., Du, C., Zuo, Q., Su, S., & Fang, B. (2020). *A survey on access control in the age of internet of things.* Academic Press.

Qiu, J., Tian, Z., Du, C., Zuo, Q., Su, S., & Fang, B. (2020). A survey on access control in the age of internet of things. *IEEE Internet of Things Journal,* 7(6), 4682–4696. 10.1109/JIOT.2020.2969326

Qose, S., & Zoltán, R. (2024). Supply Chain in the Context of 5G Technology Security and Legal Aspects. *2024 IEEE 22nd World Symposium on Applied Machine Intelligence and Informatics (SAMI),* 143-148. 10.1109/SAMI60510.2024.10432844

Radoglou Grammatikis, P. I., Sarigiannidis, P. G., & Moscholios, I. D. (2019). Securing the Internet of Things: Challenges, threats and solutions. *Internet of Things : Engineering Cyber Physical Human Systems,* 5, 41–70. 10.1016/j.iot.2018.11.003

Raghunandan, K., Gagnani, L., Amarendra, K., & Santhosh Krishna, B. (2020). Product key activation for software products using Collatz Conjuncture and asymmetric key cryptography. *Materials Today: Proceedings.* https://doi. . MATPR, 907org/10.1016/J

Ragothaman, K., Wang, Y., Rimal, B., & Lawrence, M. (2023). Access Control for IoT: A Survey of Existing Research, Dynamic Policies and Future Directions. *Sensors (Basel),* 23(4), 1–24. 10.3390/s2304180536850403

Rahman, T., Rohan, R., Pal, D., & Kanthamanon, P. (2021). *Human factors in cybersecurity: a scoping review.* Paper presented at the 12th International Conference on Advances in Information Technology. 10.1145/3468784.3468789

Rahmantyo, D. T., Erfianto, B., & Satrya, G. B. (2021). *Deep Residual CNN for Preventing Botnet Attacks on The Internet of Things.* Advance online publication. 10.1109/IC2IE53219.2021.9649314

Raj, S., & Walia, N. K. (2020). *A study on metasploit framework: A pen-testing tool. 2020 international conference on computational performance evaluation (compe).*

Ramachandra, M. N., Srinivasa Rao, M., Lai, W. C., Parameshachari, B. D., Ananda Babu, J., & Hemalatha, K. L. (2022). An efficient and secure big data storage in cloud environment by using triple data encryption standard. *Big Data and Cognitive Computing*, 6(4), 101. 10.3390/bdcc6040101

Ramteke, B., & Dongre, S. (2022). IoT Based Smart Automated Poultry Farm Management System. *2022 10th International Conference on Emerging Trends in Engineering and Technology-Signal and Information Processing (ICETET-SIP-22)*, 1-4.

RankRed. (n.d.). *17 fastest supercomputers in the world — in 2024.* Retrieved from https://www.rankred.com/fastest-supercomputers-in-the-world/

Rapuzzi, R., & Repetto, M. (2018). Building situational awareness for network threats in fog/edge computing: Emerging paradigms beyond the security perimeter model. *Future Generation Computer Systems*, 85, 235–249. 10.1016/j.future.2018.04.007

Raschke, W., Zilli, M., Baumgartner, P., Loinig, J., Steger, C., & Kreiner, C. (2014). Supporting evolving security models for an agile security evaluation. *2014 IEEE 1st International Workshop on Evolving Security and Privacy Requirements Engineering, ESPRE 2014 - Proceedings.* 10.1109/ESPRE.2014.6890525

Rashed Mohassel, R., Fung, A., Mohammadi, F., & Raahemifar, K. (2014). A survey on advanced metering infrastructure. *International Journal of Electrical Power & Energy Systems*, 63, 473–484. 10.1016/j.ijepes.2014.06.025

Ravidas, S., Lekidis, A., Paci, F., & Zannone, N. (2019). Access control in Internet-of-Things. Academic Press.

Razzaq, M. A., Gill, S. H., Qureshi, M. A., & Ullah, S. (2020). Security issues in the Internet of Things (IoT): A comprehensive study. *Mechanical Systems and Signal Processing*, 136, 106436.

Reddivari, S. (2022). An Agile Framework for Security Requirements: A Preliminary Investigation. *Proceedings - 2022 IEEE 46th Annual Computers, Software, and Applications Conference, COMPSAC 2022.* 10.1109/COMPSAC54236.2022.00076

Rescorla, E. (2018). *The Transport Layer Security (TLS) Protocol Version 1.3.* RFC 8446.

Riisom, K. R., Hubel, M. S., Alradhi, H. M., Nielsen, N. B., Kuusinen, K., & Jabangwe, R. (2018). Software security in agile software development: A literature review of challenges and solutions. *ACM International Conference Proceeding Series, Part F147763.* 10.1145/3234152.3234189

Rindell, K., Hyrynsalmi, S., & Leppänen, V. (2018). Aligning security objectives with agile software development. *ACM International Conference Proceeding Series, Part F147763.* 10.1145/3234152.3234187

Ring, M., Landes, D., & Hotho, A. (2018). *Detection of slow port scans in flow-based network traffic.* Academic Press.

Rivest, R. L., Shamir, A., & Adleman, L. M. (1978). A Method for Obtaining Digital Signatures and Public-Key Cryptosystems. *Communications of the ACM*, 21(2), 120–126. 10.1145/359340.359342

Rizvi, S., Campbell, S., & Alden, K. (2020). *Why compliance is needed for internet of things? In 2020 international conference on software security and assurance (icssa).* IEEE.

Rodriguez-Gomez, R. A., Macia-Fernandez, G., & Garcia-Teodoro, P. (2013). Survey and taxonomy of botnet research through life-cycle. *ACM Computing Surveys*, 45(4), 1–33. Advance online publication. 10.1145/2501654.2501659

Rogowski, W. (2013). *The right approach to data loss prevention*. Academic Press.

Rohan, R., Funilkul, S., Pal, D., & Chutimaskul, W. (2021). *Understanding of human factors in cybersecurity: A systematic literature review*. Paper presented at the 2021 International Conference on Computational Performance Evaluation (ComPE). 10.1109/ComPE53109.2021.9752358

Rohan, R., Funilkul, S., Pal, D., & Thapliyal, H. (2021). *Humans in the loop: cybersecurity aspects in the consumer IoT context*. Academic Press.

Rose Sebastian, S., & Babu, B. (2022). Are we Cyber aware? A cross sectional study on the prevailing Cyber practices among adults from Thiruvalla, Kerala. *International Journal of Community Medicine and Public Health*, 10(1), 235. 10.18203/2394-6040.ijcmph20223550

Rose, Borchert, Mitchell, & Connelly. (2020). *Zero Trust Architecture: NIST SP 800-207*. 10.6028/NIST.SP.800-207

Rosenthal, G., Kdosha, O. E., Cohen, K., Freund, A., Bartik, A., & Ron, A. (2020). ARBA: Anomaly and Reputation Based Approach for Detecting Infected IoT Devices. *IEEE Access : Practical Innovations, Open Solutions*, 8, 145751–145767. 10.1109/ACCESS.2020.3014619

Rosenzweig, A., Steinberg, Y., & Shamai, S. (2005). On channels with partial channel state information at the transmitter. *IEEE Transactions on Information Theory*, 51(5), 1817–1830. 10.1109/TIT.2005.846422

Rührmair, U., & Holcomb, D. E. (2014). PUFs at a glance. In *Design, Automation & Test in Europe Conference & Exhibition, DATE 2014*. European Design and Automation Association.

Sabou, M., Biffl, S., Einfalt, A., Krammer, L., Kastner, W., & Ekaputra, F. J. (2020). Semantics for cyber-physical systems: A cross-domain perspective. *Semantic Web*, 11(1), 115–124. 10.3233/SW-190381

Sadhu, P. K., Yanambaka, V. P., & Abdelgawad, A. (2022). Internet of things: Security and solutions survey. *Sensors (Basel)*, 22(19), 7433. 10.3390/s2219743336236531

Sadhwani, S., Modi, U. K., Muthalagu, R., & Pawar, P. M. (2024). Smartsentry: Cyber threat intelligence in industrial iot. *IEEE Access : Practical Innovations, Open Solutions*, 12, 34720–34740. 10.1109/ACCESS.2024.3371996

Sagirlar, G., Carminati, B., & Ferrari, E. (2018). AutoBotCatcher: Blockchain-based P2P botnet detection for the Internet of Things. *Proceedings - 4th IEEE International Conference on Collaboration and Internet Computing, CIC 2018*, 1–8. 10.1109/CIC.2018.00-46

Sajjad, S. M., Yousaf, M., Afzal, H., & Mufti, M. R. (2020). EMUD: Enhanced manufacturer usage description for IoT botnet prevention on home wifi routers. *IEEE Access : Practical Innovations, Open Solutions*, 8, 164200–164213. 10.1109/ACCESS.2020.3022272

Samonas, S., & Coss, D. (2014). The cia strikes back: Redefining confidentiality, integrity and availability in security. *Journal of Information System Security*, 10(3).

Santos, H., Oliveira, A., Soares, L., Satis, A., & Santos, A. (2021). Information Security Assessment and Certification within Supply Chains. In *Proceedings of the 16th International Conference on Availability, Reliability and Security (ARES '21)*. Association for Computing Machinery. 10.1145/3465481.3470078

Saqib, M., & Moon, A. H. (2023). A Systematic Security Assessment and Review of Internet of Things in the Context of Authentication. *Computers & Security*, 125, 103053. 10.1016/j.cose.2022.103053

Sayed, A., Kinlany, S., Zaki, A., & Mahfouz, A. (2023). VeriFace: Defending against Adversarial Attacks in Face Verification Systems. *Computers, Materials & Continua*, 76(3), 3151–3166. 10.32604/cmc.2023.040256

Schmidt, N., Zöller, B., & Rosenkranz, C. (2016). *The clash of cultures in information technology outsourcing relationships: An institutional logics perspective.* Paper presented at the Shared Services and Outsourcing: A Contemporary Outlook: 10th Global Sourcing Workshop 2016, Val d'Isère, France.

Schniederjans, D. G., Curado, C., & Khalajhedayati, M. (2020). Supply chain digitization trends: An integration of knowledge management. *International Journal of Production Economics*, 220, 107439. 10.1016/j.ijpe.2019.07.012

Schroff, F., Kalenichenko, D., & Philbin, J. (2015). FaceNet: A unified embedding for face recognition and clustering. *Proceedings of the IEEE Computer Society Conference on Computer Vision and Pattern Recognition*, 815–823. 10.1109/CVPR.2015.7298682

Seals, T. (2022). *Zero-Trust For All: A Practical Guide.* Available: https://docs.microsoft.com/en-us/azure/active-directory/conditional-access/overview

Seaman, J. (2020). *Pci dss: an integrated data security standard guide.* Apress. 10.1007/978-1-4842-5808-8

Sedjelmaci, H., Senouci, S. M., & Taleb, T. (2017). An accurate security game for low-resource IoT devices. *IEEE Transactions on Vehicular Technology*, 66(10), 9381–9393. 10.1109/TVT.2017.2701551

Sedrati, A., Mezrioui, A., & Ouaddah, A. (2022). Iot governance: A state of the art and a comparative analysis. In *2022 13th international conference on information and communication systems (icics)* (pp. 76–81). IEEE. 10.1109/ICICS55353.2022.9811219

Sedrati, A., Mezrioui, A., & Ouaddah, A. (2023). Iot-gov: A structured framework for internet of things governance. *Computer Networks*, 233, 109902. Advance online publication. 10.1016/j.comnet.2023.109902

Sektor, C. E. R. T. (2023). *The attack against danish, critical infrastructure.* https://sektorcert.dk/wp-content/uploads/2023/11/SektorCERT-The-attack-against-Danish-critical-infrastructure-TLP-CLEAR.pdf

Sengupta, J., Ruj, S., & Das Bit, S. (2020). A Comprehensive Survey on Attacks, Security Issues and Blockchain Solutions for IoT and IIoT. *Journal of Network and Computer Applications, 149*, 102481. 10.1016/j.jnca.2019.102481

Senthilkumar, K., & Easwaramoorthy, S. (2017). A Survey on Cyber Security awareness among college students in Tamil Nadu. *IOP Conference Series. Materials Science and Engineering*, 263(4), 042043. 10.1088/1757-899X/263/4/042043

Shafiei, H., Khonsari, A., Derakhshi, H., & Mousavi, P. (2014). Detection and mitigation of sinkhole attacks in wireless sensor networks. *Journal of Computer and System Sciences*, 80(3), 644–653. 10.1016/j.jcss.2013.06.016

Shafik, W. (2023b). Cyber security perspectives in public spaces: Drone case study. *Handbook of Research on Cybersecurity Risk in Contemporary Business Systems.* 10.4018/978-1-6684-7207-1.ch004

Shafik, W. (2023c). Making Cities Smarter: IoT and SDN Applications, Challenges, and Future Trends. *Opportunities and Challenges of Industrial IoT in 5G and 6G Networks.* 10.4018/978-1-7998-9266-3.ch004

Shafik, W. (2023a). A Comprehensive Cybersecurity Framework for Present and Future Global Information Technology Organizations. In *Effective Cybersecurity Operations for Enterprise-Wide Systems* (pp. 56–79). IGI Global., 10.4018/978-1-6684-9018-1.ch002

Shafiq, M., Tian, Z., Bashir, A. K., Du, X., & Guizani, M. (2021). CorrAUC: A Malicious Bot-IoT Traffic Detection Method in IoT Network Using Machine-Learning Techniques. *IEEE Internet of Things Journal*, 8(5), 3242–3254. 10.1109/JIOT.2020.3002255

Shah, T., & Venkatesan, S. (2019). A method to secure IoT devices against botnet attacks. In *Lecture Notes in Computer Science (including subseries Lecture Notes in Artificial Intelligence and Lecture Notes in Bioinformatics): Vol. 11519 LNCS.* Springer International Publishing. 10.1007/978-3-030-23357-0_3

Shah, K., Sharma, M., & Joshi, S. (2023). Digital Supply Chain Management: A Comprehensive Review Using Cluster Analysis, with Future Directions and Open Challenges. *International Journal of Supply and Operations Management, 10*(3), 337–364.

Shahraki, A., & Haugen, Ø. (2018). Social ethics in internet of things: An outline and review. *2018 IEEE Industrial Cyber-Physical Systems (ICPS)*, 509–516.

Sha, K., Yang, T. A., Wei, W., & Davari, S. (2020). A survey of Edge Computing-based designs for IOT Security. *Digital Communications and Networks, 6*(2), 195–202. 10.1016/j.dcan.2019.08.006

Shamsi, K., Li, M., Plaks, K., Fazzari, S., Pan, D. Z., & Jin, Y. (2019). *IP Protection and Supply Chain Security through Logic Obfuscation: A Systematic Overview. ACM Trans. Des. Autom. Electron. Syst., 24*(6), Article 65. 10.1145/3342099

Shannon, C. E. (1949). Communication Theory of Secrecy Systems. *The Bell System Technical Journal, 28*(4), 656–715. 10.1002/j.1538-7305.1949.tb00928.x

Shao, R., Perera, P., Yuen, P. C., & Patel, V. M. (2022). Federated Generalized Face Presentation Attack Detection. *IEEE Transactions on Neural Networks and Learning Systems.* Advance online publication. 10.1109/TNNLS.2022.317231635609091

Sharafi, M., Fotouhi-Ghazvini, F., Shirali, M., & Ghassemian, M. (2019). A low power cryptography solution based on chaos theory in wireless sensor nodes. *IEEE Access : Practical Innovations, Open Solutions, 7*, 8737–8753. 10.1109/ACCESS.2018.2886384

Sharma, Goar, Kuri, & Chowdhary. (2023). *Supply Chain Management Using Blockchain Security Enhancement.* 10.1007/978-981-19-9888-1_15

Shelby, Z., Hartke, K., & Bormann, C. (2014). *The Constrained Application Protocol (CoAP).* RFC 7252.

Shen, W., Qin, J., Yu, J., Hao, R., Hu, J., & Ma, J. (2019). Data integrity auditing without private key storage for secure cloud storage. *IEEE Transactions on Cloud Computing, 9*(4), 1408–1421. 10.1109/TCC.2019.2921553

Shi, C., Wang, Y., Chen, Y., Saxena, N., & Wang, C. (2020). WearID: Low-Effort Wearable-Assisted Authentication of Voice Commands via Cross-Domain Comparison without Training. In *ACM International Conference Proceeding Series* (Vol. 1, Issue 1). Association for Computing Machinery. 10.1145/3427228.3427259

Shi, C., Liu, J., Liu, H., & Chen, Y. (2017). Smart User authentication through actuation of daily activities leveraging wifi-enabled IoT. *Proceedings of the International Symposium on Mobile Ad Hoc Networking and Computing (MobiHoc), Part F1291*, 1–10. 10.1145/3084041.3084061

Shi, C., Liu, J., Liu, H., & Chen, Y. (2021). WiFi-Enabled User Authentication through Deep Learning in Daily Activities. *ACM Transactions on Internet of Things, 2*(2), 1–25. 10.1145/3448738

Shi, D., Tao, D., Wang, J., Yao, M., Wang, Z., Chen, H., & Helal, S. (2021). Fine-Grained and Context-Aware Behavioral Biometrics for Pattern Lock on Smartphones. *Proceedings of the ACM on Interactive, Mobile, Wearable and Ubiquitous Technologies, 5*(1), 1–30. 10.1145/3448080

Shi, Z., Yao, W., Li, Z., Zeng, L., Zhao, Y., Zhang, R., Tang, Y., & Wen, J. (2020). Artificial intelligence techniques for stability analysis and control in smart grids: Methodologies, applications, challenges and future directions. *Applied Energy, 278*, 115733. 10.1016/j.apenergy.2020.115733

Shrestha, M., Johansen, C., Noll, J., & Roverso, D. (2020). A methodology for security classification applied to smart grid infrastructures. *International Journal of Critical Infrastructure Protection*, 28, 100342. 10.1016/j.ijcip.2020.100342

Shu, F., Wang, Z., Chen, R., Wu, Y., & Wang, J. (2018). Two high-performance schemes of transmit antenna selection for secure spatial modulation. *IEEE Transactions on Vehicular Technology*, 67(9), 8969–8973. 10.1109/TVT.2018.2844401

Siddiqi, M. A., Pak, W., & Siddiqi, M. A. (2022). *A study on the psychology of social engineering-based cyberattacks and existing countermeasures*. Academic Press.

Sigl, G., Gross, M., & Pehl, M. (2018). Where Technology Meets Security: Key Storage and Data Separation for System-on-Chips. In *44th IEEE European Solid State Circuits Conference, ESSCIRC 2018*. IEEE. 10.1109/ESSCIRC.2018.8494319

Silva, S., Lima, S. M. L., Pinheiro, R. P., Abreu, L. M. S., Lima, R. D. T., & Fernandes, S. M. M. (2023). *Antivirus Solution to IoT Malware Detection with Authorial Next-Generation Sandbox*. Academic Press.

Singh, J., & Singh, J. (2021). *A survey on machine learning-based malware detection in executable files*. Academic Press.

Singh, N., Patel, P., & Datta, S. (2021). A survey on security and human-related challenges in agile software deployment. *Proceedings - 2021 International Conference on Computational Science and Computational Intelligence, CSCI 2021*. 10.1109/CSCI54926.2021.00365

Singh, P., Tapaswi, S., & Gupta, S. (2020). Malware detection in pdf and office documents. 10.1080/19393555.2020.1723747

Singla, T., Anandayuvaraj, D., Kalu, K. G., Schorlemmer, T. R., & Davis, J. C. (2023). An Empirical Study on Using Large Language Models to Analyze Software Supply Chain Security Failures. In *Proceedings of the 2023 Workshop on Software Supply Chain Offensive Research and Ecosystem Defenses (SCORED '23)*. Association for Computing Machinery. 10.1145/3605770.3625214

Sinha, S. R., Park, Y., Sinha, S. R., & Park, Y. (2017). Dealing with security, privacy, access control, and compliance. *Building an Effective IoT Ecosystem for Your Business*, 155-176.

Sinha, S., & Arora, D. Y. (2020). Ethical hacking: the story of a white hat hacker. *International Journal of Innovative Research in Computer Science & Technology*.

Siniosoglou, I., Radoglou-Grammatikis, P., Efstathopoulos, G., Fouliras, P., & Sarigiannidis, P. (2021). A unified deep learning anomaly detection and classification approach for smart grid environments. *IEEE Transactions on Network and Service Management*, 18(2), 1137–1151. 10.1109/TNSM.2021.3078381

Sisinni, E., Saifullah, A., Han, S., Jennehag, U., & Gidlund, M. (2018). Industrial internet of things: Challenges, opportunities, and directions. *IEEE Transactions on Industrial Informatics*, 14(11), 4724–4734. 10.1109/TII.2018.2852491

Sivasankari, N., & Kamalakkannan, S. (2022). *Detection and prevention of man-in-the-middle attack in iot network using regression modeling*. Academic Press.

Smith, M., & Hans, M. (2004). Sensor-Enhanced Authentication Token for Dynamic Identity Management Sensor-Enhanced Authentication Token for Dynamic Identity Management. *Hp*.

Sobb, T., Turnbull, B., & Moustafa, N. (2020). Supply Chain 4.0: A Survey of Cyber Security Challenges, Solutions and Future Directions. *Electronics (Basel)*, 9(11), 1864. 10.3390/electronics9111864

Solis, W. V., Marcelo Parra-Ullauri, J., & Kertesz, A. (2024). Exploring the Synergy of Fog Computing, Blockchain, and Federated Learning for IoT Applications: A Systematic Literature Review. *IEEE Access : Practical Innovations, Open Solutions*, 12, 68015–68060. 10.1109/ACCESS.2024.3398034

Somsuk, K., & Thakong, M. (2020). Authentication system for e-certificate by using RSA's digital signature. *TELKOM-NIKA*, 18(6), 2948–2955. 10.12928/telkomnika.v18i6.17278

Sonia, A. S., & Banati, H. (2014). FISA-XP: An Agile-based Integration of Security Activities with Extreme Programming. *Software Engineering Notes*, 39(3). Advance online publication. 10.1145/2597716.2597728

Spathoulas, G., Giachoudis, N., Damiris, G. P., & Theodoridis, G. (2019). Collaborative blockchain-based detection of distributed denial of service attacks based on Internet of things botnets. *Future Internet*, 11(11), 226. Advance online publication. 10.3390/fi11110226

Sriram, S., Vinayakumar, R., Alazab, M., & Soman, K. P. (2020). Network flow-based IoT botnet attack detection using deep learning. *IEEE INFOCOM 2020 - IEEE Conference on Computer Communications Workshops, INFOCOM WK-SHPS 2020*, 189–194. 10.1109/INFOCOMWKSHPS50562.2020.9162668

Stafford, V. (2020). Zero trust architecture. *NIST Special Publication, 800*, 207.

Stoyanova, M., Nikoloudakis, Y., Panagiotakis, S., Pallis, E., & Markakis, E. (2020). A Survey on the Internet of Things (IoT) Forensics: Challenges, Approaches and Open Issues. *IEEE Communications Surveys & Tutorials*. 10.1109/COMST.2019.2962586

Stylios, I., Chatzis, S., Thanou, O., & Kokolakis, S. (2023). Continuous authentication with feature-level fusion of touch gestures and keystroke dynamics to solve security and usability issues. *Computers & Security*, 132, 103363. 10.1016/j.cose.2023.103363

Subahi, A., & Theodorakopoulos, G. (2018). *Ensuring compliance of IoT devices with their Privacy Policy Agreement.* Paper presented at the 2018 IEEE 6th International Conference on Future Internet of Things and Cloud (FiCloud). 10.1109/FiCloud.2018.00022

Sudheera, K. L. K., Divakaran, D. M., Singh, R. P., & Gurusamy, M. (2021). ADEPT: Detection and Identification of Correlated Attack Stages in IoT Networks. *IEEE Internet of Things Journal*, 8(8), 6591–6607. 10.1109/JIOT.2021.3055937

Suh, G. E., & Devadas, S. (2007). Physical Unclonable Functions for Device Authentication and Secret Key Generation. In *Proceedings of the 44th Design Automation Conference, DAC 2007*. IEEE.

Sun, Z., Quan, Z., Yu, S., Zhang, L., & Mao, D. (2024). A Knowledge-driven Framework for Software Supply Chain Security Analysis. In *Proceedings of the 2024 8th International Conference on Control Engineering and Artificial Intelligence (CCEAI '24)*. Association for Computing Machinery. 10.1145/3640824.3640866

Swarna Sugi, S. S., & Ratna, S. R. (2020). Investigation of machine learning techniques in an intrusion detection system for IoT network. *Proceedings of the 3rd International Conference on Intelligent Sustainable Systems, ICISS 2020*, 1164–1167. 10.1109/ICISS49785.2020.9315900

Syed, D., Refaat, S. S., & Bouhali, O. (2020). Privacy preservation of data-driven models in smart grids using homomorphic encryption. *Information (Basel)*, 11(7), 357. 10.3390/info11070357

Syed, N. F., Shah, S. W., Shaghaghi, A., Anwar, A., Baig, Z., & Doss, R. (2022). Zero Trust Architecture (ZTA): A Comprehensive Survey. *IEEE Access : Practical Innovations, Open Solutions*, 10, 57143–57179. 10.1109/ACCESS.2022.3174679

Szymonik, A., & Stanisławski, R. (2022). *Supply Chain Security: How to Support Safety and Reduce Risk in Your Supply Chain Process*. Productivity Press.

Tabassum, K., Ibrahim, A., & El Rahman, S. A. (2019). Security Issues and Challenges in IoT. *2019 International Conference on Computer and Information Sciences (ICCIS)*, 1–5. 10.1109/ICCISci.2019.8716460

Taigman, Y., Yang, M., Ranzato, M., & Wolf, L. (2014). DeepFace: Closing the gap to human-level performance in face verification. *Proceedings of the IEEE Computer Society Conference on Computer Vision and Pattern Recognition*, 1701–1708. 10.1109/CVPR.2014.220

Takebayashi, T., Tsuda, H., Hasebe, T., & Masuoka, R. (2010). *Data loss prevention technologies*. Academic Press.

Talab, H. R., & Flayyih, H. H. (2023). An empirical study to measure the impact of information technology governance under the control objectives for information and related technologies on financial performance. *International Journal of Professional Business Review*, 8(4), 25.

Tambe, A., Aung, Y. L., Sridharan, R., Ochoa, M., Tippenhauer, N. O., Shabtai, A., & Elovici, Y. (2019). Detection of threats to IoT devices using scalable VPN-forwarded honeypots. *Proceedings of the Ninth ACM Conference on Data and Application Security and Privacy*. 10.1145/3292006.3300024

Tandon, A., & Nayyar, A. (2019). *A comprehensive survey on ransomware attack: A growing havoc cyberthreat*. Academic Press.

Tankard, C. (2016). What the gdpr means for businesses. *Network Security*, 2016(6), 5–8. 10.1016/S1353-4858(16)30056-3

Tawalbeh, L., Muheidat, F., Tawalbeh, M., & Quwaider, M. (2020). Iot privacy and security: Challenges and solutions. *Applied Sciences (Basel, Switzerland)*, 10(12), 4102. 10.3390/app10124102

Taylor, D., Perrin, T., Wu, T., & Mavrogiannopoulos, N. (2007). *Using the Secure Remote Password (SRP) Protocol for TLS Authentication*. RFC 5054.

Tchórzewski, J. & Jakóbik, A. (2019). Theoretical and experimental analysis of cryptographic hash functions. *Journal of Telecommunications and Information Technology*, 125-133.

Team, N. (n.d.). *IIoT Explained: Examples, Technologies, Benefits and Challenges*. https://www.emqx.com/en/blog/iiot-explained-examples-technologies-benefits-and-challenges

The Rise of Operational Technology: Why Businesses Need to Focus on OT Now More Than Ever. (n.d.). https://www.linkedin.com/pulse/rise-operational-technology-ot-why-businesses-need-focus-padam-kafle/

Thubert, P., Bormann, C., Toutain, L., & Cragie, R. (2017). *IPv6 over Low-Power Wireless Personal Area Network (6LoWPAN) Routing Header*. RFC 8138.

Tianfield, H. (2017). Cyber security situational awareness. *2016 IEEE International Conference on Internet of Things (iThings) and IEEE Green Computing and Communications (GreenCom) and IEEE Cyber, Physical and Social Computing (CPSCom) and IEEE Smart Data (SmartData)*, 782–787. 10.1109/iThings-GreenCom-CPSCom-SmartData.2016.165

Timčenko, V., Rakas, S. B., Kabović, M., & Kabović, A. (2023). Digitalization in power energy sector: Principles of cybersecurity. In *2023 30th international conference on systems, signals and image processing (iwssip)* (pp. 1–5). Academic Press.

Todos, I. (2023). *Ensuring the security of the supply chain through the implementation of ISO 28001.* .10.53486/icspm2023.11

Tolba, A., & Al-Makhadmeh, Z. (2021). A cybersecurity user authentication approach for securing smart grid communications. *Sustainable Energy Technologies and Assessments*, 46, 101284. 10.1016/j.seta.2021.101284

Tolosana, R., Vera-Rodriguez, R., & Fierrez, J. (2020). BioTouchPass: Handwritten Passwords for Touchscreen Biometrics. *IEEE Transactions on Mobile Computing*, 19(7), 1532–1543. 10.1109/TMC.2019.2911506

Toma, C., Boja, C., Popa, M., Doinea, M., & Ciurea, C. (2021). *Viruses, Exploits, Malware and Security Issues on IoT Devices.* Paper presented at the International Conference on Information Technology and Communications Security.

Tøndel, I. A., & Cruzes, D. S. (2022). Continuous software security through security prioritisation meetings. *Journal of Systems and Software*, 194, 111477. Advance online publication. 10.1016/j.jss.2022.111477

Tøndel, I. A., Cruzes, D. S., Jaatun, M. G., & Sindre, G. (2022). Influencing the security prioritisation of an agile software development project. *Computers & Security*, 118, 102744. Advance online publication. 10.1016/j.cose.2022.102744

Tøndel, I. A., Jaatun, M. G., Cruzes, D. S., & Williams, L. (2019). Collaborative security risk estimation in agile software development. *Information and Computer Security*, 26(4), 508–535. Advance online publication. 10.1108/ICS-12-2018-0138

TOP500. (n.d.). Retrieved from https://www.top500.org/lists/top500/2022/06/

Traditional IT Systems: A Comprehensive Analysis of Their Drawbacks. (n.d.). https://www.linkedin.com/pulse/traditional-systems-comprehensive-analysis-drawbacks-muntakim-pwvqc/

Trajanovski, T., & Zhang, N. (2021). An Automated and Comprehensive Framework for IoT Botnet Detection and Analysis (IoT-BDA). *IEEE Access : Practical Innovations, Open Solutions*, 9, 124360–124383. 10.1109/ACCESS.2021.3110188

Triplett, W. (2022). *Addressing human factors in cybersecurity leadership.* Academic Press.

Tschofenig, H. & Eronen, P. (2005). *Pre-Shared Key Ciphersuites for Transport Layer Security (TLS).* RFC 4279.

Tufail, S., Parvez, I., Batool, S., & Sarwat, A. (2021). A survey on cybersecurity challenges, detection, and mitigation techniques for the smart grid. *Energies*, 14(18), 5894. 10.3390/en14185894

Türksönmez, H., & Ozcanhan, M. (2023). Enhancing Security of RFID-Enabled IoT Supply Chain. *Malaysian Journal of Computer Science*, 36(3), 289–307. 10.22452/mjcs.vol36no3.5

Tyagi, A. K. (2024). Blockchain and artificial intelligence for cyber security in the era of internet of things and industrial internet of things applications. In *Ai and blockchain applications in industrial robotics* (pp. 171–199). IGI Global.

Tyagi, A. K., & Aghila, G. (2011). A Wide Scale Survey on Botnet. *International Journal of Computer Applications*, 34(9), 9–22.

Tzafestas, S. G. (2018). Ethics and law in the internet of things world. *Smart Cities*, 1(1), 98–120.

Tzagkarakis, C., Petroulakis, N., & Ioannidis, S. (2019). Botnet attack detection at the IoT edge is based on sparse representation. *Global IoT Summit, GIoTS 2019 - Proceedings.* 10.1109/GIOTS.2019.8766388

U.S. Institute of Peace. (2021). *Israeli Sabotage of Iran's Nuclear Program.* Available online: https://iranprimer.usip.org/blog/2021/apr/12/israeli-sabotage-iran%E2%80%99s-nuclear-program (accessed on 12 April 2021).

Ullah, I., & Mahmoud, Q. H. (2021). Design and Development of a Deep Learning-Based Model for Anomaly Detection in IoT Networks. *IEEE Access : Practical Innovations, Open Solutions*, 9, 103906–103926. 10.1109/ACCESS.2021.3094024

Ullah, S., Zheng, J., Din, N., Hussain, M. T., Ullah, F., & Yousaf, M. (2023). Elliptic curve cryptography; applications, challenges, recent advances, and future trends: A comprehensive survey. *Computer Science Review*, 47, 100530. 10.1016/j.cosrev.2022.100530

Umam, M. S. (2019). Orientasi Etika dan Cyber Security Awareness (Studi Kasus pada UMKM di Bantul). *Akmenika: Jurnal Akuntansi Dan Manajemen*, 16(2), 2. Advance online publication. 10.31316/akmenika.v16i2.394

Upadhya, A., & Srinivas, B. (2020). *A Survey on different Port Scanning Methods and the Tools used to perform them.* Academic Press.

Valdés-Rodríguez, Y., Hochstetter-Diez, J., Díaz-Arancibia, J., & Cadena-Martínez, R. (2023). Towards the Integration of Security Practices in Agile Software Development: A Systematic Mapping Review. *Applied Sciences (Basel, Switzerland)*, 13(7), 4578. Advance online publication. 10.3390/app13074578

Valero, J. M. J., Sánchez, P. M. S., Lekidis, A., Hidalgo, J. F., Pérez, M. G., Siddiqui, M. S., Celdrán, A. H., & Pérez, G. M. (2022). Design of a Security and Trust Framework for 5G Multi-domain Scenarios. *Journal of Network and Systems Management*, 30(1), 7. 10.1007/s10922-021-09623-7

Van Der Heijden, A., Broasca, C., & Serebrenik, A. (2018). An empirical perspective on security challenges in large-scale agile software development. *International Symposium on Empirical Software Engineering and Measurement*. 10.1145/3239235.3267426

Varadharajan, V., & Bansal, S. (2016). Data security and privacy in the internet of things (iot) environment. *Connectivity Frameworks for Smart Devices: The Internet of Things from a Distributed Computing Perspective*, 261-281.

Vashisth, M., & Verma, S. K. (2023). State of the Art Different Security Challenges, Solutions on Supply Chain: A Review. *2023 International Conference on Innovative Data Communication Technologies and Application (ICIDCA)*, 427-431. 10.1109/ICIDCA56705.2023.10099966

Verma, S., Pokharna, M., & Mishra, V. (2022). Identifying and analyzing risk mitigation strategies in iot devices using light weight symmetric encryption algorithms. *International Journal for Research in Applied Science and Engineering Technology*, 10(9), 638–646. Advance online publication. 10.22214/ijraset.2022.46697

Vhaduri, S., & Poellabauer, C. (2019). Multi-modal biometric-based implicit authentication of wearable device users. *IEEE Transactions on Information Forensics and Security*, 14(12), 3116–3125. 10.1109/TIFS.2019.2911170

Villamizar, H., Kalinowski, M., Viana, M., & Fernández, D. M. (2018). A systematic mapping study on security in agile requirements engineering. *Proceedings - 44th Euromicro Conference on Software Engineering and Advanced Applications, SEAA 2018.* https://doi.org/10.1109/SEAA.2018.00080

Villamizar, H., Kalinowski, M., Garcia, A., & Mendez, D. (2020). An efficient approach for reviewing security-related aspects in agile requirements specifications of web applications. *Requirements Engineering*, 25(4), 439–468. Advance online publication. 10.1007/s00766-020-00338-w

Vishwakarma, R., & Jain, A. K. (2019). A honeypot with a machine learning-based detection framework for defending IoT-based botnet DDoS attacks. *Proceedings of the International Conference on Trends in Electronics and Informatics, ICOEI 2019, Icoei*, 1019–1024. 10.1109/ICOEI.2019.8862720

Von Zezschwitz, E., Dunphy, P., & De Luca, A. (2013). Patterns in the wild: A field study of the usability of pattern and PIN-based authentication on mobile devices. *MobileHCI 2013 - Proceedings of the 15th International Conference on Human-Computer Interaction with Mobile Devices and Services*, 261–270. 10.1145/2493190.2493231

Vuppala, A., Roshan, R. S., Nawaz, S., & Ravindra, J. (2020). An efficient optimization and secured triple data encryption standard using enhanced key scheduling algorithm. *Procedia Computer Science*, 171, 1054–1063. 10.1016/j.procs.2020.04.113

Wang, F., Xiang, X., Cheng, J., & Yuille, A. L. (2017). NormFace: L2 hypersphere embedding for face verification. *MM 2017 - Proceedings of the 2017 ACM Multimedia Conference*, 1041–1049. 10.1145/3123266.3123359

Wang, H., & Sua, S. (2023). *Enhancing supply chain security with automated machine learning.* 10.21203/rs.3.rs-3317886/v1

Wang, M., Santillan, J., & Kuipers, F. (2018). *ThingPot: an interactive Internet-of-Things honeypot.* Academic Press.

Wang, Z., Zhu, H., & Sun, L. (2021). *Social engineering in cybersecurity: Effect mechanisms, human vulnerabilities and attack methods*. Academic Press.

Wang, B., Dou, Y., Sang, Y., Zhang, Y., & Huang, J. (2020). IoTCMal: Towards A Hybrid IoT Honeypot for Capturing and Analyzing Malware. *IEEE International Conference on Communications*. 10.1109/ICC40277.2020.9149314

Wang, C., Wang, Y., Chen, Y., Liu, H., & Liu, J. (2020). User authentication on mobile devices: Approaches, threats and trends. *Computer Networks*, 170, 107118. 10.1016/j.comnet.2020.107118

Wang, H., & Wu, B. (2019). SDN-based hybrid honeypot for attack capture. *Proceedings of 2019 IEEE 3rd Information Technology, Networking, Electronic and Automation Control Conference, ITNEC 2019, Itnec*, 1602–1606. 10.1109/ITNEC.2019.8729425

Wang, L., Bashar, S., Wei, Y., & Li, R. (2015). Secrecy enhancement analysis against unknown eavesdropping in spatial modulation. *IEEE Communications Letters*, 19(8), 1351–1354. 10.1109/LCOMM.2015.2440353

Wang, Y., Gou, G., Liu, C., Cui, M., Li, Z., & Xiong, G. (2021). Survey of security supervision on blockchain from the perspective of technology. *Journal of Information Security and Applications*, 60, 102859. 10.1016/j.jisa.2021.102859

Wang, Y., Han, J. H., & Beynon-Davies, P. (2019). Understanding blockchain technology for future supply chains: A systematic literature review and research agenda. *Supply Chain Management*, 24(1), 62–84. 10.1108/SCM-03-2018-0148

Wazid, M., Das, A. K., Shetty, S., Gope, P., & Rodrigues, J. J. (2021). Security in 5G-enabled Internet of Things communication: Issues, challenges, and future research roadmap. *IEEE Access : Practical Innovations, Open Solutions*, 9, 4466–4489. 10.1109/ACCESS.2020.3047895

Wazzan, M., Algazzawi, D., Bamasaq, O., Albeshri, A., & Cheng, L. (2021). Internet of Things botnet detection approaches: Analysis and recommendations for future research. *Applied Sciences (Basel, Switzerland)*, 11(12), 5713. Advance online publication. 10.3390/app11125713

Weiser, M. (1995). The computer for the 21st century. In *Human-computer interaction* (pp. 993–940). Morgan Kaufmann Publishers Inc.

What Is the Internet of Things (IoT) & Why Is It Important? (n.d.). IMD business school for management and leadership courses. https://www.imd.org/reflections/internet-of-things/

White, G. B., & Sjelin, N. (2022). The nist cybersecurity framework. In *Research anthology on business aspects of cybersecurity* (pp. 39–55). IGI Global. 10.4018/978-1-6684-3698-1.ch003

Williams, T. J. (1994). The purdue enterprise reference architecture. *Computers in Industry*, 24(2-3), 141–158. 10.1016/0166-3615(94)90017-5

Winckless, C., & MacDonald, N. (2021). *Quick Answer: How to Explain Zero Trust Technology to Executives*. Available: www.gartner.com

Winckless, C., & Olyaei, S. (2022). *How to Decipher Zero Trust for Your Business*. Available: www.gartner.com

Woody, C. (2013). *Agile Security – Review of Current Research and Pilot Usage*. SEI White Paper. https://insights.sei.cmu.edu/documents/366/2013_019_001_70236.pdf

Wright, S. A. (2019). *Privacy in iot blockchains: with big data comes big responsibility*. Paper presented at the 2019 IEEE International Conference on Big Data (Big Data). 10.1109/BigData47090.2019.9006341

Wu, C., Xiao, Y., & Yang, P. (2020). Covert information embedded spatial modulation. *IEEE Communications Letters*, 24(11), 2426–2430. 10.1109/LCOMM.2020.3008430

Xia, G., Lin, Y., Liu, T., Shu, F., & Hanzo, L. (2020). Transmit antenna selection and beamformer design for secure spatial modulation with rough CSI of eve. *IEEE Transactions on Wireless Communications*, 19(7), 4643–4656. 10.1109/TWC.2020.2985968

Xiao, L., Wan, X., Lu, X., Zhang, Y., & Wu, D. (2018). IoT Security Techniques Based on Machine Learning: How Do IoT Devices Use AI to Enhance Security? *IEEE Signal Processing Magazine*, 35(5), 41–49. 10.1109/MSP.2018.2825478

Xiao, Y., Jia, Y., Liu, C., Cheng, X., Yu, J., & Lv, W. (2019). Edge computing security: State of the art and challenges. *Proceedings of the IEEE*, 107(8), 1608–1631. 10.1109/JPROC.2019.2918437

Xie, K., Yang, D., Ozbay, K., & Yang, H. (2019). Use of real-world connected vehicle data in identifying high-risk locations based on a new surrogate safety measure. *Accident; Analysis and Prevention*, 125, 311–319. 10.1016/j.aap.2018.07.00229983165

Xing, Y., Shu, H., Zhao, H., Li, D., & Guo, L. (2021). Survey on Botnet Detection Techniques: Classification, Methods, and Evaluation. *Mathematical Problems in Engineering*, 2021, 1–24. Advance online publication. 10.1155/2021/6640499

Xu, W., Shen, Y., Zhang, Y., Bergmann, N., & Hu, W. (2017). Gait-watch: A context-aware authentication system for smart watch based on gait recognition. *Proceedings - 2017 IEEE/ACM 2nd International Conference on Internet-of-Things Design and Implementation, IoTDI 2017 (Part of CPS Week)*, 59–70. 10.1145/3054977.3054991

Xu, Y., Jiang, Y., Yu, L., & Li, J. (2021). Brief industry paper: Catching IoT malware in the wild using HoneyIoT. *Proceedings of the IEEE Real-Time and Embedded Technology and Applications Symposium, RTAS*, 433–436. 10.1109/RTAS52030.2021.00045

Xu, Z., Liu, W., Huang, J., Yang, C., Lu, J., & Tan, H. (2020). Artificial Intelligence for securing IOT services in Edge computing: A survey. *Security and Communication Networks*, 2020, 1–13. 10.1155/2020/8872586

Yamaguchi, S. (2020). Botnet Defense System and Its Basic Strategy against Malicious Botnet. *2020 IEEE International Conference on Consumer Electronics - Taiwan, ICCE-Taiwan 2020*, 1–2. 10.1109/ICCE-Taiwan49838.2020.9258257

Yang, N., Wang, L., Geraci, G., Elkashlan, M., Yuan, J., & Di Renzo, M. (2015). Safeguarding 5G wireless communication networks using physical layer security. *IEEE Communications Magazine*, 53(4), 20–27. 10.1109/MCOM.2015.7081071

Yang, W., Wang, S., Sahri, N. M., Karie, N. M., Ahmed, M., & Valli, C. (2021). Biometrics for internet-of-things security: A review. *Sensors (Basel)*, 21(18), 1–26. 10.3390/s2118616334577370

Yang, Y., & Guizani, M. (2018). Mapping-varied spatial modulation for physical layer security: Transmission strategy and secrecy rate. *IEEE Journal on Selected Areas in Communications*, 36(4), 877–889. 10.1109/JSAC.2018.2824598

Yaokumah, W., Appati, J. K., & Kumah, D. (2021). Machine Learning Methods for Detecting Internet-of-Things (IoT) Malware. *International Journal of Cognitive Informatics and Natural Intelligence*, 15(4), 1–18. 10.4018/IJCINI.286768

Yassin, W., Abdullah, R., Abdollah, M. F., Mas, Z., & Bakhari, F. A. (2019). *An IoT Botnet Prediction Model Using Frequency-based Dependency Graph : Proof-of-concept*. Academic Press.

Yastrebova, A., Kirichek, R., Koucheryavy, Y., Borodin, A., & Koucheryavy, A. (2018). Future Networks 2030: Architecture & Requirements. *2018 10th International Congress on Ultra Modern Telecommunications and Control Systems and Workshops (ICUMT)*. 10.1109/ICUMT.2018.8631208

Yeboah-Ofori, A., Islam, S., Lee, S. W., Shamszaman, Z. U., Muhammad, K., Altaf, M., & Al-Rakhami, M. S. (2021). Cyber Threat Predictive Analytics for Improving Cyber Supply Chain Security. *IEEE Access : Practical Innovations, Open Solutions*, 9, 94318–94337. 10.1109/ACCESS.2021.3087109

Yee, C. K., & Zolkipli, M. F. (2021). Review on confidentiality, integrity and availability in information security. *Journal of ICT in Education*, 8(2), 34–42. 10.37134/jictie.vol8.2.4.2021

Yener, A., & Ulukus, S. (2015). Wireless physical-layer security: Lessons learned from information theory. *Proceedings of the IEEE*, 103(10), 1814–1825. 10.1109/JPROC.2015.2459592

Yerrapragada, A. K., Eisman, T., & Kelley, B. (2021). Physical layer security for beyond 5G: Ultra secure low latency communications. *IEEE Open Journal of the Communications Society*, 2, 2232–2242. 10.1109/OJCOMS.2021.3105185

Yilmaz, Y., & Uludag, S. (2017). Mitigating IoT-based cyberattacks on the smart grid. *Proceedings - 16th IEEE International Conference on Machine Learning and Applications, ICMLA 2017*, 517–522. 10.1109/ICMLA.2017.0-109

Yin, M., Yang, Y., & Jiao, B. (2020). Security-oriented trellis code design for spatial modulation. *IEEE Transactions on Wireless Communications*, 20(3), 1875–1888. 10.1109/TWC.2020.3037146

Yousuf, H., Lahzi, M., Salloum, S. A. & Shaalan, K. (2020). Systematic review on fully homomorphic encryption scheme and its application. *Recent Advances in Intelligent Systems and Smart Applications*, 537-551.

Yu, H., Duan, W., Zhang, G., Ji, Y., Zhu, X., & Choi, J. (2019). A near optimal power allocation scheme for cooperative relay networking with NOMA. *China Communications*, 16(3), 122–131.

Yu, L., Fan, P., & Han, Z. (2019). Maximizing spectral efficiency for scma systems with codebooks based on star-qam signaling constellations. *IEEE Wireless Communications Letters*, 8(4), 1163–1166. 10.1109/LWC.2019.2909913

Yuliadi, Y., Hamdani, F., Fitriana, Y. B., & Oper, N. (2023). Analisis keamanan website terhadap serangan ddos menggunakan metode national institute of standards and technology (nist). *KLIK: Kajian Ilmiah Informatika dan Komputer*, 3(6), 1296–1302.

Yungaicela-Naula, N. M., Vargas-Rosales, C., Pérez-Díaz, J. A., & Zareei, M. (2022). Towards security automation in software defined networks. *Computer Communications*, 183, 64–82. 10.1016/j.comcom.2021.11.014

Zahedi, Y., Ngah, R., Nunoo, S., Mokayef, M., Alavi, S. E., & Amiri, I. S. (2016). Experimental measurement and statistical analysis of the RMS delay spread in time-varying ultra-wideband communication channel. *Measurement*, 89, 179–188. 10.1016/j.measurement.2016.04.009

Zaidi, A. Z., Chong, C. Y., Jin, Z., Parthiban, R., & Sadiq, A. S. (2021). Touch-based continuous mobile device authentication: State-of-the-art, challenges and opportunities. *Journal of Network and Computer Applications*, 191(June), 103162. 10.1016/j.jnca.2021.103162

Zaimy, N. A., Zolkipli, M. F., Katuk, N., Zaimy, N. A., Zolkipli, M. F., & Katuk, N. (2023). A review of hacking techniques in IoT systems and future trends of hacking on IoT environment. *World Journal of Advanced Research and Reviews*, 17(2), 2. Advance online publication. 10.30574/wjarr.2023.17.2.0310

Zarpelão, B. B., Miani, R. S., Kawakani, C. T., & de Alvarenga, S. C. (2017). A survey of intrusion detection in Internet of Things. *Journal of Network and Computer Applications*, 84(January), 25–37. 10.1016/j.jnca.2017.02.009

Zeadally, S., Das, A. K., & Sklavos, N. (2021). Cryptographic technologies and protocol standards for Internet of Things. *Internet of Things : Engineering Cyber Physical Human Systems*, 14, 100075. 10.1016/j.iot.2019.100075

Zeilenga, K. & Melnikov, A. (2006). *Simple Authentication and Security Layer (SASL)*. RFC 4422.

Zetter, K. (2010). *Inside the Cunning, Unprecedented Hack of Ukraine's Power Grid*. Available online: https://www.wired.com/2016/03/inside-cunning-unprecedented-hack-ukraines-power-grid/

Zhang, T.-Y., & Ye, D. (2020). *False data injection attacks with complete stealthiness in cyber–physical systems: A self-generated approach.* Academic Press.

Zhang, X., Chen, L., Fan, J., Wang, X., & Wang, Q. (2021). Power IoT security protection architecture based on zero trust framework. *Proceedings of the 2021 IEEE 5th International Conference on Cryptography, Security and Privacy (CSP).*

Zhang, Z., Zhang, Y.-Q., Chu, X., & Li, B. (2004). *An overview of virtual private network (VPN): IP VPN and optical VPN.* Academic Press.

Zhang, H., Nakamura, T., & Sakurai, K. (2019). Security and Trust Issues on Digital Supply Chain. *2019 IEEE Intl Conf on Dependable, Autonomic and Secure Computing, Intl Conf on Pervasive Intelligence and Computing, Intl Conf on Cloud and Big Data Computing, Intl Conf on Cyber Science and Technology Congress (DASC/PiCom/CBDCom/CyberSciTech),* 338-343. 10.1109/DASC/PiCom/CBDCom/CyberSciTech.2019.00069

Zhang, J., Li, Z., Zhang, H., Zhang, W., Ling, Z., & Yang, M. (2023). Sensor-based implicit authentication through learning user physiological and behavioral characteristics. *Computer Communications,* 208(March), 244–255. 10.1016/j.comcom.2023.06.016

Zhang, L., Tan, S., & Yang, J. (2017). Hearing Your Voice is Not Enough: An Articulatory gesture based liveness detection for voice authentication. *Proceedings of the ACM Conference on Computer and Communications Security,* 57–71. 10.1145/3133956.3133962

Zhang, L., Xiong, H., Huang, Q., Li, J., Choo, K.-K. R., & Li, J. (2019). Cryptographic solutions for cloud storage: Challenges and research opportunities. *IEEE Transactions on Services Computing,* 15(1), 567–587. 10.1109/TSC.2019.2937764

Zhang, W., Zhang, B., Zhou, Y., He, H., & Ding, Z. (2020). An IoT Honeynet Based on Multiport Honeypots for Capturing IoT Attacks. *IEEE Internet of Things Journal,* 7(5), 3991–3999. 10.1109/JIOT.2019.2956173

Zhou, M., Wang, Q., Yang, J., Li, Q., Xiao, F., Wang, Z., & Chen, X. (2018). PatternListener: Cracking android pattern lock using acoustic signals. *Proceedings of the ACM Conference on Computer and Communications Security,* 1775–1787. 10.1145/3243734.3243777

Zimmermann, V., & Gerber, N. (2020). The password is dead, long live the password – A laboratory study on user perceptions of authentication schemes. *International Journal of Human Computer Studies,* 133, 26–44. 10.1016/j.ijhcs.2019.08.006

Zou, Q., Wang, Y., Wang, Q., Zhao, Y., & Li, Q. (2020). Deep Learning-Based Gait Recognition Using Smartphones in the Wild. *IEEE Transactions on Information Forensics and Security,* 15, 3197–3212. 10.1109/TIFS.2020.2985628

About the Contributors

Qasem Abu Al-Haija received his Ph.D. from Tennessee State University (TSU), USA, in 2020. He is an Assistant Professor at the Department of Cybersecurity, Faculty of Computer & Information Technology, Jordan University of Science and Technology, Irbid, Jordan. He authorizes more than 200 scientific research papers and book chapters. His research interests include Artificial Intelligence (AI), Cybersecurity and Cryptography, the Internet of Things (IoT), Cyber-Physical Systems (CPS), Time Series Analysis (TSA), and Computer Arithmetic. Recently, he was listed as one of the world's top 2% of scientists list released publicly by Stanford University and Elsevier Publisher.

* * *

Anas Abu Taleb received a Ph.D. from the University of Bristol, UK, 2010, an MSc. from the University of the West of England, UK, 2007 and a BSc. degree from Princess Sumaya University for Technology, Jordan, 2004. In addition to wireless sensor networks, he is interested in network fault tolerance, routing algorithms, and cloud computing.

Nizar Al Daradkeh is a DevSecOps Engineer with a background in Network and Information Security Engineering. A graduate of Princess Sumaya University for Technology, his interests primarily include data privacy and information security.

Tareq Alhajahjeh is currently engaged in advanced research as a PhD student at the Cyber Security Centre of De Montfort University (DMU), where he delves into cutting-edge issues in cyber security. Alongside his studies, Tareq is also a dedicated lecturer in computer engineering at Khawarizmi University Technical College, where he imparts his considerable knowledge and expertise to the next generation of tech professionals.

Asser Ali Al-Jarallah received the bachelor's degree in health services administration and the master's degree in health and hospital administration from King Saud University, and the Ph.D. degree in business administration from the University of Hull, U.K. He is currently a Vice Rector of AlMaarefa University, an Assistant Professor of Quality Management with the College of Business Administration, Majmaah University, and the Chairperson of the Scientific Committee with the Saudi Society for Health Administration. He has participated and consulted in various sectors. His research interests include quality and entrepreneurship. He is a member of five teams of patent inventors and won four gold medal.

Hussein M. K. Al-Masri (S'14, M'16, SM'22) received the B.Sc. and M.S. degrees in electrical power engineering from Yarmouk University, Irbid, Jordan, in 2010 and 2012, respectively, and the Ph.D. degree in electrical engineering from Texas A&M University, College Station, TX, USA, in 2016. He was a Lab Manager and Researcher at the Sustainable Energy and Vehicle Engineering Program, Power Electronics and Motor Drives Laboratory, Texas A&M University. He is currently an Associate Professor with the Electrical Power Engineering Department, Yarmouk University. His research interests include renewable energy retrofitting systems, power electronics and photovoltaic applications, and the applications of artificial intelligence techniques to solve power system problems. Dr. Al-Masri received the 2016 Outstanding Graduate Teaching Fellowship from the Department of Electrical Engineering at Texas A&M University. Dr. Hussein has been promoted to an Associate Professor at Yarmouk University based on the Fast Track as he received distinguished comments for his research work from the external reviewers. Currently, Dr. Hussein is in a sabbatical leave working as an associate professor in Electrical Engineering at the American University of the Middle East, Kuwait.

Abdullah S. Alshra'a obtained his Ph.D. from Technische Universität Ilmenau in Germany. He works as a postdoctoral fellow at Friedrich-Alexander-Universität. His research focuses on cybersecurity in Smart Grids and the application of Network Calculus to ensure performance guarantees for Smart Grid Services.

Shahad Al-Tamimi, Masters student, Cybersecurity Department, Princess Sumaya University for Technology (PSUT), Amman-Jordan, ORCiD: https://orcid.org/0009-0005-3270-8200, received the B.S degree in computer information systems from University of Jordan. Jordan, in 2022, She is currently a student MS, Princess Sumaya University for Technology, Amman, Jordan. She's research interests include cybersecurity, Information systems, Intrusion Detection System (IDS), the Internet of Things (IoT), Machin Learning, and Artificial Intelligence.

Francisco Aparicio-Navarro is an Associate Professor in Cyber Security and Programme Leader for the BSc (Hons) Digital Technology Solutions Professional Degree Apprenticeship. He is an expert in Computer Network Security and Intrusion Detection. His research has advanced the state-of-the-art of network security by developing novel unsupervised Intrusion Detection Systems, and proposing statistical approaches to integrate Contextual Information and Situational Awareness into the cyber-attack detection process.

Justice Kwame Appati is a lecturer in the School of Physical and Mathematical Science (SPMS) and the Department of Computer Science. He began his teaching career at Kwame Nkrumah University of Science and Technology in Kumasi as a graduate assistant and then later moved to the University of Ghana in 2017 as a lecturer. Justice earned a PhD in Applied Mathematics from Kwame Nkrumah University Science and Technology in 2016. He also graduated in 2010 and 2013 with a BSc. Mathematics and MPhil Applied Mathematics from the same institution. His current research includes data science, mathematical intelligence, image processing and scientific computing, He has singly and jointly supervised undergraduate and postgraduate students from Kwame Nkrumah University of Science and Technology (KNUST), National Institute of Mathematical Sciences (NIMS), African Institute of Mathematical Sciences (AIMS) and the University of Ghana. Currently, Justice handles course including Design and Analysis of Algorithm, Artificial Intelligence, Formal Methods and Computer Vision. He looks forward to working with everyone interested in his field of study more especially, Intelligence and Data Science.

Walaa R. Ayyad received her B.Sc and M.Sc. in Computer Engineering from Yarmouk University in 2014 and 2022, respectively. She is a Teaching Assistant at the Department of Cyber Security at Jordan University of Science and Technology, Irbid, Jordan. Her research interests include parallel processing using FPGAs, GPU, IoT, cybersecurity, machine learning, artificial intelligence, computer networks, and computer vision.

Akashdeep Bhardwaj is working as Professor (Cyber Security & Digital Forensics) and Head of Cybersecurity Center of Excellence at University of Petroleum & Energy Studies (UPES), Dehradun, India. An eminent IT Industry expert with over 28 years of experience in areas such as Cybersecurity, Digital Forensics and IT Operations, Dr. Akashdeep mentors graduate, masters and doctoral students and leads several projects. Dr. Akashdeep is a Post-Doctoral from Majmaah University, Saudi Arabia, Ph.D. in Computer Science, Post Graduate Diploma in Management (equivalent to MBA), and holds an Engineering Degree in Computer Science. Dr. Akashdeep has published over 120 research works (including copyrights, patent, papers, authored & edited books) in international journals. Dr. Akashdeep worked as Technology Leader for several multinational organizations during his time in the IT industry. Dr. Akashdeep is certified in multiple technologies including Compliance Audits, Cybersecurity, and industry certifications in Microsoft, Cisco, and VMware technologies.

Stéphanie Chollet is an Associate Professor in computer science at Grenoble Institute of Technology. She received her PhD from Grenoble University in 2009. Her research focuses on the integration of security in software development for IoT applications, encompassing all aspects from devices to the cloud.

Arthur Desuert received a Ph.D. degree in Computer Science in 2023 and a Master's degree in Computer Science in 2020, both from the Université Grenoble Alpes, in France. His research is about the secure integration of connected devices in pervasive applications; understanding the implied challenges, the benefits and limitations of current solutions to design new ways of securing IoT.

Khadiga Eltira received the B.Sc. and M.Sc. degrees in electrical and electronics engineering from the University of Benghazi, Benghazi, Libya, in 2014 and 2021, respectively. She was teaching assistant at the Faculty of Medical Technology - Benghazi from 2019 to 2021. Currently, she is a faculty member of the Electrical and Electronics Engineering Department at University of Benghazi, since May 2021. Her main research interests are in the area of wireless communication with a particular focus on multiple-input multiple-output (MIMO) wireless communications, cooperative communication, and multiple access techniques.

About the Contributors

Ajay B. Gadicha is working as HOD AI&DS, Dean Research and Development, Associate Professor in Department of Artificial Intelligence & Data Science, P. R. Pote College of Engineering and Management Amravati. He has completed Honorary Doctor of Science in Computer Science and Engineering from (Dana Brain Health Institute & Iranian Neuroscience Society-Fars Chapter, Iran). He has done Post-PhD Pilot Research Project from Vietnam in Video Summarization. He has completed PhD in Computer Science and Engineering from Sant Gadge Baba Amravati University. He has 13 years of experience in the field of Computer Forensics and Information Technology. He is Visiting Scientist in National Kaohsiung University of Science and Technology IOT Cyber security Lab Taiwan. He became First Merit & University Topper in Master of Engineering in Information Technology in 2011. He has published 75 research papers in National and International Journal and conferences. He has published 4 books (online) and 14 book chapters in Scopus index book. He has 34 patents (on IPR India) and 15 Copyrights in the field of Computer Forensics and Machine Learning. He has a field of interest in Video Forensics, Network Security, Image Processing, and Video Summarization. Dr. Gadicha received Recognization and Honor from Hon. Deputy Chief Minister of Maharashtra Shri Devendraji Fandavis for Pitching Best Idea in Computer Science and Engineering at Patent –Fest on 14 Aug 2023, Nagpur. Dr. Gadicha is working as Board of Studies Member (Computer Science & Engineering) Sant Gadge Baba Amravati University. Dr. Gadicha is working as Board of Studies Member (Computer Science & Engineering) Jhulelal Institute of Technology (Autonomous) Nagpur. Dr. Gadicha currently worked in 180 editorial and 50 + Reviewer boards of various national and international bodies & communities including ISTE, CSI, IAENG, IEEE, ACM, IFERP etc. Dr. Gadicha received International Association for Science and Technology Education Awarded "Best Young Research Award-2017" at Tamil Nadu. Dr. Gadicha Received "Best Researcher Award-2019" by Vivekanandha College of Arts and Science for Women (Autonomous), Tiruchengode, Tamil Nadu, India. Dr. Gadicha Received "Young Researcher in Computer Science and Engineering on 31 July 2019" by Global Outreach Research & Education Association Bangalore. Dr. Gadicha received Token of Appreciation from Google Developers Students Clubs (GDSC-India)for being MENTOR of GDSC-P R Pote Patil COE&M, Amravati for the session 2023-24.

Sara Hamad is currently pursuing her B.Sc. in Networks and Information Security Engineering at Princess Sumaya University for Technology, expected to graduate in 2024. Her academic interests primarily focus on addressing security challenges and enhancing data privacy within the realms of Information Security, Network Security, and Systems Security.

David Hély is a Professor of Electrical and Computer Engineering at Grenoble Institute of Technology – Univ. Grenoble Alpes. He has a Ph.D. in Microelectronics and computer engineering, from the University of Montpellier. His research and education activities span hardware cybersecurity, processors and cyberphysical systems security, verification and test of secure systems.

Vishal Ashok Ingole is working as an Assistant Professor in the Department of Management, P.R. Pote Patil College of Engg. & Management, Amravati, Maharashtra. He has pursing Ph.D in subject Digital Marketing. He has more than 13 years of teaching and 17 years of as Industrialist Corporate experience. He has published 2 book and more than 12 papers Research papers in various National and International Journals and Proceedings in National Conferences.

Raed Mesleh is currently on unpaid leave at Princess Sumaya University for Technology (PSUT) where he serves as the Dean of King Abdullah I School of Graduate Studies and Scientific Research. He is also a Professor in the Communication Engineering / IoT Department at King Abdullah II School of Engineering. He is a Tenured Faculty Member in the Electrical Engineering Department at the Ger- man Jordanian University (GJU) and served as the Dean and the Vice Dean of the school of Electrical Engineering and Information Technology for about six years. He received his PhD in 2007 from Jacobs University in Bremen, Germany, and was a Postdoctoral Fellow at Jacobs University from 2007 to 2010. He was with the Electrical Engineering Department at University of Tabuk in Saudi Arabia from 2010 to 2015, where he held the positions of Department Chair and the Director of research excellence and intellectual property units at the deanship of scientific research. He has been a Visiting Scholar at Boston University, The University of Edinburgh, and Herriot-Watt University. His current research interests include MIMO techniques, terahertz and millimeter wave communications, cell-free systems, physical layer security, Steiner triple systems, graph theory, and optical wireless communication. He is the inventor and co-inventor of 10 patents and has published more than 200 articles in prestigious scientific journals and international conferences. He has an overall citation count of over 13000 with an H-index of 45. He has received Distinguished Researcher Awards from University of Tabuk in 2013 and from GJU in 2016 and 2019. In December 2016, he was honored with the Arab Scientific award from the Arab Thought Foundation.

Ammar Odeh received his Ph.D. from University of Bridgeport (UB), USA, in 2015. He is an Associate Professor at the Department of Computer Science, Faculty of King Hussein School of Computing Sciences, Princess Sumaya University for Technology, Amman, Jordan. His research interests include Cybersecurity and Cryptography, the Internet of Things (IoT).

Wasswa Shafik (Member, IEEE) received the Bachelor of Science degree in information technology engineering with a minor in mathematics from Ndejje University, Kampala, Uganda, a Master of Engineering degree in information technology engineering from Yazd University, Iran, and a Ph.D. degree in computer science with the School of Digital Science, Universiti Brunei Darussalam, Brunei Darussalam. He is also the Founder and a Principal Investigator of the Dig Connectivity Research Laboratory (DCRLab) after serving as a Research Associate at Network Interconnectivity Research Laboratory, Yazd University. Prior to this, he worked as a Community Data Analyst at Population Services International (PSI-Uganda), Community Data Officer at Programme for Accessible Health Communication (PACE-Uganda), Research Assistant at the Socio-Economic Data Centre (SEDC-Uganda), Prime Minister's Office, Kampala, Uganda, an Assistant Data Officer at TechnoServe, Kampala, IT Support at Thurayya Islam Media, Uganda, and Asmaah Charity Organization. He has more than 60 publications in renowned journals and conferences. Interests include computer vision, AI-enabled IoT/IoMTs, the IoT/IIoT/OT security, cyber security, and privacy.

Winfred Yaokumah is a researcher and senior faculty at the Department of Computer Science of the University of Ghana. He has published several articles in highly rated journals including Information and Computer Security, Information Resources Management Journal, IEEE Xplore, International Journal of Human Capital and Information Technology, International Journal of Human Capital and Information Technology Professionals, International Journal of Technology and Human Interaction, International Journal of e-Business Research, International Journal of Enterprise Information Systems, Journal of Information Technology Research, International Journal of Information Systems in the Service Sector, and Education and Information Technologies. His research interest includes cyber security, cyber ethics, network security, and information systems security and governance. He serves as a member of the International Review Board for the International Journal of Technology Diffusion.

Abdelhamid Younis is currently on a research visit at the German Jordanian University as part of a research mobility program funded by the Arab-German Young Academy (AGYA) where he has been a member since 2020, and he is an associate professor at the Department of Electrical and Electronics Engineering, University of Benghazi where he joined the department in 2015. He received the B.Sc. (with honors) in 2007 from the University of Benghazi, and the M.Sc. (with distinction) and Ph.D. in 2009 and 2014, respectively, from The University of Edinburgh, U.K. He was the dean of Engineering at the University of Benghazi until 2023 and a Research Associate at the Institute of Digital Communications at the University of Edinburgh from 2013 to 2014. Dr. Younis received the Overseas Research Student Award in 2010, Best Student Paper Award at the 78th IEEE Vehicular Technology Conference (VTC) in Las Vegas, Sep. 2013, the Graphical System Design Achievement Awards Category: Radio Frequency (RF) and Communications from National Instruments (NI) and holds the Almadar Aljadid R&D grant titled "Millimeter-wave large-scale MIMO: ABER and capacity analysis". His main research interests are in the area of wireless communication and digital signal processing with a particular focus on spatial modulation, MIMO wireless communications, and optical wireless communications. He is the Co-author of a book entitle Space Modulation Techniques published by Wiley in 2018.

Index

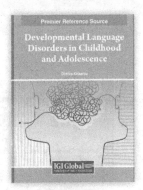

  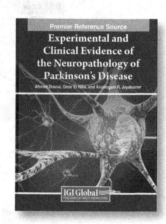 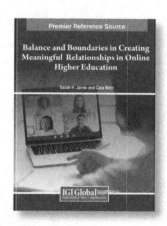

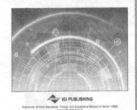

Printed in the United States
by Baker & Taylor Publisher Services